Taking SIDES

Clashing Views on Controversial Legal Issues

Seventh Edition

Edited, Selected, and with Introductions by

M. Ethan Katsh
University of Massachusetts–Amherst

Dushkin Publishing Group/Brown & Benchmark Publishers
McGraw-Hill Higher Education Group

To Beverly

Photo Acknowledgments

Part 1   Supreme Court Historical Society
Part 2   AP/Wide World
Part 3   United Nations/John Robaton

Cover Art Acknowledgment

Charles Vitelli

Manufactured in the United States of America

Seventh Edition

10   9   8   7   6   5   4   3   2   1

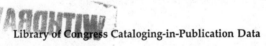

Library of Congress Cataloging-in-Publication Data

Main entry under title:
     Taking sides: clashing views on controversial legal issues/edited, selected, and with intro-
     ductions by M. Ethan Katsh.—7th ed.
        Includes bibliographical references and index.
        1. Law—Social aspects—United States. 2. United States—Constitutional law. 3. Justice,
     Administration of—United States. I. Katsh, M. Ethan, *comp.*

                                                                                340'.115
     0-697-35717-1   96-85787

Printed on Recycled Paper

PREFACE

The study of law should be introduced as part of a liberal education, to train and enrich the mind. . . . I am convinced that, like history, economics, and metaphysics—and perhaps even to a greater degree than these—the law could be advantageously studied with a view to the general development of the mind.

—Justice Louis D. Brandeis

The general study of law in colleges, universities, and even high schools has grown rapidly during the last 10 years. Accompanying this development has been the publication of new curriculum materials that go beyond the analysis of legal cases and doctrines that make up much of professional law study in law schools. This book is part of the effort to view and study law as an institution that continuously interacts with other social institutions. Law should be examined from an interdisciplinary perspective and be accessible to all students.

This book focuses on a series of controversial issues involving law and the legal system. It is, I believe, an appropriate starting point for law study since controversy and conflict are inherent in law. Law is based on an adversary approach to conflict resolution, in which two advocates representing opposing sides are pitted against each other. Judicial decisions often contain both majority and dissenting opinions, which reveal some of the arguments that went on in the judges' chambers. Perhaps most relevant to a discussion of the place of controversy in the legal system is the First Amendment guarantee of freedom of speech and press, which presumes that we all benefit by a vigorous debate of important issues.

Since many of the issues in *Taking Sides* are often in the news, you probably already have opinions on them. What you should remember, however, is that there is usually more to learn about any given issue, and the topics discussed here are best approached with an open mind. You should not be surprised if your views change as you read the selections.

Organization of the book   This book contains 36 selections presented in a pro and con format that debate 18 legal issues. Each issue has an issue *introduction*, which sets the stage for the debate as it is argued in the YES and NO selections. Each issue concludes with a *postscript* that makes some final observations, points the way to other questions related to the issue, and provides some *suggestions for further reading* on the issue. Also in the postscript are Internet site addresses (URLs) that should prove useful as starting points for further research. A good general resource and introduction to law on the World Wide Web can be found at http://www.umass.edu/legal/hyper.html. At the back of the book is a listing of all the *contributors to this volume*, which provides information on the legal scholars, commentators, and judges whose views are debated here.

Changes to this edition   This seventh edition represents a considerable revision. There are six completely new issues: *Are Term Limits for Elected Officials Unconstitutional?* (Issue 4); *Is Drug Use Testing of Student Athletes Permitted Under the Fourth Amendment?* (Issue 5); *Is Flag Burning Protected by the First Amendment?* (Issue 7); *Is the Regulation of Pornography on the Internet Unconstitutional?* (Issue 10); *Are Restrictions on Physician-Assisted Suicide Unconstitutional?* (Issue 12); and *Are Laws Restricting Gay Rights Legislation Unconstitutional?* (Issue 13). I have also revised Issue 18, *Should Drug Use Be Legalized?* so completely that I feel I should count it as brand new. In all, there are 14 new selections in this edition.

A word to the instructor   An *Instructor's Manual With Test Questions* (multiple-choice and essay) is available through the publisher for the instructor using *Taking Sides* in the classroom. And a general guidebook, *Using Taking Sides in the Classroom*, which discusses methods and techniques for integrating the pro-con approach into any classroom setting, is also available.

Taking Sides: Clashing Views on Controversial Legal Issues is only one title in the Taking Sides series; the others are listed on the back cover. If you are interested in seeing the table of contents for any of the other titles, please visit the Taking Sides Web site at http://www.dushkin.com/takingsides.

Acknowledgments   I received helpful comments and suggestions from the many users of *Taking Sides* across the United States and Canada. Their suggestions have markedly enhanced the quality of this edition of the book and are reflected in the six totally new issues and the updated selection.

Special thanks go to those who responded with specific suggestions for the seventh edition:

Maria T. Arroyo-Tabin
Chapman College

Gerald Blasi
State University of New York
   at Binghamton

E. Keith Bramlett
University of North Carolina
   at Asheville

Phillip Brown
University of California,
   Santa Barbara

Adeyemi Ejire
Shaw University

R. J. Kinkel
University of Michigan at
   Dearborn

John L. Krauss
Indiana University–Purdue
  University at Indianapolis

Douglas W. Scott
Troy State University

John Morser
University of
  Wisconsin–Stevens Point

A note on case citations   Throughout this book you will see references to judicial opinions. The judge's opinion or decision refers to the written statement of reasons the judge provides when making an interpretation of law or deciding a case. These opinions are printed and distributed in books called *reporters*, which can be found in law libraries and many university libraries. There are separate reporters for federal and state cases. When you see a reference to a case such as *Brown v. Board of Education*, 347 U.S. 483 (1954), it means that the case with that name can be found in volume 347 of the *United States Reports* on page 483 and that the case was decided in 1954. When you see a legal citation with a series of numbers and words, the first number is always the volume number and the last number is the page number.

M. Ethan Katsh
University of Massachusetts–Amherst

CONTENTS IN BRIEF

CONTENTS

Professor of law Harry I. Subin argues that greater responsibility should be placed on lawyers not to pervert the truth to help their clients. Attorney John B. Mitchell disputes the contention that the goal of the criminal justice process is to seek the truth and argues that it is essential that there be independent defense attorneys to provide protection against government oppression.

Penelope E. Bryan, a professor in the School of Law at the University of Denver, asserts that the process of mediation in divorce cases works more to the benefit of men than women. Stephen K. Erickson, a practicing divorce mediator, argues that all parties benefit from a process that is less adversarial, namely, mediation, and which is not controlled by lawyers.

Professor of philosophy Kenneth Kipnis argues that plea bargaining often subverts the cause of justice. District Attorney Nick Schweitzer finds that plea bargaining is fair, useful, desirable, necessary, and practical.

Supreme Court justice John Paul Stevens argues that the Framers intended the Constitution to establish fixed qualifications for members of Congress and that the power to add qualifications, such as term limits, is not reserved to the states by the Tenth Amendment. Supreme Court justice Clarence Thomas argues that the federal Constitution permits states to add qualifications for electing members of Congress because it does not explicitly prohibit them from doing so.

Supreme Court justice Antonin Scalia finds that nothing in the Constitution bars a random urinalysis requirement for students participating in interscholastic athletics. Supreme Court justice Sandra Day O'Connor asserts that such a requirement weakens the Fourth Amendment.

Supreme Court justice Antonin Scalia finds that the St. Paul ordinance punishing "hate speech" cannot be constitutional because it regulates speech depending on the subject the speech addresses. Justice John Paul Stevens argues that this particular ordinance is perhaps simply overbroad.

Supreme Court justice William J. Brennan, Jr., argues that burning the American flag to express displeasure at the government is behavior that is protected by the First Amendment. Supreme Court chief justice William H. Rehnquist argues that a congressional prohibition against flag burning is justified.

Supreme Court justice David H. Souter maintains that a New York statute that established a school serving only a single religious community violates the establishment clause of the First Amendment. Justice Antonin Scalia argues that the school is secular in nature and does not violate the First Amendment.

Supreme Court justice Sandra Day O'Connor upholds a woman's constitutional right to abortion under most circumstances. Chief Justice William

H. Rehnquist argues that Pennsylvania regulations on abortion should be upheld and that it is appropriate to overrule *Roe v. Wade.*

Judge Dolores K. Sloviter argues that the Communications Decency Act (CDA) violates the First Amendment rights of all people by restricting access to material on the Internet. The U.S. Department of Justice contends that limitations on minors' access to indecent materials in cyberspace are no different from constitutionally upheld limitations in other communications media.

William L. Taylor, a lawyer, and Susan M. Liss, the deputy assistant attorney general of the U.S. Department of Justice, believe that affirmative action policies have been very effective in providing new opportunities for education and economic advancement. Wm. Bradford Reynolds, a senior litigation partner, argues that any preference provided on the basis of race, gender, religion, or national origin is inconsistent with the ideal of equality.

Judge Stephen Reinhardt argues that forbidding physician-assisted suicide in the cases of competent, terminally ill patients violates the due process clause of the Constitution. Judge Robert Beeser maintains that although patients have the right to refuse life-sustaining treatment, physician-assisted suicide is not constitutionally protected.

Supreme Court justice Anthony Kennedy argues that a Colorado amendment denying certain legal protections for homosexuals violates the Constitution. Supreme Court justice Antonin Scalia asserts that the Colorado amendment denies homosexuals special treatment on the basis of their sexual orientation and that there is no constitutional reason to prohibit such a law.

Former Supreme Court justice Harry A. Blackmun argues that the application of the death penalty has been arbitrary and discriminatory. Attorney James C. Anders argues that the death penalty is the appropriate punishment for some crimes and that it should not be abolished.

U.S. Court of Appeals judge Malcolm Richard Wilkey raises objections to the exclusionary rule on the grounds that it may suppress evidence and allow the guilty to go free. Professor of law Yale Kamisar argues that the exclusionary rule is necessary to prevent abuses by police and to protect citizens' rights.

Sarah Brady, head of a citizens' lobby for gun control, argues that a waiting period for purchasing a weapon does not change who is lawfully allowed to buy a gun and that it would prevent many crimes. James Jay Baker, director of federal affairs for the National Rifle Association, claims that waiting periods do not work and that criminals would still be able to obtain weapons.

Editor Jonathan Rowe examines the insanity defense as it is now administered and finds that its application is unfair and leads to unjust results. Professor of law Richard Bonnie argues that the abolition of the insanity defense would be immoral and would leave no alternative for those who are not responsible for their actions.

Steven B. Duke, a professor of law of science and technology, contends that the war on drugs has led to an increase in criminal behavior and that the costs of drug prohibition are enormous. Therefore, he recommends decriminalization and government regulation of drugs. Associate professor Gregory A. Loken asserts that the war on drugs has successfully reduced crime and that legalization would have devastating consequences, particularly for children.

INTRODUCTION

The Role of Law

M. Ethan Katsh

Two hundred years ago, Edmund Burke, the influential British statesman and orator, commented that "in no other country perhaps in the world, is the law so general a study as it is in the United States." Today, in America, general knowledge about law is at a disappointing level. One study conducted several years ago concluded that "the general public's knowledge of and direct experience with courts is low."[1] Three out of four persons surveyed admitted that they knew either very little or nothing at all about state and local courts. More than half believed that the burden of proving innocence in a criminal trial is on the accused, and 72 percent thought that every decision made by a state could be reviewed by the Supreme Court. In a 1990 study, 59 percent could not name at least one current justice of the Supreme Court.

One purpose of this volume is to provide information about some specific and important legal issues. In your local newspaper today, there is probably at least one story concerning an issue in this book. The quality of your life will be directly affected by how many of these issues are resolved. But gun control (Issue 16), the insanity defense (Issue 17), drug legalization (Issue 18), abortion (Issue 9), legal ethics (Issue 1), and other issues in this book are often the subject of superficial, misleading, or inaccurate statements. *Taking Sides* is designed to encourage you to become involved in the public debate on these issues and to raise the level of the discussion on them.

The issues that are debated in this book represent some of the most important challenges our society faces. How they are dealt with will influence what kind of society we will have in the future. While it is important to look at and study them separately, it is equally necessary to think about their relationship to each other and about the fact that there is a tool called "law," which is being called upon to solve a series of difficult conflicts. The study of discrete legal issues should enable you to gain insight into some broad theoretical questions about law. This introduction, therefore, will focus on several basic characteristics of law and the legal process that you should keep in mind as you read this book.

THE NATURE OF LAW

The eminent legal anthropologist E. Adamson Hoebel once noted that the search for a definition of law is as difficult as the search for the Holy Grail. Law is certainly complicated, and trying to define it precisely can be frustrating. What follows, therefore, is not a definition of law but a framework or perspective for looking at and understanding law.

Law as a Body of Rules

One of the common incorrect assumptions about law is that it is merely a body of rules invoked by those who need them and then applied by a judge. Under this view, the judge is essentially a machine whose task is simply to find and apply the right rule to the dispute in question. This perspective makes the mistake of equating law with the rules of law. It is sometimes even assumed that there exists somewhere in the libraries of lawyers and judges one book with all the rules or laws in it, which can be consulted to answer legal questions. As may already be apparent, such a book could not exist. Rules alone do not supply the solutions to many legal problems. The late Supreme Court justice William O. Douglas once wrote, "The law is not a series of calculating machines where definitions and answers come tumbling out when the right levers are pushed." As you read the debates about the issues in this book, you will see that much more goes into a legal argument than the recitation of rules.

Law as a Process

A more meaningful way of thinking about law is to look at it as a process or system, keeping in mind that legal rules are one of the elements in the process. This approach requires a considerably broader vision of law: to think not only of the written rules but also of the judges, the lawyers, the police, and all the other people in the system. It requires an even further consideration of all the things that influence these people, such as their values and economic status.

"Law," one legal commentator has stated, "is very like an iceberg; only one-tenth of its substance appears above the social surface in the explicit form of documents, institutions, and professions, while the nine-tenths of its substance that supports its visible fragment leads a sub-aquatic existence, living in the habits, attitudes, emotions and aspirations of men."[2]

In reading the discussions of controversial issues in this book, try to identify what forces are influencing the content of the rules and the position of the writers. Three of the most important influences on the nature of law are economics, moral values, and public opinion.

Law and Economics

Laws that talk about equality, such as the Fourteenth Amendment, which guarantees that no state shall "deny to any person ... equal protection of the laws," suggest that economic status is irrelevant in the making and application of the law. As Anatole France, the nineteenth-century French satirist, once wrote, however, "The law, in its majestic equality, forbids the rich as well as the poor to sleep under bridges, to beg in streets, and to steal bread." Sometimes the purpose and effect of the law cannot be determined merely from the words of the law.

Marxist critics of law in capitalistic societies assert that poverty results from the manipulation of the law by the wealthy and powerful. It is possible to look at several issues in this book and make some tentative judgments about the influence of economic power on law. For example, what role does economics play in the debate over drug legalization (Issue 18)? Is the controversy over the fight against drugs one of social concerns or one of economics, in that it costs the government billions of dollars each year? In considering whether or not pornography on the Internet should be regulated (Issue 10), is the controversy purely over morality and values, or is it related to the proliferation of pornography up for sale on the Internet? Plea bargaining (Issue 3), which mostly affects poor persons who cannot afford bail, also involves the question of whether or not the law is responsible for or perpetuates poverty and economic classes.

Law and Values

The relationship between law and values has been a frequent theme of legal writers and a frequent source of debate. Clearly, there is in most societies some relationship between law and morality. One writer has summarized the relationship as follows:

1. *There is a moral order in society.* Out of the many different and often conflicting values of the individuals and institutions that make up society may emerge a dominant moral position, a "core" of the moral order. The position of this core is dynamic, and as it changes, the moral order of society moves in the direction of that change.
2. *There is a moral content to the law.* The moral content of law also changes over time, and as it changes, the law moves in the direction of that change.
3. *The moral content of the law and moral order in society are seldom identical.*
4. *A natural and necessary affinity exists between the two "bodies" of law and moral order.*
5. *When there is a gap between the moral order of society and the law, some movement to close the gap is likely.* The law will move closer to the moral order of society, or the moral order will move closer to the law, or each will move toward the other. The likelihood of the movement to close the gap between law and moral order depends upon the size of the gap between the two bodies and the perceived significance of the subject matter concerning which the gap exists.[3]

Law and morality will not be identical in a pluralistic society, but there will also be attempts by dominant groups to insert their views of what is right into the legal code. The First Amendment prohibition against establishment of religion and the guarantee of freedom of religion are designed to protect those whose beliefs are different. Yet there have also been many historical examples of legal restrictions or limitations being imposed on minorities or of laws being ineffective because of the resistance of powerful groups. Prayers in the public schools, for example, which have been forbidden since the early 1960s, are still said in a few local communities.

Of the topics in this book, the insertion of morality into legal discussions has occurred most frequently in the abortion and capital punishment debates

(Issues 9 and 14). It is probably fair to say that these issues remain high on the agenda of public debate because they involve strongly held values and beliefs. The nature of the debates is also colored by strong feelings that are held by the parties. Although empirical evidence about public health and abortion or about deterrence and capital punishment does exist, the debates are generally more emotional than objective.

Public Opinion and the Law

It is often claimed that the judicial process is insulated from public pressures. Judges are elected or appointed for long terms or for life, and the theory is that they will, therefore, be less subject to the force of public opinion. As a result, the law should be uniformly applied in different places, regardless of the nature of the community. It is fair to say that the judicial process is less responsive to public sentiment than is the political process, but that is not really saying much. What is important is that the legal process is not totally immune from public pressure. The force of public opinion is not applied directly through lobbying, but it would be naive to think that the force of what large numbers of people believe and desire never gets reflected in what happens in court. The most obvious examples are trials in which individuals are tried as much for their dissident beliefs as for their actions. Less obvious is the fact that the outcomes of cases may be determined in some measure by popular will. Judicial complicity in slavery or the internment of Japanese Americans during World War II are blatant examples of this.

Many of the issues selected for this volume are controversial because a large group is opposed to some practice sanctioned by the courts. Does this mean that the judges have taken a courageous stand and ignored public opinion? Not necessarily. Only in a few of the issues have courts adopted an uncompromising position. In most of the other issues, the trend of court decisions reflects a middle-of-the-road approach that could be interpreted as trying to satisfy everyone but those at the extremes. For example, in capital punishment (Issue 14), the original decision declaring the death penalty statutes unconstitutional was followed by the passing of new state laws, which were then upheld and which have led to a growing number of executions. Similarly, in affirmative action (Issue 11), the *Bakke* decision, while generally approving of affirmative action, was actually won by Bakke and led to the abolition of all such programs that contained rigid quotas.

ASSESSING INFLUENCES ON THE LAW

This summary of what can influence legal decisions is not meant to suggest that judges consciously ask what the public desires when interpretations of law are made. Rather, as members of society and as individuals who read newspapers and magazines and form opinions on political issues, there are subtle forces at work on judges that may not be obvious in any particular opinion but that can be discerned in a line of cases over a period of time.

This may be explicitly denied by judges, such as in this statement by Justice Harry A. Blackmun in his majority opinion for the landmark *Roe v. Wade* abortion case: "Our task, of course, is to resolve the issue by constitutional measurement, free of emotion and predilection." However, a reading of that opinion raises the question of whether or not Blackmun succeeds in being totally objective in his interpretation of law and history.

Do these external and internal influences corrupt the system, create injustice, inject bias and discrimination, and pervert the law? Or do these influences enable judges to be flexible, to treat individual circumstances, and to fulfill the spirit of the law? Both of these ends are possible and do occur. What is important to realize is that there are so many points in the legal system where discretion is employed that it is hopeless to think that we could be governed by rules alone. "A government of laws, not men," aside from the sexism of the language, is not a realistic possibility, and it is not an alternative that many would find satisfying either.

On the other hand, it is also fair to say that the law, in striving to get the public to trust in it, must persuade citizens that it is more than the whim of those who are in power. While it cannot be denied that the law may be used in self-serving ways, there are also mechanisms at work that are designed to limit abuses of discretionary power. One quality of law that is relevant to this problem is that the legal process is fundamentally a conservative institution, which is, by nature, resistant to radical change. Lawyers are trained to give primary consideration in legal arguments to precedent—previous cases involving similar facts. As attention is focused on how the present case is similar to or different from past cases, some pressure is exerted on new decisions to be consistent with old ones and on the law to be stable. Thus, the way in which a legal argument is constructed tends to reduce the influence of currently popular psychological, sociological, philosophical, or anthropological theories. Prior decisions will reflect ideologies, economic considerations, and ethical values that were influential when these decisions were made and, if no great change has occurred in the interim, the law will tend to preserve the status quo, both perpetuating old injustices and protecting traditional freedoms.

LEGAL PROCEDURE

The law's great concern with the procedure of decision making is one of its more basic and important characteristics. Any discussion of the law that did not note the importance of procedure would be inadequate. Legal standards are often phrased not in terms of results but in terms of procedure. For example, it is not unlawful to convict the innocent if the right procedures are used (and it is unlawful to convict the guilty if the wrong procedures are followed). The law feels that it cannot guarantee that the right result will always be reached and that only the guilty will be caught, so it minimizes the risk of reaching the wrong result or convicting the innocent by specifying procedural steps to be followed. Lawyers, more than most people, are satisfied if the right procedures are followed even if there is something disturbing about the outcome. Law, therefore, has virtually eliminated the word *justice* from its vocabulary and has substituted the phrase *due process*, meaning that the proper procedures, such as right to counsel, right to a public trial, and right to cross-examine witnesses, have been followed. This concern with method is one of the pillars upon which law is based. It is one of the characteristics of law that distinguishes it from nonlegal methods of dispute resolution, where the atmosphere will be more informal and there may be no set procedures. It is a trait of the law that is illustrated in Issue 1 (*Should Lawyers Be Prohibited from Presenting a False Case?*).

CONCLUSION

There is an often-told anecdote about a client who walks into a lawyer's office and asks the receptionist if the firm has a one-armed lawyer. The receptionist asks why in the world anyone would have such a preference. The client responds that he has already visited several lawyers to discuss his problem but could not get a definite answer from any of them. Their stock reply to his question of whether or not he would win his case began, "On the one hand this could happen and on the other hand...."

You may feel similarly frustrated as you examine the issues in this book. The subjects are not simple or amenable to simple solutions. The legal approach to problem solving is usually methodical and often slow. We frequently become frustrated with this process and, in fact, it may be an inappropriate way to deal with some problems. For the issues in this book, however, an approach that pays careful attention to the many different aspects of these topics will be the most rewarding. Many of the readings provide historical, economic, and sociological data as well as information about law. The issues examined in *Taking Sides* involve basic cultural institutions such as religion, schools, and the family as well as basic cultural values such as privacy, individualism, and equality. While the law takes a narrow approach to problems, reading these issues should broaden your outlook on the problems discussed and, perhaps, encourage you to do further reading on those topics that are of particular interest to you.

NOTES

1. Yankelovich, Skelly, and White, Inc., *The Public Image of Courts* (National Center for State Courts, 1978).
2. Iredell Jenkins, *Social Order and the Limits of Law* (Princeton University Press, 1980), p. xi.
3. Wardle, "The Gap Between Law and Moral Order: An Examination of the Legitimacy of the Supreme Court Abortion Decisions," *Brigham Young University Law Review* (1980), pp. 811–835.

PART 1

The Operation of Legal Institutions

According to much of what appears in the mass media, the public is increasingly disenchanted with many of the institutions that are part of the legal process. Critics complain about the proliferation of needless lawsuits, about lawyers and their tactics, and about courts that seem too lenient in their sentencing of serious criminals.

In this section we examine issues that involve our legal institutions, and the picture that emerges from these debates will reveal realities with which you may not be familiar.

- Should Lawyers Be Prohibited from Presenting a False Case?

- Does Mediation in Divorce Cases Hurt Women?

- Should Plea Bargaining Be Abolished?

- Are Term Limits for Elected Officials Unconstitutional?

ISSUE 1

Should Lawyers Be Prohibited from Presenting a False Case?

YES: Harry I. Subin, from "The Criminal Lawyer's 'Different Mission': Reflections on the 'Right' to Present a False Case," *Georgetown Journal of Legal Ethics* (vol. 1, 1987)

NO: John B. Mitchell, from "Reasonable Doubts Are Where You Find Them: A Response to Professor Subin's Position on the Criminal Lawyer's 'Different Mission,'" *Georgetown Journal of Legal Ethics* (vol. 1, 1987)

ISSUE SUMMARY

YES: Professor of law Harry I. Subin examines the ethical responsibilities of criminal defense lawyers and argues that greater responsibility should be placed on lawyers not to pervert the truth to help their clients.

NO: Attorney John B. Mitchell disputes the contention that the goal of the criminal justice process is to seek the truth and argues that it is essential that there be independent defense attorneys to provide protection against government oppression.

In 1732 Georgia was founded as a colony that was to have no lawyers. This was done with the goal of having a "happy, flourishing colony ... free from that pest and scourge of mankind called lawyers." While there are no serious efforts to abolish the legal profession today, public opinion surveys reveal that lawyers still are not held in the highest esteem. The public today may feel a little more positive about lawyers than did citizens of colonial America, and large numbers of students aspire to become lawyers, but hostility and criticism of what lawyers are and what they do are still common.

Part of the reason for the public's ambivalent attitude about lawyers concerns the adversary system and the lawyer's role in it. The adversary system requires that the lawyer's main responsibility be to the client. Except in rare instances, the lawyer is not to consider whether the client's cause is right or wrong and is not to allow societal or public needs to affect the manner in which the client is represented. The adversary system assumes that someone other than the client's lawyer is responsible for determining truth and guaranteeing justice.

The code of ethics of the legal profession instructs lawyers not to lie. However, it is permissible to mislead opponents—indeed, to do anything short of lying, if done to benefit the client. We have a system of "legal ethics" because some things lawyers are obligated to do for their clients would violate traditional standards of ethical behavior. As one legal scholar has written, "Where the attorney-client relationship exists, it is often appropriate and many times even obligatory for the attorney to do things that, all other things being equal, an ordinary person need not, and should not, do" (Richard W. Wasserstrom, "Lawyers as Professionals: Some Moral Issues," 5 *Human Rights* 1 [1975]).

In a highly publicized case that occurred a few years ago, two criminal defense lawyers learned from their client that, in addition to the crimes he was charged with, the client had murdered two girls who were missing. The lawyers discovered where the bodies were but refused to provide the parents of the missing children with any of this information. There was a public outcry when it was later discovered what the lawyers had done, but their position was generally felt to be consistent with standards of legal ethics.

Why do we have a legal system that allows truth to be concealed? Is a diminished concern with truth necessary in order to preserve the status and security of the individual? What should be the limits as to how one-sided legal representation should be? Would it be desirable to require lawyers to be more concerned with truth, so that they would be prohibited from putting forward positions they know are false? In the following selections, Harry I. Subin and John B. Mitchell debate whether or not increasing the attorney's "truth" function would be both desirable and feasible. As you read the selections, determine whether Subin's suggestion is a dangerous first step toward a more powerful state and less protection for the individual or whether it would increase public respect toward the legal system and the legal profession with little cost.

At the heart of the adversary system's attention to the relationship between client and counsel is the belief that there is something more important than discovering truth in every case. Finding the guilty and punishing them is not the sole goal of the criminal justice process. We rely on the criminal process, particularly trials, to remind us that our liberty depends on placing restrictions on the power of the state. The argument on behalf of the adversary model is that increasing the power of the state to find truth in one case may hurt all of us in the future. As you read the following selections, it will be difficult not to be troubled by the lawyer's dilemma; you may wonder if there is any acceptable middle ground when state power and individual rights clash.

YES

Harry I. Subin

THE CRIMINAL LAWYER'S "DIFFERENT MISSION": REFLECTIONS ON THE "RIGHT" TO PRESENT A FALSE CASE

I. THE INQUIRY

Should the criminal lawyer be permitted to represent a client by putting forward a defense the lawyer knows is false? . . .

Presenting a "false defense," as used here, means attempting to convince the judge or jury that facts established by the state and known to the attorney to be true are not true, or that facts known to the attorney to be false are true. While this can be done by criminal means—e.g., perjury, introduction of forged documents, and the like—I exclude these acts from the definition of false defense used here. I am not concerned with them because such blatant criminal acts are relatively uninteresting ethically, and both the courts and bar have rejected their use.[1]

My concern, instead, is with the presently legal means for the attorney to reach favorable verdict even if it is completely at odds with the facts. The permissible techniques include: (1) cross-examination of truthful government witnesses to undermine their testimony or their credibility; (2) direct presentation of testimony, not itself false, but used to discredit the truthful evidence adduced by the government, or to accredit a false theory; and (3) argument to the jury based on any of these acts. One looks in vain in ethical codes or case law for a definition of "perjury" or "false evidence" that includes these acts, although they are also inconsistent with the goal of assuring a truthful verdict.

To the extent that these techniques of legal truth-subversion have been addressed at all, most authorities have approved them. The American Bar Association's *Standards for Criminal Justice*,[2] for example, advises the criminal defense attorney that it is proper to destroy a truthful government witness when essential to provide the defendant with a defense, and that failure to do so would violate the lawyer's duty under the *Model Code of Professional*

From Harry I. Subin, "The Criminal Lawyer's 'Different Mission': Reflections on the 'Right' to Present a False Case," *Georgetown Journal of Legal Ethics*, vol. 1 (1987), pp. 125–138, 141–153. Copyright © 1987 by *Georgetown Journal of Legal Ethics*. Reprinted by permission. Some notes omitted.

Responsibility to represent the client zealously.[3] The *Standards for Criminal Justice* cite as authority for this proposition an opinion by Justice White in *United States v. Wade*,[4] which, in the most emphatic form, is to the same effect. In *Wade*, the Court held that in order to assure the reliability of the pretrial line-up, the right to counsel must be extended to the defendant compelled to participate in one.[5] Justice White warned that the presence of counsel would not necessarily assure that the identification procedure would be more accurate than if the police were left to conduct it themselves. The passage dealing with this issue, which includes the phrase that inspired the title of this piece, is worth repeating at length:

> Law enforcement officers have the obligation to convict the guilty and to make sure they do not convict the innocent. They must be dedicated to making the criminal trial a procedure for the ascertainment of the true facts surrounding the commission of the crime. To this extent, our so-called adversary system is not adversary at all; nor should it be. But defense counsel has no comparable obligation to ascertain or present the truth. Our system assigns him a different mission. He must be and is interested in preventing the conviction of the innocent, but... we also insist that he defend his client whether he is innocent or guilty. The State has the obligation to present evidence. Defense counsel need present nothing, even if he knows what the truth is. He need not furnish any witnesses to the police, or reveal any confidences of his client, or furnish any other information to help the prosecution's case. If he can confuse a witness, even a truthful one, or make him appear at a disadvantage, unsure or indecisive, that will be his normal course. Our interest in not convicting the innocent permits counsel to put the State to its proof, to put the State's case in the worst possible light, regardless of what he thinks or knows to be the truth. Undoubtedly there are some limits which defense counsel must observe but more often than not, defense counsel will cross-examine a prosecution witness, and impeach him if he can, even if he thinks the witness is telling the truth, just as he will attempt to destroy a witness who he thinks is lying. In this respect, as part of our modified adversary system and as part of the duty imposed on the most honorable defense counsel, we countenance or require conduct which in many instances has little, if any, relation to the search for truth.[6]

... The article begins with a description of a case I handled some years ago, one that I believe is a good illustration of the false defense problem. I next address the threshold question of the attorney's knowledge. It has been argued that the attorney cannot "know" what the truth is, and therefore is free to present any available defense theory. I attempt to demonstrate that the attorney can, in fact, know the truth, and I propose a process to determine when the truth is known.

I then analyze the arguments that have been advanced in support of the "different mission" theory: that the defense attorney, even if he or she knows the truth, remains free to disregard it in presenting a defense. I argue that neither the right to a defense nor the needs of the adversary system justify the presentation of a false defense. Finally, I describe a new standard that explicitly prohibits the defense attorney from asserting a false defense. I conclude with some thoughts as to why this rule would produce a generally more just system.

II. TRUTH SUBVERSION IN ACTION: THE PROBLEM ILLUSTRATED

A. The Accusation

About fifteen years ago I represented a man charged with rape and robbery. The victim's account was as follows: Returning from work in the early morning hours, she was accosted by a man who pointed a gun at her and took a watch from her wrist. He told her to go with him to a nearby lot, where he ordered her to lie down on the ground and disrobe. When she complained that the ground was hurting her, he took her to his apartment, located across the street. During the next hour there, he had intercourse with her. Ultimately, he said that they had to leave to avoid being discovered by the woman with whom he lived.[7] The complainant responded that since he had gotten what he wanted, he should give her back her watch. He said that he would.

As the two left the apartment, he said he was going to get a car. Before leaving the building, however, he went to the apartment next door, leaving her to wait in the hallway. When asked why she waited, she said that she was still hoping for the return of her watch, which was a valued gift, apparently from her boyfriend.

She never did get the watch. When they left the building, the man told her to wait on the street while he got the car. At that point she went to a nearby police precinct and reported the incident. She gave a full description of the assailant that matched my client. She also accurately described the inside of his apartment. Later, in response to a note left at his apartment by the police, my client came to the precinct, and the complainant identified him. My client was released at that time but was arrested soon thereafter at his apartment, where a gun was found.[8] No watch was recovered.

My client was formally charged, at which point I entered the case. At our initial interview and those that followed it, he insisted that he had nothing whatever to do with the crime and he had never seen the woman before.[9] He stated that he had been in several places during the night in question: visiting his aunt earlier in the evening, then traveling to a bar in New Jersey, where he was during the critical hours. He gave the name of a man there who would corroborate this. He said that he arrived home early the next morning and met a friend. He stated that he had no idea how this woman had come to know things about him such as what the apartment looked like, that he lived with a woman, and that he was a musician, or how she could identify him. He said that he had no reason to rape anyone, since he already had a woman, and that in any event he was recovering from surgery for an old gun shot wound and could not engage in intercourse. He said he would not be so stupid as to bring a woman he had robbed and was going to rape into his own apartment.

I felt that there was some strength to these arguments, and that there were questionable aspects to the complainant's story. In particular, it seemed strange that a man intending rape would be as solicitous of the victim's comfort as the woman said her assailant was at the playground. It also seemed that a person who had just been raped would flee when she had the chance to, and in any case would not be primarily concerned with the return of her watch. On balance, however, I suspected that my client was not telling me the truth. I thought the complaining witness could not possibly have known what she knew about him and his apartment, if she had not had any contact with him. True, someone else could have posed as him, and used his apartment. My client, however, could suggest no one who could have done so.[10] Moreover, that hypothesis did not explain the complainant's accurate description of him to the police. Although the identification procedure used by the police, a one person "show up," was suggestive,[11] the woman had ample opportunity to observe her assailant during the extended incident. I could not believe that the complainant had selected my client randomly to accuse falsely of rape. By both her and my client's admission, the two had not had any previous association.

That my client was probably lying to me had two possible explanations. First, he might have been lying because he was guilty and did not see any particular advantage to himself in admitting it to me. It is embarrassing to admit that one has committed a crime, particularly one of this nature. Moreover, my client might well have feared to tell me the truth. He might have believed that I would tell others what he said, or, at the very least, that I might not be enthusiastic about representing him.

He also might have lied not because he was guilty of the offense, but because he thought the concocted story was the best one under the circumstances. The sexual encounter may have taken place voluntarily, but the woman complained to the police because she was angry at my client for refusing to return the valued wrist watch, perhaps not stolen, but left, in my client's apartment. My client may not have been able to admit this, because he had other needs that took precedence over the particular legal one

that brought him to me. For example, the client might have felt compelled to deny any involvement in the incident because to admit to having had a sexual encounter might have jeopardized his relationship with the woman with whom he lived. Likewise, he might have decided to "play lawyer," and put forward what he believed to be his best defense. Not understanding the heavy burden of proof on the state in criminal cases, he might have thought that any version of the facts that showed that he had contact with the woman would be fatal because it would simply be a case of her word against his.

I discussed all of these matters with the client on several occasions. Judging him a man of intelligence, with no signs of mental abnormality, I became convinced that he understood both the seriousness of his situation, and that his exculpation did not depend upon maintaining his initial story. In ensuring that he did understand that, in fact, I came close enough to suggesting the "right" answers to make me a little nervous about the line between subornation of perjury and careful witness preparation, known in the trade as "horseshedding."[12] In the end, however, he held to his original account.

B. The Investigation

At this point the case was in equipoise for me. I had my suspicions about both the complainant's and the client's version of what had occurred, and I supposed a jury would as well. That problem was theirs, however, not mine. All I had to do was present my client's version of what occurred in the best way that I could.

Or was that all that was required? Committed to the adversarial spirit reflected in Justice White's observations about my role, I decided that it was not. The "different mission" took me beyond the task of presenting my client's position in a legally correct and persuasive manner, to trying to untrack the state's case in any lawful way that occurred to me, regardless of the facts.

With that mission in mind, I concluded that it would be too risky to have the defendant simply take the stand and tell his story, even if it were true. Unless we could create an iron-clad alibi, which seemed unlikely given the strength of the complainant's identification, I thought it was much safer to attack the complainant's story, even if it were true. I felt, however, that since my client had persisted in his original story I was obligated to investigate the alibi defense, although I was fairly certain that I would not use it. My students and I therefore interviewed everyone he mentioned, traveled and timed the route he said he had followed, and attempted to find witnesses who may have seen someone else at the apartment. We discovered nothing helpful. The witness my client identified as being at the bar in New Jersey could not corroborate the client's presence there. The times the client gave were consistent with his presence at the place of the crime when the victim claimed it took place. The client's aunt verified that he had been with her, but much earlier in the evening.

Because the alibi defense was apparently hopeless, I returned to the original strategy of attempting to undermine the complainant's version of the facts. I demanded a preliminary hearing, in which the complainant would have to testify under oath to the events in question. Her version was precisely as I have described it, and she told it in an objective manner that, far from seeming contrived, convinced me that she was telling the truth. She seemed a person who, if not at home with the meanness of the streets, was re-

signed to it. To me that explained why she was able to react in what I perceived to be a nonstereotypical manner to the ugly events in which she had been involved.

I explained to my client that we had failed to corroborate his alibi, and that the complainant appeared to be a credible witness. I said that in my view the jury would not believe the alibi, and that if we could not obtain any other information, it might be appropriate to think about a guilty plea, which would at least limit his exposure to punishment. The case, then in the middle of the aimless drift towards resolution that typifies New York's criminal justice system, was left at that.

Some time later, however, my client called me and told me that he had new evidence; his aunt, he said, would testify that he had been with her at the time in question. I was incredulous. I reminded him that at no time during our earlier conversations had he indicated what was plainly a crucial piece of information, despite my not too subtle explanation of an alibi defense. I told him that when the aunt was initially interviewed with great care on this point, she stated that he was not with her at the time of the crime. Ultimately, I told him that I thought he was lying, and that in my view even if the jury heard the aunt's testimony, they would not believe it.

Whether it was during that session or later that the client admitted his guilt I do not recall. I do recall wondering whether, now that I knew the truth, that should make a difference in the way in which the case was handled. I certainly wished that I did not know it and began to understand, psychologically if not ethically, lawyers who do not want to know their clients' stories.[13]

I did not pause very long to ponder the problem, however, because I concluded that knowing the truth in fact did not make a difference to my defense strategy, other than to put me on notice as to when I might be suborning perjury. Because the mission of the defense attorney was to defeat the prosecution's case, what I knew actually happened was not important otherwise. What did matter was whether a version of the "facts" could be presented that would make a jury doubt the client's guilt.

Viewed in this way, my problem was not that my client's story was false, but that it was not credible, and could not be made to appear so by legal means. To win, we would therefore have to come up with a better theory than the alibi, avoiding perjury in the process. Thus, the defense would have to be made out without the client testifying, since it would be a crime for him to assert a fabricated exculpatory theory under oath.[14] This was not a serious problem, however, because it would not only be possible to prevail without the defendant's testimony, but it would probably be easier to do so. Not everyone is capable of lying successfully on the witness stand, and I did not have the sense that my client would be very good at it.

There were two possible defenses that could be fabricated. The first was mistaken identity. We could argue that the opportunity of the victim to observe the defendant at the time of the original encounter was limited, since it had occurred on a dark street. The woman could be made out to have been in great emotional distress during the incident.[15] Expert testimony would have to be adduced to show the hazards of eyewitness identification.[16] We could demonstrate that an unreliable identification procedure had been used at the precinct.[17] On the other hand, given that the complainant had spent considerable time

with the assailant and had led the police back to the defendant's apartment, it seemed doubtful that the mistaken identification ploy would be successful.

The second alternative, consent, was clearly preferable. It would negate the charge of rape and undermine the robbery case.[18] To prevail, all we would have to do would be to raise a reasonable doubt as to whether he had compelled the woman to have sex with him. The doubt would be based on the scenario that the woman and the defendant met, and she voluntarily returned to his apartment. Her watch, the subject of the alleged robbery, was either left there by mistake or, perhaps better, was never there at all.

The consent defense could be made out entirely through cross-examination of the complainant, coupled with the argument to the jury about her lack of credibility on the issue of force. I could emphasize the parts of her story that sounded the most curious, such as the defendant's solicitude in taking his victim back to his apartment, and her waiting for her watch when she could have gone immediately to the nearby precinct that she went to later. I could point to her inability to identify the gun she claimed was used (although it was the one actually used), that the allegedly stolen watch was never found, there was no sign of physical violence, and no one heard screaming or any other signs of a struggle. I could also argue as my client had that even if he were reckless enough to rob and rape a woman across the street from his apartment, he would not be so foolish as to bring the victim there. I considered investigating the complainant's background, to take advantage of the right, unencumbered at the time, to impeach her on the basis of her prior unchastity.[19] I did not pursue this, however, because to me this device, although lawful, was fundamentally wrong. No doubt in that respect I lacked zeal, perhaps punishably so.

Even without assassinating this woman's character, however, I could argue that this was simply a case of a casual tryst that went awry. The defendant would not have to prove whether the complainant made the false charge to account for her whereabouts that evening, or to explain what happened to her missing watch. If the jury had reason to doubt the complainant's charges it would be bound to acquit the defendant.

How all of this would have played out at trial cannot be known. Predictably, the case dragged on so long that the prosecutor was forced to offer the unrefusable plea of possession of a gun.[20] As I look back, however, I wonder how I could justify doing what I was planning to do had the case been tried. I was prepared to stand before the jury posing as an officer of the court in search of the truth, while trying to fool the jurors into believing a wholly fabricated story, i.e., that the woman had consented, when in fact she had been forced at gunpoint to have sex with the defendant. I was also prepared to demand an acquittal because the state had not met its burden of proof when, if it had not, it would have been because I made the truth look like a lie. If there is any redeeming social value in permitting an attorney to do such things, I frankly cannot discern it. . . .

III. CAN LAWYERS "KNOW" THE TRUTH?

A. "The Adversary System" Excuse[21]
A principle argument in favor of the propriety of asserting a "false" defense

is that there is, for the lawyer, no such thing. The "truth," insofar as it is relevant to the lawyer, is what the trier of the fact determines it to be.[22] The role of the lawyer in the adversary system is not to interpose his or her own belief about what the facts are.[23] Instead, the truth will emerge through a dialectical process, in which the vigorous advocacy of thesis and antithesis will equip the neutral arbiter to synthesize the data and reach a conclusion. . . .

Suppose, for example, that I had interviewed the neighbor into whose apartment the defendant had gone following the rape—and who was unknown to the police. Suppose that he had told me that at the time of the incident he heard screams, and the sound of a struggle, and that my client had made incriminating remarks to him about what had occurred. It may be that there are reasons of policy that permit me to conceal these facts from the prosecution. It is ludicrous to assert, however, that because I can conceal them I do not know them. It is also ludicrous to suggest that if in addition I use my advocacy skills—and rights—to advance the thesis that there were no witnesses to the crime, I have engaged in a truth finding process.[24]

The argument that the attorney cannot know the truth until a court decides it fails. Either it is sophistry, designed to simplify the moral life of the attorney,[25] or it rests on a confusion between "factual truth" and "legal truth." The former relates to historical fact. The latter relates to the principle that a fact cannot be acted upon by the legal system until it is proven in accordance with legal rules. Plainly one can know the factual truth, for example, that one's client forced a woman to have sex with him, without or before knowing the legal truth that he is punishable for the crime of rape. The question is not whether an attorney can know the truth, but what standards should be applied in determining what the truth is. . . .

IV. DOES THE TRUTH MATTER? APPRAISING THE DIFFERENT MISSION

We confront at last the "Different Mission" argument we set out initially to examine. It is that the defense attorney has a broader function than protecting the innocent against wrongful conviction. Equally important is the task of protecting the factually guilty individual against overreaching by the state. The defense attorney may well be able to know the truth, but can be indifferent to it because it is the state's case, not the client's with which he or she is concerned. Professor Freedman puts it this way:

> The point . . . is not that the lawyer cannot know the truth, or that the lawyer refuses to recognize the truth, but rather that the lawyer is told: "You, personally, may very well know the truth, but your personal knowledge is irrelevant. In your capacity as an advocate (and, if you will, as an officer of the court) you are forbidden to act upon your personal knowledge of the truth, as you might want to do as a private person, because the adversary system could not function properly if lawyers did so."

The adversary system must function because it is our basic protection against governmental overreaching. The danger of such overreaching is so great, moreover, that we must allow the defense attorney broad latitude in disrupting that case, even by presenting a spurious defense.

Two principal arguments have been advanced to explain why the needs of the adversary system permit the attorney to assert a defense not founded upon the truth. The first is that a false defense may have to be asserted to protect the defendant's right in a particular case right to have a defense at all. The second argument is that it may be necessary to subvert the truth in a particular case as a way of demonstrating the supremacy of the autonomous individual in the face of the powerful forces of organized society.

A. Subverting the Truth to Protect the Defendant's Right to a Defense

The most commonly offered justification for a right to undermine a truthful case is that if there were no such right, the guilty defendant would effectively be deprived of a defense. All defendants, it is asserted, are entitled to have the state prove the case against them, whether they are factually innocent or guilty. If the spurious defense were not allowed it would be impossible to represent persons who had confessed their guilt to their lawyers, or who, in accordance with rules of the sort I advanced in the last section, were "found" guilty by them. The trial, if there were one at all, would not be an occasion to test the government's case, but a kind of elaborate plea of guilty. I believe that this argument fails for two reasons: first, because it proves too much, and second, because it is based on an erroneous assumption as to what the defendant's rights are.

If it were true that a false defense must be allowed to assure that the guilty defendant has a defense, it would seem to follow that presently established constraints on the defense attorney representing the guilty person, let alone an innocent person against whom the state had incriminating evidence, should be removed. An exception to the criminal laws prohibiting the deliberate introduction of false evidence would have to be adopted. Some have argued that a criminal defendant has a right to commit perjury, and that the defense attorney has a concomitant duty not to interfere with such testimony, or for that matter with even more extraordinary means of prevailing at trial.

The notion of a right to commit perjury, however, has been forcefully rejected by the courts[26] and by the organized bar, albeit less forcefully.[27] I suggest, however, that it cannot logically be rejected by those who espouse the Different Mission theory in defense of subverting the truth. If the right to mount a defense is paramount, and if the only conceivable defense which the guilty defendant can mount involves the defendant, or his or her witnesses committing perjury, and the defense attorney arguing that that perjury is true, then it follows that the restraints of the penal law should not be conceded to be applicable.[28] ...

The extravagant notion of the right to put on a defense is the second fallacy in the argument supporting a right to assert a false defense. Again, a moment's reflection on prevailing penal law limitations on advocacy will demonstrate that the defendant is not entitled to gain an acquittal by any available means.[29] Unless we abandon completely the notion that verdicts should be based upon the truth, we must accept the fact that there may simply be no version of the facts favorable to the defense worthy of assertion in a court. In such cases, the role of the defense attorney should be limited to assuring that the state adduces sufficient legally competent evidence to sustain its burden of proof. ...

Subverting the Truth to Preserve Individual Autonomy Against Encroachment by the State

The second prong of the "different mission" theory is that the truth must be sacrificed in individual cases as a kind of symbolic act designed to reaffirm our belief in the supremacy of the individual. This theory in turn is argued in several different ways.

The false defense may be necessary to preserve the individual's access to the legal system.

This argument is based on the proposition that because the legal system is so complex, meaningful access requires representation by an attorney. An attorney cannot perform his or her function unless the client provides the facts. The client will not do that if the facts will be used against the client, as, in this context, by not providing an available false defense. Thus it is necessary to permit the attorney to conceal harmful information obtained from the client and to act as if it did not exist.

As I have argued elsewhere, the importance of confidentiality to the performance of the lawyer's role has been greatly overstated. Even conceding its value, it does not seem to me that permitting the attorney to achieve the client's ends by subverting the truth advances the cause of individual autonomy. The legitimate concern of those who advance the autonomy argument is that the government must be prevented from interfering wrongfully or unnecessarily with individual freedom, not that there should be no interference with individual liberty at all. Here we are positing that the government has behaved reasonably, and the lawyer knows it. In my view, permitting such a case to be undermined by false evidence glorifies winning, but has very little to do with assuring justice.[30]

A false defense may be necessary to preserve the rigorous process by which guilt is determined.

Those taking this view see the criminal process not as a truth-seeking one, but a "screening system" designed to assure the utmost certainty before the criminal sanction is imposed. Only by permitting the defense attorney to use all of the tools which we have described here can we be certain that the prosecution will be put to its proof in all cases. The argument seems to be that if the prosecutor knows that the defense attorney will attempt to demolish the government's case, the prosecutor will in a sense be kept on his or her toes, and will seek the strongest evidence possible.[31]

This position is difficult to understand. In the situation under discussion here the prosecution has presented the strongest case possible, i.e., the truthful testimony of the victim of a crime. In any case, it is one thing to attack a weak government case by pointing out its weakness. It is another to attack a strong government case by confusing the jury with falsehoods. Finally, as a proponent of this "screening theory" concedes, there may be a danger that if the prosecutor sees that the truth alone is inadequate, he or she may be inspired to embellish it. That, of course, is not likely to make the screening mechanism work better.

For others, the desirability of prevailing against the state seems to be seen not as a means to assure that the prosecution will strive for high standards of proof, but as a positive good in its own right. The goal, as Professor Schwartz has put it, is to prevent the "behemoth" state from becoming a "juggernaut."[32] Schwartz states

that "[c]ross-examination to give the impression that [witnesses] are telling falsehoods may be justified as a way of keeping the state from overreaching,"[33] but we are not told what precise danger this will avert, or how it will do so. I cannot discern these, either, unless one takes the view that the exercise of a particular state power is inherently wrong, justifying resistence by any means. Otherwise, it would seem sufficient to insure that the defendant had a right to make a good faith challenge to the state's allegations.

V. ACCOMPLISHING THE DEFENSE ATTORNEY'S DIFFERENT MISSION—MORALLY

I propose a system in which the defense attorney would operate not with the right to assert defenses known to be untrue, but under the following rule:

> It shall be improper for an attorney who knows beyond a reasonable doubt the truth of a fact established in the state's case to attempt to refute that fact through the introduction of evidence, impeachment of evidence, or argument.

In the face of this rule, the attorney who knew there were no facts to contest would be limited to the "monitoring" role. Assuming that a defendant in my client's situation wanted to assert his right to contest the evidence against him, the attorney would work to assure that all of the elements of the crime were proven beyond a reasonable doubt, on the basis of competent and admissible evidence. This would include enforcing the defendant's rights to have privileged or illegally obtained evidence excluded: The goal sought here is not the elimination of all rules that result in the suppression of truth, but only those not supported by sound policy. It would also be appropriate for the attorney to argue to the jury that the available evidence is not sufficient to sustain the burden of proof. It would not, however, be proper for the attorney to use any of the presently available devices to refute testimony known to be truthful. I wish to make clear, however, that this rule would not prevent the attorney from challenging *inaccurate* testimony, even though the attorney knew that the defendant was guilty. Again, the truth-seeking goal is not applicable when a valid policy reason exists for ignoring it. Forcing the state to prove its case is such a reason.[34]

Applying these principles to my rape case, I would engage fully in the process of testing the admissibility of the state's evidence, moving to suppress testimony concerning the suggestive "show-up" identification at the precinct, and the gun found in the defendant's apartment after a warrantless search, should the state attempt to offer either piece of evidence. At the trial, I would be present to assure that the complainant testified in accordance with the rules of evidence.

Assuming that she testified at trial as she had at the preliminary hearing, however, I would not cross-examine her, because I would have no good faith basis for impeaching either her testimony or her character, since I "knew" that she was providing an accurate account of what had occurred.[35] Nor would I put on a defense case. I would limit my representation at that stage to putting forth the strongest argument I could that the facts presented by the state did not sustain its burden. In these ways, the defendant would receive the services of an attorney in subjecting the state's case to the final stage of the screening process provided by the system to insure against

unjust convictions. That, however, would be all that the defense attorney could do....

VI. CONCLUSION

...If this proposal seems radical, consider that it is essentially an adaptation of what today is the principal function of the defense attorney in every criminal justice system of significance in this nation. That function is not to create defenses out of whole cloth to present to juries, but to guide the defendant through a process that will usually end in a guilty plea. It will so end, at least when competent counsel are involved, very frequently because the defense attorney has concluded after thorough analysis that there is no answer to the state's case. If that role can be played in out of court resolution of the matter there seems to be no reason why it cannot be played in court, when the defendant insists upon his right to a trial. The important point is that the right to a trial does not embody the right to present to the tribunal any evidence at all, no matter how fictitious it is.

NOTES

1. *Nix v. Whiteside*, 106 S. Ct. 988 (1986) (criminal defendant not denied effective assistance of counsel when attorney refused to allow him to present perjured testimony);...

2. Standard 4-7.6 (2d ed. 1980 & Supp. 1986). The ABA apparently has had a complete reversal in its view of this matter. *See* ABA STANDARDS RELATING TO THE ADMINISTRATION OF CRIMINAL JUSTICE, Compilation, at 132 (1974). Standard 4-7.6 states that the lawyer "should not misuse the power of cross-examination or impeachment by employing it to discredit or undermine a witness if he knows the witness is testifying truthfully."

3. MODEL CODE DR 7-101(A)(1) and EC 7-1. DR 7-102 appears on its face to be to the contrary, prohibiting lawyers from, *inter alia*, conducting a defense merely to harass another (subd. (1));

knowingly using false evidence (subd. (3)); making a false statement of fact (subd. (5)); creating or preserving false evidence (subd. (6)); or assisting the client in fraudulent conduct (subd. (7)). None of the noncriminal acts with which this article is concerned, however, have, to the author's knowledge, been cited by the bar as coming within the proscription of DR 7-102.

A similar conclusion can be reached with respect to the *Model Rules*. Rule 3.3 is an adaptation of DR 7-102, *see* rule 3.3, model code comparison. Rule 3.1 suggests that the drafters approved of the precise conduct under discussion here, at least for criminal lawyers. The rule prohibits assertion or controversion of an issue at trial unless there is a reasonable basis for doing so, except in criminal cases. The criminal case exception is based upon the drafter's conclusion, mistaken in my view, that the constitutional requirement that the state shoulder the burden of proof requires that the defense attorney be permitted to "put the prosecution to its proof even if there is no 'reasonable basis' for the defense." MODEL RULES Rule 3.1 model code comparison.

4. 388 U.S. 218, 250 (1967) (White, J., joined by Harlan and Stewart, J.J., dissenting in part and concurring in part).

5. *Id.* at 236–37.

6. *Id.* at 256–58 (footnotes omitted).

7. She also said that he told her that he was a musician. The significance of this remark will appear shortly.

8. The woman was not able to make a positive identification of the gun as the weapon used in the incident.

9. A student working on the case with me photographed the complainant on the street. My client stated that he could not identify her.

10. The woman had indicated that her assailant opened the door with a key. There was no evidence of a forced entry.

11. *Cf. Stovall v. Denno*, 338 U.S. 293 (1967) (identification in which murder suspect shown alone to and positively identified by bedridden, hospitalized victim not unnecessarily suggestive and therefore did not deny defendant due process).

12. The dilemma faced by the lawyer is whether, in explaining to the client the legal implications of conduct, he or she is shaping the client's version of the facts. The issue was put dramatically in R. TRAVER, ANATOMY OF A MURDER (1958), in which the attorney explained the facts needed to establish an insanity defense to an apparently normal person accused of murder. *Id.* at 44–47. Whether I was quite as blatant I frankly cannot remember, but it is clear that I did more than simply listen to what the client said. I explained how one would make out an alibi defense, and I made sure that he understood both that consent was a defense to rape,

and that corroboration was necessary to support a rape conviction.

13. *See* Mitchell, *The Ethics of the Criminal Defense Attorney—New Answers to Old Questions*, 32 STAN L. REV. 293 n. 12 (1980) (author properly analogizes lawyer's preference not to know of the client's guilt to the doctrine of "conscious avoidance," which constitutes "knowledge" under criminal law).

14. The notion that the defendant in a criminal case has a right to commit perjury was finally put to rest in *Nix v. Whiteside*, 106 S. Ct. 988 (1986) (criminal defendant not denied effective assistance of counsel when attorney refused to allow him to present perjured testimony).

15. This would be one of those safe areas in cross-examination, where the witness was damned no matter what she answered. If she testified that she was distressed, it would make my point that she was making an unreliable identification; if she testified that she was calm, no one would believe her. Perhaps this is why cross-examination has been touted as "beyond any doubt the greatest legal engine ever invented for the discovery of truth." 5 J. WIGMORE, EVIDENCE § 1367 (J. Chadbourn rev. ed. 1974). Another commentator makes similar claims for his art, and while he acknowledges in passing that witnesses might tell the truth, he at no point suggests what the cross-examiner should do when faced with such a situation. F. WELLMAN, THE ART OF CROSS-EXAMINATION 7 (4th ed. 1936). The cross-examiner's world, rather, seems to be divided into two types of witnesses: those whose testimony is harmless and those whose testimony must be destroyed on pain of abandoning "all hope for a jury verdict." *Id.* at 9.

16. On the dangers of misidentification, *see, e.g., United States v. Wade*, 388 U.S. 218 (1967). The use of experts to explain the misidentification problem to the jury is well established. *See generally* E. LOFTUS, EYEWITNESS TESTIMONY 191–203 (1979) (discussing ways expert testimony on eye witness testimony can be used and problems arising from its use).

17. *See Watkins v. Sowders*, 499 U.S. 341 (1981) (identification problems properly attacked during cross-examination at trial; no per se rule compelling judicial determination outside presence of jury concerning admissibility of identification evidence).

18. Consent is a defense to a charge of rape. *E.g.*, N.Y. PENAL LAW § 130.05 (McKinney 1975 & Supp. 1987). While consent is not a defense to a robbery charge, N.Y. PENAL LAW § § 160.00–15 (McKinney 1975 & Supp. 1987), if the complainant could be made out to be a liar about the rape, there was a good chance that the jury would not believe her about the stolen watch either.

19. When this case arose it was common practice to impeach the complainant in rape cases by eliciting details of her prior sexual activities. Subsequently the rules of evidence were amended

to require a specific showing of relevance to the facts of the case. N.Y. CRIM. PROC. LAW § 60.42 (McKinney 1981 & Supp. 1987).

20. The client, who had spent time in jail awaiting trial, was not given an additional prison sentence.

21. The phrase is the title of David Luban's essay, *The Adversary System Excuse*, in THE GOOD LAWYER: LAWYERS' ROLES AND LAWYERS' ETHICS 83 (D. Luban ed. 1983).

22. *See* M. FRANKEL, PARTISAN JUSTICE, *supra* note 43, at 24. Judge Frankel, who is critical of this theory, quotes the famous answer of Samuel Johnson to the question how he can represent a bad cause: "Sir, you do not know it to be good or bad till the judge determines it." *Id.* (quoting J. BOSWELL, THE LIFE OF SAMUEL JOHNSON 366 (1925)).

23. MODEL CODE DR 7-106©(4) provides in part that a lawyer shall not "[a]ssert his personal opinion as to the justness of a cause, as to the credibility of a witness... or as to the guilt or innocence of an accused...."

24. My "proof" that there were no witnesses to the crime would come in the form of an "accrediting" cross-examination of the complainant and/or a police officer who testified. I could inquire of both concerning whether they saw or otherwise became aware of the presence of any witnesses, and then argue to the jury that their negative answers established that there were none.

25. As all lawyers who are honest with themselves know, occasions arise when doubts about a client turn into suspicion and then moral certainty that a client is lying. Although his professional role may require a lawyer to take a detached attitude of unbelief, the law of lawyering does not permit a lawyer to escape all accountability by suspending his intelligence and common sense. A lawyer may try to persuade himself that he is not absolutely sure whether his client is committing perjury.... But all authorities agree... that there comes a point when only brute rationalization, moral irresponsibility, and pure sophistry can support the contention that the lawyer does not "know" what the situation is.

G. HAZARD & W. HODES, THE LAW OF LAWYERING: A HANDBOOK ON THE MODEL RULES OF PROFESSIONAL CONDUCT 343 (1985) (citing M. FREEDMAN, *supra* note 6, at 52–55, 71–76 (1975)).

26. *Nix v. Whiteside*, 106 S. Ct. 988 (1986) (criminal defendant not denied effective assistance of counsel when attorney refused to permit him to present perjured testimony).

27. The *Model Code* prohibits the knowing introduction of perjured testimony or false evidence. MODEL CODE DR 7-102(A)(4). The *Model Code* essentially eliminates, however, the duty of the attorney to disclose the client's attempt to commit these crimes, by prohibiting such disclosure if it would reveal a protected privileged communication. MODEL CODE DR 7-102(B)(1). The *Model Rules*, however, prohibit the introduction of false testimony, and appear to modify the restriction on disclosure of client misconduct in this area. The *Model Rules* require the attorney to disclose to the court that false evidence has been introduced. MODEL RULES Rule 3.3. The disclosure requirement ends, however, if the criminal conduct of the client is not discovered until after the proceeding has ended.

28. For example, if in my rape case there were incontrovertible evidence that force had been used on the complainant, the consent defense would have been impossible. I would then have had to revert to the mistaken identification defense. Given the strength of the complainant's identification testimony, the defendant's or his aunt's perjurious testimony might have been necessary to provide a defense at all.

29. In addition to the laws against perjury, there are laws, for example, against tampering with witnesses, 18 U.S.C. §§ 1512–14 (1982 & Supp. 1985) and bribery, 18 U.S.C. § 201 (1982).

30. It is ironic that some who have supported the right to put on a false defense do so as part of the argument that defending the guilty teaches a lesson to the defendant, especially the indigent defendant, that the system is fair.... Again, the problem is the failure to distinguish between the right to a defense and the right to a false defense. Commenting on the criminal justice system in general, Jonathan Casper has observed that it "not only fails to teach [defendants] moral lessons, but reinforces the idea that the system has no moral content." Casper, *Did You Have A Lawyer When You Went to Court? No, I Had A Public Defender*, 1 YALE REV. L. & SOC. ACTION 4, 9 (1971). The same could very well be said of a method of representation in which the defendant sees the lawyer, an official of the system, attempting to win by engaging in conduct similar to that which may have brought the defendant to court.

31. The cross-examination of the "truthful" witness is justified... [because] [w]eaknesses in the witness' testimony brought out on cross-examination will make the prosecution understand the range in "quality" of evidence for subsequent cases so that in the future he or she will recognize and seek the best evidence possible.

Mitchell, *supra* note 34, at 312 n.67.

32. Schwartz, *The Zeal of the Civil Advocate*, 1983 AM. B. FOUND. RES. J. 543, 554.

33. *Id.*

34. My colleague Stephen Gillers, for whose thoughtful criticism of my view I am indebted, called my attention to this illustrative case, ruled

on by the Michigan State Bar Committee on Professional and Judicial Ethics:

A defendant is charged with armed robbery. The victim testifies that the defendant robbed him at 1:00 p.m. The defendant has confessed to his lawyer. In fact, the robbery took place at 1:30 p.m. The victim is in error about the time. The defendant has a solid and truthful alibi witness who will testify that the defendant was with the witness at 1:00 p.m.

The question presented was whether the defense could call the alibi witness. The Bar Committee answered affirmatively. Michigan State Bar Committee of Professional and Judicial Ethics Op. CI-1164, Jan. 23, 1987, *reported in* 3 LAWYER'S MANUAL ON PROFESSIONAL CONDUCT (ABA/BNA) No. 3, at 44 (March 4, 1987). I would agree. The state's proof of the time of the crime was incorrect, and therefore subject to impeachment. I would not, however, permit the defense to offer evidence that the crime occurred at 1:00 p.m. if the victim correctly testified that it occurred at 1:30 p.m.

35. I recently made an informal presentation of this position to a group of my colleagues, who beseiged me with hypotheticals, the most provocative of which were these: (A) A witness not wearing her glasses, identifies my client as having been at a certain place. If my client were in fact at that place, could I cross-examine the witness on the grounds that she was not wearing her glasses? The answer is yes: The witness' ability to perceive affects the quality of the state's proof, and the fact that she happened to be correct is irrelevant. (B) In the same situation, except here I knew that the witness was wearing her glasses. Could I cross-examine the witness in an effort to show that she was not? The answer is no: The state had adduced reliable evidence, and that is all that it was required to do.

I was also asked whether I would apply the same truth based rule and refuse, in the situation described in (B), to impeach the witness if I knew that my client were innocent. My first response was something of a dodge: If I knew that, it was difficult for me to see why I would have to impeach this witness. Ultimately (albeit tentatively) I would conclude that it was too dangerous to adopt the notion that even these ends justified subverting the truth, and I would not cross-examine on that point.

NO

John B. Mitchell

REASONABLE DOUBTS ARE WHERE YOU FIND THEM: A RESPONSE TO PROFESSOR SUBIN'S POSITION ON THE CRIMINAL LAWYER'S "DIFFERENT MISSION"

I. INTRODUCTION

In *A Criminal Lawyer's "Different Mission": Reflections on the "Right" to Present a False Case*,[1] Professor Harry I. Subin attempts to draw what he considers to be the line between attorney as advocate, and attorney as officer of the court. Specifically, he "attempts to define the limits on the methods a lawyer should be willing to use when his client's goals are inconsistent with truth."[2] This is no peripheral theme in professional responsibility. Quite the contrary, Professor Subin has chosen a difficult issue which touches upon the very nature of our criminal justice system, the role of the attorney in that system, the relationship of the individual to the state, and the Constitution. Further, Professor Subin takes a tough and controversial stand on this issue and, although I disagree with him, I respect his position....

II. PROFESSOR SUBIN'S ASSUMPTIONS

Professor Subin rests his entire analysis on two basic premises: (1) the principle goal of the criminal justice system is "truth"; and (2) it is contrary to the goal of "truth" to permit a criminal defense attorney to put on a "false defense." In Subin's terms, a false defense is an attempt to "convince the judge or jury that facts established by the state and known to the attorney to be true are not true, or that the facts known to the attorney to be false are true." Such a defense is put on by: " ... (1) cross-examination of truthful government witnesses to undermine their testimony or their credibility; (2) direct presentation of testimony, not in itself false, but used to discredit the truthful evidence adduced by the government, or to accredit a false theory; and, (3) argument to the jury based on any of these acts." I take exception to both of these premises, as set out below.[3]

A. The Principal Concern of the Criminal Justice System Is Not "Truth"

The idea that the focus of the criminal justice system is not "truth" may initially sound shocking. I have valued truth throughout my life and do not condone lying in our legal system. But the job of our criminal justice system is simply other than determining "truth." ...

A system focused on truth would first collect all information relevant to the inquiry. In our system, the defendant is generally the best source of information in the dispute, but he is not available unless he so chooses. The police may not question him. He may not be called to the stand with his own lawyer beside him and with a judge controlling questioning under the rules of evidence. The prosecutor may not even comment to the jury about the defendant's failure to testify, even though fair inferences may be drawn from the refusal to respond to serious accusations.

A system focused on truth would have the factfinder look at all the information and then decide what it believed had occurred. In our system, the inquiry is dramatically skewed against finding guilt. "Beyond a reasonable doubt" expresses the deep cultural value that "it is better to let ten guilty men go than convict one innocent man." It is a system where, after rendering a verdict of not guilty, jurors routinely approach defense counsel and say, "I thought your guy was guilty, but that prosecutor did not prove it to me beyond a reasonable doubt." What I have just described is not a "truth system" in any sense in which one could reasonably understand that term.[4] Truth may play a role, but it is not a dominant role; there is something else afoot.[5] The criminal defense attorney does not have a "different mission";[6] the system itself has a "different mission." ...

Put directly, the criminal justice system protects the individual from the police power of the executive branch of government. Between the individual citizen and the enormous governmental power residing in the executive stands a panel of that individual's peers—a jury. Through them, the executive must pass. Only if it proves its case "beyond a reasonable doubt," thereby establishing legal guilt, may the executive then legitimately intrude into the individual citizen's life. Thus, "factual" guilt or innocence, or what Professor Subin would call "truth," is not the principle issue in the system. Our concern is with the legitimate use of the prosecutor's power as embodied in the concept of "legal guilt." ...

B. A Defense Attorney Acting in a Manner Meeting with Subin's Disapproval Is Not Putting on a "False Defense"

When placed in the "reasonable doubt" context, Professor Subin's implicit distinction between "true" and "false" defenses misportrays both how a defense attorney may actually function in a case, and the very nature of evidence in that case. His categories are too imprecise to capture the subtle middle ground of a pure reasonable doubt defense, in which counsel presents the jury with alternative possibilities that counsel knows are false, without asserting the truth of those alternatives.

For example, imagine I am defending a young woman accused of shoplifting a star one places on top of Christmas trees. I interview the store manager and find that he stopped my client when he saw her walk straight through the store, star in hand, and out the door. When he stopped her and asked why she had taken the star without paying, she made no reply and burst into tears. He was then about to take her inside to the security office when an employee called out, "There's a fire!" The manager rushed inside and dealt with a small blaze in the camera section. Five minutes later he came out to find my client sitting where he had left her. He then took her back to the security room and asked if she would be willing to empty her pockets so that he could see if she had taken anything else. Without a word, she complied. She had a few items not belonging to the store and a ten-dollar bill. The star was priced at $1.79.

In an interview with my client, she admitted trying to steal the star: "It was so pretty, and would have looked so nice on the tree. I would have bought it, but I also wanted to make a special Christmas dinner for Mama and didn't have enough money to do both. I've been saving for that dinner and I know it will make her so happy. But that star.... I could just see the look in Mama's eyes if she saw that lovely thing on our tree."

At trial, the manager tells the same story he told me, except he *leaves out* the part about her waiting during the fire and having a ten-dollar bill. If I bring out these two facts on cross-examination and argue for an acquittal based upon my client "accidentally" walking out of the store with the star, surely Professor Subin will accuse me of raising a "false defense." I have brought out testimony, not itself false, to accredit a false theory and have argued to the jury based on this act. But I am not really arguing a false theory in Professor Subin's sense.

My defense is not that the defendant accidentally walked out, but rather that the prosecution cannot prove the element of intent to permanently deprive beyond

a reasonable doubt. Through this theory, I am raising "doubt" in the prosecution's case, and therefore questioning the legitimacy of the government's lawsuit for control over the defendant. In my effort to carry out this legal theory, I will *not assert* that facts known by me to be true are false or those known to be false are true. As a defense attorney, I do not have to prove what *in fact* happened. That is an advantage in the process I would not willingly give up. Under our constitutional system, I do not need to try to convince the factfinder about the truth of any factual propositions. I need only try to convince the factfinder that the prosecution has not met its burden. Again, I will not argue that particular facts are true or false. Thus, in this case I will not claim that my client walked out of the store with innocent intent (a fact which I know is false); rather, I will argue:

> The prosecution claims my client stole an ornament for a Christmas tree. The prosecution further claims that when my client walked out of that store she intended to keep it without paying. Now, maybe she did. None of us were there. On the other hand, she had $10.00 in her pocket, which was plenty of money with which to pay for the ornament without the risk of getting caught stealing. Also, she didn't try to conceal what she was doing. She walked right out of the store holding it in her hand. Most of us have come close to innocently doing the same thing. So, maybe she didn't. But then she cried the minute she was stopped. She might have been feeling guilty. So, maybe she did. On the other hand, she might just have been scared when she realized what had happened. After all, she didn't run away when she was left alone even though she knew the manager was going to be occupied with the fire inside. So, maybe she didn't. The

point is that, looking at all the evidence, you're left with "maybe she intended to steal, maybe she didn't." But, you knew that before the first witness was even sworn. The prosecution has the burden, and he simply can't carry any burden let alone "beyond a reasonable doubt" with a maybe she did, maybe she didn't case....

Is this a "false defense" for Professor Subin? Admittedly, I am trying to raise a doubt by persuading the jury to appreciate "possibilities" other than my client's guilt. Perhaps Professor Subin would say it is "false" because I know the possibilities are untrue. But if that is so, Professor Subin will have taken a leap from defining "false defense" as the assertion that true things are false and false things are true, for I am doing neither of those things here. The fact that one cannot know how Subin would reach this "pure" reasonable doubt case only reinforces my initial statement that Professor Subin's categories are imprecise.

Another perspective from which to look at the function of a defense attorney involves understanding that function in the context of the nature of evidence at trial. Professor Subin speaks of facts and the impropriety of trying to make "true facts" look false and "false facts" look true. But in a trial there are no such things as facts. There is only information, lack of information, and chains of inferences therefrom. In the courtroom there will be no crime, no store, no young girl with a star in her hand. All there will be is a collection of witnesses who are strangers to the jury, giving information which may include physical evidence and documents. For example, most people would acknowledge the existence of eyewitness identifications; however, in an evidentiary sense they do not exist. Rather, a particular person with particular perceptual abilities and motives and biases will recount an observation made under particular circumstances and utter particular words on the witness stand (e.g., "That's the man"). From this mass of information, the prosecution will argue, in story form, in favor of the inference that the defendant is their man (e.g., "The victim was on her way home, when...."). The defense will not then argue that the defendant is the wrong man in a *factual* sense, but instead will attack the persuasiveness of the criminal inference and resulting story (e.g., "The sun was in the witness' eyes; she was on drugs").

In our shoplifting example, the prosecution will elicit that the defendant burst into tears when stopped by the manager. From this information will run a chain of inferences: defendant burst into tears, people without a guilty conscience would explain their innocence, not cry; defendant has a guilty conscience; her guilty conscience is likely motivated by having committed a theft. Conversely, if the defense brings out that the manager was shaking a lead pipe in his hand when he stopped the defendant, defense counsel is *not asserting* that defendant did not have a guilty conscience when stopped. Counsel is merely *weakening* the persuasiveness of the prosecution's inference by raising the "possibility" that she was crying not from guilt, but from fear. By raising such "possibilities," the defense is making arguments against the ability of the prosecution's inferences to meet their burden of "beyond a reasonable doubt." The defense is not arguing what are true or false facts (i.e., that the tears were from fear as opposed to guilt). Whatever Professor Subin cares to call it, this commentary on the prosecution's case, complete with raising possibilities which weaken the persuasiveness of central inferences in that case, is in no ethical sense a "false case." "False case" is plainly a misnomer. In a system where factual guilt is not at issue, Professor Subin's "falsehoods" are, in fact, "reasonable doubts."

C. Even If Criminal Defense Attorneys Do Raise a "False Defense," the Role of the Defense Attorney in the Criminal Justice System Permits Such a Defense

Professor Subin does not seek to eliminate all impediments to truth, just those based upon sound policy. In failing to appreciate fully the institutional role of the defense attorney, he glosses over a major countervailing policy: even if the attorney is putting forth what Subin would term "false defense," this defense is the side effect, not the goal or function of the defense attorney's role in the criminal justice system.

Subin apparently believes that the principal position he must overcome from his opponents who seek leeway with the "truth" is that such leeway is necessary to protect the adversary system, and the adversary system, in turn, is necessary to protect the factually guilty from "overreaching by the state."[7] My position, however, does not rest on these ideas. Though the adversary system serves to protect the factually guilty from state overreaching, my position is principally based upon the criminal justice system—a system with rationales different from the general adversary system, including the protection of the factually innocent.[8]

Our criminal justice system is more appropriately defined as a screening system than as a truth-seeking one.[9] The ultimate objective of this screening system is to determine who are the proper subjects of criminal sanction. The process goes on continually. Someone notices a window which looks pried open or a suspicious-looking stranger. Neighbor talks to neighbor, and information filters to the police. The police comb the streets gathering information, focusing upon those whose behavior warrants special attention. Those selected by the police for special attention are then placed in the hands of prosecutors, courts, and juries who constantly sift through this "residue" to make final determinations about who is to be subjected to criminal sanction.

The criminal justice system is itself composed of a series of "screens," of which trial is but one. These screens help keep innocents out of the process and, at the same time, limit the intrusion of the state into people's lives. Each of these screens functions to protect the values of human dignity and autonomy, while enforcing our criminal laws. Further, to ensure that the intrusion of the state into the individual's life will be halted at the soonest possible juncture, our system provides a separate screen at each of the several stages of the criminal process. At any screen, the individual may be taken out of the criminal process and returned to society with as little disruption as possible.

By pushing hard in every case (whether the client is factually guilty or not) and thereby raising "reasonable doubts" in the prosecution's case whenever possible, the defense attorney helps "make the screens work" and thus protects the interests of the factually innocent.[10]...

III. PROFESSOR SUBIN'S APPROACH

... My analysis in this section will focus upon Professor Subin's basic approach to "defin[ing] the limits on the methods a lawyer should be willing to use when his or her client's goals are inconsistent with the truth"; i.e., distinguishing between the role of what Subin calls a "monitor" and the more familiar role of "advocate." ...

To illustrate, imagine I am representing a defendant accused of robbery. I have seen the victim at a preliminary hearing, and based upon the circumstances of the identification and my overall impression of the witness, I am certain that he is truthful and accurate. My client has confessed his factual guilt. And therefore I "know" (in Professor Subin's sense) beyond a reasonable doubt that my client has been accurately identified.

In his direct examination, the victim states, "The defendant had this big, silvery automatic pistol right up near my face the whole time he was asking for money." In accordance with Professor Subin's view that defense counsel can "persuade the jury that there are legitimate reasons to doubt the state's evidence," may I raise the general vagaries of eyewitness identification?

> All of us have had some stranger come up to us, call us by an unfamiliar name, and indicate they thought we were someone they knew. We have been with a friend who points to someone a few tables over exclaiming, "Isn't she an exact double of Sue Smith? Could be her twin," and we think to ourselves that other than the hair color, there is no resemblance at all.

Perhaps Subin would say I cannot make the misidentification argument. He might argue that the "legitimacy" of reasons to doubt the state's evidence is not to be judged from the perspective of a reasonable juror hearing the prosecution's evidence but from my subjective knowledge. Since I "know" that there was no difficulty with the identification, I cannot put forward a "legitimate" reason to doubt. If this is Professor Subin's meaning, I, as monitor, am left with the following closing argument: "Ladies and gentlemen, thank you for your attention to this case. Remember, the prosecution must prove each element beyond a reasonable doubt. Thank you." The Constitution aside (and in my view this would be putting the Constitution aside), it is hard to imagine this is Subin's intended result.

"Legitimate reason" to doubt must refer to a reasonable juror's perception of the state's evidence, not to the defense attorney's private knowledge. Bringing out reasonable doubts in the state's evidence concerning the identification therefore must be legitimate, and yet this would seem to raise a "false defense" (i.e., mistaken identification). Presumably, Subin would permit this defense because of a greater policy than "truth," i.e., the right to have the state prove guilt beyond a reasonable doubt. If this is permissible in Subin's view, it is difficult to understand why it would not be permissible to call an expert on eyewitness identification to testify.

In the hypothetical case described above, I should also be permitted to bring specific evidence about the gun into my closing argument because it offers a "legitimate" reason to doubt the accuracy of the identification (e.g., "The eyewitness was not someone sitting calmly in a restaurant looking at someone else a few tables away. Here, the eyewitness had a gun in his face.") Of course, if I can bring the gun into my closing, I presumably can do it in a manner I believe most effective; for I don't believe Professor Subin's position is that you are permitted to do it, but not very well:

> And did he notice that gun? Was he staring at that big... silvery... automatic? Wouldn't you? Not knowing if this assailant was going to beat or kill you. Wouldn't your mind turn inward? Inward to that gun, to calming your fear of death, to not provoking this spectre who could end your life in a moment? Would you be thinking "Let me see. His eyes are hazel... I want to get a good look at him so I can identify him later"? Would you want to do anything to make that person with a big... silvery... automatic gun in your face think you could identify him?...

What then is Subin really saying? Subin could not mean by his reference to the "state's evidence" that I can use evidence of the gun to raise a reasonable doubt in aid of the "false defense" of misidentification if the information is elicited on *the state's direct examination,* but that I am not permitted to bring out the information through cross-examination or defense witnesses. He could not mean that information I thus actively elicit is not "legitimate" for raising doubts. Yet, the only mechanisms he lists for putting on a "false defense" are defense cross-examination, defense witnesses, and arguments therefrom. If this distinction between information elicited by the prosecution and that elicited by the defense is really what he intends to divine the legitimate from the illegitimate, it is a strange structure upon which to rest a principle of ethical guidance, especially given the nature of the trial process. As a practical matter, this structure would allow conviction or acquittal to rest on such fortuitous circumstances as whether, when asked on direct examination if he saw a weapon in the hands of the robber, the witness in our hypothetical answered:

— "Yes."
— "Yes. Pointing at me."
— "Yes. Pointing at my face."
— "Yes. A big, silvery, automatic pointing at my face."

Much of cross-examination emphasizes points elicited in the direct examination (e.g., "Now, this gun was pointing at you?") and expands upon helpful points made during the direct (e.g., "You said on direct the gun was pointing at you. Where exactly was it pointing?"). If Professor Subin would not let me aid the "false defense" of mistaken identification by this type of cross-examination, then my client's chances for acquittal will vary with which of these responses happens to flow from the witness' mouth during direct examination on the day of trial.

Statements, however, do not just, "flow from" witnesses' mouths on direct examination. Witnesses are often coached regarding their testimony. That reality is at the core of my next point. If the content of the prosecution's direct examination limits the range of my ethical behavior, then my adversary controls my client's fate by deciding what to ask in the direct examination (e.g., "When I ask you in your direct examination about the gun, be certain you *do not* mention that it was directly pointed at you, and especially *do not* say it was pointed at your face."). Is this prosecutorial manipulation, in conjunction with the serendipity of answers proffered on the prosecution's direct examination, the basis for Professor Subin's ethical standards for criminal defense? If not, and if I may fully cross-examine in support of my "false defense" of misidentification, then it is difficult to see Professor Subin's point.

It is possible Subin was thinking about a situation where a defense attorney argues that the crime did not occur at all. For example, assume that when asked by the prosecution where he was going with a wallet full of money, the robbery victim's testimony is that he was going to get his wife a gift because she was angry at him for wasting his paycheck gambling the previous week. In closing, the defense argues an alternative explanation for the information the prosecution has presented, one based on the possibility that the victim had created the entire robbery story to cover up further gambling losses. While this would be a "false defense," there appears no real difference between a "false defense" that seeks acquittal by raising doubts that the defendant committed the crime (questioning identification evidence), which Professor Subin would seem to sanction, and one which raises doubts, as in this example, that the crime occurred at all. The former more closely tracks the prosecution's theory that there *was* a robbery, but this is a distinction of no apparent significance. In both examples, the defense counsel takes information in the case and arranges it differently than the prosecution to present alternative "possibilities" which resonate with reasonable doubts. Both are equally "false" in Subin's sense. Once Subin allows the defense attorney to argue reasonable doubts in support of a "false" defense, the line between the permissible and the impermissible is blurred and is definable only in terms of the false dichotomy between evidence brought in by the prosecution and evidence elicited by the defense.

Another indication that Subin would not adhere to the "stark" definition of lawyer as monitor is that he would allow the defense to demonstrate the inaccuracy of information that may be harmful to its case. Imagine that the robbery victim in my hypothetical testifies that Bloogan's Department Store, directly across the street from where the nighttime robbery occurred, had all of its lights on at the time of the robbery. In fact, I find out in investigation that Bloogan's was closed for remodeling that evening. Subin would undoubtedly allow me to bring this out. What, after all, would a "truth" theory be if I were not permitted to confront "lies" and "misperceptions." If Professor Subin permits me to bring out this "inaccuracy" on cross-examination and/or through other witnesses, he must also allow me to use it in closing or my initial access to this information would be meaningless. In closing, my only real use for this information would be in support of my "false defense" of mistaken identification. The line between advocate and monitor is again blurred.

Another example of the unworkability of his distinction between advocate and monitor is reflected in the defense lawyer's use of inaccurate information brought out in the prosecution's case that is helpful to the defense. The victim of the robbery now testifies that the robbery took place at 10 p.m. My client has a strong alibi for 10 p.m. I "know," however, that the robbery actually took place at 10:30 p.m. May I put on my alibi in support of my "false defense," raising doubts that my client was the robber? Subin would say yes. In a similar set of circumstances Subin stated: "The state's proof of the time of the crime was incorrect, and therefore subject to impeachment." This, however, is not "impeachment." The probative value of the information is not being questioned. Quite the contrary, the incorrect information is being embraced as true. A prosecution witness has simply made a "mistake" and Professor Subin allows the defense attorney to take advantage of it, furthering a "false defense." Without some analysis tied to the rationales for the advocate-monitor distinction in the first place, the distinction seems to depend on ad hoc judgments....

A. A Reevaluation of a Monitor's Role in Subin's Rape Case

To summarize, our monitor may bring in information and draw inferences which support "false defense" if the information or inferences fall within any one of six categories: (1) quality, (2) reliability, (3) mistakes in the prosecution's case, (4) adequacy, (5) inaccuracy, or (6) legitimate reasons to doubt. These broad, imprecise categories are not very confining for a profession which makes its living developing plausible positions for filing things into categories. It is instructive focusing on Subin's principal example, the rape case in which he "knows" his client is factually guilty, with these categories in mind.

In that case, two principal pieces of information emerged which were potentially helpful for the defense: 1) the victim stated that the defendant took her to his apartment; and 2) the victim was left alone for a time in a hallway after the rape but did not try to flee. Professor Subin recognized the significance of these and other miscellaneous pieces of information for the defense:

> I could emphasize the parts of her story that sounded the most curious, such as the defendant's solicitude in taking his victim back to his apartment, and her waiting for her watch when she could have gone immediately to the nearby

precinct that she went to later. I could point to her inability to identify the gun she claimed was used (although it was the one actually used), that the allegedly stolen watch was never found, that there was no sign of physical violence, and no one heard screaming or any other signs of a struggle. I could also argue as my client had that even if he were reckless enough to rob and rape a woman across the street from his apartment, he would not be so foolish as to bring the victim there.

However, Subin is unclear as to what he would have done with this information. He claims he would have had no right to raise the "false defense" of consent. He would not have cross-examined the victim or put on defense witnesses. Instead, Subin would "limit my representation at that stage to putting forth the strongest argument I could that the facts presented by the state did not sustain its burden." Assuming sufficient information was elicited on the victim's direct examination to make the two helpful points above, what "strong argument" would defense counsel Subin make? Without using any of the information helpful to the defense, his argument could not have been other than: "Thank you, the prosecution has the burden."

Imagine instead he had taken the information and argued as follows:

> This just doesn't make sense. If he took her to his apartment, he'd have to know he'd be identified within hours. There's no evidence he blindfolded her or in any other way made an effort to conceal the identity and location of the apartment. And here she'd just been raped at gunpoint by a man who, for all she knew, might now kill her, and she was alone in the hallway, neighbors around, a staircase 10 feet away leading to the outside and safety. Yet her testimony is

she just sat there and waited for the defendant. None of this makes sense, and the prosecution cannot carry its burden if the story it is presenting does not make sense.

Would this have been a "false defense" for Professor Subin? The argument raises "legitimate" doubts. The fact that the prosecution's underlying story does not make sense goes to the quality, reliability, and adequacy of the prosecution's case. Maybe the line would have been crossed if as defense counsel he had added:

> Who knows from this evidence what really happened? Maybe she consented and then felt guilty—afraid to acknowledge the truth to herself and her boyfriend. Who knows? All we know is that the story does not make sense.

Does even mentioning the possibility of consent really cross Subin's line between the ethical and unethical? One major shortcoming in Subin's presentation is his failure to illustrate what a monitor in this rape case *may* do. He tells us what he would do, but does not show us what his "monitor's" closing argument would really look like.

Subin has left us in a quandary. The "stark" definition of monitor may have been at odds with the nature of the criminal justice system and the Constitution, but at least it was consistent with an unmitigated desire for truth. This current wavering line between advocates and monitors, based as it is on permissible versus impermissible information and inferences, is somewhat more in step with the Constitution and the justice system, but hopelessly vague and uncertain.

B. Bigger Problems: Constitutional Concerns and Jeopardizing an Independent Defense Bar

If Professor Subin's approach is more than a statement of his own private ethics, the vagueness and uncertainty of the line which divides the advocate from the monitor presents a serious problem. First, constitutional concerns additional to those already expressed may arise. Criminal defense representation touches significant interests: 1) protection of the individual from the state; 2) the freedom of the defendant in a nation which values liberty; and 3) significant constitutional rights (fourth, fifth, sixth, eighth, and fourteenth amendments). It is within these areas that the impreciseness in Professor Subin's categories comes to the fore. To the extent defense attorneys are guided by ethical rules which are vague about what conduct is proper, the representation of the clients is hampered. Counsel, uncertain as to appropriate behavior, may fall into a "conflict" between pushing the client's interests as far as is legitimate and protecting himself against charges of unethical conduct. Attorneys' decisions may then tend to fall on the self-protective side, raising constitutional concerns regarding zealous representation.

Second, if Subin's approach were enforced as a rule of professional conduct, the independent defense bar would be seriously jeopardized. Professor Subin may or may not be correct that the public and the bar have a low view of the criminal defense bar. Nonetheless, the independence of that bar has provided all citizens with significant protection against government oppression.[11] With Professor Subin's approach, however, if an acquittal were gained by a defense attorney who was a thorn in the government's side, the prosecutor's office might be tempted to file an ethical complaint stating that defense counsel should have known he put on a "false defense." Subin's position now becomes a weapon of repression in the hands of the government. Even if vindication follows upon a disciplinary hearing, time, expense, and public humiliation might ensue. This will deliver a powerful message to defense attorneys. Don't risk fighting, plead your clients guilty.

IV. CONCLUSION

Discussions of "monitors," "advocates," and "false defenses," while interesting, are premature. If the legal profession is ever to develop meaningful guidelines for criminal and civil attorneys, the focus must be on certain basic premises. Specifically, we must consider: What is the relationship between our criminal and civil systems, and what is the implication of that relationship for those practicing in the two systems? Is the criminal justice system primarily a truth system? Is it primarily a screening system intended as a check on governmental power? It seems to me that here is where we must begin.

NOTES

1. Subin, *The Criminal Lawyer's "Different Mission": Reflections on the "Right" to Present a False Case,* 1 GEO. J. LEGAL ETHICS 125 (1987).
2. Subin, *supra* note 1, at 125.
3. For a very well-thought out recent discussion which generally takes the position that the defense attorney's knowledge of the client's guilt should have no bearing upon that attorney's representation, *see* Kaplan, *Defending Guilty People,* 7 U. BRIDGEPORT L. REV. 223 (1986).
4. Mitchell, *supra* note 3, at 300–01.
5. For an interesting discussion of various justifications for the truth-dysfunctional nature of the criminal trial which implicitly leads one to conclude that Professor Subin's quest for factual truth is the least of what is going on, *see* Goodpaster, *On the Theory of American Adversary Criminal Trials,* 78 J. CRIM. L. & CRIMINOLOGY 118 (1987).
6. Subin, *supra* note 1, at 127–29, 143. As the title presages, Professor Subin makes this concept of a "different mission" the metaphorical focus of his article.
7. Subin, *supra* note 1, at 143.
8. For a defense of the lawyer's position as an "amoral" actor on behalf of a client which does not rely on the adversary system rationale, *see* Pepper, *The Lawyer's Amoral Ethical Role: A Defense, A Problem, and Some Possibilities,* A.B.A. RESEARCH J. 613 (1986).
9. Mitchell, *supra* note 3, at 299–302.
10. *Id.* at 302–21.
11. They did after all defend strikers in the early labor movement, were present during the McCarthy hearings and the Smith Act prosecutions and defended those voicing objections to the government's policies in Vietnam. Most of us take comfort in thinking they will be there in the future. *Cf.* Babcock, *Defending the Guilty,* 32 CLEV. ST. L. REV. 175 (1983–84) (discussing reasons to defend a person one knows is guilty).

POSTSCRIPT

Should Lawyers Be Prohibited from Presenting a False Case?

During the last 30 years, the legal profession has experienced unprecedented change. The most frequently publicized development of this period has been the great increase in the size of the profession. The United States now has almost 1,000,000 lawyers, nearly triple the number in 1970.

In addition to larger numbers of lawyers, recent years have seen the following significant changes take place: (1) A decline in the number of lawyers practicing independently or in firms and an increase in the number of lawyers employed by corporations and institutions. As a result, "a profession that was 85 percent self-employed in 1948 and about 60 percent self-employed in 1980 soon may be more than half employees." (2) Elimination of some anticompetitive practices previously enjoyed by the profession, such as minimum fee schedules and restrictions on advertising. (3) An increase in the size of law firms. The largest firms now have hundreds of lawyers with offices in many states. (4) Increasing heterogeneity of the legal profession. Due to the recent growth of the bar, members of the profession are younger, with more women and minorities. There are more fields of specialization and types of practice. (5) Increases in the number and use of paraprofessionals. (6) Challenges to the profitability of some large law firms.

Clearly, the legal profession is not as stable as it once was. The work that lawyers do and how they do it is changing. This may have an impact on the ethical standards of lawyers. One of the characteristics of a profession is that it sets its own standards. But what happens when, because of changes in the makeup of the profession, it becomes harder to do this?

For further insight into the role and nature of the legal profession and of legal ethics, see Peter Joy, "What We Talk About When We Talk About Professionalism," 7 *Georgetown Journal of Legal Ethics* 987 (Spring 1994); R. Abel, *American Lawyers* (Oxford University Press, 1989); and Babcock, "Defending the Guilty," 32 *Cleveland State Law Review* 175 (1983). *Bates v. State Bar of Arizona*, 97 S. Ct. 2691 (1977) permitted lawyers to advertise. Recent cases involving the ethical practices of lawyers are *Florida Bar v. Went for It, Inc.*, 115 S. Ct. 2371 (1995); *Shapero v. Kentucky Bar Association*, 108 S. Ct. 1916 (1988), allowing lawyers to use mailing lists to advertise their services to potential clients; and *Nix v. Whiteside*, 106 S. Ct. 988 (1986), which held that it is not a violation of the right to counsel for an attorney to threaten to resign if the client insists on lying while testifying. Two Internet sites related to lawyers' ethics in this age of changing technology are http://www.legalethics.com/ and http://journal.law.ufl.edu/~techlaw/1/hankins.html.

ISSUE 2

Does Mediation in Divorce Cases Hurt Women?

YES: Penelope E. Bryan, from "Killing Us Softly: Divorce Mediation and the Politics of Power," *Buffalo Law Review* (vol. 40, 1992)

NO: Stephen K. Erickson, from "ADR and Family Law," *Hamline Journal of Public Law and Policy* (Spring 1991)

ISSUE SUMMARY

YES: Penelope E. Bryan, a professor in the School of Law at the University of Denver, asserts that the process of mediation in divorce cases works more to the benefit of men than women and preserves a dominant position for husbands.

NO: Stephen K. Erickson, a practicing divorce mediator, argues that all parties benefit from a process that is less adversarial—namely, mediation—and that is not controlled by lawyers.

Mediation is a method of resolving disputes and conflicts and is being used increasingly in the United States. Unlike the adversary process, where a lawyer's only aim is to help his or her client win, mediation stresses compromise and agreement between the parties. In mediation, all parties to a dispute are given the opportunity to actively participate in the settlement of their problems without being involved in a formal judicial proceeding.

Mediation is one of several techniques for settling disputes that are alternatives to litigation; collectively, these techniques are known as alternative dispute resolution (or ADR). Supporters of ADR consider litigation to be a costly and time-consuming process, which typically ends with one party the winner and the other the loser, and which often makes the parties more hostile to each other at the end than they were at the beginning.

There was extraordinary growth in the use of alternatives to litigation in the 1980s. There are thousands of mediation programs in the United States today, as compared to only a handful that existed in the late 1970s. The most common ADR processes are negotiation, arbitration, and mediation. These processes differ from litigation in a number of ways.

1. They are more informal than litigation. Lawyers are often not present and rules of evidence do not have to be followed. Cases are settled more quickly and more cheaply.

2. They are generally held in private and the proceedings are confidential.
3. They are often voluntary, with the parties coming together because of a desire to settle the dispute out of court.
4. There is usually no appeal from a settlement reached through ADR.

There are also significant differences among the various ADR techniques, some of which are as different from each other as they are from litigation. Some ADR methods, for example, have some of the features of litigation and others do not. Negotiation is the ADR process that is least like litigation. There is no third party present to assist in the resolution of the problem and the parties are free to leave and break off negotiations at any time. Arbitration, on the other hand, is an ADR process that has some qualities in common with litigation. The parties agree ahead of time that the arbitrator has the authority to issue rulings and decide the case. Lawyers are often involved in presenting the case to the arbitrator. Typically, arbitration will still be quicker than litigation and proceed in a less legalistic fashion.

Mediation differs from arbitration in that a mediator does not have the power to issue rulings. Like negotiation, mediation works only when the settlement that is reached is acceptable to the parties. If any party is dissatisfied, there will be no settlement. Mediators will have different styles and some are more comfortable than others in making suggestions and indicating to the parties what they feel is fair. But what is most important in increasing the likelihood that any settlement will last and that the parties will walk away pleased with the outcome is for the parties in conflict to believe that they have contributed to the nature of the settlement. The best settlements are those where the parties come to understand the motives and needs of their opponents and have worked out a solution that benefits all sides. The mediator is much more interested than a judge in promoting communication, understanding, and a complete airing of the circumstances that contributed to the dispute.

Should more cases be resolved through mediation and fewer through the court system? Would anything be lost if cases that might have been resolved through litigation are instead diverted to a mediation project? What kinds of cases are best handled through mediation and what kinds should be litigated? The following selections focus on the use of mediation in family law cases. The use of mediation has been heavily promoted in divorce cases since it has been assumed that mediation would lead to more creative problem solving and there would be less hostility during the process of distributing assets and arranging custody. In the first selection, however, law professor Penelope E. Bryan argues that mediation places women at a distinct disadvantage. The appropriateness of ADR is defended by Stephen K. Erickson, a practicing divorce mediator, in the second selection.

YES

Penelope E. Bryan

KILLING US SOFTLY: DIVORCE MEDIATION AND THE POLITICS OF POWER

Divorce mediation's seductive marketing rhetoric masks a political agenda: entrenchment. Recently reformed divorce law confers greater economic rights upon divorcing women. Custody law also favors women. Negotiating lawyers rely upon these legal entitlements and craft divorce agreements reflecting them, thereby loosening the control men traditionally wield over economic resources and the socialization of children. While mediation proponents employ the obscuring rhetoric of relatedness, mediation unobtrusively reduces this threat to patriarchy by returning men to their former dominant position. This article explains how mediation accomplishes this feat....

DISTRIBUTION OF POWER BETWEEN HUSBANDS AND WIVES

During negotiation the parties explore their relative power and reach agreements reflecting their strengths and weaknesses. Since the husband and wife negotiate directly with each other in divorce mediation, absent active mediator intervention, outcomes should reflect power differences between them....

Throughout this article, the mediation model I contemplate offers an informal conflict resolution process in which a neutral mediator helps the husband and wife negotiate the disputed issues in their divorce. The mediator guards the process, while the parties determine the substance of the divorce agreement. Substantive law does not control the divorce settlement's terms. Rather the mediator encourages the couple to design an agreement that reflects their particular needs and interests. While some variation exists, this model captures most divorce mediation. Moreover, because most divorce mediation occurs in court affiliated programs and most divorce mediators have mental health backgrounds, this article anticipates a mediation program with these characteristics....

Tangible Resources

The spouse with greater income has several advantages in negotiation. He more easily can hire experts to advise him on how to negotiate or how to structure an agreement to maximize his, and minimize the other party's, interests. Moreover, due to greater self-sufficiency, he more credibly can threaten to terminate or extend the length of negotiations if the other party fails to meet his demands. Income disparity between negotiating spouses then affects their negotiating strength.

In the United States men earn much more than women. The wage gap between husbands and wives is even wider than between men and women generally. Approximately fifty percent of married women and married women with children in the home earn no income because they do not participate in the paid labor force. Even when married women work outside the home, they average less than half the income of married men. More specifically, in 1980 wives' earnings, on the average, accounted for only twenty-six percent of total family income, and the median contribution to the total family income of wives with full-time, year round employment was only thirty-eight percent. Wives with children whose births are spaced over many years and wives with many children have the lowest wages of all wives. While certainly some spouses will have equivalent incomes and a few wives' incomes will exceed that of their husbands, most marriages will reflect the pattern these statistics reveal: the wife, if employed at all, will earn much less than her husband. The husband thus is better able to purchase expert advice and to threaten termination or extension of negotiations....

Educational superiority also can create negotiating power. The individual with more education may have important knowledge, such as the tax consequences of property distribution, that enables him to negotiate an agreement more favorable to him than the other spouse suspects. Advanced education also might provide training in negotiation skills. Moreover, the better educated individual can control outcomes because his exposure to a wider range of ideas helps him generate more alternatives during negotiation. Higher education, too, implies a superior ability to understand what occurs in mediation. Tellingly, in one custody mediation program, only the women with graduate educations and/or women over forty-five years of age failed to complain of jumbled and confused thoughts during negotiations with their husbands.

In the United States men and women tend to marry those of similar educational levels. However, where a difference exists, women more than men marry people with higher educational attainment. When this occurs the husband has further advantages in divorce mediation. One's occupation also can increase one's negotiating strength by providing training or information relevant to divorce issues. If the husband is an attorney or a corporate financial officer, his occupation provides him knowledge of legal rights and finances. Moreover, some occupations require negotiation skills. A construction foreman, for instance, must negotiate....

Effects of Tangible Resource Power on Mediated Outcomes

... Research on marital negotiations shows that the greater income and education and the higher occupational level of husbands, compared to wives, confers upon husbands greater power over routine decisions and decisions on issues over which the couple frequently disagrees. Moreover, husbands believe they control decisions over important financial issues, whereas they perceive as shared or wife-dominated less important financial decisions or mundane decisions requiring time to implement. That employed wives have more decisional power relative to their husbands than unemployed wives, further illustrates the importance of tangible resources to marital negotiating power.

Tangible resources probably create more power for the husband in divorce negotiations than marital decisionmaking research indicates. Spouses inevitably develop psychological and emotional interdependencies. A wife then has some power over her husband during marriage because of his dependence on her for emotional and psychological support, as well as sexual gratification. At divorce these sources of power evaporate. Thus, tangible resources probably have even more influence in divorce than in marital negotiations.

In summary, marital decisionmaking research suggests that, unless the mediator intervenes, the husband's greater tangible resources will grant him the lion's share of power in divorce negotiations, particularly over critical financial issues. Differences in possession of tangible resources, however, are only one source of inequality between spouses. Intangible factors such as status, dominance, depression, self esteem, reward expectation and fear of achievement further empower the husband during divorce mediation....

Mediator Coercion on Child Issues

In divorce mediation the wife confronts a mental health mediator surrounded by an aura of professional expertise regarding the children's best interests. Mediators claim expert authority by describing their training and experience to the couple and by sharing their allegedly expert knowledge on children's developmental needs. The wife's legitimate authority over the children pales in the shadow of the professional's expert authority.

If the expert mediator remained neutral, the wife still could use her child-centered power in direct negotiation with her husband. Or, if the formal law that recognized the caretaking mother's superior right to children remained relevant in mediation, it might enhance the wife's power over child issues. But formal law does not dictate mediated outcomes and mental health mediators do not remain neutral. Emboldened and legitimated by their professional expertise, divorce mediators abandon their prescribed neutrality and zealously intervene to protect defenseless children from the custody and visitation decisions of their allegedly destructive parents. Mediator intervention results in custody arrangements more favorable to fathers than fathers could obtain in direct negotiations with their authoritative wives.

Divorce mediators have a strong bias in favor of joint custody and coerce divorcing mothers into this arrangement. Irving and Benjamin unwittingly provide an illustrative case. At mediation's beginning, the mother requested sole custody of the couple's two girls, aged ten and six. The case report nowhere indicates the mother's unfitness. The mother, however, did raise some question about the quality of the father's prior involvement with the girls. During the course of the mediation, the mediators convinced the mother that, irrespective of the father's past behavior, the children "needed" and "loved" their father and suggested the mother should behave in accordance with the children's best interests. In seeking to persuade the mother, the mediators engaged the children in the mediation as well as the maternal grandmother who, at the outset, had insisted the girls' mother should have sole custody. At mediation's end, the agreement reflected a joint physical custody arrangement with the girls spending weekdays with their mother and weekends with their father. The couple, however, continued having difficulty and returned for follow-up mediation. With the mediator's assistance, the couple arrived at a new custody arrangement: the girls would stay with their father two evenings per week as well as the weekends, leaving them with their mother only three days per week.

Only the mother's resistance offers to control a biased mediator's imposition of joint custody. However, the mother's insistence upon sole custody or her threat to walk out of mediation seems unlikely because of the mental health professional's expert authority and because the mother's sex role socialization makes her susceptible to manipulation by the mediator. Her belief in her responsibility to maintain familial relationships predisposes her to joint custody because mediators present that arrangement as the one best designed to preserve the children's relationship with their father. Moreover, as the above case illustrates, mediators appeal to the traditional mother's care orientation by emphasizing the father's emotional importance to the children. The traditional mother then falls victim to a skillful mediator armed with such rhetoric. Unsurprisingly, mediation produces a significantly greater percentage of joint custody arrangements than

any other process of custody dispute resolution.

The joint custody agreements reached in mediation, however, more commonly seem to reflect joint legal, rather than joint physical, custody. In contrast to joint physical custody where the child spends extended periods of time living with each parent, joint legal custody requires the parents only to share control over important child related decisions. Because this form of custody superficially seems less threatening to mothers, its subtle political implications frequently go unnoticed. Joint legal custody often perpetuates the preexisting patriarchal family structure by allocating the day-to-day care of the children to the mother, while solidifying the ex-husband's power over important child related decisions. The mother can make decisions as long as they reflect her ex-husband's wishes. The moment, however, her opinion differs from his, he has veto power. This veto power, or the threat of its use, invades the ex-wife's consciousness and makes her ex-husband, and the male control he represents, an ever-present force with which to contend. The message is clear: she may escape the marriage but will remain subject to male domination. This implicit, yet powerful, message keeps women aware of their required submissiveness and thus strengthens patriarchy.

The effect joint legal or physical custody has on the children of divorce also reinforces existing hierarchy between men and women. The father's absence from the family unit interferes with socialization of the children into patriarchal patterns. How, for instance, does a little girl learn proper submissiveness to male authority in the absence of a powerful male figure and in the presence of an independently decisive mother. Likewise, how can a little boy learn proper domination of women if he lacks his father's modeling, his mother dominates the household, and he observes his mother operating as an autonomous adult. While certainly children's exposure to patriarchal patterns in other areas of life will influence them, the absence of these patterns in their homes makes their socialization less effective. Joint legal and joint physical custody reintroduce male power into the post-divorce family and ensure that children remain aware of male dominance. The significant increase in joint custody, whether physical or legal, generated by mediation thus reflects a corresponding increase in the male dominance characteristic of patriarchy.

Not only does mediator bias in favor of joint custody reinforce patriarchy through custody arrangements, it also further weakens the wife's already precarious financial position in divorce mediation by eliminating the wife's ability to use her child-centered power during negotiations over financial issues. Moreover, a mother intent upon sole custody despite mediator coercion might attempt to circumvent the mediator and appeal directly to the father by offering to accept a grossly inequitable financial arrangement in exchange for sole custody. While those working in family law recognize that fathers frequently threaten to dispute custody in order to strengthen their financial position, the mediator's advocacy of joint custody enhances the father's coercive power.

Considering the foregoing, women's highly ambivalent response to custody mediation causes no surprise:

> Although a complete analysis is not available, there is reason to think that

women are significantly more likely to regard mediation as threatening and balanced against them than are men. While women did report that mediation helped them in understanding themselves and their spouses, they were also far more likely than men to report a sense of being pressured into agreement, a lack of comfort in expressing their feelings, anger during mediation sessions, and a sense that mediators essentially dictated the terms of the agreement.

In conclusion, traditional sex role ideology enhances the husband's power over financial issues and, when coupled with mediator bias for joint custody, strengthens the father's position in custody matters as well. . . .

PROTECTION FOR THE DISADVANTAGED WIFE

Balancing the Power: A Rhetorical Smokescreen

Mediator Self-Interested Ignorance on Power Issues. Given the importance of power balancing, divorce mediation literature carefully should explain the factors that create power, how those factors normally are distributed among husbands and wives, and methods for detecting these factors as well as techniques for correcting power disparities rooted in different factors. As I mentioned earlier, however, the literature proves insensitive to power issues. Characteristically, a recent book on divorce mediation devotes only sixteen of over four hundred pages to power imbalances. In those sixteen pages the authors deny the existence of power imbalances or suggest that if they exist they do not affect mediation.

Divorce mediation training programs show equivalent insensitivity to power issues. The better divorce mediation training programs require trainees to devote a maximum of forty hours, usually over a five day period, to becoming a mediator. In that short time the program director attempts to instill in the trainees an expertise in basic mediation skills, the psychology of divorce, child psychology, and the complex financial and legal issues presented in divorce. During this ambitious agenda, power issues remain unacknowledged or receive scant attention.

Because mediation literature and training fail to address and explain power adequately, mediators can avoid acknowledging the seriousness of unequal power between divorcing spouses and the need for mediator intervention. Moreover, because of insufficient training, even those who do recognize the need to power balance have knowledge and skills inadequate to the task. Deficient in both skills and awareness, mediators lack the motivation and the ability to power balance.

More importantly, the mediation profession cannot be expected to correct its inadequate response to power issues: their ignorance serves their purposes. Candid exposition of the depth, breadth, and tenacity of power disparities between spouses threatens the survival of this budding profession because it suggests the impossibility of power balancing. In order to alter a power disparity, a mediator must first be able to detect its existence. Yet diagnosis of a disparity based on intangible power factors or sex role ideology proves difficult. For instance, if a highly educated professional wife earns a high income and the husband does not make obvious his greater power during mediation by dominating conversation, the mediator has little reason to suspect an imbalance. This wife, however, may agree to her husband's inadequate financial proposal because her adherence to traditional sex role ideology, her depression, and her low self-esteem override her more obvious tangible power bases. The mediator, insensitive to the wife's low power based on intangible factors, will assure the wife freely has chosen to accept her husband's proposal and will see no need to power balance. Because many of the bases for power disparity remain elusive, the need to power balance frequently will go unrecognized. Without this recognition power balancing cannot occur.

Moreover, the severity and complexity of power disparities between most spouses suggest that power balancing requires skills most mediators do not and cannot have. It defies imagination to think of the skill and knowledge required to empower a depressed wife with low self-esteem who believes in traditional sex role ideology, fears confronting her husband, and has no occupation outside the home. Certainly the mediator cannot alter the wife's occupation during mediation. Nor can the mediator significantly improve the wife's psychological and emotional state. Even if the mediator has knowledge of counseling psychology, mediation focuses on the task of reaching agreement, rather than on therapy for troubled spouses. The extensive therapy required to balance a power disparity grounded in a wife's low self-esteem, depression, fear of confrontation, and traditional sex role ideology would require a mediator willing to redefine mediation and develop complex skills.

Even if a sufficiently talented mediator was willing to assume this task, the efficiency rationale justifying court affiliated mediation programs makes therapy a practical impossibility. The efficiency focus of these programs pressures the mediator to produce agreements quickly. For instance, studies indicate that custody mediation in court affiliated programs takes an average of four hours. In contrast, two therapeutic mediators in a private mediation program acknowledged that "detection" of the twenty percent of their clients who were totally inappropriate for mediation and the other fifty percent who needed a therapeutic "premediation" stage to prepare them for mediation, required an approximately six hour assessment stage. Mediator power balancing through extensive therapy thus proves a practical impossibility.

In summary, full exploration of power issues by mediation proponents would require the corresponding admission that detection difficulties, lack of skill, and program constraints make power balancing impossible for most, if not all, mediators. With power balancing no longer available as a rhetorical safeguard, judicial administrators and the public would understand mediation for what it is: an informal process that places the low powered spouse, usually the wife, fully at the mercy of her more powerful husband. This recognition might cause the demise of this new profession. Mediation proponents thus have a vested interest in remaining ignorant of power issues.

THE COMPARATIVE EFFECTIVENESS OF LAWYER NEGOTIATION

Divorce agreements negotiated by lawyers will be more favorable to wives than mediated agreements for several reasons. While mediators must remain substantively neutral, lawyers have a professional obligation to pursue and protect the client's interests during negotiations. The lawyer advocate also insulates the disadvantaged wife from her husband and prevents the tangible, intangible, and sex role differences between them from dictating the terms of the agreement. By forcing the husband and wife to deal directly with one another, mediation, in contrast, sharpens the wife's disadvantages. Even lawyers who might compromise their clients' concerns in order to fulfill their own interests have an advocacy role and professional ethic to constrain their self-interested behaviors. The mediator, as a neutral, has no counterbalancing role or ethical prescription to mitigate the mediator's interest in obtaining an agreement irrespective of its substance. The lawyer's advocacy role thus differs markedly from mediator neutrality and offers far greater protection for a low power spouse.

Market factors provide the lawyer additional motivation to protect the low powered wife's interests. An attorney's ability to generate business turns upon whether professional peers and clients see her as competent in protecting client interests. To remain in business the mediator in a court affiliated program, on the other hand, need only produce many agreements quickly. Market factors suggest then that negotiating lawyers will provide much more protection for client interests than will mediators.

In addition to role and market factors, liability for professional malpractice helps motivate the lawyer to seek legally defined client interests during negotiations. The possibility of a malpractice claim for failure to secure the wife's legal entitlement to part of her husband's pension plan, for instance, motivates the lawyer to negotiate assertively to secure that right in the divorce settlement. In contrast, the mediator, who lacks accountability for the mediated agreement's substance, will have less difficulty allowing the wife to relinquish her right to a portion of the pension plan.

The above observation invites recognition of the importance of legal rights in determining the substance of a lawyer negotiated, as opposed to a mediated, divorce agreement. Women's ability to avoid substantive law in mediation might seem attractive to a group these laws consistently have treated unfairly. However, as argued throughout this article, movement out of a dispute resolution system in which law is relevant into an informal system where it is not limits law's ability to constrain power abuses and ensures that preexisting power disparities, rather than law, will dictate the divorce agreement's terms. In contrast, substantive legal norms form the expectations of negotiating lawyers and create a foundation from which they can begin to judge the acceptability of the negotiated agreement. Thus, while formal substantive law may not reflect true distributive justice for divorcing women, because of power disparities and the lack of meaningful safeguards in mediation women will obtain more advantageous outcomes when negotiating lawyers rely on law than when mediators rely on vague and biased equity norms.

CONCLUSION

Today custody law still favors women and recent reforms in family law create new economic rights for divorcing women. Lawyers negotiating divorce settlements concern themselves with implementing these legal entitlements. Mediation proponents believe the lawyer's focus on rights generates hostility among divorcing parties and unnecessarily infringes upon the couple's right to order their post divorce lives. In contrast they maintain mediation preserves relationships, empowers the parties, and generates good feelings. Legal rights fade into the shadows of informality.

This shift in focus from rights to relatedness, however, endangers divorcing women and reinforces male dominance. Mediation proponents seductively appeal to women's socialized values by speaking softly of relatedness. Yet mediation exploits wives by denigrating their legal entitlements, stripping them of authority, encouraging unwarranted compromise, isolating them from needed support, and placing them across the table from their more powerful husbands and demanding that they fend for themselves. The process thus perpetuates patriarchy by freeing men to use their power to gain greater control over children, to implant more awareness of male dominance into women's consciousness, and to retain more of the marital financial assets than men would obtain if lawyers negotiated divorce agreements.

The insidious nature of mediation for divorcing women, though, remains hidden beneath its carefully crafted marketing rhetoric. This article looks beneath that rhetoric. The effects upon women of the political agenda disclosed should inspire critical debate on the propriety of divorce mediation. At the very least those who structure court affiliated programs, as well as mediators, now should recognize their complicity in the continued oppression of women and their dependent children.

NO

Stephen K. Erickson

ADR AND FAMILY LAW

INTRODUCTION

Shakespeare's oft-quoted phrase, "First thing, let's kill all the lawyers," commits the cardinal sin by attacking the person rather than the problem. Mediators argue that it is necessary to attack the problem, rather than the person; therefore, if Shakespeare really wanted to find a solution, he should have said: "First thing, let's kill the system and design something that protects the parties, is less costly and works better." Mediators would say "You don't have to kill the system; let's just learn to live side by side in harmony."

...The purpose of this article is to attempt to show how mediation creates different ground rules and an entirely different environment so that settlement can occur more easily. These new rules permit the professional to avoid getting caught up in the couple's battle, focusing rather on how to end the battle in a constructive manner....

MEDIATION DEFINED

Jay Folberg, Dean of the San Francisco University Law School, attempts to define mediation as:

> An alternative to violence, self-help, or litigation that differs from the processes of counseling, negotiation, and arbitration. It can be defined as the process by which the participants, together with the assistance of a neutral person or persons, systematically isolate disputed issues in order to develop options, consider alternatives, and reach a consensual settlement that will accommodate their needs. Mediation is a process that emphasizes the participants' own responsibility for making decisions that affect their lives.

Folberg continues by pointing out that a competitive process of conflict resolution focuses on the parties' differences, while a mediation process focuses on the parties' similarities.

Mediation is best thought of as a process of conflict resolution whereby the parties are encouraged to find the best result they can for themselves by using cooperative negotiation rules rather than a competitive or adversarial

From Stephen K. Erickson, "ADR and Family Law," *Hamline Journal of Public Law and Policy* (Spring 1991). Copyright © 1991 by Stephen K. Erickson. Reprinted by permission. Notes omitted.

process. One of the main points of the co-operative mediation process is an effort to resolve the underlying aspects of the divorce dispute through focusing on the things couples really want, rather than focusing on who is more powerful or who is right. William Ury's recent book, *Getting Disputes Resolved*, suggests that there are three methods people have traditionally used to resolve conflict: power, rights, and interests. A power-based system of conflict resolution focuses on who has the most power. A rights-based system focuses on who is right and who is wrong using certain relevant standards or guideposts for a fair outcome. However, the parties may also choose to resolve disputes by trying to reconcile their underlying interests. Ury argues that a system that reconciles people's underlying interests, while not invariably better than focusing on rights and power, "simply means that it tends to result in lower transaction costs, greater satisfaction with outcomes, less strain on the relationship and less recurrence of disputes."

Perhaps influenced by Fisher and Ury's 1981 book, *Getting to Yes*, mediators in this country have tended to use an interest based approach to conflict resolution. This makes sense, because most couples have already failed at power-based negotiations within the relationship, and most couples lack the ability to understand and apply the complex legal principles of divorce law (rights). By focusing on the underlying interests of the couple, mediators have created a conceptual framework that attempts to reconcile both parties' need to have a good relationship with their children, the need to obtain some measure of financial security after the divorce, and the need to create a fair division of the accumulated property of the marriage relationship.

ACCEPTANCE OF MEDIATION BY THE PUBLIC AND THE JUDICIARY

The ABA Standing Committee on Dispute Resolution reports there are approximately 4,500 jurisdictions requiring mediation in family custody and visitation disputes, whereas no such requirement existed in any jurisdiction in 1977. The Academy of Family Mediators, founded in 1981 as a non-profit Minnesota corporation, now has 1,400 practicing members nationwide and in Canada. Most popular magazines have run articles about divorce mediation and in 1984, ABC Television News' *Nightline* featured live interviews with two Minneapolis couples telling Sam Donaldson about their wonderful experiences in mediation....

HOW COOPERATION IS ACHIEVED IN THE MEDIATION ROOM

Mediators do not have the power to wave a magic wand and suddenly people begin to cooperate. However, mediators do have the ability to influence what goes on in the room in a number of powerful ways.

Asking Different Questions
It has been said that the person who defines the problem has a great deal of power over the resolution of the problem. This is nowhere more evident than in custody battles. If you really think about it only the adversarial system asks the question "Who will have custody of the minor children?" This question, by its very nature, creates a competitive battle for "ownership" of the minor children.

Just the words "custody" and "visitation" also create problems. The only other place in our language where "custody" is frequently used is in prisons. The word "visitation" is also used in connection with funerals. The words and the questions asked create a situation where parties fight over who will get the children. Mediators can reduce the fighting by simply asking a different question: Not who is a better or worse parent, but when will each of you care for the children.

The Idaho Supreme Court, in the case of *Stockwell v. Stockwell*, recognized this concept. Justice Robert Huntley, writing for the Idaho Supreme Court, described the child custody case as "unusually acrimonious and expensive," and directed the parties to participate under the auspices of the district court, in "a mediation process wherein all concerned focus on seeking the interests of the children."

With regard to mediation, the court stated:

> It is obvious that the parties have expended thousands of dollars in attorney fees, travel expenses, and loss of time from employment, while pursuing interests other than those which might be expected to be in the best interests of the child as distinguished from the best interests of the parents and their respective families. It is a case where all might benefit if they were to cooperate in seeking a mutually satisfactory resolution through a mediation process wherein all concerned focus on seeking the best interests of the children.

The court directed the trial court, prior to conducting further custody hearings, to require the parties to "undergo a mediation process under the auspices of the district court before a qualified mediator."

Justice Johnson, concurring, referred the trial court and the parties to J. Folberg and A. Milne, *Divorce Mediation: Theory and Practice*. He also quoted at some length from on of the articles in that volume, S. Erickson, "The Legal Dimension of Divorce Mediation." Justice Johnson quoted in part:

> The legal adversarial system asks, "Who will be awarded custody of the minor children?" ...
>
> ... A more appropriate question to ask the divorcing couple is, "What future parenting arrangements can you agree to, so that each of you can continue to be involved, loving parents?" This version of the custody question creates a different focus and a very different outcome. First, the question is mutual, and answering it requires cooperation. Asking "Who shall have custody?" creates a competitive focus and is likely to produce an adversarial or fighting response, but asking the couple to agree to certain parenting arrangements requires collaborative discussions and mutual planning.
>
> Second, the question is future oriented. Mediation pushes couples to look more to the future because it can be controlled and changed.

Couples can usually discuss future parenting arrangements with little conflict because they are prevented from fighting over who was a more faulty parent in the past. This becomes easier to accomplish when a different question is asked.

Focusing on the Future

Divorce trials, by their very nature, focus on information about the past. Some time must be spent establishing factual data about incomes, expenses, and the nature of marital assets. However, once this is accomplished, the real focus must then be on the future. An interest-based approach to conflict resolution deals primarily with solving future problems. In divorce, these problems are always: 1) How will both of you be able to act as good, loving parents in the future, even though you are living separately? 2) How will it be possible to achieve some measure of economic security for both of you, given the fact that it now costs more money to live in two separate residences? 3) How can the property be fairly divided in order to meet your future needs for housing, transportation, and financial security? A rights-based approach, with its requirements of applying legal standards of fairness, tends to keep people in the past. An interest-based approach tends to focus people on the future, thereby eliminating a good measure of blaming and fault-finding, because the future can be shaped and controlled hundreds of different ways, and the past can only be fought about.

Discourage Blaming and Fault Finding

Conflict tends to escalate when parties seek to fix blame over some past events. Cooperation is easier to achieve when parties are told by the mediator: "No one in this room has the power to change the past; therefore, it is important to avoid using time and effort trying to determine who was more at fault for your present problems. Rather, let's try to turn past problems into an opportunity to find solutions that will prevent these problems from occurring again." This is a difficult task to accomplish with an angry, highly conflicted couple, but it creates a much better environment for cooperative problem solving.

Avoiding Positional Bargaining

When a parent in mediation states: "I want custody of the minor children," that person's underlying interest is in trying to avoid losing the children. More important, it is a positional statement that says, "My position is that I don't want to lose my relationship with the children; therefore, my solution is to demand custody." Positions can only be met in one way—either custody is won, or it is lost. By moving the couple to talk about their real underlying interest in remaining good, loving parents, the mediator can explore a range of options and eventually find some way to achieve resolution. A positional statement can only be solved in one way. An interest statement can be solved in hundreds of different ways. Therefore, opening statements are avoided and the future needs of the parties, rather than the past problems are stressed, and options, rather than positions, are discussed.

CONCLUSION

The exciting aspect of mediation is that it allow professionals to avoid getting bruised in acrimonious family law battles. To represent couples in mediation, or to act as a neutral in cooperation with the parties' attorneys, requires understanding of the underlying principles of mediation. Different rules, different questions, and effective control of the process make mediation more than another hoop to jump through for the attorney who hears the judge order a client into mediation. It presents a better opportunity for the client than could be obtained in litigation, especially when the financial and emotional cost of the contested trial are considered.

POSTSCRIPT

Does Mediation in Divorce Cases Hurt Women?

These articles raise a question on legal ethics—namely, what are the goals of the legal process? The attractiveness of mediation is that it does an excellent job of fostering communication between hostile parties and of allowing them to work through their differences. But, as Bryan argues, law is designed to do more than help the particular disputants in a case. The resolution of disputes through law sends a message to all of us indicating what the norms of our society are and should be, what is acceptable behavior and what is not. When disputes are mediated privately, as occurs with most ADR processes, the public is left out. Having read the preceding articles, consider whether this is a problem that is insurmountable or whether there are ways to determine which kinds of problems should be settled in court and which might be resolved through ADR.

Several decades ago, a common rallying cry was the phrase "law and order." The solution to disorder and to conflict was to have more law. It would have been inconceivable for many to believe that one could have more order with less law. Since that time, we have become more skeptical about the power of our institutions. We are also more knowledgeable about the strengths and weaknesses of the law. The growth of ADR reflects this increased level of both skepticism and knowledge. The increased use of ADR presents us with more choices in how disputes may be settled. It also provides us with a more complicated system of dispute resolution, since we no longer automatically run to court to solve a problem but instead ask which of several available methods is most appropriate.

Modern life is characterized by increased options and choices. Our range of alternatives in both ideas and material goods has been expanded, and making choices is not easy. We are no longer able to react to some social problem or dispute with the attitude of "there ought to be a law." We are more sensitive today to the limits of the law and to the strengths of some alternatives to law. We also have to be very careful to know when it is appropriate to use some alternative in lieu of law and when it is not.

Further information about the practice and theory of ADR can be found in Bush and Folger, *The Promise of Mediation* (1994); Jonathan Shailor, *Empowerment in Dispute Resolution* (1994); Deborah Kolb, *When Talk Works: Profiles of Mediators* (1993); Goldberg, Green, and Sander, *Dispute Resolution* (1985); Auerbach, *Justice Without Law* (1983); and Fisher and Ury, *Getting to Yes* (1981). Family mediation is discussed in Robert Dingwall and John Eekelaar, *Divorce Mediation and the Legal Process* (1988) and Jay Folberg and Ann Milne, eds., *Divorce Mediation: Theory and Practice* (1988). Alternative dispute resolution has surfaced as an intriguing option for settling on-line disputes. Several Internet sites offer ADR services, including the Online Ombuds Office at `http://www.ombuds.org/` and the Virtual Magistrate Project at `http://vmag.law.vill.edu:8080`.

ISSUE 3

Should Plea Bargaining Be Abolished?

YES: Kenneth Kipnis, from "Criminal Justice and the Negotiated Plea," *Ethics* (vol. 86, 1976)

NO: Nick Schweitzer, from "Plea Bargaining: A Prosecutor's View," *Wisconsin Bar Bulletin* (October 1988)

ISSUE SUMMARY

YES: Professor of philosophy Kenneth Kipnis makes the case that justice cannot be traded on the open market and that plea bargaining often subverts the cause of justice.

NO: District Attorney Nick Schweitzer finds that plea bargaining is fair, useful, desirable, necessary, and practical.

One of the most common myths fostered by television programs about lawyers concerns the place of the trial in the American legal system. The television lawyer, who is invariably a criminal trial lawyer, defends an innocent individual and, at a particularly dramatic point in the trial, achieves vindication for the client. One can now watch "Court TV," a cable channel, and see trials at almost any hour. In 1994 and 1995, the O. J. Simpson trial dominated public attention and attracted huge audiences.

If you visit a courthouse, you may be able to find a trial being held that resembles what you have seen on television. The lawyer may be less dramatic, the judge less dour, and the defendant less appealing, but the main elements of the television version of justice, such as cross-examination of witnesses, opening and closing arguments, and, perhaps, a jury verdict, will be present. What is important to understand, however, is that of the cases processed by the criminal justice system, only a handful are disposed of in this manner. Instead, as many as 90 percent of the cases are resolved through plea bargaining.

Plea bargaining is a method of avoiding trials by securing guilty pleas from defendants. It occurs primarily because trials are expensive and time-consuming. In plea bargaining, the defendant agrees to plead guilty in exchange for an agreement by the prosecutor to reduce the charges or recommend a lenient sentence. The defendant essentially has a choice between going to trial and possibly being found guilty on a more serious charge or pleading guilty and suffering less severe consequences.

This is a difficult choice for any defendant, and at the center of the debate over the legitimacy of plea bargaining is the question of whether or not the defendant, in these circumstances, is making a voluntary choice. In the following selections, Kenneth Kipnis argues that there is too much coercion involved for the choice to be considered voluntary, that the process is inherently unjust, and that innocent individuals may be coerced into pleading guilty. District Attorney Nick Schweitzer believes that the system is not at fault and that if the standard legal procedures are followed, plea bargaining is not only indispensable but also just and desirable.

Plea bargaining has been upheld by the Supreme Court, but only when the Court was persuaded that the plea was made voluntarily. Yet it is rare for a convicted defendant to make a successful challenge to the voluntariness of a guilty plea because the defendant must admit in open court, prior to making the plea, that it is being made voluntarily. In every courtroom in which plea bargaining occurs, the judge asks the defendant the following questions:

1. Do you understand the charges against you and the maximum penalties authorized by law?
2. Are you, in fact, guilty of the charge you are pleading guilty to?
3. Are you pleading guilty voluntarily?
4. Do you understand that you have the right to a trial by jury and that you are waiving that right?

The judge will not accept a plea unless the defendant answers yes to all of these questions. For a plea of guilty to be challenged later, therefore, the defendant must persuade a higher court that he was coerced into lying when he was asked these questions.

Another important issue in the controversy over plea bargaining is the fact that plea bargaining is mainly a poor person's problem. The reason for this is that the greatest incentive to plead guilty exists for those persons who are in jail awaiting trial and cannot afford bail. Their choice is to plead guilty now and get out of jail immediately, or at some definite future date, or to insist on a trial, stay in jail until the trial occurs, and risk a long sentence if convicted. As you read the following selections, you should consider how important this factor is in making a decision about whether or not plea bargaining should be abolished.

CRIMINAL JUSTICE AND THE
NEGOTIATED PLEA

In recent years it has become apparent to many that, in practice, the criminal justice system in the United States does not operate as we thought it did. The conviction secured through jury trial, so familiar in countless novels, films, and television programs, is beginning to be seen as the aberration it has become. What has replaced the jury's verdict is the negotiated plea. In these "plea bargains" the defendant agrees to plead guilty in exchange for discretionary consideration on the part of the state. Generally, this consideration amounts to some kind of assurance of a minimal sentence....

Plea bargaining involves negotiations between the defendant (through an attorney in the standard case) and the prosecutor as to the conditions under which the defendant will enter a guilty plea.[1] Both sides have bargaining power in these negotiations. The prosecutor is ordinarily burdened with cases and does not have the wherewithal to bring more than a fraction of them to trial. Often there is not sufficient evidence to ensure a jury's conviction. Most important, the prosecutor is typically under administrative and political pressure to dispose of cases and to secure convictions as efficiently as possible. If the defendant exercises the constitutional right to a jury trial, the prosecutor must decide whether to drop the charges entirely or to expend scarce resources to bring the case to trial. Since neither prospect is attractive, prosecutors typically exercise their broad discretion to induce defendants to waive trial and to plead guilty.

From the defendant's point of view, such prosecutorial discretion has two aspects; it darkens the prospect of going to trial as it brightens the prospect of pleading guilty. Before negotiating, a prosecutor may improve his bargaining position by "overcharging" defendants[2] or by developing a reputation for severity in the sentences he recommends to judges. Such steps greatly increase the punishment that the defendant must expect if convicted at trial. On the other hand, the state may offer to reduce or to drop some charges, or to recommend leniency to the judge if the defendant agrees to plead guilty. These steps minimize the punishment that will result from a guilty plea. Though the exercise of prosecutorial discretion to secure pleas of guilty may differ somewhat in certain jurisdictions and in particular cases, the broad outlines are as described.

Of course a defendant can always reject any offer of concessions and challenge the state to prove its case. A skilled defense attorney can do much to force the prosecutor to expend resources in bringing a case to trial.[3] But the trial route is rarely taken by defendants. Apart from prosecutorial pressure, other factors may contribute to a defendant's willingness to plead guilty: feelings of guilt which may or may not be connected with the charged crime; the discomforts of the pretrial lockup as against the comparatively better facilities of a penitentiary; the costs of going to trial as against the often cheaper option of consenting to a plea; a willingness or unwillingness to lie; and the delays which are almost always present in awaiting trial, delays which the defendant may sit out in jail in a kind of preconviction imprisonment which may not be credited to a postconviction sentence. It is not surprising that the right to a trial by jury is rarely exercised....

I

As one goes through the literature on plea bargaining one gets the impression that market forces are at work in this unlikely context. The terms "bargain" and "negotiation" suggest this. One can see the law of supply and demand operating in that, other things being equal, if there are too many defendants who want to go to trial, prosecutors will have to concede more in order to get the guilty pleas that they need to clear their case load. And if the number of prosecutors and courts goes up, prosecutors will be able to concede less. Against this background it is not surprising to find one commentator noting:[4] "In

some places a 'going rate' is established under which a given charge will automatically be broken down to a given lesser offense with the recommendation of a given lesser sentence." Prosecutors, like retailers before them, have begun to appreciate the efficiency of the fixed-price approach.

The plea bargain in the economy of criminal justice has many of the important features of the contract in commercial transactions. In both institutions offers are made and accepted, entitlements are given up and obtained, and the notion of an exchange, ideally a fair one, is presented to both parties. Indeed one detects something of the color of consumer protection law in a few of the decisions on plea bargaining. In *Baily v. MacDougal*[5] the court held that "a guilty plea cannot be accepted unless the defendant understands its consequences." And in *Santo Bello v. New York*[6] the court secured a defendant's entitlement to a prosecutorial concession when a second prosecutor replaced the one who had made the promise. Rule 11 of the Federal Rules of Criminal Procedure requires that "if a plea agreement has been reached by the parties which contemplates entry of a plea of guilty or nolo contendere in the expectation that a specific sentence will be imposed or that other charges before the court will be dismissed, the court shall require the disclosure of the agreement in open court at the time the plea is offered." These procedures all have analogues in contract law. Though plea bargains may not be seen as contracts by the parties, agreements like them are the stuff of contract case law. While I will not argue that plea bargains are contracts (or even that they should be treated as such), I do think it proper to look to contract law for help in evaluating the justice of such agreements....

Judges have long been required to see to it that guilty pleas are entered voluntarily. And one would expect that, if duress is present in the plea-bargaining situation, then, just as the handing over of cash to the gunman is void of legal effect (as far as entitlement to the money is concerned), so no legal consequences should flow from the plea of guilty which is the product of duress. However, Rule 11 of the Federal Rules of Criminal Procedure requires the court to insure that a plea of guilty (or nolo contendere) is voluntary by "addressing the defendant personally in open court, determining that the plea is voluntary and not the result of force or promises *apart from a plea agreement*" (emphasis added). In two important cases (*North Carolina v. Alford* and *Brady v. United States*)[7] defendants agreed to plead guilty in order to avoid probable death sentences. Both accepted very long prison sentences. In both cases the Supreme Court decided that guilty pleas so entered were voluntary (through Brennan, Douglas, and Marshall dissented). In his dissent in *Alford*, Brennan writes: "... the facts set out in the majority opinion demonstrate that Alford was 'so gripped by fear of the death penalty' that his decision to plead guilty was not voluntary but was the 'product of duress as much so as choice reflecting physical constraint.'" In footnote 2 of the *Alford* opinion, the Court sets out the defendant's testimony given at the time of the entry of his plea of guilty before the trial court. That testimony deserves examination: "I pleaded guilty on second degree murder because they said there is too much evidence, but I ain't shot no man, but I take the fault for the other man. We never had an argument in our life and I just pleaded guilty because they said if I didn't they would gas me for it, and that is all." The rule to be followed in such cases is set out in *Brady:* "A plea of guilty entered by one fully aware of the direct consequences, including the actual value of any commitments made to him by the court, prosecutor or his own counsel, must stand unless induced by threats (or promises to discontinue improper harassment), misrepresentation (including unfilled or unfillable promises), or perhaps by promises that are by their very nature improper as having no proper relationship to the prosecutor's business (e.g. bribes)." Case law and the Federal Rules both hold that the standard exercise of prosecutorial discretion in order to secure a plea of guilty cannot be used to prove that such a plea is involuntary. Even where the defendant enters a guilty plea in order to avert his death at the hands of the state, as in *Alford*, the Court has not seen involuntariness. Nevertheless, it may be true that some guilty pleas are involuntary in virtue of prosecutorial inducement considered proper by the Supreme Court.

Regarding the elements of duress, let us compare the gunman situation with an example of plea bargaining in order to examine the voluntariness of the latter. Albert W. Alschuler, author of one of the most thorough studies of plea bargaining, describes an actual case:

San Francisco defense attorney Benjamin M. Davis recently represented a man charged with kidnapping and forcible rape. The defendant was innocent, Davis says, and after investigating the case Davis was confident of an acquittal. The prosecutor, who seems to have shared the defense attorney's opinion on this point, offered to permit a guilty plea to simple battery. Conviction on this charge would not have led to a greater sentence than thirty days' imprisonment, and there was every likelihood that the defendant would be granted probation. When Davis informed his client of this offer, he emphasized that conviction at trial seemed highly improbable. The defendant's reply was simple: "I can't take the chance."[8]

Both the gunman and the prosecutor require persons to make hard choices between a very certain smaller imposition and an uncertain greater imposition. In the gunman situation I must choose between the very certain loss of my money and the difficult-to-assess probability that my assailant is willing and able to kill me if I resist. As a defendant I am forced to choose between a very certain smaller punishment and a substantially greater punishment with a difficult-to-assess probability. As the size of the certain smaller imposition comes down and as the magnitude and probability of the larger imposition increases, it becomes more and more reasonable to choose the former. This is what seems to be occurring in Alschuler's example: "Davis reports that he is uncomfortable when he permits innocent defendants to plead guilty; but in this case it would have been playing God to stand in the defendant's way. The attorney's assessment of the outcome at trial can always be wrong, and it is hard to tell a defendant that 'professional ethics' require a course that may ruin his life." Davis's client must decide whether to accept a very certain, very minor punishment or to chance a ruined life. Of course the gunman's victim can try to overpower his assailant and the defendant can attempt to clear himself at trial. But the same considerations that will drive reasonable people to give in to the gunman compel one to accept the prosecutor's offer. Applying the second and third ele-ments of duress, one can see that, like the gunman's act, the acts of the prosecutor can "operate coercively upon the will of the plaintiff, judged subjectively," and both the gunman's victim and the defendant may "have no adequate remedy to avoid the coercion except to give in." In both cases reasonable persons might well conclude (after considering the gunman's lethal weapon or the gas chamber) "I can't take the chance." A spineless person would not need to deliberate....

One might argue that not all "hard choices" are examples of duress. A doctor could offer to sell vital treatment for a large sum. After the patient has been cured it will hardly do for her to claim that she has been the victim of duress. The doctor may have forced the patient to choose between a certain financial loss and the risk of death. But surely doctors are not like gunmen.

Two important points need to be made in response to this objection. First, the doctor is not, one assumes, responsible for the diseased condition of the patient. The patient would be facing death even if she had never met the doctor. But this is not true in the case of the gunman, where both impositions are his work. And in this respect the prosecutor offering a plea bargain in a criminal case is like the gunman rather than like the doctor. For the state forces a choice between adverse consequences that it imposes. And, of course, one cannot say that in the defendant's wrongdoing he has brought his dreadful dilemma upon himself. To do so would be to ignore the good reasons there are for the presumption of innocence in dispositive criminal proceedings.

Second, our laws do not prohibit doctors from applying their healing skills to maximize their own wealth. They are free to contract to perform services in return for a fee. But our laws do severely restrict the state in its prosecution of criminal defendants. Those who framed our constitution were well aware of the great potential for abuse that the criminal law affords. Much of the constitution (especially the Bill of Rights) checks the activity of the state in this area. In particular, the Fifth Amendment provides that no person "shall be compelled in any criminal case to be a witness against himself." If I am right in judging that defendants like Alford and Davis's client do not act freely in pleading guilty to the facts of their cases, that the forced choice of the prosecutor may be as coercive as the forced choice of the gunman, that a defendant may be compelled to speak against himself (or herself) by a prosecutor's discretion inducing him to plead guilty, then, given the apparent constitutional prohibition of such compulsion, the prosecutor acts wrongfully in compelling such pleas. And in this manner it may be that the last element of duress, wrongfulness, can be established. But it is not my purpose here to establish the unconstitutionality of plea bargaining, for it is not necessary to reach unconstitutionality to grasp the wrongfulness of that institution. One need only reflect upon what justice amounts to in our system of criminal law. This is the task I will take up in the final section of this paper.

II

Not too long ago plea bargaining was an officially prohibited practice. Court procedures were followed to ensure that no concessions had been given to defendants in exchange for guilty pleas. But gradually it became widely known that these procedures had become charades of perjury, shysterism, and bad faith involving judges, prosecutors, defense attorneys and defendants. This was scandalous. But rather than cleaning up the practice in order to square it with the rules, the rules were changed in order to bring them in line with the practice. There was a time when it apparently seemed plain that the old rules were the right rules. One finds in the *Restatement of Contracts:*[9] " ... even if the accused is guilty and the process valid, so that as against the State the imprisonment is lawful, it is a wrongful means of inducing the accused to enter into a transaction. To overcome the will of another for the prosecutor's advantage is *an abuse of the criminal law which was made for another purpose"* (emphasis added). The authors of the *Restatement* do not tell us what they were thinking when they spoke of the purpose of the criminal law. Nonetheless it is instructive to conjecture and to inquire along the lines suggested by the *Restatement.*

Without going deeply into detail, I believe that it can be asserted without controversy that the liberal-democratic approach to criminal justice—and in particular the American criminal justice system—is an institutionalization of two principles. The first principle refers to the intrinsic point of systems of criminal justice.

> A. Those (and only those) individuals who are clearly guilty of certain serious specified wrongdoings deserve an officially administered punishment which is proportional to their wrongdoing.

In the United States it is possible to see this principle underlying the activities of legislators specifying and grading wrongdoings which are serious enough to warrant criminalization and, further, determining the punishment appropriate to each offense; the activities of policemen and prosecutors bringing to trial those who are suspected of having committed such wrongdoings; the activities of jurors determining if defendants are guilty beyond a reasonable doubt; the activities of defense attorneys insuring that relevant facts in the defendant's favor are brought out at trial; the activities of judges seeing to it that proceedings are fair and that those who are convicted receive the punishment they deserve; and the activities of probation officers, parole officers, and prison personnel executing the sentences of the courts. All of these people play a part in bringing the guilty to justice.

But in liberal-democratic societies not everything is done to accomplish this end. A second principle makes reference to the limits placed upon the power of the state to identify and punish the guilty.

B. Certain basic liberties shall not be violated in bringing the guilty to justice.

This second principle can be seen to underlie the constellation of the constitutional checks on the activities of virtually every person playing a role in the administration of the criminal justice system.

Each of these principles is related to a distinctive type of injustice that can occur in the context of criminal law. An injustice can occur in the outcome of the criminal justice procedure. That is, an innocent defendant may be convicted and punished, or a guilty defendant may be acquitted or, if convicted, he or she may receive more or less punishment than is deserved. Because these injustices occur in the meting out of punishment to defendants who are being processed by the system, we can refer to them as internal injustices. They are violations of the first principle. On the other hand, there is a type of injustice which occurs when basic liberties are violated in the operation of the criminal justice system. It may be true that Star Chamber proceedings, torture, hostages, bills of attainder, dragnet arrests, unchecked searches, *ex post facto* laws, unlimited invasions of privacy, and an arsenal of other measures could be employed to bring more of the guilty to justice. But these steps lead to a dystopia where our most terrifying nightmares can come true. However we limit the activity of the criminal justice system in the interest of basic liberty, that limit can be overstepped. We can call such infringements upon basic liberties external injustices. They are violations of the second principle. If, for example, what I have suggested in the previous section is correct, then plea bargaining can bring about an external injustice with respect to a basic liberty secured by the Fifth Amendment. The remainder of this section will be concerned with internal injustice or violations of the first principle.

It is necessary to draw a further distinction between aberrational and systemic injustice. It may very well be that in the best criminal justice system that we are capable of devising human limitations will result in some aberrational injustice. Judges, jurors, lawyers, and legislators with the best of intentions may make errors in judgment that result in mistakes in the administration of punishment. But despite the knowledge that an unknown percentage of all dispositions of criminal cases are, to some extent, miscarriages of justice, it may still be reasonable to believe that a certain system of criminal justice is well calculated to avoid such results within the limits referred to by the second principle.[10] We can refer to these incorrect outcomes of a sound system of criminal justice as instances of aberrational injustice. In contrast, instances of systemic injustice are those that result from structural flaws in the criminal justice system itself. Here incorrect outcomes in the operations of the system are not the result of human error. Rather, the system itself is not well calculated to avoid injustice. What would be instances of aberrational injustice in a sound system are not aberrations in an unsound system: they are a standard result.

... [L]et us look at a particular instance of plea bargaining recently described by a legal aid defense attorney.[11] Ted Alston has been charged with armed robbery. Let us assume that persons who have committed armed robbery (in the way Alston is accused of having committed it) deserve five to seven years of prison. Alston's attorney sets out the options for him: "I told Alston it was possible, perhaps even probable, that if he went to trial he would be convicted and get a prison term of perhaps five to seven years. On the other hand, if he agreed to plead guilty to a low-grade felony, he would get a probationary sentence and not go to prison. The choice was his." Let us assume that Alston accepts the terms of the bargain and pleads guilty to a lesser offense. If Alston did commit the armed robbery, there is a violation of the first principle in that he receives far less punishment than he deserves. On the other hand, if Alston did not commit the armed robbery, there is still a violation of the first principle in that he is both convicted of and punished for a crime that he did not commit, a crime that no one seriously believes to be his distinctive wrongdoing. It is of course possible that while Alston did not commit the armed robbery, he did commit the lesser offense. But though justice would be done here, it would be an accident. Such a serendipitous result is a certain sign that what we have here is systemic injustice.

If we assume that legislatures approximate the correct range of punishment for each offense, that judges fairly sentence those who are convicted by juries, and that prosecutors reasonably charge defendants, then, barring accidents, justice will *never* be the outcome of the plea-bargaining procedure: the defendant who "cops a plea" will never receive the punishment which is deserved. Of course legislatures can set punishments too high, judges can oversentence those who are convicted by juries, and prosecutors can overcharge defendants. In these cases the guilty can receive the punishment they deserve through plea bargaining. But in these cases we compensate for one injustice by introducing others that unfairly jeopardize the innocent and those that demand trials.

In contrast to plea bargaining, the disposition of criminal cases by jury trial seems well calculated to avoid internal injustices even if these may sometimes occur. Where participants take their responsibilities seriously we have good reason to believe that the outcome is just, even when this may not be so. In contrast, with plea bargaining we have no reason to believe that the outcome is just even when it is.

I think that the appeal that plea bargaining has is rooted in our attitude toward bargains in general. Where both parties are satisfied with the terms of an agreement, it is improper to interfere. Generally speaking, prosecutors and defendants are pleased with the advantages they gain by negotiating a plea. And courts, which gain as well, are reluctant to vacate negotiated pleas where only "proper" inducements have been applied and where promises have been understood and kept. Such judicial neutrality may be commendable where entitlements are being exchanged. But the criminal justice system is not such a context. Rather it is one in which persons are justly given, not what they have bargained for, but what they deserve, irrespective of their bargaining position.

To appreciate this, let us consider another context in which desert plays a familiar role; the assignment of grades in an academic setting. Imagine a "grade bargain" negotiated between a grade-conscious student and a harried instructor. A term paper has been submitted and, after glancing at the first page, the instructor says that if he were to read the paper carefully, applying his usually rigid standards, he would probably decide to give the paper a grade of D. But if the student were to waive his right to a careful reading and conscientious critique, the instructor would agree to a grade of B. The grade-point average being more important to him than either education or justice in grading, the student happily accepts the B, and the instructor enjoys a reduced workload.

One strains to imagine legislators and administrators commending the practice of grade bargaining because it permits more students to be processed by fewer instructors. Teachers can be freed from the burden of having to read and to criticize every paper. One struggles to envision academicians arguing for grade bargaining in the way that jurists have defended plea bargaining, suggesting that a quick assignment of a grade is a more effective influence on the behavior of students, urging that grade bargaining is necessary to the efficient functioning of the schools. There can be no doubt that students who have negotiated a grade are more likely to accept and to understand the verdict of the instructor. Moreover, in recognition of a student's help to the

school (by waiving both the reading and the critique), it is proper for the instructor to be lenient. Finally, a quickly assigned grade enables the guidance personnel and the registrar to respond rapidly and appropriately to the student's situation.

What makes all of this laughable is what makes plea bargaining outrageous. For grades, like punishments, should be deserved. Justice in retribution, like justice in grading, does not require that the end result be acceptable to the parties. To reason that because the parties are satisfied the bargain should stand is to be seriously confused. For bargains are out of place in contexts where persons are to receive what they deserve. And the American courtroom, like the American classroom, should be such a context.

In this section, until now I have been attempting to show that plea bargaining is not well calculated to insure that those guilty of wrongdoing will receive the punishment they deserve. But a further point needs to be made. While the conviction of the innocent would be a problem in any system we might devise, it appears to be a greater problem under plea bargaining. With the jury system the guilt of the defendant must be established in an adversary proceeding and it must be established beyond a reasonable doubt to each of the twelve jurors. This is very staunch protection against an aberrational conviction. But under plea bargaining the foundation for conviction need only include a factual basis for the plea (in the opinion of the judge) and the guilty plea itself. Considering the coercive nature of the circumstances surrounding the plea, it would be a mistake to attach much reliability to it. Indeed, as we have seen in *Alford*, guilty pleas are acceptable even when accompanied by a denial of guilt.

And in a study of 724 defendants who had pleaded guilty, only 13.1 percent admitted guilt to an interviewer, while 51.6 percent asserted their innocence.[12] This leaves only the factual basis for the plea to serve as the foundation for conviction. Now it is one thing to show a judge that there are facts which support a plea of guilty and quite another to prove to twelve jurors in an adversary proceeding guilt beyond a reasonable doubt. Plea bargaining substantially erodes the standards for guilt and it is reasonable to assume that the sloppier we are in establishing guilt, the more likely it is that innocent persons will be convicted. So apart from having no reason whatever to believe that the guilty are receiving the punishment they deserve, we have far less reason to believe that the convicted are guilty in the first place than we would after a trial.

In its coercion of criminal defendants, in its abandonment of desert as the measure of punishment, and in its relaxation of the standards for conviction, plea bargaining falls short of the justice we expect of our legal system. I have no doubt that substantial changes will have to be made if the institution of plea bargaining is to be obliterated or even removed from its central position in the criminal justice system. No doubt we need more courts and more prosecutors. Perhaps ways can be found to streamline the jury trial procedure without sacrificing its virtues.[24] Certainly it would help to decriminalize the host of victimless crimes —drunkenness and other drug offenses, illicit sex, gambling and so on—in order to free resources for dealing with more serious wrongdoings. And perhaps crime itself can be reduced if we begin to attack seriously those social and economic injustices that have for too long sent their victims to our prisons in disproportionate numbers. In any case, if we are to expect our citizenry to respect the law, we must take care to insure that our legal institutions are worthy of that respect. I have tried to show that plea bargaining is not worthy, that we must seek a better way. Bargain justice does not become us.

NOTES

1. Often the judge will play an important role in these discussions, being called upon, for example, to indicate a willingness to go along with a bargain involving a reduction in sentence. A crowded calendar will make the bench an interested party.

2. In California, for example, armed robbers are technically guilty of kidnapping if they point a gun at their victim and tell him to back up. Thus, beyond the charge of armed robbery, they may face a charge of kidnapping which will be dropped upon entry of a guilty plea (see Albert W. Alschuler, "The Prosecutor's Role in Plea Bargaining," *University of Chicago Law Review* 36 (Fall 1968): 88).

3. Arthur Rosett, "The Negotiated Guilty Plea," *Annals of the American Academy of Political and Social Science* 374 (November 1967): 72.

4. Rosett, p. 71.

5. 392 F.2d 155 (1968).

6. 404 U.S. 257 (1971).

7. 400 U.S. 25 (1970) and 397 U.S. 742 (1970), respectively.

8. Alschuler, p. 61.

9. American Law Institute, *Restatement of Contracts* (Saint Paul, 1933), p. 652.

10. My discussion here owes much to John Rawls's treatment of "imperfect procedural justice" in his *A Theory of Justice* (Cambridge, 1971), pp. 85–86.

11. Robert Hermann, "The Case of the Jamaican Accent," *New York Times Magazine* (December 1, 1974), p. 93 (© The New York Times Company).

12. Abraham S. Blumberg, *Criminal Justice* (Chicago, 1967), p. 91.

13. John Langbein has suggested that we look to the German legal system to see how this might be done. See his "Controlling Prosecutorial Discretion in Germany," *University of Chicago Law Review* 41 (Spring 1974): 439.

NO

Nick Schweitzer

PLEA BARGAINING:
A PROSECUTOR'S VIEW

More than nine out of every ten cases I handle are disposed of by plea bargaining. And, to the best of my knowledge, except for Marco Polo-like reports from exotic foreign jurisdictions like Alaska and New Orleans, that ratio holds true for all prosecutors. Yet, despite the pervasiveness of the practice, plea bargaining often is criticized as improper—a conspiracy to emasculate the criminal justice system.

Plea bargaining is a useful, nay vital, tool. It is a response to a court system that never could accord the luxury of a trial to every criminal charge and civil suit brought before it. It is a practical way to dispose of matters that do not require the full solemnity of legal procedure. Plea bargaining in criminal cases is the equivalent of negotiation and mediation in civil cases. While the latter are praised and encouraged, the former is frequently condemned. Why?

At one level, academicians and other legal thinkers disapprove of prosecutors' unbridled discretion as not fitting into an orderly scheme. But, I see the criticism more often arising out of dissatisfaction with a particular case and expanding to the generalization that plea bargaining is bad. I find two basic reasons for such criticism. The first is that a particular plea-bargain genuinely may be "bad," which means that an offender is offered either a charge reduction or a sentence concession, or both, which is unmerited by the offender and unjustified by any necessity. Experience shows that such "bad" plea-bargains do occur in a small number of cases—generally for expedience, as explained later. The second source of criticism is much more common. This is where an interested party is dissatisfied with the outcome, finding it wholly inadequate to salve his or her injured feelings. I find that this is as likely to occur with a "good" plea-bargain, which is reasoned, conscientious and practical, as it is with a "bad" one.

The reason, I believe, lies in the differing expectations held by experienced criminal attorneys and the general public. Experienced attorneys know the inherent constraints and time-honored practices of our criminal justice system, which imposed practical limits on the punishment of an offender even if she or he were convicted at trial. However, if the case happens to be

From Nick Schweitzer, "Plea Bargaining: A Prosecutor's View," *Wisconsin Bar Bulletin* (October 1988). Copyright © 1988 by *Wisconsin Bar Bulletin*. Reprinted by permission of *Wisconsin Bar Bulletin*, the official publication of the State Bar of Wisconsin.

disposed of by a negotiated plea, critics may ascribe all their frustrations and disappointments to the plea-bargain.

LOOKING AHEAD TO SENTENCING

Strange as it sounds, and despite all the criticism, an essential aspect of plea bargaining is the need to be fair. Plea negotiations, like the sentencing discretion of judges, reflect the need to individualize justice. Only the most naive person would think that a single determinate sentence awaits the end of any particular prosecution. For any given defendant, on any given charge, there is a range of penalties. Most criminal statutes carry a maximum penalty, and some a minimum penalty. However, all Wisconsin statutes, except that for first-degree murder, permit a range. In addition, sentencing options may include community service and probation as well as conditions on probation such as counseling, restitution, jail time and alcohol and drug treatment. Except in certain categories of cases for which sentencing guidelines have been set,[1] sentencing is a human decision. At some stage, some person must decide what sentence will deter future acts by this offender and by other potential offenders without being unduly harsh and at the same time sufficiently assuage the victim.

The sentencing decision is not the function of a trial. A trial is held to determine facts and the essential facts are truly at issue in only a small fraction of criminal cases. The majority of people charged with crimes are guilty and know it, but before they plead guilty or no contest, they want to know what punishment they face. Often, the only argument is over one or more mitigating factors that do not rise to the level of legal defenses, so a trial in most criminal cases would be a waste of time. Sentencing is the bottom line for most defendants. If they can live with the sentence, most defendants are happy to save the court system and themselves the trouble of a trial. Generally, a bargain can be struck when the advantage to the defendant of an acceptable, known, sentence meets the advantage to the prosecutor of concluding the case for what it realistically is worth.

THE PROSECUTOR'S ROLE

The responsibility for sentencing ultimately lies with a judge. However, no judge has the time to check into the details of every felony, misdemeanor and ordinance that comes before the court. Court calendars being what they are, most judges want a recommendation from someone who already has taken the time to investigate the offense, the situation of any victims and the background of the defendant. A judge can accomplish this by ordering the local probation office to conduct a presentence investigation, but resources limit this option to only the more serious cases.

The prosecution and defense attorneys are in a position to review the offense, check the defendant's record and character, contact any victims and recommend an appropriate sentence. The prosecuting attorney knows the details of the offense and the defendant's prior record. The defense attorney knows the defendant and any mitigating factors. In most routine cases, these two lawyers are in the best position early on to discuss the merits of the case and are best able to find the time to negotiate before trial. If these two sides can reach agreement, the judge's decision can reasonably be reduced to review and ratification.

Another important reason for negotiation to take place at this level is the prosecutor's exclusive discretion to reduce or amend charges. A charge may be totally dismissed only with the court's approval.[2] However, the judge has no mandate to amend or reduce a charge. The discretion to amend charges is vested in the prosecutor to cover those rare cases where the wrong charge is issued.[3] This authority turns out to be even more useful in the frequent cases where some penalty is inappropriate. As an example, cooperative first offenders usually are offered some alternative, such as a county ordinance, that allows them to avoid a criminal record. This discretion to amend adds a second dimension to plea negotiations; the parties can consider not only the range of penalties associated with the original charge, but also the ranges associated with all related charges.

There are other reasons for a prosecutor to make concessions in return for a guilty or no contest plea. More often than not, a prosecutor will dismiss or read in one or more offenses for a defendant facing multiple charges. Usually, the prosecutor still will insist on a sentence consistent with the total number of offenses, but there is a general belief that reducing the number of convictions on the defendant's record will induce the defendant not to tie up the court system by trying all the cases. There also are cases in which the prosecutor faces some obstacle to conviction, other than the defendant's innocence, such as an unavailable witness or a witness who would be compromised or traumatized by having to testify. In such cases, any conviction, even on a reduced charge, generally is seen as better than a dismissal, an acquit-

tal or a Pyrrhic conviction. Then, there are the infrequent cases in which a concession is necessary to secure a defendant's testimony against a co-defendant in an unrelated case. Plea bargaining also can be used to expedite cases that would drag on for months or years. A prosecutor may agree to a charge or sentence concession in return for a speedy disposition that benefits a victim or quickly takes an offender out of circulation.

THE QUALITY OF THE BARGAIN

For all the above reasons, cases will continue to be settled at the trial attorneys' level. The real issue is the quality of the decisions made. Plea bargaining is a tool and its mark largely depends on the skill and care of the crafter. If the product is flawed, the fault lies less with the tool than with the user. The quality of the plea-bargain depends on the values, interests and abilities of the attorneys. If both sides are interested in finding a "just" sentence, the result is as likely to be "good" as that made by a conscientious judge. But if one or both sides are mainly interested in expedience, primarily want to "win" or have priorities unrelated to the merits of the defendant and the case, then the bargain may well be "bad." Unfortunately, it is true that prosecutors and defense attorneys make some "bad" plea-bargains. It also is true that judges can make sentencing decisions that are injudicious. Since the majority of cases are disposed of by negotiated plea, the opportunity for a "bad" decision by prosecutors is that much greater.

Two weaknesses exist in the plea bargaining process. First, it can become routine and thereby an end rather than a means. As stated earlier, very few cases crossing a prosecutor's desk deserve a trial. The majority of cases do settle and prosecutors develop a strong work habit of managing their caseload that way. As a result, a holdout case may be seen as a nuisance, causing plea bargaining to deteriorate into coercion, concession and compromise without regard for the merits of the case. The indiscriminate use of plea bargaining to clear court calendars justly has been condemned. But under pressure, a prosecutor's definition of a "reasonable" plea-bargain has an unfortunate tendency to expand.

Second, plea bargaining does not encourage participation by the victim. The criminal justice system historically has treated victims cavalierly. It is only with the recent development of victim/witness programs that victims' involvement is being encouraged.

Most victims want to have a voice in the outcome of a case, but this very seldom happens when cases are plea-bargained. Victims generally are left out because negotiations often are informal and unscheduled and talking to victims can be time-consuming and painful, as a victim's viewpoint often is very different from that of an experienced criminal attorney. Victims have difficulty accepting the concept of "what a case is worth" in criminal justice terms and understanding the realistic limitations on punishment. The prosecutor risks becoming the focus of the victim's anger, disappointment and abuse.

SUGGESTIONS

There are no standards or checks imposed on plea bargaining by statute or case law. In fact, courts strictly have avoided involvement in the process.[4] Whether to subject plea-bargaining to some degree of quality control is a policy decision balancing discretion and accountability. However, I offer a few suggestions to district attorneys and judges.

First, have set guidelines as have some D.A. offices. Well-understood policies for reductions and sentencing recommendations can limit very effectively the possibilities for poor judgment. Guidelines could be developed statewide, similar to the sentencing guidelines for judges, which set standard dispositions yet allow departure from the standards for good reason.

Second, plea-bargains could be reduced to writing and reviewed within the D.A.'s office before final agreement. Although this would add a step or two to the process, it would go a long way toward establishing uniformity, avoiding bad decisions and, if part of the policy, assuring that victims' views are considered.

Finally, any judge who is concerned about the quality of the plea-bargains brought before the court could develop questions for accepting a plea bargain, similar to those for the taking of a guilty plea. This allows the judge to play a more active role, or at least to signal that certain aspects of plea bargaining are open to scrutiny, without taking part in the actual negotiations. One question might ask the attorneys for justification of any reduction or sentencing recommendation. Another might ask whether a victim was involved and, if so, whether the victim has been consulted.

CONCLUSION

Despite my reservations about the potential and occasional weaknesses of plea bargaining, I defend the practice as a practical solution to some of the needs and pressures of today's criminal justice system. Plea bargaining is a vital part of the complex system of powers and responsibilities that has evolved in our efforts to make justice as equal, fair and efficient as resources permit. Without it, other parts of the system would have to absorb increased stress. Specifically, if we wanted judges to make all the decisions (even assuming that their decisions would uniformly be better), we would need more judges, more courtrooms, more jurors and more trials. This is not because defendants want trials but largely because most defendants will "plead in" only if they know ahead of time what sentence is likely to be imposed. Plea bargaining is essential until society decides to allocate sufficient resources to these ends. When exercised with a due regard to the case, the victim and the defendant, plea-bargains can result in outcomes as "just" as any available in our current system.

NOTES

1. State of Wisconsin Sentencing Commission, "Wisconsin Sentencing Guidelines Manual," (1985).

2. *State v. Kenyon*, 85 Wis. 2d 36, 270 N.W.2d 160 (1978).

3. Wis. Stat. § 971.29.

4. *See In the Matter of the Amendment of Rules of Civil & Criminal Procedure: Sections 971.07 & 971.08, Stats.*, 128 Wis. 2d 422, 383 N.W.2d 496 (1986); *State v. Erickson*, 53 Wis. 2d 474, 192 N.W.2d 872 (1972); *Rahhal v. State*, 52 Wis. 2d 144, 187 N.W.2d 800 (1971); *State v. Wolfe*, 46 Wis. 2d 478, 175 N.W.2d 216 (1970).

POSTSCRIPT

Should Plea Bargaining Be Abolished?

Plea bargaining, former Supreme Court chief justice Warren E. Burger has stated, "is an essential component of the administration of criminal justice." What is more debatable is another statement by Burger that "properly administered, it is to be encouraged." We do not know how many innocent persons have pleaded guilty in order to avoid a trial. On the other hand, abolitionists have difficulty describing what a workable replacement for plea bargaining would be like.

Interesting experiments to reform or abolish plea bargaining have taken place in Texas, as seen in Weninger, "The Abolition of Plea Bargaining: A Case Study of El Paso County, Texas," 35 *UCLA Law Review* 265 (1987) and Callan, "An Experiment in Justice Without Plea Negotiation," 13 *Law and Society Review*, pp. 327–347 (1979); Alaska, as seen in Carns, "Alaska's Ban on Plea Bargaining Reevaluated," 75 *Judicature* 310 (1992) and Rubinstein and White, "Plea Bargaining: Can Alaska Live Without It?" *Judicature* (December–January, 1979); and Arizona, as seen in Berger, "The Case Against Plea Bargaining," *ABA Journal*, p. 621 (1976). These and other alternatives to the plea bargaining system are examined in Alschuler, "Implementing the Criminal Defendant's Right to Trial: Alternatives to the Plea Bargaining System," 50 *University of Chicago Law Review* 931 (1983); Cohen and Doob, "Public Attitudes to Plea Bargaining," 32 *Criminal Law Quarterly* 85 (1989); "The Victim's Veto: A Way to Increase Victim Impact on Criminal Case Dispositions," 77 *California Law Review* 417 (1989); Fine, "Plea Bargaining: An Unnecessary Evil," 70 *Marquette Law Review* 615 (1987); Schulhofer, "Plea Bargaining as Disaster," 101 *Yale Law Journal* 1979 (1992); and Note, "Constitutional Alternatives to Plea Bargaining: A New Waive," 132 *University of Pennsylvania Law Review* 327 (1984).

Plea bargaining has been the subject of a considerable number of Supreme Court cases. Among the most noteworthy are *Boykin v. Alabama*, 395 U.S. 238 (1969); *Brady v. U.S.*, 397 U.S. 742 (1970); *North Carolina v. Alford*, 400 U.S. 25 (1970); *Santobello v. New York*, 404 U.S. 257 (1971); and *Bordenkircher v. Hayes*, 434 U.S. 357 (1978). Each of these cases describes the plight of a particular defendant, but probably the most vivid account of the plea bargaining process is a journalist's description. See Mills, "I Have Nothing to Do With Justice," *Life* (March 12, 1971), reprinted in Bonsignore et al., *Before the Law: An Introduction to the Legal Process* (Houghton Mifflin, 1979). Two Internet sites that discuss in detail lawsuits and trial procedures are http://www.lawlead.com/minnesota/business/chapters/b04.html and http://www.ojp.usdoj.gov/BJA/html/victsguide.htm.

ISSUE 4

Are Term Limits for Elected Officials Unconstitutional?

YES: John Paul Stevens, from Majority Opinion, *U.S. Term Limits, Inc., et al. v. Ray Thornton et al.,* U.S. Supreme Court (1995)

NO: Clarence Thomas, from Dissenting Opinion, *U.S. Term Limits, Inc., et al. v. Ray Thornton et al.,* U.S. Supreme Court (1995)

ISSUE SUMMARY

YES: Supreme Court justice John Paul Stevens, representing the majority opinion, reaffirms the Court's belief that the Framers intended the Constitution to establish fixed qualifications for members of Congress and that the power to add qualifications, such as term limits, is not reserved to the states by the Tenth Amendment.

NO: Supreme Court justice Clarence Thomas argues that the federal Constitution permits states to add qualifications for electing members of Congress because it does not explicitly prohibit them from doing so.

Citizen dissatisfaction with electoral politics has recently manifested itself in the form of both national and grassroots movements advocating term limits for state and federal legislators. With the historic midterm elections of 1994, in which the Republican party gained control of both houses of the U.S. Congress for the first time in 40 years, the term limits movement attained new levels of interest and success. In a two-year period (1992–1994), 20 states decided, by popular vote, to impose restrictions on how long their elected representatives could serve in Congress. In addition, voters have placed restrictions on the terms of service of state and local legislators.

The modern term limits movement had its origins in California's populist politics of the late 1970s and early 1980s. The focus initially was on local politicians—mayors and city council members. It developed a more national perspective as public cynicism increased. Many critics of American electoral politics have long observed that the most needed reform was in how we financed elections. However, the appeal of term limits was simple and straightforward; it is captured in the old political epithet "Throw the bums out." By the 1990s opinion polls suggested that politicians had sunk to new levels of disrepute. The public seemed to conflate current social and economic problems with the shortcomings of "career" politicians and their susceptibility to the pressures of monied special interest groups. Term limits seemed to many the best solution.

Certainly, distrust of government and a skeptical attitude toward the intentions of those in public office are not new phenomena in American political life. As the following selections by Supreme Court justices John Paul Stevens and Clarence Thomas indicate, such concerns permeated the Federalist/Anti-Federalist debates over the ratification of the Constitution; they continued, with varying degrees of intensity, in the ensuing years.

Proponents of term limits contend that such restrictions are necessary in order to return real choice to the electorate. The power of incumbency has become so great, it is argued, that challengers for a congressional seat face little real chance of success. The result is that many qualified potential candidates have declined to run for office; elections have lost a sense of real competitiveness, of providing real choice; and voter interest and turnout has decreased. The consequence of all this, it is claimed, is that democracy itself is threatened. A recent convert to the term limits side, the conservative political commentator George Will, argues that "[l]imits are required to institute healthy competition in the political market just as anti-trust intervention in economic markets can serve the values of a basically free market economy." (*Restoration*, Free Press, 1992). Opponents of term limits argue that legally mandated restrictions on terms of office are fundamentally undemocratic, serving actually to limit the electorate's choice by removing popular legislators from the candidate pool, for no reason other than length of service. Opponents are also fond of reminding advocates of term limits that such limits have been in place from the beginning of the republic; it is the very purpose of an election. Moreover, opponents argue that state-imposed term limits for members of the House of Representatives are unconstitutional. The Supreme Court, although sharply divided, has now decided the issue in favor of the opponents of term limits. The reader may note that beyond compelling issues of representative politics, the term limits debate raises constitutional questions fundamental to the U.S. federal system—the power of the states relative to the national government.

Arkansas was typical of many of the states in which an angry and disaffected populism had developed. There, voters approved a state constitutional amendment that prohibited the appearance on state ballots of the name of any candidate who had been elected for three or more terms to the Arkansas delegation to the U.S. House of Representatives or who had been elected for two or more terms to the U.S. Senate. The amendment did allow voters to write in the name of any candidate otherwise covered under its terms. Before its effective date, however, Arkansas resident Bobbie E. Hill challenged the constitutionality of the amendment and sought a declaratory judgment in the Arkansas state court system. The state courts held that the ballot-access prohibition was in violation of the "qualifications" provisions of the U.S. Constitution (Article I, Section 2, Clause 2, and Article I, Section 3, Clause 3). The Supreme Court affirmed the decision of the Arkansas courts.

YES

John Paul Stevens

MAJORITY OPINION

U.S. TERM LIMITS, INC. *v.* THORNTON

The Constitution sets forth qualifications for membership in the Congress of the United States. Article I, Sec. 2, cl. 2, which applies to the House of Representatives, provides:

> "No Person shall be a Representative who shall not have attained to the Age of twenty five Years, and been seven Years a Citizen of the United States, and who shall not, when elected, be an Inhabitant of that State in which he shall be chosen."

Article I, Sec. 3, cl. 3, which applies to the Senate, similarly provides:

> "No Person shall be a Senator who shall not have attained to the Age of thirty Years, and been nine Years a Citizen of the United States, and who shall not, when elected, be an Inhabitant of that State for which he shall be chosen."

Today's cases present a challenge to an amendment to the Arkansas State Constitution that prohibits the name of an otherwise-eligible candidate for Congress from appearing on the general election ballot if that candidate has already served three terms in the House of Representatives or two terms in the Senate. The Arkansas Supreme Court held that the amendment violates the Federal Constitution. We agree with that holding. Such a state-imposed restriction is contrary to the "fundamental principle of our representative democracy," embodied in the Constitution, that "the people should choose whom they please to govern them." *Powell v. McCormack*, 395 U.S. 486, 547 (1969). Allowing individual States to adopt their own qualifications for congressional service would be inconsistent with the Framers' vision of a uniform National Legislature representing the people of the United States. If the qualifications set forth in the text of the Constitution are to be changed, that text must be amended.

... [T]he constitutionality of Amendment 73 depends critically on the resolution of two distinct issues. The first is whether the Constitution forbids States from adding to or altering the qualifications specifically enumerated in the Constitution. The second is, if the Constitution does so forbid, whether

From *U.S. Term Limits, Inc., et al. v. Ray Thornton et al.*, 115 S. Ct. 1842, 131 L.Ed.2d 881 (1995). Notes and some case citations omitted.

the fact that Amendment 73 is formulated as a ballot access restriction rather than as an outright disqualification is of constitutional significance. Our resolution of these issues draws upon our prior resolution of a related but distinct issue: whether Congress has the power to add to or alter the qualifications of its Members.

Twenty-six years ago, in *Powell v. McCormack*, 395 U.S. 486, we reviewed the history and text of the Qualifications Clauses in a case involving an attempted exclusion of a duly elected Member of Congress. The principal issue was whether the power granted to each House in Art. I, Sec. 5, to judge the "Qualifications of its own Members" includes the power to impose qualifications other than those set forth in the text of the Constitution. In an opinion by Chief Justice Warren for eight Members of the Court, we held that it does not. Because of the obvious importance of the issue, the Court's review of the history and meaning of the relevant constitutional text was especially thorough....

[O]ur historical analysis in *Powell* was both detailed and persuasive. We thus conclude now, as we did [then], that history shows that, with respect to Congress, the Framers intended the Constitution to establish fixed qualifications.

Powell's Reliance on Democratic Principles

In *Powell*, of course, we did not rely solely on an analysis of the historical evidence, but instead complemented that analysis with "an examination of the basic principles of our democratic system." *Id.*, at 548. We noted that allowing Congress to impose additional qualifications would violate that "fundamental principle of our representative democracy... 'that the

people should choose whom they please to govern them.'" *Id.*, at 547, quoting 2 Elliot's Debates 257 (A. Hamilton, New York).

Our opinion made clear that this broad principle incorporated at least two fundamental ideas. First, we emphasized the egalitarian concept that the opportunity to be elected was open to all. We noted in particular Madison's statement in The Federalist that "'[u]nder these reasonable limitations [enumerated in the Constitution], the door of this part of the federal government is open to merit of every description, whether native or adoptive, whether young or old, and without regard to poverty or wealth, or to any particular profession of religious faith.'" *Powell*, 395 U.S. at 540, n. 74, quoting The Federalist No. 52, at 326. Similarly, we noted that Wilson Carey Nicholas defended the Constitution against the charge that it "violated democratic principles" by arguing: "'It has ever been considered a great security to liberty, that very few should be excluded from the right of being chosen to the legislature. This Constitution has amply attended to this idea. We find no qualifications required except those of age and residence.'" 395 U.S. at 541, quoting 3 Elliot's Debates 8.

Second, we recognized the critical postulate that sovereignty is vested in the people, and that sovereignty confers on the people the right to choose freely their representatives to the National Government. For example, we noted that "Robert Livingston... endorsed this same fundamental principle: 'The people are the best judges who ought to represent them. To dictate and control them, to tell them whom they shall not elect, is to abridge their natural rights.'" 395 U.S. at 541, n. 76, quoting 2 Elliot's Debates 292-293. Similarly, we observed that "[b]efore the New York convention..., Hamilton emphasized: 'The true principle of a republic is, that the people should choose whom they please to govern them. Representation is imperfect in proportion as the current of popular favor is checked. This great source of free government, popular election, should be perfectly pure, and the most unbounded liberty allowed.'" 395 U.S. at 540–541, quoting 2 Elliot's Debates 257. Quoting from the statement made in 1807 by the Chairman of the House Committee on Elections, we noted that "restrictions upon the people to choose their own representatives must be limited to those 'absolutely necessary for the safety of the society.'" 395 U.S. at 543, quoting 17 Annals of Cong. 874 (1807). Thus, in *Powell*, we agreed with the sentiment... "'[T]hat the right of the electors to be represented by men of their own choice, was so essential for the preservation of all their other rights, that it ought to be considered as one of the most sacred parts of our constitution.'" 395 U.S. at 534, n. 65, quoting 16 Parl. Hist. Eng. 589-590 (1769).

Powell thus establishes two important propositions: first, that the "relevant historical materials" compel the conclusion that, at least with respect to qualifications imposed by Congress, the Framers intended the qualifications listed in the Constitution to be exclusive; and second, that that conclusion is equally compelled by an understanding of the "fundamental principle of our representative democracy... 'that the people should choose whom they please to govern them.'" 395 U.S. at 547....

In sum, after examining *Powell*'s historical analysis and its articulation of the "basic principles of our democratic system," we reaffirm that the qualifications for service in Congress set forth in the text of the Constitution are "fixed," at least in the sense that they may not be supplemented by Congress.

III

Our reaffirmation of *Powell*, does not necessarily resolve the specific questions presented in these cases. For petitioners argue that whatever the constitutionality of additional qualifications for membership imposed by Congress, the historical and textual materials discussed in *Powell* do not support the conclusion that the Constitution prohibits additional qualifications imposed by States. In the absence of such a constitutional prohibition, petitioners argue, the Tenth Amendment and the principle of reserved powers require that States be allowed to add such qualifications....

Petitioners argue that the Constitution contains no express prohibition against state-added qualifications, and that Amendment 73 is therefore an appropriate exercise of a State's reserved power to place additional restrictions on the choices that its own voters may make. We disagree for two independent reasons. First, we conclude that the power to add qualifications is not within the "original powers" of the States, and thus is not reserved to the States by the Tenth Amendment. Second, even if States possessed some original power in this area, we conclude that the Framers intended the Constitution to be the exclusive source of qualifications for members of Congress, and that the Framers thereby "divested" States of any power to add qualifications.

The "plan of the convention" as illuminated by the historical materials, our opinions, and the text of the Tenth Amendment, draws a basic distinction between the powers of the newly created Federal Government and the powers retained by the pre-existing sovereign States. As Chief Justice Marshall explained, "it was neither necessary nor proper to define the powers retained by the States. These powers proceed, not from the people of America, but from the people of the several States; and remain, after the adoption of the constitution, what they were before, except so far as they may be abridged by that instrument."

This classic statement by the Chief Justice endorsed Hamilton's reasoning in The Federalist No. 32 that the plan of the Constitutional Convention did not contemplate "an entire consolidation of the States into one complete national sovereignty," but only a partial consolidation in which "the State governments would clearly retain all the rights of sovereignty which they before had, and which were not, by that act, exclusively delegated to the United States." The Federalist No. 32, at 198. The text of the Tenth Amendment unambiguously confirms this principle:

"The powers not delegated to the United States by the Constitution, nor prohibited by it to the States, are reserved to the States respectively, or to the people."

As we have frequently noted, "the States unquestionably do retain a significant measure of sovereign authority. They do so, however, only to the extent that the Constitution has not divested them of their original powers and transferred those powers to the Federal Government." *Garcia v. San Antonio Metropoli-*

tan Transit Authority, 469 U.S. 528, 549 (1985).

Source of the Power

Contrary to petitioners' assertions, the power to add qualifications is not part of the original powers of sovereignty that the Tenth Amendment reserved to the States. Petitioners' Tenth Amendment argument misconceives the nature of the right at issue because that Amendment could only "reserve" that which existed before. As Justice Story recognized, "the states can exercise no powers whatsoever, which exclusively spring out of the existence of the national government, which the constitution does not delegate to them.... No state can say, that it has reserved, what it never possessed." 1 Story Sec. 627.

Justice Story's position thus echoes that of Chief Justice Marshall in *McCulloch v. Maryland,* 17 U.S. 316, 4 Wheat. 316, 4 L.Ed. 579 (1819). In *McCulloch,* the Court rejected the argument that the Constitution's silence on the subject of state power to tax corporations chartered by Congress implies that the States have "reserved" power to tax such federal instrumentalities. As Chief Justice Marshall pointed out, an "original right to tax" such federal entities "never existed, and the question whether it has been surrendered, cannot arise." *id.,* at 430. In language that presaged Justice Story's argument, Chief Justice Marshall concluded: "This opinion does not deprive the States of any resources which they originally possessed." 4 Wheat., at 436.

With respect to setting qualifications for service in Congress, no such right existed before the Constitution was ratified. The contrary argument overlooks the revolutionary character of the government that the Framers conceived. Prior to the adoption of the Constitution, the States had joined together under the Articles of Confederation. In that system, "the States retained most of their sovereignty, like independent nations bound together only by treaties." After the Constitutional Convention convened, the Framers were presented with, and eventually adopted a variation of, "a plan not merely to amend the Articles of Confederation but to create an entirely new National Government with a National Executive, National Judiciary, and a National Legislature." In adopting that plan, the Framers envisioned a uniform national system, rejecting the notion that the Nation was a collection of States, and instead creating a direct link between the National Government and the people of the United States. In that National Government, representatives owe primary allegiance not to the people of a State, but to the people of the Nation. As Justice Story observed, each Member of Congress is "an officer of the union, deriving his powers and qualifications from the constitution, and neither created by, dependent upon, nor controllable by, the states.... Those officers owe their existence and functions to the united voice of the whole, not of a portion, of the people." 1 Story Sec. 627. Representatives and Senators are as much officers of the entire union as is the President. States thus "have just as much right, and no more, to prescribe new qualifications for a representative, as they have for a president.... It is no original prerogative of state power to appoint a representative, a senator, or president for the union." *Ibid.*

We believe that the Constitution reflects the Framers' general agreement with the approach later articulated by Justice Story. For example, Art. I, Sec. 5, cl. 1 provides: "Each House shall be the Judge of the Elections, Returns and Qualifications of its own Members." The text of the Constitution thus gives the representatives of all the people the final say in judging the qualifications of the representatives of any one State. For this reason, the dissent falters when it states that "the people of Georgia have no say over whom the people of Massachusetts select to represent them in Congress." ...

In short, as the Framers recognized, electing representatives to the National Legislature was a new right, arising from the Constitution itself. The Tenth Amendment thus provides no basis for concluding that the States possess reserved power to add qualifications to those that are fixed in the Constitution. Instead, any state power to set the qualifications for membership in Congress must derive not from the reserved powers of state sovereignty, but rather from the delegated powers of national sovereignty. In the absence of any constitutional delegation to the States of power to add qualifications to those enumerated in the Constitution, such a power does not exist.

The Preclusion of State Power

Even if we believed that States possessed as part of their original powers some control over congressional qualifications, the text and structure of the Constitution, the relevant historical materials, and, most importantly, the "basic principles of our democratic system" all demonstrate that the Qualifications Clauses were intended to preclude the States from exercising any such power and to fix as exclusive the qualifications in the Constitution....

The available affirmative evidence indicates the Framers' intent that States have no role in the setting of qualifications. In Federalist Paper No. 52, dealing with the House of Representatives, Madison addressed the "qualifications of the electors and the elected." The Federalist No. 52, at 325. Madison first noted the difficulty in achieving uniformity in the qualifications for electors, which resulted in the Framers' decision to require only that the qualifications for federal electors be the same as those for state electors. Madison argued that such a decision "must be satisfactory to every State, because it is comfortable to the standard already established, or which may be established, by the State itself." Id., at 326. Madison then explicitly contrasted the state control over the qualifications of electors with the lack of state control over the qualifications of the elected:

"The qualifications of the elected, being less carefully and properly defined by the State constitutions, and being at the same time more susceptible of uniformity, have been very properly considered and regulated by the convention. A representative of the United States must be of the age of twenty-five years; must have been seven years a citizen of the United States; must, at the time of his election be an inhabitant of the State he is to represent; and, during the time of his service must be in no office under the United States. Under these reasonable limitations, the door of this part of the federal government is open to merit of every description, whether native or adoptive, whether young or old, and without regard to poverty or wealth, or to any particular profession of religious faith." Ibid.

Madison emphasized this same idea in Federalist 57:

"Who are to be the objects of popular choice? Every citizen whose merit may recommend him to the esteem and confidence of his country. No qualification of wealth, of birth, of religious faith, or of civil profession is permitted to fetter the judgment or disappoint the inclination of the people." The Federalist No. 57, at 351.

The provisions in the Constitution governing federal elections confirm the Framers' intent that States lack power to add qualifications. The Framers feared that the diverse interests of the States would undermine the National Legislature, and thus they adopted provisions intended to minimize the possibility of state interference with federal elections. For example, to prevent discrimination against federal electors, the Framers required in Art. I, Sec. 2, cl. 1, that the qualifications for federal electors be the same as those for state electors. As Madison noted, allowing States to differentiate between the qualifications for state and federal electors "would have rendered too dependent on the State governments that branch of the federal government which ought to be dependent on the people alone." The Federalist No. 52, at 326. Similarly, in Art. I, Sec. 4, cl. 1, though giving the States the freedom to regulate the "Times, Places and Manner of holding Elections," the Framers created a safeguard against state abuse by giving Congress the power to "by Law make or alter such Regulations." The Convention debates make clear that the Framers' overriding concern was the potential for States' abuse of the power to set the "Times, Places and Manner" of elections. Madison noted that "it was impossible to foresee all the abuses that might be made of the discretionary power." 2 Farrand 240. Gouverneur Morris feared "that the States might make false returns and then make no provisions for new elections." Id., at 241. When Charles Pinckney and John Rutledge moved to strike the congressional safeguard, the motion was soundly defeated. *Id.,* at 240-241. As Hamilton later noted: "Nothing can be more evident than that an exclusive power of regulating elections for the national government, in the hands of the State legislatures, would leave the existence of the Union entirely at their mercy." The Federalist No. 59, at 363. . . .

In light of the Framers' evident concern that States would try to undermine the National Government, they could not have intended States to have the power to set qualifications. Indeed, one of the more anomalous consequences of petitioners' argument is that it accepts federal supremacy over the procedural aspects of determining the times, places, and manner of elections while allowing the states carte blanche with respect to the substantive qualifications for membership in Congress. . . .

We find further evidence of the Framers' intent in Art. 1, Sec. 5, cl. 1, which provides: "Each House shall be the Judge of the Elections, Returns and Qualifications of its own Members." That Art. I, Sec. 5 vests a federal tribunal with ultimate authority to judge a Member's qualifications is fully consistent with the understanding that those qualifications are fixed in the Federal Constitution, but not with the understanding that they can be altered by the States. If the States had the right to prescribe additional qualifications—such as property, educational, or professional qualifications—for their own representatives, state law would provide the standard for judging a Member's eligibility. . . . The Constitution's provision for each House to be the judge of its own qualifications thus provides further evidence that the Framers believed that the primary source

of those qualifications would be federal law.

We also find compelling the complete absence in the ratification debates of any assertion that States had the power to add qualifications. In those debates, the question whether to require term limits, or "rotation," was a major source of controversy. The draft of the Constitution that was submitted for ratification contained no provision for rotation. In arguments that echo in the preamble to Arkansas' Amendment 73, opponents of ratification condemned the absence of a rotation requirement, noting that "there is no doubt that senators will hold their office perpetually; and in this situation, they must of necessity lose their dependence, and their attachments to the people." Even proponents of ratification expressed concern about the "abandonment in every instance of the necessity of rotation in office." At several ratification conventions, participants proposed amendments that would have required rotation.

The Federalists' responses to those criticisms and proposals addressed the merits of the issue, arguing that rotation was incompatible with the people's right to choose. As we noted above, Robert Livingston argued:

> "The people are the best judges who ought to represent them. To dictate and control them, to tell them whom they shall not elect, is to abridge their natural rights. This rotation is an absurd species of ostracism." 2 Elliot's Debates 292-293.

Similarly, Hamilton argued that the representatives' need for reelection rather than mandatory rotation was the more effective way to keep representatives responsive to the people, because "when a man knows he must quit his station, let his merit be what it may, he will turn his attention chiefly to his own emolument." *Id.*, at 320.

Regardless of which side has the better of the debate over rotation, it is most striking that nowhere in the extensive ratification debates have we found any statement by either a proponent or an opponent of rotation that the draft constitution would permit States to require rotation for the representatives of their own citizens. If the participants in the debate had believed that the States retained the authority to impose term limits, it is inconceivable that the Federalists would not have made this obvious response to the arguments of the pro-rotation forces. The absence in an otherwise freewheeling debate of any suggestion that States had the power to impose additional qualifications unquestionably reflects the Framers' common understanding that States lacked that power.

In short, if it had been assumed that States could add additional qualifications, that assumption would have provided the basis for a powerful rebuttal to the arguments being advanced. The failure of intelligent and experienced advocates to utilize this argument must reflect a general agreement that its premise was unsound, and that the power to add qualifications was one that the Constitution denied the States....

Our conclusion that States lack the power to impose qualifications vindicates the same "fundamental principle of our representative democracy" that we recognized in *Powell*, namely that "the people should choose whom they please to govern them." *Id.*, at 547.

As we noted earlier, the *Powell* Court recognized that an egalitarian ideal— that election to the National Legislature should be open to all people of merit —provided a critical foundation for the Constitutional structure. This egalitarian theme echoes throughout the constitutional debates. In The Federalist No. 57, for example, Madison wrote:

"Who are to be the objects of popular choice? Every citizen whose merit may recommend him to the esteem and confidence of his country. No qualification of wealth, of birth, of religious faith, or of civil profession is permitted to fetter the judgment or disappoint the inclination of the people." The Federalist No. 57, at 351.

... Similarly, we believe that state-imposed qualifications, as much as congressionally imposed qualifications, would undermine the second critical idea recognized in *Powell*: that an aspect of sovereignty is the right of the people to vote for whom they wish. Again, the source of the qualification is of little moment in assessing the qualification's restrictive impact.

Finally, state-imposed restrictions, unlike the congressionally imposed restrictions at issue in *Powell*, violate a third idea central to this basic principle: that the right to choose representatives belongs not to the States, but to the people. From the start, the Framers recognized that the "great and radical vice" of the Articles of Confederation was "the principle of LEGISLATION for STATES or GOVERNMENTS, in their CORPORATE or COLLECTIVE CAPACITIES, and as contradistinguished from the INDIVIDUALS of whom they consist." The Federalist No. 15, at 108 (Hamilton). Thus the Framers, in perhaps their most important contribution, conceived of a Federal Government directly responsible to the people, possessed of direct power over the people, and chosen directly, not by States, but by the people. The Framers implemented this ideal most clearly in the provision, extant from the beginning of the Republic, that calls for the Members of the House of Representatives to be "chosen every second Year by the People of the several States." Art. I, Sec. 2, cl. 1. Following the adoption of the 17th Amendment in 1913, this ideal was extended to elections for the Senate. The Congress of the United States, therefore, is not a confederation of nations in which separate sovereigns are represented by appointed delegates, but is instead a body composed of representatives of the people. As Chief Justice John Marshall observed: "The government of the union, then, ... is, emphatically, and truly, a government of the people. In form and in substance it emanates from them. Its powers are granted by them, and are to be exercised directly on them, and for their benefit." *McCulloch v. Maryland*, 4 Wheat., at 404–405. Ours is a "government of the people, by the people, for the people." A. Lincoln, Gettysburg Address (1863)....

Consistent with these views, the constitutional structure provides for a uniform salary to be paid from the national treasury, allows the States but a limited role in federal elections, and maintains strict checks on state interference with the federal election process. The Constitution also provides that the qualifications of the representatives of each State will be judged by the representatives of the entire Nation. The Constitution thus creates a uniform national body representing the interests of a single people.

Permitting individual States to formulate diverse qualifications for their representatives would result in a patchwork of state qualifications, undermining the uniformity and the national character that

the Framers envisioned and sought to ensure....

The merits of term limits, or "rotation," have been the subject of debate since the formation of our Constitution, when the Framers unanimously rejected a proposal to add such limits to the Constitution. The cogent arguments on both sides of the question that were articulated during the process of ratification largely retain their force today. Over half the States have adopted measures that impose such limits on some offices either directly or indirectly, and the Nation as a whole, notably by constitutional amendment, has imposed a limit on the number of terms that the President may serve. Term limits, like any other qualification for office, unquestionably restrict the ability of voters to vote for whom they wish. On the other hand, such limits may provide for the infusion of fresh ideas and new perspectives, and may decrease the likelihood that representatives will lose touch with their constituents. It is not our province to resolve this longstanding debate.

We are, however, firmly convinced that allowing the several States to adopt term limits for congressional service would effect a fundamental change in the constitutional framework. Any such change must come not by legislation adopted either by Congress or by an individual State, but rather—as have other important changes in the electoral process—through the Amendment procedures set forth in Article V. The Framers decided that the qualifications for service in the Congress of the United States be fixed in the Constitution and be uniform throughout the Nation. That decision reflects the Framers' understanding that Members of Congress are chosen by separate constituencies, but that they become, when elected, servants of the people of the United States. They are not merely delegates appointed by separate, sovereign States; they occupy offices that are integral and essential components of a single National Government. In the absence of a properly passed constitutional amendment, allowing individual States to craft their own qualifications for Congress would thus erode the structure envisioned by the Framers, a structure that was designed, in the words of the Preamble to our Constitution, to form a "more perfect Union."

NO

Clarence Thomas

DISSENTING OPINION OF CLARENCE THOMAS

It is ironic that the Court bases today's decision on the right of the people to "choose whom they please to govern them." Under our Constitution, there is only one State whose people have the right to "choose whom they please" to represent Arkansas in Congress. The Court holds, however, that neither the elected legislature of that State nor the people themselves (acting by ballot initiative) may prescribe any qualifications for those representatives. The majority therefore defends the right of the people of Arkansas to "choose whom they please to govern them" by invalidating a provision that won nearly 60% of the votes cast in a direct election and that carried every congressional district in the State.

I dissent. Nothing in the Constitution deprives the people of each State of the power to prescribe eligibility requirements for the candidates who seek to represent them in Congress. The Constitution is simply silent on this question. And where the Constitution is silent, it raises no bar to action by the States or the people.

I

Because the majority fundamentally misunderstands the notion of "reserved" powers, I start with some first principles. Contrary to the majority's suggestion, the people of the States need not point to any affirmative grant of power in the Constitution in order to prescribe qualifications for their representatives in Congress, or to authorize their elected state legislators to do so.

A

Our system of government rests on one overriding principle: all power stems from the consent of the people. To phrase the principle in this way, however, is to be imprecise about something important to the notion of "reserved" powers. The ultimate source of the Constitution's authority is the consent of

From *U.S. Term Limits, Inc., et al. v. Ray Thornton et al.,* 115 S. Ct. 1842, 131 L.Ed.2d 881 (1995). Notes and some case citations omitted.

the people of each individual State, not the consent of the undifferentiated people of the Nation as a whole.

The ratification procedure erected by Article VII makes this point clear. The Constitution took effect once it had been ratified by the people gathered in convention in nine different States. But the Constitution went into effect only "between the States so ratifying the same," Art. VII; it did not bind the people of North Carolina until they had accepted it. In Madison's words, the popular consent upon which the Constitution's authority rests was "given by the people, not as individuals composing one entire nation, but as composing the distinct and independent States to which they respectively belong." The Federalist No. 39, p. 243 (C. Rossiter ed. 1961) (hereinafter The Federalist). Accord, 3 Debates in the Several State Conventions on the Adoption of the Federal Constitution 94 (J. Elliot 2d ed. 1876) (hereinafter Elliot) (remarks of James Madison at the Virginia convention).

When they adopted the Federal Constitution, of course, the people of each State surrendered some of their authority to the United States (and hence to entities accountable to the people of other States as well as to themselves). They affirmatively deprived their States of certain powers, see, e.g., Art. I, Sec. 10, and they affirmatively conferred certain powers upon the Federal Government, see, e.g., Art. I, Sec. 8. Because the people of the several States are the only true source of power, however, the Federal Government enjoys no authority beyond what the Constitution confers: the Federal Government's powers are limited and enumerated. In the words of Justice Black, "the United States is entirely a creature of the Constitution.

Its power and authority have no other source."

In each State, the remainder of the people's powers—"the powers not delegated to the United States by the Constitution, nor prohibited by it to the States," Amdt. 10—are either delegated to the state government or retained by the people. The Federal Constitution does not specify which of these two possibilities obtains; it is up to the various state constitutions to declare which powers the people of each State have delegated to their state government. As far as the Federal Constitution is concerned, then, the States can exercise all powers that the Constitution does not withhold from them. The Federal Government and the States thus face different default rules: where the Constitution is silent about the exercise of a particular power—that is, where the Constitution does not speak either expressly or by necessary implication—the Federal Government lacks that power and the States enjoy it.

These basic principles are enshrined in the Tenth Amendment, which declares that all powers neither delegated to the Federal Government nor prohibited to the States "are reserved to the States respectively, or to the people." With this careful last phrase, the Amendment avoids taking any position on the division of power between the state governments and the people of the States: it is up to the people of each State to determine which "reserved" powers their state government may exercise. But the Amendment does make clear that powers reside at the state level except where the Constitution removes them from that level. All powers that the Constitution neither delegates to the Federal Government nor prohibits to the States are controlled by the people of each State.

To be sure, when the Tenth Amendment uses the phrase "the people," it does not specify whether it is referring to the people of each State or the people of the Nation as a whole. But the latter interpretation would make the Amendment pointless: there would have been no reason to provide that where the Constitution is silent about whether a particular power resides at the state level, it might or might not do so. In addition, it would make no sense to speak of powers as being reserved to the undifferentiated people of the Nation as a whole, because the Constitution does not contemplate that those people will either exercise power or delegate it. The Constitution simply does not recognize any mechanism for action by the undifferentiated people of the Nation. Thus, the amendment provision of Article V calls for amendments to be ratified not by a convention of the national people, but by conventions of the people in each State or by the state legislatures elected by those people. Likewise, the Constitution calls for Members of Congress to be chosen State by State, rather than in nationwide elections. Even the selection of the President—surely the most national of national figures—is accomplished by an electoral college made up of delegates chosen by the various States, and candidates can lose a Presidential election despite winning a majority of the votes cast in the Nation as a whole. See also Art. II, Sec. 1, cl. 3 (providing that when no candidate secures a majority of electoral votes, the election of the President is thrown into the House of Representatives, where "the Votes shall be taken by States, the Representatives from each State having one Vote"); Amdt. 12 (same).

In short, the notion of popular sovereignty that undergirds the Constitution does not erase state boundaries, but rather tracks them. The people of each State obviously did trust their fate to the people of the several States when they consented to the Constitution; not only did they empower the governmental institutions of the United States, but they also agreed to be bound by constitutional amendments that they themselves refused to ratify. See Art. V (providing that proposed amendments shall take effect upon ratification by three-quarters of the States). At the same time, however, the people of each State retained their separate political identities. As Chief Justice Marshall put it, "[n]o political dreamer was ever wild enough to think of breaking down the lines which separate the States, and of compounding the American people into one common mass." *McCulloch v. Maryland,* 4 Wheat. 316, 403 (1819).

Any ambiguity in the Tenth Amendment's use of the phrase "the people" is cleared up by the body of the Constitution itself. Article I begins by providing that the Congress of the United States enjoys "[a]ll legislative Powers herein granted," Sec. 1, and goes on to give a careful enumeration of Congress' powers, Sec. 8. It then concludes by enumerating certain powers that are prohibited to the States. The import of this structure is the same as the import of the Tenth Amendment: if we are to invalidate Arkansas' Amendment 73, we must point to something in the Federal Constitution that deprives the people of Arkansas of the power to enact such measures.

B

The majority disagrees that it bears this burden. But its arguments are unpersuasive.

1

The majority begins by announcing an enormous and untenable limitation on the principle expressed by the Tenth Amendment. According to the majority, the States possess only those powers that the Constitution affirmatively grants to them or that they enjoyed before the Constitution was adopted; the Tenth Amendment "could only 'reserve' that which existed before." From the fact that the States had not previously enjoyed any powers over the particular institutions of the Federal Government established by the Constitution, the majority derives a rule precisely opposite to the one that the Amendment actually prescribes: " '[T]he states can exercise no powers whatsoever, which exclusively spring out of the existence of the national government, which the constitution does not delegate to them.' " Ibid. (quoting 1 J. Story, Commentaries on the Constitution of the United States, Sec. 627 (3d ed. 1858)).

The majority's essential logic is that the state governments could not "reserve" any powers that they did not control at the time the Constitution was drafted. But it was not the state governments that were doing the reserving. The Constitution derives its authority instead from the consent of the people of the States. Given the fundamental principle that all governmental powers stem from the people of the States, it would simply be incoherent to assert that the people of the States could not reserve any powers that they had not previously controlled.

The Tenth Amendment's use of the word "reserved" does not help the majority's position. If someone says that the power to use a particular facility is reserved to some group, he is not saying anything about whether that group has previously used the facility. He is merely saying that the people who control the facility have designated that group as the entity with authority to use it. The Tenth Amendment is similar: the people of the States, from whom all governmental powers stem, have specified that all powers not prohibited to the States by the Federal Constitution are reserved "to the States respectively, or to the people."

The majority is therefore quite wrong to conclude that the people of the States cannot authorize their state governments to exercise any powers that were unknown to the States when the Federal Constitution was drafted. Indeed, the majority's position frustrates the apparent purpose of the Amendment's final phrase. The Amendment does not preempt any limitations on state power found in the state constitutions, as it might have done if it simply had said that the powers not delegated to the Federal Government are reserved to the States. But the Amendment also does not prevent the people of the States from amending their state constitutions to remove limitations that were in effect when the Federal Constitution and the Bill of Rights were ratified.

In an effort to defend its position, the majority points to language in *Garcia v. San Antonio Metropolitan Transit Authority*, 469 U.S. 528 (1985), which it takes to indicate that the Tenth Amendment covers only "the original powers of [state] sovereignty." But *Garcia* dealt with an entirely different issue: the extent to which principles of state sovereignty implicit in our federal system curtail Congress' authority to exercise its enumerated powers. When we are asked to decide whether a congressional statute that appears to have been authorized by

Article I is nonetheless unconstitutional because it invades a protected sphere of state sovereignty, it may well be appropriate for us to inquire into what we have called the "traditional aspects of state sovereignty." The question raised by the present case, however, is not whether any principle of state sovereignty implicit in the Tenth Amendment bars congressional action that Article I appears to authorize, but rather whether Article I bars state action that it does not appear to forbid. The principle necessary to answer this question is express on the Tenth Amendment's face: unless the Federal Constitution affirmatively prohibits an action by the States or the people, it raises no bar to such action.

The majority also seeks support for its view of the Tenth Amendment in *McCulloch v. Maryland*, 4 Wheat. 316 (1819). But this effort is misplaced. *McCulloch* did make clear that a power need not be "expressly" delegated to the United States or prohibited to the States in order to fall outside the Tenth Amendment's reservation; delegations and prohibitions can also arise by necessary implication. True to the text of the Tenth Amendment, however, *McCulloch* indicated that all powers as to which the Constitution does not speak (whether expressly or by necessary implication) are "reserved" to the state level. Thus, in its only discussion of the Tenth Amendment, *McCulloch* observed that the Amendment "leaves the question, whether the particular power which may become the subject of contest has been delegated to the one government, or prohibited to the other, to depend on a fair construction of the whole [Constitution]." *McCulloch* did not qualify this observation by indicating that the question also turned on whether the States had enjoyed the power before the fram-

ing. To the contrary, *McCulloch* seemed to assume that the people had "conferred on the general government the power contained in the constitution, and on the States the whole residuum of power." ...

For the past 175 years, *McCulloch* has been understood to rest on the proposition that the Constitution affirmatively barred Maryland from imposing its tax on the Bank's operations.... For the majority, however, *McCulloch* apparently turned on the fact that before the Constitution was adopted, the States had possessed no power to tax the instrumentalities of the governmental institutions that the Constitution created. This understanding of *McCulloch* makes most of Chief Justice Marshall's opinion irrelevant; according to the majority, there was no need to inquire into whether federal law deprived Maryland of the power in question, because the power could not fall into the category of "reserved" powers anyway.

Despite the majority's citation of *Garcia* and *McCulloch*, the only true support for its view of the Tenth Amendment comes from Joseph Story's 1833 treatise on constitutional law. See 2 J. Story, Commentaries on the Constitution of the United States, Sec. 623-628. Justice Story was a brilliant and accomplished man, and one cannot casually dismiss his views. On the other hand, he was not a member of the Founding generation, and his Commentaries on the Constitution were written a half century after the framing. Rather than representing the original understanding of the Constitution, they represent only his own understanding. In a range of cases concerning the federal/state relation, moreover, this Court has deemed positions taken in Story's commentaries to be more nationalist than the Constitution warrants....

2

The majority also sketches out what may be an alternative (and narrower) argument. Again citing Story, the majority suggests that it would be inconsistent with the notion of "national sovereignty" for the States or the people of the States to have any reserved powers over the selection of Members of Congress. The majority apparently reaches this conclusion in two steps. First, it asserts that because Congress as a whole is an institution of the National Government, the individual Members of Congress "owe primary allegiance not to the people of a State, but to the people of the Nation." Second, it concludes that because each Member of Congress has a nationwide constituency once he takes office, it would be inconsistent with the Framers' scheme to let a single State prescribe qualifications for him.

Political scientists can debate about who commands the "primary allegiance" of Members of Congress once they reach Washington. From the framing to the present, however, the selection of the Representatives and Senators from each State has been left entirely to the people of that State or to their state legislature. See Art. I, Sec. 2, cl. 1 (providing that members of the House of Representatives are chosen "by the People of the several States"); Art. I, Sec. 3, cl. 1 (originally providing that the Senators from each State are "chosen by the Legislature thereof"); Amdt. 17 (amending Sec. 3 to provide that the Senators from each State are "elected by the people thereof"). The very name "congress" suggests a coming together of representatives from distinct entities. In keeping with the complexity of our federal system, once the representatives chosen by the people of each State assemble in Congress, they form a national body and are beyond the control of the individual States until the next election. But the selection of representatives in Congress is indisputably an act of the people of each State, not some abstract people of the Nation as a whole....

In short, while the majority is correct that the Framers expected the selection process to create a "direct link" between members of the House of Representatives and the people, the link was between the Representatives from each State and the people of that State; the people of Georgia have no say over whom the people of Massachusetts select to represent them in Congress. This arrangement must baffle the majority, whose understanding of Congress would surely fit more comfortably within a system of nationwide elections. But the fact remains that when it comes to the selection of Members of Congress, the people of each State have retained their independent political identity. As a result, there is absolutely nothing strange about the notion that the people of the States or their state legislatures possess "reserved" powers in this area.

The majority seeks support from the Constitution's specification that Members of Congress "shall receive a Compensation for their Services, to be ascertained by Law, and paid out of the Treasury of the United States." Art. I, Sec. 6, cl. 1. But the fact that Members of Congress draw a federal salary once they have assembled hardly means that the people of the States lack reserved powers over the selection of their representatives. Indeed, the historical evidence about the compensation provision suggests that the States' reserved powers may even extend beyond the selection stage. The majority itself indicates that if the Constitution had made no provision for congressional compensation, this topic would have been "left to state legislatures." Likewise, Madison specifically indicated that even with the compensation provision in place, the individual States still enjoyed the reserved power to supplement the federal salary (remarks at the Virginia ratifying convention).

As for the fact that a State has no reserved power to establish qualifications for the office of President, it surely need not follow that a State has no reserved power to establish qualifications for the Members of Congress who represent the people of that State. Because powers are reserved to the States "respectively," it is clear that no State may legislate for another State: even though the Arkansas legislature enjoys the reserved power to pass a minimum-wage law for Arkansas, it has no power to pass a minimum-wage law for Vermont. For the same reason, Arkansas may not decree that only Arkansas citizens are eligible to be President of the United States; the selection of the President is not up to Arkansas alone, and Arkansas can no more prescribe the qualifications for that office than it can set the qualifications for Members of Congress from Florida. But none of this suggests that Arkansas cannot set qualifications for Members of Congress from Arkansas.

In fact, the Constitution's treatment of Presidential elections actively contradicts the majority's position. While the individual States have no "reserved" power to set qualifications for the office of President, we have long understood that they do have the power (as far as the Federal Constitution is concerned) to set qualifications for their Presidential electors—the delegates that each State selects to represent it in the electoral college that actually chooses the Nation's chief executive. Even respondents do not dispute that the States may establish qualifications for their delegates to the electoral college, as long as those qualifications pass muster under other constitutional provisions (primarily the First and Fourteenth Amendments). As the majority cannot argue that the Constitution affirmatively grants this power, the power must be one that is "reserved" to the States. It necessarily follows that the majority's understanding of the Tenth Amendment is incorrect, for the position of Presidential elector surely "'springs out of the existence of the national government.'"

3

In a final effort to deny that the people of the States enjoy "reserved" powers over the selection of their representatives in Congress, the majority suggests that the Constitution expressly delegates to the States certain powers over congressional elections. Such delegations of power, the majority argues, would be superfluous if the people of the States enjoyed reserved powers in this area.

Only one constitutional provision— the Times, Places and Manner Clause of Article I, Sec. 4—even arguably supports the majority's suggestion. It reads:

> "The Times, Places and Manner of holding Elections for Senators and Representatives, shall be prescribed in each State by the Legislature thereof; but the Congress may at any time by Law make or alter such Regulations, except as to the Places of chusing Senators."

Contrary to the majority's assumption, however, this Clause does not delegate any authority to the States. Instead, it simply imposes a duty upon them. The majority gets it exactly right: by specifying that the state legislatures "shall" prescribe the details necessary to hold congressional elections, the Clause "expressly requires action by the States." This command meshes with one of the principal purposes of Congress' "make or alter" power: to ensure that the States hold congressional elections in the first place, so that Congress continues to exist....

Respondent Thornton seeks to buttress the majority's position with Article I, Sec. 2, cl. 1, which provides:

"The House of Representatives shall be composed of Members chosen every second Year by the People of the several States, and the Electors in each State shall have the Qualifications requisite for Electors of the most numerous Branch of the State Legislature."

According to respondent Thornton, this provision "grants States authority to prescribe the qualifications of [voters]" in congressional elections. If anything, however, the Clause limits the power that the States would otherwise enjoy. Though it does leave States with the ability to control who may vote in congressional elections, it has the effect of restricting their authority to establish special requirements that do not apply in elections for the state legislature.

Our case law interpreting the Clause affirmatively supports the view that the States enjoy reserved powers over congressional elections. We have treated the Clause as a one-way ratchet: while the requirements for voting in congressional elections cannot be more onerous than the requirements for voting in elections for the most numerous branch of the statute legislature, they can be less so. If this interpretation of the Clause is correct, it means that even with the Clause in place, States still have partial freedom to set special voting requirements for congressional elections. As this power is not granted in Article I, it must be among the "reserved" powers.

II

I take it to be established, then, that the people of Arkansas do enjoy "reserved" powers over the selection of their representatives in Congress. Purporting to exercise those reserved powers, they have agreed among themselves that the candidates covered by Sec. 3 of Amendment 73—those whom they have already elected to three or more terms in the House of Representatives or to two or more terms in the Senate—should not be eligible to appear on the ballot for re-election, but should nonetheless be returned to Congress if enough voters are sufficiently enthusiastic about their candidacy to write in their names. Whatever one might think of the wisdom of this arrangement, we may not override the decision of the people of Arkansas unless something in the Federal Constitution deprives them of the power to enact such measures.

The majority settles on "the Qualifications Clauses" as the constitutional provisions that Amendment 73 violates. Because I do not read those provisions to impose any unstated prohibitions on the States, it is unnecessary for me to decide whether the majority is correct to identify Arkansas' ballot-access restriction with laws fixing true term limits or otherwise prescribing "qualifications" for congressional office. [T]he Qualifications Clauses are merely straightforward recitations of the minimum eligibility requirements that the Framers thought it essential for every Member of Congress to meet. They restrict state power only in that they prevent the States from abolishing all eligibility requirements for membership in Congress.

Because the text of the Qualifications Clauses does not support its position, the majority turns instead to its vision of the democratic principles that animated the Framers. But the majority's analysis goes to a question that is not before us: whether Congress has the power to prescribe qualifications for its own members. [T]he democratic principles that contributed to the Framers' decision to withhold this power from Congress do not prove that the Framers also deprived the people of the States of their reserved authority to set eligibility requirements for their own representatives.

To the extent that they bear on this case, the records of the Philadelphia Convention affirmatively support my unwillingness to find hidden meaning in the Qualifications Clauses, while the surviving records from the ratification debates help neither side. As for the postratification period, five States supplemented the constitutional disqualifications in their very first election laws. The historical evidence thus refutes any notion that the Qualifications Clauses were generally understood to be exclusive. Yet the majority must establish just such an understanding in order to justify its position that the Clauses impose unstated prohibitions on the States and the people. In my view, the historical evidence is simply inadequate to warrant the majority's conclusion that the Qualifications Clauses mean anything more than what they say.

POSTSCRIPT

Are Term Limits for Elected Officials Unconstitutional?

The Supreme Court's decision in *U.S. Term Limits, Inc. v. Thornton* may have settled the constitutional question for now, but it has had little impact on the high levels of distrust toward and disaffection from all levels of the political system. Proposed legislation aimed at campaign finance reform was once again defeated in June 1996 in the U.S. Congress. "Third parties" from both the left and right wings of the American political spectrum seem to hold the potential for fielding serious candidates for national office ("serious" not in the sense of winning office but of capturing enough votes to alter the outcome of the campaign between the mainstream Democrat and Republican parties).

The literature on American electoral politics and its problems is enormous. The work directed toward the specific issue of term limits is much more manageable. Unfortunately, too often it is polemical in nature, reflecting the political ideology that has given rise to the right-wing populism that has spawned much of the current distrust of "government." For a more balanced overview of some of the key issues, see Gerald Benjamin and Michael Malbin, eds., *Limiting Legislative Terms* (Congressional Quarterly Press, 1992) and Alan Grant, "Legislative Careerism and the Term Limitation Movement," in Grant, ed., *Contemporary American Politics* (Dartmouth, 1995). One may also usefully consult George Will's *Restoration: Congress, Term Limits, and the Recovery of Deliberative Democracy* (Free Press, 1992). For a brief statement of the arguments for and against term limits, see "Debate: The Federalist and the Contemporary Debate on Term Limits," *Harvard Journal of Law and Public Policy* (vol. 16, 1993), which also contains articles by William Kristol, "Term Limitations: Breaking Up the Iron Triangle," and Nelson Polsby, "Some Arguments Against Congressional Term Limitations."

More information on term limits and the workings of the U.S. Congress can be found on the Internet at `http://www.termlimits.org/homepage.shtml` and `http://policy.net/capweb/congress.html`.

PART 2

Law and Social Values

In any democratic society, the laws must reflect some consensus concerning the values of that society. Some of these values are clearly and easily determined. Laws against murder and theft, for example, command respect and acceptance and reflect widely held values.

In an increasingly complex, diverse, and technologically advanced society, however, questions of how best to protect individual rights of minorities and those with unpopular views inspire intense emotional debate, as evidenced by the issues in this section.

- Is Drug Use Testing of Student Athletes Permitted Under the Fourth Amendment?

- Is "Hate Speech" Fully Protected by the Constitution?

- Is Flag Burning Protected by the First Amendment?

- Are School Districts Created for Religious Reasons a Violation of the Constitution?

- Is Abortion Protected by the Constitution?

- Is the Regulation of Pornography on the Internet Unconstitutional?

- Should Affirmative Action Policies Be Continued?

- Are Restrictions on Physician-Assisted Suicide Unconstitutional?

- Are Laws Restricting Gay Rights Legislation Unconstitutional?

ISSUE 5

Is Drug Use Testing of Student Athletes Permitted Under the Fourth Amendment?

YES: Antonin Scalia, from Majority Opinion, *Vernonia School District v. Wayne Acton et ux, Guardians ad Litem for James Acton*, U.S. Supreme Court (1995)

NO: Sandra Day O'Connor, from Dissenting Opinion, *Vernonia School District v. Wayne Acton et ux, Guardians ad Litem for James Acton*, U.S. Supreme Court (1995)

ISSUE SUMMARY

YES: Supreme Court justice Antonin Scalia, representing the majority opinion, finds that nothing in the Constitution bars a random urinalysis requirement for students participating in interscholastic athletics.

NO: Supreme Court justice Sandra Day O'Connor accuses the majority of needlessly invading privacy and weakening the Fourth Amendment.

Assume that you have recently completed your education and have applied for a job at a local public high school. You submit a written application and are invited for an interview. When you appear at school department headquarters, the receptionist tells you that prior to the interview you will have to provide a urine sample, which will be tested for the presence of drugs. If the test shows traces of certain drugs, your application for employment will be denied. What would be your response to such a request? Would you take the test? Do you have any objections or concerns about such tests? Do you think such practices should be allowed?

As public concern about drug abuse in this country has grown, drug use testing has become increasingly common. Many *Fortune* 500 companies test employees for drug use. The U.S. Department of Defense began mandatory urinalysis for members of the armed forces in 1982, and it claims that drug use has been cut in half as a result. In Supreme Court cases decided in 1989, the Court allowed drug testing of customs officials and train engineers.

In trying to develop a legal response to expanded proposals for drug use testing, consider the circumstances that courts might find significant in the hypothetical example above:

1. *Private or public institution*—The case described above involves a government agency as employer. The Constitution provides more protection to

citizens from governmental invasions of privacy than from similar acts by private employers. Even if the Fourth Amendment, which protects against unreasonable searches and seizures, were held to bar drug use testing by the government, private employers might still be allowed to conduct such tests. Unless privacy or civil rights laws are found to be applicable, legislation, either by states or by Congress, would probably be necessary to regulate private drug testing.

2. *Test reliability*—Some urine tests may give false positive results between 5 and 20 percent of the time. In addition, some over-the-counter drugs and even some foods have been known to trigger positive readings. Thus, urine tests will identify all illegal users but will also direct suspicion on some innocent persons. More expensive follow-up tests can be used to separate the legal from the illegal drug users, but sometimes action is taken merely on the basis of the first urine screen. Should this be permitted? How much suspicion of drug use should be required before some action is allowed to be taken?

3. *Privacy*—In thinking about the drug testing process, you might be concerned with two different privacy issues. The most obvious is the intrusiveness of the testing procedure itself. In addition, however, drug use testing raises the question of whether or not school officials or employers have a legitimate interest in the out-of-school or off-the-job activities of students and employees. A positive reading by the most commonly used urine tests will not reveal when the drug was used. Drug traces may remain in the urine for days or weeks. Should it be lawful for school officials or employers to concern themselves with the off-hours activities of students or employees, even if they are illegal?

Drug use testing is becoming increasingly common. Many, if not most, individuals can live their lives without being fingerprinted or experiencing a lie detector test, but drug use testing is something that is becoming more difficult to avoid. In the following opinion by Justice Antonin Scalia, a majority of the Supreme Court finds that nothing in the Constitution bars a random urinalysis requirement for students participating in interscholastic athletics. In a vigorous response, Justice Sandra Day O'Connor accuses the majority of needlessly invading privacy and weakening the Fourth Amendment.

YES

Antonin Scalia

MAJORITY OPINION

VERNONIA SCHOOL DISTRICT v. ACTON

Justice SCALIA delivered the opinion of the Court.

The Student Athlete Drug Policy adopted by School District 47J in the town of Vernonia, Oregon, authorizes random urinalysis drug testing of students who participate in the District's school athletics programs. We granted *certiorari* to decide whether this violates the Fourth and Fourteenth Amendments to the United States Constitution.

I
A

Petitioner Vernonia School District 47J (District) operates one high school and three grade schools in the logging community of Vernonia, Oregon. As elsewhere in small-town America, school sports play a prominent role in the town's life, and student athletes are admired in their schools and in the community.

Drugs had not been a major problem in Vernonia schools. In the mid-to-late 1980's, however, teachers and administrators observed a sharp increase in drug use. Students began to speak out about their attraction to the drug culture, and to boast that there was nothing the school could do about it. Along with more drugs came more disciplinary problems. Between 1988 and 1989 the number of disciplinary referrals in Vernonia schools rose to more than twice the number reported in the early 1980's, and several students were suspended. Students became increasingly rude during class; outbursts of profane language became common.....

Initially, the District responded to the drug problem by offering special classes, speakers, and presentations designed to deter drug use. It even brought in a specially trained dog to detect drugs, but the drug problem persisted. According to the District Court:

"[T]he administration was at its wits end and ... a large segment of the student body, particularly those involved in interscholastic athletics, was in a state of

From *Vernonia School District v. Wayne Acton et ux, Guardians ad Litem for James Acton*, 115 S. Ct. 2386, 132 L.Ed.2d 564 (1995). Notes and some case citations omitted.

rebellion. Disciplinary problems had reached 'epidemic proportions.' The coincidence of an almost three-fold increase in classroom disruptions and disciplinary reports along with the staff's direct observations of students using drugs or glamorizing drug and alcohol use led the administration to the inescapable conclusion that the rebellion was being fueled by alcohol and drug abuse as well as the student's misperceptions about the drug culture." *Ibid*.

At that point, District officials began considering a drug-testing program. They held a parent "input night" to discuss the proposed Student Athlete Drug Policy (Policy), and the parents in attendance gave their unanimous approval. The school board approved the Policy for implementation in the fall of 1989. Its expressed purpose is to prevent student athletes from using drugs, to protect their health and safety, and to provide drug users with assistance programs.

B

The Policy applies to all students participating in interscholastic athletics. Students wishing to play sports must sign a form consenting to the testing and must obtain the written consent of their parents. Athletes are tested at the beginning of the season for their sport. In addition, once each week of the season the names of the athletes are placed in a "pool" from which a student, with the supervision of two adults, blindly draws the names of 10% of the athletes for random testing. Those selected are notified and tested that same day, if possible.

The student to be tested completes a specimen control form which bears an as-signed number. Prescription medications that the student is taking must be identified by providing a copy of the prescription or a doctor's authorization. The student then enters an empty locker room accompanied by an adult monitor of the same sex. Each boy selected produces a sample at a urinal, remaining fully clothed with his back to the monitor, who stands approximately 12 to 15 feet behind the student. Monitors may (though do not always) watch the student while he produces the sample, and they listen for normal sounds of urination. Girls produce samples in an enclosed bathroom stall, so that they can be heard but not observed. After the sample is produced, it is given to the monitor, who checks it for temperature and tampering and then transfers it to a vial.

The samples are sent to an independent laboratory, which routinely tests them for amphetamines, cocaine, and marijuana. Other drugs, such as LSD, may be screened at the request of the District, but the identity of a particular student does not determine which drugs will be tested. The laboratory's procedures are 99.94% accurate. The District follows strict procedures regarding the chain of custody and access to test results. The laboratory does not know the identity of the students whose samples it tests. It is authorized to mail written test reports only to the superintendent and to provide test results to District personnel by telephone only after the requesting official recites a code confirming his authority. Only the superintendent, principals, vice-principals, and athletic directors have access to test results, and the results are not kept for more than one year.

If a sample tests positive, a second test is administered as soon as possible to confirm the result. If the second test is negative, no further action is taken. If the second test is positive, the athlete's parents are notified, and the school principal convenes a meeting with the student and his parents, at which the student is given the option of (1) participating for six weeks in an assistance program that includes weekly urinalysis, or (2) suffering suspension from athletics for the remainder of the current season and the next athletic season. The student is then retested prior to the start of the next athletic season for which he or she is eligible. The Policy states that a second offense results in automatic imposition of option (2); a third offense in suspension for the remainder of the current season and the next two athletic seasons.

C

In the fall of 1991, respondent James Acton, then a seventh-grader, signed up to play football at one of the District's grade schools. He was denied participation, however, because he and his parents refused to sign the testing consent forms. The Actons filed suit, seeking declaratory and injunctive relief from enforcement of the Policy on the grounds that it violated the Fourth and Fourteenth Amendments to the United States Constitution and Article I, sec. 9, of the Oregon Constitution. After a bench trial, the District Court entered an order denying the claims on the merits and dismissing the action. 796 F.Supp., at 1355. The United States Court of Appeals for the Ninth Circuit reversed, holding that the Policy violated both the Fourth and Fourteenth Amendments and Article I, sec. 9, of the Oregon Constitution. 23 F.3d 1514 (1994). We granted *certiorari*.

II

The Fourth Amendment to the United States Constitution provides that the Federal Government shall not violate "[t]he right of the people to be secure in their persons, houses, papers, and effects, against unreasonable searches and seizures...." We have held that the Fourteenth Amendment extends this constitutional guarantee to searches and seizures by state officers, *Elkins v. United States*, 364 U.S. 206 (1960), including public school officials, *New Jersey v. T.L.O.*, 469 U.S. 325, 336-337, 105 S.Ct. 733, 740, 83 L.Ed.2d 720 (1985). In *Skinner v. Railway Labor Executives' Assn.*, 489 U.S. 602 (1989), we held that state-compelled collection and testing of urine, such as that required by the Student Athlete Drug Policy, constitutes a "search" subject to the demands of the Fourth Amendment. See also *Treasury Employees v. Von Raab*, 489 U.S. 656, 665 (1989).

As the text of the Fourth Amendment indicates, the ultimate measure of the constitutionality of a governmental search is "reasonableness." At least in a case such as this, where there was no clear practice, either approving or disapproving the type of search at issue, at the time the constitutional provision was enacted, whether a particular search meets the reasonableness standard " 'is judged by balancing its intrusion on the individual's Fourth Amendment interests against its promotion of legitimate governmental interests.' " *Skinner, supra,* at 619 (quoting *Delaware v. Prouse,* 440 U.S. 648 (1979)). Where a search is undertaken by law enforcement officials to discover evidence of criminal wrongdoing, this Court has said that reasonableness generally requires the obtaining of a judicial warrant, *Skinner, supra,* at 619. Warrants cannot be issued, of course, without the showing of probable cause required by the Warrant Clause. But a warrant is not required to establish the reasonableness of *all* government searches; and when a warrant is not required (and the Warrant Clause therefore not applicable), probable cause is not invariably required either. A search unsupported by probable cause can be constitutional, we have said, "when special needs, beyond the normal need for law enforcement, make the warrant and probable-cause requirement impracticable." *Griffin v. Wisconsin*, 483 U.S. 868 (1987).

We have found such "special needs" to exist in the public-school context. There, the warrant requirement "would unduly interfere with the maintenance of the swift and informal disciplinary procedures [that are] needed," and "strict adherence to the requirement that searches be based upon probable cause" would undercut "the substantial need of teachers and administrators for freedom to maintain order in the schools." *T.L.O.*, 469 U.S. 325, 340 (1985). The school search we approved in *T.L.O.*, while not based on probable cause, *was* based on individualized *suspicion* of wrongdoing. As we explicitly acknowledged, however, "'the Fourth Amendment imposes no irreducible requirement of such suspicion,'" *id.*, at 342, n. 8, 105 S.Ct., at 743, n. 8 (quoting *United States v. Martinez-Fuerte*, 428 U.S. 543, 560-561 (1976)). We have upheld suspicionless searches and seizures to conduct drug testing of railroad personnel involved in train accidents, see *Skinner, supra;* to conduct random drug testing of federal customs officers who carry arms or are involved in drug interdiction, see *Von Raab, supra;* and to maintain automobile checkpoints looking for illegal immigrants and contraband, *Martinez-Fuerte, supra,* and drunk drivers, *Michigan Dept. of State Police v. Sitz,* 496 U.S. 444 (1990).

III

The first factor to be considered is the nature of the privacy interest upon which the search here at issue intrudes. The Fourth Amendment does not protect all subjective expectations of privacy, but only those that society recognizes as "legitimate." *T.L.O.*, 469 U.S., at 338. What expectations are legitimate varies, of course, with context, *id.*, at 337, depending, for example, upon whether the individual asserting the privacy interest is at home, at work, in a car, or in a public park. In addition, the legitimacy of certain privacy expectations vis-a-vis the State may depend upon the individual's legal relationship with the State.... Central, in our view, to the present case is the fact that the subjects of the Policy are (1) children, who (2) have been committed to the temporary custody of the State as schoolmaster.

Traditionally at common law, and still today, unemancipated minors lack some of the most fundamental rights of self-determination—including even the right of liberty in its narrow sense, i.e., the right to come and go at will. They are subject, even as to their physical freedom, to the control of their parents or guardians. When parents place minor children in private schools for their education, the teachers and administrators of those schools stand in *loco parentis* over the children entrusted to them....

In *T.L.O.* we rejected the notion that public schools, like private schools, exercise only parental power over their students, which of course is not subject to constitutional constraints. Such a view of things, we said, "is not entirely 'consonant with compulsory education laws,'" and is inconsistent with our prior decisions treating school officials as state actors for purposes of the Due Process and Free Speech Clauses. But while denying that the State's power over schoolchildren is formally no more than the delegated power of their parents, T.L.O. did not deny, but indeed emphasized, that the nature of that power is custodial and tutelary, permitting a degree of supervision and control that could not be exercised over free adults. "[A] proper educational environment requires close supervision of schoolchildren, as well as the enforcement of rules against conduct that would be perfectly permissible if undertaken by an adult." 469 U.S., at 339. While we do not, of course, suggest that public schools as a general matter have such a degree of control over children as to give rise to a constitutional "duty to protect," we have acknowledged that for many purposes "school authorities ac[t] in *loco parentis*," *Bethel School Dist. No. 403 v. Fraser,* 478 U.S. 675, 684 (1986), with the power and indeed the duty to "inculcate the habits and manners of civility," *id.,* at 681. Thus, while children assuredly do not "shed their constitutional rights... at the schoolhouse gate," *Tinker v. Des Moines Independent Community School Dist.,* 393 U.S. 503, 506 (1969), the nature of those rights is what is appropriate for children in school....

Fourth Amendment rights, no less than First and Fourteenth Amendment rights, are different in public schools than elsewhere; the "reasonableness" inquiry cannot disregard the schools' custodial and tutelary responsibility for children. For their own good and that of their classmates, public school children are routinely required to submit to various physical examinations, and to be vaccinated against various diseases....

Legitimate privacy expectations are even less with regard to student athletes. School sports are not for the bashful. They require "suiting up" before each practice or event, and showering and changing afterwards. Public school locker rooms, the usual sites for these activities, are not notable for the privacy they afford. The locker rooms in Vernonia are typical: no individual dressing rooms are provided; shower heads are lined up along a wall, unseparated by any sort of partition or curtain; not even all the toilet stalls have doors. As the United States Court of Appeals for the Seventh Circuit has noted, there is "an element of 'communal undress' inherent in athletic participation," *Schaill by Kross v. Tippecanoe County School Corp.,* 864 F.2d 1309, 1318 (1988).

There is an additional respect in which school athletes have a reduced expectation of privacy. By choosing to "go out for the team," they voluntarily subject themselves to a degree of regulation even higher than that imposed on students generally. In Vernonia's public schools, they must submit to a preseason physical exam (James testified that his included the giving of a urine sample, App. 17), they must acquire adequate insurance coverage or sign an insurance waiver, maintain a minimum grade point average, and comply with any "rules of conduct, dress, training hours and related matters as may be established for each sport by the head coach and athletic director with the principal's approval." Record, Exh. 2, p. 30, P 8. Somewhat like adults who choose to participate in a "closely regulated industry," students who voluntarily participate in school athletics have reason to expect intrusions upon normal rights and privileges, including privacy.

IV

Having considered the scope of the legitimate expectation of privacy at issue here, we turn next to the character of the intrusion that is complained of. We recognized in *Skinner* that collecting the samples for urinalysis intrudes upon "an excretory function traditionally shielded by great privacy." *Skinner,* 489 U.S., at 626. We noted, however, that the degree of intrusion depends upon the manner in which production of the urine sample is monitored. Under the District's Policy, male students produce samples at a urinal along a wall. They remain fully clothed and are only observed from behind, if at all. Female students produce samples in an enclosed stall, with a female monitor standing outside listening only for sounds of tampering. These conditions are nearly identical to those typically encountered in public restrooms, which men, women, and especially school children use daily. Under such conditions, the privacy interests compromised by the process of obtaining the urine sample are in our view negligible....

Respondents argue, however, that the District's Policy is in fact more intrusive than this suggests, because it requires the students, if they are to avoid sanctions for a falsely positive test, to identify in advance prescription medications they are taking. We agree that this raises some cause for concern.... On the other hand, we have never indicated that requiring advance disclosure of medications is per se unreasonable. Indeed, in *Skinner* we held that it was not "a significant invasion

of privacy." *Skinner,* 489 U.S., at 626, n. 7....

The General Authorization Form that respondents refused to sign, which refusal was the basis for James's exclusion from the sports program, said only (in relevant part): "I ... authorize the Vernonia School District to conduct a test on a urine specimen which I provide to test for drugs and/or alcohol use. I also authorize the release of information concerning the results of such a test to the Vernonia School District and to the parents and/or guardians of the student." While the practice of the District seems to have been to have a school official take medication information from the student at the time of the test, that practice is not set forth in, or required by, the Policy, which says simply: "Student athletes who... are or have been taking prescription medication must provide verification (either by a copy of the prescription or by doctor's authorization) prior to being tested." It may well be that, if and when James was selected for random testing at a time that he was taking medication, the School District would have permitted him to provide the requested information in a confidential manner—for example, in a sealed envelope delivered to the testing lab. Nothing in the Policy contradicts that, and when respondents choose, in effect, to challenge the Policy on its face, we will not assume the worst. Accordingly, we reach the same conclusion as in *Skinner:* that the invasion of privacy was not significant.

V

Finally, we turn to consider the nature and immediacy of the governmental concern at issue here, and the efficacy of this means for meeting it. In both

Skinner and *Von Raab*, we characterized the government interest motivating the search as "compelling." *Skinner, supra,* 489 U.S., at 628 (interest in preventing railway accidents); *Von Raab, supra,* 489 U.S., at 670 (interest in insuring fitness of customs officials to interdict drugs and handle firearms). Relying on these cases, the District Court held that because the District's program also called for drug testing in the absence of individualized suspicion, the District "must demonstrate a 'compelling need' for the program." 796 F.Supp., at 1363. The Court of Appeals appears to have agreed with this view. See 23 F.3d, at 1526. It is a mistake, however, to think that the phrase "compelling state interest," in the Fourth Amendment context, describes a fixed, minimum quantum of governmental concern, so that one can dispose of a case by answering in isolation the question: Is there a compelling state interest here? Rather, the phrase describes an interest which appears important enough to justify the particular search at hand, in light of other factors which show the search to be relatively intrusive upon a genuine expectation of privacy. Whether that relatively high degree of government concern is necessary in this case or not, we think it is met.

That the nature of the concern is important—indeed, perhaps compelling —can hardly be doubted. Deterring drug use by our Nation's schoolchildren is at least as important as enhancing efficient enforcement of the Nation's laws against the importation of drugs, which was the governmental concern in *Von Raab,* or deterring drug use by engineers and trainmen, which was the governmental concern in *Skinner.* School years are the time when the physical, psychological, and addictive effects of drugs are most severe.... And of course the effects of a drug-infested school are visited not just upon the users, but upon the entire student body and faculty, as the educational process is disrupted. In the present case, moreover, the necessity for the State to act is magnified by the fact that this evil is being visited not just upon individuals at large, but upon children for whom it has undertaken a special responsibility of care and direction. Finally, it must not be lost sight of that this program is directed more narrowly to drug use by school athletes, where the risk of immediate physical harm to the drug user or those with whom he is playing his sport is particularly high....

As for the immediacy of the District's concerns: We are not inclined to question —indeed, we could not possibly find clearly erroneous—the District Court's conclusion that "a large segment of the student body, particularly those involved in interscholastic athletics, was in a state of rebellion," that "[d]isciplinary actions had reached 'epidemic proportions,'" and that "the rebellion was being fueled by alcohol and drug abuse as well as by the student's misperceptions about the drug culture." 796 F.Supp., at 1357. That is an immediate crisis of greater proportions than existed in *Skinner,* where we upheld the Government's drug testing program based on findings of drug use by railroad employees nationwide, without proof that a problem existed on the particular railroads whose employees were subject to the test....

As to the efficacy of this means for addressing the problem: It seems to us self-evident that a drug problem largely fueled by the "role model" effect of athletes' drug use, and of particular danger to athletes, is effectively addressed by making sure that athletes do not use drugs. Respondents argue that a "less intrusive means to the same end" was available, namely, "drug testing on suspicion of drug use." Brief for Respondents 45-46. We have repeatedly refused to declare that only the "least intrusive" search practicable can be reasonable under the Fourth Amendment. Respondents' alternative entails substantial difficulties—if it is indeed practicable at all. It may be impracticable, for one thing, simply because the parents who are willing to accept random drug testing for athletes are not willing to accept accusatory drug testing for all students, which transforms the process into a badge of shame. Respondents' proposal brings the risk that teachers will impose testing arbitrarily upon troublesome but not drug-likely students. It generates the expense of defending lawsuits that charge such arbitrary imposition, or that simply demand greater process before accusatory drug testing is imposed. And not least of all, it adds to the ever-expanding diversionary duties of schoolteachers the new function of spotting and bringing to account drug abuse, a task for which they are ill prepared, and which is not readily compatible with their vocation. . . .

VI

Taking into account all the factors we have considered above—the decreased expectation of privacy, the relative unobtrusiveness of the search, and the severity of the need met by the search—we conclude Vernonia's Policy is reasonable and hence constitutional.

We caution against the assumption that suspicionless drug testing will readily pass constitutional muster in other contexts. The most significant element in this case is the first we discussed: that the Policy was undertaken in furtherance of the government's responsibilities, under a public school system, as guardian and tutor of children entrusted to its care. Just as when the government conducts a search in its capacity as employer (a warrantless search of an absent employee's desk to obtain an urgently needed file, for example), the relevant question is whether that intrusion upon privacy is one that a reasonable employer might engage in, see *O'Connor v. Ortega*, 480 U.S. 709 (1987); so also when the government acts as guardian and tutor the relevant question is whether the search is one that a reasonable guardian and tutor might undertake. Given the findings of need made by the District Court, we conclude that in the present case it is.

We may note that the primary guardians of Vernonia's schoolchildren appear to agree. The record shows no objection to this districtwide program by any parents other than the couple before us here —even though, as we have described, a public meeting was held to obtain parents' views. We find insufficient basis to contradict the judgment of Vernonia's parents, its school board, and the District Court, as to what was reasonably in the interest of these children under the circumstances. . . .

We therefore vacate the judgment, and remand the case to the Court of Appeals for further proceedings consistent with this opinion.

It is so ordered.

NO

Sandra Day O'Connor

DISSENTING OPINION OF SANDRA DAY O'CONNOR

Justice O'CONNOR, with whom Justice STEVENS and Justice SOUTER join, dissenting.

The population of our Nation's public schools, grades 7 through 12, numbers around 18 million. By the reasoning of today's decision, the millions of these students who participate in interscholastic sports, an overwhelming majority of whom have given school officials no reason whatsoever to suspect they use drugs at school, are open to an intrusive bodily search.

In justifying this result, the Court dispenses with a requirement of individualized suspicion on considered policy grounds. First, it explains that precisely because every student athlete is being tested, there is no concern that school officials might act arbitrarily in choosing who to test. Second, a broad-based search regime, the Court reasons, dilutes the accusatory nature of the search. In making these policy arguments, of course, the Court sidesteps powerful, countervailing privacy concerns. Blanket searches, because they can involve "thousands or millions" of searches, "pos[e] a greater threat to liberty" than do suspicion-based ones, which "affec[t] one person at a time," *Illinois v. Krull*, 480 U.S. 340 (1987) (O'CONNOR, J., dissenting). Searches based on individualized suspicion also afford potential targets considerable control over whether they will, in fact, be searched because a person can avoid such a search by not acting in an objectively suspicious way. And given that the surest way to avoid acting suspiciously is to avoid the underlying wrongdoing, the costs of such a regime, one would think, are minimal.

But whether a blanket search is "better" than a regime based on individualized suspicion is not a debate in which we should engage. In my view, it is not open to judges or government officials to decide on policy grounds which is better and which is worse. For most of our constitutional history, mass, suspicionless searches have been generally considered per se unreasonable within the meaning of the Fourth Amendment. And we have allowed exceptions in recent years only where it has been clear that a suspicion-based regime would be ineffectual. Because that is not the case here, I dissent.

From *Vernonia School District v. Wayne Acton et ux, Guardians ad Litem for James Acton*, 115 S Ct. 2386, 132 L.Ed.2d 564 (1995). Notes and some case citations omitted.

I

A

In *Carroll v. United States*, 267 U.S. 132 (1925), the Court explained that "[t]he Fourth Amendment does not denounce all searches or seizures, but only such as are unreasonable." *Id.*, at 147. Applying this standard, the Court first held that a search of a car was not unreasonable merely because it was warrantless; because obtaining a warrant is impractical for an easily movable object such as a car, the Court explained, a warrant is not required. The Court also held, however, that a warrantless car search was unreasonable unless supported by some level of individualized suspicion, namely probable cause. Significantly, the Court did not base its conclusion on the express probable cause requirement contained in the Warrant Clause, which, as just noted, the Court found inapplicable. Rather, the Court rested its views on "what was deemed an unreasonable search and seizure when [the Fourth Amendment] was adopted" and "[what] will conserve public interests as well as the interests and rights of individual citizens." *Id.*, at 149. With respect to the "rights of individual citizens," the Court eventually offered the simple yet powerful intuition that "those lawfully within the country, entitled to use the public highways, have a right to free passage without interruption or search unless there is known to a competent official authorized to search, probable cause for believing that their vehicles are carrying contraband or illegal merchandise." *Id.*, at 154.

More important for the purposes of this case, the Court clearly indicated that evenhanded treatment was no substitute for the individualized suspicion requirement:

> "It would be intolerable and unreasonable if a prohibition agent were authorized to stop every automobile on the chance of finding liquor and thus subject all persons lawfully using the highways to the inconvenience and indignity of such a search." *Id.*, at 153–154.

... [I]t remains the law that the police cannot, say, subject to drug testing every person entering or leaving a certain drug-ridden neighborhood in order to find evidence of crime. 3 W. LaFave, *Search and Seizure* sec. 9.5(b), pp. 551–553 (2d ed. 1987) (hereinafter LaFave). And this is true even though it is hard to think of a more compelling government interest than the need to fight the scourge of drugs on our streets and in our neighborhoods. Nor could it be otherwise, for if being evenhanded were enough to justify evaluating a search regime under an open-ended balancing test, the Warrant Clause, which presupposes that there is some category of searches for which individualized suspicion is nonnegotiable, see 2 LaFave sec. 4.1, at 118, would be a dead letter.

Outside the criminal context, however, in response to the exigencies of modern life, our cases have upheld several evenhanded blanket searches, including some that are more than minimally intrusive, after balancing the invasion of privacy against the government's strong need. Most of these cases, of course, are distinguishable insofar as they involved searches either not of a personally intrusive nature, such as searches of closely regulated businesses, see, *e.g.*, *New York v. Burger*, 482 U.S. 691 (1987); *cf.* Cuddihy 1501 ("Even the states with the strongest constitutional restrictions on general searches had long exposed commercial establishments to warrantless inspection"), or arising in unique contexts such as prisons, see, e.g., [Bell v.] Wolfish, supra, 441 U.S., at 558–560 (visual body cavity searches of prisoners following contact visits); cf. Cuddihy 1516–1519, 1552–1553 (indicating that searches incident to arrest and prisoner searches were the only common personal searches at time of founding). This certainly explains why Justice Scalia, in his dissent in our recent [Treasury Employees v.] Von Raab decision, found it significant that "[u]ntil today this Court had upheld a bodily search separate from arrest and without individualized suspicion of wrong-doing only with respect to prison inmates, relying upon the uniquely dangerous nature of that environment." Von Raab, supra, 489 U.S., at 680 (citation omitted).

In any event, in many of the cases that can be distinguished on the grounds suggested above and, more important, in all of the cases that cannot, see, e.g., Skinner, supra (blanket drug testing scheme); Von Raab, supra (same); cf. Camara v. Municipal Court of San Francisco, 387 U.S. 523, 87 S.Ct. 1727, 18 L.Ed.2d 930 (1967) (area-wide searches of private residences), we upheld the suspicionless search only after first recognizing the Fourth Amendment's longstanding preference for a suspicion-based search regime, and then pointing to sound reasons why such a regime would likely be ineffectual under the unusual circumstances presented. In Skinner, for example, we stated outright that " 'some quantum of individualized suspicion' " is "usually required" under the Fourth Amendment, Skinner, supra, at 624, quoting [United States v.] Martinez-Fuerte, 428 U.S., at 560, and we built the requirement into the test we announced:

"In limited circumstances, where the privacy interests implicated by the search are minimal, and where an important governmental interest furthered by the intrusion *would be placed in jeopardy by a requirement of individualized suspicion*, a search may be reasonable despite the absence of such suspicion." Ibid. (emphasis added). The obvious negative implication of this reasoning is that, if such an individualized suspicion requirement would not place the government's objectives in jeopardy, the requirement should not be forsaken. See also Von Raab, supra, at 665–666.

Accordingly, we upheld the suspicionless regime at issue in Skinner on the firm understanding that a requirement of individualized suspicion for testing train operators for drug or alcohol impairment following serious train accidents would be unworkable because "the scene of a serious rail accident is chaotic." Skinner, 489 U.S., at 631....

Moreover, an individualized suspicion requirement was often impractical in these cases because they involved situations in which even one undetected instance of wrongdoing could have injurious consequences for a great number of people. See, e.g., Camara, supra, at 535 (even one safety code violation can cause "fires and epidemics [that] ravage large urban areas"); Skinner, supra, 489 U.S., at 628, (even one drug- or alcohol-impaired train operator can lead to the "disastrous consequences" of a train wreck, such as "great human loss"); Von Raab, supra, at 670, 674, 677, (even one customs official caught up in drugs can, by virtue of impairment, susceptibility to bribes, or indifference, result in the noninterdiction of a "sizable drug shipmen[t]," which eventually injures the lives of thousands, or to a breach of "national security"); [United

States v.] Edwards, supra, at 500 (even one hijacked airplane can destroy " 'hundreds of human lives and millions of dollars of property' ").

B

The instant case stands in marked contrast. One searches today's majority opinion in vain for recognition that history and precedent establish that individualized suspicion is "usually required" under the Fourth Amendment (regardless of whether a warrant and probable cause are also required) and that, in the area of intrusive personal searches, the only recognized exception is for situations in which a suspicion-based scheme would be likely ineffectual. Far from acknowledging anything special about individualized suspicion, the Court treats a suspicion-based regime as if it were just any run-of-the-mill, less intrusive alternative—that is, an alternative that officials may bypass if the lesser intrusion, in their reasonable estimation, is outweighed by policy concerns unrelated to practicability.

... [H]aving misconstrued the fundamental role of the individualized suspicion requirement in Fourth Amendment analysis, the Court never seriously engages the practicality of such a requirement in the instant case. And that failure is crucial because nowhere is it less clear that an individualized suspicion requirement would be ineffectual than in the school context. In most schools, the entire pool of potential search targets—students—is under constant supervision by teachers and administrators and coaches, be it in classrooms, hallways, or locker rooms. See *T.L.O.,* 469 U.S., at 339 ("[A] proper educational environment requires close supervision of schoolchildren").

The record here indicates that the Vernonia schools are no exception. The great irony of this case is that most (though not all) of the evidence the District introduced to justify its suspicionless drug-testing program consisted of first- or second-hand stories of particular, identifiable students acting in ways that plainly gave rise to reasonable suspicion of in-school drug use—and thus that would have justified a drug-related search under our *T.L.O.* decision. See *id.,* at 340–342 (warrant and probable cause not required for school searches; reasonable suspicion sufficient). Small groups of students, for example, were observed by a teacher "passing joints back and forth" across the street at a restaurant before school and during school hours. Another group was caught skipping school and using drugs at one of the students' houses. Several students actually admitted their drug use to school officials (some of them being caught with marijuana pipes). One student presented himself to his teacher as "clearly obviously inebriated" and had to be sent home. Still another was observed dancing and singing at the top of his voice in the back of the classroom; when the teacher asked what was going on, he replied, "Well, I'm just high on life." To take a final example, on a certain road trip, the school wrestling coach smelled marijuana smoke in a hotel room occupied by four wrestlers, an observation that (after some questioning) would probably have given him reasonable suspicion to test one or all of them....

In light of all this evidence of drug use by particular students, there is a substantial basis for concluding that a vigorous regime of suspicion-based testing (for which the District appears already to have rules in place, see Record, Exh. 2, at 14, 17) would have gone a long way toward solving Vernonia's school drug problem while preserving the Fourth Amendment rights of James Acton and others like him. And were there any doubt about such a conclusion, it is removed by indications in the record that suspicion-based testing could have been supplemented by an equally vigorous campaign to have Vernonia's parents encourage their children to submit to the District's *voluntary* drug testing program. See *id.*, at 32 (describing the voluntary program); *ante*, at 2396 (noting widespread parental support for drug testing). In these circumstances, the Fourth Amendment dictates that a mass, suspicionless search regime is categorically unreasonable.

I recognize that a suspicion-based scheme, even where reasonably effective in controlling in-school drug use, may not be as effective as a mass, suspicionless testing regime. In one sense, that is obviously true—just as it is obviously true that suspicion-based law enforcement is not as effective as mass, suspicionless enforcement might be. "But there is nothing new in the realization" that Fourth Amendment protections come with a price. *Arizona v. Hicks*, 480 U.S. 321, 329 (1987). Indeed, the price we pay is higher in the criminal context, given that police do not closely observe the entire class of potential search targets (all citizens in the area) and must ordinarily adhere to the rigid requirements of a warrant and probable cause.

The principal counterargument to all this, central to the Court's opinion, is that the Fourth Amendment is more lenient with respect to school searches. That is no doubt correct, for, as the Court explains, schools have traditionally had special guardian-like responsibilities for children that necessitate a degree of constitutional leeway. This principle explains the considerable Fourth Amendment leeway we gave school officials in *T.L.O.* In that case, we held that children at school do not enjoy two of the Fourth Amendment's traditional categorical protections against unreasonable searches and seizures: the warrant requirement and the probable cause requirement. See *T.L.O.*, 469 U.S., at 337–343. And this was true even though the same children enjoy such protections "in a nonschool setting." *Id.*, at 348 (Powell, J., concurring).

The instant case, however, asks whether the Fourth Amendment is even more lenient than that, *i.e.*, whether it is *so* lenient that students may be deprived of the Fourth Amendment's only remaining, and most basic, categorical protection: its strong preference for an individualized suspicion requirement, with its accompanying antipathy toward personally intrusive, blanket searches of mostly innocent people. It is not at all clear that people in prison lack this categorical protection, see *Wolfish*, 441 U.S., at 558–560 (upholding certain suspicionless searches of prison inmates); but *cf. supra*, at 2401 (indicating why suspicion requirement was impractical in *Wolfish*), and we have said "we are not yet ready to hold that the schools and the prisons need be equated for purposes of the Fourth Amendment." *T.L.O.*, *supra*, at 338–339. Thus, if we are to mean what we often proclaim—that students do not "shed their constitutional rights ... at the schoolhouse gate," *Tinker v. Des Moines Independent Community School Dist.*, 393 U.S. 503, 506 (1969)—the answer must plainly be no....

I find unpersuasive the Court's reliance on the widespread practice of physical examinations and vaccinations, which are both blanket searches of a sort. Of course, for these practices to have *any* Fourth Amendment significance, the Court has to assume that these physical exams and vaccinations are typically "required" to a similar extent that urine testing and collection is required in the instant case, *i.e.*, that they are required regardless of parental objection and that some meaningful sanction attaches to the failure to submit. In any event, without forming any particular view of such searches, it is worth noting that a suspicion requirement for vaccinations is not merely impractical; it is nonsensical, for vaccinations are not searches *for anything in particular* and so there is nothing about which to be suspicious. Nor is this saying anything new; it is the same theory on which, in part, we have repeatedly upheld certain inventory searches. See, *e.g.*, *South Dakota v. Opperman*, 428 U.S. 364, 370, n. 5 (1976) ("The probable-cause approach is unhelpful when analysis centers upon the reasonableness of routine administrative caretaking functions"). As for physical examinations, the practicability of a suspicion requirement is highly doubtful because the conditions for which these physical exams ordinarily search, such as latent heart conditions, do not manifest themselves in observable behavior the way school drug use does.

It might also be noted that physical exams (and of course vaccinations) are not searches for conditions that reflect wrongdoing on the part of the student, and so are wholly nonaccusatory and have no consequences that can be regarded as punitive. These facts may explain the absence of Fourth Amendment challenges to such searches. By contrast, although I agree with the Court that the accusatory nature of the District's testing program is *diluted* by making it a blanket one, any testing program that

searches for conditions plainly reflecting serious wrongdoing can never be made wholly nonaccusatory from the student's perspective, the motives for the program notwithstanding; and for the same reason, the substantial consequences that can flow from a positive test, such as suspension from sports, are invariably —and quite reasonably—understood as punishment. The best proof that the District's testing program is to *some* extent accusatory can be found in James Acton's own explanation on the witness stand as to why he did not want to submit to drug testing: "Because I feel that they have no reason to think I was taking drugs." Tr. 13 (Apr. 29, 1992). It is hard to think of a manner of explanation that resonates more intensely in our Fourth Amendment tradition than this.

II

I do not believe that suspicionless drug testing is justified on these facts. But even if I agreed that some such testing were reasonable here, I see two other Fourth Amendment flaws in the District's program. First, and most serious, there is virtually no evidence in the record of a drug problem at the Washington Grade School, which includes the 7th and 8th grades, and which Acton attended when this litigation began. This is not surprising, given that, of the four witnesses who testified to drug-related incidents, three were teachers and/or coaches at the high school, see Tr. 65; *id.*, at 86; *id.*, at 99, and the fourth, though the principal of the grade school at the time of the litigation, had been employed as principal of the high school during the years leading up to (and beyond) the implementation of the drug testing policy. See *id.*, at 17. The only evidence of a grade school drug problem that my review of the record uncovered is a "guarantee" by the late-arriving grade school principal that "our problems we've had in '88 and '89 didn't start at the high school level. They started in the elementary school." *Id.*, at 43. But I would hope that a single assertion of this sort would not serve as an adequate basis on which to uphold mass, suspicionless drug testing of two entire grades of student-athletes—in Vernonia and, by the Court's reasoning, in other school districts as well. Perhaps there is a drug problem at the grade school, but one would not know it from this record. At the least, then, I would insist that the parties and the District Court address this issue on remand.

Second, even as to the high school, I find unreasonable the school's choice of student athletes as the class to subject to suspicionless testing—a choice that appears to have been driven more by a belief in what would pass constitutional muster, see *id.*, at 45–47 (indicating that the original program was targeted at students involved in any extracurricular activity), than by a belief in what was required to meet the District's principal disciplinary concern. Reading the full record in this case, as well as the District Court's authoritative summary of it, 796 F.Supp. 1354, 1356–1357 (Or. 1992), it seems quite obvious that the true driving force behind the District's adoption of its drug testing program was the need to combat the rise in drug-related disorder and disruption in its classrooms and around campus. I mean no criticism of the strength of that interest. On the contrary, where the record demonstrates the existence of such a problem, that interest seems self-evidently compelling. "Without first establishing discipline and maintaining order, teachers cannot begin to educate their students." *T.L.O.*, 469 U.S., at 350 (Powell, J., concurring). And the record in this case surely demonstrates there was a drug-related discipline problem in Vernonia of "'epidemic proportions.'" 796 F.Supp., at 1357. The evidence of a drug-related sports injury problem at Vernonia, by contrast, was considerably weaker.

On this record, then, it seems to me that the far more reasonable choice would have been to focus on the class of students found to have violated published school rules against severe disruption in class and around campus, see Record, Exh. 2, at 9, 11—disruption that had a strong nexus to drug use, as the District established at trial. Such a choice would share two of the virtues of a suspicion-based regime: testing dramatically fewer students, tens as against hundreds, and giving students control, through their behavior, over the likelihood that they would be tested. Moreover, there would be a reduced concern for the accusatory nature of the search, because the Court's feared "badge of shame," *ante*, at 2396, would already exist, due to the antecedent accusation and finding of severe disruption. In a lesser known aspect of *Skinner*, we upheld an analogous testing scheme with little hesitation. See *Skinner*, 489 U.S., at 611 (describing "'Authorization to Test for Cause'" scheme, according to which train operators would be tested "in the event of certain specific rule violations, including noncompliance with a signal and excessive speeding").

III

It cannot be too often stated that the greatest threats to our constitutional

NO Sandra Day O'Connor / 105

freedoms come in times of crisis. But we must also stay mindful that not all government responses to such times are hysterical overreactions; some crises are quite real, and when they are, they serve precisely as the compelling state interest that we have said may justify a measured intrusion on constitutional rights. The only way for judges to mediate these conflicting impulses is to do what they should do anyway: stay close to the record in each case that appears before them, and make their judgments based on that alone. Having reviewed the record here, I cannot avoid the conclusion that the District's suspicionless policy of testing all student-athletes sweeps too broadly, and too imprecisely, to be reasonable under the Fourth Amendment.

POSTSCRIPT

Is Drug Use Testing of Student Athletes Permitted Under the Fourth Amendment?

The pressure to pursue drug testing programs is political, economic, and technological. Drug abuse has surfaced as a principal domestic concern of voters. In 1992 the U.S. Office of Management and Budget estimated that drug abuse costs the nation $300 billion annually in lost productivity, crime, health care, and accidents. Seventy-four million Americans acknowledge using illegal drugs; 6 million are believed to be so seriously addicted that they require treatment. As many as 375,000 babies are born after being exposed to drugs in the womb every year; many of them are permanently damaged by their mothers' drug use. In addition, technologies for drug testing that are cheaper and more revealing but that seem less intrusive are being developed. Would the objection to drug testing be as strong if the test consisted of cutting and analyzing one or two hairs rather than obtaining a urine specimen? The new technologies that will become available for testing and the new technologies that already exist for communicating private information guarantee that there will be a growing amount of litigation during the next few years.

The number of cases involving the legality of drug use testing is proliferating. Courts have allowed drug tests for college athletes, *Hill v. National Collegiate Athletic Association*, 865 P.2d 633 (1994); jockeys, *Shoemaker v. Handel*, 795 F.2d 1136 (1986); prison employees, *McDonell v. Hunter*, 809 F.2d 1302 (1987); and school bus drivers, *Division 241 Amalgamated Transit Union v. Sucsy*, 538 F.2d 1264 (1976). For a state court case that applied a state law to limit drug testing for employees, see *Webster v. Motorola*, 637 N.E.2d 203 (1994). For a case that found that teachers may not be tested without particularized suspicion, see *Patchogue-Medford Congress of Teachers v. Board of Education*, 70 N.Y.2d 57, 517 N.Y.S.2d 456, 510 N.E.2d 325 (1987). A landmark case that allowed blood samples to be forcibly obtained in drunk driving arrests is *Schmerber v. California*, 86 S. Ct. 1826 (1966).

An excellent source of recent writings about legal issues associated with the drug problem is the 1994 symposium issue of the *University of Chicago Legal Forum* entitled "Toward a Rational Drug Policy." Recent analyses of drug use testing can be found in "Alternative Challenges to Drug Testing of Government Employees: Options After *Von Raab* and *Skinner*," 58 *George Washington Law Review* 148 (1989); "Testing for Drug Use in the American Workplace: A Symposium," 11 *Nova Law Review* 291 (1987); Morrow, "Drug Testing in the Workplace: Issues for the Arbitrator," 4 *Journal of Dispute Res-*

olution 273 (1989); and Yale Kamisar, "The Fourth Amendment in an Age of Drug and AIDS Testing," *New York Times Magazine* (September 13, 1987). J. M. Chaiken and M. R. Chaiken, in *Varieties of Criminal Behavior* (Rand, 1982), report their study of the history of drug abuse among career criminals. For information on the Drug Enforcement Administration, see the Internet site `http://www.usdoj.gov/dea/`.

ISSUE 6

Is "Hate Speech" Fully Protected by the Constitution?

YES: **Antonin Scalia**, from Majority Opinion, *R. A. V. v. City of St. Paul, Minnesota*, U.S. Supreme Court (1992)

NO: **John Paul Stevens**, from Concurring Opinion, *R. A. V. v. City of St. Paul, Minnesota*, U.S. Supreme Court (1992)

ISSUE SUMMARY

YES: Supreme Court justice Antonin Scalia finds that the St. Paul ordinance punishing "hate speech" cannot be constitutional because it regulates speech depending on the subject the speech addresses.

NO: Supreme Court justice John Paul Stevens concurs that this particular ordinance is not constitutional, but he argues that it is perhaps simply overbroad.

There are certain well-defined and narrowly limited classes of speech, the prevention and punishment of which have never been thought to raise any Constitutional problem. These include the lewd and obscene, the profane, the libelous, and the insulting or "fighting" words—those which by their very utterance inflict injury or tend to incite an immediate breach of the peace. It has been well observed that such utterances are no essential part of any exposition of ideas, and are of such slight social value as a step to truth that any benefit that may be derived from them is clearly outweighed by the social interest in order and morality.

—Chaplinsky v. New Hampshire

Seven hundred eighty-three hate crimes were recorded in Los Angeles County in 1993, which is over a hundred more than were recorded in 1991. For the first time since 1980, when the county began tracking hate crimes, gay men supplanted blacks as the primary target. Jews constitute only 5 percent of the Los Angeles County population but account for 89.5 percent of all victims of religious hate crimes. According to the FBI, 7,684 hate crimes were reported to law enforcement agencies in the United States in 1993. Even that figure is low, since police agencies contributing to the study represented only 56 percent of the population. Klanwatch, a project of the Southern Poverty Law Center in Montgomery, Alabama, reported a record number of white supremacist groups—346—actively operating in 1991 and a doubling of reported incidents of cross burnings, from 50 in 1990 to 101 in 1991.

We do not live in particularly tranquil, quiet, or harmonious times. Even on college campuses, controversies over courses of study or "political correctness" seem to have a more strident tone than they used to. In 1990 Congress enacted the "Hate Crimes Statistics Act," which requires the FBI to compile data tracking the frequency of hate crimes. (This Act expired recently but may be reenacted.) And cities and universities have dealt with situations in which speech is racist or sexist or denigrating and offensive to someone or some group by enacting regulations that punish such speech.

Typical of hate speech codes at universities is the excerpt below, which was enacted at the University of Wisconsin and then declared unconstitutional by a court.

The university may discipline a student in nonacademic matters in the following situations:

(2)(a) For racist or discriminatory comments, epithets or other expressive behavior directed at an individual or on separate occasions at different individuals, or for physical conduct, if such comments, epithets or other expressive behavior or physical conduct intentionally:

1. Demean the race, sex, religion, color, creed, disability, sexual orientation, national origin, ancestry or age of the individual or individuals and
2. Create an intimidating, hostile or demeaning environment for education, university-related work, or other university-authorized activity.

Current First Amendment law allows regulation over a very limited class of expressions, among them obscenity, fighting words, and libel. Advocates of hate speech codes argue that hate speech causes deep and permanent injury, that words can at times injure as much as sticks and stones. Opponents argue that the best antidote for hate speech is not to punish speech, but to produce more speech. As Benno Schmidt, former president of Yale University, has stated, "It is precisely societies that are diverse, pluralistic, and contentious that most urgently need freedom of speech." In addition, opponents claim that it is not really possible to distinguish the worst hate speech from that which is moderately disagreeable and offensive.

Are there other avenues for institutions to confront racism, sexism, anti-Semitism and homophobia? Would hate speech codes lead us down the slippery slope toward uniformity of thought? Or is the dehumanization that occurs with such speech too harmful to tolerate? The following opinions constitute a fairly strong warning to state and local governmental bodies and institutions to be extremely careful in trying to restrict speech. The majority opinion, by Justice Antonin Scalia, indicates that it is unlikely that any hate speech codes could be found to be constitutional in the future. The concurring opinion, by Justice John Paul Stevens, agrees with the result in this particular case; however, he suggests that a more narrowly drawn code might be approved.

YES

Antonin Scalia

MAJORITY OPINION

R. A. V. v. ST. PAUL

JUSTICE SCALIA delivered the opinion of the Court.

In the predawn hours of June 21, 1990, petitioner and several other teenagers allegedly assembled a crudely-made cross by taping together broken chair legs. They then allegedly burned the cross inside the fenced yard of a black family that lived across the street from the house where petitioner was staying. Although this conduct could have been punished under any of a number of laws, one of the two provisions under which respondent city of St. Paul chose to charge petitioner (then a juvenile) was the St. Paul Bias-Motivated Crime Ordinance, St. Paul, Minn. Legis. Code Sec. 292.02 (1990), which provides:

> "Whoever places on public or private property a symbol, object, appellation, characterization or graffiti, including, but not limited to, a burning cross or Nazi swastika, which one knows or has reasonable grounds to know arouses anger, alarm or resentment in others on the basis of race, color, creed, religion or gender commits disorderly conduct and shall be guilty of a misdemeanor." ...

I

In construing the St. Paul ordinance, we are bound by the construction given to it by the Minnesota court. *Posadas de Puerto Rico Associates v. Tourism Co. of Puerto Rico*, 478 U.S. 328, 339 (1986); *New York v. Ferber*, 458 U.S. 747, 769, n. 24 (1982); *Terminiello v. Chicago*, 337 U.S. 1, 4 (1949). Accordingly, we accept the Minnesota Supreme Court's authoritative statement that the ordinance reaches only those expressions that constitute "fighting words" within the meaning of *Chaplinsky.* 464 N. W. 2d, at 510–511. Petitioner and his *amici* urge us to modify the scope of the Chaplinsky formulation, thereby invalidating the ordinance as "substantially overbroad," *Broadrick v. Oklahoma*, 413 U.S. 601, 610 (1973). We find it unnecessary to consider this issue. Assuming, *arguendo*, that all of the expression reached by the ordinance is proscribable under the "fighting words" doctrine, we nonetheless conclude that the

From *R. A. V. v. City of St. Paul, Minnesota*, 60 L.W. 4667 (1992). Notes and some case citations omitted.

ordinance is facially unconstitutional in that it prohibits otherwise permitted speech solely on the basis of the subjects the speech addresses.

The First Amendment generally prevents government from proscribing speech, or even expressive conduct, because of disapproval of the ideas expressed. Content-based regulations are presumptively invalid. From 1791 to the present, however, our society, like other free but civilized societies, has permitted restrictions upon the content of speech in a few limited areas, which are "of such slight social value as a step to truth that any benefit that may be derived from them is clearly outweighed by the social interest in order and morality." *Chaplinsky, supra,* at 572. We have recognized that "the freedom of speech" referred to by the First Amendment does not include a freedom to disregard these traditional limitations. See, e.g., *Roth v. United States,* 354 U.S. 476 (1957) (obscenity); *Beauharnais v. Illinois,* 343 U.S. 250 (1952) (defamation); *Chaplinsky v. New Hampshire, supra,* ("fighting words"); see generally *Simon & Schuster, supra,* at _____ (KENNEDY, J., concurring in judgment) (slip op., at 4). Our decisions since the 1960's have narrowed the scope of the traditional categorical exceptions for defamation, see *New York Times Co. v. Sullivan,* 376 U.S. 254 (1964); *Gertz v. Robert Welch, Inc.,* 418 U.S. 323 (1974); see generally *Milkovich v. Lorain Journal Co.,* 497 U.S. 1, 13–17 (1990), and for obscenity, see *Miller v. California,* 413 U.S. 15 (1973), but a limited categorical approach has remained an important part of our First Amendment jurisprudence.

We have sometimes said that these categories of expression are "not within the area of constitutionally protected speech," or that the "protection of the First Amendment does not extend" to them. Such statements must be taken in context, however, and are no more literally true than is the occasionally repeated shorthand characterizing obscenity "as not being speech at all," Sunstein, Pornography and the First Amendment, 1986 Duke L. J. 589, 615, n. 146. What they mean is that these areas of speech can, consistently with the First Amendment, be regulated *because of their constitutionally proscribable content* (obscenity, defamation, etc.)—not that they are categories of speech entirely invisible to the Constitution, so that they may be made the vehicles for content discrimination unrelated to their distinctively proscribable content. Thus, the government may proscribe libel; but it may not make the further content discrimination of proscribing only libel critical of the government. We recently acknowledged this distinction in *Ferber,* 458 U.S., at 763, where, in upholding New York's child pornography law, we expressly recognized that there was no "question here of censoring a particular literary theme...."

Our cases surely do not establish the proposition that the First Amendment imposes no obstacle whatsoever to regulation of particular instances of such proscribable expression, so that the government "may regulate [them] freely," *post,* at 4 (WHITE, J., concurring in judgment). That would mean that a city council could enact an ordinance prohibiting only those legally obscene works that contain criticism of the city government or, indeed, that do not include endorsement of the city government. Such a simplistic, all-or-nothing-at-all approach to First Amendment protection is at odds with common sense and with our jurisprudence as well. It is not true that "fighting words" have at most a "de minimis" expressive content, *ibid.*, or that their content is *in all respects* "worthless and undeserving of constitutional protection"; sometimes they are quite expressive indeed. We have not said that they constitute "*no* part of the expression of ideas," but only that they constitute "no *essential* part of any exposition of ideas." *Chaplinsky*, 315 U.S., at 572 (emphasis added).

The proposition that a particular instance of speech can be proscribable on the basis of one feature (e.g., obscenity) but not on the basis of another (e.g., opposition to the city government) is commonplace, and has found application in many contexts. We have long held, for example, that nonverbal expressive activity can be banned because of the action it entails, but not because of the ideas it expresses—so that burning a flag in violation of an ordinance against outdoor fires could be punishable, whereas burning a flag in violation of an ordinance against dishonoring the flag is not. See *Johnson*, 491 U.S., at 406–407. Similarly, we have upheld reasonable "time, place, or manner" restrictions, but only if they are "justified without reference to the content of the regulated speech." *Ward v. Rock Against Racism*, 491 U.S. 781, 791 (1989); see also *Clark v. Community for Creative Non-Violence*, 468 U.S. 288, 298 (1984) (noting that the *O'Brien* test differs little from the standard applied to time, place, or manner restrictions). And just as the power to proscribe particular speech on the basis of a noncontent element (e.g., noise) does not entail the power to proscribe the same speech on the basis of a content element; so also, the power to proscribe it on the basis of *one* content element (e.g., obscenity) does not entail the power to proscribe it on the basis of *other* content elements.

In other words, the exclusion of "fighting words" from the scope of the First Amendment simply means that, for purposes of that Amendment, the unprotected features of the words are, despite their verbal character, essentially a "non-speech" element of communication. Fighting words are thus analogous to a noisy sound truck: Each is, as Justice Frankfurter recognized, a "mode of speech," *Niemotko v. Maryland*, 340 U.S. 268, 282 (1951) (Frankfurter, J., concurring in result); both can be used to convey an idea; but neither has, in and of itself, a claim upon the First Amendment. As with the sound truck, however, so also with fighting words: The government may not regulate use based on hostility—or favoritism—towards the underlying message expressed. Compare *Frisby v. Schultz*, 487 U.S. 474 (1988) (upholding, against facial challenge, a content-neutral ban on targeted residential picketing) with *Carey v. Brown*, 447 U.S. 455 (1980) (invalidating a ban on residential picketing that exempted labor picketing)....

When the basis for the content discrimination consists entirely of the very reason the entire class of speech at issue is proscribable, no significant danger of idea or viewpoint discrimination exists. Such a reason, having been adjudged neutral enough to support exclusion of the entire class of speech from First Amendment protection, is also neutral enough to form the basis of distinction within the class. To illustrate: A State might choose to prohibit only that obscenity which is the most patently offensive *in its prurience*—i.e., that which involves the most lascivious displays of sexual activity. But it may not prohibit, for example, only that obscenity which includes offensive *political* messages. And the Federal Government can criminalize only those threats of violence that are directed against the President, see 18 U.S.C. sec. 871—since the reasons why threats of violence are outside the First Amendment (protecting individuals from the fear of violence, from the disruption that fear engenders, and from the possibility that the threatened violence will occur) have special force when applied to the person of the President. See *Watts v. United States*, 394 U.S. 705, 707 (1969) (upholding the facial validity of § 871 because of the "overwhelmin[g] interest in protecting the safety of [the] Chief Executive and in allowing him to perform his duties without interference from threats of physical violence"). But the Federal Government may not criminalize only those threats against the President that mention his policy on aid to inner cities. And to take a final example (one mentioned by Justice Stevens, *post*, at 6–7), a State may choose to regulate price advertising in one industry but not in others, because the risk of fraud (one of the characteristics of commercial speech that justifies depriving it of full First Amendment protection, see *Virginia Pharmacy Bd. v. Virginia Citizens Consumer Council, Inc.*, 425 U.S. 748, 771–772 (1976)) is in its view greater there. But a State may not prohibit only that commercial advertising that depicts men in a demeaning fashion.

Another valid basis for according differential treatment to even a content-defined subclass of proscribable speech is that the subclass happens to be associated with particular "secondary effects" of the speech, so that the regulation is "justified without reference to the content of the... speech," *Renton v. Playtime Theatres, Inc.*, 475 U.S. 41, 48 (1986). A State could, for example, permit all obscene live performances except those involving minors. Moreover, since words can in some circumstances violate laws directed not against speech but against conduct (a law against treason, for example, is violated by telling the enemy the nation's defense secrets), a particular content-based subcategory of a proscribable class of speech can be swept up incidentally within the reach of a statute directed at conduct rather than speech. Thus, for example, sexually derogatory "fighting words," among other words, may produce a violation of Title VII's general prohibition against sexual discrimination in employment practices, 42 U.S.C. § 2000e-2; 29 CFR § 1604.11 (1991). See also 18 U.S.C. § 242; 42 U.S.C. § 1981, 1982. Where the government does not target conduct on the basis of its expressive content, acts are not shielded from regulation merely because they express a discriminatory idea or philosophy.

These bases for distinction refute the proposition that the selectivity of the restriction is "even arguably 'conditioned upon the sovereign's agreement with what a speaker may intend to say.'" *Metromedia, Inc. v. San Diego*, 453 U.S. 490, 555 (1981) (STEVENS, J., dissenting in part) (citation omitted). There may be other such bases as well. Indeed, to validate such selectivity (where totally proscribable speech is at issue) it may not even be necessary to identify any particular "neutral" basis, so long as the nature of the content discrimination is such that there is no realistic possibility that official suppression of ideas is afoot. (We cannot think of any First Amendment interest that would stand in the way of a State's prohibiting only those obscene motion pictures with blue-eyed actresses.) Save for that limitation, the regulation of "fighting words," like the regulation of noisy speech, may address some offensive instances and leave other, equally offensive, instances alone.

II

Applying these principles to the St. Paul ordinance, we conclude that, even as narrowly construed by the Minnesota Supreme Court, the ordinance is facially unconstitutional. Although the phrase in the ordinance, "arouses anger, alarm or resentment in others," has been limited by the Minnesota Supreme Court's construction to reach only those symbols or displays that amount to "fighting words," the remaining, unmodified terms make clear that the ordinance applies only to "fighting words" that insult, or provoke violence, "on the basis of race, color, creed, religion or gender." Displays containing abusive invective, no matter how vicious or severe, are permissible unless they are addressed to one of the specified disfavored topics. Those who wish to use "fighting words" in connection with other ideas—to express hostility, for example, on the basis of political affiliation, union membership, or homosexuality—are not covered. The First Amendment does not permit St. Paul to impose special prohibitions on those speakers who express views on disfavored subjects.

In its practical operation, moreover, the ordinance goes even beyond mere content discrimination, to actual viewpoint discrimination. Displays containing some words—odious racial epithets, for example—would be prohibited to proponents of all views. But "fighting words" that do not themselves invoke race, color, creed, religion, or gender—aspersions upon a person's mother, for example—would seemingly be usable *ad libitum* in the placards of those arguing *in favor* of racial, color, etc., tolerance and equality, but could not be used by that speaker's opponents. One could hold up a sign saying, for example, that all "anti-Catholic bigots" are misbegotten; but not that all "papists" are, for that would insult and provoke violence "on the basis of religion." St. Paul has no such authority to license one side of a debate to fight freestyle, while requiring the other to follow Marquis of Queensbury Rules.

What we have here, it must be emphasized, is not a prohibition of fighting words that are directed at certain persons or groups (which would be *facially* valid if it met the requirements of the Equal Protection Clause); but rather, a prohibition of fighting words that contain (as the Minnesota Supreme Court repeatedly emphasized) messages of "bias-motivated" hatred and in particular, as applied to this case, messages "based on virulent notions of racial supremacy." 464 N. W. 2d, at 508, 511. One must wholeheartedly agree with the Minnesota Supreme Court that "[i]t is the responsibility, even the obligation, of diverse communities to confront such notions in whatever form they appear," *ibid.*, but the manner of that confrontation cannot consist of selective limitations upon speech. St. Paul's brief asserts that a general "fighting words" law would not meet the city's needs because only a content-specific measure can communicate to minority groups that the "group hatred" aspect of such speech "is not condoned by the majority." Brief for Respondent 25. The point of the First Amendment is that majority preferences must be expressed in some fashion other than silencing speech on the basis of its content.

Despite the fact that the Minnesota Supreme Court and St. Paul acknowledge that the ordinance is directed at expression of group hatred, Justice Stevens suggests that this "fundamentally misreads" the ordinance. It is directed, he claims, not to speech of a particular content, but to particular "injur[ies]" that are "qualitatively different" from other injuries. This is word-play. What makes the anger, fear, sense of dishonor, etc. produced by violation of this ordinance distinct from the anger, fear, sense of dishonor, etc. produced by other fighting words is nothing other than the fact that it is caused by a distinctive idea, conveyed by a distinctive message. The First Amendment cannot be evaded that easily. It is obvious that the symbols which will arouse "anger, alarm or resentment in others on the basis of race, color, creed, religion or gender" are those symbols that communicate a message of hostility based on one of these characteristics. St. Paul concedes in its brief that the ordinance applies only to "racial, religious, or gender-specific symbols" such as "a burning cross, Nazi swastika or other instrumentality of like import." Brief for Respondent 8. Indeed, St. Paul argued in the Juvenile Court that "[t]he burning of a cross does express a message and it is, in fact, the content of that message which the St. Paul Ordinance attempts to legislate." Memorandum from the Ramsey County Attorney to the Honorable Charles A. Flinn, Jr., dated July 13, 1990, in *In re Welfare of R. A. V.*, No. 89-D-1231 (Ramsey Cty. Juvenile Ct.), p. 1, reprinted in App. to Brief for Petitioner C-1.

The content-based discrimination reflected in the St. Paul ordinance comes within neither any of the specific exceptions to the First Amendment prohibition we discussed earlier, nor within a more general exception for content discrimination that does not threaten censorship of ideas. It assuredly does not fall within the exception for content discrimination based on the very reasons why the particular class of speech at issue (here, fighting words) is proscribable. As explained earlier, the reason why fighting words are categorically excluded from the protection of the First Amendment is not that their content communicates any particular idea, but that their content embodies a particularly intolerable (and socially unnecessary) *mode* of expressing *whatever* idea the speaker wishes to convey. St. Paul has not singled out an especially offensive mode of expression—it has not, for example, selected for prohibition only those fighting words that communicate ideas in a threatening (as opposed to a merely obnoxious) manner. Rather, it has proscribed fighting words of whatever manner that communicate messages of racial, gender, or religious intolerance. Selectivity of this sort creates the possibility that the city is seeking to handicap the expression of particular ideas. That possibility would alone be enough to render the ordinance presumptively invalid, but St. Paul's comments and concessions in this case elevate the possibility to a certainty.

St. Paul argues that the ordinance comes within another of the specific exceptions we mentioned, the one that allows content discrimination aimed only at the "secondary effects" of the speech. According to St. Paul, the ordinance is intended, "not to impact on [sic] the right of free expression of the accused," but rather to "protect against the victimization of a person or persons who are particularly vulnerable because of their membership in a group that historically has been discriminated against." Brief for Respondent 28. Even assuming that an ordinance that completely proscribes, rather than merely regulates, a specified category of speech can ever be considered to be directed only to the secondary effects of such speech, it is clear that the St. Paul ordinance is not directed to secondary effects within the meaning of *Renton*. As we said in *Boos v. Barry*, 485 U.S. 312 (1988), "listeners' reactions to speech are not the type of 'secondary effects' we referred to in *Renton*." *Id.*, at 321. "The emotive impact of speech on its audience is not a 'secondary effect.' "

It hardly needs discussion that the ordinance does not fall within some more general exception permitting *all* selectivity that for any reason is beyond the suspicion of official suppression of ideas. The statements of St. Paul in this very case afford ample basis for, if not full confirmation of, that suspicion.

Finally, St. Paul and its *amici* defend the conclusion of the Minnesota Supreme Court that, even if the ordinance regulates expression based on hostility towards its protected ideological content, this discrimination is nonetheless justified because it is narrowly tailored to serve compelling state interests. Specifically, they assert that the ordinance helps to ensure the basic human rights of members of groups that have historically been subjected to discrimination, including the right of such group members to live in peace where they wish. We do not doubt that these interests are compelling, and that the ordinance can be said to promote them. But the "danger of censorship" presented by a facially content-based statute requires that that weapon be employed only where it is "*necessary* to serve the asserted [compelling] interest," (emphasis added). The existence of adequate content-neutral alternatives thus "undercut[s] significantly" any defense of such a statute, casting considerable doubt on the government's protestations that "the asserted justification is in fact an accurate description of the purpose and effect of the law." The dispositive question in this case, therefore, is whether content discrimination is reasonably necessary to achieve St. Paul's compelling interests; it plainly is not. An ordinance not limited to the favored topics, for example, would have precisely the same beneficial effect. In fact the only interest distinctively served by the content limitation is that of displaying the city council's special hostility towards the particular biases thus singled out. That is precisely what the First Amendment forbids. The politicians of St. Paul are entitled to express that hostility—but not through the means of imposing unique limitations upon speakers who (however benightedly) disagree.

Let there be no mistake about our belief that burning a cross in someone's front yard is reprehensible. But St. Paul has sufficient means at its disposal to prevent such behavior without adding the First Amendment to the fire.

The judgment of the Minnesota Supreme Court is reversed, and the case is remanded for proceedings not inconsistent with this opinion.

It is so ordered.

NO

John Paul Stevens

OPINION OF JOHN PAUL STEVENS

Concurring opinion by Justice Stevens:

Conduct that creates special risks or causes special harms may be prohibited by special rules. Lighting a fire near an ammunition dump or a gasoline storage tank is especially dangerous; such behavior may be punished more severely than burning trash in a vacant lot. Threatening someone because of her race or religious beliefs may cause particularly severe trauma or touch off a riot, and threatening a high public official may cause substantial social disruption; such threats may be punished more severely than threats against someone based on, say, his support of a particular athletic team. There are legitimate, reasonable, and neutral justifications for such special rules.

This case involves the constitutionality of one such ordinance. Because the regulated conduct has some communicative content—a message of racial, religious or gender hostility—the ordinance raises two quite different First Amendment questions. Is the ordinance "overbroad" because it prohibits too much speech? If not, is it "underbroad" because it does not prohibit enough speech? . . .

I

Fifty years ago, the Court articulated a categorical approach to First Amendment jurisprudence.

> "There are certain well-defined and narrowly limited classes of speech, the prevention and punishment of which have never been thought to raise any Constitutional problem. . . . It has been well observed that such utterances are no essential part of any exposition of ideas, and are of such slight social value as a step to truth that any benefit that may be derived from them is clearly outweighed by the social interest in order and morality." *Chaplinsky v. New Hampshire*, 315 U.S. 568, 571-572 (1942).

We have, as Justice White observes, often described such categories of expression as "not within the area of constitutionally protected speech." *Roth v. United States*, 354 U.S. 476, 483 (1957).

From *R. A. V. v. City of St. Paul, Minnesota*, 60 L.W. 4667 (1992). Some notes and case citations omitted.

The Court today revises this categorical approach. It is not, the Court rules, that certain "categories" of expression are "unprotected," but rather that certain "elements" of expression are wholly "proscribable." To the Court, an expressive act, like a chemical compound, consists of more than one element. Although the act may be regulated because it contains a proscribable element, it may not be regulated on the basis of another (nonproscribable) element it also contains. Thus, obscene antigovernment speech may be regulated because it is obscene, but not because it is antigovernment. It is this revision of the categorical approach that allows the Court to assume that the St. Paul ordinance proscribes *only* fighting words, while at the same time concluding that the ordinance is invalid because it imposes a content-based regulation on expressive activity.

As an initial matter, the Court's revision of the categorical approach seems to me something of an adventure in a doctrinal wonderland, for the concept of "obscene antigovernment" speech is fantastical. The category of the obscene is very narrow; to be obscene, expression must be found by the trier of fact to "appea[l] to the prurient interest, ... depic[t] or describ[e], in a patently offensive way, sexual conduct, [and] taken as a whole, *lac[k] serious literary, artistic, political or scientific value." Miller v. California*, 413 U.S. 15, 24 (1973) (emphasis added). "Obscene antigovernment" speech, then, is a contradiction in terms: If expression is antigovernment, it does not "lac[k] serious... political... value" and cannot be obscene.

The Court attempts to bolster its argument by likening its novel analysis to that applied to restrictions on the time, place, or manner of expression or on expressive conduct. It is true that loud speech in favor of the Republican Party can be regulated because it is loud, but not because it is pro-Republican; and it is true that the public burning of the American flag can be regulated because it involves public burning and not because it involves the flag. But these analogies are inapposite. In each of these examples, the two elements (e.g., loudness and pro-Republican orientation) can coexist; in the case of "obscene antigovernment" speech, however, the presence of one element ("obscenity") by definition means the absence of the other. To my mind, it is unwise and unsound to craft a new doctrine based on such highly speculative hypotheticals.

I am, however, even more troubled by the second step of the Court's analysis—namely, its conclusion that the St. Paul ordinance is an unconstitutional content-based regulation of speech. Drawing on broadly worded *dicta*, the Court establishes a near-absolute ban on content-based regulations of expression and holds that the First Amendment prohibits the regulation of fighting words by subject matter. Thus, while the Court rejects the "all-or-nothing-at-all" nature of the categorical approach, it promptly embraces an absolutism of its own: within a particular "proscribable" category of expression, the Court holds, a government must either proscribe *all* speech or no speech at all. This aspect of the Court's ruling fundamentally misunderstands the role and constitutional status of content-based regulations on speech, conflicts with the very nature of First Amendment jurisprudence, and disrupts well-settled principles of First Amendment law.

Although the Court has, on occasion, declared that content-based regulations of speech are "never permitted," *Police*

Dept. of Chicago v. Mosley, 408 U.S. 92, 99 (1972), such claims are overstated. Indeed, in *Mosley* itself, the Court indicated that Chicago's selective proscription of nonlabor picketing was not *per se* unconstitutional, but rather could be upheld if the City demonstrated that nonlabor picketing was "clearly more disruptive than [labor] picketing." *Id.*, at 100. Contrary to the broad *dicta* in *Mosley* and elsewhere, our decisions demonstrate that content-based distinctions, far from being presumptively invalid, are an inevitable and indispensable aspect of a coherent understanding of the First Amendment.

This is true at every level of First Amendment law. In broadest terms, our entire First Amendment jurisprudence creates a regime based on the content of speech. The scope of the First Amendment is determined by the content of expressive activity: Although the First Amendment broadly protects "speech," it does not protect the right to "fix prices, breach contracts, make false warranties, place bets with bookies, threaten, [or] extort." Schauer, Categories and the First Amendment: A Play in Three Acts, 34 Vand. L. Rev. 265, 270 (1981). Whether an agreement among competitors is a violation of the Sherman Act or protected activity under the *Noerr-Pennington* doctrine hinges upon the content of the agreement. Similarly, "the line between permissible advocacy and impermissible incitation to crime or violence depends, not merely on the setting in which the speech occurs, but also on exactly what the speaker had to say." *Young v. American Mini Theatres, Inc.*, 427 U.S. 50, 66 (1976) (plurality opinion).

Likewise, whether speech falls within one of the categories of "unprotected" or "proscribable" expression is determined,

in part, by its content. Whether a magazine is obscene, a gesture a fighting word, or a photograph child pornography is determined, in part, by its content. Even within categories of protected expression, the First Amendment status of speech is fixed by its content. *New York Times Co. v. Sullivan*, 376 U.S. 254 (1964), and *Dun & Bradstreet, Inc. v. Greenmoss Builders, Inc.*, 472 U.S. 749 (1985), establish that the level of protection given to speech depends upon its subject matter: speech about public officials or matters of public concern receives greater protection than speech about other topics. It can, therefore, scarcely be said that the regulation of expressive activity cannot be predicated on its content: much of our First Amendment jurisprudence is premised on the assumption that content makes a difference.

Consistent with this general premise, we have frequently upheld content-based regulations of speech. For example, in *Young v. American Mini Theatres*, the Court upheld zoning ordinances that regulated movie theaters based on the content of the films shown. In *FCC v. Pacifica Foundation*, 438 U.S. 726 (1978) (plurality opinion), we upheld a restriction on the broadcast of *specific* indecent words. In *Lehman v. City of Shaker Heights*, 418 U.S. 298 (1974) (plurality opinion), we upheld a city law that permitted commercial advertising, but prohibited political advertising, on city buses. In *Broadrick v. Oklahoma*, 413 U.S. 601 (1973), we upheld a state law that restricted the speech of state employees, but only as concerned partisan political matters. We have long recognized the power of the Federal Trade Commission to regulate misleading advertising and labeling, and the National Labor Relations Board's power to regulate an employer's election-related speech on the basis of its content. It is also beyond question that the Government may choose to limit advertisements for cigarettes, see 15 U.S.C. § 1331–1340, but not for cigars; choose to regulate airline advertising, but not bus advertising; or choose to monitor solicitation by lawyers, see *Ohralik v. Ohio State Bar Assn.*, 436 U.S. 447 (1978), but not by doctors.

All of these cases involved the selective regulation of speech based on content—precisely the sort of regulation the Court invalidates today. Such selective regulations are unavoidably content based, but they are not, in my opinion, "presumptively invalid." As these many decisions and examples demonstrate, the prohibition on content-based regulations is not nearly as total as the *Mosley* dictum suggests.

Disregarding this vast body of case law, the Court today goes beyond even the overstatement in *Mosley* and applies the prohibition on content-based regulation to speech that the Court had until today considered wholly "unprotected" by the First Amendment—namely, fighting words. This new absolutism in the prohibition of content-based regulations severely contorts the fabric of settled First Amendment law.

Our First Amendment decisions have created a rough hierarchy in the constitutional protection of speech. Core political speech occupies the highest, most protected position; commercial speech and nonobscene, sexually explicit speech are regarded as a sort of second-class expression; obscenity and fighting words receive the least protection of all. Assuming that the Court is correct that this last class of speech is not wholly "unprotected," it certainly does not follow that fighting words and obscenity receive the *same* sort of protection afforded core political speech. Yet in ruling that proscribable speech cannot be regulated based on subject matter, the Court does just that. Perversely, this gives fighting words *greater* protection than is afforded commercial speech. If Congress can prohibit false advertising directed at airline passengers without also prohibiting false advertising directed at bus passengers and if a city can prohibit political advertisements in its buses while allowing other advertisements, it is ironic to hold that a city cannot regulate fighting words based on "race, color, creed, religion or gender" while leaving unregulated fighting words based on "union membership or homosexuality." The Court today turns First Amendment law on its head: Communication that was once entirely unprotected (and that still can be wholly proscribed) is now entitled to greater protection than commercial speech—and possibly greater protection than core political speech.

Perhaps because the Court recognizes these perversities, it quickly offers some ad hoc limitations on its newly extended prohibition on content-based regulations. First, the Court states that a content-based regulation is valid "[w]hen the content discrimination is based upon the very reason the entire class of speech… is proscribable." In a pivotal passage, the Court writes

"the Federal Government can criminalize only those physical threats that are directed against the President, see 18 U.S.C. § 871—since the reasons why threats of violence are outside the First Amendment (protecting individuals from the fear of violence, from the disruption that fear engenders, and from the possibility that the threatened violence will occur) have special force when applied to the… President."

As I understand this opaque passage, Congress may choose from the set of unprotected speech (all threats) to proscribe only a subset (threats against the President) because those threats are particularly likely to cause "fear of violence," "disruption," and actual "violence."

Precisely this same reasoning, however, compels the conclusion that St. Paul's ordinance is constitutional. Just as Congress may determine that threats against the President entail more severe consequences than other threats, so St. Paul's City Council may determine that threats based on the target's race, religion, or gender cause more severe harm to both the target and to society than other threats. This latter judgment—that harms caused by racial, religious, and gender-based invective are qualitatively different from that caused by other fighting words —seems to me eminently reasonable and realistic.

Next, the Court recognizes that a State may regulate advertising in one industry but not another because "the risk of fraud (one of the characteristics that justifies depriving [commercial speech] of full First Amendment protection...)" in the regulated industry is "greater" than in other industries. Again, the same reasoning demonstrates the constitutionality of St. Paul's ordinance. "[O]ne of the characteristics that justifies" the constitutional status of fighting words is that such words "by their very utterance inflict injury or tend to incite an immediate breach of the peace." *Chaplinsky*, 315 U.S., at 572. Certainly a legislature that may determine that the risk of fraud is greater in the legal trade than in the medical trade may determine that the risk of injury or breach of peace created by race-

based threats is greater than that created by other threats....

In sum, the central premise of the Court's ruling—that "[c]ontent-based regulations are presumptively invalid"— has simplistic appeal, but lacks support in our First Amendment jurisprudence. To make matters worse, the Court today extends this overstated claim to reach categories of hitherto unprotected speech and, in doing so, wreaks havoc in an area of settled law. Finally, although the Court recognizes exceptions to its new principle, those exceptions undermine its very conclusion that the St. Paul ordinance is unconstitutional. Stated directly, the majority's position cannot withstand scrutiny....

III

As the foregoing suggests, I disagree with both the Court's and part of Justice White's analysis of the constitutionality [of the] St. Paul ordinance. Unlike the Court, I do not believe that all content-based regulations are equally infirm and presumptively invalid; unlike Justice White, I do not believe that fighting words are wholly unprotected by the First Amendment. To the contrary, I believe our decisions establish a more complex and subtle analysis, one that considers the content and context of the regulated speech, and the nature and scope of the restriction on speech. Applying this analysis and assuming *arguendo* (as the Court does) that the St. Paul ordinance is *not* overbroad, I conclude that such a selective, subject-matter regulation on proscribable speech is constitutional.

Not all content-based regulations are alike; our decisions clearly recognize that some content-based restrictions raise more constitutional questions than others. Although the Court's analysis of content-based regulations cannot be reduced to a simple formula, we have considered a number of factors in determining the validity of such regulations.

First, as suggested above, the scope of protection provided expressive activity depends in part upon its content and character. We have long recognized that when government regulates political speech or "the expression of editorial opinion on matters of public importance," *FCC v. League of Women Voters of California*, 468 U.S. 364, 375–376 (1984), "First Amendment protectio[n] is 'at its zenith.'" *Meyer v. Grant*, 486 U.S. 414, 425 (1988). In comparison, we have recognized that "commercial speech receives a limited form of First Amendment protection," *Posadas de Puerto Rico Associates v. Tourism Co. of Puerto Rico*, 478 U.S. 328, 340 (1986), and that "society's interest in protecting [sexually explicit films] is of a wholly different, and lesser magnitude than [its] interest in untrammeled political debate." *Young v. American Mini Theatres*, 427 U.S., at 70; see also *FCC v. Pacifica Foundation*, 438 U.S. 726 (1978). The character of expressive activity also weighs in our consideration of its constitutional status. As we have frequently noted, "the government generally has a freer hand in restricting expressive conduct than it has in restricting the written or spoken word." *Texas v. Johnson*, 491 U.S. 397, 406 (1989); see also *United States v. O'Brien*, 391 U.S. 367 (1968).

The protection afforded expression turns as well on the context of the regulated speech. We have noted, for example, that "[a]ny assessment of the precise scope of employer expression, of course, must be made in the context of its labor relations setting... [and]

must take into account the economic dependence of the employees on their employers." *NLRB v. Gissel Packing Co.*, 395 U.S., at 617. Similarly, the distinctive character of a university environment or a secondary school environment, see *Hazelwood School Dist. v. Kuhlmeier*, 484 U.S. 260 (1988), influences our First Amendment analysis. The same is true of the presence of a " 'captive audience, [one] there as a matter of necessity, not of choice.'" *Lehman v. City of Shaker Heights*, 418 U.S., at 302 (citation omitted). Perhaps the most familiar embodiment of the relevance of context is our "fora" jurisprudence, differentiating the levels of protection afforded speech in different locations.

The nature of a contested restriction of speech also informs our evaluation of its constitutionality. Thus, for example, "[a]ny system of prior restraints of expression comes to this Court bearing a heavy presumption against its constitutional validity." *Bantam Books, Inc. v. Sullivan*, 372 U.S. 58, 70 (1963). More particularly to the matter of content-based regulations, we have implicitly distinguished between restrictions on expression based on *subject matter* and restrictions based on *viewpoint*, indicating that the latter are particularly pernicious. "If there is a bedrock principle underlying the First Amendment, it is that the Government may not prohibit the expression of an idea simply because society finds the idea itself offensive or disagreeable." *Texas v. Johnson*, 491 U.S., at 414. "Viewpoint discrimination is censorship in its purest form," *Perry Education Assn. v. Perry Local Educators' Assn.*, 460 U.S. 37, 62 (1983) (Brennan, J., dissenting), and requires particular scrutiny, in part because such regulation often indicates a legislative effort to skew public debate on an issue. See, e.g., *Schacht v. United States*, 398 U.S. 58, 63 (1970). "Especially where ... the legislature's suppression of speech suggests an attempt to give one side of a debatable public question an advantage in expressing its views to the people, the First Amendment is plainly offended." *First National Bank of Boston v. Bellotti*, 435 U.S. 765, 785–786 (1978). Thus, although a regulation that on its face regulates speech by subject matter may in some instances effectively suppress particular viewpoints, in general, viewpoint-based restrictions on expression require greater scrutiny than subject-matter based restrictions.

Finally, in considering the validity of content-based regulations we have also looked more broadly at the scope of the restrictions. For example, in *Young v. American Mini Theatres*, 427 U.S., at 71, we found significant the fact that "what [was] ultimately at stake [was] nothing more than a limitation on the place where adult films may be exhibited." Similarly, in *FCC v. Pacifica Foundation*, the Court emphasized two dimensions of the limited scope of the FCC ruling. First, the ruling concerned only broadcast material which presents particular problems because it "confronts the citizen ... in the privacy of the home"; second, the ruling was not a complete ban on the use of selected offensive words, but rather merely a limitation on the times such speech could be broadcast. 438 U.S., at 748–750.

All of these factors play some role in our evaluation of content-based regulations on expression. Such a multi-faceted analysis cannot be conflated into two dimensions. Whatever the allure of absolute doctrines, it is just too simple to declare expression "protected" or "un-protected" or to proclaim a regulation "content-based" or "content-neutral."

In applying this analysis to the St. Paul ordinance, I assume *arguendo*—as the Court does—that the ordinance regulates *only* fighting words and therefore is *not* overbroad. Looking to the content and character of the regulated activity, two things are clear. First, by hypothesis the ordinance bars only low-value speech, namely, fighting words. By definition such expression constitutes "no essential part of any exposition of ideas, and [is] of such slight social value as a step to truth that any benefit that may be derived from [it] is clearly outweighed by the social interest in order and morality." *Chaplinsky*, 315 U.S., at 572. Second, the ordinance regulates "expressive conduct [rather] than ... the written or spoken word." *Texas v. Johnson*, 491 U.S., at 406.

Looking to the context of the regulated activity, it is again significant that the statute (by hypothesis) regulates *only* fighting words. Whether words are fighting words is determined in part by their context. Fighting words are not words that merely cause offense; fighting words must be directed at individuals so as to "by their very utterance inflict injury." By hypothesis, then, the St. Paul ordinance restricts speech in confrontational and potentially violent situations. The case at hand is illustrative. The cross-burning in this case—directed as it was to a single African-American family trapped in their home—was nothing more than a crude form of physical intimidation. That this cross-burning sends a message of racial hostility does not automatically endow it with complete constitutional protection.

Significantly, the St. Paul ordinance regulates speech not on the basis of its subject matter or the viewpoint expressed, but rather on the basis of the *harm* the speech causes. In this regard, the Court fundamentally misreads the St. Paul ordinance. The Court describes the St. Paul ordinance as regulating expression "addressed to one of [several] specified disfavored *topics*," as policing "disfavored *subjects*," and as "prohibit[ing] ... speech solely on the basis of the *subjects* the speech addresses" (emphasis supplied). Contrary to the Court's suggestion, the ordinance regulates only a subcategory of expression that causes *injuries based* on race, color, creed, religion or gender," not a subcategory that involves discussions that concern those characteristics.[1] The ordinance, as construed by the Court, criminalizes expression that "one knows ... [by its very utterance inflicts injury on] others on the basis of race, color, creed, religion or gender." In this regard, the ordinance resembles the child pornography law at issue in *Ferber,* which in effect singled out child pornography because those publications caused far greater harms than pornography involving adults.

Moreover, even if the St. Paul ordinance did regulate fighting words based on its subject matter, such a regulation would, in my opinion, be constitutional. As noted above, subject-matter based regulations on commercial speech are widespread and largely unproblematic. As we have long recognized, subject-matter regulations generally do not raise the same concerns of government censorship and the distortion of public discourse presented by viewpoint regulations. Thus, in upholding subject-matter regulations we have carefully noted that viewpoint-based discrimination was not implicated.... Indeed, some subject-matter restrictions are a functional necessity in contemporary governance: "The

First Amendment does not require States to regulate for problems that do not exist."

Contrary to the suggestion of the majority, the St. Paul ordinance does *not* regulate expression based on viewpoint. The Court contends that the ordinance requires proponents of racial intolerance to "follow the Marquis of Queensbury Rules" while allowing advocates of racial tolerance to "fight freestyle." The law does no such thing.

The Court writes:

"One could hold up a sign saying, for example, that all 'anti-Catholic bigots' are misbegotten; but not that all 'papists' are, for that would insult and provoke violence 'on the basis of religion.'"

This may be true, but it hardly proves the Court's point. The Court's reasoning is asymmetrical. The response to a sign saying that "all [religious] bigots are misbegotten" is a sign saying that "all advocates of religious tolerance are misbegotten." Assuming such signs could be fighting words (which seems to me extremely unlikely), neither sign would be banned by the ordinance for the attacks were not "based on... religion" but rather on one's beliefs about tolerance. Conversely (and again assuming such signs are fighting words), just as the ordinance would prohibit a Muslim from hoisting a sign claiming that all Catholics were misbegotten, so the ordinance would bar a Catholic from hoisting a similar sign attacking Muslims.

The St. Paul ordinance is evenhanded. In a battle between advocates of tolerance and advocates of intolerance, the ordinance does not prevent either side from hurling fighting words at the other on the basis of their conflicting ideas, but it does bar *both* sides from hurling such words on the basis of the target's "race, color, creed, religion or gender." To extend the Court's pugilistic metaphor, the St. Paul ordinance simply bans punches "below the belt"—*by either party*. It does not, therefore, favor one side of any debate.

Finally, it is noteworthy that the St. Paul ordinance is, as construed by the Court today, quite narrow. The St. Paul ordinance does not ban all "hate speech," nor does it ban, say, all cross-burnings or all swastika displays. Rather it only bans a subcategory of the already narrow category of fighting words. Such a limited ordinance leaves open and protected a vast range of expression on the subjects of racial, religious, and gender equality. As construed by the Court today, the ordinance certainly does not " 'raise the specter that the Government may effectively drive certain ideas or viewpoints from the marketplace.' " Petitioner is free to burn a cross to announce a rally or to express his views about racial supremacy, he may do so on private property or public land, at day or at night, so long as the burning is not so threatening and so directed at an individual as to "by its very [execution] inflict injury." Such a limited proscription scarcely offends the First Amendment.

In sum, the St. Paul ordinance (as construed by the Court) regulates expressive activity that is wholly proscribable and does so not on the basis of viewpoint, but rather in recognition of the different harms caused by such activity. Taken together, these several considerations persuade me that the St. Paul ordinance is not an unconstitutional content-based regulation of speech. Thus, were the ordinance not overbroad, I would vote to uphold it.

NOTES

1. The Court contends that this distinction is "wordplay," reasoning that "[w]hat makes [the harms caused by race-based threats] distinct from [the harms] produced by other fighting words is... the fact that [the former are] caused by a *distinctive idea*" (emphasis added). In this way, the Court concludes that regulating speech based on the injury it causes is no different from regulating speech based on its subject matter. This analysis fundamentally miscomprehends the role of "race, color, creed, religion [and] gender" in contemporary American society. One need look no further than the recent social unrest in the Nation's cities to see that race-based threats may cause more harm to society and to individuals than other threats. Just as the statute prohibiting threats against the President is justifiable because of the place of the President in our social and political order, so a statute prohibiting race-based threats is justifiable because of the place of race in our social and political order. Although it is regrettable that race occupies such a place and is so incendiary an issue, until the Nation matures beyond that condition, laws such as St. Paul's ordinance will remain reasonable and justifiable.

POSTSCRIPT

Is "Hate Speech" Fully Protected by the Constitution?

Law professor Rodney Smolla has inquired, "Should an open culture tolerate speech designed to spread intolerance? This may be the hardest free speech question of all, because an open culture is largely built on the ethos of tolerance." Smolla's question becomes even more significant because the principal arena where hate speech codes have been put into place has been college campuses, arguably the institution in our society that is most tolerant of deviant speech.

Hundreds of college campuses had hate speech codes in place at the time of the *R. A. V.* decision. A 1993 study showed that 36 percent of 384 colleges surveyed still had hate speech rules, many of which were probably unconstitutional. The challenge in drafting codes is to distinguish between actions and conduct, such as hate crimes, which are not protected by the First Amendment, and speech, which is protected.

The Supreme Court decision in *R. A. V.* was not all that surprising, given the breadth of the St. Paul statute. Judges have more experience with First Amendment theory than do campus administrators or politicians. They are more likely to have a clearer historical perspective, and they are certainly removed from the pressures facing those who have enacted such codes. The traditional answer of the courts to disturbing speech has been that the antidote is more speech and counterprotests that will educate the public and not simply punish those who have caused anger and hurt. Whether or not this is an appropriate response to hate speech, which degrades and injures and which seems to be on the increase, will, in spite of the opinions you have just read, continue to challenge us.

A recent case allowing stiffer sentences in cases of hate crimes is *Wisconsin v. Todd Mitchell*, 113 S. Ct. 2194 (1993). The University of Wisconsin code was declared unconstitutional in *UWM Post v. Regents*, 774 F. Supp. 1163 (1991). Readings that discuss hate speech include R. Smolla, *Free Speech in an Open Society* (Alfred A. Knopf, 1992); L. Bollinger, *The Tolerant Society* (Oxford University Press, 1986); Matsuda, "Public Response to Racist Speech: Considering the Victim's Story," 87 *Michigan Law Review* 2320 (1989); and Minow, "Speaking and Writing Against Hate," 11 *Cardozo Law Review* 1393 (1990). A famous case involving a plan by a Nazi group to march in the largely Jewish community of Skokie, Illinois, is recounted in D. Downs, *Nazis in Skokie* (University of Notre Dame Press, 1985), and in *Skokie v. National*

Socialist Party of America, 373 N.E.2d 21 (1978) and *Collin v. Smith,* 578 F.2d 1197 (7th Cir. 1978).

Two good sites on the Internet from which to begin exploring more about hate and censorship are `http://www.law.harvard.edu/library/guides/hateweb/hate.html` and `http://www.nizkor.eye.net/other-sites/related-legal.html`.

ISSUE 7

Is Flag Burning Protected by the First Amendment?

YES: William J. Brennan, Jr., from Majority Opinion, *Texas v. Johnson*, U.S. Supreme Court (1989)

NO: William H. Rehnquist, from Dissenting Opinion, *Texas v. Johnson*, U.S. Supreme Court (1989)

ISSUE SUMMARY

YES: Supreme Court justice William J. Brennan, Jr., representing the majority opinion, argues that burning the American flag to express displeasure at the government is behavior that is protected by the First Amendment.

NO: Supreme Court chief justice William H. Rehnquist argues that the American flag has become such a historically significant symbol of the United States that a congressional prohibition against flag burning is justified.

When a dispute gets to court, the issues before the court tend to be framed differently from the way they are stated in the popular press or in discussions among laypeople. Courts may be concerned with matters that the public considers unimportant, such as the procedure that a particular agency followed or whether or not an agency had the right or authority to do something. At the same time, the substantive question of what the result should be in a particular case—the kind of debate that one often finds on editorial pages of newspapers—may not be the main question presented to the court.

The flag-burning controversy is the kind of dispute where legal and media concerns may be quite different. For citizens, the paramount issue may be what flag burning symbolizes. The more one sees the flag as representing a country and a way of life, rather than as simply a piece of cloth with a distinctive pattern, the harder it is to accept its desecration. On the other hand, the more one focuses on the purpose and context in which the act takes place, the more the First Amendment seems relevant.

The case *Texas v. Johnson*—the majority opinion and a dissenting opinion of which are excerpted in the following selections—arose out of a protest during the 1984 Republican National Convention in Dallas, Texas. Gregory Lee Johnson participated in a political protest against the policies of the Reagan administration and some Dallas-based corporations. At the end of the demonstration, and in front of the Dallas City Hall, Johnson unfurled and burned an American flag, while the protesters chanted, "America, the red, white, and blue, we spit on you." Several witnesses to the demonstration later testified that they had been seriously offended by the incident, and one witness testified that he had gathered the remains of the flag for a proper burial in his backyard.

Johnson was arrested and charged with violating a Texas flag desecration statute that made it a crime for any person to "deface, damage or otherwise physically mistreat [the flag] in any way that the actor knows will seriously offend one or more persons likely to observe or discover his action." After a trial, Johnson was convicted, sentenced to one year in prison, and fined $2,000. The Court of Appeals for the Fifth District of Texas affirmed Johnson's conviction, but the Texas Supreme Court of Criminal Appeals reversed, holding that, given the facts of this case, the state's punishment of Johnson would violate the First Amendment. In a 5–4 vote, the U.S. Supreme Court affirmed the judgment of the Texas Court of Criminal Appeals and held that the Texas statute violated the First Amendment as applied to Johnson's acts. Justice William J. Brennan, Jr., delivered the majority opinion. Justices Byron R. White and Sandra Day O'Connor joined a dissent by Chief Justice William H. Rehnquist. Justice John Paul Stevens dissented separately.

Texas v. Johnson was not the first flag case and probably will not be the last. In one of the most important flag cases, the Court ruled that West Virginia could not require students in public schools to salute the flag (*West Virginia State Board of Education v. Barnette*, 319 U.S. 624, 1943). This overturned a decision handed down only three years earlier, in which refusal to salute the flag was not protected (*Minersville School District v. Gobitis*, 310 U.S. 586, 1940).

YES

William J. Brennan, Jr.

MAJORITY OPINION

TEXAS *v.* JOHNSON

JUSTICE BRENNAN delivered the opinion of the Court.

After publicly burning an American flag as a means of political protest, Gregory Lee Johnson was convicted of desecrating a flag in violation of Texas law. This case presents the question whether his conviction is consistent with the First Amendment. We hold that it is not....

II

Johnson was convicted of flag desecration for burning the flag rather than for uttering insulting words. This fact somewhat complicates our consideration of his conviction under the First Amendment. We must first determine whether Johnson's burning of the flag constituted expressive conduct, permitting him to invoke the First Amendment in challenging his conviction. If his conduct was expressive, we next decide whether the State's regulation is related to the suppression of free expression. See, *e.g.*, *United States v. O'Brien*, 391 U.S. 367, 377 (1968). If the State's regulation is not related to expression, then the less stringent standard we announced in *United States v. O'Brien* for regulations of noncommunicative conduct controls. If it is, then we are outside of *O'Brien's* test, and we must ask whether this interest justifies Johnson's conviction under a more demanding standard. A third possibility is that the State's asserted interest is simply not implicated on these facts, and in that event the interest drops out of the picture.

The First Amendment literally forbids the abridgment only of "speech," but we have long recognized that its protection does not end at the spoken or written word. While we have rejected "the view that an apparently limitless variety of conduct can be labeled 'speech' whenever the person engaging in the conduct intends thereby to express an idea," *United States v. O'Brien, supra*, at 376, we have acknowledged that conduct may be "sufficiently imbued with elements of communication to fall within the scope of the First and Fourteenth Amendments."

From *Texas v. Johnson*, 491 U.S. 397 (1989). Notes and some case citations omitted.

In deciding whether particular conduct possesses sufficient communicative elements to bring the First Amendment into play, we have asked whether "[a]n intent to convey a particularized message was present, and [whether] the likelihood was great that the message would be understood by those who viewed it." Hence, we have recognized the expressive nature of students' wearing of black armbands to protest American military involvement in Vietnam, *Tinker v. Des Moines Independent Community School Dist.*, 393 U.S. 503, 505 (1969)....

Especially pertinent to this case are our decisions recognizing the communicative nature of conduct relating to flags. Attaching a peace sign to the flag, *Spence [v. Washington], supra*, at 409–410; refusing to salute the flag, *[West Virginia Board of Education v.] Barnette*, 319 U.S., at 632; and displaying a red flag, *Stromberg v. California*, 283 U.S. 359, 368–369 (1931), we have held, all may find shelter under the First Amendment.... That we have had little difficulty identifying an expressive element in conduct relating to flags should not be surprising. The very purpose of a national flag is to serve as a symbol of our country; it is, one might say, "the one visible manifestation of two hundred years of nationhood." ... Thus, we have observed:

> "[T]he flag salute is a form of utterance. Symbolism is a primitive but effective way of communicating ideas.The use of an emblem or flag to symbolize some system, idea, institution, or personality, is a short cut from mind to mind. Causes and nations, political parties, lodges and ecclesiastical groups seek to knit the loyalty of their followings to a flag or banner, a color or design." *Barnette, supra*, at 632.

Pregnant with expressive content, the flag as readily signifies this Nation as does the combination of letters found in "America."

We have not automatically concluded, however, that any action taken with respect to our flag is expressive. Instead, in characterizing such action for First Amendment purposes, we have considered the context in which it occurred....

The State of Texas conceded for purposes of its oral argument in this case that Johnson's conduct was expressive conduct.... Johnson burned an American flag as part—indeed, as the culmination—of a political demonstration that coincided with the convening of the Republican Party and its renomination of Ronald Reagan for President. The expressive, overtly political nature of this conduct was both intentional and overwhelmingly apparent. At his trial, Johnson explained his reasons for burning the flag as follows: "The American Flag was burned as Ronald Reagan was being renominated as President. And a more powerful statement of symbolic speech, whether you agree with it or not, couldn't have been made at that time. It's quite a just position [juxtaposition]. We had new patriotism and no patriotism." In these circumstances, Johnson's burning of the flag was conduct "sufficiently imbued with elements of communication," to implicate the First Amendment.

III

The government generally has a freer hand in restricting expressive conduct than it has in restricting the written or spoken word. It may not, however, proscribe particular conduct *because* it has expressive elements. "[W]hat might be termed the more generalized guarantee of freedom of expression makes the communicative nature of conduct an inadequate *basis* for singling out that conduct for proscription. A law directed at the communicative nature of conduct must, like a law *directed* at speech itself, be justified by the substantial showing of need that the First Amendment requires." It is, in short, not simply the verbal or nonverbal nature of the expression, but the governmental interest at stake, that helps to determine whether a restriction on that expression is valid.

Thus, although we have recognized that where " 'speech' and 'nonspeech' elements are combined in the same course of conduct, a sufficiently important governmental interest in regulating the nonspeech element can justify incidental limitations on First Amendment freedoms," we have limited the applicability of O'Brien's relatively lenient standard to those cases in which "the governmental interest is unrelated to the suppression of free expression." In stating, moreover, that O'Brien's test "in the last analysis is little, if any, different from the standard applied to time, place, or manner restrictions," we have highlighted the requirement that the governmental interest in question be unconnected to expression in order to come under O'Brien's less demanding rule.

In order to decide whether O'Brien's test applies here, therefore, we must decide whether Texas has asserted an interest in support of Johnson's conviction that is unrelated to the suppression of expression. If we find that an interest asserted by the State is simply not implicated on the facts before us, we need not ask whether O'Brien's test applies. The State offers two separate interests to justify this conviction: preventing breaches of the peace and preserving the flag as a symbol of nationhood and national unity. We hold that the first interest is not implicated on this record and that the second is related to the suppression of expression.

A

Texas claims that its interest in preventing breaches of the peace justifies Johnson's conviction for flag desecration. However, no disturbance of the peace actually occurred or threatened to occur because of Johnson's burning of the flag. Although the State stresses the disruptive behavior of the protestors during their march toward City Hall, it admits that "no actual breach of the peace occurred at the time of the flagburning or in response to the flagburning." The State's emphasis on the protestors' disorderly actions prior to arriving at City Hall is not only somewhat surprising given that no charges were brought on the basis of this conduct, but it also fails to show that a disturbance of the peace was a likely reaction to Johnson's conduct. The only evidence offered by the State at trial to show the reaction to Johnson's actions was the testimony of several persons who had been seriously offended by the flag burning.

The State's position, therefore, amounts to a claim that an audience that takes serious offense at particular expression is necessarily likely to disturb the peace and that the expression may be prohibited on this basis. Our precedents do not countenance such a presumption. On the contrary, they recognize that a principal "function of free speech under our system of government is to invite dispute. It may indeed best serve its high purpose when it induces a condition of unrest, creates dissatisfaction with conditions as they are, or even stirs people to anger." *Terminiello v. Chicago*, 337 U.S. 1, 4 (1949).

It would be odd indeed to conclude *both* that "if it is the speaker's opinion that gives offense, that consequence is a reason for according it constitutional protection," *and* that the government may ban the expression of certain disagreeable ideas on the unsupported presumption that their very disagreeableness will provoke violence.

Thus, we have not permitted the government to assume that every expression of a provocative idea will incite a riot, but have instead required careful consideration of the actual circumstances surrounding such expression, asking whether the expression "is directed to inciting or producing imminent lawless action and is likely to incite or produce such action." *Brandenburg v. Ohio*, 395 U.S. 444, 447 (1969). To accept Texas' arguments that it need only demonstrate "the potential for a breach of the peace," and that every flag burning necessarily possesses that potential, would be to eviscerate our holding in *Brandenburg.* This we decline to do.

Nor does Johnson's expressive conduct fall within that small class of "fighting words" that are "likely to provoke the average person to retaliation, and thereby cause a breach of the peace." *Chaplinsky v. New Hampshire*, 315 U.S. 568, 574 (1942). No reasonable onlooker would have regarded Johnson's generalized expression of dissatisfaction with the policies of the Federal Government as a direct personal insult or an invitation to exchange fisticuffs.

We thus conclude that the State's interest in maintaining order is not implicated on these facts....

B

The State also asserts an interest in preserving the flag as a symbol of nationhood and national unity. In *Spence*, we acknowledged that the government's interest in preserving the flag's special symbolic value "is directly related to expression in the context of activity" such as affixing a peace symbol to a flag. We are equally persuaded that this interest is related to expression in the case of Johnson's burning of the flag. The State, apparently, is concerned that such conduct will lead people to believe either that the flag does not stand for nationhood and national unity, but instead reflects other, less positive concepts, or that the concepts reflected in the flag do not in fact exist, that is, that we do not enjoy unity as a Nation. These concerns blossom only when a person's treatment of the flag communicates some message, and thus are related "to the suppression of free expression" within the meaning of *O'Brien.* We are thus outside of *O'Brien's* test altogether.

IV

It remains to consider whether the State's interest in preserving the flag as a symbol of nationhood and national unity justifies Johnson's conviction.

As in *Spence*, "[w]e are confronted with a case of prosecution for the expression of an idea through activity," and "[a]ccordingly, we must examine with particular care the interests advanced by [petitioner] to support its prosecution." Johnson was not, we add, prosecuted for the expression of just any idea; he was prosecuted for his expression of dissatisfaction with the policies of this country, expression situated at the core of our First Amendment values.

Moreover, Johnson was prosecuted because he knew that his politically charged expression would cause "serious offense." If he had burned the flag as a means of disposing of it because it was dirty or torn, he would not have been convicted of flag desecration under this Texas law: federal law designates burning as the preferred means of disposing of a flag "when it is in such condition that it is no longer a fitting emblem for display," 36 U.S.C. sec. 176(k), and Texas has no quarrel with this means of disposal. The Texas law is thus not aimed at protecting the physical integrity of the flag in all circumstances, but is designed instead to protect it only against impairments that would cause serious offense to others.…

Whether Johnson's treatment of the flag violated Texas law thus depended on the likely communicative impact of his expressive conduct. Our decision in *Boos v. Barry* tells us that this restriction on Johnson's expression is content based. In *Boos*, we considered the constitutionality of a law prohibiting "the display of any sign within 500 feet of a foreign embassy if that sign tends to bring that foreign government into 'public odium' or 'public disrepute.'" Rejecting the argument that the law was content neutral because it was justified by "our international law obligation to shield diplomats from speech that offends their dignity," we held that "[t]he emotive impact of speech on its audience is not a 'secondary effect'" unrelated to the content of the expression itself.

According to the principles announced in *Boos*, Johnson's political expression was restricted because of the content of the message he conveyed. We must there- fore subject the State's asserted interest in preserving the special symbolic character of the flag to "the most exacting scrutiny." …

The State's argument is not that it has an interest simply in maintaining the flag as a symbol of *something*, no matter what it symbolizes; indeed, if that were the State's position, it would be difficult to see how that interest is endangered by highly symbolic conduct such as Johnson's. Rather, the State's claim is that it has an interest in preserving the flag as a symbol of *nationhood* and *national unity*, a symbol with a determinate range of meaning. According to Texas, if one physically treats the flag in a way that would tend to cast doubt on either the idea that nationhood and national unity are the flag's referents or that national unity actually exists, the message conveyed thereby is a harmful one and therefore may be prohibited.

If there is a bedrock principle underlying the First Amendment, it is that the government may not prohibit the expression of an idea simply because society finds the idea itself offensive or disagreeable.

We have not recognized an exception to this principle even where our flag has been involved. In *Street v. New York*, 394 U.S. 576 (1969), we held that a State may not criminally punish a person for uttering words critical of the flag. Rejecting the argument that the conviction could be sustained on the ground that Street had "failed to show the respect for our national symbol which may properly be demanded of every citizen," we concluded that "the constitutionally guaranteed 'freedom to be intellectually … diverse or even contrary,' and the 'right to differ as to things that touch the heart of the existing order,' encompass the freedom to express publicly one's opinions about our flag, including those opinions which are defiant or contemptuous." Nor may the government, we have held, compel conduct that would evince respect for the flag. "To sustain the compulsory flag salute we are required to say that a Bill of Rights which guards the individual's right to speak his own mind, left it open to public authorities to compel him to utter what is not in his mind." ...

In short, nothing in our precedents suggests that a State may foster its own view of the flag by prohibiting expressive conduct relating to it. To bring its argument outside our precedents, Texas attempts to convince us that even if its interest in preserving the flag's symbolic role does not allow it to prohibit words or some expressive conduct critical of the flag, it does permit it to forbid the outright destruction of the flag. The State's argument cannot depend here on the distinction between written or spoken words and nonverbal conduct. That distinction, we have shown, is of no moment where the nonverbal conduct is expressive, as it is here, and where the regulation of that conduct is related to expression, as it is here. ...

Texas' focus on the precise nature of Johnson's expression, moreover, misses the point of our prior decisions: their enduring lesson, that the government may not prohibit expression simply because it disagrees with its message, is not dependent on the particular mode in which one chooses to express an idea. If we were to hold that a State may forbid flag burning wherever it is likely to endanger the flag's symbolic role, but allow it wherever burning a flag promotes that role—as where, for example, a person ceremoniously burns a dirty flag—we would be saying that

when it comes to impairing the flag's physical integrity, the flag itself may be used as a symbol—as a substitute for the written or spoken word or a "short cut from mind to mind"—only in one direction. We would be permitting a State to "prescribe what shall be orthodox" by saying that one may burn the flag to convey one's attitude toward it and its referents only if one does not endanger the flag's representation of nationhood and national unity.

We never before have held that the Government may ensure that a symbol be used to express only one view of that symbol or its referents. ...

To conclude that the government may permit designated symbols to be used to communicate only a limited set of messages would be to enter territory having no discernible or defensible boundaries. Could the government, on this theory, prohibit the burning of state flags? Of copies of the Presidential seal? Of the Constitution? In evaluating these choices under the First Amendment, how would we decide which symbols were sufficiently special to warrant this unique status? To do so, we would be forced to consult our own political preferences, and impose them on the citizenry, in the very way that the First Amendment forbids us to do.

There is, moreover, no indication—either in the text of the Constitution or in our cases interpreting it—that a separate juridical category exists for the American flag alone. Indeed, we would not be surprised to learn that the persons who framed our Constitution and wrote the Amendment that we now construe were not known for their reverence for the Union Jack. The First Amendment does not guarantee that other concepts virtually sacred to our

Nation as a whole—such as the principle that discrimination on the basis of race is odious and destructive—will go unquestioned in the marketplace of ideas. We decline, therefore, to create for the flag an exception to the joust of principles protected by the First Amendment....

The way to preserve the flag's special role is not to punish those who feel differently about these matters. It is to persuade them that they are wrong. And, precisely because it is our flag that is involved, one's response to the flag burner may exploit the uniquely persuasive power of the flag itself.... We do not consecrate the flag by punishing its desecration, for in doing so we dilute the freedom that this cherished emblem represents.

V

Johnson was convicted for engaging in expressive conduct. The State's interest in preventing breaches of the peace does not support his conviction because Johnson's conduct did not threaten to disturb the peace. Nor does the State's interest in preserving the flag as a symbol of nationhood and national unity justify his criminal conviction for engaging in political expression. The judgment of the Texas Court of Criminal Appeals is therefore *Affirmed*.

NO

William H. Rehnquist

DISSENTING OPINION OF WILLIAM H. REHNQUIST

CHIEF JUSTICE REHNQUIST, with whom JUSTICE WHITE and JUSTICE O'CONNOR join, dissenting.

In holding this Texas statute unconstitutional, the Court ignores Justice Holmes' familiar aphorism that "a page of history is worth a volume of logic." *New York Trust Co. v. Eisner*, 256 U.S. 345, 349 (1921). For more than 200 years, the American flag has occupied a unique position as the symbol of our Nation, a uniqueness that justifies a governmental prohibition against flag burning in the way respondent Johnson did here.

At the time of the American Revolution, the flag served to unify the Thirteen Colonies at home, while obtaining recognition of national sovereignty abroad. Ralph Waldo Emerson's "Concord Hymn" describes the first skirmishes of the Revolutionary War in these lines:

> "By the rude bridge that arched the flood
> Their flag to April's breeze unfurled,
> Here once the embattled farmers stood
> And fired the shot heard round the world."

During that time, there were many colonial and regimental flags, adorned with such symbols as pine trees, beavers, anchors, and rattlesnakes, bearing slogans such as "Liberty or Death," "Hope," "An Appeal to Heaven," and "Don't Tread on Me." The first distinctive flag of the Colonies was the "Grand Union Flag"—with 13 stripes and a British flag in the left corner—which was flown for the first time on January 2, 1776, by troops of the Continental Army around Boston. By June 14, 1777, after we declared our independence from England, the Continental Congress resolved:

> "That the flag of the thirteen United States be thirteen stripes, alternate red and white: that the union be thirteen stars, white in a blue field, representing a new constellation." 8 *Journal of the Continental Congress* 1774–1789, p. 464 (W. Ford ed. 1907).

From *Texas v. Johnson*, 491 U.S. 397 (1989). Notes and some case citations omitted.

One immediate result of the flag's adoption was that American vessels harassing British shipping sailed under an authorized national flag. Without such a flag, the British could treat captured seamen as pirates and hang them summarily; with a national flag, such seamen were treated as prisoners of war.

During the War of 1812, British naval forces sailed up Chesapeake Bay and marched overland to sack and burn the city of Washington. They then sailed up the Patapsco River to invest the city of Baltimore, but to do so it was first necessary to reduce Fort McHenry in Baltimore Harbor. Francis Scott Key, a Washington lawyer, had been granted permission by the British to board one of their warships to negotiate the release of an American who had been taken prisoner. That night, waiting anxiously on the British ship, Key watched the British fleet firing on Fort McHenry. Finally, at daybreak, he saw the fort's American flag still flying; the British attack had failed. Intensely moved, he began to scribble on the back of an envelope the poem that became our national anthem:

"O say can you see by the dawn's
   early light,
What so proudly we hail'd at the
   twilight's last gleaming,
Whose broad stripes & bright stars,
   thro' the perilous fight
O'er the ramparts we watch'd were so
   gallantly streaming?
And the rocket's red glare, the bomb
   bursting in air,
Gave proof through the night that our
   flag was still there,
O say does that star-spangled banner
   yet wave

O'er the land of the free & the home of
   the brave?"

The American flag played a central role in our Nation's most tragic conflict, when the North fought against the South. The lowering of the American flag at Fort Sumter was viewed as the start of the war. G. Preble, *History of the Flag of the United States of America* 453 (1880). The Southern States, to formalize their separation from the Union, adopted the "Stars and Bars" of the Confederacy. The Union troops marched to the sound of "Yes We'll Rally Round The Flag Boys, We'll Rally Once Again." President Abraham Lincoln refused proposals to remove from the American flag the stars representing the rebel States, because he considered the conflict not a war between two nations but an attack by 11 States against the National Government. *Id.*, at 411. By war's end, the American flag again flew over "an indestructible union, composed of indestructible states." *Texas v. White*, 74 U.S. (7 Wall.) 700, 725, 19 L.Ed. 227 (1869)....

No other American symbol has been as universally honored as the flag. In 1931, Congress declared "The Star-Spangled Banner" to be our national anthem. 36 U.S.C. sec. 170. In 1949, Congress declared June 14th to be Flag Day. sec. 157. In 1987, John Philip Sousa's "The Stars and Stripes Forever" was designated as the national march. Pub.L. 101–186, 101 Stat. 1286. Congress has also established "The Pledge of Allegiance to the Flag" and the manner of its deliverance. 36 U.S.C. sec. 172. The flag has appeared as the principal symbol on approximately 33 United States postal stamps and in the design of at least 43 more, more times than any other symbol.

United States Postal Service, Definitive Mint Set 15 (1988).

Both Congress and the States have enacted numerous laws regulating misuse of the American flag. Until 1967, Congress left the regulation of misuse of the flag up to the States. Now, however, 18 U.S.C. sec. 700(a) provides that:

"Whoever knowingly casts contempt upon any flag of the United States by publicly mutilating, defacing, defiling, burning, or trampling upon it shall be fined not more than $1,000 or imprisoned for not more than one year, or both."

Congress has also prescribed, *inter alia*, detailed rules for the design of the flag, 4 U.S.C. sec. 1, the time and occasion of flag's display, 36 U.S.C. sec. 174, the position and manner of its display, sec. 175, respect for the flag, sec. 176, and conduct during hoisting, lowering, and passing of the flag, sec. 177. With the exception of Alaska and Wyoming, all of the States now have statutes prohibiting the burning of the flag. Most of the state statutes are patterned after the Uniform Flag Act of 1917, which in sec. 3 provides: "No person shall publicly mutilate, deface, defile, defy, trample upon, or by word or act cast contempt upon any such flag, standard, color, ensign or shield." Proceedings of National Conference of Commissioners on Uniform State Laws 323–324 (1917). Most were passed by the States at about the time of World War I. Rosenblatt, *Flag Desecration Statutes: History and Analysis*, 1972 Wash. U.L.Q. 193, 197.

The American flag ... throughout more than 200 years of our history, has come to be the visible symbol embodying our Nation. It does not represent the views of any particular political party, and it does not represent any particular political philosophy. The flag is not simply another "idea" or "point of view" competing for recognition in the marketplace of ideas. Millions and millions of Americans regard it with an almost mystical reverence regardless of what sort of social, political, or philosophical beliefs they may have. ...

More than 80 years ago in *Halter v. Nebraska*, 205 U.S. 34, 27 S.Ct. 419, 51 L.Ed. 696 (1907), this Court upheld the constitutionality of a Nebraska statute that forbade the use of representations of the American flag for advertising purposes upon articles of merchandise. The Court there said:

"For that flag every true American has not simply an appreciation but a deep affection. ... Hence, it has often occurred that insults to a flag have been the cause of war, and indignities put upon it, in the presence of those who revere it, have often been resented and sometimes punished on the spot." *Id.*

Only two Terms ago, in *San Francisco Arts & Athletics, Inc. v. United States Olympic Committee*, 483 U.S. 522, 107 S.Ct. 2971, 97 L.Ed.2d 427 (1987), the Court held that Congress could grant exclusive use of the word "Olympic" to the United States Olympic Committee. The Court thought that this "restrictio[n] on expressive speech properly [was] characterized as incidental to the primary congressional purpose of encouraging and rewarding the USOC's activities." *Id.*, at 536, 107 S.Ct., at 2981. As the Court stated, "when a word [or symbol] acquires value 'as the result of organization and the expenditure of labor, skill, and money' by an entity, that entity constitutionally may obtain a limited property right in the word [or symbol]." *Id.*, at 532, 107 S.Ct., at 2974, quoting *International News Service v. Associated Press*, 248 U.S. 215, 239, 39 S.Ct. 68, 72, 63 L.Ed. 211 (1918). Surely Congress or the States may recognize a similar interest in the flag.

But the Court insists that the Texas statute prohibiting the public burning of the American flag infringes on respondent Johnson's freedom of expression. Such freedom, of course, is not absolute. See *Schenck v. United States*, 249 U.S. 47, 39 S.Ct. 247, 63 L.Ed. 470 (1919). In *Chaplinsky v. New Hampshire*, 315 U.S. 568, 62 S.Ct. 766, 86 L.Ed. 1031 (1942), a unanimous Court said:

> "Allowing the broadest scope to the language and purpose of the Fourteenth Amendment, it is well understood that the right of free speech is not absolute at all times and under all circumstances. There are certain well-defined and narrowly limited classes of speech, the prevention and punishment of which have never been thought to raise any Constitutional problem. These include the lewd and obscene, the profane, the libelous, and the insulting or 'fighting' words— those which by their very utterance inflict injury or tend to incite an immediate breach of the peace. It has been well observed that such utterances are no essential part of any exposition of ideas, and are of such slight social value as a step to truth that any benefit that may be derived from them is clearly outweighed by the social interest in order and morality." *Id.*, at 571–572.

The Court upheld Chaplinsky's conviction under a state statute that made it unlawful to "address any offensive, derisive or annoying word to any person who is lawfully in any street or other public place." *Id.*, at 569. Chaplinsky had told a local marshal, " ' "You are a God damned racketeer" and a "damned Fascist and the whole government of Rochester are Fascists or agents of Fascists." ' " *Ibid.*

Here it may equally well be said that the public burning of the American flag by Johnson was no essential part of any exposition of ideas, and at the same time it had a tendency to incite a breach of the peace. Johnson was free to make any verbal denunciation of the flag that he wished; indeed, he was free to burn the flag in private. He could publicly burn other symbols of the Government or effigies of political leaders. He did lead a march through the streets of Dallas, and conducted a rally in front of the Dallas City Hall. He engaged in a "die-in" to protest nuclear weapons. He shouted out various slogans during the march, including: "Reagan, Mondale which will it be? Either one means World War III"; "Ronald Reagan, killer of the hour, Perfect example of U.S. power"; and "red, white and blue, we spit on you, you stand for plunder, you will go under." Brief for Respondent 3. For none of these acts was he arrested or prosecuted; it was only when he proceeded to burn publicly an American flag stolen from its rightful owner that he violated the Texas statute.

The Court could not, and did not, say that Chaplinsky's utterances were not expressive phrases—they clearly and succinctly conveyed an extremely low opinion of the addressee. The same may be said of Johnson's public burning of the flag in this case; it obviously did convey Johnson's bitter dislike of his country. But his act, like Chaplinsky's provocative words, conveyed nothing that could not have been conveyed and was not conveyed just as forcefully in a dozen different ways. As with "fighting words," so with flag burning, for purposes of the First Amendment: It is "no essential part of any exposition of ideas, and [is] of such slight social value as a step to truth that any benefit that may be derived from [it] is clearly outweighed" by the public interest in avoiding a probable breach of the peace. The highest courts of several States have upheld state statutes prohibiting the public burning of the flag on the grounds that it is so inherently inflammatory that it may cause a breach of public order. See, *e.g., State v. Royal,* 113 N.H. 224, 229, 305 A.2d 676, 680 (1973); *State v. Waterman,* 190 N.W.2d 809, 811-812 (Iowa 1971); see also *State v. Mitchell,* 32 Ohio App.2d 16, 30, 288 N.E.2d 216, 226 (1972).

The result of the Texas statute is obviously to deny one in Johnson's frame of mind one of many means of "symbolic speech." Far from being a case of "one picture being worth a thousand words," flag burning is the equivalent of an inarticulate grunt or roar that, it seems fair to say, is most likely to be indulged in not to express any particular idea, but to antagonize others. Only five years ago we said in *City Council of Los Angeles v. Taxpayers for Vincent,* 466 U.S. 789, 812, (1984), that "the First Amendment does not guarantee the right to employ every conceivable method of communication at all times and in all places." The Texas statute deprived Johnson of only one rather inarticulate symbolic form of protest— a form of protest that was profoundly offensive to many—and left him with a full panoply of other symbols and every conceivable form of verbal expression to express his deep disapproval of national policy. Thus, in no way can it be said that Texas is punishing him because his hearers—or any other group of people— were profoundly opposed to the message that he sought to convey. Such opposition is no proper basis for restricting speech or expression under the First Amendment. It was Johnson's use of this particular symbol, and not the idea that he sought to convey by it or by his many other expressions, for which he was punished.

Our prior cases dealing with flag desecration statutes have left open the question that the Court resolves today. In *Street v. New York,* 394 U.S. 576, 579 (1969), the defendant burned a flag in the street, shouting "We don't need no damned flag" and "[i]f they let that happen to Meredith we don't need an American flag." The Court ruled that since the defendant might have been convicted solely on the basis of his words, the conviction could not stand, but it expressly reserved the question whether a defendant could constitutionally be convicted for burning the flag. *Id.,* at 581.

Chief Justice Warren, in dissent, stated: "I believe that the States and Federal Government do have the power to protect the flag from acts of desecration and disgrace.... [I]t is difficult for me to imagine that, had the Court faced this issue, it would have concluded otherwise." *Id.,* at 605.

In *Spence v. Washington,* 418 U.S. 405 (1974), the Court reversed the conviction of a college student who displayed the flag with a peace symbol affixed to it by means of removable black tape from the window of his apartment. Unlike the instant case, there was no risk of a breach of the peace, no one other than the arresting officers saw the flag, and the defendant owned the flag in question. The Court concluded that the student's conduct was protected under the First Amendment, because "no interest the State may have in preserving the physical integrity of a privately owned flag was significantly impaired on these facts." *Id.,* at 415. The Court was careful to note, however, that the defendant "was not charged under the desecration statute, nor did he permanently disfigure the flag or destroy it." *Ibid.*

In another related case, *Smith v. Goguen*, 415 U.S. 566 (1974), the appellee, who wore a small flag on the seat of his trousers, was convicted under a Massachusetts flag-misuse statute that subjected to criminal liability anyone who "publicly... treats contemptuously the flag of the United States." *Id.*, at 568–569. The Court affirmed the lower court's reversal of appellee's conviction, because the phrase "treats contemptuously" was unconstitutionally broad and vague. *Id.*, at 576. The Court was again careful to point out that "[c]ertainly nothing prevents a legislature from defining with substantial specificity what constitutes forbidden treatment of United States flags." *Id.*, at 581–582. See also *id.*, at 587 (WHITE, J., concurring in judgment) ("The flag is a national property, and the Nation may regulate those who would make, imitate, sell, possess, or use it. I would not question those statutes which proscribe mutilation, defacement, or burning of the flag or which otherwise protect its physical integrity, without regard to whether such conduct might provoke violence.... There would seem to be little question about the power of Congress to forbid the mutilation of the Lincoln Memorial.... The flag is itself a monument, subject to similar protection"); *id.*, at 591 (BLACKMUN, J., dissenting) ("Goguen's punishment was constitutionally permissible for harming the physical integrity of the flag by wearing it affixed to the seat of his pants").

But the Court today will have none of this. The uniquely deep awe and respect for our flag felt by virtually all of us

are bundled off under the rubric of "designated symbols," *ante*, at 417, that the First Amendment prohibits the government from "establishing." But the government has not "established" this feeling; 200 years of history have done that. The government is simply recognizing as a fact the profound regard for the American flag created by that history when it enacts statutes prohibiting the disrespectful public burning of the flag.

The Court concludes its opinion with a regrettably patronizing civics lecture, presumably addressed to the Members of both Houses of Congress, the members of the 48 state legislatures that enacted prohibitions against flag burning, and the troops fighting under that flag in Vietnam who objected to its being burned: "The way to preserve the flag's special role is not to punish those who feel differently about these matters. It is to persuade them that they are wrong." The Court's role as the final expositor of the Constitution is well established, but its role as a Platonic guardian admonishing those responsible to public opinion as if they were truant school-children has no similar place in our system of government. The cry of "no taxation without representation" animated those who revolted against the English Crown to found our Nation—the idea that those who submitted to government should have some say as to what kind of laws would be passed. Surely one of the high purposes of a democratic society is to legislate against conduct that is regarded as evil and profoundly offensive to the majority of people—whether it be murder, embezzlement, pollution, or flag burning.

Our Constitution wisely places limits on powers of legislative majorities to act, but the declaration of such limits by this Court "is, at all times, a question of much delicacy, which ought seldom, if ever, to be decided in the affirmative, in a doubtful case." *Fletcher v. Peck*, 6 Cranch 87, 128 (1810). Uncritical extension of constitutional protection to the burning of the flag risks the frustration of the very purpose for which organized governments are instituted. The Court decides that the American flag is just another symbol, about which not only must opinions pro and con be tolerated, but for which the most minimal public respect may not be enjoined. The government may conscript men into the Armed Forces where they must fight and perhaps die for the flag, but the government may not prohibit the public burning of the banner under which they fight. I would uphold the Texas statute as applied in this case.

POSTSCRIPT

Is Flag Burning Protected by the First Amendment?

The political response to the Supreme Court's decision of *Texas v. Johnson* was immediate and overwhelming; both houses of Congress passed resolutions expressing "profound disappointment" with the *Johnson* decision. In the Senate, the resolution passed by a vote of 97–3; in the House, the resolution passed by a vote of 411–5.

Shortly thereafter, Congress passed the Flag Protection Act of 1989, which made it a crime for any person to knowingly mutilate, deface, burn, maintain on the floor or ground, or trample upon any flag of the United States. Congress asserted the constitutionality of the statute on the grounds that it was directed at protecting the "physical integrity" of the flag and that it did not create a content-based restriction targeting "expressive conduct" as did the Texas statute at issue in *Johnson*. The Supreme Court disagreed, however, and in *United States v. Eichman*, 496 U.S. 310 (1990), a 5–4 decision invalidated the act. Justice William J. Brennan, Jr., delivered the opinion of the Court. Justice John Paul Stevens filed a dissenting opinion that was joined by Chief Justice William H. Rehnquist and Justices Byron R. White and Sandra Day O'Connor.

The *Johnson* and *Eichman* cases impose significant limits on the power of states to punish flag burning. Pressure on Congress, however, has continued, and proposals to amend the Constitution have been introduced. Attempts to pass the constitutional amendment failed in 1990, but since then the American Legion has spearheaded a petition drive that has resulted in 49 states passing resolutions calling on Congress to approve the legislation.

Interesting readings about flag burning include Robert Justin Goldstein, *Saving "Old Glory": The History of the Flag Desecration Controversy* (Westview Press, 1995); Geoffrey R. Stone, "Flag Burning and the Constitution," 75 *Iowa Law Review* 111 (1989); Kenneth L. Karst, "Faiths, Flags, and Family Values: The Constitution of the Theater State," 41 *UCLA Law Review* 1 (1993); Kent Greenawalt, "O'er the Land of the Free: Flag Burning as Speech," 37 *UCLA Law Review* 925 (1990); and Jeff Rosen, "Was the Flag Burning Amendment Unconstitutional?" 100 *Yale Law Journal* 1073 (1991).

Sites on the Internet that are relevant to the issue of flag burning include http://www.indirect.com/user/warren/flag.html and http://www.cfa-inc.org/cfafaq.htm.

ISSUE 8

Are School Districts Created for Religious Reasons a Violation of the Constitution?

YES: David H. Souter, from Majority Opinion, *Board of Education of Kiryas Joel Village School District v. Louis Grumet et al.*, U.S. Supreme Court (1994)

NO: Antonin Scalia, from Dissenting Opinion, *Board of Education of Kiryas Joel Village School District v. Louis Grumet et al.*, U.S. Supreme Court (1994)

ISSUE SUMMARY

YES: Supreme Court justice David H. Souter maintains that a New York statute that established a school serving only a single religious community violates the establishment clause of the First Amendment.

NO: Supreme Court justice Antonin Scalia argues that the New York public school, run by a local school district, is secular in nature and does not violate the First Amendment.

An Easter egg hunt on the White House lawn. Christmas as a national holiday. Prayers opening legislative sessions of state legislatures. If you were a judge and the above practices were challenged as being unconstitutional, how would you rule?

The First Amendment to the Constitution states that "Congress shall make no law respecting an establishment of religion, or prohibiting the free exercise thereof." Interpreting these words and applying them in particular cases has been exceedingly difficult for the courts. What, for example, does "respecting an establishment of religion" mean? Is any governmental involvement or support for religion, direct or indirect, small or great, barred by this phrase?

While the courts have struggled to keep church and state separate, they have also recognized that it would be impossible to have an absolute prohibition on the celebration of religious values and holidays. Cases continue to be brought, therefore, challenging the courts to determine how the words of the Constitution and the standards of prior cases should be applied to the facts of the new case.

The clearest and most well known of the establishment of religion cases are the school prayer decisions. In 1963, in *School District of Abington Township, Pennsylvania v. Schempp*, 374 U.S. 203, the Supreme Court ruled that it was unconstitutional to require students to open the school day by reading biblical passages and reciting the Lord's Prayer. A year earlier, in *Engel v. Vitale*, 370 U.S. 421 (1962), the Supreme Court had ruled that recitation of the New York Regent's Prayer was unconstitutional. This prayer read, "Almighty God, we acknowledge our dependence upon Thee, and we beg thy blessings upon us, our parents, our teachers, and our country."

The Supreme Court has attempted to make its decisions in this area appear less subjective by considering the following three questions:

1. Does the statute have a secular legislative purpose?
2. Does its principal effect advance or inhibit religion?
3. Does the statute foster an excessive governmental entanglement with religion?

Using this standard, the courts have upheld some questionable practices, such as blue laws (regulating business on Sundays) and the loaning of secular textbooks to parochial schools. However, they have struck down other statutes, such as the Kentucky law that required posting the Ten Commandments in the classroom (see *Stone v. Graham*, 101 S. Ct. 192, 1980). More generally, the Supreme Court has upheld prayers at the beginning of a legislative session, the existence of after-school religious clubs, and tuition tax credits for parochial schools. Yet, using the same test, it has held unconstitutional a statute requiring a moment of silence in public schools, remedial programs for parochial schools, and a law requiring the teaching of "creation science" whenever evolution was taught.

The many cases involving religion that have been considered by the Supreme Court in the past 25 years indicate that the task of defining precisely what role religion should have in government-sponsored activities is extraordinarily difficult. Religion has not been banned from public life. "In God We Trust" appears on our coins, prayers are said at presidential inaugurations, Christmas is a national holiday, the lighting of the national Christmas tree at the White House is a newsworthy event, and tax exemptions are given to religious institutions. As a Supreme Court justice once wrote, "We are a religious people whose institutions presuppose a Supreme Being." It is also true, however, that many religious activities may not be sponsored by the government.

The following case is the most recent Supreme Court decision to consider what "establishment of religion" means. Some observers had predicted that the court might abandon the three-part test mentioned above. It did not do so, and more religion cases, probably involving schools in some way, can be expected to come before the Court.

YES

David H. Souter

MAJORITY OPINION

BOARD OF EDUCATION v. GRUMET

SOUTER, J., announced the judgment of the Court and delivered the opinion of the Court. . . .

The Village of Kiryas Joel in Orange County, New York, is a religious enclave of Satmar Hasidim, practitioners of a strict form of Judaism. The village fell within the Monroe-Woodbury Central School District until a special state statute passed in 1989 carved out a separate district, following village lines, to serve this distinctive population. The question is whether the Act creating the separate school district violates the Establishment Clause of the First Amendment, binding on the States through the Fourteenth Amendment. Because this unusual act is tantamount to an allocation of political power on a religious criterion and neither presupposes nor requires governmental impartiality toward religion, we hold that it violates the prohibition against establishment.

I

The Satmar Hasidic sect takes its name from the town near the Hungarian and Romanian border where, in the early years of this century, Grand Rebbe Joel Teitelbaum molded the group into a distinct community. After World War II and the destruction of much of European Jewry, the Grand Rebbe and most of his surviving followers moved to the Williamsburg section of Brooklyn, New York. Then, 20 years ago, the Satmars purchased an approved but undeveloped subdivision in the town of Monroe and began assembling the community that has since become the Village of Kiryas Joel. When a zoning dispute arose in the course of settlement, the Satmars presented the Town Board of Monroe with a petition to form a new village within the town, a right that New York's Village Law gives almost any group of residents who satisfy certain procedural niceties. Neighbors who did not wish to secede with the Satmars objected strenuously, and after arduous negotiations the proposed boundaries of the Village of Kiryas Joel were drawn to include

From *Board of Education of Kiryas Joel Village School District v. Louis Grumet et al.*, 114 S. Ct. 2481 (1994). Notes and some case citations omitted.

just the 320 acres owned and inhabited entirely by Satmars. The village, incorporated in 1977, has a population of about 8,500 today. Rabbi Aaron Teitelbaum, eldest son of the current Grand Rebbe, serves as the village rov (chief rabbi) and rosh yeshivah (chief authority in the parochial schools).

The residents of Kiryas Joel are vigorously religious people who make few concessions to the modern world and go to great lengths to avoid assimilation into it. They interpret the Torah strictly; segregate the sexes outside the home; speak Yiddish as their primary language; eschew television, radio, and English-language publications; and dress in distinctive ways that include headcoverings and special garments for boys and modest dresses for girls. Children are educated in private religious schools, most boys at the United Talmudic Academy where they receive a thorough grounding in the Torah and limited exposure to secular subjects, and most girls at Bais Rochel, an affiliated school with a curriculum designed to prepare girls for their roles as wives and mothers.

These schools do not, however, offer any distinctive services to handicapped children, who are entitled under state and federal law to special education services even when enrolled in private schools. Starting in 1984 the Monroe-Woodbury Central School District provided such services for the children of Kiryas Joel at an annex to Bais Rochel, but a year later ended that arrangement in response to our decisions in *Aguilar v. Felton*, 473 U.S. 402 (1985), and *School Dist. of Grand Rapids v. Ball*, 473 U.S. 373 (1985). Children from Kiryas Joel who needed special education (including the deaf, the mentally retarded, and others suffering from a range of physical, mental, or emotional disor-

ders) were then forced to attend public schools outside the village, which their families found highly unsatisfactory. Parents of most of these children withdrew them from the Monroe-Woodbury secular schools, citing "the panic, fear and trauma [the children] suffered in leaving their own community and being with people whose ways were so different," and some sought administrative review of the public-school placements. *Board of Ed. of Monroe-Woodbury Central School Dist. v. Wieder*, 72 N.Y.2d 174, 180–181, 527 N.E.2d 767, 770 (1988).

Monroe-Woodbury, for its part, sought a declaratory judgment in state court that New York law barred the district from providing special education services outside the district's regular public schools. *Id.*, at 180, 527 N.E.2d, at 770. The New York Court of Appeals disagreed, holding that state law left Monroe-Woodbury free to establish a separate school in the village because it gives educational authorities broad discretion in fashioning an appropriate program. *Id.*, at 186–187, 527 N.E.2d, at 773. The court added, however, that the Satmars' constitutional right to exercise their religion freely did not require a separate school, since the parents had alleged emotional trauma, not inconsistency with religious practice or doctrine, as the reason for seeking separate treatment. *Id.*, at 189, 527 N.E.2d, at 775.

By 1989, only one child from Kiryas Joel was attending Monroe-Woodbury's public schools; the village's other handicapped children received privately funded special services or went without. It was then that the New York Legislature passed the statute at issue in this litigation, which provided that the Village of Kiryas Joel "is constituted a separate school district, . . . and shall have and enjoy all the powers and duties of a union free school district...." 1989 N.Y. Laws, ch. 748. The statute thus empowered a locally elected board of education to take such action as opening schools and closing them, hiring teachers, prescribing textbooks, establishing disciplinary rules, and raising property taxes to fund operations. N.Y. Educ. Law § 1709 (McKinney 1988). In signing the bill into law, Governor Cuomo recognized that the residents of the new school district were "all members of the same religious sect," but said that the bill was "a good faith effort to solve th[e] unique problem" associated with providing special education services to handicapped children in the village. Memorandum filed with Assembly Bill Number 8747 (July 24, 1989), App. 40–41.

Although it enjoys plenary legal authority over the elementary and secondary education of all school-aged children in the village, the Kiryas Joel Village School District currently runs only a special education program for handicapped children. The other village children have stayed in their parochial schools, relying on the new school district only for transportation, remedial education, and health and welfare services. If any child without handicap in Kiryas Joel were to seek a public-school education, the district would pay tuition to send the child into Monroe-Woodbury or another school district nearby. Under like arrangements, several of the neighboring districts send their handicapped Hasidic children into Kiryas Joel, so that two thirds of the full-time students in the village's public school come from outside. In all, the new district serves just over 40 full-time students, and two or three times that many parochial school students on a part-time basis.

Several months before the new district began operations, the New York State School Boards Association and respondents Grumet and Hawk brought this action against the State Education Department and various state officials, challenging Chapter 748 under the national and state constitutions as an unconstitutional establishment of religion. The State Supreme Court for Albany County allowed the Kiryas Joel Village School District and the Monroe-Woodbury Central School District to intervene as parties defendant and accepted the parties' stipulation discontinuing the action against the original state defendants, although the Attorney General of New York continued to appear to defend the constitutionality of the statute. On cross-motions for summary judgment, the trial court ruled for the plaintiffs (respondents here), finding that the statute failed all three prongs of the test in *Lemon v. Kurtzman*, 403 U.S. 602 (1971), and was thus unconstitutional under both the National and State Constitutions. *Grumet v. New York State Ed. Dept.*, 151 Misc.2d 60, 579 N.Y.S.2d 1004 (1992).

A divided Appellate Division affirmed on the ground that Chapter 748 had the primary effect of advancing religion, in violation of both constitutions, 187 App. Div.2d 16, 592 N.Y.S.2d 123 (1992), and the state Court of Appeals affirmed on the federal question, while expressly reserving the state constitutional issue, 81 N.Y.2d 518, 618 N.E.2d 94 (1993). Judge Smith wrote for the court in concluding that because both the district's public school population and its school board would be exclusively Hasidic, the statute created a "symbolic union of church and state" that was "likely to be perceived by the Satmarer Hasidim as an endorsement of their religious choices, or by nonadherents as a disapproval" of their own. *Id.*, at 529, 618 N.E.2d, at 100. As a result, said the majority, the statute's primary effect was an impermissible advancement of religious belief....

We stayed the mandate of the Court of Appeals, 509 U.S. (1993), and granted certiorari, 510 U.S. (1993).

II

"A proper respect for both the Free Exercise and the Establishment Clauses compels the State to pursue a course of 'neutrality' toward religion," *Committee for Public Ed. & Religious Liberty v. Nyquist*, 413 U.S. 756, 792–793 (1973), favoring neither one religion over others nor religious adherents collectively over nonadherents. Chapter 748, the statute creating the Kiryas Joel Village School District, departs from this constitutional command by delegating the State's discretionary authority over public schools to a group defined by its character as a religious community, in a legal and historical context that gives no assurance that governmental power has been or will be exercised neutrally.

Larkin v. Grendel's Den, Inc., 459 U.S. 116 (1982), provides an instructive comparison with the litigation before us. There, the Court was requested to strike down a Massachusetts statute granting religious bodies veto power over applications for liquor licenses. Under the statute, the governing body of any church, synagogue, or school located within 500 feet of an applicant's premises could, simply by submitting written objection, prevent the Alcohol Beverage Control Commission from issuing a license. In spite of the State's valid interest in protecting churches, schools, and like institutions from "'the hurly-burly' associated with liquor outlets," *id.*, at 123 (internal quotation marks omitted), the Court found that in two respects the statute violated

"the wholesome 'neutrality' of which this Court's cases speak," *School Dist. of Abington v. Schempp*, 374 U.S. 203, 222 (1963). The Act brought about a "'fusion of governmental and religious functions'" by delegating "important, discretionary governmental powers" to religious bodies, thus impermissibly entangling government and religion. 459 U.S., at 126, 127 (quoting *Abington School Dist. v. Schempp, supra*, at 222); see also *Lemon v. Kurtzman, supra*, at 613. And it lacked "any 'effective means of guaranteeing' that the delegated power '[would] be used exclusively for secular, neutral, and nonideological purposes,'" 459 U.S., at 125 (quoting Committee for *Public Ed. & Religious Liberty v. Nyquist, supra*, at 780); this, along with the "significant symbolic benefit to religion" associated with "the mere appearance of a joint exercise of legislative authority by Church and State," led the Court to conclude that the statute had a "'primary' and 'principal' effect of advancing religion," 459 U.S., at 125–126; see also *Lemon v. Kurtzman, supra*, at 612. Comparable constitutional problems inhere in the statute before us.

A

Larkin presented an example of united civic and religious authority, an establishment rarely found in such straightforward form in modern America, and a violation of "the core rationale underlying the Establishment Clause," 459 U.S., at 126....

The Establishment Clause problem presented by Chapter 748 is more subtle, but it resembles the issue raised in *Larkin* to the extent that the earlier case teaches that a State may not delegate its civic authority to a group chosen according to a religious criterion. Authority over public schools belongs to the State, N.Y. Const., Art. XI, § 1 (McKinney 1987), and cannot be delegated to a local school district defined by the State in order to grant political control to a religious group. What makes this litigation different from *Larkin* is the delegation here of civic power to the "qualified voters of the village of Kiryas Joel," 1989 N.Y. Laws, ch. 748, as distinct from a religious leader such as the village rov, or an institution of religious government like the formally constituted parish council in Larkin. In light of the circumstances of this case, however, this distinction turns out to lack constitutional significance.

It is, first, not dispositive that the recipients of state power in this case are a group of religious individuals united by common doctrine, not the group's leaders or officers. Although some school district franchise is common to all voters, the State's manipulation of the franchise for this district limited it to Satmars, giving the sect exclusive control of the political subdivision. In the circumstances of this case, the difference between thus vesting state power in the members of a religious group as such instead of the officers of its sectarian organization is one of form, not substance....

It is undisputed that those who negotiated the village boundaries when applying the general village incorporation statute drew them so as to exclude all but Satmars, and that the New York Legislature was well aware that the village remained exclusively Satmar in 1989 when it adopted Chapter 748. The significance of this fact to the state legislature is indicated by the further fact that carving out the village school district ran counter to customary districting practices in the State. Indeed, the trend in New York is not toward dividing school districts but toward consolidating them. The thousands of small common school districts laid out in the early 19th century have been combined and recombined, first into union free school districts and then into larger central school districts, until only a tenth as many remain today. Most of these cover several towns, many of them cross county boundaries, and only one remains precisely coterminous with an incorporated village. The object of the State's practice of consolidation is the creation of districts large enough to provide a comprehensive education at affordable cost, which is thought to require at least 500 pupils for a combined junior-senior high school. The Kiryas Joel Village School District, in contrast, has only 13 local, full-time students in all (even including out-of-area and part-time students leaves the number under 200), and in offering only special education and remedial programs it makes no pretense to be a full-service district....

Because the district's creation ran uniquely counter to state practice, following the lines of a religious community where the customary and neutral principles would not have dictated the same result, we have good reasons to treat this district as the reflection of a religious criterion for identifying the recipients of civil authority. Not even the special needs of the children in this community can explain the legislature's unusual Act, for the State could have responded to the concerns of the Satmar parents without implicating the Establishment Clause, as we explain in some detail further on. We therefore find the legislature's Act to be substantially equivalent to defining a political subdivision and hence the qualification for its franchise by a religious test, resulting in a purposeful and forbidden "fusion of governmental and religious functions." *Larkin v. Grendel's Den,* 459 U.S., at 126 (internal quotation marks and citation omitted).

B

The fact that this school district was created by a special and unusual Act of the legislature also gives reason for concern whether the benefit received by the Satmar community is one that the legislature will provide equally to other religious (and nonreligious) groups. This is the second malady the *Larkin* Court identified in the law before it, the absence of an "effective means of guaranteeing" that governmental power will be and has been neutrally employed. But whereas in *Larkin* it was religious groups the Court thought might exercise civic power to advance the interests of religion (or religious adherents), here the threat to neutrality occurs at an antecedent stage.

The fundamental source of constitutional concern here is that the legislature itself may fail to exercise governmental authority in a religiously neutral way. The anomalously case-specific nature of the legislature's exercise of state authority in creating this district for a religious community leaves the Court without any direct way to review such state action for the purpose of safeguarding a principle at the heart of the Establishment Clause, that government should not prefer one religion to another, or religion to irreligion. See *Wallace v. Jaffree,* 472 U.S., at 52–54; *Epperson v. Arkansas,* 393 U.S., at 104; *School Dist. of Abington v. Schempp,* 374 U.S., at 216–217. Because the religious community of Kiryas Joel did not receive its new governmental authority simply as one of many communities eligible for equal treatment under a general

law, we have no assurance that the next similarly situated group seeking a school district of its own will receive one; unlike an administrative agency's denial of an exemption from a generally applicable law, which "would be entitled to a judicial audience," *Olsen v. Drug Enforcement Admin.,* 878 F.2d 1458, 1461 (CADC 1989) (R. B. Ginsburg, J.), a legislature's failure to enact a special law is itself unreviewable. Nor can the historical context in this case furnish us with any reason to suppose that the Satmars are merely one in a series of communities receiving the benefit of special school district laws. Early on in the development of public education in New York, the State rejected highly localized school districts for New York City when they were promoted as a way to allow separate schooling for Roman Catholic children. R. Church & M. Sedlak, *Education in the United States* 162, 167–169 (1976). And in more recent history, the special Act in this case stands alone. The general principle that civil power must be exercised in a manner neutral to religion is one the *Larkin* Court recognized, although it did not discuss the specific possibility of legislative favoritism along religious lines because the statute before it delegated state authority to any religious group assembled near the premises of an applicant for a liquor license, as well as to a further category of institutions not identified by religion. But the principle is well grounded in our case law, as we have frequently relied explicitly on the general availability of any benefit provided religious groups or individuals in turning aside Establishment Clause challenges. In *Walz v. Tax Comm'n of New York City,* 397 U.S. 664, 673 (1970), for example, the Court sustained a property tax exemption for religious properties in part because the State had "not singled out one particular church or religious group or even churches as such," but had exempted "a broad class of property owned by non-profit, quasi-public corporations." ...

C

In finding that Chapter 748 violates the requirement of governmental neutrality by extending the benefit of a special franchise, we do not deny that the Constitution allows the state to accommodate religious needs by alleviating special burdens. Our cases leave no doubt that in commanding neutrality the Religion Clauses do not require the government to be oblivious to impositions that legitimate exercises of state power may place on religious belief and practice. Rather, there is "ample room under the Establishment Clause for 'benevolent neutrality which will permit religious exercise to exist without sponsorship and without interference,'" *Corporation of Presiding Bishop of Church of Jesus Christ of Latter-day Saints v. Amos*, 483 U.S. 327, 334 (1987) (quoting *Walz v. Tax Comm'n, supra*, at 673); "government may (and sometimes must) accommodate religious practices and ... may do so without violating the Establishment Clause." *Hobbie v. Unemployment Appeals Comm'n of Fla.*, 480 U.S. 136, 144–145 (1987). The fact that Chapter 748 facilitates the practice of religion is not what renders it an unconstitutional establishment. *Cf. Lee v. Weisman*, 505 U.S., (1992) (SOUTER, J., concurring) (*slip op.*, at 19) ("That government must remain neutral in matters of religion does not foreclose it from ever taking religion into account"); *School Dist. of Abington v. Schempp*, 374 U.S., at 299 (Brennan, J., concurring) ("[H]ostility, not neutrality, would characterize the refusal to provide chaplains and places of worship for pris-

oners and soldiers cut off by the State from all civilian opportunities for public communion").

But accommodation is not a principle without limits, and what petitioners seek is an adjustment to the Satmars' religiously grounded preferences that our cases do not countenance. Prior decisions have allowed religious communities and institutions to pursue their own interests free from governmental interference, see *Corporation of Presiding Bishop v. Amos, supra*, at 336–337 (government may allow religious organizations to favor their own adherents in hiring, even for secular employment); *Zorach v. Clauson*, 343 U.S. 306 (1952) (government may allow public schools to release students during the school day to receive off-site religious education), but we have never hinted that an otherwise unconstitutional delegation of political power to a religious group could be saved as a religious accommodation. Petitioners' proposed accommodation singles out a particular religious sect for special treatment, and whatever the limits of permissible legislative accommodations may be, compare *Texas Monthly, Inc. v. Bullock, supra* (striking down law exempting only religious publications from taxation), with *Corporation of Presiding Bishop v. Amos, supra* (upholding law exempting religious employers from Title VII), it is clear that neutrality as among religions must be honored. See *Larson v. Valente*, 456 U.S., at 244–246.

This conclusion does not, however, bring the Satmar parents, the Monroe-Woodbury school district, or the State of New York to the end of the road in seeking ways to respond to the parents' concerns. Just as the Court in *Larkin* observed that the State's interest in protecting religious meeting places could be "readily accomplished by other means," 459 U.S., at 124, there are several alternatives here for providing bilingual and bicultural special education to Satmar children. Such services can perfectly well be offered to village children through the Monroe-Woodbury Central School District. Since the Satmars do not claim that separatism is religiously mandated, their children may receive bilingual and bicultural instruction at a public school already run by the Monroe-Woodbury district. Or if the educationally appropriate offering by Monroe-Woodbury should turn out to be a separate program of bilingual and bicultural education at a neutral site near one of the village's parochial schools, this Court has already made it clear that no Establishment Clause difficulty would inhere in such a scheme, administered in accordance with neutral principles that would not necessarily confine special treatment to Satmars. See *Wolman v. Walter*, 433 U.S., at 247–248....

III

Justice Cardozo once cast the dissenter as "the gladiator making a last stand against the lions." B. Cardozo, *Law and Literature* 34 (1931). JUSTICE SCALIA's dissent is certainly the work of a gladiator, but he thrusts at lions of his own imagining. We do not disable a religiously homogeneous group from exercising political power conferred on it without regard to religion. Unlike the states of Utah and New Mexico (which were laid out according to traditional political methodologies taking account of lines of latitude and longitude and topographical features, see F. Van Zandt, *Boundaries of the United States and the Several States* 250–257 (1966)), the reference line chosen for the Kiryas Joel Village School District was one purposely drawn to separate Satmars from non-Satmars. Nor do we impugn the motives of the New York Legislature, which no doubt intended to accommodate the Satmar community without violating the Establishment Clause; we simply refuse to ignore that the method it chose is one that aids a particular religious community, rather than all groups similarly interested in separate schooling. The dissent protests [that] it is novel to insist "up front" that a statute not tailor its benefits to apply only to one religious group, but if this were so, *Texas Monthly, Inc.* would have turned out differently, see 489 U.S., at 14–15 (plurality opinion); *id.,* at 28 (BLACKMUN, J., concurring in judgment), and language in *Walz v. Tax Comm'n of New York City,* 397 U.S., at 673, and *Bowen v. Kendrick,* 487 U.S., at 608, purporting to rely on the breadth of the statutory schemes would have been mere surplusage. Indeed, under the dissent's theory, if New York were to pass a law providing school buses only for children attending Christian day schools, we would be constrained to uphold the statute against Establishment Clause attack until faced by a request from a non-Christian family for equal treatment under the patently unequal law. Cf. *Everson v. Board of Ed. of Ewing,* 330 U.S., at 17 (upholding school bus service provided all pupils). And to end on the point with which JUSTICE SCALIA begins, the license he takes in suggesting that the Court holds the Satmar sect to be New York's established church, is only one symptom of his inability to accept the fact that this Court has long held that the First Amendment reaches more than classic, 18th century establishments. See *Torcaso v. Watkins,* 367 U.S., at 492–495.

Our job, of course would be easier if the dissent's position had prevailed with the Framers and with this Court over the years. An Establishment Clause diminished to the dimensions acceptable to JUSTICE SCALIA could be enforced by a few simple rules, and our docket would never see cases requiring the application of a principle like neutrality toward religion as well as among religious sects. But that would be as blind to history as to precedent, and the difference between JUSTICE SCALIA and the Court accordingly turns on the Court's recognition that the Establishment Clause does comprehend such a principle and obligates courts to exercise the judgment necessary to apply it.

In this case we are clearly constrained to conclude that the statute before us fails the test of neutrality. It delegates a power this Court has said "ranks at the very apex of the function of a State," *Wisconsin v. Yoder*, 406 U.S. 205, 213 (1972), to an electorate defined by common religious belief and practice, in a manner that fails to foreclose religious favoritism. It therefore crosses the line from permissible accommodation to impermissible establishment. The judgment of the Court of Appeals of the State of New York is accordingly

Affirmed.

NO

Antonin Scalia

DISSENTING OPINION OF ANTONIN SCALIA

JUSTICE SCALIA, with whom THE CHIEF JUSTICE and JUSTICE THOMAS join, dissenting.

The Court today finds that the Powers That Be, up in Albany, have conspired to effect an establishment of the Satmar Hasidim. I do not know who would be more surprised at this discovery: the Founders of our Nation or Grand Rebbe Joel Teitelbaum, founder of the Satmar. The Grand Rebbe would be astounded to learn that after escaping brutal persecution and coming to America with the modest hope of religious toleration for their ascetic form of Judaism, the Satmar had become so powerful, so closely allied with Mammon, as to have become an "establishment" of the Empire State. And the Founding Fathers would be astonished to find that the Establishment Clause —which they designed "to insure that no one powerful sect or combination of sects could use political or governmental power to punish dissenters," *Zorach v. Clauson*, 343 U.S. 306, 319 (1952) (Black, J., dissenting)—has been employed to prohibit characteristically and admirably American accommodation of the religious practices (or more precisely, cultural peculiarities) of a tiny minority sect. I, however, am not surprised. Once this Court has abandoned text and history as guides, nothing prevents it from calling religious toleration the establishment of religion.

I

Unlike most of our Establishment Clause cases involving education, these cases involve no public funding, however slight or indirect, to private religious schools. They do not involve private schools at all. The school under scrutiny is a public school specifically designed to provide a public secular education to handicapped students. The superintendent of the school, who is not Hasidic, is a 20-year veteran of the New York City public school system, with expertise in the area of bilingual, bicultural, special education. The teachers and therapists at the school all live outside the village of Kiryas Joel. While the village's private schools are profoundly religious and strictly

From *Board of Education of Kiryas Joel Village School District v. Louis Grumet et al.*, 114 S. Ct. 2481 (1994). Notes and some case citations omitted.

segregated by sex, classes at the public school are co-ed and the curriculum secular. The school building has the bland appearance of a public school, unadorned by religious symbols or markings; and the school complies with the laws and regulations governing all other New York State public schools. There is no suggestion, moreover, that this public school has gone too far in making special adjustments to the religious needs of its students. In sum, these cases involve only public aid to a school that is public as can be. The only thing distinctive about the school is that all the students share the same religion.

None of our cases has ever suggested that there is anything wrong with that. In fact, the Court has specifically approved the education of students of a single religion on a neutral site adjacent to a private religious school. See *Wolman v. Walter*, 433 U.S. 229, 247–248 (1977). In that case, the Court rejected the argument that "any program that isolates the sectarian pupils is impermissible," *id.*, at 246, and held that, "[t]he fact that a unit on a neutral site on occasion may serve only sectarian pupils does not provoke [constitutional] concerns," *id.*, at 247. And just last Term, the Court held that the State could permit public employees to assist students in a Catholic school. See *Zobrest v. Catalina Foothills School Dist.*, 509 U.S. (1993) (*slip op.*, at 11–12) (sign-language translator for deaf student). If a State can furnish services to a group of sectarian students on a neutral site adjacent to a private religious school, or even within such a school, how can there be any defect in educating those same students in a public school? As the Court noted in *Wolman*, the constitutional dangers of establishment arise "from the nature of the institution, not from the nature of the pupils," *Wolman, supra,* at 248. There is no danger in educating religious students in a public school.

For these very good reasons, JUSTICE SOUTER's opinion does not focus upon the school, but rather upon the school district and the New York Legislature that created it. His arguments, though sometimes intermingled, are two: that reposing governmental power in the Kiryas Joel School District is the same as reposing governmental power in a religious group; and that in enacting the statute creating the district, the New York State Legislature was discriminating on the basis of religion, i.e., favoring the Satmar Hasidim over others. I shall discuss these arguments in turn.

II

For his thesis that New York has unconstitutionally conferred governmental authority upon the Satmar sect, JUSTICE SOUTER relies extensively, and virtually exclusively, upon *Larkin v. Grendel's Den, Inc.*, 459 U.S. 116 (1982). JUSTICE SOUTER believes that the present case "resembles" *Grendel's Den* because that case "teaches that a state may not delegate its civic authority to a group chosen according to a religious criterion." That misdescribes both what that case taught (which is that a state may not delegate its civil authority to a church), and what this case involves (which is a group chosen according to cultural characteristics). The statute at issue there gave churches veto power over the State's authority to grant a liquor license to establishments in the vicinity of the church. The Court had little difficulty finding the statute unconstitutional. "The Framers did not set up a system of government in which important, discretionary governmental powers

NO Antonin Scalia / 159

would be delegated to or shared with religious institutions." *Id.*, at 127.

JUSTICE SOUTER concedes that *Grendel's Den* "presented an example of united civic and religious authority, an establishment rarely found in such straightforward form in modern America." The uniqueness of the case stemmed from the grant of governmental power directly to a religious institution, and the Court's opinion focused on that fact, remarking that the transfer of authority was to "churches" (10 times), the "governing body of churches" (twice), "religious institutions" (twice) and "religious bodies" (once). Astonishingly, however, JUSTICE SOUTER dismisses the difference between a transfer of government power to citizens who share a common religion as opposed to "the officers of its sectarian organization"—the critical factor that made *Grendel's Den* unique and "rar[e]" —as being "one of form, not substance."

JUSTICE SOUTER's steamrolling of the difference between civil authority held by a church, and civil authority held by members of a church, is breathtaking. To accept it, one must believe that large portions of the civil authority exercised during most of our history were unconstitutional, and that much more of it than merely the Kiryas Joel School District is unconstitutional today. The history of the populating of North America is in no small measure the story of groups of people sharing a common religious and cultural heritage striking out to form their own communities. See, e.g., W. Sweet, *The Story of Religion in America* 9 (1950). It is preposterous to suggest that the civil institutions of these communities, separate from their churches, were constitutionally suspect. And if they were, surely JUSTICE SOUTER cannot mean that the inclusion of one or two nonbelievers in the community would have been enough to eliminate the constitutional vice. If the conferral of governmental power upon a religious institution as such (rather than upon American citizens who belong to the religious institution) is not the test of *Grendel's Den* invalidity, there is no reason why giving power to a body that is overwhelmingly dominated by the members of one sect would not suffice to invoke the Establishment Clause. That might have made the entire States of Utah and New Mexico unconstitutional at the time of their admission to the Union, and would undoubtedly make many units of local government unconstitutional today.

JUSTICE SOUTER's position boils down to the quite novel proposition that any group of citizens (say, the residents of Kiryas Joel) can be invested with political power, but not if they all belong to the same religion. Of course such disfavoring of religion is positively antagonistic to the purposes of the Religion Clauses, and we have rejected it before. In *McDaniel v. Paty*, 435 U.S. 618 (1978), we invalidated a state constitutional amendment that would have permitted all persons to participate in political conventions, except ministers. We adopted James Madison's view that the State could not " 'punis[h] a religious profession with the privation of a civil right.' " *Id.*, at 626 (opinion of Burger, C. J.), quoting 5 *Writings of James Madison* 288 (G. Hunt ed. 1904). Or as Justice Brennan put it in his opinion concurring in judgment: "Religionists no less than members of any other group enjoy the full measure of protection afforded speech, association, and political activity generally." *Id.*, at 641; see also *Widmar v. Vincent*, 454 U.S. 263 (1981). I see no reason why it is any less pernicious to deprive a group rather than an individual of its rights simply because of its religious beliefs.

Perhaps appreciating the startling implications for our constitutional jurisprudence of collapsing the distinction between religious institutions and their members, JUSTICE SOUTER tries to limit his "unconstitutional conferral of civil authority" holding by pointing out several features supposedly unique to the present case: that the "boundary lines of the school district divide residents according to religious affiliation"; that the school district was created by "a special act of the legislature"; and that the formation of the school district ran counter to the legislature's trend of consolidating districts in recent years. Assuming all these points to be true (and they are not), they would certainly bear upon whether the legislature had an impermissible religious motivation in creating the district (which is JUSTICE SOUTER's next point, in the discussion of which I shall reply to these arguments). But they have nothing to do with whether conferral of power upon a group of citizens can be the conferral of power upon a religious institution. It can not. Or if it can, our Establishment Clause jurisprudence has been transformed.

III

I turn, next, to JUSTICE SOUTER's second justification for finding an establishment of religion: his facile conclusion that the New York Legislature's creation of the Kiryas Joel School District was religiously motivated. But in the Land of the Free, democratically adopted laws are not so easily impeached by unelected judges. To establish the unconstitutionality of a facially neutral law on the mere basis of its asserted religiously preferential (or discriminatory) effects—or at least to establish it in conformity with our precedents—JUSTICE SOUTER "must be able to show the absence of a neutral, secular basis" for the law. *Gillette v. United States*, 401 U.S. 437, 452 (1971); see also *Arlington Heights v. Metropolitan Housing Development Corp.*, 429 U.S. 252, 266 (1977) (facially race-neutral laws can be invalidated on the basis of their effects only if "unexplainable on grounds other than race").

There is of course no possible doubt of a secular basis here. The New York Legislature faced a unique problem in Kiryas Joel: a community in which all the non-handicapped children attend private schools, and the physically and mentally disabled children who attend public school suffer the additional handicap of cultural distinctiveness. It would be troublesome enough if these peculiarly dressed, handicapped students were sent to the next town, accompanied by their similarly clad but unimpaired classmates. But all the unimpaired children of Kiryas Joel attend private school. The handicapped children suffered sufficient emotional trauma from their predicament that their parents kept them home from school. Surely the legislature could target this problem, and provide a public education for these students, in the same way it addressed, by a similar law, the unique needs of children institutionalized in a hospital. See e.g., 1970 N.Y. Laws, ch. 843 (authorizing a union free school district for the area owned by Blythedale Children's Hospital).

Since the obvious presence of a neutral, secular basis renders the asserted preferential effect of this law inadequate to invalidate it, JUSTICE SOUTER is required to come forward with direct evidence that religious preference was the objective. His case could scarcely be weaker. It consists, briefly, of this: The People of New York created the Kiryas Joel Village School District in order to further the Satmar religion, rather than for any proper secular purpose, because (1) they created the district in an extraordinary manner —by special Act of the legislature, rather than under the State's general laws governing school-district reorganization; (2) the creation of the district ran counter to a State trend toward consolidation of school districts; and (3) the District includes only adherents of the Satmar religion. On this indictment, no jury would convict.

One difficulty with the first point is that it is not true. There was really nothing so "special" about the formation of a school district by an Act of the New York Legislature. The State has created both large school districts, see e.g., 1972 N.Y. Laws, ch. 928 (creating the Gananda School District out of land previously in two other districts), and small specialized school districts for institutionalized children, see e.g., 1972 N.Y. Laws, ch. 559 (creating a union free school district for the area owned by Abbott House), through these special Acts. But in any event all that the first point proves, and the second point as well (countering the trend toward consolidation), is that New York regarded Kiryas Joel as a special case, requiring special measures. I should think it obvious that it did, and obvious that it should have. But even if the New York Legislature had never before created a school district by special statute (which is not true), and even if it had done nothing but consolidate school districts for over a century (which is not true), how could the departure from those past

practices possibly demonstrate that the legislature had religious favoritism in mind? It could not. To be sure, when there is no special treatment there is no possibility of religious favoritism; but it is not logical to suggest that when there is special treatment there is proof of religious favoritism.

JUSTICE SOUTER's case against the statute comes down to nothing more, therefore, than his third point: the fact that all the residents of the Kiryas Joel Village School District are Satmars. But all its residents also wear unusual dress, have unusual civic customs, and have not much to do with people who are culturally different from them. (The Court recognizes that "the Satmars prefer to live together 'to facilitate individual religious observance and maintain social, cultural and religious values,' but that it is not 'against their religion' to interact with others." On what basis does JUSTICE SOUTER conclude that it is the theological distinctiveness rather than the cultural distinctiveness that was the basis for New York State's decision? The normal assumption would be that it was the latter, since it was not theology but dress, language, and cultural alienation that posed the educational problem for the children. JUSTICE SOUTER not only does not adopt the logical assumption, he does not even give the New York Legislature the benefit of the doubt. The following is the level of his analysis: "Not even the special needs of the children in this community can explain the legislature's unusual Act, for the State could have responded to the concerns of the Satmar parents [by other means]." In other words, we know the legislature must have been motivated by the desire to favor the Satmar Hasidim religion, because it could have met the needs of these children by a method that did not place the Satmar Hasidim in a separate school district. This is not a rational argument proving religious favoritism; it is rather a novel Establishment Clause principle to the effect that no secular objective may be pursued by a means that might also be used for religious favoritism if some other means is available.

I have little doubt that JUSTICE SOUTER would laud this humanitarian legislation if all of the distinctiveness of the students of Kiryas Joel were attributable to the fact that their parents were nonreligious commune-dwellers, or American Indians, or gypsies. The creation of a special, one-culture school district for the benefit of those children would pose no problem. The neutrality demanded by the Religion Clauses requires the same indulgence toward cultural characteristics that are accompanied by religious belief. "The Establishment Clause does not license government to treat religion and those who teach or practice it, simply by virtue of their status as such, as... subject to unique disabilities." *McDaniel v. Paty, supra*, at 641 (Brennan, J., concurring in judgment).

Even if JUSTICE SOUTER could successfully establish that the cultural distinctiveness of the Kiryas Joel students (which is the problem the New York Legislature addressed) was an essential part of their religious belief rather than merely an accompaniment of their religious belief, that would not discharge his heavy burden. In order to invalidate a facially neutral law, JUSTICE SOUTER would have to show not only that legislators were aware that religion caused the problems addressed, but also that the legislature's proposed solution was motivated by a desire to disadvantage or benefit a religious group (i.e., to disadvantage or benefit them because of their religion). For example, if the city of Hialeah, knowing of the potential health problems raised by the Santeria religious practice of animal sacrifice, were to provide by ordinance a special, more frequent, municipal garbage collection for the carcasses of dead animals, we would not strike the ordinance down just because the city council was aware that a religious practice produced the problem the ordinance addressed. See *Church of Lukumi Babalu Aye, Inc. v. Hialeah*, 508 U.S. (1993) (*slip op.*, at 15–19). Here a facially neutral statute extends an educational benefit to the one area where it was not effectively distributed. Whether or not the reason for the ineffective distribution had anything to do with religion, it is a remarkable stretch to say that the Act was motivated by a desire to favor or disfavor a particular religious group. The proper analogy to Chapter 748 is not the Court's hypothetical law providing school buses only to Christian students, but a law providing extra buses to rural school districts (which happen to be predominantly Southern Baptist).

At various times JUSTICE SOUTER intimates, though he does not precisely say, that the boundaries of the school district were intentionally drawn on the basis of religion. He refers, for example, to "[t]he State's manipulation of the franchise for this district..., giving the sect exclusive control of the political subdivision," *ante*, at 10—implying that the "giving" of political power to the religious sect was the object of the "manipulation." There is no evidence of that. The special district was created to meet the special educational needs of distinctive handicapped children, and the geographical boundaries selected for that district were (quite logically) those that already existed for the village. It sometimes appears as though the shady "manipulation" JUSTICE SOUTER has in mind is that which occurred when the village was formed, so that the drawing of its boundaries infected the coterminous boundaries of the district. He says, for example, that "[i]t is undisputed that those who negotiated the village boundaries when applying the general village incorporation statute drew them so as to exclude all but Satmars." It is indeed. But non-Satmars were excluded, not (as he intimates) because of their religion, but—as JUSTICE O'CONNOR clearly describes—because of their lack of desire for the high-density zoning that Satmars favored. It was a classic drawing of lines on the basis of communality of secular governmental desires, not communality of religion. What happened in the creation of the village is in fact precisely what happened in the creation of the school district, so that the former cannot possibly infect the latter, as JUSTICE SOUTER tries to suggest. Entirely secular reasons (zoning for the village, cultural alienation of students for the school district) produced a political unit whose members happened to share the same religion. There is no evidence (indeed, no plausible suspicion) of the legislature's desire to favor the Satmar religion, as opposed to meeting distinctive secular needs or desires of citizens who happened to be Satmars. If there were, JUSTICE SOUTER would say so; instead, he must merely insinuate.

IV

But even if Chapter 748 were intended to create a special arrangement for the Satmars because of their religion (not including, as I have shown in Part I, any

conferral of governmental power upon a religious entity), it would be a permissible accommodation. "This Court has long recognized that the government may (and sometimes must) accommodate religious practices and that it may do so without violating the Establishment Clause." *Hobbie v. Unemployment Appeals Comm'n of Fla.*, 480 U.S. 136, 144–145 (1987). Moreover, "there is ample room for accommodation of religion under the Establishment Clause," *Corporation for Presiding Bishop of Church of Jesus of Latter-day Saints v. Amos*, 483 U.S. 327, 338 (1987), and for "play in the joints [flexibility in interpretation] productive of a benevolent neutrality which will permit religious exercise to exist without sponsorship and without interference," *Walz v. Tax Comm'n of N. Y. City*, 397 U.S. 664, 669 (1970). Accommodation is permissible, moreover, even when the statute deals specifically with religion, see, e.g., *Zorach v. Clauson*, 343 U.S., at 312–315, and even when accommodation is not commanded by the Free Exercise Clause, see, e.g., *Walz, supra,* at 673.

When a legislature acts to accommodate religion, particularly a minority sect, "it follows the best of our traditions." *Zorach, supra,* at 314. The Constitution itself contains an accommodation of sorts. Article VI, cl. 3, prescribes that executive, legislative and judicial officers of the Federal and State Governments shall bind themselves to support the Constitution "by Oath or Affirmation." Although members of the most populous religions found no difficulty in swearing an oath to God, Quakers, Moravians, and Mennonites refused to take oaths based on Matthew 5:34's injunction "swear not at all." The option of affirmation was added to accommodate these minority religions and enable their members to serve in government. See 1 A. Stokes, *Church and State in the United States* 524–527 (1950). Congress, from its earliest sessions, passed laws accommodating religion by refunding duties paid by specific churches upon the importation of plates for the printing of Bibles, see 6 Stat. 116 (1813), vestments, 6 Stat. 346 (1816), and bells, 6 Stat. 675 (1836). Congress also exempted church property from the tax assessments it levied on residents of the District of Columbia; and all 50 States have had similar laws. See *Walz, supra,* at 676–678.

This Court has also long acknowledged the permissibility of legislative accommodation. In one of our early Establishment Clause cases, we upheld New York City's early release program, which allowed students to be released from public school during school hours to attend religious instruction or devotional exercises. See *Zorach, supra,* at 312–315. We determined that the early release program "accommodates the public service to... spiritual needs," and noted that finding it unconstitutional would "show a callous indifference to religious groups." 343 U.S., at 314. In *Walz, supra,* we upheld a property tax exemption for religious organizations, observing that it was part of a salutary tradition of "permissible state accommodation to religion." *Id.,* at 672–673. And in *Presiding Bishop, supra,* we upheld a section of the Civil Rights Act of 1964 exempting religious groups from the antidiscrimination provisions of Title VII. We concluded that it was "a permissible legislative purpose to alleviate significant governmental interference with the ability of religious organizations to define and carry out their religious missions." *Id.,* at 335.

In today's opinion, however, the Court seems uncomfortable with this aspect of our constitutional tradition. Although it acknowledges the concept of accommodation, it quickly points out that it is "not a principle without limits," *ante,* at 18, and then gives reasons why the present case exceeds those limits, reasons which simply do not hold water. "[W]e have never hinted," the Court says, "that an otherwise unconstitutional delegation of political power to a religious group could be saved as a religious accommodation." *Ante,* at 19. Putting aside the circularity inherent in referring to a delegation as "otherwise unconstitutional" when its constitutionality turns on whether there is an accommodation, if this statement is true, it is only because we have never hinted that delegation of political power to citizens who share a particular religion could be unconstitutional. This is simply a reply of the argument we rejected in Part II, *supra.*

The second and last reason the Court finds accommodation impermissible is, astoundingly, the mere risk that the State will not offer accommodation to a similar group in the future, and that neutrality will therefore not be preserved. Returning to the ill fitted crutch of *Grendel's Den,* the Court suggests that by acting through this special statute the New York Legislature has eliminated any " 'effective means of guaranteeing' that governmental power will be and has been neutrally employed." *Ante,* at 15, quoting *Grendel's Den,* 459 U.S., at 125. How misleading. That language in *Grendel's Den* was an expression of concern not (as the context in which it is quoted suggests) about the courts' ability to assure the legislature's future neutrality, but about the legislature's ability to assure the neutrality of the churches to which it had transferred legislative power. That concern is inapposite here; there is no doubt about the legislature's capacity to control what transpires in a public school.

At bottom, the Court's "no guarantee of neutrality" argument is an assertion of this Court's inability to control the New York Legislature's future denial of comparable accommodation. We have "no assurance," the Court says, "that the next similarly situated group seeking a school district of its own will receive one," since "a legislature's failure to enact a special law is... unreviewable." *Ante*, at 16; see also *ante*, at 6 (O'CONNOR, J., concurring in part and concurring in judgment). That is true only in the technical (and irrelevant) sense that the later group denied an accommodation may need to challenge the grant of the first accommodation in light of the later denial, rather than challenging the denial directly. But one way or another, "even if [an administrative agency is] not empowered or obliged to act, [a litigant] would be entitled to a judicial audience. Ultimately the courts cannot escape the obligation to address [a] plea that the exemption [sought] is mandated by the first amendment's religion clauses." *Olsen v. Drug Enforcement Admin.*, 878 F.2d 1458, 1461 (CADC 1989) (R. B. Ginsburg, J.).

The Court's demand for "up front" assurances of a neutral system is at war with both traditional accommodation doctrine and the judicial role. As we have described, *supra*, at 15, Congress's earliest accommodations exempted duties paid by specific churches on particular items. See, e.g., 6 Stat. 346 (1816) (exempting vestments imported by "bishop of Bardstown"). Moreover, most efforts at accommodation seek to solve a problem that applies to members of only one or a few religions. Not every religion uses wine in its sacraments, but that does not make an exemption from Prohibition for sacramental wine-use impermissible, *accord, Church of Lukumi Babalu Aye, Inc. v. Hialeah*, 508 U.S., at n. 2 (*slip op.*, at 3, n. 2) (SOUTER, J., concurring in judgment), nor does it require the State granting such an exemption to explain in advance how it will treat every other claim for dispensation from its controlled-substances laws. Likewise, not every religion uses peyote in its services, but we have suggested that legislation which exempts the sacramental use of peyote from generally applicable drug laws is not only permissible, but desirable, see *Employment Div., Ore. Dept of Human Resources v. Smith*, 494 U.S. 872, 890 (1990), without any suggestion that some "up front" legislative guarantee of equal treatment for sacramental substances used by other sects must be provided. The record is clear that the necessary guarantee can and will be provided, after the fact, by the courts. See, e.g., *Olsen v. Drug Enforcement Admin.*, supra, (rejecting claim that peyote exemption requires marijuana exemption for Ethiopian Zion Coptic Church); *Olsen v. Iowa*, 808 F.2d 652 (CA8 1986) (same); *Kennedy v. Bureau of Narcotics and Dangerous Drugs*, 459 F.2d 415 (CA9 1972) (accepting claim that peyote exemption for Native American Church requires peyote exemption for other religions that use that substance in their sacraments).

Contrary to the Court's suggestion, *ante*, at 20–22, I do not think that the Establishment Clause prohibits formally established "state" churches and nothing more. I have always believed, and all my opinions are consistent with the view, that the Establishment Clause prohibits the favoring of one religion over others. In this respect, it is the Court that attacks lions of straw. What I attack is the Court's imposition of novel "up front" procedural requirements on state legislatures. Making law (and making exceptions) one case at a time, whether through adjudication or through highly particularized rulemaking or legislation, violates, *ex ante,* no principle of fairness, equal protection, or neutrality, simply because it does not announce in advance how all future cases (and all future exceptions) will be disposed of. If it did, the manner of proceeding of this Court itself would be unconstitutional. It is presumptuous for this Court to impose—out of nowhere—and unheard-of prohibition against proceeding in this manner upon the Legislature of New York State. I never heard of such a principle, nor has anyone else, nor will it ever be heard of again. Unlike what the New York Legislature has done, this is a special rule to govern only the Satmar Hasidim.

* * *

The Court's decision today is astounding. Chapter 748 involves no public aid to private schools and does not mention religion. In order to invalidate it, the Court casts aside, on the flimsiest of evidence, the strong presumption of validity that attaches to facially neutral laws, and invalidates the present accommodation because it does not trust New York to be as accommodating toward other religions (presumably those less powerful than the Satmar Hasidim) in the future. This is unprecedented—except that it continues, and takes to new extremes, a recent tendency in the opinions of this Court to turn the Establishment Clause into a repealer of our Nation's tradition of religious toleration. I dissent.

POSTSCRIPT

Are School Districts Created for Religious Reasons a Violation of the Constitution?

Why should church and state be separate? Is there any danger to be feared from public religious displays? Does religion bring us to a higher level of existence, or is it a system that will oppress dissidents, nonbelievers, and members of minority faiths? Almost everyone has an opinion on this question, and most can find some historical support for their positions. Ironically, the same historical circumstance may even be used to support opposing points of view. For example, at a congressional hearing on school prayer, the following testimony was introduced.

> When I was educated in German public schools, they provided as part of the regular curriculum separate religious instruction for children of the three major faiths. At that time, all children in public schools from the ages of 6 to 18 were required not merely to recite a prayer at the beginning of each school session but to receive religious instruction twice a week. That system continued in the following decades. (Statement by Joachim Prinz, quoted in testimony of Nathan Dershowitz, *Hearings on Prayer in Public Schools and Buildings*, Committee on the Judiciary, House of Representatives, August 19, 1980.)

Did that program effectively teach morality to the German people? If it did, it would be difficult to explain the rise of Hitler and the total moral collapse and even depravity of the German people, which resulted in the torture and death of millions of Jews and Christians.

Yet another witness, however, testifying in support of prayer in the schools, quoted the report of the President's Commission on the Holocaust, which wrote that "the Holocaust could not have occurred without the collapse of certain religious norms; increasing secularity fueled a devaluation of the image of the human being created in the likeness of God." (Statement of Judah Glasner, *Hearings on Prayer in Public Schools and Buildings*, Committee on the Judiciary, House of Representatives, July 30, 1980.)

Relevant cases concerning religion in the public schools are *McCollum v. Board of Education*, 333 U.S. 203 (1948), about religious instruction on school property; *Zorach v. Clauson*, 343 U.S. 306 (1952), regarding free time from school for religious instruction off school property; and *Board of Education of the Westside Community Schools v. Mergens*, 110 S. Ct. 2356 (1990), regarding the use of school premises for an after-school religious club. The Separation of Church and State Home Page can be found on the Internet at http://www.louisville.edu/~tnpete01/church/index.htm.

ISSUE 9

Is Abortion Protected by the Constitution?

YES: Sandra Day O'Connor, from Majority Opinion, *Planned Parenthood of Southeastern Pennsylvania et al. v. Robert P. Casey et al.,* U.S. Supreme Court (1992)

NO: William H. Rehnquist, from Dissenting Opinion, *Planned Parenthood of Southeastern Pennsylvania et al. v. Robert P. Casey et al.,* U.S. Supreme Court (1992)

ISSUE SUMMARY

YES: Supreme Court justice Sandra Day O'Connor upholds a woman's constitutional right to abortion under most circumstances and reaffirms the central holding of *Roe v. Wade.*

NO: Supreme Court chief justice William H. Rehnquist argues that Pennsylvania regulations on abortion should be upheld and that it is appropriate to overrule *Roe v. Wade.*

One of the strengths of the American judicial process, lawyers often claim, is that it encourages logical and objective solutions to problems and reduces the influence of emotion and whim. By proceeding slowly, by applying abstract legal rules, by relying on professional lawyers and restricting the layperson's role, it is asserted that impartiality and neutrality will be achieved and that explosive issues will be defused. The legal process works this kind of magic often, but it has clearly failed to do so with regard to the issue of abortion. Abortion remains as newsworthy and important a subject today as it was when the landmark case of *Roe v. Wade* was decided in 1973.

Perceptions of the abortion issue differ. For the courts, it is a constitutional issue, meaning that the focus is on whether or not laws restricting abortion deny a woman due process of law under the Fourteenth Amendment. Part of the reason courts have been unable to defuse the abortion issue is that they have not persuaded the public to see the subject only in these terms. How we define or categorize an issue frequently determines our conclusions about the subject.

For example, do we view abortion as an issue primarily affecting women and thus see outlawing it as an example of sex discrimination? Or do we think firstly of the fetus and thus conclude that abortion is murder? Do we look at abortion from a religious perspective, thinking of how the legal codes of Western religions treat the subject? Or is it a question of privacy and of preventing the state from intruding into the affairs and personal decisions of citizens? Is it a matter of health, of preventing injuries and death to women who undergo illegal abortions? Is it an issue of discrimination against the poor, who may need the state to subsidize abortions, or even racial discrimination, because a higher proportion of poor women are black? How abortion is described can be all-important. One writer, for example, has written, "The real question is not, 'How can we justify abortion?' but, 'How can we justify compulsory childbearing?' " See Cisler, "Unfinished Business: Birth Control and Women's Liberation," in Morgan, ed., *Sisterhood is Powerful: An Anthology of Writings from the Women's Movement* (Random House, 1970).

The landmark decision of *Roe v. Wade*, 410 U.S. 113 (1973) was handed down on January 23, 1973. In the majority opinion, Justice Harry A. Blackmun wrote that states may not prohibit abortions during the first trimester, that some abortions may be regulated but not prohibited during the second trimester, and that abortions may be prohibited during the last trimester.

In the years since *Roe v. Wade* there have been many attempts to circumvent, narrow, delay, or avoid the Court's ruling. In *Harris v. McCrae*, 100 S. Ct. 2671 (1980), for example, in a 5–4 decision, the Supreme Court upheld a federal law that prohibited the federal government from reimbursing states for providing Medicaid abortions to women, except under specified circumstances. The majority held that the law did not illegally discriminate against the poor, nor did it violate the doctrines of separation of church and state merely because the restrictions coincided with Roman Catholic religious beliefs. In 1991 further limits on the use of federal funds were approved by the Court in *Rust v. Sullivan*, 111 S. Ct. 1759 (1991). In that case, regulations prohibiting abortion counseling in programs receiving federal funds for family planning were upheld.

More recently, in *Webster v. Reproductive Health Services*, 109 S. Ct. 3040 (1989), the Court refused to overturn *Roe v. Wade*, but it allowed states to impose more restrictions, such as one that required doctors, when a woman is more than 20 weeks pregnant, to perform tests "to determine if the unborn child is viable." The five-member majority included four votes to overturn *Roe*. Justice Sandra Day O'Connor, the critical fifth vote, was unwilling to overturn *Roe* but felt the Missouri law was constitutional since it did not place an "undue burden" on the woman's abortion rights.

The following selections are from the most recent and, in all likelihood, the most significant abortion decision since *Roe v. Wade*. The majority refused to overturn *Roe* but was also willing to allow some Pennsylvania restrictions involving parental notification and waiting periods. It also parted ways with the trimester model of *Roe*. The decision was neither a clear victory nor a clear defeat for either the pro-choice or pro-life movements. And as you read, you should ask whether or not the Court has finally articulated a position that will be an acceptable middle ground.

YES

Sandra Day O'Connor

MAJORITY OPINION

PLANNED PARENTHOOD v. CASEY

JUSTICE O'CONNOR, JUSTICE KENNEDY, and JUSTICE SOUTER announced the judgment of the Court.

I

Liberty finds no refuge in a jurisprudence of doubt. Yet 19 years after our holding that the Constitution protects a woman's right to terminate her pregnancy in its early stages, *Roe v. Wade*, 410 U.S. 113 (1973), that definition of liberty is still questioned. Joining the respondents as *amicus curiae*, the United States, as it has done in five other cases in the last decade, again asks us to overrule *Roe.*

At issue in these cases are five provisions of the Pennsylvania Abortion Control Act of 1982 as amended in 1988 and 1989. 18 Pa. Cons. Stat. Sec. 3203–3220 (1990). The Act requires that a woman seeking an abortion give her informed consent prior to the abortion procedure, and specifies that she be provided with certain information at least 24 hours before the abortion is performed. For a minor to obtain an abortion, the Act requires the informed consent of one of her parents, but provides for a judicial bypass option if the minor does not wish to or cannot obtain a parent's consent. Another provision of the Act requires that, unless certain exceptions apply, a married woman seeking an abortion must sign a statement indicating that she has notified her husband of her intended abortion. The Act exempts compliance with these three requirements in the event of a "medical emergency," which is defined in Sec. 3203 of the Act. In addition to the above provisions regulating the performance of abortions, the Act imposes certain reporting requirements on facilities that provide abortion services.

Before any of these provisions took effect, the petitioners, who are five abortion clinics and one physician representing himself as well as a class of physicians who provide abortion services, brought this suit seeking declaratory and injunctive relief. Each provision was challenged as unconstitutional

From *Planned Parenthood of Southeastern Pennsylvania et al. v. Robert P. Casey et al.*, 505 U.S. 833, 60 U.S.L.W. 4795 (1992). Some case citations omitted.

on its face. The District Court entered a preliminary injunction against the enforcement of the regulations, and, after a 3-day bench trial, held all the provisions at issue here unconstitutional, entering a permanent injunction against Pennsylvania's enforcement of them. 744 F. Supp 1323 (ED Pa. 1990). The Court of Appeals for the Third Circuit affirmed in part and reversed in part, upholding all of the regulations except for the husband notification requirement. 947 F.2d 682 (1991). We granted certiorari.

... [A]t oral argument in this Court, the attorney for the parties challenging the statute took the position that none of the enactments can be upheld without overruling *Roe v. Wade*. We disagree with that analysis; but we acknowledge that our decisions after *Roe* cast doubt upon the meaning and reach of its holding. Further, the Chief Justice admits that he would overrule the central holding of *Roe* and adopt the rational relationship test as the sole criterion of constitutionality. State and federal courts as well as legislatures throughout the Union must have guidance as they seek to address this subject in conformance with the Constitution. Given these premises, we find it imperative to review once more the principles that define the rights of the woman and the legitimate authority of the State respecting the termination of pregnancies by abortion procedures.

After considering the fundamental constitutional questions resolved by *Roe*, principles of institutional integrity, and the rule of *stare decisis*, we are led to conclude this: the essential holding of *Roe v. Wade* should be retained and once again reaffirmed.

It must be stated at the outset and with clarity that *Roe*'s essential holding, the holding we reaffirm, has three parts.

First is a recognition of the right of the woman to choose to have an abortion before viability and to obtain it without undue interference from the State. Before viability, the State's interests are not strong enough to support a prohibition of abortion or the imposition of a substantial obstacle to the woman's effective right to elect the procedure. Second is a confirmation of the State's power to restrict abortions after fetal viability, if the law contains exceptions for pregnancies which endanger a woman's life or health. And third is the principle that the State has legitimate interests from the outset of the pregnancy in protecting the health of the woman and the life of the fetus that may become a child. These principles do not contradict one another; and we adhere to each.

II

... Men and women of good conscience can disagree, and we suppose some always shall disagree, about the profound moral and spiritual implications of terminating a pregnancy, even in its earliest stage. Some of us as individuals find abortion offensive to our most basic principles of morality, but that cannot control our decision. Our obligation is to define the liberty of all, not to mandate our own moral code. The underlying constitutional issue is whether the State can resolve these philosophic questions in such a definitive way that a woman lacks all choice in the matter, except perhaps in those rare circumstances in which the pregnancy is itself a danger to her own life or health, or is the result of rape or incest....

Our law affords constitutional protection to personal decisions relating to marriage, procreation, contraception, family relationships, child rearing, and education. *Carey v. Population Services International*, 431 U.S., at 685. Our cases recognize "the right of the *individual*, married or single, to be free from unwarranted governmental intrusion into matters so fundamentally affecting a person as the decision whether to bear or beget a child." *Eisenstadt v. Baird, supra*, at 453. Our precedents "have respected the private realm of family life which the state cannot enter." *Prince v. Massachusetts*, 321 U.S. 158, 166 (1944). These matters, involving the most intimate and personal choices a person may make in a lifetime, choices central to personal dignity and autonomy, are central to the liberty protected by the Fourteenth Amendment. At the heart of liberty is the right to define one's own concept of existence, of meaning, of the universe, and of the mystery of human life. Beliefs about these matters could not define the attributes of personhood were they formed under compulsion of the State.

These considerations begin our analysis of the woman's interest in terminating her pregnancy but cannot end it, for this reason: though the abortion decision may originate within the zone of conscience and belief, it is more than a philosophic exercise. Abortion is a unique act. It is an act fraught with consequences for others: for the woman who must live with the implications of her decision; for the persons who perform and assist in the procedure; for the spouse, family, and society which must confront the knowledge that these procedures exist, procedures some deem nothing short of an act of violence against innocent human life; and, depending on one's beliefs, for the life or potential life that is aborted. Though abortion is conduct, it does not follow that the State is entitled to proscribe it in all instances.

That is because the liberty of the woman is at stake in a sense unique to the human condition and so unique to the law. The mother who carries a child to full term is subject to anxieties, to physical constraints, to pain that only she must bear. That these sacrifices have from the beginning of the human race been endured by woman with a pride that ennobles her in the eyes of others and gives to the infant a bond of love cannot alone be grounds for the State to insist she make the sacrifice. Her suffering is too intimate and personal for the State to insist, without more, upon its own vision of the woman's role, however dominant that vision has been in the course of our history and our culture. The destiny of the woman must be shaped to a large extent on her own conception of her spiritual imperatives and her place in society.

It should be recognized, moreover, that in some critical respects the abortion decision is of the same character as the decision to use contraception, to which *Griswold v. Connecticut, Eisenstadt v. Baird*, and *Carey v. Population Services International*, afford constitutional protection. We have no doubt as to the correctness of those decisions. They support the reasoning in *Roe* relating to the woman's liberty because they involve personal decisions concerning not only the meaning of procreation but also human responsibility and respect for it. As with abortion, reasonable people will have differences of opinion about these matters. One view is based on such reverence for the wonder of creation that any pregnancy ought to be welcomed and carried to full term no matter how difficult it will be to provide for the child and ensure its well-being. Another is that the inability to provide for the nurture and care of the infant is a cruelty to the child and an anguish to the parent. These are intimate views with infinite variations, and their deep, personal character underlay our decisions in *Griswold, Eisenstadt,* and *Carey.* The same concerns are present when the woman confronts the reality that, perhaps despite her attempts to avoid it, she has become pregnant.

It was this dimension of personal liberty that *Roe* sought to protect, and its holding invoked the reasoning and the tradition of the precedents we have discussed, granting protection to substantive liberties of the person. *Roe* was, of course, an extension of those cases and, as the decision itself indicated, the separate States could act in some degree to further their own legitimate interests in protecting prenatal life. The extent to which the legislatures of the States might act to outweigh the interests of the woman in choosing to terminate her pregnancy was a subject of debate both in *Roe* itself and in decisions following it.

While we appreciate the weight of the arguments made on behalf of the State in the case before us, arguments which in their ultimate formulation conclude that *Roe* should be overruled, the reservations any of us may have in reaffirming the central holding of *Roe* are outweighed by the explication of individual liberty we have given combined with the force of *stare decisis.* We turn now to that doctrine.

III
A

... [W]hen this Court reexamines a prior holding, its judgment is customarily informed by a series of prudential and pragmatic considerations designed to test the consistency of overruling a prior decision with the ideal of the rule of law, and to gauge the respective costs of reaffirming and overruling a prior case. Thus, for example, we may ask whether the rule has proved to be intolerable simply in defying practical workability; whether the rule is subject to a kind of reliance that would lend a special hardship to the consequences of overruling and add inequity to the cost of repudiation; whether related principles of law have so far developed as to have left the old rule no more than a remnant of abandoned doctrine; or whether facts have so changed or come to be seen so differently, as to have robbed the old rule of significant application or justification.

So in this case we may inquire whether *Roe*'s central rule has been found unworkable; whether the rule's limitation on state power could be removed without serious inequity to those who have relied upon it or significant damage to the stability of the society governed by the rule in question; whether the law's growth in the intervening years has left *Roe*'s central rule a doctrinal anachronism discounted by society; and whether *Roe*'s premises of fact have so far changed in the ensuing two decades as to render its central holding somehow irrelevant or unjustifiable in dealing with the issue it addressed.

1

Although *Roe* has engendered opposition, it has in no sense proven "unworkable," see *Garcia v. San Antonio Metropolitan Transit Authority,* 469 U.S. 528, 546 (1985), representing as it does a simple limitation beyond which a state law is unenforceable. While *Roe* has, of course, required judicial assessment of state laws affecting the exercise of the choice guaranteed against government infringement, and although the need for such review will remain as a consequence of today's decision, the required determinations fall within judicial competence.

2

... [F]or two decades of economic and social developments, people have organized intimate relationships and made choices that define their views of themselves and their places in society, in reliance on the availability of abortion in the event that contraception should fail. The ability of women to participate equally in the economic and social life of the Nation has been facilitated by their ability to control their reproductive lives. See, e.g., R. Petchesky, Abortion and Woman's Choice 109, 133, n. 7 (rev. ed. 1990). The Constitution serves human values, and while the effect of reliance on Roe cannot be exactly measured, neither can the certain cost of overruling Roe for people who have ordered their thinking and living around that case be dismissed.

3

No evolution of legal principle has left Roe's doctrinal footings weaker than they were in 1973. No development of constitutional law since the case was decided has implicitly or explicitly left Roe behind as a mere survivor of obsolete constitutional thinking.

It will be recognized, of course, that Roe stands at an intersection of two lines of decisions, but in whichever doctrinal category one reads the case, the result for present purposes will be the same. The Roe Court itself placed its holding in the succession of cases most prominently exemplified by Griswold v. Connecticut, 381 U.S. 479 (1965), see Roe, 410 U.S., at 152–153. When it is so seen, Roe is clearly in no jeopardy, since subsequent constitutional developments have neither disturbed, nor do they threaten to diminish, the scope of recognized protection accorded to the liberty relating to intimate relationships, the family, and decisions about whether or not to beget or bear a child. See, e.g., Carey v. Population Services International, 431 U.S. 678 (1977); Moore v. East Cleveland, 431 U.S. 678 (1977).

Roe, however, may be seen not only as an exemplar of Griswold liberty but as a rule (whether or not mistaken) of personal autonomy and bodily integrity, with doctrinal affinity to cases recognizing limits on governmental power to mandate medical treatment or to bar its rejection. If so, our cases since Roe accord with Roe's view that a State's interest in the protection of life falls short of justifying any plenary override of individual liberty claims....

4

We have seen how time has overtaken some of Roe's factual assumptions: advances in maternal health care allow for abortions safe to the mother later in pregnancy than was true in 1973, and advances in neonatal care have advanced viability to a point somewhat earlier. But these facts go only to the scheme of time limits on the realization of competing interests, and the divergences from the factual premises of 1973 have no bearing on the validity of Roe's central holding, that viability marks the earliest point at which the State's interest in fetal life is constitutionally adequate to justify a legislative ban on nontherapeutic abortions. The soundness or unsoundness of that constitutional judgment in no sense turns on whether viability occurs at approximately 28 weeks, as was usual at the time of *Roe*, at 23 to 24 weeks, as it sometimes does today, or at some moment even slightly earlier in pregnancy, as it may if fetal respiratory capacity can somehow be enhanced in the future. Whenever it may occur, the attainment of viability may continue to serve as the critical fact, just as it has done since *Roe* was decided; which is to say that no change in *Roe*'s factual underpinning has left its central holding obsolete, and none supports an argument for overruling it.

5

The sum of the precedential inquiry to this point shows *Roe*'s underpinnings unweakened in any way affecting its central holding. While it has engendered disapproval, it has not been unworkable. An entire generation has come of age free to assume *Roe*'s concept of liberty in defining the capacity of women to act in society, and to make reproductive decisions; no erosion of principle going to liberty or personal autonomy has left *Roe*'s central holding a doctrinal remnant; *Roe* portends no developments at odds with other precedent for the analysis of personal liberty; and no changes of fact have rendered viability more or less appropriate as the point at which the balance of interests tips. Within the bounds of normal *stare decisis* analysis, then, and subject to the considerations on which it customarily turns, the stronger argument is for affirming *Roe*'s central holding, with whatever degree of personal reluctance any of us may have, not for overruling it....

Our analysis would not be complete... without explaining why overruling *Roe*'s central holding would not only reach an unjustifiable result under principles of *stare decisis*, but would seriously weaken the Court's capacity to exercise the judicial power and to function as the Supreme Court of a Nation dedicated to the rule of law. To understand why this would be so it is necessary to understand the source of this Court's authority, the conditions necessary for its preservation, and its relationship to the country's understanding of itself as a constitutional Republic.

The root of American governmental power is revealed most clearly in the instance of the power conferred by the Constitution upon the Judiciary of the United States and specifically upon this Court. As Americans of each succeeding generation are rightly told, the Court cannot buy support for its decisions by spending money and, except to a minor degree, it cannot independently coerce obedience to its decrees. The Court's power lies, rather, in its legitimacy, a product of substance and perception that shows itself in the people's acceptance of the Judiciary as fit to determine what the Nation's law means and to declare what it demands.

The underlying substance of this legitimacy is of course the warrant for the Court's decisions in the Constitution and the lesser sources of legal principle on which the Court draws. That substance is expressed in the Court's opinions, and our contemporary understanding is such that a decision without principled justification would be no judicial act at all. But even when justification is furnished by apposite legal principle, something more is required. Because not every conscientious claim of principled justification will be accepted as such, the justification claimed must be beyond dispute. The Court must take care to speak and act in ways that allow people to accept its decisions on the terms the Court claims for them, as grounded truly in principle, not as compromises with social and political pressures having, as such, no bearing on the principled choices that the Court is obliged to make. Thus, the Court's legitimacy depends on making legally principled decisions under circumstances in which their principled character is sufficiently plausible to be accepted by the Nation.

The need for principled action to be perceived as such is implicated to some degree whenever this, or any other appellate court, overrules a prior case. This is not to say, of course, that this Court cannot give a perfectly satisfactory explanation in most cases. People understand that some of the Constitution's language is hard to fathom and that the Court's Justices are sometimes able to perceive significant facts or to understand principles of law that eluded their predecessors and that justify departures from existing decisions. However upsetting it may be to those most directly affected when one judicially derived rule replaces another, the country can accept some correction of error without necessarily questioning the legitimacy of the Court.

In two circumstances, however, the Court would almost certainly fail to receive the benefit of the doubt in overruling prior cases. There is, first, a point beyond which frequent overruling would overtax the country's belief in the Court's good faith. Despite the variety of reasons that may inform and justify a decision to overrule, we cannot forget that such a decision is usually perceived (and perceived correctly) as, at the least, a statement that a prior decision was wrong. There is a limit to the amount of error that can plausibly be imputed to prior courts. If that limit should be exceeded, disturbance of prior rulings would be taken as evidence that justifiable reexamination of principle had given way to drives for particular results in the short term. The legitimacy of the Court would fade with the frequency of its vacillation.

That first circumstance can be described as hypothetical; the second is to the point here and now. Where, in the performance of its judicial duties, the Court decides a case in such a way as to resolve the sort of intensely divisive controversy reflected in *Roe* and those rare, comparable cases, its decision has a dimension that the resolution of the normal case does not carry. It is the dimension present whenever the Court's interpretation of the Constitution calls the contending sides of a national controversy to end their national division by accepting a common mandate rooted in the Constitution.

The Court is not asked to do this very often, having thus addressed the Nation only twice in our lifetime, in the decisions of *Brown* and *Roe*. But when the Court does act in this way, its decision requires an equally rare precedential force to counter the inevitable efforts to overturn it and to thwart its implementation. Some of those efforts may be mere unprincipled emotional reactions; others may proceed from principles worthy of profound respect. But whatever the premises of opposition may be, only the most convincing justification under accepted standards of precedent could suffice to demonstrate that a later decision overruling the first was anything but a surrender to political pressure, and an unjustified repudiation of the principle on which the Court staked its authority in the first instance. So to overrule under fire in the absence of the most compelling reason to reexamine a watershed decision would subvert the Court's legitimacy beyond any serious question....

The Court's duty in the present case is clear. In 1973, it confronted the already-divisive issue of governmental power to limit personal choice to undergo abortion, for which it provided a new resolution based on the due process guaranteed by the Fourteenth Amendment. Whether or not a new social consensus is developing on that issue, its divisiveness is no less today than in 1973, and pressure to overrule the decision, like pressure to retain it, has grown only more intense. A decision to overrule *Roe's* essential holding under the existing circumstances would address error, if error there was, at the cost of both profound and unnecessary damage to the Court's legitimacy, and to the Nation's commitment to the rule of law. It is therefore imperative to adhere to the essence of Roe's original decision, and we do so today.

IV

From what we have said so far it follows that it is a constitutional liberty of the woman to have some freedom to terminate her pregnancy. We conclude that the basic decision in *Roe* was based on a constitutional analysis which we cannot now repudiate. The woman's liberty is not so unlimited, however, that from the outset the State cannot show its concern for the life of the unborn, and at a later point in fetal development the State's interest in life has sufficient force so that the right of the woman to terminate the pregnancy can be restricted.

That brings us, of course, to the point where much criticism has been directed at *Roe*, a criticism that always inheres when the Court draws a specific rule from what in the Constitution is but a general standard. We conclude, however, that the urgent claims of the woman to retain the ultimate control over her destiny and her body, claims implicit in the meaning of liberty, require us to perform that function. Liberty must not be extinguished for want of a line that is clear. And it falls to us to give some real substance to the woman's liberty to determine whether to carry her pregnancy to full term.

We conclude the line should be drawn at viability, so that before that time the woman has a right to choose to terminate her pregnancy. We adhere to this principle for two reasons. First, as we have said, is the doctrine of *stare decisis*. Any judicial act of line-drawing may seem somewhat arbitrary, but *Roe* was a reasoned statement, elaborated with great care. We have twice reaffirmed it in the face of great opposition. See *Thornburgh v. American College of Obstetricians & Gynecologists,* 476 U.S., at 759; *Akron I,* 462 U.S., at 419–420. Although we must overrule those parts of *Thornburgh* and *Akron I* which, in our view, are inconsistent with *Roe's* statement that the State has a legitimate interest in promoting the life or potential life of the unborn, the central premise of those cases represents an unbroken commitment by this Court to the essential holding of *Roe.* It is that premise which we reaffirm today.

The second reason is that the concept of viability, as we noted in *Roe,* is the time at which there is a realistic possibility of maintaining and nourishing a life outside the womb, so that the independent existence of the second life can in reason and all fairness be the object of state protection that now overrides the rights of the woman. See *Roe v. Wade,* 410 U.S., at

163. Consistent with other constitutional norms, legislatures may draw lines which appear arbitrary without the necessity of offering a justification. But courts may not. We must justify the lines we draw. And there is no line other than viability which is more workable. To be sure, as we have said, there may be some medical developments that affect the precise point of viability, but this is an imprecision within tolerable limits given that the medical community and all those who must apply its discoveries will continue to explore the matter. The viability line also has, as a practical matter, an element of fairness. In some broad sense it might be said that a woman who fails to act before viability has consented to the State's intervention on behalf of the developing child.

The woman's right to terminate her pregnancy before viability is the most central principle of Roe v. Wade. It is a rule of law and a component of liberty we cannot renounce.

On the other side of the equation is the interest of the State in the protection of potential life. The Roe Court recognized the State's "important and legitimate interest in protecting the potentiality of human life." Roe, supra, at 162. The weight to be given this state interest, not the strength of the woman's interest, was the difficult question faced in Roe. We do not need to say whether each of us, had we been Members of the Court when the valuation of the State interest came before it as an original matter, would have concluded, as the Roe Court did, that its weight is insufficient to justify a ban on abortions prior to viability even when it is subject to certain exceptions. The matter is not before us in the first instance, and coming as it does after nearly 20 years of litigation in Roe's wake we are satisfied that the immediate question is not the soundness of Roe's resolution of the issue, but the precedential force that must be accorded to its holding. And we have concluded that the essential holding of Roe should be reaffirmed.

Yet it must be remembered that Roe v. Wade speaks with clarity in establishing not only the woman's liberty but also the State's "important and legitimate interest in potential life." Roe, supra, at 163. That portion of the decision in Roe has been given too little acknowledgement and implementation by the Court in its subsequent cases....

Roe established a trimester framework to govern abortion regulations. Under this elaborate but rigid construct, almost no regulation at all is permitted during the first trimester of pregnancy; regulations designed to protect the woman's health, but not to further the State's interest in potential life, are permitted during the second trimester; and during the third trimester, when the fetus is viable, prohibitions are permitted provided the life or health of the mother is not at stake. Roe v. Wade, supra, at 163–166. Most of our cases since Roe have involved the application of rules derived from the trimester framework.

The trimester framework no doubt was erected to ensure that the woman's right to choose not become so subordinate to the State's interest in promoting fetal life that her choice exists in theory but not in fact. We do not agree, however, that the trimester approach is necessary to accomplish this objective. A framework of this rigidity was unnecessary and in its later interpretation sometimes contradicted the State's permissible exercise of its powers.

Though the woman has a right to choose to terminate or continue her pregnancy before viability, it does not at all follow that the State is prohibited from taking steps to ensure that this choice is thoughtful and informed. Even in the earliest stages of pregnancy, the State may enact rules and regulations designed to encourage her to know that there are philosophic and social arguments of great weight that can be brought to bear in favor of continuing the pregnancy to full term and that there are procedures and institutions to allow adoption of unwanted children as well as a certain degree of state assistance if the mother chooses to raise the child herself. " '[T]he Constitution does not forbid a State or city, pursuant to democratic processes, from expressing a preference for normal childbirth.' " *Webster v. Reproductive Health Services,* 492 U.S., at 511 (opinion of the Court) (quoting *Poelker v. Doe,* 432 U.S. 519, 521 (1977)). It follows that States are free to enact laws to provide a reasonable framework for a woman to make a decision that has such profound and lasting meaning. This, too, we find consistent with *Roe's* central premises, and indeed the inevitable consequence of our holding that the State has an interest in protecting the life of the unborn.

We reject the trimester framework, which we do not consider to be part of the essential holding of *Roe.* Measures aimed at ensuring that a woman's choice contemplates the consequences for the fetus do not necessarily interfere with the right recognized in *Roe,* although those measures have been found to be inconsistent with the rigid trimester framework announced in that case. A logical reading of the central holding in *Roe* itself, and a necessary reconciliation of the liberty of the woman and the interest of the State in promoting prenatal life, re-

quire, in our view, that we abandon the trimester framework as a rigid prohibition on all previability regulation aimed at the protection of fetal life. The trimester framework suffers from these basic flaws: in its formulation it misconceives the nature of the pregnant woman's interest; and in practice it undervalues the State's interest in potential life, as recognized in *Roe.*

As our jurisprudence relating to all liberties save perhaps abortion has recognized, not every law which makes a right more difficult to exercise is, *ipso facto,* an infringement of that right. An example clarifies the point. We have held that not every ballot access limitation amounts to an infringement of the right to vote. Rather, the States are granted substantial flexibility in establishing the framework within which voters choose the candidates for whom they wish to vote. *Anderson v. Celebrezze,* 460 U.S. 780, 788 (1983); *Norman v. Reed,* 502 U.S. ____ (1992).

The abortion right is similar. Numerous forms of state regulation might have the incidental effect of increasing the cost or decreasing the availability of medical care, whether for abortion or any other medical procedure. The fact that a law which serves a valid purpose, one not designed to strike at the right itself, has the incidental effect of making it more difficult or more expensive to procure an abortion cannot be enough to invalidate it. Only where state regulation imposes an undue burden on a woman's ability to make this decision does the power of the State reach into the heart of the liberty protected by the Due Process Clause....

A finding of an undue burden is a shorthand for the conclusion that a state regulation has the purpose or effect of placing a substantial obstacle in the path of a woman seeking an abortion of a nonviable fetus. A statute with this purpose is invalid because the means chosen by the State to further the interest in potential life must be calculated to inform the woman's free choice, not hinder it. And a statute which, while furthering the interest in potential life or some other valid state interest, has the effect of placing a substantial obstacle in the path of a woman's choice cannot be considered a permissible means of serving its legitimate ends. To the extent that the opinions of the Court or of individual Justices use the undue burden standard in a manner that is inconsistent with this analysis, we set out what in our view should be the controlling standard.... Understood another way, we answer the question, left open in previous opinions discussing the undue burden formulation, whether a law designed to further the State's interest in fetal life which imposes an undue burden on the woman's decision before fetal viability could be constitutional. The answer is no.

Some guiding principles should emerge. What is at stake is the woman's right to make the ultimate decision, not a right to be insulated from all others in doing so. Regulations which do no more than create a structural mechanism by which the State, or the parent or guardian of a minor, may express profound respect for the life of the unborn are permitted, if they are not a substantial obstacle to the woman's exercise of the right to choose. Unless it has that effect on her right of choice, a state measure designed to persuade her to choose childbirth over abortion will be upheld if reasonably related to that goal. Regulations designed to foster the health of a woman seeking an abortion are valid if they do not constitute an undue burden.

Even when jurists reason from shared premises, some disagreement is inevitable. That is to be expected in the application of any legal standard which must accommodate life's complexity. We do not expect it to be otherwise with respect to the undue burden standard. We give this summary:

1. To protect the central right recognized by *Roe v. Wade* while at the same time accommodating the State's profound interest in potential life, we will employ the undue burden analysis as explained in this opinion. An undue burden exists, and therefore a provision of law is invalid, if its purpose or effect is to place a substantial obstacle in the path of a woman seeking an abortion before the fetus attains viability.

2. We reject the rigid trimester framework of *Roe v. Wade*. To promote the State's profound interest in potential life, throughout pregnancy the State may take measures to ensure that the woman's choice is informed, and measures designed to advance this interest will not be invalidated as long as their purpose is to persuade the woman to choose childbirth over abortion. These measures must not be an undue burden on the right.

3. As with any medical procedure, the State may enact regulations to further the health or safety of a woman seeking an abortion. Unnecessary health regulations that have the purpose or effect of presenting a substantial obstacle to a woman seeking an abortion impose an undue burden on the right.

4. Our adoption of the undue burden analysis does not disturb the central holding of *Roe v. Wade*, and we reaffirm that holding. Regardless of

whether exceptions are made for particular circumstances, a State may not prohibit any woman from making the ultimate decision to terminate her pregnancy before viability.

5. We also reaffirm *Roe's* holding that "subsequent to viability, the State in promoting its interest in the potentiality of human life may, if it chooses, regulate, and even proscribe, abortion except where it is necessary, in appropriate medical judgment, for the preservation of the life or health of the mother." *Roe v. Wade,* 410 U.S., at 164–165.

NO

William H. Rehnquist

DISSENTING OPINION OF WILLIAM H. REHNQUIST

CHIEF JUSTICE REHNQUIST, with whom JUSTICE WHITE, JUSTICE SCALIA, and JUSTICE THOMAS join, concurring in the judgment in part and dissenting in part.

... We believe that *Roe* was wrongly decided, and that it can and should be overruled consistently with our traditional approach to *stare decisis* in constitutional cases. We would adopt the approach of the plurality in *Webster v. Reproductive Health Services*, 492 U.S. 490 (1989), and uphold the challenged provisions of the Pennsylvania statute in their entirety.

I

... In *Roe v. Wade*, the Court recognized a "guarantee of personal privacy" which "is broad enough to encompass a woman's decision whether or not to terminate her pregnancy." 410 U.S., at 152–153. We are now of the view that, in terming this right fundamental, the Court in *Roe* read the earlier opinions upon which it based its decision much too broadly. Unlike marriage, procreation and contraception, abortion "involves the purposeful termination of potential life." *Harris v. McRae*, 448 U.S. 297, 325 (1980). The abortion decision must therefore "be recognized as *sui generis*, different in kind from the others that the Court has protected under the rubric of personal or family privacy and autonomy." *Thornburgh v. American College of Obstetricians and Gynecologists, supra*, at 792 (White, J., dissenting). One cannot ignore the fact that a woman is not isolated in her pregnancy, and that the decision to abort necessarily involves the destruction of a fetus. *See Michael H. v. Gerald D., supra*, at 124, n. 4 (To look "at the act which is assertedly the subject of a liberty interest in isolation from its effect upon other people [is] like inquiring whether there is a liberty interest in firing a gun where the case at hand happens to involve its discharge into another person's body").

Nor do the historical traditions of the American people support the view that the right to terminate one's pregnancy is "fundamental." The common law which we inherited from England made abortion after "quickening" an

From *Planned Parenthood of Southeastern Pennsylvania et al. v. Robert P. Casey et al.*, 505 U.S. 833, 60 U.S.L.W. 4795 (1992). Notes and some case citations omitted.

offense. At the time of the adoption of the Fourteenth Amendment, statutory prohibitions or restrictions on abortion were commonplace; in 1868, at least 28 of the then-37 States and 8 Territories had statutes banning or limiting abortion. J. Mohr, Abortion in America 200 (1978). By the turn of the century virtually every State had a law prohibiting or restricting abortion on its books. By the middle of the present century, a liberalization trend had set in. But 21 of the restrictive abortion laws in effect in 1868 were still in effect in 1973 when *Roe* was decided, and an overwhelming majority of the States prohibited abortion unless necessary to preserve the life or health of the mother. *Roe v. Wade*, 410 U.S., at 139–140; *id.*, at 176–177, n. 2 (Rehnquist, J., dissenting). On this record, it can scarcely be said that any deeply rooted tradition of relatively unrestricted abortion in our history supported the classification of the right to abortion as "fundamental" under the Due Process Clause of the Fourteenth Amendment.

We think, therefore, both in view of this history and of our decided cases dealing with substantive liberty under the Due Process Clause, that the Court was mistaken in *Roe* when it classified a woman's decision to terminate her pregnancy as a "fundamental right" that could be abridged only in a manner which withstood "strict scrutiny." In so concluding, we repeat the observation made in *Bowers v. Hardwick*, 478 U.S. 186 (1986):

> "Nor are we inclined to take a more expansive view of our authority to discover new fundamental rights imbedded in the Due Process Clause. The Court is most vulnerable and comes nearest to illegitimacy when it deals with judge-made constitutional law having little or no cog-

nizable roots in the language or design of the Constitution." *Id.*, at 194.

We believe that the sort of constitutionally imposed abortion code of the type illustrated by our decisions following Roe is inconsistent "with the notion of a Constitution cast in general terms, as ours is, and usually speaking in general principles, as ours does." *Webster v. Reproductive Health Services*, 492 U.S., at 518 (plurality opinion). The Court in *Roe* reached too far when it analogized the right to abort a fetus to the rights involved in *Pierce*, *Meyer*, *Loving*, and *Griswold*, and thereby deemed the right to abortion fundamental.

II

The joint opinion of Justices O'Connor, Kennedy, and Souter cannot bring itself to say that *Roe* was correct as an original matter, but the authors are of the view that "the immediate question is not the soundness of *Roe*'s resolution of the issue, but the precedential force that must be accorded to its holding." Instead of claiming that *Roe* was correct as a matter of original constitutional interpretation, the opinion therefore contains an elaborate discussion of *stare decisis*. This discussion of the principle of *stare decisis* appears to be almost entirely dicta, because the joint opinion does not apply that principle in dealing with Roe. Roe decided that a woman had a fundamental right to an abortion. The joint opinion rejects that view. *Roe* decided that abortion regulations were to be subjected to "strict scrutiny" and could be justified only in the light of "compelling state interests." The joint opinion rejects that view. *Roe* analyzed abortion regulation under a rigid trimester framework, a framework which has guided this Court's decisionmaking for 19 years. The joint opinion rejects that framework.... In our view, authentic principles of *stare decisis* do not require that any portion of the reasoning in *Roe* be kept intact. "*Stare decisis* is not ... a universal, inexorable command," especially in cases involving the interpretation of the Federal Constitution. *Burnet v. Coronado Oil & Gas Co.*, 285 U.S. 393, 405 (1932) (Brandeis, J., dissenting). Erroneous decisions in such constitutional cases are uniquely durable, because correction through legislative action, save for constitutional amendment, is impossible. It is therefore our duty to reconsider constitutional interpretations that "depar[t] from a proper understanding" of the Constitution.... Our constitutional watch does not cease merely because we have spoken before on an issue; when it becomes clear that a prior constitutional interpretation is unsound we are obliged to reexamine the question.

The joint opinion discusses several *stare decisis* factors which, it asserts, point toward retaining a portion of *Roe*. Two of these factors are that the main "factual underpinning" of *Roe* has remained the same, and that its doctrinal foundation is no weaker now than it was in 1973. Of course, what might be called the basic facts which gave rise to *Roe* have remained the same—women become pregnant, there is a point somewhere, depending on medical technology, where a fetus becomes viable, and women give birth to children. But this is only to say that the same facts which gave rise to *Roe* will continue to give rise to similar cases. It is not a reason, in and of itself, why those cases must be decided in the same incorrect manner as was the first case to deal with the question. And surely there is no requirement, in considering whether to depart from *stare decisis* in a constitutional case, that a decision be more wrong now than it was at the time it was rendered. If that were true, the most outlandish constitutional decision could survive forever, based simply on the fact that it was no more outlandish later than it was when originally rendered.

Nor does the joint opinion faithfully follow this alleged requirement. The opinion frankly concludes that *Roe* and its progeny were wrong in failing to recognize that the State's interests in maternal health and in the protection of unborn human life exist throughout pregnancy. But there is no indication that these components of *Roe* are any more incorrect at this juncture than they were at its inception....

The joint opinion thus turns to what can only be described as an unconventional—and unconvincing—notion of reliance, a view based on the surmise that the availability of abortion since *Roe* has led to "two decades of economic and social developments" that would be undercut if the error of *Roe* were recognized. The joint opinion's assertion of this fact is undeveloped and totally conclusory. In fact, one can not be sure to what economic and social developments the opinion is referring. Surely it is dubious to suggest that women have reached their "places in society" in reliance upon *Roe*, rather than as a result of their determination to obtain higher education and compete with men in the job market, and of society's increasing recognition of their ability to fill positions that were previously thought to be reserved only for men.

In the end, having failed to put forth any evidence to prove any true reliance, the joint opinion's argument is based solely on generalized assertions about the national psyche, on a belief that the people of this country have grown accustomed to the *Roe* decision over the last 19 years and have "ordered their thinking and living around" it. As an initial matter, one might inquire how the joint opinion can view the "central holding" of *Roe* as so deeply rooted in our constitutional culture, when it so casually uproots and disposes of that same decision's trimester framework. Furthermore, at various points in the past, the same could have been said about this Court's erroneous decisions that the Constitution allowed "separate but equal" treatment of minorities, see *Plessy v. Ferguson*, 163 U.S. 537 (1896), or that "liberty" under the Due Process Clause protected "freedom of contract." See *Adkins v. Children's Hospital of D. C.*, 261 U.S. 525 (1923); *Lochner v. New York*, 198 U.S. 45 (1905). The "separate but equal" doctrine lasted 58 years after *Plessy*, and *Lochner*'s protection of contractual freedom lasted 32 years. However, the simple fact that a generation or more had grown used to these major decisions did not prevent the Court from correcting its errors in those cases, nor should it prevent us from correctly interpreting the Constitution here.

Apparently realizing that conventional *stare decisis* principles do not support its position, the joint opinion advances a belief that retaining a portion of *Roe* is necessary to protect the "legitimacy" of this Court. Because the Court must take care to render decisions "grounded truly in principle," and not simply as political and social compromises, the joint opinion properly declares it to be this Court's duty to ignore the public criticism and protest that may arise as a result of a decision. Few would quarrel with this statement, although it may be doubted that Members of this Court, holding their tenure as they do during constitutional "good behavior," are at all likely to be intimidated by such public protests....

The joint opinion also agrees that the Court acted properly in rejecting the doctrine of "separate but equal" in *Brown*. In fact, the opinion lauds *Brown* in comparing it to *Roe*. This is strange, in that under the opinion's "legitimacy" principle the Court would seemingly have been forced to adhere to its erroneous decision in *Plessy* because of its "intensely divisive" character. To us, adherence to *Roe* today under the guise of "legitimacy" would seem to resemble more closely adherence to *Plessy* on the same ground. Fortunately, the Court did not choose that option in *Brown*, and instead frankly repudiated *Plessy*. The joint opinion concludes that such repudiation was justified only because of newly discovered evidence that segregation had the effect of treating one race as inferior to another. But it can hardly be argued that this was not urged upon those who decided *Plessy*, as Justice Harlan observed in his dissent that the law at issue "puts the brand of servitude and degradation upon a large class of our fellow-citizens, our equals before the law." *Plessy v. Ferguson*, 163 U.S., at 562 (Harlan, J., dissenting). It is clear that the same arguments made before the Court in *Brown* were made in *Plessy* as well. The Court in *Brown* simply recognized, as Justice Harlan had recognized beforehand, that the Fourteenth Amendment does not permit racial segregation. The rule of *Brown* is not tied to popular opinion about the evils of segregation; it is a judgment that the Equal Protection Clause does not permit racial segregation, no matter whether the public might come to believe that it is beneficial. On that ground it stands, and on that ground alone the Court was justified in properly concluding that the *Plessy* Court had erred. . . .

There are other reasons why the joint opinion's discussion of legitimacy is unconvincing as well. In assuming that the Court is perceived as "surrender[ing] to political pressure" when it overrules a controversial decision, the joint opinion forgets that there are two sides to any controversy. The joint opinion asserts that, in order to protect its legitimacy, the Court must refrain from overruling a controversial decision lest it be viewed as favoring those who oppose the decision. But a decision to *adhere* to prior precedent is subject to the same criticism, for in such a case one can easily argue that the Court is responding to those who have demonstrated in favor of the original decision. The decision in *Roe* has engendered large demonstrations, including repeated marches on this Court and on Congress, both in opposition to and in support of that opinion. A decision either way on *Roe* can therefore be perceived as favoring one group or the other. But this perceived dilemma arises only if one assumes, as the joint opinion does, that the Court should make its decisions with a view toward speculative public perceptions. If one assumes instead, as the Court surely did in both *Brown* and *West Coast Hotel*, that the Court's legitimacy is enhanced by faithful interpretation of the Constitution irrespective of public opposition, such self-engendered difficulties may be put to one side.

Roe is not this Court's only decision to generate conflict. Our decisions in some recent capital cases, and in *Bowers v. Hardwick*, 478 U.S. 186 (1986), have also engendered demonstrations in opposition. The joint opinion's message to such protesters appears to be that they must cease their activities in order to serve their cause, because their protests will only cement in place a decision which by normal standards of *stare decisis* should be reconsidered. Nearly a century ago, Justice David J. Brewer of this Court, in an article discussing criticism of its decisions, observed that "many criticisms may be, like their authors, devoid of good taste, but better all sorts of criticism than no criticism at all." Justice Brewer on "The Nation's Anchor," 57 Albany L.J. 166, 169 (1898). This was good advice to the Court then, as it is today. Strong and often misguided criticism of a decision should not render the decision immune from reconsideration, lest a fetish for legitimacy penalize freedom of expression.

The end result of the joint opinion's paeans of praise for legitimacy is the enunciation of a brand new standard for evaluating state regulation of a woman's right to abortion—the "undue burden" standard. As indicated above, *Roe v. Wade* adopted a "fundamental right" standard under which state regulations could survive only if they met the requirement of "strict scrutiny." While we disagree with that standard, it at least had a recognized basis in constitutional law at the time *Roe* was decided. The same cannot be said for the "undue burden" standard, which is created largely out of whole cloth by the authors of the joint opinion. It is a standard which even today does not command the support of a majority of this Court. And it will not, we believe, result in the sort of "simple limitation," easily applied, which the joint opinion anticipates. In sum, it is a standard which is not built to last. . . .

The sum of the joint opinion's labors in the name of *stare decisis* and "legitimacy" is this: *Roe v. Wade* stands as a sort of judicial Potemkin Village, which may be pointed out to passers by as a monument to the importance of adhering to precedent. But behind the facade, an entirely new method of analysis, without any roots in constitutional law, is imported to decide the constitutionality of state laws regulating abortion. Neither *stare decisis* nor "legitimacy" are truly served by such an effort.…

III
E

Finally, petitioners challenge the medical emergency exception provided for by the Act. The existence of a medical emergency exempts compliance with the Act's informed consent, parental consent, and spousal notice requirements. See 18 Pa. Cons. Stat. sec. 3205(a), 3206(a), 3209(c) (1990). The Act defines a "medical emergency" as

> "[t]hat condition which, on the basis of the physician's good faith clinical judgment, so complicates the medical condition of a pregnant woman as to necessitate the immediate abortion of her pregnancy to avert her death or for which a delay will create serious risk of substantial and irreversible impairment of major bodily function." sec. 3203.

Petitioners argued before the District Court that the statutory definition was inadequate because it did not cover three serious conditions that pregnant women can suffer—preeclampsia, inevitable abortion, and prematurely ruptured membrane. The District Court agreed with petitioners that the medical emergency exception was inadequate, but the Court of Appeals reversed this holding. In construing the medical emer-

gency provision, the Court of Appeals first observed that all three conditions do indeed present the risk of serious injury or death when an abortion is not performed, and noted that the medical profession's uniformly prescribed treatment for each of the three conditions is an immediate abortion. See 947 F.2d, at 700–701. Finding that "[t]he Pennsylvania legislature did not choose the wording of its medical emergency exception in a vacuum," the court read the exception as intended "to assure that compliance with its abortion regulations would not in any way pose a significant threat to the life or health of a woman." *Id.*, at 701. It thus concluded that the exception encompassed each of the three dangerous conditions pointed to by petitioners.

We observe that Pennsylvania's present definition of medical emergency is almost an exact copy of that State's definition at the time of this Court's ruling in *Thornburgh*, one which the Court made reference to with apparent approval. 476 U.S., at 771 ("It is clear that the Pennsylvania Legislature knows how to provide a medical-emergency exception when it chooses to do so"). We find that the interpretation of the Court of Appeals in this case is eminently reasonable, and that the provision thus should be upheld. When a woman is faced with any condition that poses a "significant threat to [her] life or health," she is exempted from the Act's consent and notice requirements and may proceed immediately with her abortion.

IV

For the reasons stated, we therefore would hold that each of the challenged provisions of the Pennsylvania statute is consistent with the Constitution. It bears emphasis that our conclusion in this regard does not carry with it any necessary approval of these regulations. Our task is, as always, to decide only whether the challenged provisions of a law comport with the United States Constitution. If, as we believe, these do, their wisdom as a matter of public policy is for the people of Pennsylvania to decide.

POSTSCRIPT

Is Abortion Protected by the Constitution?

In spite of the majority's refusal to overturn *Roe*, the constitutional right is still not absolutely secure. This was, after all, a 5–4 decision. In 1993 Justice Harry A. Blackmun wrote, "I am 83 years old. I cannot remain on this Court forever, and when I do step down, the confirmation process for my successor well may focus on the issue before us today." In 1994 Justice Blackmun did step down and Justice Stephen Breyer was confirmed to take his place. Justice Breyer's confirmation hearings did not focus on abortion and were relatively free of conflict. Whether or not *Roe v. Wade* is overturned is, however, still only partly a matter of legal analysis. It is also a matter of politics, of personality, of values, and of judicial philosophy.

What would be the consequences of a decision overturning *Roe*? The current state of great controversy over abortion would likely increase. The reason for this is that reversing *Roe* would mean that each state could permit or restrict abortion as it wished. The main contention of the justices who wish to overturn *Roe* is not necessarily that abortion should be banned but that this decision should be left to the states, and that it is not a constitutional issue. Such a position means that the political process will have to deal with the issue more than it does now, which is not likely to defuse the issue.

Even without overturning *Roe*, conflict will continue. Courts will be faced with determining whether or not state regulations constitute an "undue burden." Congress will wrestle with federal legislation that would restrict state regulations, such as the Freedom of Choice Act. New technologies, such as RU-486, the so-called abortion pill, which is not approved for use in the United States, will raise legal challenges as will groups, such as Operation Rescue, that employ methods that are at the boundary of permissible protests.

Recent writings about abortion include Dworkin, *Life's Dominion: An Argument About Abortion, Euthanasia, and Individual Freedom* (Alfred A. Knopf, 1993); Tribe, *Abortion: The Clash of Absolutes* (W. W. Norton, 1990); Note, "Judicial Restraint and the Non-Decision in *Webster v. Reproductive Health Services*," 13 *Harvard Journal of Law and Public Policy* 263 (1990); and Novick, "Justice Holmes and *Roe v. Wade*," 25 *Trial* 58 (December 1989). The story of the *Roe* case is recounted in Faux, *Roe v. Wade: The Untold Story of the Landmark Supreme Court Decision That Made Abortion Legal* (NAL, 1988). Information on both sides of the debate can be found on the Internet at http://www.naral.org/ and http://www.prolife.org/ultimate/. The home page for Planned Parenthood Federation of America is at http://www.ppfa.org/ppfa/index.html.

ISSUE 10

Is the Regulation of Pornography on the Internet Unconstitutional?

YES: Dolores K. Sloviter, from *American Civil Liberties Union v. Janet Reno,* U.S. District Court for the Eastern District of Pennsylvania (1996)

NO: Department of Justice, from *American Civil Liberties Union v. Janet Reno,* U.S. District Court for the Eastern District of Pennsylvania (1996)

ISSUE SUMMARY

YES: Dolores K. Sloviter, a judge in the Court of Appeals for the Third Circuit in Philadelphia, Pennsylvania, argues that although the government has a compelling interest to protect minors from indecent material, the Communications Decency Act (CDA) violates the First Amendment rights of all people by restricting access to material on the Internet.

NO: The U.S. Department of Justice contends that limitations on minors' access to indecent materials in cyberspace are no different from constitutionally upheld limitations in other communications media and that the enormous number of children surfing the Internet requires that the CDA be upheld.

The Internet is a collection of computer networks that allows people to share, communicate, and work with information in novel ways. The Internet began in 1969 but, for its first 25 years, was largely unknown to the general public. Currently, however, talk of cyberspace is everywhere, and it is hard to ignore the impact of the Internet and the World Wide Web.

Even if you do not have an e-mail account and have only read about "surfing the Web," you may have an impression of what kind of information is available on the Internet and of how people are using it. The popular media consider the Internet and cyberspace to be a highly newsworthy topic. Politicians talk about it, and movies such as *The Net* and *Mission Impossible* depict individuals using the Internet.

In July 1995 *Time* devoted its cover story to a recently published study of pornography on the Internet. The study, conducted by Martin Rimm, an undergraduate at Carnegie Mellon University, asserted that pornography was rampant and easily accessible on the Internet. As it turned out, the Rimm study was highly flawed, seriously distorted how much pornography was on the Internet, and mischaracterized how easy it was to obtain such images. Yet the study remained politically significant and provided support to legislation, particularly the Communications Decency Act (CDA), which had been proposed to regulate sexually oriented material on the Internet.

The Communications Decency Act was included in the Telecommunications Reform Act that was passed by Congress and signed into law in February 1996. Shortly thereafter, the American Civil Liberties Union and several other organizations brought suit challenging the constitutionality of the act.

There were two sections of the act that were the focus of the lawsuit: Section 223 (a)(1)(B), which prohibited using a "telecommunications device" for making, creating, or soliciting "any comment, request, suggestion, proposal, image, or other communication which is obscene or indecent, knowing that the recipient of the communication is under 18 years of age, regardless of whether the maker of such communication placed the call or initiated the communication"; and Section 223(d) of the act, which provided that whoever "uses any interactive computer service to display in a manner available to a person under 18 years of age, any comment, request, suggestion, proposal, image, or other communication that, in context, depicts or describes, in terms patently offensive as measured by contemporary community standards, sexual or excretory activities or organs, regardless of whether the user of such service placed the call or initiated the communication" would be fined, imprisoned, or both.

In June 1996 a three-judge federal court ruled that the act was unconstitutional. Each of the three judges agreed with this conclusion, and the following selections include the opinion of Judge Dolores K. Sloviter as well as the Justice Department's brief arguing in support of the law. After the court decision, the Justice Department announced that it would appeal the case to the U.S. Supreme Court. The CDA has a clause requiring the Court to accept the case, so a ruling can be expected from the Supreme Court during its 1996–1997 term.

At the heart of the challenge to the CDA is the existing legal model for regulating obscenity and pornography. These terms are often used synonymously by laypeople, but the courts distinguish between them, and, as a consequence, obscenity can be punished in any medium while pornographic communications, no matter how offensive they may be to some people, may not be barred. When the issue in a case, such as the one that follows, involves material that is pornographic or indecent but not obscene, what becomes significant is whether or not the court will recognize another exception to the First Amendment.

YES

Dolores K. Sloviter

OPINION OF DOLORES K. SLOVITER

AMERICAN CIVIL LIBERTIES UNION v. RENO

The government asserts that shielding minors from access to indecent materials is the compelling interest supporting the CDA [Communications Decency Act]. It cites in support the statements of the Supreme Court that "[i]t is evident beyond the need for elaboration that a State's interest in 'safeguarding the physical and psychological well-being of a minor' is 'compelling,'" *New York v. Ferber*, 458 U.S. 747, 757 (1982)(quoting *Globe Newspaper Co. v. Superior Court*, 457 U.S. 596, 607 (1982)), and "there is a compelling interest in protecting the physical and psychological well-being of minors. This interest extends to shielding minors from the influence of literature that is not obscene by adult standards." *Sable [Communications of California v. FCC,]* 492 U.S. at 126. It also cites the similar quotation appearing in *Fabulous Assoc., Inc. v. Pennsylvania Public Utility Comm'n*, 896 F.2d 780, 787 (3d Cir. 1990).

Those statements were made in cases where the potential harm to children from the material was evident. *Ferber* involved the constitutionality of a statute which prohibited persons from knowingly promoting sexual performances by children under 16 and distributing material depicting such performances. *Sable* and *Fabulous* involved the FCC's ban on "dial-a-porn" (dealing by definition with pornographic telephone messages). In contrast to the material at issue in those cases, at least some of the material subject to coverage under the "indecent" and "patently offensive" provisions of the CDA may contain valuable literary, artistic or educational information of value to older minors as well as adults. The Supreme Court has held that "minors are entitled to a significant measure of First Amendment protection, and only in relatively narrow and well-defined circumstances may government bar public dissemination of protected materials to them." *Erznoznik v. City of Jacksonville*, 422 U.S. 205, 212-213 (1975) (citations omitted).

In *Erznoznik*, the Court rejected an argument that an ordinance prohibiting the display of films containing nudity at drive-in movie theatres served a compelling interest in protecting minor passersby from the influence of such films. The Court held that the prohibition was unduly broad, and explained

From *American Civil Liberties Union v. Janet Reno*, 1996 U.S. Dist. Lexis 7919.

that "[s]peech that is neither obscene as to youths nor subject to some other legitimate proscription cannot be suppressed solely to protect the young from ideas or images that a legislative body thinks unsuitable for them." 422 U.S. at 213–14. As Justice Scalia noted in *Sable*, "[t]he more pornographic what is embraced within the... category of 'indecency,' the more reasonable it becomes to insist upon greater assurance of insulation from minors." *Sable*, 492 U.S. at 132 (Scalia, J., concurring). It follows that where non-pornographic, albeit sexually explicit, material also falls within the sweep of the statute, the interest will not be as compelling.

In part, our consideration of the government's showing of a "compelling interest" trenches upon the vagueness issue, discussed in detail in Judge Buckwalter's opinion but equally pertinent to First Amendment analysis. Material routinely acceptable according to the standards of New York City, such as the Broadway play *Angels in America* which concerns homosexuality and AIDS portrayed in graphic language, may be far less acceptable in smaller, less cosmopolitan communities of the United States. Yet the play garnered two Tony Awards and a Pulitzer prize for its author, and some uninhibited parents and teachers might deem it to be material to be read or assigned to eleventh and twelfth graders. If available on the Internet through some libraries, the text of the play would likely be accessed in that manner by at least some students, and it would also arguably fall within the scope of the CDA.

There has been recent public interest in the female genital mutilation routinely practiced and officially condoned in some countries. News articles have been descriptive, and it is not stretching to assume that this is a subject that occupies news groups and chat rooms on the Internet. We have no assurance that these discussions, of obvious interest and relevance to older teenage girls, will not be viewed as patently offensive—even in context—in some communities.

Other illustrations abound of non-obscene material likely to be available on the Internet but subject to the CDA's criminal provisions. Photographs appearing in *National Geographic* or a travel magazine of the sculptures in India of couples copulating in numerous positions, a written description of a brutal prison rape, or Francesco Clemente's painting "Labirinth," all might be considered to "depict or describe, in terms patently offensive as measured by contemporary community standards, sexual or excretory activities or organs." 47 U.S.C. sec. 223(d)(1). But the government has made no showing that it has a compelling interest in preventing a seventeen-year-old minor from accessing such images.

By contrast, plaintiffs presented testimony that material that could be considered indecent, such as that offered Stop Prisoner Rape or Critical Path AIDS project, may be critically important for certain older minors. For example, there was testimony that one quarter of all new HIV infections in the United States is estimated to occur in young people between the ages of 13 and 20, an estimate the government made no effort to rebut. The witnesses believed that graphic material that their organizations post on the Internet could help save lives, but were concerned about the CDA's effect on their right to do so.

The government counters that this court should defer to legislative conclusions about this matter. However, where First Amendment rights are at stake, "[d]eference to a legislative finding cannot limit judicial inquiry." Sable, 492 U.S. at 129 (quoting Landmark Communications, Inc. v. Virginia, 435 U.S. 829, 843 (1978)). "[W]hatever deference is due legislative findings would not foreclose our independent judgment of the facts bearing on an issue of constitutional law." Id.

Moreover, it appears that the legislative "findings" the government cites concern primarily testimony and statements by legislators about the prevalence of obscenity, child pornography, and sexual solicitation of children on the Internet. Similarly, at the hearings before us the government introduced exhibits of sexually explicit material through the testimony of Agent Howard Schmidt, which consisted primarily of the same type of hard-core pornographic materials (even if not technically obscene) which concerned Congress and which fill the shelves of "adult" book and magazine stores. Plaintiffs emphasize that they do not challenge the Act's restrictions on speech not protected by the First Amendment, such as obscenity, child pornography or harassment of children. Their suit is based on their assertion, fully supported by their evidence and our findings, that the CDA reaches much farther.

I am far less confident than the government that its quotations from earlier cases in the Supreme Court signify that it has shown a compelling interest in regulating the vast range of online material covered or potentially covered by the CDA. Nonetheless, I acknowledge that there is certainly a compelling government interest to shield a substantial number of minors from some of the online material that motivated Congress to enact the CDA, and do not rest my decision on the inadequacy of the government's showing in this regard.

THE REACH OF THE STATUTE

Whatever the strength of the interest the government has demonstrated in preventing minors from accessing "indecent" and "patently offensive" material online, if the means it has chosen sweeps more broadly than necessary and thereby chills the expression of adults, it has overstepped onto rights protected by the First Amendment. Sable, 492 U.S. at 131.

The plaintiffs argue that the CDA violates the First Amendment because it effectively bans a substantial category of protected speech from most parts of the Internet. The government responds that the Act does not on its face or in effect ban indecent material that is constitutionally protected for adults. Thus one of the factual issues before us was the likely effect of the CDA on the free availability of constitutionally protected material. A wealth of persuasive evidence, referred to in detail in the Findings of Fact, proved that it is either technologically impossible or economically prohibitive for many of the plaintiffs to comply with the CDA without seriously impeding their posting of online material which adults have a constitutional right to access.

With the possible exception of an e-mail to a known recipient, most content providers cannot determine the identity and age of every user accessing their material. Considering separately content providers that fall roughly into two categories, we have found that no technology exists which allows those posting on the category of newsgroups, mail exploders or chat rooms to screen for age. Speakers using those forms of communication cannot control who receives the communication, and in most instances are not aware of the identity of the recipients. If it is not feasible for speakers who communicate via these forms of communication to conduct age screening, they would have to reduce the level of communication to that which is appropriate for children in order to be protected under the statute. This would effect a complete ban even for adults of some expression, albeit "indecent," to which they are constitutionally entitled, and thus would be unconstitutional under the holding in *Sable*, 492 U.S. at 131.

Even as to content providers in the other broad category, such as the World Wide Web, where efforts at age verification are technically feasible through the use of Common Gateway Interface (cgi) scripts (which enable creation of a document that can process information provided by a Web visitor), the Findings of Fact show that as a practical matter, non-commercial organizations and even many commercial organizations using the Web would find it prohibitively expensive and burdensome to engage in the methods of age verification proposed by the government, and that even if they could attempt to age verify, there is little assurance that they could successfully filter out minors.

The government attempts to circumvent this problem by seeking to limit the scope of the statute to those content providers who are commercial pornographers, and urges that we do likewise in our obligation to save a congressional enactment from facial unconstitutionality wherever possible. But in light of its plain language and its legislative history, the CDA cannot reasonably be read as limited to commercial pornographers. A court may not impose a narrowing construction on a statute unless it is "readily susceptible" to such a construction. *Virginia v. American Booksellers Ass'n*, 484

U.S. 383, 397 (1988). The court may not "rewrite a . . . law to conform it to constitutional requirements." *Id.* Although we may prefer an interpretation of a statute that will preserve the constitutionality of the statutory scheme, *United States v. Clark*, 445 U.S. 23, 27 (1980), we do not have license to rewrite a statute to "create distinctions where none were intended." *American Tobacco Co. v. Patterson*, 456 U.S. 63, 72 n. 6 (1982); see also *Consumer Party v. Davis*, 778 F.2d 140, 147 (3d Cir. 1985). The Court has often stated that "absent a clearly expressed legislative intention to the contrary, [statutory] language must ordinarily be regarded as conclusive." *Escondido Mut. Water Co. v. La Jolla Band of Mission Indians*, 466 U.S. 765, 772 (1984)(quoting *North Dakota v. United States*, 460 U.S. 300, 312 (1983)).

It is clear from the face of the CDA and from its legislative history that Congress did not intend to limit its application to commercial purveyors of pornography. Congress unquestionably knew how to limit the statute to such entities if that was its intent, and in fact it did so in provisions relating to dial-a-porn services. See 47 U.S.C. sec. 223(b)(2)(A) (criminalizing making any indecent telephone communication "for commercial purposes"). It placed no similar limitation in the CDA. Moreover, the Conference Report makes clear that Congress did not intend to limit the application of the statute to content providers such as those which make available the commercial material contained in the government's exhibits, and confirms that Congress intended "content regulation of both commercial and non-commercial providers." Conf. Rep. at 191. See also, 141 Cong. Rec. S8089 (daily ed. June 9, 1995) (Statement of Senator Exon).

The scope of the CDA is not confined to material that has a prurient interest or appeal, one of the hallmarks of obscenity, because Congress sought to reach farther. Nor did Congress include language that would define "patently offensive" or "indecent" to exclude material of serious value. It follows that to narrow the statute in the manner the government urges would be an impermissible exercise of our limited judicial function, which is to review the statute as written for its compliance with constitutional mandates.

I conclude inexorably from the foregoing that the CDA reaches speech subject to the full protection of the First Amendment, at least for adults. In questions of the witnesses and in colloquy with the government attorneys, it became evident that even if "indecent" is read as parallel to "patently offensive," the terms would cover a broad range of material from contemporary films, plays and books showing or describing sexual activities (*e.g.*, [the film] *Leaving Las Vegas*) to controversial contemporary art and photographs showing sexual organs in positions that the government conceded would be patently offensive in some communities (*e.g.*, a Robert Mapplethorpe photograph depicting a man with an erect penis).

We have also found that there is no effective way for many Internet content providers to limit the effective reach of the CDA to adults because there is no realistic way for many providers to ascertain the age of those accessing their materials. As a consequence, we have found that "[m]any speakers who display arguably indecent content on the Internet must choose between silence and the risk of prosecution." Such a choice, forced by sections 223(a) and (d) of the CDA, strikes at the heart of speech of adults as well as minors.

WHETHER CDA IS NARROWLY TAILORED

In the face of such a patent intrusion on a substantial category of protected speech for adults, there is some irony in considering whether the statute is narrowly tailored or, as sometimes put, whether Congress has used the least restrictive means to achieve a compelling government interest. See *Sable*, 492 U.S. at 126. It would appear that the extent of the abridgement of the protected speech of adults that it has been shown the CDA would effect is too intrusive to be outweighed by the government's asserted interest, whatever its strength, in protecting minors from access to indecent material. Nonetheless, the formulation of the inquiry requires that we consider the government's assertion that the statute is narrowly drafted, and I proceed to do so.

In this case, the government relies on the statutory defenses for its argument of narrow tailoring. There are a number of reasons why I am not persuaded that the statutory defenses can save the CDA from a conclusion of facial unconstitutionality.

First, it is difficult to characterize a criminal statute that hovers over each content provider, like the proverbial sword of Damocles, as a narrow tailoring. Criminal prosecution, which carries with it the risk of public obloquy as well as the expense of court preparation and attorneys' fees, could itself cause incalculable harm. No provider, whether an individual, non-profit corporation, or even large publicly held corporation, is likely to willingly subject itself to prosecution for a miscalculation of the prevalent community standards or for an error in judgment as to what is indecent. A successful defense to a criminal prosecution would be small solace indeed.

Credit card and adult verification services are explicitly referred to as defenses in sec. 223(e)(5)(B) of the CDA. As is set forth fully in the detailed Findings of Fact, these defenses are not technologically or economically feasible for most providers.

The government then falls back on the affirmative defense to prosecution provided in sec. 223(e)(5)(A) for a person who "has taken, in good faith, reasonable, effective, and appropriate actions under the circumstances to restrict or prevent access by minors to a communication specified in such subsections... including any method which is feasible under available technology." The government emphasizes that "effective" does not require 100% restriction, and that this defense is "open-ended" and requires only reasonable efforts based on current technology.

But, as the evidence made clear, there is no such technology at this time. The government proffered as one option that would constitute a valid affirmative defense under sec. 223(e)(5)(A) a "tagging" scheme conceived by Dr. Olsen in response to this lawsuit whereby a string of characters would be imbedded in all arguably indecent or patently offensive material. Our Findings of Fact set forth fully the reasons why we found that the feasibility and effectiveness of tagging in the manner proposed by the government has not been established. All parties agree that tagging alone does nothing to prevent children from accessing potentially indecent material, because it depends upon the cooperation of third parties to block the material on which

the tags are embedded. Yet these third parties, over which the content providers have no control, are not subject to the CDA. I do not believe a statute is narrowly tailored when it subjects to potential criminal penalties those who must depend upon third parties for the effective operation of a statutory defense.

Most important, the government's "tagging" proposal is purely hypothetical and offers no currently operative defense to Internet content providers. At this time, there is no agreed-upon "tag" in existence, and no web browsers or user-based screening systems are now configured to block tagged material. Nor, significantly, has the government stipulated that a content provider could avoid liability simply by tagging its material.

Third, even if the technology catches up, as the government confidently predicts, there will still be a not insignificant burden attached to effecting a tagging defense, a burden one should not have to bear in order to transmit information protected under the constitution. For example, to effect tagging content providers must review all of their material currently published online, as well as all new material they post in the future, to determine if it could be considered "patently offensive" in any community nationwide. This would be burdensome for all providers, but for the many not-for-profit entities which currently post thousands of Web pages, this burden would be one impossible to sustain.

Finally, the viability of the defenses is intricately tied to the clarity of the CDA's scope. Because, like Judge Buckwalter, and for many of the reasons he gives, I believe that "indecent" and "patently offensive" are inherently vague, particularly in light of the government's inability to identify the relevant community by whose standards the material will be judged, I am not persuaded by the government that the statutory defenses in sec. 223(e) provide effective protection from the unconstitutional reach of the statute.

Minors would not be left without any protection from exposure to patently unsuitable material on the Internet should the challenged provisions of the CDA be preliminarily enjoined. Vigorous enforcement of current obscenity and child pornography laws should suffice to address the problem the government identified in court and which concerned Congress. When the CDA was under consideration by Congress, the Justice Department itself communicated its view that it was not necessary because it was prosecuting online obscenity, child pornography and child solicitation under existing laws, and would continue to do so. It follows that the CDA is not narrowly tailored, and the government's attempt to defend it on that ground must fail.

PRELIMINARY INJUNCTION

When Congress decided that material unsuitable for minors was available on the Internet, it could have chosen to assist and support the development of technology that would enable parents, schools, and libraries to screen such material from their end. It did not do so, and thus did not follow the example available in the print media where non-obscene but indecent and patently offensive books and magazines abound. Those responsible for minors undertake the primary obligation to prevent their exposure to such material. Instead, in the CDA Congress chose to place on the speakers the obligation of screening the material that would possibly offend some communities.

Whether Congress' decision was a wise one is not at issue here. It was unquestionably a decision that placed the CDA in serious conflict with our most cherished protection—the right to choose the material to which we would have access.

The government makes what I view as an extraordinary argument in its brief. It argues that blocking technology needed for effective parental control is not yet widespread but that it "will imminently be in place." Government's Post-hearing Memorandum at 66. It then states that if we uphold the CDA, it "will likely unleash the 'creative genius' of the Internet community to find a myriad of possible solutions." I can imagine few arguments less likely to persuade a court to uphold a criminal statute than one that depends on future technology to cabin the reach of the statute within constitutional bounds.

The government makes yet another argument that troubles me. It suggests that the concerns expressed by the plaintiffs and the questions posed by the court reflect an exaggerated supposition of how it would apply the law, and that we should, in effect, trust the Department of Justice to limit the CDA's application in a reasonable fashion that would avoid prosecution for placing on the Internet works of serious literary or artistic merit. That would require a broad trust indeed from a generation of judges not far removed from the attacks on James Joyce's *Ulysses* as obscene. See *United States v. One Book Entitled Ulysses*, 72 F.2d 705 (2d Cir. 1934); see also *Book Named "John Cleland's Memoirs of a Woman of Pleasure" v. Attorney General of Mass.*, 383 U.S. 413 (1966). Even if we were to place

YES Dolores K. Sloviter / 199

confidence in the reasonable judgment of the representatives of the Department of Justice who appeared before us, the Department is not a monolithic structure, and individual U.S. Attorneys in the various districts of the country have or appear to exercise some independence, as reflected by the Department's tolerance of duplicative challenges in this very case.

But the bottom line is that the First Amendment should not be interpreted to require us to entrust the protection it affords to the judgment of prosecutors. Prosecutors come and go. Even federal judges are limited to life tenure. The First Amendment remains to give protection to future generations as well. I have no hesitancy in concluding that it is likely that plaintiffs will prevail on the merits of their argument that the challenged provisions of the CDA are facially invalid under both the First and Fifth Amendments.

NO

Department of Justice

BRIEF FILED BY DEPARTMENT
OF JUSTICE

A. Congress Has Regulated Access by Minors to Indecent Materials in Several Communications Media.

The Communications Decency Act [CDA] is the latest in a long line of congressional efforts to protect children from exposure to indecent material. Congress has acted to regulate the exposure to children of indecent material in the broadcast medium. See 18 U.S.C. Section 1464. This includes broadcast of indecent material on the radio, see *FCC v. Pacifica Foundation*, 438 U.S. 726 (1978), as well as on television. *Action for Children's Television v. FCC*, 58 F.3d 654 (D.C. Cir. 1995) ("ACT III"), cert. denied, 116 S.Ct. 701 (1996) (upholding ban on television broadcast of indecent materials from 10 p.m. to 6 a.m.).

Congress has also regulated access by minors to indecent "dial-a-porn" telephone messages 47 U.S.C. 223(c); see *Dial Information Services v. Thornburgh*, 938 F.2d 1535 (2d Cir. 1991), cert. denied, 502 U.S. 1072 (1992); *Information Providers' Coalition For Defense of the First Amendment v. FCC*, 928 F.2d 866 (9th Cir. 1991) (upholding criminal prohibition on transmission of indecent communication to persons under 18 through telephone facilities). In addition, Congress has regulated access by minors to indecent material transmitted over certain cable television channels. *Alliance for Community Media v. FCC*, 56 F.3d 105, 129 (D.C. Cir. 1995), cert. granted, 116 S.Ct. 471 (1995) (upholding requirement that indecent programming on leased access channels be blocked to prevent access by minors).

B. Interactive Computer Services and the Internet.

The newly established section 223(d) of Title 47 continues this well-established regulation of indecent materials, applying it next to the most rapidly evolving communications medium—"interactive computer services." ...

Common examples of interactive computer services include those provided by commercial entities such as America Online, Prodigy, and CompuServe that, in addition to providing subscribers with access to information in their

From *American Civil Liberties Union v. Janet Reno*, 1996 U.S. Dist. Lexis 7919. Notes omitted.

200

own databases, provide access to the Internet. Interactive computer services also include other entities called Internet Service Providers ("ISP"), which provide software and a direct connection to the Internet. In addition, so-called bulletin board services ("BBS") are separate computer sites that can be logged onto through a telephone modem, and from which text and graphical images can be downloaded to a home computer.

The Communications Decency Act defines "the Internet" as "the international computer network of both Federal and non-Federal interoperable packet switched data networks." 47 U.S.C. Section 230(e)(1). In simpler terms, "the Internet is an international, cooperative computer network of networks, which links many types of users, such as governments, schools, libraries, corporations, hospitals, individuals, and others." See Rita Tehan, *Welcome to Cyberia: An Internet Guide,* Congressional Research Service, Library of Congress, May 12, 1994 at 1 (hereafter "CRS"). The Internet provides access to a vast source of information world-wide on all manner of topics, from world events, politics, education, art, sports, hobbies, entertainment, science, healthcare, and law....

C. Children "Surfing the Net".

During the debate on the CDA, the Senate was informed that "[o]f the 6.8 million homes with online accounts currently available, 35 percent have children under the age of 18." Remarks of Senator Coats, 141 Cong. Record S8333 (June 14, 1995). Online computer services, including the Internet, have an array of information and material directed at informing, educating, and entertaining children. For example, one publication describing material for children on the Internet lists such items as "Disney"— information about Disneyland, lyrics to Disney songs, EuroDisney reports, and other material form the Magic Kingdom. See Hahn & Stout, *The Internet Yellow Pages* (Osborne McGraw-Hill: 2d ed. 1995) at 371. There is also a related "chat" channel to talk about "all things Disney." *Id.* Another listing for "Kids Internet Delight" is a "gathering of sites children might enjoy, such as dinosaurs, sports information, and links to elementary schools across the country." *Id.* at 372. Sites are also listed for "youth" that concern scouting and nature activities. *Id.* at 739–40.

The Internet is a place where millions of children are online looking for information on fun and games, educational interests, and hobbies. More and more households are purchasing computers to enable their children to access, as effectively as possible, educational and recreational materials.

D. Availability of Obscene and Indecent Materials Online.

As the Senate debate on the Communications Decency Act made graphically clear, there is also a very seamy side of the Internet and related computer services. The range of such material runs from the extreme of the most graphic obscenity and child pornography, to less extreme pornography. As the Act's chief sponsor, Senator James Exon, put it:

It is no exaggeration to say that the most disgusting, repulsive pornography is only a few clicks away from any child with a computer. I am not talking just about *Playboy* and *Penthouse* magazines.... I am talking about the most hardcore, perverse types of pornography, photos, and stories featuring torture, child abuse, and bestiality.

... Senator Exon's observations are verified by a cursory look at publicly available sources. For example, *The Internet Yellow Pages* contains many listings for "sex" and "X-rated" sites online. This includes materials on various sexual fetishes, masturbation, and Playboy Centerfolds. *Id.* at 601–602. There are web sites for locating "X-rated pornographic photos." *Id.* at 602. There is a site for a "cyber-brothel" available for exchanging erotic mail and pictures. *Id.* at 732. There is a long list of "newsgroup" sites called "alt.binaries" and "alt.sex" where erotic pictures and stories can be downloaded over a computer. *Id.*

None of this array of sexual and X-rated materials was discussed in plaintiffs' papers. But it was the major cause of concern that led to enactment of the CDA....

It is against the backdrop of this information that the provisions—and the constitutionality—of the CDA must be initially assessed in deciding plaintiffs' request for a TRO [temporary restraining order]....

Section 223(d), as amended, is a lawful exercise of Congress' authority to restrict access to indecent speech by children. Although indecent images and texts (including non-obscene pornography) are not outside the realm of the First Amendment, and Congress may not proscribe them totally, indecent communications have such little social value that they are at the bottom of the scale of protected speech. See *Pacifica*, 438 U.S. at 743 (patently offensive references to sexual or excretory activities or organs "surely lie at the periphery of First Amendment concern"); *Young v. American Mini Theatres*, 427 U.S. 50, 70 (1976) (Stevens, J., concurring) (with respect to sexually explicit, non-obscene

speech, "society's interest in protecting this type of expression is of a wholly different, and lesser, magnitude than the interest in untrammeled political debate..."). Thus, Congress' authority to restrict indecent speech is greater than its authority to restrict other forms of speech.

In analyzing the constitutional validity of Congress' effort to restrict online indecency, the Court should bear in mind that "differences in the characteristics of new media justify differences in the First Amendment standards applied to them." *Red Lion Broadcasting v. FCC*, 395 U.S. 367, 386 (1969); see also *Pacifica*, 438 U.S. at 748 ("each medium of expression presents special First Amendment problems"). However, as Congress made clear in the legislative history of section 223(d), this Court may be fairly guided by a substantial body of First Amendment case law in the area of broadcasting (radio and television), cable television, and telephone communications—most notably in the so-called "dial-a-porn" cases—in making a determination that Congress has acted within its constitutional authority to restrict transmission or posting of patently offensive images and texts regarding sexual or excretory activities or organs made available to minors over computer networks.

Assuming, *arguendo*, that this Court is to apply "strict scrutiny" under the First Amendment to Congress' enactment of section 223(d), the standard as articulated is whether, in "regulat[ing] the content of constitutionally protected speech in order to promote a compelling interest," the government "chooses the least restrictive means to further the articulated interest."

Sable Communications, 492 U.S. at 126. As the Court in *Sable* went on to state:

> The Government may serve this... interest, but to withstand constitutional scrutiny, it must do so by narrowly drawn regulations designed to serve those interests without unnecessarily interfering with First Amendment freedoms. It is not enough to show that the Government's ends are compelling; the means must be carefully tailored to achieve those ends....

1. Congress Has a Compelling Interest in Preventing Minors from Obtaining Access to Online Indecency.

"A democratic society rests, for its continuance, upon the healthy, well-rounded growth of young people into full maturity as citizens, with all that implies." *Prince v. Massachusetts*, 321 U.S. 158, 168 (1944). Thus, the Supreme Court has often affirmed that the government has a "compelling interest in protecting the physical and psychological well-being of minors," *Sable Communications*, 492 U.S. at 126, an interest that "extends to shielding minors from the influence of literature [and other indecent forms of expression] that is not obscene by adult standards." *Id.* See *Bethel School District No. 403 v. Fraser*, 478 U.S. 675, 684 (1986) ("First Amendment jurisprudence has acknowledged limitations on the otherwise absolute interest of the speaker in reaching an unlimited audience where the speech is sexually explicit and the audience may include children."); *New York v. Ferber*, 458 U.S. 747, 756–64 (1982) (individuals may be prosecuted for distribution of pornographic materials using depictions of sexually explicit conduct by children, even if materials are not legally obscene); *Ginsberg v. New York*, 390 U.S. 629, 638–640 (1968) (court upheld conviction of store owner for selling a non-obscene "girlie" magazine to a minor, recognizing that the power of the state to regulate conduct of minors is greater than control of conduct of adults). Collectively, these cases stand for the proposition that the government may take steps to restrict the distribution of indecent materials to minors— including provision for criminal penalties—even though access to such materials could not constitutionally be denied to adults.

Moreover, apart from the government's "independent interest in the well-being of its youth," *Ginsberg*, 390 U.S. at 640; *Sable Communications [of California v. FCC,]* 492 U.S. at 126; *Ferber*, 458 U.S. at 756-57, the government has an equally compelling interest in helping parents exercise "authority in their own household to direct the rearing of their children." *Ginsberg*, 390 U.S. at 639; see *ACT III*, 58 F.3d at 661. The interest of parents in the "care, custody, and management" of children "occupies a unique place in our legal culture, given the centrality of family life as the focus for personal meaning and responsibility." *Lassiter v. Department of Social Services*, 452 U.S. 18, 38 (1981) (Blackmun, J., dissenting) (quoting *Stanley v. Illinois*, 405 U.S. 645, 651 (1972)).

... [T]his case has compelling parallels to *Pacifica*, where the Court held that indecent broadcasts could be regulated based on factors including the "uniquely pervasive presence" of radio, and the fact that such broadcasts were "uniquely accessible to children." 438 U.S. at 748–49. Plaintiffs would be hard pressed to discount that home computers have become commonplace; that millions of homes are "online"; that there are large numbers of juveniles and children who have developed computer literacy (in many cases far beyond the simple act of pointing and clicking to get into World Wide Web pages, or newsgroups); and that, in general, there is a generational gap between children and their less computer-sophisticated parents. (Indeed, a number of plaintiffs' declarants highlight the fact that minors do indeed access their services.) To paraphrase *Pacifica*, "[t]he ease with which children may obtain access to [online indecent] material, coupled with the concerns recognized in *Ginsberg*, amply justify special treatment [of the online medium]." 438 U.S. at 750....

In the end, plaintiffs cannot dispute that a large and growing amount of pornography is presently available online and easily accessible to children in the home, far exceeding anything available prior to the advent of online computer services. Given this fact, Congress' bedrock concern for the protection of children takes on paramount importance.

2. Congress Has Provided for the "Least Restrictive Means" by Which Online Indecency May Continue to Be Made Available to Adults Although Inaccessible to Minors.

Contrary to plaintiffs' contention, Congress neither purported to ban, nor effectively ban, online indecency in all its various forms. *Cf. Sable Communications*, 492 U.S. at 127 (statute denied adults as well as children access to indecent "dial-a-porn" messages). Rather, in several narrowly tailored provisions located in section 223(e), Congress acted in a sophisticated way to provide "information content providers" with broad defenses to criminal liability for the posting of indecent material, provided that they have employed one or more technical means of blocking access to minors as set forth in section 223(e)(5)(A) & (B). Thus, those who create or "post" indecent images or texts in cyberspace are on notice that they are free to do so, so long as they have taken reasonable and appropriate measures to block access to children effectively.

As the Congressional history makes clear, Congress borrowed from a solid foundation of case law upholding similar measures in formulating a scheme which places the burden on the information content provider to restrict access to indecent communications.

a. The Defenses to Criminal Liability Provided for in Section 223(e)(5)(B) Incorporate Valid Restrictions Which Have Been Upheld in the "Dial-A-Porn" Context.

Section 223(e)(5)(B) provides that it is a complete defense to prosecution for a content provider to have restricted access to indecent communications "by requiring use of a verified credit card, debit account, adult access code, or adult personal identification number." 47 U.S.C. Section 223(e)(5)(B). As such, Congress has done no more than incorporate the standards for blocking access to "dial-a-porn" messages—which were developed by the FCC in response to 47 U.S.C. Section 223(b), as amended in 1989, and which have been subsequently upheld by the Courts—as one option that content providers may take to ensure against children's online access to posted indecent material. See 47 C.F.R. Section 64.201; *Dial Information Services, supra; Information Providers' Coalition, supra.*

Plaintiffs do not dispute that such measures are feasible and are being employed in a variety of areas in "cyberspace." See, e.a., Hauman Aff., paragraph 9 ("BiblioFile Books on Computer" currently requires credit card for purchase of electronic books); Pls.' Mem. at 11 n. 26

("computer bulletin board systems that specialize in adult material generally require identification and payment and screen out minors, and are thus not at issue in this case"). Certainly, with respect to content providers to bulletin boards, Internet web pages, and other sites, who have the technical means to control and block access to their content, it should be undisputed that section 223(e)(5)(B) constitutes a sufficient "least restrictive means" of regulating indecency.

Other individuals and entities that communicate patently offensive material may likewise utilize such measures that allow for the identification of adults prior to obtaining access to particular Internet web pages and other online sites. There is simply insufficient evidence of record—especially at this early stage of the proceedings—to suggest that such measures would be so unduly burdensome on any of the plaintiffs, so as to justify invalidating this provision on constitutional grounds.

b. Section 223(e)(5)(A) Provides for Additional "Safe Harbors" from Liability for Providers of Online Indecency. Going one step further than the "dial-a-porn" regulations, Congress has included a second, broadly worded "safe harbor" provision, allowing for a good faith defense to liability if a person has taken "reasonable, effective, and appropriate actions" to "restrict or prevent" access by minors to indecent material, based on any appropriate measure or method which is "feasible under available technology." 47 U.S.C. Section 223(e)(5)(A).

In addition to whatever is feasible now, the legislative history makes clear that Congress understood that "content selection standards" and other technologies "currently under development" may be developed which provide for effective restrictions on access by minors to online indecency. See Conf. Rep. at 190. Congress also does not expect perfection; the conference report makes clear that the statutory term "effective" is to be given "its common meaning and does not require an absolute 100% restriction of access to be judged effective." Id....

At bottom, plaintiffs are demanding that unlike physical space, cyberspace be free of any form of "cyberzoning" of indecent speech—even if that means unlimited availability of pornography and indecency to minors in the home. This position flies in the face of a body of precedent in which the Supreme Court has upheld reasonable time, place, and manner limitations on indecency in "public" spaces. See, e.g., Bethel School District, 478 U.S. at 675–87 (upholding restrictions on indecent speech in a political address by high school student); City of Renton v. Playtime Theatres, 475 U.S. 41 (1986) (upholding zoning restrictions on location of adult theatres); City of Newport v. Iacobucci, 479 U.S. 92 (1986) (upholding statute forbidding non-obscene nude or nearly nude dancing in pubs); see also American Booksellers Ass'n, Inc. v. Virginia, 882 F.2d 125 (4th Cir. 1989), cert. denied, 494 U.S. 1056 (1990) (upholding statute prohibiting the display of sexually explicit materials to juveniles in a manner whereby they may examine and peruse them). The Constitution does not forbid the legislature from requiring libraries and bookstores to shield adult magazines from minors, and similarly, plaintiffs have failed to provide a constitutional justification for requiring the application of a different rule in cyberspace....

B. The Indecency Standard Is Not Void-for-Vagueness.

It Is Settled Law That the CDA's Indecency Standard Is Not Unconstitutionally Vague. Perhaps the heart of plaintiffs' complaint is that the indecency standard set forth in the Communications Decency Act is impermissibly vague. They argue that " '[i]ndecency' ... is a completely imprecise term—wholly subjective and dependent on individual values and attitudes that no person engaged in speech can be expected to anticipate." Through the collection of a number of parties, plaintiffs seek to set forth hypothetically impermissible applications of the indecency standard to literary, artistic, educational, health-related, or political speech. Indeed, plaintiffs' theory appears to be that the government cannot constitutionally regulate access by minors to any materials, unless they meet the standard of legally obscene or its variant of "harmful to minors." ...

Several courts have specifically upheld the indecency standard against vagueness challenges. To begin with, the Supreme Court in *Pacifica* upheld an FCC adjudication that an afternoon radio broadcast of the now-famous "seven dirty words" monologue by George Carlin was indecent. The FCC indecency standard at issue in *Pacifica* was defined as "language that describes, in terms patently offensive as measured by contemporary community standards for the broadcast medium, sexual or excretory activities and organs." 438 U.S. at 732. Section 223 (d) of the CDA mirrors the language at issue in Pacifica. It regulates the knowing transmission of "any comment, request, suggestion, proposal, image, or other communication that, in context, depicts or describes, in terms patently offensive as measured by contemporary community standards, sexual or excretory activities or organs." 47 U.S.C. Section 223 (d)(l)....

2. The Patent Offensiveness Standard Is Not Unconstitutionally Vague.

Aside from the fact that no court has ever declared the indecency standard void-for-vagueness, the question remains as to whether the standard could be found to be impermissibly vague.

Although due process requires that a criminal statute be "clearly defined," *Grayned v. City of Rockford*, 408 U.S. 104, 108 (1972), the Supreme Court has recognized that "we can never expect mathematical certainty from our language." *Id.* at 110. Accordingly, "due process does not require 'impossible standards' of clarity," *Kolender v. Lawson*, 461 U.S. 352, 361 (1983) (quoting *United States v. Petrillo*, 332 U.S. 1, 7–8 (1947)), but rather that a criminal statute "give the person of ordinary intelligence a reasonable opportunity to know what is prohibited, so that he may act accordingly." *Grayned*, 408 U.S. at 108.

This holds true even in the First Amendment context. "[Language's] inherent limitations obtain in a speech-laden, First Amendment setting as in any other." *United States v. Thomas*, 864 F.2d 188, 195 (D.C. Cir. 1988). Courts do not require that "an enactment touching on First Amendment interests set forth the precise line dividing proscribed from permitted behavior, or that a person contemplating a course of behavior know with certainty whether his or her act will be found to violate the proscription." *Id.* Rather, "even in this sensitive area the Due Process Clause requires that the enactment be drafted with reasonable specificity sufficient to provide fair notice." *Id.*

Plaintiffs' contention that the indecency standard is so subjective as to leave the public guessing as to what is proscribed, or as to invite arbitrary law enforcement, Pls.' Mem. at 34–42, is built on a foundation of speculation unsupported by existing authority in this area.

The Supreme Court in *Pacifica* stressed that "indecency is largely a function of context—it cannot be adequately judged in the abstract." 438 U.S. at 742. The Court specifically rejected *Pacifica*'s request to invalidate the FCC's indecency regulation entirely "on the basis of hypothetical applications not before the Court." *Id.* at 743. The Court emphasized that its decision to uphold the FCC's specific adjudication as to the indecent "seven dirty words" monologue did not mean the indecency standard could be widely applied to any speech that included offensive or sexually-related language.

Rather, the Court indicated that a consideration of context includes a consideration of the merit of the work's content. At issue in *Pacifica* was a broadcast that the Court found was indisputably "vulgar," "offensive," and "shocking." *Id.* at 747. The Court distinguished the "Filthy Words" monologue at issue there from "a telecast of an Elizabethan comedy," *id.* at 750, or "a prime-time recitation of Geoffrey Chaucer's Miller's Tale." *Id.* at 750 n. 29. Putting aside the fact that most works of such literary merit do not contain proscribed communications, for those works that might, *Pacifica* indicates that their merit is included in the statute's calculus with its command that communications be adjudged "in context."

In adopting the indecency standard in the CDA, Congress likewise expressed a clear intent that the standard consider works "in context." Distinguishing "material with redeeming value," the conference report states that in applying the indecency standard, "it will be imperative to consider the context and the nature of the material in question when determining its 'patent offensiveness.'" Conf. Rep. at 189. . . .

In sum, notwithstanding the fact that *Pacifica* indicates that the indecency standard must be understood and applied in the context of the work; or that courts have applied the indecency standard in the context of "adult" fare such as "dial-a-porn"; or that Congress was prompted to act to control access by minors to explicit pornography online, plaintiffs ask the Court to enjoin an Act of Congress based on an academic reading of a statute which they theorize might be applied generally to literary, scientific, or health-care related communications that concerns sexuality or may contain offensive words. Plaintiffs point to no authority supporting their position that the indecency standard would be applied so broadly. As such, they have not demonstrated the likelihood of success on the merits of this issue necessary to obtain a temporary restraining order.

C. The Indecency Standard Is Not Unconstitutionally Overbroad.

Plaintiffs' overbreadth argument is a strange one. They contend that section · 223(d) is overbroad because it keeps from minors materials that, plaintiffs assert, they have a First Amendment right to obtain. Relying on cases in which the governing authority employed a "harmful to minors" standard instead of an "indecency" standard, plaintiffs suggest that the former establishes the outer limit of what may be kept from minors without violating their rights. They contend that the indecency standard therefore violates minors' rights by prohibiting access to materials that, although patently offensive in their depictions of sexual and excretory organs, do not meet the "harmful to minors" test. See *id.*

As the Supreme Court has made clear, facial invalidation for overbreadth is "strong medicine" to be used "with hesitation, and then only as a last resort." *New York v. Ferber*, 458 U.S. at 769 (internal quotation marks omitted); see also *United States v. Knox*, 32 F.3d 733, 751–52 (3d Cir. 1994). The potential for some troublesome applications is not enough. A statute can be found overbroad only if it has a "substantial number of impermissible applications." *Id.* at 771; *New York State Club Ass'n. v. City of New York*, 487 U.S. 1, 14 (1988); *Brockett v. Spokane Arcades. Inc.*, 472 U.S. 491, 503 n. 12 (1985); *Broadrick v. Oklahoma*, 413 U.S. at 615.

Plaintiffs' contention that Congress is constitutionally precluded from barring access by minors through the indecency standard may be disposed of easily. "[E]ven where there is an invasion of protected freedoms the power of the state to control the conduct of children reaches beyond the scope of its authority over adults." *Ginsberg,* 390 U.S. at 638 (1968). (internal quotations omitted). Although the Supreme Court has upheld the "harmful to minors" test as a valid limit on minors' rights to access, see *id.* at 635, there is no indication that this standard constitutes the outer limit of what may be prohibited. In *Pacifica* itself,

the Court upheld application of the indecency standard as applied to minors in the limited context of broadcast media, 438 U.S. at 750, and suggested that the standard might be applied even more widely. *Id.* at 749 ("bookstores and motion picture theaters, for example, may be prohibited from making indecent material available to children"). Likewise, in *Sable Communications,* the Court recognized "the compelling interest of preventing minors from being exposed to indecent telephone messages." 492 U.S. at 131; see also *Fabulous Associates,* 896 F.2d at 787 ("[t]here is little question that the interest of the state in shielding its youth from exposure to indecent materials is a compelling state interest").

Indeed, three circuits have now upheld the use of the "indecency" standard as applied to minors. See *ACT III, supra* ("indecency" standard applied to restrict minors' access to television broadcasts); *Alliance for Community Media, supra* (same); *Dial Information Services, supra* (same, in dial-a-porn context); *Information Providers' Coalition, supra* (dial-a-porn).

The idea, then, that the CDA is overbroad because it applies an indecency standard and not a "harmful to minors" one is clearly wrong....

CONCLUSION

For the foregoing reasons, plaintiffs' motion for a temporary restraining order should be denied.

POSTSCRIPT

Is the Regulation of Pornography on the Internet Unconstitutional?

Supreme Court decisions cannot be predicted with certainty, but it would be quite surprising if Judge Sloviter's decision were reversed. Yet this will probably not mean the end to conflict about communication over the Internet. While the courts have generally resisted attempts to restrict offensive art and expression, political pressure to combat pornography has been increasing. There have been frequent newsworthy attempts to suppress a wide variety of forms of expression, such as the exhibition of sexually explicit photographs by the late Robert Mapplethorpe. Efforts have been made to require special warning labels on record albums that contain explicit lyrics, to prosecute some television executives for transmitting allegedly obscene films by satellite to Alabama, and to impose restrictions on controversial artists who receive grants from the National Endowment for the Arts. These examples suggest that courts will continue to be very busy trying to distinguish protected from unprotected forms of expression.

Recent writings on the problem of pornography include MacKinnon, *Only Words* (1993); Lacombe, *Blue Politics: Pornography and the Law in the Age of Feminism* (1994); Sunstein, *Democracy and the Problem of Free Speech* (1993); Hunt, *The Invention of Pornography* (1993); and Strossen, "A Feminist Critique of 'the' Feminist Critique of Pornography," 79 *Virginia Law Review* 1099 (1993). Child pornography was dealt with by the Supreme Court in *New York v. Ferber*, 458 U.S. 747. The most relevant obscenity case is *Miller v. California*, 413 U.S. 15 (1974). Dial-a-porn was the subject of *Sable Communications, Inc. v. FCC*, 492 U.S. 115 (1989) and 492 U.S. 889 (1989). Indecent radio communications was considered in *FCC v. Pacifica Foundation*, 438 U.S. 726 (1978).

The impact of computers and electronic communication on the First Amendment is discussed in E. Katsh, *The Electronic Media and the Transformation of Law* (Oxford University Press, 1989); *Law in a Digital World* (Oxford University Press, 1995); Symposium, "Emerging Media Technology and the First Amendment," 104 *Yale Law Journal* 1805 (1995); Donald Lively, "The Information Superhighway: A First Amendment Roadmap," 35 *Boston College Law Review* 1067 (1994); and Debra D. Burke, "Cybersmut and the First Amendment: A Call for a New Obscenity Standard," 9 *Harvard Journal of Law and Technology* 87 (1996). On the Internet itself, information about government regulation can be found at the following sites: `http://www.vtw.org/`; `http://epic.org/`; `http://www.eff.org/pub/Alerts/`; `http://www.cdt.org/cda.html`; and `http://www.umassp.edu/legal/hyper3.html`.

ISSUE 11

Should Affirmative Action Policies Be Continued?

YES: William L. Taylor and Susan M. Liss, from "Affirmative Action in the 1990s: Staying the Course," *The Annals of the American Academy of Political and Social Science* (September 1992)

NO: Wm. Bradford Reynolds, from "Affirmative Action and Its Negative Repercussions," *The Annals of the American Academy of Political and Social Science* (September 1992)

ISSUE SUMMARY

YES: William L. Taylor, a lawyer specializing in civil rights, and Susan M. Liss, the deputy assistant attorney general of the U.S. Department of Justice, believe that affirmative action policies have been very effective in providing new opportunities for education and economic advancement.

NO: Wm. Bradford Reynolds, a senior litigation partner with a Washington, D.C., law firm, argues that any preference provided on the basis of race, gender, religion, or national origin is inconsistent with the ideal of equality.

The most widely publicized Supreme Court case of the late 1970s was *Regents of the University of California v. Allan Bakke* 438 U.S. 265 (1978). Bakke had been denied admission to the medical school of the University of California, Davis, even though he had ranked higher than some minority applicants who were admitted to the school. He sued, asserting that the affirmative action program, which reserved 16 of 100 places for minority students, discriminated against him because of his race and that "reverse discrimination" of this sort violated his constitutional right to equal protection of the laws.

In its decision, the Supreme Court held that Bakke should prevail and be admitted to the medical school. Rigid quotas, it ruled, were indeed prohibited by the Constitution. More important, however, the Court also indicated that affirmative action programs that did not impose quotas would be permissible. Thus, if the University of California had an admissions program that gave some preference to an ethnic or racial group and that took race or sex into account along with test scores, geographical origins, extracurricular activities, and so on, it would have been upheld.

The *Bakke* case, as often occurs with Supreme Court decisions, raised as many questions as it answered. *Bakke* inevitably led to cases involving the validity of affirmative action programs in a variety of contexts. In *United Steel-*

workers v. Weber, 443 U.S. 193 (1979), the Steelworkers Union and the Kaiser Aluminum and Chemical Company negotiated a collective bargaining agreement that set aside 50 percent of trainee positions for blacks, until their low percentage (2 percent) among Kaiser craft employees rose to approximate their percentage (39 percent) in the local labor force. This case included a strict quota, but the Supreme Court upheld the program since it did not involve state action and was, according to Justice Lewis P. Powell, Jr., "adopted voluntarily."

In 1989, in a case that did involve government, the Court ruled that a municipal public works program that allotted 30 percent of its funds for minority contractors was unconstitutional (*City of Richmond v. J. A. Croson Co.*, 109 S. Ct. 706, 1989). In the absence of some specific evidence of discrimination, such a program was held to violate the white contractors' rights to equal protection of the law. The case has been a major blow to local governmental efforts to increase minority involvement in construction. In *Adarand Constructors, Inc. v. Pena*, 115 S. Ct. 2097 (1995), the Supreme Court invalidated a similar *federal* minority set-aside program. *City of Richmond* and *Adarand* now constitute the principal statements by the Supreme Court concerning the constitutional validity of race-conscious governmental programs that have been designed to remedy contemporary racial disparities allegedly resulting from historical patterns of racial discrimination.

More is involved in these cases than the development of a consistent body of law, and more is involved than the determination of whether or not a particular individual should be employed or admitted to an academic institution. Affirmative action is an experiment that tests the power of the law. In his exceptional book about the 1954 school desegregation cases, *Simple Justice* (Alfred A. Knopf, 1976), Richard Kluger describes discussions that took place in 1929 about what strategies could be used to promote the legal rights of southern blacks. At that time, Roger Baldwin of the American Civil Liberties Union expressed some skepticism that the law could be used to this end "because forces that keep the Negro under subjection will find some way of accomplishing their purposes, law or no law." Such an attitude toward affirmative action programs and their real impact upon institutions might not be inappropriate today. In March 1996 a federal court of appeals ruled in *Hopwood v. Texas*, 78 F.3d 932 (1996) that admissions programs employed by the University of Texas Law School that took race into account were unconstitutional. This ruling appeared to negate the *Bakke* decision and, if it were upheld on appeal, would probably end affirmative action programs. In June 1996, however, the Supreme Court declined to hear the appeal. The *Hopwood* ruling, therefore, only applies to a few states in the South.

Should the law permit otherwise equal applicants to be treated differently on the basis of sex, race, or ethnic background? The authors of the following selections come to different conclusions about the impact of and need for affirmative action programs.

YES

William L. Taylor and Susan M. Liss

AFFIRMATIVE ACTION IN THE 1990s: STAYING THE COURSE

The phrase "affirmative action," while capable of fairly narrow definition,[1] also serves as the line that divides people who have starkly different views on the nation's most enduring problem—how American society should treat people of color. On one side of that line are the messengers of the last 12 years who argue that discrimination is no longer to be viewed as a serious problem in this nation; what occurred in the past does not have any impact on the present. Their claim is that it is time to wipe the slate clean, to assume, in an extension of Lyndon Johnson's vivid imagery, that everyone who is now at the starting line is unburdened by any chains and has an equal chance. Government may have a continuing duty to see to it that no flagrant fouls are committed against minority competitors in the running of the race, but that is the limit of its responsibility.

On the other side of the line are those who believe that the vestiges of past discrimination are continuing barriers to the opportunities of the present generation of black people, that discrimination is still an active problem, and that substantial progress will not be made without affirmative government.

Defined in these terms, affirmative action is a touchstone for defining the role of government. Will government, acting affirmatively, extend a helping hand to those who need special assistance in order to achieve their potential, or will government, in the posture of neutrality, leave to the vagaries of the marketplace those who continue to be affected by the legacy of discrimination?

This article will assess the efficacy and fairness of affirmative action policies, review the legal standards that have guided our policymakers and courts in crafting affirmative remedies for discrimination, and conclude with a few observations about future directions for affirmative action policies.

THE LINK BETWEEN AFFIRMATIVE ACTION AND BLACK PROGRESS

A critical question about affirmative action policies is whether they have been effective, that is, whether they have worked in conjunction with other policies to provide opportunities for education and economic advancement that had previously been unavailable.

Affirmative Action Policies

Beginning with the passage of the Civil Rights Act of 1964, rules barring racial discrimination in the private sector began to be enforced, and affirmative remedies were developed to prevent or redress violations of the law. Particularly after the 1971 Supreme Court decision in *Griggs v. Duke Power*,[2] which prohibited practices that deny opportunities to minorities even when the practices are not intentionally discriminatory, courts finding the existence of pervasive patterns or practices of discrimination ordered strong affirmative remedies.[3]

Toward the end of the decade, the Supreme Court ratified lower-court interpretations of Title VII to permit employers and unions to enter into voluntary agreements that made conscious use of race to eliminate "old patterns of racial segregation and hierarchy."[4] . . .

Progress

As evidence that affirmative action policies have not been effective in addressing the needs of black Americans, critics of affirmative action like to point to the fact that in overall terms the economic progress of blacks relative to whites peaked in the early 1970s and since has stagnated or deteriorated. But no proponent of affirmative action has claimed that economic advancement for minorities can be divorced from the economic health of the nation. The issue is not whether affirmative action policies are sufficient conditions for progress but rather whether they are necessary and important conditions.

In fact, there have been a number of studies that demonstrate the effectiveness of affirmative action policies, particularly during the period of the 1970s when civil rights and affirmative action polices were being vigorously implemented.[5] Studies of the contract compliance program have indicated that companies subject to goals and timetable requirements had greater success during the 1970s in increasing minority employment in several job categories than did companies not subject to such requirements.[6] Other evidence can be gathered from examining changes in the employment patterns of companies subject to civil rights litigation. For example, studies of the huge Bell Telephone system conducted after the company entered into a Title VII consent decree in 1973 calling for the use of numerical goals and timetables showed that black workers had made substantial gains in entering managerial and skilled-craft positions.[7]

Similarly, the rapid growth in the enrollment and completion rates of black students in colleges and universities in the 1970s must be attributed in part to the application of affirmative action policies encouraging institutions of higher education to seek out minorities, as well as to the improved preparation of black students that came about through school desegregation and other improvements in educational opportunity.[8] In addition, affirmative action had an impact on the growth in minority business development that took place in skill-intensive areas of business services, finance, insurance, and real estate, areas outside the traditional realm of entrepreneurship.[9]

Mobility

Some critics of affirmative action argue that even if there are some benefits from the policy, those benefits flow largely to minorities who are already advantaged or middle class. Thus, they say, the policy is at best selective and at worse unneeded since middle-class people might advance without the aid of affirmative action.

This view is contradicted by studies showing, for example, that, of the increased enrollment of minority students in medical schools in the 1970s, significant numbers were from families of low income and job status, indicating that affirmative action policies have resulted in increased mobility, not simply in changing occupational preferences among middle-class minority families.[10] Moreover, many of the gains have come in occupations and trades not usually associated with advantaged status, such as law enforcement, fire fighting, and skilled construction work.[11]

For those seeking to achieve professional status, affirmative action has been applied at the gateway points, namely, at college and professional school admissions. Admissions policies designed to encourage minority participation in the professions may offer those who are otherwise qualified an equal chance at success in occupations with a more advantaged status. But affirmative action does not guarantee success for those who would not otherwise succeed as professionals; it merely provides the opportunity to compete.

Other critics of affirmative action have argued that there is a "creaming process" in which those most likely to seize the opportunities provided by affirmative action are apt to be the most motivated in the less advantaged group.[12] This may well be the case. Affirmative action is unlikely to be sufficient for those who are truly bereft of educational, social, and material resources. Other initiatives are called for to address the urgent needs of this group.

THE LEGAL STANDARDS GOVERNING AFFIRMATIVE ACTION

In assessing the legality of affirmative action under both the Constitution and statutes, the courts have struggled conscientiously to balance competing interests in order to meet a test of practical fairness to all parties. Cases such as *University of California Regents v. Bakke*, which invalidated an affirmative action plan for minority admissions to the medical school at the University of California,[13] and *United Steelworkers v. Weber*, which upheld a voluntary plan to remedy past discrimination in occupations traditionally closed to minorities,[14] reflect a pragmatic approach by the courts to the difficult legal and policy questions posed by affirmative action.

Using a pragmatic approach, the Supreme Court has ruled that black workers may be denied positions they would have held "but for" the discriminatory practices of an employer if awarding the positions would require the displacement of an incumbent white worker.[15] The test, as articulated in *Weber*, is whether race-conscious remedies "unnecessarily trammel the interest of the white employees." In employing this test, courts have drawn lines between actions that disappoint the expectations of whites and those that uproot them from a status that already has been vested.[16]

This practical approach to balancing competing rights may have been ushered out by a 1989 decision invalidating a minority business set-aside program adopted by the city of Richmond, *City of Richmond v. Croson.*[17] In that case, the Supreme Court, having grown more conservative and increasingly hostile to affirmative action as justices appointed by President Reagan joined the Court, applied new constitutional ground rules for state and local affirmative action programs, requiring that localities demonstrate an evidentiary predicate for affirmative action that may be nearly impossible for most state and local governments to meet.[18] During the term following the *Croson* decision, a majority of the Court in *Metro Broadcasting v. FCC*[19] rejected the applicability of the *Croson* standards to affirmative action programs mandated by Congress. Nevertheless, with the subsequent retirements of Justices Brennan and Marshall, the legal standards for assessing the validity of affirmative action are likely to be guided increasingly by ideology rather than the pragmatism of the last decade.

THE FUTURE OF AFFIRMATIVE ACTION

Affirmative action is under siege in the 1990s. The courts are no longer a friendly forum for deprived and powerless citizens who in the past were often able to find redress when it was denied in the more political arenas. The pragmatic efforts of the Supreme Court in *Bakke*, *Weber*, and other cases to strike a balance between the legitimate needs and expectations of white and minority workers may soon be replaced by an ideological commitment to color blindness, a cruel irony when it results in the courts' turn-ing a blind eye to the legacy of past and continuing discrimination.

The situation also is bleak in the more explicitly political arenas. During the debate over the Civil Rights Act of 1991, the Bush administration found political gold in labeling civil rights requirements of the legislation as "quota" provisions, seeking in a flagging economy to channel the discontent of many white workers toward the scapegoating of minority workers and Democratic advocates of affirmative action. The administration was pulled back from the brink only through the efforts of moderate and conservative Republican senators concerned about the long-range consequences of their party's being seen as having made common cause with David Duke and his fellow racists. But the administration has not taken any pledge of moral sobriety, threatening even on the eve of the signing ceremony for the Civil Rights Act to dismantle long-standing federal affirmative action programs. The difficulties of defenders of affirmative action are compounded by the fact that their ability to persuade depends on reasoned explication, not easily reducible to the 30-second sound bites used effectively by their opponents.[20]

In these circumstances, some observers have suggested that goals and timetables and other effective affirmative action measures be abandoned in favor of other ameliorative approaches. Paul Starr has proposed, for example, that the response to a Supreme Court reversal of the *Weber* decision should not be a legislative struggle for restoration but a dual effort "toward the reconstruction of civil society in minority communities and toward the promotion of broad policies for economic opportunity and security that benefit low- and middle-income

Americans, black and white alike."[21] However well-intentioned the proposal to view civil rights and economic and social programs as alternatives may be, several questions need to be asked.

One is whether legislative efforts to secure such "economic opportunit[ies]" through greater public investments in education, job training, and national health and welfare reform have been stymied by continued adherence to affirmative action policies and whether affirmative action will be an impediment in the future. While there have been facile suggestions that this is the case, the evidence does not support it. Legislation to fully fund Head Start, to provide family and medical leave, and to accomplish other economic and social goals has been threatened by the same kinds of attitudinal barriers founded on race and class as undergird the resistance to affirmative action.

A second question is whether sufficient progress has been made in eliminating racial discrimination to warrant a conclusion that the forms of affirmative action that have occasioned the greatest controversy are no longer necessary. If indeed discrimination is a sporadic phenomenon that is no longer the norm, a case can be made for changing course. But here again, despite the progress that has been made, the evidence points in another direction. Studies by the Urban Institute of the treatment of black and white job seekers, by the Department of Housing and Urban Development of the treatment of black and white home seekers, by the Federal Reserve and several newspapers of the persistence of redlining by financial institutions all strongly suggest that discrimination remains a pervasive and institutional problem. Given these facts, individual lawsuits are simply inadequate;

the rationale for affirmative action policy —that it is necessary to counter the effects of past, as well as ongoing, discrimination —continues to have vitality.

Ultimately, the question is whether it is possible to develop effective measures to assure that all people will have the opportunity to develop to their full potential without confronting the nation's most entrenched social problem—racial oppression and inequality. Again, those who propose that racial issues be finessed have little evidence to suggest that such evasions will be productive.

Interestingly, the current debate over affirmative action is taking place at a time when the antigovernment binge of the Reagan era appears to be losing force. There appears to be a growing recognition that if the productivity of the private sector of the U.S. economy is to be restored, government must play an affirmative role in investing in human resources. That recognition, if coupled with a recommitment to the unredeemed national promise of racial justice, may yet yield tangible opportunity for all. Now is not the time to lose our nerve.

NOTES

1. One definition is that affirmative action encompasses "any measure, beyond simple termination of a discriminatory practice, adopted to correct or compensate for past or present discrimination or to prevent discrimination from recurring in the future." U.S., Commission on Civil Rights, *Statement on Affirmative Action*, Oct. 1977, p. 2.

2. 401 U.S. 424 (1971).

3. In particularly blatant cases of discrimination, courts restrained employers from hiring new white employees until proportionate numbers of qualified minority employees were hired. See, for example, *Boston Chapter, NAACP v. Beecher*, 504 F.2d 1017 (1st Cir. 1974), *cert. denied*, 421 U.S. 910 (1975).

4. *United Steelworkers of America v. Weber*, 443 U.S. 193 (1979).

5. See Gerald David Jaynes and Robin M. Williams, Jr., eds., *A Common Destiny: Blacks*

and *American Society* (Washington, DC: National Academy Press, 1989), pp. 269–329. See also *Affirmative Action to Open the Doors of Job Opportunity* (Washington, DC: Citizens' Commission on Civil Rights, 1984), 121–47.

6. See, for example, J. Leonard, *The Effectiveness of Equal Employment Law and Affirmative Action Regulation* (Berkeley: University of California, School of Business Administration, 1985).

7. See statement of economist Bernard Anderson in U.S., Congress, House, Committee on Education and Labor, Subcommittee on Employment Opportunities, *Oversight Hearings on Equal Employment Opportunity*, 97th Cong., 1st sess., 1981, pt. 1, pp. 219, 221. For a report on similar progress following a consent decree in the steel industry, see statement of Phyllis Wallace, in ibid., pp. 528–29.

8. See studies summarized in W. Taylor, *Brown, Equal Protection and the Isolation of the Poor, Yale Law Journal*, 95:1709-10 (1986).

9. See Jaynes and Williams, eds., *Common Destiny*, p. 314.

10. See M. Alexis, "The Effect of Admission Procedures on Minority Enrollment in Graduate and Professional Schools," in *Working Papers: Bakke, Weber and Affirmative Action* (New York: Rockefeller Foundation, 1979), pp. 52–71.

11. In law enforcement, the numbers of black police officers nearly doubled from 1970 to 1980. In Philadelphia, after the initiation of the goals and timetables program for federal contractors, the percentage of skilled minority construction workers rose from less than 1 percent to more than 12 percent of the total.

12. See William Julius Wilson, *The Truly Disadvantaged* (Chicago: University of Chicago Press, 1989), pp. 114–15.

13. 438 U.S. 265 (1978).

14. 443 U.S. 193 (1979).

15. See, for example, the statement of Justice White that even a person adversely affected by discrimination "is not automatically entitled to have a non-minority employee laid off to make room for him." *Firefighters Local Union No. 1784 v. Stotts*, 104 S.Ct. 2576, 2588 (1984). The Court in *Stotts* decided that the benefits of an affirmative action plan would have to be negated by laying off recently hired black firefighters rather than displacing more senior white workers.

16. See 443 U.S. at 208 (1979).

17. 488 U.S. 469 (1989).

18. For a comprehensive analysis of the Court's standards in the *Croson* case, see Michael Small, "The New Legal Regime: Affirmative Action after *Croson* and *Metro*," in *Lost Opportunities: The Civil Rights Record of the Bush Administration Mid-Term*, ed. S. M. Liss and W. L. Taylor (Washington, DC: Citizens' Commission on Civil Rights, 1991).

19. 110 S.Ct. 2997 (1990).

20. The problem may be illustrated by the television ad used by Senator Jesse Helms in his successful 1990 reelection campaign. The ad depicted a white worker denied a job because the employer used a quota system to hire black applicants. Of course, an alternative explanation in many situations is that the white applicant lacked the requisite qualifications. Indeed, critics of civil rights enforcement have charged that minority workers are being encouraged to think of themselves as victims rather than to examine the need to upgrade their skills and develop self-discipline. Yet, without any conscious irony, Senator Helms and other affirmative action bashers do precisely the same thing by encouraging whites to view themselves as victims. For understandable reasons, however, few politicians would seek to counter a Helms attack by suggesting that some white applicants may lack the qualifications.

21. Paul Starr, "Civil Reconstruction: What to Do without Affirmative Action," *American Prospect*, Winter 1992, p. 7.

NO

Wm. Bradford Reynolds

AFFIRMATIVE ACTION AND ITS NEGATIVE REPERCUSSIONS

The phrase "affirmative action" has been so much a part of civil rights policy over the past three decades that it rarely is defined or explained by those who use it. For the most part, the omission is calculated. Few dare to quarrel with a program offered to promote civil rights objectives and described simply as "affirmative action."

Yet it is just such programs that have energized much of the debate in the field of civil rights since the early 1960s. First introduced by President John F. Kennedy in Executive Order No. 10925,[1] "affirmative action" was originally defined in terms of active recruitment and outreach measures aimed at enhancing employment opportunities for all Americans. Its race-neutral character could not have been more clearly expressed: employers contracting with the federal government were directed to "take affirmative action to ensure that the applicants are employed, and that employees are treated during employment, without regard to race, creed, color or national origin."[2]

It should come as no surprise that in the early 1960s, measures devised to tear down racial barriers and affirmatively promote equal opportunity were required to be themselves indifferent to racial distinctions. Discrimination on account of skin color was, after all, the evil identified as constitutionally intolerable in the Supreme Court's landmark decision in *Brown v. Board of Education*.[3] "At stake," wrote Chief Justice Earl Warren for the full Court in *Brown II*, "is the personal interest of plaintiffs' admission to public schools . . . on a [racially] nondiscriminatory basis."[4] What the school children were seeking, their counsel Thurgood Marshall argued, was the assignment of students to the public schools "without regard to race or color."[5]

The Supreme Court's dramatic reversal of its half-century precedent of *Plessy v. Ferguson*[6] precipitated an outpouring of condemnation directed at all forms of racial segregation. During the next decade, the color line that had officially divided Americans came under stinging attack from all quarters. Racial distinctions, declared the High Court, were by their very nature "odious to a free people whose institutions are founded upon the doctrine of equality."[7]

From Wm. Bradford Reynolds, "Affirmative Action and Its Negative Repercussions," *The Annals of the American Academy of Political and Social Science* (September 1992). Copyright © 1992 by The American Academy of Political and Social Science. Reprinted by permission of Sage Publications, Inc.

Thus the visible barriers of everyday life that had for so long kept blacks out began to tumble, one by one. Water fountains, restrooms, hotels, restaurants, trolley cars, lunch counters, movie theaters, and department stores all were finally opened to blacks and whites alike throughout the 1960s and into the 1970s.

The congressional response to *Brown* was no less emphatic. With enactment of the Civil Rights Acts of 1957, 1960, and 1964,[8] the Voting Rights Act of 1965,[9] and the Fair Housing Act of 1968,[10] Congress demanded removal of the race factor in the work force, the classroom, places of public accommodation, the voting booth, and the housing market. The message was that public and private decision makers in the areas covered were to be wholly blind to color differences.

The legislative debates of that era underscored the wholesale nature of this neutrality mandate. Significantly, much of the discussion leading up to the 1964 act centered on the issue of preferential treatment, that is, whether the measure under consideration, while condemning racial discrimination, would countenance race-conscious hiring and promotion practices. Proponents of the bill's employment provisions—Title VII of the act—uniformly and unequivocally denied that the legislation should or could be so interpreted. Favoring black employees in the selection process would violate Title VII "just as much as a 'white only' employment policy," declared Senator Harrison Williams.[11] "How can the language of equality," he asked, "favor one race or one religion over another? Equality can have only one meaning, and that meaning is self-evident to reasonable men. Those who say that equality means favoritism do violence to common sense."[12]

Senator Edmund Muskie, another key supporter of the 1964 act, expressed a similar understanding of the legislation. "Every American citizen," said Muskie, "has the right to equal treatment—not favored treatment, not complete individual equality—just equal treatment."[13] Senator Hubert Humphrey agreed. The principal force behind the passage of the 1964 Civil Rights Act in the Senate, Humphrey repeatedly stated that Title VII would prohibit any consideration of race in employment matters. On one occasion he used these words:

> The title does not provide that any preferential treatment in employment shall be given to Negroes or to any other persons or groups. It does not provide that any quota system may be established to maintain racial balance in employment. In fact, the title would prohibit preferential treatment for any particular group, and any person, whether or not a member of any minority group, would be permitted to file a complaint of discriminatory employment practices.[14]

The leadership of the civil rights movement echoed the same view. Appearing at congressional hearings during consideration of the 1964 civil rights laws, Roy Wilkins, executive director of the National Association for the Advancement of Colored People (NAACP), stated unabashedly, "Our association has never been in favor of a quota system."[15] "We believe the quota system is unfair whether it is used for Negroes or against Negroes," he testified.[16] "We feel people ought to be hired because of their ability, irrespective of their color.... We want equality, equality of opportunity and employment on the basis of ability."[17]

The same theme was sounded by Jack Greenberg, then director counsel of the NAACP Legal Defense Fund, in his successful 1964 argument to the Supreme Court in *Anderson v. Martin*,[18] urging that a state statute requiring the ballot designation of a candidate's race be invalidated. "The fact that this statute might operate to benefit a Negro candidate and against a white candidate... is not relevant," he insisted, "for... the state has a duty under the fifteenth amendment and the fourteenth amendment to be 'color-blind' and not to act so as to encourage racial discrimination... against any racial group."[19]

Color blindness was, in fact, the banner under which the civil rights movement marched, largely in unison, through most of the 1960s. Those who joined in—both black and white—drew legal strength from the Supreme Court's landmark decision in *Brown*, policy support from the recent acts of Congress, and moral inspiration from the words and deeds of Dr. Martin Luther King, Jr. His dream became America's dream on that summer afternoon in 1963, as he stood at the foot of the Washington Monument and, with millions of Americans watching, challenged a country to bring about the day when his children would at last be judged "by the content of their character" and measure of their abilities, not "the color of their skin."[20]

As we moved through the decade of the 1960s, there were innumerable signs of progress as the "whites only" signs were removed. The outlawing of racial discrimination in employment, coupled with the government impetus behind affirmative action recruitment and outreach efforts, introduced blacks into a significant number of workplaces previously having white employees only. With increasing regularity, the courts began issuing orders that white public schools open their doors to black students. The

message of equal opportunity had broken through.

There was, however, a growing undercurrent of discontent. Many in the civil rights movement began to express dissatisfaction over the pace of desegregation initiatives. By the early 1970s, a perception had set in that the momentum had peaked and was even slipping backward. The policymakers could have pointed out that educational and economic disparities between blacks and whites due to the long history of segregation made inevitable the sort of slowdown that followed the dramatic first-wave breakthrough. It is painfully obvious that many blacks forced into segregated classrooms in the South had been denied a quality education—some had received almost no education at all; they could hardly have been expected to compete effectively with better-educated whites for employment.

Yet, to focus on this systemwide failing and face it forthrightly was seen by many as too prolonged an effort to satisfy the political demands of the time. Instead, the policymakers sought a quick fix, without giving serious thought to its long-term repercussions or implications. The concept of racial neutrality gave way to a concept of racial balance, on the representation that the former could not be fully realized unless the latter was achieved.

In the employment arena, the principal tool used was affirmative action, not in its original race-neutral sense but now endorsing racial preference. The claim was that regulation and allocation by race were not wrong per se; rather, their validity depended upon who was being regulated, on what was being allocated, and on the purpose of the arrangement. If a racial preference would produce the desired statistical result, it was argued, its discriminatory feature could be tolerated as an unfortunate but necessary consequence of remedying the effects of past discrimination. Using race "to get beyond racism" was the way one Supreme Court Justice explained it.[21]

Once again, the use of race as a criterion for governmental classification became acceptable during the decade of the 1970s. Having been rescued in *Brown* from the insidious policy of separate but equal, the country found itself only two short decades later drifting steadily toward the policy of separate but proportional: separate avenues to school, separate employment lines, separate contract-bid procedures, all inspired by the objective of achieving proportional representation by race in the classroom, in the work force, and on the job site.

Proponents of preferential affirmative action soon discarded the precept that a race-based employment preference was constitutionally permissible only when necessary to place an individual victim of proven discrimination in a position he or she would have attained but for the discrimination. Instead they focused on entire groups of individuals said to be disadvantaged because of race.[22] Quotas, goals and timetables, and other race-conscious techniques gained increasing acceptance among federal bureaucrats and judges, and by the decade's end, racial considerations influenced public employment decisions of every kind, from hirings to layoffs.

It did not seem to matter that those favored solely because of race frequently had never been wronged by the employer or that the preferential treatment afforded them was at the expense of other employees who were themselves admittedly innocent of any discrimination or other wrongdoing. The preoccupation was on removing from the work force any racial imbalance between employees in a discrete job unit, no matter how large or small. Lost in the scramble for strictly numerical solutions was the fundamental truth that "no discrimination based on race is benign,... no action disadvantaging a person because of color is affirmative."[23]

By the early 1980s, the use of race in the distribution of the country's limited economic and educational resources had sadly led to the creation of a kind of racial spoils system in America, fostering competition not only between individual members of contending groups, but between the groups themselves. The color-blind ideal had largely given way to a color-conscious mentality, one that encouraged stereotyping and that invited people to view others as possessors of racial characteristics, not as unique individuals. Thus the policy of preferential affirmative action had effectively submerged the vitality of personality under the deadening prejudgments of race. The very purpose intended to be served was being defeated, for race-based preferences cut against the grain of equal opportunity. In the broadest sense, color consciousness and racial polarization pose the greatest threat to members of minority groups because it is they who are, by definition, outnumbered. As individuals, members of all racial groups suffer, because an individual's energy, ability, and dedication can take him or her no further than permitted by the group's allotment or quota.

What began as a pursuit for equality of opportunity became, therefore, through preferential affirmative action, a forfeiture of opportunity in absolute terms. Individual opportunity was diminished in order to achieve group equality, measured solely in terms of proportional representation and numerically balanced results. Yet, as Justice Powell stated in his *Bakke* concurrence, "Nothing in the Constitution supports the notion that individuals may be asked to suffer otherwise impermissible burdens in order to enhance the societal standing of their ethnic groups."[24]

Justice Powell's view was not shared by all of his colleagues on the High Court, however. Indeed, in many respects, the public debate in the late 1970s over whether use of racial preferences was affirmative or negative action was mirrored in the Supreme Court's opinions. Alan Bakke won admission to the University of California Medical School on the ground that a minority preference program designed to benefit all but Caucasian applicants excluded him unconstitutionally because of race. But the Court was sharply divided, and no single opinion could command a majority.[25]

The heart of the judicial controversy did not appear to be a difference of view as to the fundamental commitment to eradicate all forms of racial discrimination. As Justice Marshall made clear in his opinion for the Court in *McDonald v. Santa Fe Trail Transportation Co.*, color-conscious bias was condemned by law with equal force whether it operated in forward gear or reverse.[26] Rather, the break point came over whether and to what extent the antidiscrimination principle should be compromised on the strength of a promise that its equal protection guarantee would be thereby more likely to be achieved.

The signals sent by the Court were at best mixed and invariably muddled.[27] At one end of the compendium, there was the view expressed by Justice Blackmun in *Bakke* that the use of race was necessary "to get beyond racism."[28] On the other end, then Associate Justice Rehnquist argued no less forcefully that to compromise the principle of nondiscrimination, no matter how slightly, was to lose it forever to the emerging compromise.[29] Between the two was the rationale commanding the most support in *United Steelworkers v. Weber*.[30] In upholding the minority training program favoring in-plant black employees over their white counterparts for 50 percent of the openings, Justice Brennan stressed the restricted nature of the affirmative action preference that was allowed to stand: its adoption was intended to correct persistent racial exclusion from the work force; it was of limited duration; and it was tailored to remedy the identified exclusionary practices, not to maintain racial balance or skin-color proportionality.[31]

When the affirmative action issue came again to the Court two years later in a constitutional setting, the split between the justices was no less pronounced. The case was *Fullilove v. Klutznick*,[32] and, again, enough votes were pulled together to uphold a minority set-aside provision enacted by Congress. The 10 percent contracting preference survived judicial scrutiny, however, only because a majority of the justices regarded it to be (1) remedially "compelled" in order to counter persistent, industrywide discrimination and (2) "narrowly tailored" as to duration, scope, and application.[33]

If such program constraints had been endorsed by the full Court, they undoubtedly would have been taken more seriously by the lower federal courts. But, precisely because the Supreme Court spoke with many voices, a number of appellate court judges took it upon themselves to read both *Fullilove* and *Weber* expansively and assign undeserved weight to dictum in *Bakke*.[34] As a consequence, the racial preference acquired a respectability it did not justifiably deserve.[35]

Such programs, however, have been unable to sustain lasting support—a consequence that, in the final analysis, is as much a tribute to the Supreme Court as the flirtation with a racial-quota policy was one of the Court's more noticeable embarrassments. The issue of preference revisited the High Court repeatedly in the 1980s, and by the end of the decade there emerged a far clearer understanding of its acceptable use. Wholesale return to the days in the early 1960s—when "affirmative action" was a neutral phrase that demanded outreach efforts aimed at all Americans without regard to race—has not occurred.[36] But neither is it any longer the case that a racial solution can be fashioned to correct a statistical imbalance in the workplace that is attributed to discrimination in the past, not the present.[37]

Rather, in a series of decisions authorized by justices on both sides of the philosophical spectrum, affirmative action preferences have been assigned a modest, albeit not unimportant, role in the fight against discrimination. They are available not as a first-resort measure but as a remedy of last resort, to be used when—and only when—compelled by racially exclusionary practices that persist notwithstanding concerted efforts, nonracial in character, to bring them to a halt.[38] Even then, the race-conscious alternative must be narrowly tailored to the remedial purpose it is intended to serve, so as not to intrude needlessly on the rights of others who have done no wrong or last longer than necessary to correct the discrimination.[39]

Accordingly, there is good reason to believe that we are entering an era when government will no longer feel the need to rely so heavily on racial classifications. To be sure, there are those who still insist that minorities are bound to remain on the sidelines without some racial-preference measure to get them into the game. Rather than demanding rigid quotas, however, they claim to be content with goals and timetables.

But racial goals, tied to short- or long-term timetables, offer no solution to the real problems at hand. Whether racial preference is enforced by the raw racism of a quota program or guided by the more subtle hand of a flexible goal, it still confers benefits on some while denying them to others for the worst of reasons: because of skin color or ethnic origin. The unfortunate reality is that under either regime, the specter of racial inferiority is kept alive; behind every goal and timetable lurks the message that minorities cannot make it under the same rules, that they need a special set of privileges that come with being members of a particular race.

The recently concluded debates over the Civil Rights Act of 1991 reverberated around that theme. The advocates of racial preference lobbied hard for codification of a legal standard that would effectively define discrimination in terms of proportional representation—not just in terms of race and ethnicity, but also with respect to gender and religion. Any work force imbalance as to one or more of the designated groupings was, under their proposal, presumptively unlawful, and the traditional defense of merit selection would be unacceptable against any claimant minimally qualified for the job in question.

Those who opposed and ultimately defeated this measure were not far off the mark to call it a quota bill. Unless companies hired and promoted by race, gender, ethnic background, and religion, work force proportionality would simply not be achievable and therefore litigation would be a virtual certainty.[40] The most cost-effective corporate response would thus be to maintain separate lists of applicants and select new hires or promotees proportionately according to skin color, sex, ethnicity, and religious beliefs. Self-imposition of employee quotas to avoid presumptive liability was the unstated, but fully understood, objective of the offered legislation.

What finally was passed by Congress and signed by President Bush was the product of compromise and, in candor, probably eases the quota pressure on corporate America to some degree, even if it does not eliminate it altogether. The presumption of discriminatory selection procedures on a showing of work force disproportionately remained in the final bill.[41] But the employer—who, under the 1991 act, inherits the burden of proof once a *prima facie* showing of racial, gender, ethnic, or religious disparity has been made[42]—can rebut the presumption on a showing that its alleged discriminatory procedure is related to the job in question and necessary to the business.[43] In other words, proof that the selection process was designed to, and did in fact, produce the best-qualified candidates for the particular job is an acceptable defense.

To be sure, the new statute lacks definition in a number of important respects,[44] but that has become an expected character flaw in virtually all congressional legislation that is the product of extended debate and compromise. In this instance, the shortcoming probably bodes well for the forces whose understanding of civil rights continues to rest, at bottom, on the color-blind ideal of equal opportunity for all Americans and not just a preferred group or groups. For it is they who now seem to have the ear of a majority of the Supreme Court justices as well as many lower federal court judges who will be called upon to resolve definitional disputes and matters of statutory interpretation.[45]

That is the more gratifying news. An immediate legislative threat to an eventual return to race neutrality has been diverted. The new civil rights legislation at least pays symbolic deference to a principled assault on the evils of discrimination, and nothing it says provides a basis for any more expansive use of the remedy of racial—or ethnic or gender or religious—preference than has been permitted by the Supreme Court. Affirmative action measures thus are readily available as a remedial tool to respond to acts of bias and prejudice, but they must remain unconscious to color differences except as a "narrowly tailored," last-resort effort to rid a work force of persistent discrimination.[46]

This is not to suggest that the 1991 act deserves no criticism. Its new provisions on punitive damages,[47] standing,[48] limitation periods,[49] attorney and witness fees,[50] and retroactivity each raise questions that are already subject to litigation or soon will be. As a consequence, the real beneficiaries of the compromise that emerged from the prolonged legislative battle are, for now, likely to be the lawyers who will, predictably, further clog the courts' crowded dockets with numerous new lawsuits seeking to exploit the damages and fee-recovery provisions —the beneficiaries will not be the ever-expanding minority population, which is still waiting, largely in vain, for the employment opportunities promised in the Civil Rights Act of 1964. That promise has, for most, too long been thwarted by the policy of racial preference. The real disappointment is that its prospects under the new act are only marginally brighter, even on the best of assumptions that preferential affirmative action has been caged and will henceforth be available only for tailored, last-resort, remedial use.

NOTES

1. 3 CFR 1959-63, pp. 448–54.

2. Ibid.

3. 347 U.S. 483 (1954).

4. *Brown v. Board of Education*, 349 U.S. 296, 300 (1955).

5. Reprinted in *O. Brown, Argument: The Oral Argument before the Supreme Court in Brown v. Board of Education of Topeka, 1952–55*, ed. L. Friedman (New York: Walter, 1969), p. 47.

6. 163 U.S. 537 (1894). The case involved a suit by Plessy, petitioner, a "resident of the State of Louisiana, of mixed descent, in the proportion of seven-eighths Caucasian and one-eighth African blood," against the Honorable John H. Ferguson, judge of the Parish of Orleans. Ibid., p. 538. While seated in the "white race" section of an East Louisiana railway passenger train, Plessy was required by the conductor to vacate the seat and find another in a section of the train "for persons not of the white race." Ibid. Upon his refusal to move, Plessy was ejected, arrested, and charged with a criminal violation. Ibid. He was convicted and thereafter appealed the constitutionality of the Louisiana law "providing for separate railway carriage for white and colored races." Ibid., p. 539. In its now roundly criticized opinion, delivered by Justice Brown, the Court affirmed the conviction, ruling the law within the bounds of the Fourteenth Amendment. Ibid., p. 540. Laws providing for "separate but equal" public accommodations were thereby given the stamp of constitutionality. Ibid., p. 550. But see ibid., p. 559 (Harlan, J., dissenting) ("Our constitution is color-blind, and neither knows nor tolerates classes among citizens.... The law regards man as man, and takes no account of his surroundings or of his color").

7. See *Loving v. Virginia*, 388 U.S. 1, 11 (1966) (quoting *Hirabayashi v. United States*, 320 U.S. 81, 100 (1943)).

8. Civil Rights Act of 1957, Pub. L. 85-315, 71 Stat. 634 (codified as amended in scattered sections of 42 U.S.C.).

9. Pub. L. 89-110, 79 Stat. 437 (codified as amended at 42 U.S.C. §§ 1971, 1973 to 1973 bb-l (1982)).

10. Pub. L. 90-284, 82 Stat. 81 (codified as amended at 42 U.S.C. § § 3601-19 (1982)).

11. 110 Cong. Rec. 8921 (1964).

12. Ibid.

13. Ibid., p. 12,614.

14. Ibid., p. 11,848. At another point, Senator Humphrey's exasperation with the opposition's preference argument prompted him to make the following offer: "If... in the title VII... any language [can be found] which provides that an employer will have to hire on the basis of percentage or quota related to color... I will start eating the pages [of the bill] one after another...." Ibid., p. 7,420.

15. Statement of Roy Wilkins, in U.S., Congress, House, Committee on the Judiciary, Subcommittee no. 5, *Miscellaneous Proposals Regarding the Civil Rights of Persons within the Jurisdiction of the United States, 1963: Hearings on H.R. 7152.* 88th Cong., 1st sess., 1963, p. 2,144.

16. Ibid.

17. Ibid.

18. See *Anderson v. Martin*, 375 U.S. 399 (1964), a case involving a state statute requiring that the race of each candidate for public office be accurately designated on each ballot. Noting that any governmental endorsement of racial bloc voting would tend to favor the race having a numerical majority, the Court held that the state could not constitutionally encourage racial discrimination of any kind, whether it worked to the disadvantage of blacks or whites. The state's designation of candidate's race was, according to a unanimous Court, of "no relevance" in the electoral process. Ibid., pp. 401–3.

19. Jurisdictional Statement of Appellants at 11–12, *Anderson v. Martin*, 375 U.S. 399 (1964) (No. 51).

20. M. King, Jr., "I've Got a Dream," in Martin Luther King, Jr., *A Documentary... Montgomery to Memphis*, ed. F. Schulte (New York: Norton, 1976), p. 218.

21. *Board of Regents of Univ. of Cal. v. Bakke*, 438 U.S. 265, 407 (1978) (Blackmun, J., concurring). But see *DeFunis v. Odegaard*, 416 U.S. 312, 343 (1974) (Douglas, J., dissenting) ("The Equal Protection Clause commands elimination of racial barriers, not their creation in order to satisfy our theory as to how society ought to be organized").

22. Cf. *Board of Regents of Univ. of Cal. v. Bakke*, 438 U.S. at 299 (Powell, J., concurring) ("It is the individual who is entitled to judicial protection against classifications based upon racial or ethnic background because such distinctions impinge upon personal rights, rather than the individual only because of his membership in a particular group").

23. See *United Steelworkers of America v. Weber*, 443 U.S. 193, 254 (1979) (Rehnquist, J., dissenting).

24. See *Board of Regents of Univ. of Cal. v. Bakke*, 438 U.S. at 298 (Powell, J., concurring).

25. There were four separate opinions. Chief Justice Burger, joined by Justices White, Stewart, and Rehnquist, wrote the plurality opinion, as to which Justices Blackmun, Stevens, and Powell concurred separately. Justice Brennan dissented, joined by Justice Marshall.

26. 427 U.S. 273 (1976). In *McDonald*, petitioners, two white employees of respondent company, were discharged for cause while a black employee charged with the same offense was not discharged. Petitioners filed suit alleging racial discrimination in violation of Title VII. The district court dismissed petitioners' claims on the ground that Title VII was unavailable to white people. 427 U.S. at 275. The Supreme Court reversed. Ibid., p. 296. Justice Marshall, writing for the Court, stated, "We therefore hold today that Title VII prohibits racial discrimination against white petitioners in this case upon the same standards as would be applicable were they Negroes and Jackson white." Ibid., p. 280.

27. The Court was sharply divided on the preference issue in the 1970s and for most of the 1980s, often speaking through multiple opinions without a clear majority (see *Board of Regents of Univ. of Cal. v. Bakke*; *Fullilove v. Klutznick*; *United Steelworkers of America v. Weber*; *Wygant v. Jackson Bd. of Educ.*, 467 U.S. 267 (1986)) or with an exceedingly narrow (5–4) margin (see *United States v. Paradise*, 480 U.S. 149 (1987); *Local 28, Sheet Metal Workers v. EEOC*, 478 U.S. 421 (1986); *Firefighters Local Union No. 1784 v. Stotts*, 467 U.S. 561 (1984); *Wards Cove Packing Co. v. Antonio*, 490 U.S. 642 (1989).

28. See fn. 21.

29. See fn. 23.

30. 443 U.S. 193 (1979).

31. Ibid., p. 208. The Court did not elaborate on how the persistent racial exclusion was to be proven or on how the tailoring and duration of the remedy must be fashioned in relation to the proof of prior exclusion.

32. 448 U.S. 448 (1980) (plurality).

33. Ibid., p. 478. In upholding a minority set-aside provision enacted by Congress, the Court's plurality—Burger, C. J., joined by Justices White and Powell—found that "Congress had abundant historical basis from which it could conclude that traditional procurement practices, when applied to minority businesses, could perpetuate the fact of past discrimination."

34. Justice Powell suggested in his separate concurrence that "in light of the countervailing constitutional interest... of the First Amendment," 438 U.S. at 313, a university could permissibly exercise its academic freedom to consider race as one factor in promoting a diverse student body. Ibid.,

pp. 311–15. Whatever force such a reading of the Fourteenth Amendment may have to accommodate First Amendment freedoms where the two come into direct conflict, there is no countervailing First Amendment interest implicated in the usual employer-employee relationship. See generally Wm. Bradford Reynolds, "The Justice Department's Enforcement of Title VII," *Labor Law Journal*, 34:259–65 (1963).

35. See, for example, *H. K. Porter Co., Inc. v. Metropolitan Dade County*, 825 F.2d 324 (11th Cir. 1987), vacated and remanded, 489 U.S. 1062 (1989); *Higgins v. City of Vallejo*, 823 F.2d 351 (9th Cir. 1987) (rejecting constitutional and Title VII challenges to award of firefighter-engineer position to third-ranked black candidate over first-ranked white candidate); *Smith v. Hennesy*, 831 F.2d 1068 (11th Cir. 1987), aff'g, 648 F.Supp 1103 (M.D. Fla. 1986) (upholding a one-for-one policy adopted by city's firefighter department over constitutional and Title VII challenges); *Kromnick v. School Dist.*, 939 F.2d 894 (3d Cir. 1984) (upholding teacher assignment program); *South Florida Chapter, Associated General Contractors of America, Inc. v. Metropolitan Dade County*, 723 F.2d 846 (11th Cir.), cert. denied, 469 U.S. 871 (1984) (upholding local set-aside program); *Bratton v. City of Detroit*, 704 F.2d 878 (6th Cir. 1983), cert. denied, 464 U.S. 1040 (1984) (upholding voluntary police quota); *Ohio Contractors Association v. Keip*, 713 F.2d 167 (6th Cir. 1983) (upholding state set-aside); *Schmidt v. Oakland Unified School Dist.*, 662 F.2d 550 (9th Cir.) (upholding local set-aside), vacated on other grounds, 457 U.S. 594 (1982); *Geier v. Alexander*, 593 F.Supp 1263 (M.D. Tenn. 1984), aff'd, 801 F.2d 799 (6th Cir. 1986) (approving special tracking of 75 black sophomores to state professional schools); *M. C. West, Inc. v. Lewis*, 522 F.Supp 338 (M.D. Tenn. 1981) (upholding U.S. Department of Transportation set-aside regulations on the basis of *Fullilove*).

36. Only Justice Scalia has insisted that the Fourteenth Amendment is truly color-blind and tolerates no racial preferences for non-victims of discrimination, even if the stated purpose is remedial. See *City of Richmond v. Croson*, 488 U.S. 469, 520-28 (Scalia, J., concurring separately).

37. A plurality of the Court in *Wygant v. Jackson Bd. of Educ.* rejected outright the proposition that racial preferences could be constitutionally justified or remedially necessary to correct "historical" or "societal" discrimination. 476 U.S. at 274-75. See also ibid., pp. 288–89 (O'Connor, J., concurring). This conclusion was adopted by five justices in *Croson*, 488 U.S. at 496–97 (O'Connor, J., joined by the Chief Justice and Justices White and Kennedy, with Scalia, J., concurring separately).

38. See, for example, *Local 28, Sheet Metal Workers v. EEOC*, 478 U.S. at 449 ("Where an employer or union has engaged in particularly long-standing or

egregious discrimination... requiring recalcitrant employers or unions to hire and to admit qualified minorities roughly in proportion to the number of qualified minorities in the work force may be the only effective way to ensure the full enjoyment of the rights protected by Title VII"); *United States v. Paradise*, 480 U.S. at 171–72 (a promotions quota was justified by a compelling governmental interest in remedying "'long-term, open and pervasive' discrimination, including absolute exclusion of blacks from... upper ranks [of the Alabama State Troopers]"). And see *City of Richmond v. Croson*, 488 U.S. at 509 (It is only "in the extreme case [that] some form of narrowly tailored racial preference might be necessary to break down patterns of deliberate exclusion").

39. See *City of Richmond v. Croson*, 408 U.S. at 497–98; and see *Wygant v. Jackson Bd. of Educ.*, 476 U.S. at 282–84.

40. The irony is that, under the new act, the employer is put in a catch-22 position. If the hiring is done along racial, gender, ethnic, and religious lines—so as to avoid work force disparity in any or all of the designated categories—the employer faces the prospect of a Title VII lawsuit alleging intentional discrimination on account of race, sex, national origin, or religion. Conversely, if the hiring is done without regard to race, gender, or ethnic or religious affiliation—which will invariably produce disparity on one or another basis—the employer similarly faces the prospect of a Title VII lawsuit alleging impermissible disparity.

41. Despite much debate over whether the new act was or was not a quota bill—and assurances from both proponents and opponents of the legislation that quota hiring was not permitted by the language ultimately adopted—the reality is that the Civil Rights Act of 1991 makes suspect a numerical disparity in the work force based on race, gender, national origin, or religion. Pub L. 102-166, sec. 105, 42 U.S.C. § 2000e-2 (k) (1) (A) (1991).

42. The new act shifts the burden of proof to the employer upon a showing by the complainant of a racial—or other—disparity among employee hires attributable to a particular selection practice or practices utilized by the employer. Pub. L. 102-166, sec. 105(a), 42 U.S.C. § 2000-2 (k) (1) (B) (1991).

43. See Pub. L. 102-166, sec. 105(a), 42 U.S.C. § 2000e-2(k) (1) (A) (i) (1991). In order to pass statutory muster, the challenged employment practice must be "job related for the position in question and consistent with business necessity."

44. For example, the term "business necessity" is not defined. Nor does the statute explain the appropriate comparative analysis for determining that a particular statistical imbalance creates a presumption of "disparate impact."

45. See fnn. 36–39 and accompanying text.

46. See fnn. 38–39 and accompanying text.

47. See Pub. L. 102-166, sec. 102, 42 U.S.C. § 1981 A(b) (1991).

48. See Pub. L. 102-166, secs. 108, 112, 42 U.S.C. §§ 2000e-2(n) (1) (A) and (B) (1991), 2000e-5(a) (1991).

49. See Pub. L. 102-166, sec. 112, 42 U.S.C. § 2000e-5(e) (1991).

50. See Pub. L. 102-166, sec. 103, 113, 42 U.S.C. § 1988 (1991).

POSTSCRIPT

Should Affirmative Action Policies Be Continued?

One of the most significant developments of the last few years may not have been a court decision but a court appointment. The selection of Judge Clarence Thomas to the Supreme Court aroused controversy for many reasons, among them Thomas's views on affirmative action, against which he has been an outspoken opponent. Indeed, in his concurring opinion in *Adarand Constructors, Inc. v. Pena*, Justice Thomas maintained that "there is a moral and constitutional equivalence between laws designed to subjugate a race and those that distribute benefits on the basis of race in order to foster some current notion of equality. Government cannot make us equal; it can only recognize, respect, and protect us as equal before the law."

The United States is an increasingly heterogeneous society, a situation that may only exacerbate its racial conflicts. As black intellectual W.E.B. Du Bois once said, the central problem of the twentieth century will be the problem of the "color line." Another observer of American law has suggested that "the modern story of the Supreme Court has centrally been about race." In an era of rapid political, social, and economic change, where there is continuing competition over resources, we can expect to see frequent controversies and claims involving explicitly race-conscious legislation. Yet after *City of Richmond v. J. A. Croson Co.* and *Adarand*, the future of affirmative action is seriously in doubt.

The study of the question of affirmative action calls for an interdisciplinary approach. Beyond the legal and constitutional issues are philosophical problems of morality and justice, economic issues involving employment and the distribution of scarce resources, and sociological and psychological analyses of racism and sexism. Affirmative action programs force us to take an honest look at our own attitudes and at the nature of our society. What are the attitudes and practices of our institutions with respect to race and sex? What would we like such attitudes and practices to be in the future? What means should be employed to move us from the current state of affairs to where we would like to be?

Litigation in the affirmative action area is discussed in Devins, "Affirmative Action After Reagan," 68 *Texas Law Review* 1711 (1989); "Constitutional Scholars' Statement on Affirmative Action After *City of Richmond v. J. A. Croson Co.*," 98 *Yale Law Journal* 155 (1989); Fried, "Affirmative Action After *City of Richmond v. J. A. Croson Co.: A Response to the Scholars' Statement*," 99 *Yale Law Journal* 155 (1989); and Schwartz, "The 1986 and 1987 Affirmative Action Cases: It's All Over but the Shouting," 86 *Michigan Law Review* 524 (1987). One of the most enlightening law review articles defending affirmative action is Wasserstrom, "Racism, Sexism and Preferential Treatment: An Approach to the Topics," 24 *UCLA Law Review*, pp. 581, 622 (1977). A history of the *Bakke* case is found in Dreyfuss and Lawrence, *The Bakke Case: The Politics of Inequality* (Harcourt Brace Jovanovich, 1979). Interesting recent books include Lani Guinier, *The Tyranny of the Majority* (Maxwell McMillan International, 1994); Stephen L. Carter, *Reflections of an Affirmative Action Baby* (Basic Books, 1991); and Michel Rosenfeld, *Affirmative Action and Justice* (Yale University Press, 1991).

In Derrick Bell, *And We Are Not Saved* (Basic Books, 1987) and Girardeau Spann, *Race Against the Court* (New York University Press, 1991), the authors argue that civil rights activists must confront the stark reality of the persistence of racism in American society; that years of struggle in the courts have not really altered the social, political, and economic situation of the significant majority of African Americans; that when the Supreme Court has decided favorably for minorities, such decisions have inevitably benefited whites as well; and (Spann in particular) that minorities would be better off forsaking hope in the Supreme Court's protection of their interests and instead seeking gains through a more robust activity in an explicitly political sphere (i.e., legislation). These claims are given empirical support in Gerald Rosenberg's extraordinary and provocative book *The Hollow Hope: Can Courts Bring About Social Change?* (University of Chicago Press, 1991).

On the Internet, some facts and myths about affirmative action presented by the United States Student Association can be found at http://www.essential.org/ussa/foundati/aamyths.html. For 1995 remarks by President Bill Clinton on affirmative action, see http://gort.ucsd.edu/docs/presafir.html.

ISSUE 12

Are Restrictions on Physician-Assisted Suicide Unconstitutional?

YES: Stephen Reinhardt, from Majority Opinion, *Compassion in Dying v. State of Washington*, U.S. Court of Appeals for the Ninth Circuit (1996)

NO: Robert Beeser, from Dissenting Opinion, *Compassion in Dying v. State of Washington*, U.S. Court of Appeals for the Ninth Circuit (1996)

ISSUE SUMMARY

YES: Judge Stephen Reinhardt argues that forbidding physician-assisted suicide in the cases of competent, terminally ill patients violates the due process clause of the Constitution.

NO: Judge Robert Beeser maintains that although patients have the right to refuse life-sustaining treatment, physician-assisted suicide is not constitutionally protected.

To please no one will I prescribe a deadly drug, nor give advice which may cause death.

—Oath of Hippocrates

One of the most publicized legal-medical cases of the 1970s involved 21-year-old Karen Ann Quinlan. Quinlan was in a coma, her doctors did not believe she would ever come out of the coma, and all believed (erroneously it turned out) that if her respirator were removed she would stop breathing. The question the court focused on was who had authority over the respirator and who should be responsible for deciding what to do with it. The court did not answer the question of whether or not the respirator should be disconnected but left this tormenting problem to the party that prevailed in the case. Soon after the decision, Quinlan's parents authorized the removal of the respirator. Contrary to what had been predicted, this did not result in her death. She survived another nine years before succumbing in 1985.

In 1990 the Supreme Court issued its landmark ruling in *Cruzan v. Missouri Department of Health*, 497 U.S. 261 (1990). Nancy Beth Cruzan had sustained severe and irreversible injuries in an automobile accident; her condition was one commonly characterized as a "persistent vegetative state." She displayed no discernible cognitive functioning and was kept alive through the use of artificial hydration and feeding equipment. Four years after the accident,

Nancy's parents began proceedings in a Missouri state trial court so that they could withdraw all artificial means of life support.

Cruzan was one of an estimated 10,000 persons in the United States in a vegetative state. She had left no explicit directions on whether or not she wanted to continue to be fed and receive treatment if she were ever to be in such a condition. Should her parents have been allowed to make life and death decisions under such circumstances? How clear should an incompetent person's wishes be before the parents are allowed to make a decision? The trial court granted the parents' request to withdraw life support. However, the State of Missouri intervened, claiming an "unqualified governmental interest in preserving the sanctity of human life." Although the state recognized the legal validity of "living wills," in which a person would indicate what he or she would like done if the individual were no longer able to make treatment decisions, it argued that in the absence of a living will, "clear and convincing" evidence of the patient's wishes was required to authorize the removal of life-sustaining devices. Agreeing with the state, the Missouri Supreme Court reversed the trial court order directing the withdrawal of life-support equipment.

In *Cruzan*, the U.S. Supreme Court granted *certiorari* to hear, for the first time, a constitutional question concerning a "right to die." Upholding the constitutionality of Missouri's evidentiary requirements, the decision of the Missouri Supreme Court was affirmed. Chief Justice William H. Rehnquist delivered the opinion of the Court and wrote that while a "right to die" might be exercised by an individual who was able to make his or her own decisions, "clear and convincing" evidence of the individual's wishes were needed before a court could allow parents or someone else to make a decision to stop treatment or care. The Postscript to this issue describes what the consequences of this were for Cruzan and her parents.

The issues raised in the *Cruzan* case illustrate a basic distinction made by the law. The law prohibits active euthanasia, in which death results from some positive act, such as a lethal injection. "Mercy killings" fall into this category and can be prosecuted as acts of homicide. The law is more tolerant of passive euthanasia, in which death results from the failure to act or on the removal of life-saving equipment. This distinction is not always easy to apply, however. The activities of Dr. Jack Kevorkian, for example, have brought to the public attention the role of physicians in assisting individuals who are mentally competent but have physical problems that interfere with their ability to carry out their wishes.

Should physicians who assist in suicides be punished? The number of cases related to this issue will likely increase. The following selections are from the opinions of Judges Stephen Reinhardt and Robert Beeser in *Compassion in Dying v. State of Washington*. This case represents one of the first attempts to analyze whether or not the state should be able to limit physicians who feel that they are only helping their patients. The Supreme Court will consider an appeal on *Compassion in Dying* during the 1996–1997 term.

YES

Stephen Reinhardt

MAJORITY OPINION

COMPASSION IN DYING *v.* STATE OF WASHINGTON

I.

This case raises an extraordinarily important and difficult issue. It compels us to address questions to which there are no easy or simple answers, at law or otherwise. It requires us to confront the most basic of human concerns—the mortality of self and loved ones—and to balance the interest in preserving human life against the desire to die peacefully and with dignity. People of good will can and do passionately disagree about the proper result, perhaps even more intensely than they part ways over the constitutionality of restricting a woman's right to have an abortion. Heated though the debate may be, we must determine whether and how the United States Constitution applies to the controversy before us, a controversy that may touch more people more profoundly than any other issue the courts will face in the foreseeable future.

Today, we are required to decide whether a person who is terminally ill has a constitutionally-protected liberty interest in hastening what might otherwise be a protracted, undignified, and extremely painful death. If such an interest exists, we must next decide whether or not the state of Washington may constitutionally restrict its exercise by banning a form of medical assistance that is frequently requested by terminally ill people who wish to die. We first conclude that there is a constitutionally-protected liberty interest in determining the time and manner of one's own death, an interest that must be weighed against the state's legitimate and countervailing interests, especially those that relate to the preservation of human life. After balancing the competing interests, we conclude by answering the narrow question before us: We hold that insofar as the Washington statute prohibits physicians from prescribing life-ending medication for use by terminally ill, competent adults who wish to hasten their own deaths, it violates the Due Process Clause of the Fourteenth Amendment.

From *Compassion in Dying v. State of Washington,* 96 C.D.O.S. 1507 (1996).

II. PRELIMINARY MATTERS AND HISTORY OF THE CASE

... The plaintiffs do not challenge Washington statute RCW 9A.36.060 in its entirety. Specifically they do not object to the portion of the Washington statute that makes it unlawful for a person knowingly to cause another to commit suicide. Rather, they only challenge the statute's "or aids" provision. They challenge that provision both on its face and as applied to terminally ill, mentally competent adults who wish to hasten their own deaths with the help of medication prescribed by their doctors. The plaintiffs contend that the provision impermissibly prevents the exercise by terminally ill patients of a constitutionally-protected liberty interest in violation of the Due Process Clause of the Fourteenth Amendment, and also that it impermissibly distinguishes between similarly situated terminally ill patients in violation of the Equal Protection Clause....

III. OVERVIEW OF LEGAL ANALYSIS: IS THERE A DUE PROCESS VIOLATION?

In order to answer the question whether the Washington statute violates the Due Process Clause insofar as it prohibits the provision of certain medical assistance to terminally ill, competent adults who wish to hasten their own deaths, we first determine whether there is a liberty interest in choosing the time and manner of one's death—a question sometimes phrased in common parlance as: Is there a right to die? Because we hold that there is, we must then determine whether prohibiting physicians from prescribing life-ending medication for use by terminally ill patients who wish to die violates the patients' due process rights.

The mere recognition of a liberty interest does not mean that a state may not prohibit the exercise of that interest in particular circumstances, nor does it mean that a state may not adopt appropriate regulations governing its exercise. Rather, in cases like the one before us, the courts must apply a balancing test under which we weigh the individual's liberty interests against the relevant state interests in order to determine whether the state's actions are constitutionally permissible....

Defining the Liberty Interest and Other Relevant Terms

... While some people refer to the liberty interest implicated in right-to-die cases as a liberty interest in committing suicide, we do not describe it that way. We use the broader and more accurate terms, "the right to die," "determining the time and manner of one's death," and "hastening one's death" for an important reason. The liberty interest we examine encompasses a whole range of acts that are generally not considered to constitute "suicide." Included within the liberty interest we examine, is for example, the act of refusing or terminating unwanted medical treatment ... a competent adult has a liberty interest in refusing to be connected to a respirator or in being disconnected from one, even if he is terminally ill and cannot live without mechanical assistance. The law does not classify the death of a patient that results from the granting of his wish to decline or discontinue treatment as "suicide." Nor does the law label the acts of those who help the patient carry out that wish, whether by physically disconnecting the respirator or by removing an intravenous tube, as assistance in suicide. Accordingly, we believe that the broader terms—"the right to die," "controlling the time and manner of one's death," and "hastening one's death"—more accurately describe the liberty interest at issue here....

Like the Court in *Roe [v. Wade]*, we begin with ancient attitudes. In Greek and Roman times, far from being universally prohibited, suicide was often considered commendable in literature, mythology, and practice....

While Socrates counseled his disciples against committing suicide, he willingly drank the hemlock as he was condemned to do, and his example inspired others to end their lives. Plato, Socrates' most distinguished student, believed suicide was often justifiable.

He suggested that if life itself became immoderate, then suicide became a rational, justifiable act. Painful disease, or intolerable constraint were sufficient reasons to depart. And this when religious superstitions faded was philosophic justification enough.

Many contemporaries of Plato were even more inclined to find suicide a legitimate and acceptable act. In *Roe*, while surveying the attitudes of the Greeks toward abortion, the Court stated that "only the Pythagorean school of philosophers frowned on the related act of suicide," 410 U.S. at 131; it then noted that the Pythagorean school represented a distinctly minority view. *Id.*

The Stoics glorified suicide as an act of pure rational will. Cato, who killed himself to avoid dishonor when Ceasar crushed his military aspirations, was the most celebrated of the many suicides among the Stoics. Montaigne wrote of Cato: "This was a man chosen by nature to show the heights which can be attained by human steadfastness

and constancy.... Such courage is above philosophy."

Like the Greeks, the Romans often considered suicide to be acceptable or even laudable.

To live nobly also meant to die nobly and at the right time. Everything depended on a dominant will and a rational choice....

Suicide was a crime under the English common law, at least in limited circumstances, probably as early as the thirteenth century. Bracton, incorporating Roman Law as set forth in Justinian's Digest, declared that if someone commits suicide to avoid conviction of a felony, his property escheats to his lords. Bracton said "[i]t ought to be otherwise if he kills himself through madness or unwillingness to endure suffering." Despite his general fidelity to Roman law, Bracton did introduce a key innovation: "[I]f a man slays himself in weariness of life or because he is unwilling to endure further bodily pain... he may have a successor, but his movable goods [personal property] are confiscated. He does not lose his inheritance [real property], only his movable goods." Bracton's innovation was incorporated into English common law, which has thus treated suicides resulting from the inability to "endure further bodily pain" with compassion and understanding ever since a common law scheme was firmly established....

English attitudes toward suicide, including the tradition of ignominious burial, carried over to America where they subsequently underwent a transformation. By 1798, six of the 13 original colonies had abolished all penalties for suicide either by statute or state constitution. There is no evidence that any court ever imposed a punishment for suicide or attempted suicide under common law in post-revolutionary America. By the time the Fourteenth Amendment was adopted in 1868, suicide was generally not punishable, and in only nine of the 37 states is it clear that there were statutes prohibiting assisting suicide.

The majority of states have not criminalized suicide or attempted suicide since the turn of the century. The New Jersey Supreme Court declared in 1901 that since suicide was not punishable it should not be considered a crime. "[A]ll will admit that in some cases it is ethically defensible," the court said, as when a woman kills herself to escape being raped or "when a man curtails weeks or months of agony of an incurable disease." *Campbell v. Supreme Conclave Improved Order Heptasophs,* 66 N.J.L. 274, 49 A. 550, 553 (1901). Today, no state has a statute prohibiting suicide or attempted suicide; nor has any state had such a statute for at least 10 years. A majority of states do, however, still have laws on the books against assisting suicide.

Current Societal Attitudes

Clearly the absence of a criminal sanction alone does not show societal approbation of a practice. Nor is there any evidence that Americans approve of suicide in general. In recent years, however, there has been increasingly widespread support for allowing the terminally ill to hasten their deaths and avoid painful, undignified, and inhumane endings to their lives. Most Americans simply do not appear to view such acts as constituting suicide, and there is much support in reason for that conclusion.

Polls have repeatedly shown that a large majority of Americans—sometimes nearing 90%—fully endorse recent legal changes granting terminally ill patients, and sometimes their families, the prerog-

ative to accelerate their death by refusing or terminating treatment. Other polls indicate that a majority of Americans favor doctor-assisted suicide for the terminally ill. In April, 1990, the Roper Report found that 64% of Americans believed that the terminally ill should have the right to request and receive physician aid-in-dying. Another national poll, conducted in October 1991, shows that "nearly two out of three Americans favor doctor-assisted suicide and euthanasia for terminally ill patients who request it." A 1994 Harris poll found 73% of Americans favor legalizing physician-assisted suicide. Three states have held referenda on proposals to allow physicians to help terminally ill, competent adults commit suicide with somewhat mixed results. In Oregon, voters approved the carefully-crafted referendum by a margin of 51 to 49 percent in November of 1994. In Washington and California where the measures contained far fewer practical safeguards, they narrowly failed to pass, each drawing 46 percent of the's suicide. Accounts of doctors who have helped their patients end their lives have appeared both in professional journals and in the daily press. . . .

Liberty Interest Under Casey

In *[Planned Parenthood v.] Casey,* the Court surveyed its prior decisions affording "constitutional protection to personal decisions relating to marriage, procreation, contraception, family relationships, child rearing, and education," *id.* at 2807 and then said:

> These matters, involving the most intimate and personal choices a person may make in a lifetime, choices central to personal dignity and autonomy, are central to the liberty protected by the Fourteenth Amendment. At the heart of liberty is the right to define one's own concept of exis-

tence, of meaning, of the universe, and of the mystery of human life. Beliefs about these matters could not define the attributes of personhood were they formed under compulsion of the State. The district judge in this case found the Court's reasoning in *Casey* "highly instructive" and "almost prescriptive" for determining "what liberty interest may inhere in a terminally ill person's choice to commit suicide." Compassion In Dying, 850 F. Supp. at 1459. We agree.

Like the decision of whether or not to have an abortion, the decision how and when to die is one of "the most intimate and personal choices a person may make in a lifetime," a choice "central to personal dignity and autonomy." A competent terminally ill adult, having lived nearly the full measure of his life, has a strong liberty interest in choosing a dignified and humane death rather than being reduced at the end of his existence to a childlike state of helplessness, diapered, sedated, incontinent. How a person dies not only determines the nature of the final period of his existence, but in many cases, the enduring memories held by those who love him.

Prohibiting a terminally ill patient from hastening his death may have an even more profound impact on that person's life than forcing a woman to carry a pregnancy to term. The case of an AIDS patient treated by Dr. Peter Shalit, one of the physician-plaintiffs in this case, provides a compelling illustration. In his declaration, Dr. Shalit described his patient's death this way:

One patient of mine, whom I will call Smith, a fictitious name, lingered in the hospital for weeks, his lower body so swollen from oozing Kaposi's lesions that he could not walk, his genitals so swollen that he required a catheter to drain his bladder, his fingers gangrenous from clotted arteries. Patient Smith's friends stopped visiting him because it gave them nightmares. Patient Smith's agonies could not be relieved by medication or by the excellent nursing care he received. Patient Smith begged for assistance in hastening his death. As his treating doctor, it was my professional opinion that patient Smith was mentally competent to make a choice with respect to shortening his period of suffering before inevitable death. I felt that I should accommodate his request. However, because of the statute, I was unable to assist him and he died after having been tortured for weeks by the end-phase of his disease.

For such patients, wracked by pain and deprived of all pleasure, a state-enforced prohibition on hastening their deaths condemns them to unrelieved misery or torture. Surely, a person's decision whether to endure or avoid such an existence constitutes one of the most, if not the most, "intimate and personal choices a person may make in a lifetime," a choice that is "central to personal dignity and autonomy." *Casey*, 112 S.Ct. at 2807....

Cruzan stands for the proposition that there is a due process liberty interest in rejecting unwanted medical treatment, including the provision of food and water by artificial means. Moreover, the Court majority clearly recognized that granting the request to remove the tubes through which Cruzan received artificial nutrition and hydration would lead inexorably to her death. *Cruzan*, 497 U.S. at 267–68, 283. Accordingly, we conclude that *Cruzan*, by recognizing a liberty interest that includes the refusal of artificial provision of life-sustaining food and water, necessarily recognizes a liberty interest in hastening one's own death.

Summary

Casey and *Cruzan* provide persuasive evidence that the Constitution encompasses a due process liberty interest in controlling the time and manner of one's death —that there is, in short, a constitutionally recognized "right to die." Our conclusion is strongly influenced by, but not limited to, the plight of mentally competent, terminally ill adults. We are influenced as well by the plight of others, such as those whose existence is reduced to a vegetative state or a permanent and irreversible state of unconsciousness.

Our conclusion that there is a liberty interest in determining the time and manner of one's death does not mean that there is a concomitant right to exercise that interest in all circumstances or to do so free from state regulation. To the contrary, we explicitly recognize that some prohibitory and regulatory state action is fully consistent with constitutional principles.

In short, finding a liberty interest constitutes a critical first step toward answering the question before us. The determination that must now be made is whether the state's attempt to curtail the exercise of that interest is constitutionally justified.

V. RELEVANT FACTORS AND INTERESTS

To determine whether a state action that impairs a liberty interest violates an individual's substantive due process rights we must identify the factors relevant to the case at hand, assess the state's interests and the individual's liberty interest in light of those factors, and then weigh and balance the competing interests. The relevant factors generally include: 1) the importance of the various state interests, both in general and in the factual context of the case; 2) the manner in which those interests are furthered by the state law or regulation; 3) the importance of the liberty interest, both in itself and in the context in which it is being exercised; 4) the extent to which that interest is burdened by the challenged state action; and, 5) the consequences of upholding or overturning the statute or regulation. . . .

B. The Means by Which the State Furthers Its Interests

In applying the balancing test, we must take into account not only the strength of the state's interests but also the means by which the state has chosen to further those interests.

1. Prohibition—A Total Ban for the Terminally Ill

Washington's statute prohibiting assisted suicide has a drastic impact on the terminally ill. By prohibiting physician assistance, it bars what for many terminally ill patients is the only palatable, and only practical, way to end their lives. Physically frail, confined to wheelchairs or beds, many terminally ill patients do not have the means or ability to kill themselves in the multitude of ways that healthy individuals can. Often, for example, they cannot even secure the medication or devices they would need to carry out their wishes.

Some terminally ill patients stockpile prescription medicine, which they can use to end their lives when they decide the time is right. The successful use of the stockpile technique generally depends, however, on the assistance of a physician, whether tacit or unknowing (although it is possible to end one's life with over-the-counter medication). Even if the terminally ill patients are able to accumulate sufficient drugs, given the pain killers and other medication they are taking, most of them would lack the knowledge to determine what dose of any given drug or drugs they must take, or in what combination. Miscalculation can be tragic. It can lead to an even more painful and lingering death. Alternatively, if the medication reduces respiration enough to restrict the flow of oxygen to the brain but not enough to cause death, it can result in the patient's falling into a comatose or vegetative state.

Thus for many terminally ill patients, the Washington statute is effectively a prohibition. While technically it only prohibits one means of exercising a liberty interest, practically it prohibits the exercise of that interest as effectively as prohibiting doctors from performing abortions prevented women from having abortions in the days before *Roe*.

2. Regulation—A Permissible Means of Promoting State Interests

State laws or regulations governing physician-assisted suicide are both necessary and desirable to ensure against errors and abuse, and to protect legitimate state interests. Any of several model statutes might serve as an example of how these legitimate and important concerns can be addressed effectively.

By adopting appropriate, reasonable, and properly drawn safeguards Washington could ensure that people who choose to have their doctors prescribe lethal doses of medication are truly competent and meet all of the requisite standards. Without endorsing the constitutionality of any particular procedural safeguards, we note that the state might,

for example, require: witnesses to ensure voluntariness; reasonable, though short, waiting periods to prevent rash decisions; second medical opinions to confirm a patient's terminal status and also to confirm that the patient has been receiving proper treatment, including adequate comfort care; psychological examinations to ensure that the patient is not suffering from momentary or treatable depression; reporting procedures that will aid in the avoidance of abuse. Alternatively, such safeguards could be adopted by interested medical associations and other organizations involved in the provision of health care, so long as they meet the state's needs and concerns....

E. The Consequences of Upholding or Overturning the Statutory Provision

In various earlier sections of this opinion, we have discussed most of the consequences of upholding or overturning the Washington statutory provision at issue, because in this case those consequences are best considered as part of the discussion of the specific factors or interests. The one remaining consequence of significance is easy to identify: Whatever the outcome here, a host of painful and agonizing issues involving the right to die will continue to confront the courts. More important, these problems will continue to plague growing numbers of Americans of advanced age as well as their families, dependents, and loved ones. The issue is truly one which deserves the most thorough, careful, and objective attention from all segments of society.

VI. APPLICATION OF THE BALANCING TEST AND HOLDING

Weighing and then balancing a constitutionally-protected interest against the state's countervailing interests, while bearing in mind the various consequences of the decision, is quintessentially a judicial role. Despite all of the efforts of generations of courts to categorize and objectify, to create multi-part tests and identify weights to be attached to the various factors, in the end balancing entails the exercise of judicial judgment rather than the application of scientific or mathematical formulae. No legislative body can perform the task for us. Nor can any computer. In the end, mindful of our constitutional obligations, including the limitations imposed on us by that document, we must rely on our judgment, guided by the facts and the law as we perceive them.

As we have explained, in this case neither the liberty interest in choosing the time and manner of death nor the state's countervailing interests are static. The magnitude of each depends on objective circumstances and generally varies inversely with the other. The liberty interest in hastening death is at its strongest when the state's interest in protecting life and preventing suicide is at its weakest, and vice-versa.

The liberty interest at issue here is an important one and, in the case of the terminally ill, is at its peak. Conversely, the state interests, while equally important in the abstract, are for the most part at a low point here. We recognize that in the case of life and death decisions the state has a particularly strong interest in avoiding undue influence and other forms of abuse. Here, that concern is ameliorated in large measure because of the mandatory involvement in the decision-making process of physicians, who have a strong bias in favor of preserving life, and because the process itself can be carefully regulated and rigorous safeguards

adopted. Under these circumstances, we believe that the possibility of abuse, even when considered along with the other state interests, does not outweigh the liberty interest at issue.

The state has chosen to pursue its interests by means of what for terminally ill patients is effectively a total prohibition, even though its most important interests could be adequately served by a far less burdensome measure. The consequences of rejecting the as-applied challenge would be disastrous for the terminally ill, while the adverse consequences for the state would be of a far lesser order. This, too, weighs in favor of upholding the liberty interest.

We consider the state's interests in preventing assisted suicide as being different only in degree and not in kind from its interests in prohibiting a number of other medical practices that lead directly to a terminally ill patient's death. Moreover, we do not consider those interests to be significantly greater in the case of assisted suicide than they are in the case of those other medical practices, if indeed they are greater at all. However, even if the difference were one of kind and not degree, our result would be no different. For no matter how much weight we could legitimately afford the state's interest in preventing suicide, that weight, when combined with the weight we give all the other state's interests, is insufficient to outweigh the terminally ill individual's interest in deciding whether to end his agony and suffering by hastening the time of his death with medication prescribed by his physician. The individual's interest in making that vital decision is compelling indeed, for no decision is more painful, delicate, personal, important, or final than the decision how and when one's life shall end. If broad general state policies can be used to deprive a terminally ill individual of the right to make that choice, it is hard to envision where the exercise of arbitrary and intrusive power by the state can be halted. In this case, the state has wide power to regulate, but it may not ban the exercise of the liberty interest, and that is the practical effect of the program before us. Accordingly, after examining one final legal authority, we hold that the "or aids" provision of Washington statute RCW 9A.36.06 is unconstitutional as applied to terminally ill competent adults who wish to hasten their deaths with medication prescribed by their physicians. . . .

VII. CONCLUSION

We hold that a liberty interest exists in the choice of how and when one dies, and that the provision of the Washington statute banning assisted suicide, as applied to competent, terminally ill adults who wish to hasten their deaths by obtaining medication prescribed by their doctors, violates the Due Process Clause. We recognize that this decision is a most difficult and controversial one, and that it leaves unresolved a large number of equally troublesome issues that will require resolution in the years ahead. We also recognize that other able and dedicated jurists, construing the Constitution as they believe it must be construed, may disagree not only with the result we reach but with our method of constitutional analysis. Given the nature of the judicial process and the complexity of the task of determining the rights and interests comprehended by the Constitution, good faith disagreements within the judiciary should not surprise or disturb anyone who follows the development of the law. For these reasons, we express our hope that whatever debate may accompany the future exploration of the issues we have touched on today will be conducted in an objective, rational, and constructive manner that will increase, not diminish, respect for the Constitution.

There is one final point we must emphasize. Some argue strongly that decisions regarding matters affecting life or death should not be made by the courts. Essentially, we agree with that proposition. In this case, by permitting the individual to exercise the right to choose we are following the constitutional mandate to take such decisions out of the hands of the government, both state and federal, and to put them where they rightly belong, in the hands of the people. We are allowing individuals to make the decisions that so profoundly affect their very existence—and precluding the state from intruding excessively into that critical realm. The Constitution and the courts stand as a bulwark between individual freedom and arbitrary and intrusive governmental power. Under our constitutional system, neither the state nor the majority of the people in a state can impose its will upon the individual in a matter so highly "central to personal dignity and autonomy," *Casey*, 112 S.Ct. at 2807. Those who believe strongly that death must come without physician assistance are free to follow that creed, be they doctors or patients. They are not free, however, to force their views, their religious convictions, or their philosophies on all the other members of a democratic society, and to compel those whose values differ with theirs to die painful, protracted, and agonizing deaths.

Affirmed.

NO

Robert Beeser

DISSENTING OPINION OF
ROBERT BEESER

I

It is imperative that I make clear what I mean by physician-assisted suicide. The process should be distinguished definitionally from both euthanasia and the withdrawal or refusal of life-sustaining treatment.

Euthanasia occurs when the physician actually administers the agent which causes death. An example is when a physician injects the patient with a poisonous substance. A gray area between euthanasia and bona fide treatment arises when, for example, a physician administers ever-increasing doses of palliative pain-killing medication, and those doses eventually reach toxic levels.

Life-sustaining treatment is defined in [*Compassion in Dying v. State of*] *Washington* as "any medical means that uses mechanical or other artificial means, including artificially provided nutrition and hydration, to sustain, restore, or replace a vital function, which, when applied to a qualified patient, would serve only to prolong the process of dying. [It does not include treatment] deemed necessary solely to alleviate pain." RCW 70.122.020(5). A patient has a nonfundamental constitutionally protected liberty-based right to refuse or withdraw life-sustaining treatment, including respirators and artificial nutrition and hydration. See *Cruzan v. Director, Missouri Dep't of Health*, 497 U.S. 261 (1990). In *Washington*, that right is also explicitly guaranteed by the Natural Death Act, RCW 70.122.010 *et seq*.

Physician-assisted suicide encompasses the situation where a physician makes available to a patient the means for that patient intentionally to cause his or her own death. For example, physician-assisted suicide would be the proper description of a process in which a physician, with the intent to assist a patient to commit suicide, prescribes medication which, when taken by the patient in sufficient potency and quantity, is lethal. The prescription may be part of a bona fide treatment, or it may be specifically prescribed as a means by which the patient commits suicide.

In all three sorts of cases, euthanasia, withdrawal of life-sustaining treatment, and physician-assisted suicide, there is a decision that other factors

From *Compassion in Dying v. State of Washington,* 96 C.D.O.S. 1507 (1996).

outweigh the patient's continuing to live. Plaintiffs ask us to blur the line between withdrawal of life-sustaining treatment and physician-assisted suicide. At the same time, some proponents of physician-assisted suicide would maintain a conceptual distinction between physician-assisted suicide and euthanasia. Associating physician-assisted suicide with a relatively accepted procedure and dissociating it from an unpalatable one are rhetorically powerful devices, but run counter to U.S. Supreme Court precedent, Washington State statutory law, medical ethics guidelines of the American Medical Association and the American College of Physicians, and legal reasoning.

The proper place to draw the line is between withdrawing life-sustaining treatment (which is based on the right to be free from unwanted intrusion) and physician-assisted suicide and euthanasia (which implicate the assistance of others in controlling the timing and manner of death). The former is constitutionally protected (under *Cruzan*); the latter are not....

I would hold that mentally competent, terminally ill adults do not have a fundamental right to commit physician-assisted suicide. The Supreme Court has repeatedly indicated an unwillingness to expand the list of rights deemed fundamental. Physician-assisted suicide is not currently on that list. To be fundamental, a liberty interest must be central to personal autonomy or deeply rooted in history.... The second test for determining the existence of fundamental rights, whether the interest is rooted in the nation's history, similarly militates against a fundamental right to physician-assisted suicide.

I would hold that mentally competent, terminally ill adults do have an autonomy-based, nonfundamental liberty interest in committing physician-assisted suicide.

A. No New Fundamental Rights

While the list of fundamental rights has not been definitively closed to expansion, the Court has indicated an unwillingness to find new penumbral, privacy-type fundamental rights. In *Reno v. Flores*, 113 S.Ct. 1439 (1993), the Court refuses to expand the list of fundamental rights to include a right of juveniles to be released into a noncustodial setting. *Reno* states:

> We are unaware... that any court— aside from the courts below—has ever held that [the asserted fundamental right exists]. The mere novelty of such a claim is reason enough to doubt that "substantive due process" sustains it; the alleged right certainly cannot be considered "'so rooted in the traditions and conscience of our people as to be ranked as fundamental.'" *Salerno, supra,* 481 U.S., at 751, 107 S.Ct., at 2103 (quoting *Snyder v. Massachusetts*, 291 U.S. 97, 105, 54 S.Ct. 330, 332, 78 L.Ed. 674 (1934)).

113 S.Ct. at 1447. See also *Bowers v. Hardwick*, 478 U.S. 186, 190 (1986) ("[T]here should be... great resistance to expand the substantive reach of [the due process clauses of the Fifth and Fourteenth Amendments], particularly if it requires redefining the category of rights deemed fundamental.")...

VII

Whatever test is ultimately used to evaluate the constitutionality of RCW 9A.36.060, the plaintiffs' liberty interest must be compared against the state interests underlying the statute.

The State asserts three interests: (1) preventing suicide, (2) protecting vulnerable individuals from abuse or undue influence and (3) preserving and protecting the lives of its people. It asserts that the interest in preventing suicide applies equally to all the state's citizens; the State does not evaluate the quality of life among its citizenry, and preserve and protect only those whose lives are deemed "worth living."

Washington courts recognize four state interests common to end-of-life cases: (1) the preservation of life, (2) the protection of the interests of innocent third parties, (3) the prevention of suicide, and (4) the maintenance of the ethical integrity of the medical profession. *In re Guardianship of Grant*, 747 P.2d 445, 451 (Wash. 1987); *In re Colyer*, 660 P.2d 738, 743 (Wash. 1983). The Supreme Court has also recognized all four of these state interests. *Cruzan*, 497 U.S. at 271.

The four governmental interests recognized by Washington courts and endorsed by the Supreme Court are all very strong, and apply with undiminished vigor to justify RCW 9A.36.060's prohibition of physician-assisted suicide for mentally competent, terminally ill adults. Any one of these interests would be sufficient to support this application of the statute under a rational relationship test. Were it necessary for me to do so, I would even be inclined to hold that the cumulative force of all four governmental interests is sufficient to enable this application of the statute to withstand strict scrutiny....

In 1991, the Dutch Government released a report on the practice of euthanasia and physician-assisted suicide in The Netherlands. *Commissie Onderzoek Medische Praktijk Inzake Euthanasie, Medische Beslissingen Rond Het Levenseinde* (1991)

(the *Remmelink Report*). According to the Remmelink Report, 2.1% of all deaths in The Netherlands are due to physician-assisted suicide or euthanasia. Another 7% are due to the alleviation of pain or symptoms where the physician had the explicit (total or partial) purpose of shortening life. In 1990: 2300 people were euthanized upon request, 400 died as a result of physician-assisted suicide, 1000 died from involuntary euthanasia (patients were killed without their knowledge or consent), and 8100 died as a result of doctors deliberately giving them overdoses of pain medication (again, 61% of this category were killed without their knowledge or consent).

Critics of this data would respond that the Dutch experiment has focused mainly on euthanasia, rather than physician-assisted suicide. But even proponents of assisted suicide have begun to abandon the distinction between physician-assisted suicide and euthanasia:

> To confine legalized physician-assisted death to assisted suicide unfairly discriminates against patients with unbelievable suffering who resolve to end their lives but are physically unable to do so. The method chosen is less important than the careful assessment that precedes assisted death.

Franklin G. Miller et al., "Sounding Board: Regulating Physician-Assisted Death," 331 *New England J. Med.* 119, 120 (1994). Likewise, the AMA Code of Ethics section 2.211 uses identical language to condemn both euthanasia and physician-assisted suicide.

The poor, the elderly, the disabled and minorities are all at risk from undue pressure to commit physician-assisted suicide, either through direct pressure or through inadequate treatment of their pain and suffering. They cannot be adequately protected by procedural safeguards, if the Dutch experience is any indication. The only way to achieve adequate protection for these groups is to maintain a bright-line rule against physician-assisted suicide.

But it is not only people at the margins who are imperilled by the threat of a constitutional right to physician-assisted suicide. Such a right could disrupt the established legal order of wills, trusts, life insurance, annuities, pensions, and other estate planning tools employed by many Americans. Many life insurance policies have suicide clauses in them, which negate the insurer's liability if the insured commits suicide. Many states have statutes like *Washington's Slayer's Act*, which preclude participants in the unlawful killing of another person from acquiring property or receiving benefits as the result of the death. A sampling of cases demonstrates that these and related concerns are real. In *People v. Matlock*, 336 P.2d 505 (Cal. (In Bank) 1959) and *Godsparek v. State*, 1993 WL 213854 (Ala. Cr. App. 1993), the defendants were tried for killing people who had hired or requested to be killed because they wanted to die, but did not want to void their life insurance by committing suicide. In *Keddie v. Delaware Violent Crimes Compensation Board*, 1991 WL 215655 (Del Super. 1991), Ms. Keddie was denied compensation under the Compensation for Innocent Victims of Crime Act for her husband's suicide. He committed suicide at the encouragement of Anthony Sabbato, who was convicted of promoting a suicide. The court reasoned that Ms. Keddie's husband was not an innocent victim of crime, insofar as he contributed to his own death. In *Holmes v. Morgan*, 899 P.2d 738 (Or. App. 1995), a distraught young man changed the named beneficiary on his life insurance policy from his parents to a friend, who may have assisted him in a suicide attempt. He later committed suicide without assistance. The Oregon Court of Appeals held that the friend could receive the policy proceeds. Finally, in *Wilmington Trust Co. v. Clark*, 424 A.2d 744 (Md. 1981), the Maryland Supreme Court considered whether a woman could bring a contract or tort action against her former husband's estate, on the ground that his suicide deprived her of alimony.

The interests of many innocent third parties are implicated by a putative right to physician-assisted suicide. Most obviously, the poor, minorities and the disabled are at risk of suffering undue indifference or pressure to commit physician-assisted suicide. Less obviously, a right to physician-assisted suicide could severely disrupt the economic interests of the relatives, partners and associates of those who commit physician-assisted suicide. . . .

X

The issue of whether mentally competent, terminally ill adults have a constitutionally protected right to commit physician-assisted suicide is one of the most difficult, divisive and heart-wrenching issues facing the courts today. The correlative issue of whether terminally ill loved ones ought to be allowed to commit assisted suicide is likewise one of the most difficult, divisive and heart-wrenching issues facing American society. The former is a constitutional issue for the courts; the latter is a moral question for society as a whole.

The two issues are not the same. The latter requires us—all of us, not just judges—to engage in a soul-searching dialogue about our collective morals. Given the tremendous advances in twentieth-century medical technology and public health, it is now possible to live much longer than at any time in recorded history. We have controlled most of the swift and merciful diseases that caused most deaths in the past. In their place are a host of diseases that cause a slow deterioration of the human condition: cancer, Alzheimer's disease, and AIDS are but a few. This change has forced us to step back and reexamine the historic presumption that all human lives are equally and intrinsically valuable. Viewed most charitably, this reexamination may be interpreted as our struggle with the question whether we as a society are willing to excuse the terminally ill for deciding that their lives are no longer worth living. Viewed less charitably, the reexamination may be interpreted as a mere rationalization for housecleaning, cost-cutting and burden-shifting—a way to get rid of those whose lives we deem worthless. Whether the charitable or uncharitable characterization ultimately prevails is a question that must be resolved by the people through deliberative decision making in the voting booth, as in Washington in 1991, California in 1992 and Oregon in 1994, or in the legislatures, as recently undertaken in Michigan and New York. This issue we, the courts, need not—and should not—decide.

Instead, we should restrict our decision to the former issue: whether mentally competent, terminally ill adults have a constitutionally protected liberty interest in committing physician-assisted suicide. This is the first federal appellate case in our nation's history to address the issue of physician-assisted suicide. To declare a constitutional right to physician-assisted suicide would be to impose upon the nation a repeal of local laws. Such a declaration would also usurp states' rights to regulate and further the practice of medicine, insofar as a right to physician-assisted suicide flies in the face of well-established state laws governing the medical profession. Finally, the rationales under which we are asked to create this right fail adequately to distinguish physician-assisted suicide as a unique category. If physician-assisted suicide for mentally competent, terminally ill adults is made a constitutional right, voluntary euthanasia for weaker patients, unable to self-terminate, will soon follow. After voluntary euthanasia, it is but a short step to a "substituted judgment" or "best interests" analysis for terminally ill patients who have not yet expressed their constitutionally sanctioned desire to be dispatched from this world. This is the sure and inevitable path, as the Dutch experience has amply demonstrated. It is not a path I would start down....

I dissent.

POSTSCRIPT

Are Restrictions on Physician-Assisted Suicide Unconstitutional?

Nancy Cruzan died six months after the U.S. Supreme Court's ruling on her right to die. Two months after the Court's decision, the Cruzans asked for a court hearing to present new evidence from three of their daughter's co-workers. At the hearing, the co-workers testified that they recalled her saying she would never want to live "like a vegetable." At the same hearing, Cruzan's doctor called her existence a "living hell" and recommended removal of the tube. Her court-appointed guardian concurred. The judge then ruled that there was clear evidence of Cruzan's wishes and gave permission for the feeding tube to be removed. She died on December 26, 1990.

The fundamental concern of courts in right-to-die cases—indeed in most civil liberties cases—is the fear of what will happen in the next case. In other words, a judge may avoid doing what seems reasonable in one case if his ruling could be used to reach a less desirable result in a future case with slightly different facts. Lawyers refer to this as the "slippery slope." If euthanasia is justified in a case where the patient is conscious and competent, it may be allowed in a later case where, perhaps due to the pain the patient is in, competency is not perfectly clear.

Underlying the slippery slope argument in these cases is the fear of what might happen if life in some instances is not considered to be sacred. A member of the prosecution staff at the Nuremberg trials of Nazi doctors who participated in the killing of "incurables" and the "useless" traced the origin of Nazi policy to

> a subtle shift in emphasis in the basic attitude of the physicians. It started with the acceptance of the attitude, basic in the euthanasia movement, that there is such a thing as the life not worthy to be lived. This attitude in its early stages concerned itself merely with the severely and chronically sick. Gradually, the sphere of those to be included in this category was enlarged to encompass the socially unproductive, the ideologically unwanted, the racially unwanted and finally all non-Germans. But it is important to realize that the infinitely small wedged-in lever from which this entire trend received its impetus was the attitude toward the unrehabilitatable sick. (Kamisar, "Some Non-Religious Views Against Proposed 'Mercy Killing' Legislation," 42 *Minnesota Law Review* 969, 1958)

Considering the decision in the *Compassion in Dying* case, how do you feel about the slippery slope argument? Does the majority opinion, by allowing assisted suicide, start us down the slippery slope?

One effect of the *Cruzan* opinion was to encourage the use of living wills. More than 40 states and the District of Columbia have statutes permitting living wills, which allow individuals to specify in advance what treatment they would wish to receive. Since less than half of the U.S. population have regular wills, the living will is unlikely to provide a total solution to the problem.

One recent case that reached the same result as *Compassion in Dying v. State of Washington* is *Quill et al. v. Vacco et al.* 80 F.3d 716 (1996). The legal issues involved in assisting suicide are covered in a symposium in the *Ohio Northern Law Review*, p. 559 (vol. 20, 1994). Dr. Jack Kevorkian's case is discussed by his attorney, Geoffrey Fieger, in "The Persecution and Prosecution of Dr. Death and His Mercy Machine," 20 *Ohio Northern Law Review* 659 (1994). Other interesting writings in this area include Note, "Physician-Assisted Suicide and the Right to Die With Assistance," 105 *Harvard Law Review* 2021 (1992); Kamisar, "When Is There a Constitutional 'Right to Die'? When Is There No Constitutional 'Right to Live'?" 25 *Georgia Law Review* 1203 (1991); Robertson, "Assessing Quality of Life: A Response to Professor Kamisar," 25 *Georgia Law Review* 1243 (1991); and A. W. Alschuler, "The Right to Die," 141 *New Law Journal* 1637 (November 29, 1991).

Information on euthanasia, physician-assisted suicide, living wills, the right to die, and mercy killing can be found on the Internet at http://www.euthanasia.com/.

ISSUE 13

Are Laws Restricting Gay Rights Legislation Unconstitutional?

YES: Anthony Kennedy, from Majority Opinion, *Roy Romer et al. v. Richard G. Evans et al.,* U.S. Supreme Court (1996)

NO: Antonin Scalia, from Dissenting Opinion, *Roy Romer et al. v. Richard G. Evans et al.,* U.S. Supreme Court (1996)

ISSUE SUMMARY

YES: Supreme Court justice Anthony Kennedy argues that a Colorado amendment denying certain legal protections for homosexuals violates the equal protection clause of the Constitution.

NO: Supreme Court justice Antonin Scalia asserts that the Colorado amendment denies homosexuals special treatment on the basis of their sexual orientation and that there is no constitutional reason to prohibit such a law.

In *Bowers v. Hardwick,* 478 U.S. 186 (1986), the Supreme Court upheld a Georgia law that made acts of sodomy performed by anyone in any place a crime. The 5–4 decision was one of the most controversial and widely publicized Supreme Court decisions of 1986. The Georgia law had been challenged by Michael Hardwick, a homosexual who had been arrested for acts of sodomy performed in his own home. The Supreme Court refused to find that such acts, even when performed in private places, were protected by the Constitution and ruled that there was no "fundamental right to engage in homosexual sodomy."

Bowers v. Hardwick was a considerable blow to the cause of gay rights. The inability to find protection for gay rights in privacy law or in the Constitution meant that legal protection for gays would require cities and states to pass new ordinances and statutes that barred discrimination in various activities. In the years following the decision, 9 states and more than 100 municipalities passed measures relating to discrimination in housing, employment, education, public accommodations, and health and welfare services.

In Colorado groups opposed to these kinds of laws put a referendum on the ballot in 1992 to prohibit all legislative, executive, and judicial action at any level of state or local government that was designed to protect gays and lesbians. Amendment 2, as the referendum was called, was approved by a 53 percent majority. Soon after, a lawsuit was filed to declare its invalidity and enjoin its enforcement. A state judge in Denver enjoined its enforcement, and the Colorado Supreme Court struck it down as unconstitutional under the U.S. Constitution. The U.S. Supreme Court agreed to hear the case and, in a 6–3 decision, ruled that Amendment 2 violates the equal protection clause of the Constitution because it abridges "the right to participate equally in the political process."

It is normally very difficult to persuade a court that a law or regulation that treats one group differently from another violates the equal protection clause of the Constitution. The court will declare such laws unconstitutional only if "no grounds can be conceived to justify them." In other words, a program that discriminates against a group that is not protected by the civil rights laws would generally be upheld unless the court found it to be irrational. There is, however, an exception. If the court determines that the plaintiff belongs to a "suspect class," a group that has been the target of unusual discrimination, the challenged law is subjected to greater scrutiny. The court, in such cases, will look carefully at the stated objectives of the legislation and judge whether the classification is necessary to meet an important governmental purpose. Thus, any group, such as homosexuals, significantly increases its chance of winning an equal protection case if it can persuade a court that it is a "suspect class."

There is no objective test that can be used to identify "suspect classes." However, the Supreme Court has suggested four factors that such groups should possess and that must be considered in the determination. These are:

1. *Immutability*—Can the trait that characterizes the class be changed?
2. *Stereotypes*—Is the legislation based on long-held and inaccurate perceptions of the group?
3. *History of discrimination*
4. *Politically powerless minority status*

Racial minorities fit this model most clearly, and any laws that make distinctions based on race are subject to heightened scrutiny. Other suspect classes involve gender, ethnic groups, illegitimate children, and the children of aliens. On the other hand, the courts have refused to treat poor persons as a suspect class and, in general, do not seem eager to expand the number of such groups.

In the following selections from the majority and dissenting opinions of *Romer v. Evans*, Justice Anthony Kennedy finds that the equal protection clause is violated by the legislation in question, although he is not willing to declare gays to be a "suspect class." Justice Antonin Scalia argues that denying homosexuals preferential treatment is appropriate.

YES

Anthony Kennedy

MAJORITY OPINION

ROMER v. EVANS

Justice KENNEDY delivered the opinion of the Court.

One century ago, the first Justice Harlan admonished this Court that the Constitution "neither knows nor tolerates classes among citizens." *Plessy v. Ferguson*, 163 U.S. 537, 559, 16 S.Ct. 1138, 1146, 41 L.Ed. 256 (1896) (dissenting opinion). Unheeded then, those words now are understood to state a commitment to the law's neutrality where the rights of persons are at stake. The Equal Protection Clause enforces this principle and today requires us to hold invalid a provision of Colorado's Constitution....

II

The State's principal argument in defense of Amendment 2 is that it puts gays and lesbians in the same position as all other persons. So, the State says, the measure does no more than deny homosexuals special rights. This reading of the amendment's language is implausible. We rely not upon our own interpretation of the amendment but upon the authoritative construction of Colorado's Supreme Court. The state court, deeming it unnecessary to determine the full extent of the amendment's reach, found it invalid even on a modest reading of its implications. The critical discussion of the amendment, set out in Evans I, is as follows: "The immediate objective of Amendment 2 is, at a minimum, to repeal existing statutes, regulations, ordinances, and policies of state and local entities that barred discrimination based on sexual orientation. See Aspen, Colo., Mun.Code sec. 13-98 (1977) (prohibiting discrimination in employment, housing and public accommodations on the basis of sexual orientation); Boulder, Colo., Rev.Code secs. 12-1-2 to -4 (1987) (same); Denver, Colo., Rev. Mun.Code art. IV, secs. 28-91 to -116(1991) (same); Executive Order No. D0035 (December 10, 1990) (prohibiting employment discrimination for 'all state employees, classified and exempt' on the basis of sexual orientation); Colorado Insurance Code, sec. 10-3-1104, 4A C.R.S. (1992 Supp.) (forbidding health insurance providers from determining insurability

From *Roy Romer et al. v. Richard G. Evans et al.*, 116 S. Ct. 1620 (1996).

and premiums based on an applicant's, a beneficiary's, or an insured's sexual orientation); and various provisions prohibiting discrimination based on sexual orientation at state colleges. . . .

"The 'ultimate effect' of Amendment 2 is to prohibit any governmental entity from adopting similar, or more protective statutes, regulations, ordinances, or policies in the future unless the state constitution is first amended to permit such measures." 854 P.2d, at 1284–1285, and n. 26.

Sweeping and comprehensive is the change in legal status effected by this law. So much is evident from the ordinances that the Colorado Supreme Court declared would be void by operation of Amendment 2. Homosexuals, by state decree, are put in a solitary class with respect to transactions and relations in both the private and governmental spheres. The amendment withdraws from homosexuals, but no others, specific legal protection from the injuries caused by discrimination, and it forbids reinstatement of these laws and policies.

The change that Amendment 2 works in the legal status of gays and lesbians in the private sphere is far-reaching, both on its own terms and when considered in light of the structure and operation of modern anti-discrimination laws. That structure is well illustrated by contemporary statutes and ordinances prohibiting discrimination by providers of public accommodations. "At common law, innkeepers, smiths, and others who 'made profession of a public employment,' were prohibited from refusing, without good reason, to serve a customer." *Hurley v. Irish-American Gay, Lesbian and Bisexual Group of Boston, Inc.*, 115 S.Ct. 2338 (1995). The duty was a general one and did not specify protection for particular groups. The common law rules, however, proved insufficient in many instances, and it was settled early that the Fourteenth Amendment did not give Congress a general power to prohibit discrimination in public accommodations, Civil Rights Cases, 109 U.S. 3, 25, 3 S.Ct. 18, 31-32, 27 L.Ed. 835 (1883). In consequence, most States have chosen to counter discrimination by enacting detailed statutory schemes. . . .

Colorado's state and municipal laws typify this emerging tradition of statutory protection and follow a consistent pattern. The laws first enumerate the persons or entities subject to a duty not to discriminate. The list goes well beyond the entities covered by the common law. The Boulder ordinance, for example, has a comprehensive definition of entities deemed places of "public accommodation." They include "any place of business engaged in any sales to the general public and any place that offers services, facilities, privileges, or advantages to the general public or that receives financial support through solicitation of the general public or through governmental subsidy of any kind." Boulder Rev.Code sec. 12-1-1(j) (1987). The Denver ordinance is of similar breadth, applying, for example, to hotels, restaurants, hospitals, dental clinics, theaters, banks, common carriers, travel and insurance agencies, and "shops and stores dealing with goods or services of any kind." Denver Rev. Municipal Code, Art. IV, sec. 28-92.

These statutes and ordinances also depart from the common law by enumerating the groups or persons within their ambit of protection. Enumeration is the essential device used to make the duty not to discriminate concrete and to provide guidance for those who must comply. In following this approach, Colorado's state and local governments have not limited anti-discrimination laws to groups that have so far been given the protection of heightened equal protection scrutiny under our cases. See, e.g., *J.E.B. v. Alabama ex rel. T.B.*, 511 U.S.——, ——, 114 S.Ct. 1419, 1425, 128 L.Ed.2d 89 (1994) (sex); *Lalli v. Lalli*, 439 U.S. 259, 265, 99 S.Ct. 518, 523, 58 L.Ed.2d 503 (1978) (illegitimacy); *McLaughlin v. Florida*, 379 U.S. 184, 191-192, 85 S.Ct. 283, 288-289, 13 L.Ed.2d 222 (1964) (race); *Oyama v. California*, 332 U.S. 633, 68 S.Ct. 269, 92 L.Ed. 249 (1948) (ancestry). Rather, they set forth an extensive catalogue of traits which cannot be the basis for discrimination, including age, military status, marital status, pregnancy, parenthood, custody of a minor child, political affiliation, physical or mental disability of an individual or of his or her associates—and, in recent times, sexual orientation. Aspen Municipal Code sec. 13-98(a)(1) (1977); Boulder Rev.Code secs. 12-1-1 to 12-1-4 (1987); Denver Rev. Municipal Code, Art. IV, secs. 28-92 to 28-119 (1991); Colo. Rev. Stat. secs. 24-34-401 to 24-34-707(1988 and Supp. 1995).

Amendment 2 bars homosexuals from securing protection against the injuries that these public-accommodations laws address. That in itself is a severe consequence, but there is more. Amendment 2, in addition, nullifies specific legal protections for this targeted class in all transactions in housing, sale of real estate, insurance, health and welfare services, private education, and employment. See, e.g., Aspen Municipal Code secs. 13-98(b), (c) (1977); Boulder Rev.Code secs. 12-1-2, 12-1-3 (1987); Denver Rev. Municipal Code, Art. IV secs. 28-93 to 28-95, sec. 28-97 (1991).

Not confined to the private sphere, Amendment 2 also operates to repeal and forbid all laws or policies providing specific protection for gays or lesbians from discrimination by every level of Colorado government. The State Supreme Court cited two examples of protections in the governmental sphere that are now rescinded and may not be reintroduced. The first is Colorado Executive Order D0035 (1990), which forbids employment discrimination against "'all state employees, classified and exempt' on the basis of sexual orientation." 854 P.2d, at 1284. Also repealed, and now forbidden, are "various provisions prohibiting discrimination based on sexual orientation at state colleges." *Id.*, at 1284, 1285. The repeal of these measures and the prohibition against their future reenactment demonstrates that Amendment 2 has the same force and effect in Colorado's governmental sector as it does elsewhere and that it applies to policies as well as ordinary legislation.

Amendment 2's reach may not be limited to specific laws passed for the benefit of gays and lesbians. It is a fair, if not necessary, inference from the broad language of the amendment that it deprives gays and lesbians even of the protection of general laws and policies that prohibit arbitrary discrimination in governmental and private settings. See, e.g., Colo. Rev. Stat. sec. 24-4-106(7) (1988) (agency action subject to judicial review under arbitrary and capricious standard); sec. 18-8-405 (making it a criminal offense for a public servant knowingly, arbitrarily or capriciously to refrain from performing a duty imposed on him by law); sec. 10-3-1104(1)(f) (prohibiting "unfair discrimination" in insurance); 4 Colo.Code of Regulations 801-1, Policy 11-1 (1983) (prohibiting discrimination in state employment on grounds of specified traits or "other non-merit factor"). At some point in the systematic administration of these laws, an official must determine whether homosexuality is an arbitrary and thus forbidden basis for decision. Yet a decision to that effect would itself amount to a policy prohibiting discrimination on the basis of homosexuality, and so would appear to be no more valid under Amendment 2 than the specific prohibitions against discrimination the state court held invalid.

If this consequence follows from Amendment 2, as its broad language suggests, it would compound the constitutional difficulties the law creates. The state court did not decide whether the amendment has this effect, however, and neither need we. In the course of rejecting the argument that Amendment 2 is intended to conserve resources to fight discrimination against suspect classes, the Colorado Supreme Court made the limited observation that the amendment is not intended to affect many anti-discrimination laws protecting non-suspect classes, Romer II, 882 P.2d at 1346, n. 9. In our view that does not resolve the issue. In any event, even if, as we doubt, homosexuals could find some safe harbor in laws of general application, we cannot accept the view that Amendment 2's prohibition on specific legal protections does no more than deprive homosexuals of special rights. To the contrary, the amendment imposes a special disability upon those persons alone. Homosexuals are forbidden the safeguards that others enjoy or may seek without constraint. They can obtain specific protection against discrimination only by enlisting the citizenry of Colorado to amend the state constitution or perhaps, on the State's view, by trying to pass helpful laws of general applicability. This is so no matter how local or discrete the harm,

no matter how public and widespread the injury. We find nothing special in the protections Amendment 2 withholds. These are protections taken for granted by most people either because they already have them or do not need them; these are protections against exclusion from an almost limitless number of transactions and endeavors that constitute ordinary civic life in a free society.

III

The Fourteenth Amendment's promise that no person shall be denied the equal protection of the laws must co-exist with the practical necessity that most legislation classifies for one purpose or another, with resulting disadvantage to various groups or persons. *Personnel Administrator of Mass. v. Feeney*, 442 U.S. 256, 271-272, 99 S.Ct. 2282, 2292, 60 L.Ed.2d 870 (1979); *F.S. Royster Guano Co. v. Virginia*, 253 U.S. 412, 415, 40 S.Ct. 560, 561-562, 64 L.Ed. 989 (1920). We have attempted to reconcile the principle with the reality by stating that, if a law neither burdens a fundamental right nor targets a suspect class, we will uphold the legislative classification so long as it bears a rational relation to some legitimate end....

Amendment 2 fails, indeed defies, even this conventional inquiry. First, the amendment has the peculiar property of imposing a broad and undifferentiated disability on a single named group, an exceptional and, as we shall explain, invalid form of legislation. Second, its sheer breadth is so discontinuous with the reasons offered for it that the amendment seems inexplicable by anything but animus toward the class that it affects; it lacks a rational relationship to legitimate state interests.

Taking the first point, even in the ordinary equal protection case calling for the most deferential of standards, we insist on knowing the relation between the classification adopted and the object to be attained. The search for the link between classification and objective gives substance to the Equal Protection Clause; it provides guidance and discipline for the legislature, which is entitled to know what sorts of laws it can pass; and it marks the limits of our own authority. In the ordinary case, a law will be sustained if it can be said to advance a legitimate government interest, even if the law seems unwise or works to the disadvantage of a particular group, or if the rationale for it seems tenuous. See *New Orleans v. Dukes*, 427 U.S. 297, 96 S.Ct. 2513, 49 L.Ed.2d 511(1976) (tourism benefits justified classification favoring pushcart vendors of certain longevity); *Williamson v. Lee Optical of Okla., Inc.*, 348 U.S. 483, 75 S.Ct. 461, 99 L.Ed. 563 (1955) (assumed health concerns justified law favoring optometrists over opticians); *Railway Express Agency, Inc. v. New York*, 336 U.S. 106, 69 S.Ct. 463, 93 L.Ed. 533 (1949) (potential traffic hazards justified exemption of vehicles advertising the owner's products from general advertising ban); *Kotch v. Board of River Port Pilot Comm'rs for Port of New Orleans*, 330 U.S. 552, 67 S.Ct. 910, 91 L.Ed. 1093 (1947) (licensing scheme that disfavored persons unrelated to current river boat pilots justified by possible efficiency and safety benefits of a closely knit pilotage system). The laws challenged in the cases just cited were narrow enough in scope and grounded in a sufficient factual context for us to ascertain that there existed some relation between the classification and the purpose it served. By requiring that the classification bear a rational relationship to an independent and legitimate legislative end, we ensure that classifications are not drawn for the purpose of disadvantaging the group burdened by the law. See *United States Railroad Retirement Bd. v. Fritz*, 449 U.S. 166, 181, 101 S.Ct. 453, 462, 66 L.Ed.2d 368 (1980) (STEVENS, J., concurring) ("If the adverse impact on the disfavored class is an apparent aim of the legislature, its impartiality would be suspect.").

Amendment 2 confounds this normal process of judicial review. It is at once too narrow and too broad. It identifies persons by a single trait and then denies them protection across the board. The resulting disqualification of a class of persons from the right to seek specific protection from the law is unprecedented in our jurisprudence. The absence of precedent for Amendment 2 is itself instructive; "[d]iscriminations of an unusual character especially suggest careful consideration to determine whether they are obnoxious to the constitutional provision." *Louisville Gas & Elec. Co. v. Coleman*, 277 U.S. 32, 37-38, 48 S.Ct. 423, 425, 72 L.Ed. 770 (1928).

It is not within our constitutional tradition to enact laws of this sort. Central both to the idea of the rule of law and to our own Constitution's guarantee of equal protection is the principle that government and each of its parts remain open on impartial terms to all who seek its assistance. " 'Equal protection of the laws is not achieved through indiscriminate imposition of inequalities.' " *Sweatt v. Painter*, 339 U.S. 629, 635, 70 S.Ct. 848, 850–851, 94 L.Ed. 1114 (1950) (quoting *Shelley v. Kraemer*, 334 U.S. 1, 22, 68 S.Ct. 836, 846, 92 L.Ed. 1161(1948)). Respect for this principle explains why laws singling out a certain class of citizens for disfavored legal status or general hardships are rare. A law declaring that in general it shall be more difficult for one group of citizens than for all others to seek aid from the government is itself a denial of equal protection of the laws in the most literal sense. "The guaranty of 'equal protection of the laws is a pledge of the protection of equal laws.'" *Skinner v. Oklahoma ex rel. Williamson,* 316 U.S. 535, 541, 62 S.Ct. 1110, 1113, 86 L.Ed. 1655 (1942) (quoting *Yick Wo v. Hopkins,* 118 U.S. 356, 369, 6 S.Ct. 1064, 1070, 30 L.Ed. 220 (1886)).

Davis v. Beason, 133 U.S. 333, 10 S.Ct. 299, 33 L.Ed. 637 (1890), not cited by the parties but relied upon by the dissent, is not evidence that Amendment 2 is within our constitutional tradition, and any reliance upon it as authority for sustaining the amendment is misplaced. In *Davis,* the Court approved an Idaho territorial statute denying Mormons, polygamists, and advocates of polygamy the right to vote and to hold office because, as the Court construed the statute, it "simply excludes from the privilege of voting, or of holding any office of honor, trust or profit, those who have been convicted of certain offences, and those who advocate a practical resistance to the laws of the Territory and justify and approve the commission of crimes forbidden by it." *Id.,* at 347, 10 S.Ct., at 302. To the extent *Davis* held that persons advocating a certain practice may be denied the right to vote, it is no longer good law. *Brandenburg v. Ohio,* 395 U.S. 444, 89 S.Ct. 1827, 23 L.Ed.2d 430 (1969) (*per curiam*). To the extent it held that the groups designated in the statute may be deprived of the right to vote because of their status, its ruling could not stand without surviving strict scrutiny, a most doubtful outcome. *Dunn*

v. Blumstein, 405 U.S. 330, 337, 92 S.Ct. 995, 1000, 31 L.Ed.2d 274 (1972); *cf United States v. Brown,* 381 U.S. 437, 85 S.Ct. 1707, 14 L.Ed.2d 484 (1965); *United States v. Robel,* 389 U.S. 258, 88 S.Ct. 419, 19 L.Ed.2d 508 (1967). To the extent *Davis* held that a convicted felon may be denied the right to vote, its holding is not implicated by our decision and is unexceptionable. See *Richardson v. Ramirez,* 418 U.S. 24, 94 S.Ct. 2655, 41 L.Ed.2d 551 (1974).

A second and related point is that laws of the kind now before us raise the inevitable inference that the disadvantage imposed is born of animosity toward the class of persons affected. "[I]f the constitutional conception of 'equal protection of the laws' means anything, it must at the very least mean that a bare . . . desire to harm a politically unpopular group cannot constitute a legitimate governmental interest." *Department of Agriculture v. Moreno,* 413 U. S. 528, 534, 93 S.Ct. 2821, 2826, 37 L.Ed.2d 782 (1973). Even laws enacted for broad and ambitious purposes often can be explained by reference to legitimate public policies which justify the incidental disadvantages they impose on certain persons. Amendment 2, however, in making a general announcement that gays and lesbians shall not have any particular protections from the law, inflicts on them immediate, continuing, and real injuries that outrun and belie any legitimate justifications that may be claimed for it. We conclude that, in addition to the far-reaching deficiencies of Amendment 2 that we have noted, the principles it offends, in another sense, are conventional and venerable; a law must bear a rational relationship to a legitimate governmental purpose, *Kadrmas v. Dickinson Public Schools,* 487 U.S 450, 462, 108 S.Ct. 2481, 2489-2490, 101 L.Ed.2d 399 (1988), and Amendment 2 does not.

The primary rationale the State offers for Amendment 2 is respect for other citizens' freedom of association, and in particular the liberties of landlords or employers who have personal or religious objections to homosexuality. Colorado also cites its interest in conserving resources to fight discrimination against other groups. The breadth of the Amendment is so far removed from these particular justifications that we find it impossible to credit them. We cannot say that Amendment 2 is directed to any identifiable legitimate purpose or discrete objective. It is a status-based enactment divorced from any factual context from which we could discern a relationship to legitimate state interests; it is a classification of persons undertaken for its own sake, something the Equal Protection Clause does not permit. "[C]lass legislation... [is] obnoxious to the prohibitions of the Fourteenth Amendment...." Civil Rights Cases, 109 U.S., at 24, 3 S.Ct., at 30.

We must conclude that Amendment 2 classifies homosexuals not to further a proper legislative end but to make them unequal to everyone else. This Colorado cannot do. A State cannot so deem a class of persons a stranger to its laws. Amendment 2 violates the Equal Protection Clause, and the judgment of the Supreme Court of Colorado is affirmed.

It is so ordered.

NO

Antonin Scalia

DISSENTING OPINION OF ANTONIN SCALIA

Justice SCALIA, with whom THE CHIEF JUSTICE and Justice THOMAS join, dissenting.

The Court has mistaken a Kulturkampf for a fit of spite. The constitutional amendment before us here is not the manifestation of a " 'bare... desire to harm' " homosexuals, but is rather a modest attempt by seemingly tolerant Coloradans to preserve traditional sexual mores against the efforts of a politically powerful minority to revise those mores through use of the laws. That objective, and the means chosen to achieve it, are not only unimpeachable under any constitutional doctrine hitherto pronounced (hence the opinion's heavy reliance upon principles of righteousness rather than judicial holdings); they have been specifically approved by the Congress of the United States and by this Court.

In holding that homosexuality cannot be singled out for disfavorable treatment, the Court contradicts a decision, unchallenged here, pronounced only 10 years ago, see *Bowers v. Hardwick*, 478 U.S. 186, 106 S.Ct. 2841, 92 L.Ed.2d 140 (1986), and places the prestige of this institution behind the proposition that opposition to homosexuality is as reprehensible as racial or religious bias. Whether it is or not is precisely the cultural debate that gave rise to the Colorado constitutional amendment (and to the preferential laws against which the amendment was directed). Since the Constitution of the United States says nothing about this subject, it is left to be resolved by normal democratic means, including the democratic adoption of provisions in state constitutions. This Court has no business imposing upon all Americans the resolution favored by the elite class from which the Members of this institution are selected, pronouncing that "animosity" toward homosexuality is evil. I vigorously dissent.

I

Let me first discuss Part II of the Court's opinion, its longest section, which is devoted to rejecting the State's arguments that Amendment 2 "puts gays

From *Roy Romer et al. v. Richard G. Evans et al.*, 116 S. Ct. 1620 (1996).

and lesbians in the same position as all other persons," and "does no more than deny homosexuals special rights." The Court concludes that this reading of Amendment 2's language is "implausible" under the "authoritative construction" given Amendment 2 by the Supreme Court of Colorado.

In reaching this conclusion, the Court considers it unnecessary to decide the validity of the State's argument that Amendment 2 does not deprive homosexuals of the "protection [afforded by] general laws and policies that prohibit arbitrary discrimination in governmental and private settings." I agree that we need not resolve that dispute, because the Supreme Court of Colorado has resolved it for us. In *Evans v. Romer*, 882 P.2d 1335 (1994), the Colorado court stated: "[I]t is significant to note that Colorado law currently proscribes discrimination against persons who are not suspect classes, including discrimination based on age, sec. 24-34-402(1)(a), 10A C.R.S. (1994 Supp.); marital or family status, sec. 24-34-502(1)(a), 10A C.R.S. (1994 Supp.); veterans' status, sec. 28-3-506, 11B C.R.S. (1989); and for any legal, off-duty conduct such as smoking tobacco, sec. 24-34-402.5, 10A C.R.S. (1994 Supp.). Of course Amendment 2 is not intended to have any effect on this legislation, but seeks only to prevent the adoption of antidiscrimination laws intended to protect gays, lesbians, and bisexuals." *Id.*, at 1346, n. 9. The Court utterly fails to distinguish this portion of the Colorado court's opinion. Colorado Rev. Stat. sec. 24-34-402.5 (Supp. 1995), which this passage authoritatively declares not to be affected by Amendment 2, was respondents' primary example of a generally applicable law whose protections would be unavailable to homosexuals under Amendment

2. See Brief for Respondents Evans et al. 11-12. The clear import of the Colorado court's conclusion that it is not affected is that "general laws and policies that prohibit arbitrary discrimination" would continue to prohibit discrimination on the basis of homosexual conduct as well. This analysis, which is fully in accord with (indeed, follows inescapably from) the text of the constitutional provision, lays to rest such horribles, raised in the course of oral argument, as the prospect that assaults upon homosexuals could not be prosecuted. The amendment prohibits special treatment of homosexuals, and nothing more. It would not affect, for example, a requirement of state law that pensions be paid to all retiring state employees with a certain length of service; homosexual employees, as well as others, would be entitled to that benefit. But it would prevent the State or any municipality from making death-benefit payments to the "life partner" of a homosexual when it does not make such payments to the long-time roommate of a nonhomosexual employee. Or again, it does not affect the requirement of the State's general insurance laws that customers be afforded coverage without discrimination unrelated to anticipated risk. Thus, homosexuals could not be denied coverage, or charged a greater premium, with respect to auto collision insurance; but neither the State nor any municipality could require that distinctive health insurance risks associated with homosexuality (if there are any) be ignored.

Despite all of its hand-wringing about the potential effect of Amendment 2 on general antidiscrimination laws, the Court's opinion ultimately does not dispute all this, but assumes it to be true. The only denial of equal treatment it contends homosexuals have suffered is this: They may not obtain preferential treatment without amending the state constitution. That is to say, the principle underlying the Court's opinion is that one who is accorded equal treatment under the laws, but cannot as readily as others obtain preferential treatment under the laws, has been denied equal protection of the laws. If merely stating this alleged "equal protection" violation does not suffice to refute it, our constitutional jurisprudence has achieved terminal silliness.

The central thesis of the Court's reasoning is that any group is denied equal protection when, to obtain advantage (or, presumably, to avoid disadvantage), it must have recourse to a more general and hence more difficult level of political decisionmaking than others. The world has never heard of such a principle, which is why the Court's opinion is so long on emotive utterance and so short on relevant legal citation. And it seems to me most unlikely that any multilevel democracy can function under such a principle. For whenever a disadvantage is imposed, or conferral of a benefit is prohibited, at one of the higher levels of democratic decisionmaking (i.e., by the state legislature rather than local government, or by the people at large in the state constitution rather than the legislature), the affected group has (under this theory) been denied equal protection. To take the simplest of examples, consider a state law prohibiting the award of municipal contracts to relatives of mayors or city councilmen. Once such a law is passed, the group composed of such relatives must, in order to get the benefit of city contracts, persuade the state legislature— unlike all other citizens, who need only persuade the municipality. It is ridiculous to consider this a denial of equal protec-

tion, which is why the Court's theory is unheard-of.

The Court might reply that the example I have given is not a denial of equal protection only because the same "rational basis" (avoidance of corruption) which renders constitutional the substantive discrimination against relatives (i.e., the fact that they alone cannot obtain city contracts) also automatically suffices to sustain what might be called the electoral-procedural discrimination against them (i.e., the fact that they must go to the state level to get this changed). This is of course a perfectly reasonable response, and would explain why "electoral-procedural discrimination" has not hitherto been heard of: a law that is valid in its substance is automatically valid in its level of enactment. But the Court cannot afford to make this argument, for as I shall discuss next, there is no doubt of a rational basis for the substance of the prohibition at issue here. The Court's entire novel theory rests upon the proposition that there is something special—something that cannot be justified by normal "rational basis" analysis—in making a disadvantaged group (or a non-preferred group) resort to a higher decisionmaking level. That proposition finds no support in law or logic.

II

I turn next to whether there was a legitimate rational basis for the substance of the constitutional amendment—for the prohibition of special protection for homosexuals. It is unsurprising that the Court avoids discussion of this question, since the answer is so obviously yes. The case most relevant to the issue before us today is not even mentioned in the Court's opinion: In *Bowers v. Hardwick*,

478 U.S. 186, 106 S.Ct. 2841, 92 L.Ed.2d 140 (1986), we held that the Constitution does not prohibit what virtually all States had done from the founding of the Republic until very recent years—making homosexual conduct a crime. That holding is unassailable, except by those who think that the Constitution changes to suit current fashions. But in any event it is a given in the present case: Respondents' briefs did not urge overruling *Bowers,* and at oral argument respondents' counsel expressly disavowed any intent to seek such overruling, Tr. of Oral Arg. 53. If it is constitutionally permissible for a State to make homosexual conduct criminal, surely it is constitutionally permissible for a State to enact other laws merely disfavoring homosexual conduct. (As the Court of Appeals for the District of Columbia Circuit has aptly put it: "If the Court [in *Bowers*] was unwilling to object to state laws that criminalize the behavior that defines the class, it is hardly open... to conclude that state sponsored discrimination against the class is invidious. After all, there can hardly be more palpable discrimination against a class than making the conduct that defines the class criminal." *Padula v. Webster,* 822 F.2d 97, 103 (1987).) And *a fortiori* it is constitutionally permissible for a State to adopt a provision not even disfavoring homosexual conduct, but merely prohibiting all levels of state government from bestowing special protections upon homosexual conduct. Respondents (who, unlike the Court, cannot afford the luxury of ignoring inconvenient precedent) counter *Bowers* with the argument that a greater-includes-the-lesser rationale cannot justify Amendment 2's application to individuals who do not engage in homosexual acts, but are merely of homosexual "orientation." Some courts of ap-

peals have concluded that, with respect to laws of this sort at least, that is a distinction without a difference. See *Equality Foundation of Greater Cincinnati, Inc. v. Cincinnati,* 54 F.3d 261, 267 (C.A.6 1995) ("[F]or purposes of these proceedings, it is virtually impossible to distinguish or separate individuals of a particular orientation which predisposes them toward a particular sexual conduct from those who actually engage in that particular type of sexual conduct"); *Steffan v. Perry,* 41 F.3d 677, 689-690 (C.A.D.C.1994). The Supreme Court of Colorado itself appears to be of this view. See 882 P.2d, at 1349-1350 ("Amendment 2 targets this class of persons based on four characteristics: sexual orientation; conduct; practices; and relationships. Each characteristic provides a potentially different way of identifying that class of persons who are gay, lesbian, or bisexual. These four characteristics are not truly severable from one another because each provides nothing more than a different way of identifying the same class of persons")....

But assuming that, in Amendment 2, a person of homosexual "orientation" is someone who does not engage in homosexual conduct but merely has a tendency or desire to do so, *Bowers* still suffices to establish a rational basis for the provision. If it is rational to criminalize the conduct, surely it is rational to deny special favor and protection to those with a self-avowed tendency or desire to engage in the conduct....

Moreover, even if the provision regarding homosexual "orientation" were invalid, respondents' challenge to Amendment 2—which is a facial challenge—must fail. "A facial challenge to a legislative Act is, of course, the most difficult challenge to mount successfully, since the challenger must establish that no set of circumstances exists under which the Act would be valid." *United States v. Salerno*, 481 U.S. 739, 745, 107 S.Ct. 2095, 2100, 95 L.Ed.2d 697 (1987). It would not be enough for respondents to establish (if they could) that Amendment 2 is unconstitutional as applied to those of homosexual "orientation"; since, under *Bowers*, Amendment 2 is unquestionably constitutional as applied to those who engage in homosexual conduct, the facial challenge cannot succeed. Some individuals of homosexual "orientation" who do not engage in homosexual acts might successfully bring an as-applied challenge to Amendment 2, but so far as the record indicates, none of the respondents is such a person. See App. 4-5 (complaint describing each of the individual respondents as either "a gay man" or "a lesbian")....

III

The foregoing suffices to establish what the Court's failure to cite any case remotely in point would lead one to suspect: No principle set forth in the Constitution, nor even any imagined by this Court in the past 200 years, prohibits what Colorado has done here. But the case for Colorado is much stronger than that. What it has done is not only unprohibited, but eminently reasonable, with close, congressionally approved precedent in earlier constitutional practice.

First, as to its eminent reasonableness. The Court's opinion contains grim, disapproving hints that Coloradans have been guilty of "animus" or "animosity" toward homosexuality, as though that has been established as un-American. Of course it is our moral heritage that one should not hate any human being or class of human beings. But I had thought that one could consider certain conduct reprehensible—murder, for example, or polygamy, or cruelty to animals—and could exhibit even "animus" toward such conduct. Surely that is the only sort of "animus" at issue here: moral disapproval of homosexual conduct, the same sort of moral disapproval that produced the centuries-old criminal laws that we held constitutional in *Bowers*. The Colorado amendment does not, to speak entirely precisely, prohibit giving favored status to people who are homosexuals; they can be favored for many reasons—for example, because they are senior citizens or members of racial minorities. But it prohibits giving them favored status because of their homosexual conduct—that is, it prohibits favored status for homosexuality.

But though Coloradans are, as I say, entitled to be hostile toward homosexual conduct, the fact is that the degree of hostility reflected by Amendment 2 is the smallest conceivable. The Court's portrayal of Coloradans as a society fallen victim to pointless, hate-filled "gay-bashing" is so false as to be comical. Colorado not only is one of the 25 States that have repealed their antisodomy laws, but was among the first to do so. See 1971 Colo. Sess. Laws, ch. 121, sec. 1. But the society that eliminates criminal punishment for homosexual acts does not necessarily abandon the view that homosexuality is morally wrong and socially harmful; often, abolition simply reflects the view that enforcement of such criminal laws involves unseemly intrusion into the intimate lives of citizens. Cf. Brief for Lambda Legal Defense and Education Fund, Inc., et al. as Amici Curiae in *Bowers v. Hardwick*, O.T.1985, No. 85-140, p. 25, n. 21 (antisodomy statutes are "unenforceable by any but the most offensive snooping and wasteful allocation of law enforcement resources"); Kadish, The Crisis of Overcriminalization, 374 The Annals of the American Academy of Political and Social Science 157, 161 (1967) ("To obtain evidence [in sodomy cases], police are obliged to resort to behavior which tends to degrade and demean both themselves personally and law enforcement as an institution").

There is a problem, however, which arises when criminal sanction of homosexuality is eliminated but moral and social disapprobation of homosexuality is meant to be retained. The Court cannot be unaware of that problem; it is evident in many cities of the country, and occasionally bubbles to the surface of the news, in heated political disputes over such matters as the introduction into local schools of books teaching that homosexuality is an optional and fully acceptable "alternate life style." The problem (a problem, that is, for those who wish to retain social disapprobation of homosexuality) is that, because those who engage in homosexual conduct tend to reside in disproportionate numbers in certain communities, see Record, Exh. MMM, have high disposable income, see ibid.; App. 254 (affidavit of Prof. James Hunter), and of course care about homosexual-rights issues much more ardently than the public at large, they possess political power much greater than their numbers, both locally and statewide. Quite understandably, they devote this political power to achieving not merely a grudging social toleration, but full social acceptance, of homosexuality. See, e.g., Jacobs, The Rhetorical Construction of Rights: The Case of the Gay Rights Movement, 1969–1991, 72 Neb. L.Rev. 723, 724 (1993) ("[T]he task of gay rights proponents is to move the center of public discourse along a continuum from the rhetoric of disapprobation, to rhetoric of tolerance, and finally to affirmation").

By the time Coloradans were asked to vote on Amendment 2, their exposure to homosexuals' quest for social endorsement was not limited to newspaper accounts of happenings in places such as New York, Los Angeles, San Francisco, and Key West. Three Colorado cities—Aspen, Boulder, and Denver—had enacted ordinances that listed "sexual orientation" as an impermissible ground for discrimination, equating the moral disapproval of homosexual conduct with racial and religious bigotry. See Aspen Municipal Code sec. 13-98 (1977); Boulder Rev. Municipal Code secs. 12-1-1 to 12-1-11 (1987); Denver Rev. Municipal Code, Art. IV secs. 28-91 to 28-116 (1991). The phenomenon had even appeared statewide: the Governor of Colorado had signed an executive order pronouncing that "in the State of Colorado we recognize the diversity in our pluralistic society and strive to bring an end to discrimination in any form," and directing state agency-heads to "ensure non-discrimination" in hiring and promotion based on, among other things, "sexual orientation." Executive Order No. D0035 (Dec. 10, 1990). I do not mean to be critical of these legislative successes; homosexuals are as entitled to use the legal system for reinforcement of their moral sentiments as are the rest of society. But they are subject to being countered by lawful, democratic countermeasures as well.

That is where Amendment 2 came in. It sought to counter both the geographic concentration and the disproportionate political power of homosexuals by (1) resolving the controversy at the statewide level, and (2) making the election a single-issue contest for both sides. It put directly, to all the citizens of the State, the question:

Should homosexuality be given special protection? They answered no. The Court today asserts that this most democratic of procedures is unconstitutional. Lacking any cases to establish that facially absurd proposition, it simply asserts that it must be unconstitutional, because it has never happened before. "[Amendment 2] identifies persons by a single trait and then denies them protection across the board. The resulting disqualification of a class of persons from the right to seek specific protection from the law is unprecedented in our jurisprudence. The absence of precedent for Amendment 2 is itself instructive.... It is not within our constitutional tradition to enact laws of this sort. Central both to the idea of the rule of law and to our own Constitution's guarantee of equal protection is the principle that government and each of its parts remain open on impartial terms to all who seek its assistance." As I have noted above, this is proved false every time a state law prohibiting or disfavoring certain conduct is passed, because such a law prevents the adversely affected group—whether drug addicts, or smokers, or gun owners, or motorcyclists—from changing the policy thus established in "each of [the] parts" of the State. What the Court says is even demonstrably false at the constitutional level. The Eighteenth Amendment to the Federal Constitution, for example, deprived those who drank alcohol not only of the power to alter the policy of prohibition locally or through state legislation, but even of the power to alter it through state constitutional amendment or federal legislation. The Establishment Clause of the First Amendment prevents theocrats from having their way by converting their fellow citizens at the local, state, or federal statutory level; as does the Republican Form of Government Clause prevent monarchists.

But there is a much closer analogy, one that involves precisely the effort by the majority of citizens to preserve its view of sexual morality statewide, against the efforts of a geographically concentrated and politically powerful minority to undermine it. The constitutions of the States of Arizona, Idaho, New Mexico, Oklahoma, and Utah to this day contain provisions stating that polygamy is "forever prohibited." See Ariz. Const., Art. XX, par. 2; Idaho Const., Art. I, sec. 4; N.M. Const., Art. XXI, sec. 1; Okla. Const., Art. I, sec. 2; Utah Const., Art. III, sec. 1. Polygamists, and those who have a polygamous "orientation," have been "singled out" by these provisions for much more severe treatment than merely denial of favored status; and that treatment can only be changed by achieving amendment of the state constitutions. The Court's disposition today suggests that these provisions are unconstitutional, and that polygamy must be permitted in these States on a state-legislated, or perhaps even local-option, basis—unless, of course, polygamists for some reason have fewer constitutional rights than homosexuals.

The United States Congress, by the way, required the inclusion of these antipolygamy provisions in the constitutions of Arizona, New Mexico, Oklahoma, and Utah, as a condition of their admission to statehood. See Arizona Enabling Act, 36 Stat. 569; New Mexico Enabling Act, 36 Stat. 558; Oklahoma Enabling Act, 34 Stat. 269; Utah Enabling Act, 28 Stat. 108. (For Arizona, New Mexico, and Utah, moreover, the Enabling Acts required that the antipolygamy provisions be "irrevocable without the consent of the United States and the people of said State"—so that not only were "each of [the] parts" of these States not "open on impartial terms" to polygamists, but even the States as a whole were not; polygamists would have to persuade the whole country to their way of thinking.) Idaho adopted the constitutional provision on its own, but the 51st Congress, which admitted Idaho into the Union, found its constitution to be "republican in form and... in conformity with the Constitution of the United States." Act of Admission of Idaho, 26 Stat. 215. Thus, this "singling out" of the sexual practices of a single group for statewide, democratic vote—so utterly alien to our constitutional system, the Court would have us believe—has not only happened, but

has received the explicit approval of the United States Congress....

Today's opinion has no foundation in American constitutional law, and barely pretends to. The people of Colorado have adopted an entirely reasonable provision which does not even disfavor homosexuals in any substantive sense, but merely denies them preferential treatment. Amendment 2 is designed to prevent piecemeal deterioration of the sexual morality favored by a majority of Coloradans, and is not only an appropriate means to that legitimate end, but a means that Americans have employed before. Striking it down is an act, not of judicial judgment, but of political will. I dissent.

POSTSCRIPT

Are Laws Restricting Gay Rights Legislation Unconstitutional?

There appears to be an increasing number of legal cases involving gay rights issues. Partly, this is a result of more routine and more public involvement of gays in economic, social, and political activities. *Romer* does not require that new legal rights be granted, but it does establish a new backdrop against which claims of discrimination will be considered. Consider, for example, the following issues, which have received publicity recently:

1. *Same-sex marriages*—The federal "Defense of Marriage Act" specifies that states are not required to give effect to same-sex unions and bars federal benefits associated with marriage to such couples. This law is a reaction to efforts in several states to legalize same-sex marriages.
2. *Adoptions by gay couples*—Should sexual orientation be taken into account in the adoption of children or the granting of custody? Whether or not the "best interests of the child" are interfered with by the sexual orientation of a parent is discussed in *In re Petition of K.M.*, 653 N.E.2d 888 (1995).
3. *Military service*—The Clinton administration's "don't ask, don't tell" policy allows gays to serve in the military as long as they keep their sexual orientation to themselves. A soldier can be "separated" from the military if it is found that he or she has engaged or attempted to engage in homosexual acts and can be terminated for declaring his or her homosexuality unless the individual can demonstrate "no propensity or intent to engage in homosexual acts." This practice is currently being litigated.

A significant Supreme Court decision involving gay rights was the challenge to the exclusion of a gay and lesbian group from Boston, Massachusett's St. Patrick's Day Parade (*Hurley v. Irish-American Gay, Lesbian and Bisexual Group*, 115 S. Ct. 2338, 1995). The Court ruled that the group organizer's decision was protected by the First Amendment rights of expression. The decision in *Baehr v. Lewin*, 852 P.2d 44 (1993) was that Hawaii's prohibition of same-sex marriage was subject to strict scrutiny under state equal protection doctrine. Recent articles on gay rights include William E. Adams, Jr., "Whose Family Is it Anyway? The Continuing Struggle for Lesbians and Gay Men Seeking to Adopt Children," 30 *New England Law Review* 579 (1996) and Lawrence Kent Mendenhall, "Misters Korematsu and Steffan: The Japanese Internment and the Military's Ban on Gays in the Armed Forces," 70 *New York University Law Review* 196 (1995). On the Internet see
`http://www.qrd.org/QRD/www/usa/legal/lgln/lgln.html` and
`http://www.qrd.org/qrd/www/qlegal.html`.

PART 3

Law and Crime

Crime is a fact of life for many citizens in the United States, and the social, economic, and psychological costs are high for individual victims and society as a whole. Every society has to contend with those members who refuse to adhere to the established rules of behavior; how criminals are treated is often one standard for judging a society's fairness and compassion.

The debates in this section address issues concerning the treatment of criminals and the legal rights of the accused as well as the rights of citizens to be free from fear.

■ Should the Death Penalty Be Abolished?

■ Should the Exclusionary Rule Be
   Abolished?

■ Will Waiting Periods Control Gun
   Purchases?

■ Should the Insanity Defense Be Abolished?

■ Should Drug Use Be Legalized?

ISSUE 14

Should the Death Penalty Be Abolished?

YES: Harry A. Blackmun, from Dissenting Opinion, *Bruce Edwin Callins v. James A. Collins,* U.S. Supreme Court (1994)

NO: James C. Anders, from Statement Before the Committee on the Judiciary, U.S. Senate (September 19, 1989)

ISSUE SUMMARY

YES: Former Supreme Court justice Harry A. Blackmun argues that the application of the death penalty has been arbitrary and discriminatory.

NO: Attorney James C. Anders argues that the death penalty is the appropriate punishment for some crimes and that it should not be abolished even if it is not an effective deterrent.

Unlike some of the issues in this book, capital punishment has a long history. For example, in 428 B.C., Thucydides recorded the following arguments by Cleon in support of the death penalty:

> Punish them as they deserve, and teach your other allies by a striking example that the penalty of rebellion is death. Let them once understand this and you will not so often have to neglect your enemies while you are fighting with your confederates.

In response, Diodotus wrote:

> All states and individuals are alike prone to err, and there is no law that will prevent them, or why should men have exhausted the list of punishments in search of enactments to protect them from evil doers? It is probable that in early times the penalties for the greatest offenses were less severe, and that as these were disregarded, the penalty of death has been by degrees in most cases arrived at, which is itself disregarded in like manner. Either some means of terror more terrible than this must be discovered, or it must be owned that this restraint is useless....
>   We must make up our minds to look for our protection not to legal terrors but to careful administration.... Good policy against an adversary is superior to the blind attacks of brute force.

During the last two and a half decades, the Supreme Court has been confronted with death penalty cases almost every year. The most significant decision was that of *Furman v. Georgia,* 408 U.S. 238, decided in 1972. Furman, a 26-year-old black man, had killed a homeowner during a break-in and was sentenced to death. In a 5–4 decision, the Court overturned the sentence. It held that the procedure used by Georgia (and most other states at that time) was "cruel and unusual" and therefore a violation of the Eighth Amendment of the Constitution. At the heart of the case was the fact that Georgia law left it up to the discretion of the jury to decide whether or not the death penalty was appropriate in a particular case. Two justices, Thurgood Marshall and William J. Brennan, Jr., believed that the death penalty under any circumstances violated the cruel and unusual punishment clause. The three other justices in the majority, however, felt that the death penalty was not in itself unconstitutional but that the manner in which it was applied in this case was unlawful. They felt that leaving the sentence up to the jury led it to be "wantonly" and "freakishly" imposed and "pregnant with discrimination."

Since 1972, 38 states have enacted new death penalty statutes. The following cases illustrate some of the difficulties involved in developing a consistent standard through a case-by-case approach.

1. *Gregg v. Georgia*, 428 U.S. 153 (1976)—After *Furman*, Georgia enacted a new statute retaining the death penalty for murder and five other crimes. Guilt or innocence was determined at a trial and then a second hearing or trial was held for the jury to determine whether the death penalty should be applied. The law set up procedures that were intended to limit the jury's discretion and that required higher court review of the sentence with the hope that this would reduce the incidence of discrimination and prejudice. In a 7–2 decision, this law was upheld by the Supreme Court.

2. *Lockett v. Ohio*, 438 U.S. 586 (1978)—Ohio law prevented the jury from considering any mitigating circumstances other than those specifically enumerated in the statute. The Supreme Court held that this law was unconstitutional.

3. *Coker v. Georgia*, 433 U.S. 584 (1977)—The Supreme Court held that the death penalty may not be imposed on persons convicted of rape. The case suggests that the death penalty is unconstitutional if a death did not take place as a result of the defendant's actions.

What these cases indicate is that the death penalty is lawful and not "cruel and unusual" if the victim has been killed, if the statute provides the defendant the opportunity to present mitigating circumstances, if the statute lists aggravating circumstances that must be considered, and if it requires appellate review. These procedural requirements have been imposed mainly to reduce the possibility of discriminatory application of the death penalty.

The following selection, by recently retired Supreme Court justice Harry A. Blackmun, is a remarkable statement of the limits of judicial power. Blackmun does not feel that capital punishment is necessarily unconstitutional. He concludes, however, that the Court has been unable to provide a proper framework for applying the death penalty in a nonarbitrary manner and will be unable to do so. Attorney James C. Anders disagrees.

YES

Harry A. Blackmun

DISSENTING OPINION OF HARRY A. BLACKMUN

CALLINS v. COLLINS

Justice BLACKMUN, dissenting.

On February 23, 1994, at approximately 1:00 a.m., Bruce Edwin Callins will be executed by the State of Texas. Intravenous tubes attached to his arms will carry the instrument of death, a toxic fluid designed specifically for the purpose of killing human beings. The witnesses, standing a few feet away, will behold Callins, no longer a defendant, an appellant, or a petitioner, but a man, strapped to a gurney, and seconds away from extinction.

Within days, or perhaps hours, the memory of Callins will begin to fade. The wheels of justice will churn again, and somewhere, another jury or another judge will have the unenviable task of determining whether some human being is to live or die. We hope, of course, that the defendant whose life is at risk will be represented by competent counsel—someone who is inspired by the awareness that a less-than-vigorous defense truly could have fatal consequences for the defendant. We hope that the attorney will investigate all aspects of the case, follow all evidentiary and procedural rules, and appear before a judge who is still committed to the protection of defendants' rights —even now, as the prospect of meaningful judicial oversight has diminished. In the same vein, we hope that the prosecution, in urging the penalty of death, will have exercised its discretion wisely, free from bias, prejudice, or political motive, and will be humbled, rather than emboldened, by the awesome authority conferred by the State.

But even if we can feel confident that these actors will fulfill their roles to the best of their human ability, our collective conscience will remain uneasy. Twenty years have passed since this Court declared that the death penalty must be imposed fairly, and with reasonable consistency, or not at all, see *Furman v. Georgia*, 408 U.S. 238, 92 S.Ct. 2726, 33 L.Ed.2d 346 (1972), and, despite the effort of the States and courts to devise legal formulas and procedural rules to meet this daunting challenge, the death penalty remains fraught with arbitrariness, discrimination, caprice, and mistake. This is not to say that the

From *Bruce Edwin Callins v. James A. Collins*, 114 S. Ct. 1127 (1994). Some notes and case citations omitted.

problems with the death penalty today are identical to those that were present 20 years ago. Rather, the problems that were pursued down one hole with procedural rules and verbal formulas have come to the surface somewhere else, just as virulent and pernicious as they were in their original form. Experience has taught us that the constitutional goal of eliminating arbitrariness and discrimination from the administration of death can never be achieved without compromising an equally essential component of fundamental fairness—individualized sentencing. See *Lockett v. Ohio*, 438 U.S. 586, 98 S.Ct. 2954, 57 L.Ed.2d 973 (1978).

It is tempting, when faced with conflicting constitutional commands, to sacrifice one for the other or to assume that an acceptable balance between them already has been struck. In the context of the death penalty, however, such jurisprudential maneuvers are wholly inappropriate. The death penalty must be imposed "fairly, and with reasonable consistency, or not at all." *Eddings v. Oklahoma*, 455 U.S. 104, 112, 102 S.Ct. 869, 875, 71 L.Ed.2d 1 (1982).

To be fair, a capital sentencing scheme must treat each person convicted of a capital offense with that "degree of respect due the uniqueness of the individual." *Lockett v. Ohio*, 438 U.S., at 605, 98 S.Ct., at 2964 (plurality opinion). That means affording the sentencer the power and discretion to grant mercy in a particular case, and providing avenues for the consideration of any and all relevant mitigating evidence that would justify a sentence less than death. Reasonable consistency, on the other hand, requires that the death penalty be inflicted evenhandedly, in accordance with reason and objective standards, rather than by whim, caprice, or prejudice. Finally, because human error is inevitable, and because our criminal justice system is less than perfect, searching appellate review of death sentences and their underlying convictions is a prerequisite to a constitutional death penalty scheme.

On their face, these goals of individual fairness, reasonable consistency, and absence of error appear to be attainable: Courts are in the very business of erecting procedural devices from which fair, equitable, and reliable outcomes are presumed to flow. Yet, in the death penalty area, this Court, in my view, has engaged in a futile effort to balance these constitutional demands, and now is retreating not only from the *Furman* promise of consistency and rationality, but from the requirement of individualized sentencing as well. Having virtually conceded that both fairness and rationality cannot be achieved in the administration of the death penalty, see *McCleskey v. Kemp*, 481 U.S. 279, 313, n. 37, 107 S.Ct. 1756, 1778, n. 37, 95 L.Ed.2d 262 (1987), the Court has chosen to deregulate the entire enterprise, replacing, it would seem, substantive constitutional requirements with mere aesthetics, and abdicating its statutorily and constitutionally imposed duty to provide meaningful judicial oversight to the administration of death by the States.

From this day forward, I no longer shall tinker with the machinery of death. For more than 20 years I have endeavored—indeed, I have struggled—along with a majority of this Court, to develop procedural and substantive rules that would lend more than the mere appearance of fairness to the death penalty endeavor. Rather than continue to coddle the Court's delusion that the desired level of fairness has been achieved and the need for regulation eviscerated, I feel morally and intellectually obligated simply to concede that the death penalty experiment has failed. It is virtually self-evident to me now that no combination of procedural rules or substantive regulations ever can save the death penalty from its inherent constitutional deficiencies. The basic question—does the system accurately and consistently determine which defendants "deserve" to die? —cannot be answered in the affirmative. It is not simply that this Court has allowed vague aggravating circumstances to be employed, see, e.g., *Arave v. Creech*, ___ U.S. ___ 113 S.Ct. 1534, 123 L.Ed.2d 188 (1993), relevant mitigating evidence to be disregarded, see, e.g., *Johnson v. Texas*, ___ U.S. ___, 113 S.Ct. 2658, 125 L.Ed.2d 290 (1993), and vital judicial review to be blocked, see, e.g., *Coleman v. Thompson*, 501 U.S. ___, 112 S.Ct. 1845, 119 L.Ed.2d 1 (1992). The problem is that the inevitability of factual, legal, and moral error gives us a system that we know must wrongly kill some defendants, a system that fails to deliver the fair, consistent, and reliable sentences of death required by the Constitution.[1]

I

In 1971, in an opinion which has proved partly prophetic, the second Justice Harlan, writing for the Court, observed: "Those who have come to grips with the hard task of actually attempting to draft means of channeling capital sentencing discretion have confirmed the lesson taught by the history recounted above. To identify before the fact those characteristics of criminal homicides and their perpetrators which call for the death penalty, and to express these characteristics in language which can be fairly understood and applied by the sentencing authority, appear to be tasks which are beyond present human ability.... For a court to attempt to catalog the appropriate factors in this elusive area could inhibit rather than expand the scope of consideration, for no list of circumstances would ever be really complete." *McGautha v. California*, 402 U.S. 183, 204, 208, 91 S.Ct. 1454, 1466, 1467, 28 L.Ed.2d 711 (1971). In *McGautha*, the petitioner argued that a statute which left the penalty of death entirely in the jury's discretion, without any standards to govern its imposition, violated the Fourteenth Amendment. Although the Court did not deny that serious risks were associated with a sentencer's unbounded discretion, the Court found no remedy in the Constitution for the inevitable failings of human judgment.

A year later, the Court reversed its course completely in *Furman v. Georgia*, 408 U.S. 238, 92 S.Ct. 2726, 33 L.Ed.2d 346 (1972) (*per curiam*, with each of the nine Justices writing separately). The concurring Justices argued that the glaring inequities in the administration of death, the standardless discretion wielded by judges and juries, and the pervasive racial and economic discrimination, rendered the death penalty, at least as administered, "cruel and unusual" within the meaning of the Eighth Amendment. Justice White explained that, out of the hundreds of people convicted of murder every year, only a handful were sent to their deaths, and that there was "no meaningful basis for distinguishing the few cases in which [the death penalty] is imposed from the many cases in which it is not." 408 U.S., at 313, 92 S.Ct, at 2764. If any discernible basis could be identified for the selection of those few who were chosen to die, it was "the constitutionally impermissible basis of race." *Id.*, at 310, 92 S.Ct., at 2762 (Stewart, J., concurring).

I dissented in *Furman*. Despite my intellectual, moral, and personal objections to the death penalty, I refrained from joining the majority because I found objectionable the Court's abrupt change of position in the single year that had passed since *McGautha*. While I agreed that the Eighth Amendment's prohibition against cruel and unusual punishments " 'may acquire meaning as public opinion becomes enlightened by a humane justice,' " 408 U.S., at 409, 92 S.Ct., at 2814, quoting *Weems v. United States,* 217 U.S. 349, 378, 30 S.Ct. 544, 553, 54 L.Ed. 793 (1910), I objected to the "suddenness of the Court's perception of progress in the human attitude since decisions of only a short while ago." 408 U.S., at 410, 92 S.Ct., at 2814. Four years after *Furman* was decided, I concurred in the judgment in *Gregg v. Georgia,* 428 U.S. 153, 96 S.Ct. 2909, 49 L.Ed.2d 859 (1976), and its companion cases which upheld death sentences rendered under statutes passed after *Furman* was decided. See *Proffitt v. Florida,* 428 U.S. 242, 261, 96 S.Ct. 2960, 2970, 49 L.Ed.2d 913 (1976), and *Jurek v. Texas,* 428 U.S. 262, 279, 96 S.Ct. 2950, 2960, 49 L.Ed.2d 929 (1976). *Cf. Woodson v. North Carolina,* 428 U.S. 280, 307, 96 S.Ct. 2978, 2992, 49 L.Ed.2d 944 (1976), and *Roberts v. Louisiana,* 428 U.S. 325, 363, 96 S.Ct. 3001, 3020, 49 L.Ed.2d 974 (1976).

A

There is little doubt now that *Furman's* essential holding was correct. Although most of the public seems to desire, and the Constitution appears to permit, the penalty of death, it surely is beyond dispute that if the death penalty cannot be administered consistently and rationally, it may not be administered at all. *Eddings v. Oklahoma,* 455 U.S., at 112, 102 S.Ct., at 875. I never have quarreled with this principle; in my mind, the real meaning of *Furman's* diverse concurring opinions did not emerge until some years after *Furman* was decided. See *Gregg v. Georgia,* 428 U.S., at 189, 96 S.Ct., at 2932 (opinion of Stewart, Powell, and STEVENS, JJ.) ("*Furman* mandates that where discretion is afforded a sentencing body on a matter so grave as the determination of whether a human life should be taken or spared, that discretion must be suitably directed and limited so as to minimize the risk of wholly arbitrary and capricious action"). Since *Gregg,* I faithfully have adhered to the *Furman* holding and have come to believe that it is indispensable to the Court's Eighth Amendment jurisprudence.

Delivering on the *Furman* promise, however, has proved to be another matter. *Furman* aspired to eliminate the vestiges of racism and the effects of poverty in capital sentencing; it deplored the "wanton" and "random" infliction of death by a government with constitutionally limited power. *Furman* demanded that the sentencer's discretion be directed and limited by procedural rules and objective standards in order to minimize the risk of arbitrary and capricious sentences of death.

In the years following *Furman,* serious efforts were made to comply with its mandate. State legislatures and appellate courts struggled to provide judges and juries with sensible and objective guidelines for determining who should live and who should die. Some States attempted to define who is "deserving" of the death penalty through the use of carefully chosen adjectives, reserving the death penalty for those who commit crimes that are "especially heinous, atrocious, or cruel," or "wantonly vile, horrible or inhuman." ...

Unfortunately, all this experimentation and ingenuity yielded little of what *Furman* demanded. It soon became apparent that discretion could not be eliminated from capital sentencing without threatening the fundamental fairness due a defendant when life is at stake. Just as contemporary society was no longer tolerant of the random or discriminatory infliction of the penalty of death, evolving standards of decency required due consideration of the uniqueness of each individual defendant when imposing society's ultimate penalty.

This development in the American conscience would have presented no constitutional dilemma if fairness to the individual could be achieved without sacrificing the consistency and rationality promised in *Furman*. But over the past two decades, efforts to balance these competing constitutional commands have been to no avail. Experience has shown that the consistency and rationality promised in *Furman* are inversely related to the fairness owed the individual when considering a sentence of death. A step toward consistency is a step away from fairness.

B

There is a heightened need for fairness in the administration of death. This unique level of fairness is born of the appreciation that death truly is different from all other punishments a society inflicts upon its citizens. "Death, in its finality, differs more from life imprisonment than a 100-year prison term differs from one of only a year or two." *Woodson*, 428 U.S., at 305, 96 S.Ct.,

at 2991 (opinion of Stewart, Powell, and STEVENS, JJ.). Because of the qualitative difference of the death penalty, "there is a corresponding difference in the need for reliability in the determination that death is the appropriate punishment in a specific case." *Ibid.* In *Woodson*, a decision striking down mandatory death penalty statutes as unconstitutional, a plurality of the Court explained: "A process that accords no significance to relevant facets of the character and record of the individual offender or the circumstances of the particular offense excludes from consideration in fixing the ultimate punishment of death the possibility of compassionate or mitigating factors stemming from the diverse frailties of humankind." *Id.*, at 304, 96 S.Ct., at 2991.

While the risk of mistake in the determination of the appropriate penalty may be tolerated in other areas of the criminal law, "in capital cases the fundamental respect for humanity underlying the Eighth Amendment ... requires consideration of the character and record of the individual offender and the circumstances of the particular offense as a constitutionally indispensable part of the process of inflicting the penalty of death." *Ibid.* Thus, although individualized sentencing in capital cases was not considered essential at the time the Constitution was adopted, *Woodson* recognized that American standards of decency could no longer tolerate a capital sentencing process that failed to afford a defendant individualized consideration in the determination whether he or she should live or die. *Id.*, at 301, 96 S.Ct., at 2989.

The Court elaborated on the principle of individualized sentencing in *Lockett v. Ohio*, 438 U.S. 586, 98 S.Ct. 2954, 57 L.Ed.2d 973 (1978). In that case, a plurality acknowledged that strict restraints on sentencer discretion are necessary to achieve the consistency and rationality promised in *Furman*, but held that, in the end, the sentencer must retain unbridled discretion to afford mercy. Any process or procedure that prevents the sentencer from considering "as a mitigating factor, any aspect of a defendant's character or record and any circumstances of the offense that the defendant proffers as a basis for a sentence less than death," creates the constitutionally intolerable risk that "the death penalty will be imposed in spite of factors which may call for a less severe penalty." *Id.*, at 604–605, 98 S.Ct., at 2964–2965 (emphasis in original). See also *Sumner v. Shuman*, 483 U.S. 66, 107 S.Ct. 2716, 97 L.Ed.2d 56 (1987) (invalidating a mandatory death penalty statute reserving the death penalty for life-term inmates convicted of murder). The Court's duty under the Constitution therefore is to "develop a system of capital punishment at once consistent and principled but also humane and sensible to the uniqueness of the individual." *Eddings v. Oklahoma*, 455 U.S., at 110, 102 S.Ct., at 874.

C

I believe the *Woodson-Lockett* line of cases to be fundamentally sound and rooted in American standards of decency that have evolved over time. The notion of prohibiting a sentencer from exercising its discretion "to dispense mercy on the basis of factors too intangible to write into a statute," *Gregg*, 428 U.S., at 222, 96 S.Ct., at 2947 (White, J., concurring), is offensive to our sense of fundamental fairness and respect for the uniqueness of the individual....

Yet, as several Members of the Court have recognized, there is real "tension"

between the need for fairness to the individual and the consistency promised in *Furman*. On the one hand, discretion in capital sentencing must be "'controlled by clear and objective standards so as to produce non-discriminatory [and reasoned] application.'" *Gregg*, 428 U.S., at 198, 96 S.Ct., at 2936 (opinion of Stewart, Powell, and STEVENS, JJ.), quoting *Coley v. State*, 231 Ga. 829, 834, 204 S.E.2d 612, 615 (1974). On the other hand, the Constitution also requires that the sentencer be able to consider "any relevant mitigating evidence regarding the defendant's character or background, and the circumstances of the particular offense." *California v. Brown*, 479 U.S. 538, 544, 107 S.Ct. 837, 840, 93 L.Ed.2d 934 (1987) (O'CONNOR, J., concurring). The power to consider mitigating evidence that would warrant a sentence less than death is meaningless unless the sentencer has the discretion and authority to dispense mercy based on that evidence. Thus, the Constitution, by requiring a heightened degree of fairness to the individual, and also a greater degree of equality and rationality in the administration of death, demands sentencer discretion that is at once generously expanded and severely restricted.

This dilemma was laid bare in *Penry v. Lynaugh*, 492 U.S. 302, 109 S.Ct. 2934, 106 L.Ed.2d 256 (1989). The defendant in *Penry* challenged the Texas death penalty statute, arguing that it failed to allow the sentencing jury to give full mitigating effect to his evidence of mental retardation and history of child abuse. The Texas statute required the jury, during the penalty phase, to answer three "special issues"; if the jury unanimously answered "yes" to each issue, the trial court was obligated to sentence the defendant to death. Only one of the three issues—whether the defendant posed a "continuing threat to society"—was related to the evidence Penry offered in mitigation. But Penry's evidence of mental retardation and child abuse was a two-edged sword as it related to that special issue: "it diminish[ed] his blameworthiness for his crime even as it indicate[d] that there [was] a probability that he [would] be dangerous in the future." 492 U.S., at 324, 109 S.Ct., at 2949. The Court therefore reversed Penry's death sentence, explaining that a reasonable juror could have believed that the statute prohibited a sentence less than death based upon his mitigating evidence. *Id.*, at 326, 109 S.Ct., at 2950.

After *Penry*, the paradox underlying the Court's post-*Furman* jurisprudence was undeniable. Texas had complied with *Furman* by severely limiting the sentencer's discretion, but those very limitations rendered Penry's death sentence unconstitutional.

D

The theory underlying *Penry* and *Lockett* is that an appropriate balance can be struck between the *Furman* promise of consistency and the *Lockett* requirement of individualized sentencing if the death penalty is conceptualized as consisting of two distinct stages. In the first stage of capital sentencing, the demands of *Furman* are met by "narrowing" the class of death-eligible offenders according to objective, fact-bound characteristics of the defendant or the circumstances of the offense. Once the pool of death-eligible defendants has been reduced, the sentencer retains the discretion to consider whatever relevant mitigating evidence the defendant chooses to offer. . . .

Over time, I have come to conclude that even this approach is unacceptable: It simply reduces, rather than eliminates, the number of people subject to arbitrary sentencing. It is the decision to sentence a defendant to death—not merely the decision to make a defendant eligible for death—that may not be arbitrary. While one might hope that providing the sentencer with as much relevant mitigating evidence as possible will lead to more rational and consistent sentences, experience has taught otherwise. It seems that the decision whether a human being should live or die is so inherently subjective—rife with all of life's understandings, experiences, prejudices, and passions—that it inevitably defies the rationality and consistency required by the Constitution. . . .

E

The arbitrariness inherent in the sentencer's discretion to afford mercy is exacerbated by the problem of race. Even under the most sophisticated death penalty statutes, race continues to play a major role in determining who shall live and who shall die. Perhaps it should not be surprising that the biases and prejudices that infect society generally would influence the determination of who is sentenced to death, even within the narrower pool of death-eligible defendants selected according to objective standards. No matter how narrowly the pool of death-eligible defendants is drawn according to objective standards, *Furman*'s promise still will go unfulfilled so long as the sentencer is free to exercise unbridled discretion within the smaller group and thereby to discriminate. " 'The power to be lenient [also] is the power to discriminate.' " *McCleskey v. Kemp*, 481 U.S., at

312, 107 S.Ct., at 1778 quoting K. Davis, Discretionary Justice 170 (1973).

A renowned example of racism infecting a capital-sentencing scheme is documented in *McCleskey v. Kemp*, 481 U.S. 279, 107 S.Ct. 1756, 95 L.Ed.2d 262 (1987). Warren McCleskey, an African-American, argued that the Georgia capital-sentencing scheme was administered in a racially discriminatory manner, in violation of the Eighth and Fourteenth Amendments. In support of his claim, he proffered a highly reliable statistical study (the Baldus study) which indicated that, "after taking into account some 230 nonracial factors that might legitimately influence a sentencer, the jury more likely than not would have spared McCleskey's life had his victim been black." 481 U.S., at 325, 107 S.Ct., at 1784 (emphasis in original) (Brennan, J., dissenting). The Baldus study further demonstrated that blacks who kill whites are sentenced to death "at nearly 22 times the rate of blacks who kill blacks, and more than 7 times the rate of whites who kill blacks." *Id.*, at 327, 107 S.Ct., at 1785 (emphasis in original).

Despite this staggering evidence of racial prejudice infecting Georgia's capital-sentencing scheme, the majority turned its back on McCleskey's claims, apparently troubled by the fact that Georgia had instituted more procedural and substantive safeguards than most other States since *Furman*, but was still unable to stamp out the virus of racism. Faced with the apparent failure of traditional legal devices to cure the evils identified in *Furman*, the majority wondered aloud whether the consistency and rationality demanded by the dissent could ever be achieved without sacrificing the discretion which is essential to fair treatment of individual defendants: "[I]t is difficult to imagine guidelines that would pro-

duce the predictability sought by the dissent without sacrificing the discretion essential to a humane and fair system of criminal justice.... The dissent repeatedly emphasizes the need for 'a uniquely high degree of rationality in imposing the death penalty.' ... Again, no suggestion is made as to how greater 'rationality' could be achieved under any type of statute that authorizes capital punishment.... Given these safeguards already inherent in the imposition and review of capital sentences, the dissent's call for greater rationality is no less than a claim that a capital punishment system cannot be administered in accord with the Constitution." *Id.*, at 314–315, n. 37, 107 S.Ct., at 1778, n. 37.

I joined most of Justice Brennan's significant dissent which expounded McCleskey's Eighth Amendment claim, and I wrote separately, *id.*, at 345, 107 S.Ct., at 1795, to explain that McCleskey also had a solid equal protection argument under the Fourteenth Amendment. I still adhere to the views set forth in both dissents, and, as far as I know, there has been no serious effort to impeach the Baldus study. Nor, for that matter, have proponents of capital punishment provided any reason to believe that the findings of that study are unique to Georgia....

II

My belief that this Court would not enforce the death penalty (even if it could) in accordance with the Constitution is buttressed by the Court's "obvious eagerness to do away with any restriction on the States' power to execute whomever and however they please." *Herrera*, ___ U.S. ___, ___, 113 S.Ct. 853, 884, 122 L.Ed.2d 203 (BLACKMUN, J., dissenting). I have explained at length on numerous occasions that my willingness to enforce the capital punishment statutes enacted by the States and the Federal Government, "notwithstanding my own deep moral reservations... has always rested on an understanding that certain procedural safeguards, chief among them the federal judiciary's power to reach and correct claims of constitutional error on federal habeas review, would ensure that death sentences are fairly imposed." *Sawyer v. Whitley,* ___ U.S. ___, ___, 112 S.Ct. 2514, 2528, 120 L.Ed.2d 269 (1992) (BLACK-MUN, J., concurring in the judgment). See also *Herrera v. Collins,* ___ U.S., at ___, 113 S.Ct., at 880–881 (BLACKMUN, J., dissenting). In recent years, I have grown increasingly skeptical that "the death penalty really can be imposed fairly and in accordance with the requirements of the Eighth Amendment," given the now limited ability of the federal courts to remedy constitutional errors. *Sawyer,* ___ U.S., at ___, 112 S.Ct., at 2525 (BLACK-MUN, J., concurring in the judgment).

Federal courts are required by statute to entertain petitions from state prisoners who allege that they are held "in violation of the Constitution or the treaties of the United States." 28 U.S.C. §2254(a). Serious review of these claims helps to ensure that government does not secure the penalty of death by depriving a defendant of his or her constitutional rights. At the time I voted with the majority to uphold the constitutionality of the death penalty in *Gregg v. Georgia,* 428 U.S. 153, 227, 96 S.Ct. 2909, 2950 49 L.Ed.2d 859 (1976), federal courts possessed much broader authority than they do today to address claims of constitutional error on habeas review. In 1976, there were few procedural barriers to the federal judiciary's review of a State's capital sentencing scheme,

or the fairness and reliability of a State's decision to impose death in a particular case. Since then, however, the Court has "erected unprecedented and unwarranted barriers" to the federal judiciary's review of the constitutional claims of capital defendants.

The Court's refusal last term to afford Leonel Torres Herrera an evidentiary hearing, despite his colorable showing of actual innocence, demonstrates just how far afield the Court has strayed from its statutorily and constitutionally imposed obligations. See *Herrera v. Collins, supra.* In *Herrera,* only a bare majority of this Court could bring itself to state forthrightly that the execution of an actually innocent person violates the Eighth Amendment. This concession was made only in the course of erecting nearly insurmountable barriers to a defendant's ability to get a hearing on a claim of actual innocence. *Ibid.* Certainly there will be individuals who are actually innocent who will be unable to make a better showing than what was made by Herrera without the benefit of an evidentiary hearing. The Court is unmoved by this dilemma, however; it prefers "finality" in death sentences to reliable determinations of a capital defendant's guilt. Because I no longer can state with any confidence that this Court is able to reconcile the Eighth Amendment's competing constitutional commands, or that the federal judiciary will provide meaningful oversight to the state courts as they exercise their authority to inflict the penalty of death, I believe that the death penalty, as currently administered, is unconstitutional....

III

Perhaps one day this Court will develop procedural rules or verbal formulas that actually will provide consistency, fairness, and reliability in a capital-sentencing scheme. I am not optimistic that such a day will come. I am more optimistic, though, that this Court eventually will conclude that the effort to eliminate arbitrariness while preserving fairness "in the infliction of [death] is so plainly doomed to failure that it—and the death penalty—must be abandoned altogether." *Godfrey v. Georgia*, 446 U.S. 420, 442, 100 S.Ct. 1759, 1772, 64 L.Ed.2d 398 (1980) (Marshall, J., concurring in the judgment). I may not live to see that day, but I have faith that eventually it will arrive. The path the Court has chosen lessens us all. I dissent.

NOTES

1. Because I conclude that no sentence of death may be constitutionally imposed under our death penalty scheme, I do not address Callins' individual claims of error. I note, though, that the Court has stripped "state prisoners of virtually any meaningful federal review of the constitutionality of their incarceration." *Butler v. McKellar*, 494 U.S. 407, 417, 110 S.Ct. 1212, 1219, 108 L.Ed.2d 347 (1990) (Brennan, J., dissenting) (emphasis in original). Even if Callins had a legitimate claim of constitutional error, this Court would be deaf to it on federal habeas unless "the state court's rejection of the constitutional challenge was so clearly invalid under then-prevailing legal standards that the decision could not be defended by any reasonable jurist." *Id.*, at 417–418, 110 S.Ct., at 1219 (emphasis in original). That a capital defendant facing imminent execution is required to meet such a standard before the Court will remedy constitutional violations is indefensible.

NO
James C. Anders

STATEMENT OF JAMES C. ANDERS

There are in this world a number of extremely wicked people, disposed to get what they want by force or fraud, with complete indifference to the interests of others, and in ways which are totally inconsistent with the existence of civilized society.

— James Fitzjames Stephen

What is society to do with these people? I believe that in certain cases, the death penalty can be shown to be the only rational and realistic punishment for an unspeakable crime. But before embarking on a discussion on the merits of the death penalty, a fundamental philosophical question must be answered. What is the purpose of punishment? Harmonious coexistence among people in any society is dependent upon the advancement of mutually agreed upon goals for the good of the whole society. Obviously, the most basic right a citizen has is the right to be secure in his person, the right to be safe from physical or economic harm from another. Laws to protect citizens and advance the harmony of society are founded upon these principles. To enforce these laws, created in the best interest of society as a whole, there has to be a deterrent for a breach of the law. Therefore, deterrence is the first aim of a system of punishment.

Deterrence is only one side of the punishment coin, however. An equally fundamental reason to punish lies in society's compelling desire to see justice done. Punishment expresses the emotions of the society wronged, the anger and outrage felt, and it solidifies and reinforces the goals, values and norms of acceptable behavior in the society. Punishment is justified purely on the ground that wrongdoing merits punishment, and that it is morally fitting that one who does wrong suffers, and suffers in proportion to his wrongdoing.

Consider the facts of a 1977 case from my jurisdiction. Codefendants Shaw, Roach and Mahaffey spent the morning of October 29th drinking and shooting up drugs. That afternoon the three decided to, in Mahaffey's words, "see if we could find a girl to rape." They drove to a nearby baseball field where they spotted a car parked with two teenagers inside. They robbed and killed the young man on the spot. The girl was carried to a dirt road a short

From U.S. Senate. Committee on the Judiciary. *The Death Penalty.* Hearing, September 19, 1989. Washington, DC: Government Printing Office, 1989.

distance away where she was repeatedly raped and sodomized over a period of hours. When they finished with her, they forced her to place her head in a circle they had drawn in the dirt, and they executed her. Later that evening, Shaw returned by himself and sexually mutilated the girl's body.

The deterrent effect of the death penalty is the favorite criticism of the opponents of capital punishment. The social scientists' studies have been mixed at best and there is no authoritative consensus on whether or not the death penalty deters anyone from committing a crime. Threats of punishment cannot and are not meant to deter everybody all of the time. They are meant to deter most people most of the time.

The threatened punishment must be carried out—otherwise the threats are reduced to bluffs and become incredible and therefore ineffective.

— Ernest van den Haag

Therefore, the death penalty can only be a deterrent if it is meted out with a reasonable degree of consistency. The deterrent effect lies in the knowledge of the citizenry that it will more likely than not be carried out if the named crime is committed.

Even if one is not fully convinced of the deterrent effect of the death penalty, he or she would surely choose the certainty of the convicted criminal's death by execution over the possibility of the deaths of new victims. These new deaths could either be deterred by the execution, or prevented by the executed criminal's obvious incapacity. Simply put, one should opt to execute a man convicted of having caused the death of others than to put the lives of innocents at risk if there is a chance their deaths could be prevented by the deterrent effect.

Death penalty opponents argue that if life is sacred (as, presumably, we all believe) then the murderer's life, too, is sacred and for the State to punish him by execution is barbaric and causes the State to bend to the murderer's level. The only similarity between the unjustified taking of an innocent life and the carrying out of a convicted murderer's execution is the end result —death. The death penalty is a legal sentence, enacted by the legislatures of various states which presumably reflect their constituents' desires. It is a penalty that can finally be carried out only after a trial where the defendant is afforded all of his constitutional rights, and the lengthy appellate process has been exhausted. It is a penalty that has been sanctioned by the United States Supreme Court, a majority of whose members have said, regardless of their personal feelings, that the death penalty is a constitutionally valid punishment. How then can its invocation be compared to the senseless, irrational murder of an innocent victim who is afforded no rights, and is tried and convicted by his murderer for the crime of being in the wrong place at the wrong time? Legal execution and murder are no more comparable than driving a car and knowingly driving a stolen car. Although the physical act of driving either is the same, the two acts are separated by the crime involved in the latter, and that makes all the difference.

Death penalty opponents are also troubled by the studies that purport to show that the death penalty is applied capriciously, that it discriminates racially and economically. They cite these studies as justification for eliminating the penalty. Notice that they are not claiming that some innocent person may be executed, but, rather, that not all the guilty are executed. Assuming that premise for the sake of argument, is that a rational reason to abolish the death penalty? Is the fact that some guilty persons escape punishment sufficient to let all guilty persons escape it? If it is then, in practice, penalties never could be applied if we insisted that they cannot be inflicted on any guilty persons unless we are able to make sure that they are equally applied to all other guilty persons. There is no more merit in persuading the courts to let all capital defendants go because some escaped penalties than it is to say let all burglars go because some have escaped detection and imprisonment. If discrimination exists in the application of the death penalty, then the remedy is statutory reform to minimize or abolish the discrimination, not the abolition of the penalty itself.

The capricious/discriminatory complaint seems by and large to be an abolitionist sham. The abolitionists would oppose the death penalty if it could be meted out without any discretion, if it were mandatory under certain conditions. They would oppose it in a homogeneous country without racial discrimination. It is the death penalty itself, not its possible maldistribution that the abolitionists oppose. Opponents rarely raise the objection that an innocent person might be sent to the electric chair. With the sophistication of the criminal justice system today, the likelihood of convicting, let alone executing, an innocent man is all but nil. But there is another more subtle reason abolitionists no longer advance the "innocent man proposition" as a justification for their opposition to the penalty and that is because this argument

too would be a sham. Death penalty opponents would rid the world of the death penalty for everyone, including the admittedly guilty.

To defend the death penalty should not lead to one's being labeled "cold", "blood-thirsty" or "barbaric". A person who commits capital murder simply cannot and should not expect to be given a pat on the back and told to "go and sin no more." If the death penalty can deter one murder of an innocent life or if it can make a statement to the community about what will and will not be tolerated, then it is justified.

Opponents of the death penalty advocate the life sentence in prison as a viable alternative to execution. My experiences lead me to believe that life imprisonment is not a satisfactory means of dealing with the most horrid of criminals. Early release programs, furloughs, and escapes combine to place a shockingly high number of convicted murderers back on the streets in record time. Hardly a day goes by when one cannot pick up a newspaper and read a gruesome account of the crimes committed by a now liberated "lifer". But that is not the worst of it. Consider the plight of the victims' families, forced to relive the nightmare again and again each time a parole hearing is scheduled. Year after year they endure the uncertainty and agony while waiting on the decision of the parole board. Will this be the year the man who turned their lives upside down will be released to live out his life, perhaps to put another family through the same nightmare?

The life without parole sentence is no solution either. First the possibility of escape cannot be completely eliminated, even in the most secure of institutions. For example, convicted triple murderer and death row inmate Fred Kornahrens escaped with a ploy so simple it caught prison officials completely by surprise. During a body search prior to being transported to court, Kornahrens concealed a key between his index and middle fingers. When handcuffed, he simply uncuffed himself and made good his escape. Given enough time, I am certain Fred Kornahrens could escape again. Second, the life without parole sentence places a tremendous burden on prison administrators. Faced with controlling inmates who have already received the worst punishment society can mete out, they can only throw their hands up in frustration. Lastly, the true lifer is not only capable of continuing to murder, but may actually be more likely to do so. Every prison in the country has its own stories of the lifer who killed another inmate over a cigarette or a piece of chicken. In my home state this scenario was taken one step further when disenchanted crime victim Tony Cimo hired convicted mass murderer Donald "Pee Wee" Gaskins to kill another convicted murderer Rudolph Tyner, the slayer of Cimo's parents. Pee Wee Gaskins is a perfect example of why life imprisonment is never going to be an acceptable alternative to the death penalty and why the death penalty for murder by a federal prisoner serving a life term is a viable proposal.

I recently prosecuted a capital case involving the murder of a state highway patrolman. Trooper George Radford was brutally beaten and executed with his own weapon over a $218 ticket. All Trooper Radford did was show his murderer the same consideration and courtesy he exhibited to all every day on duty. Rather than handcuffing the defendant, Warren Manning, whom he had ticketed for driving under suspension, Trooper Radford allowed him to remain unhandcuffed for the twenty minute ride to the police station so that he would be more comfortable. Manning surprised Trooper Radford halfway there and callously murdered him. Law enforcement personnel deserve the additional protection and security the death penalty affords them. The scores of highway patrolmen who travelled to Camden, South Carolina, for the sentencing of Warren Manning show exactly how important the death penalty issue is to them.

Based on the foregoing analysis, the death penalty takes on special significance in deterrence and punishment of federal law violations. Serious problems exist in American society on a large scale basis or threaten to grow to such a basis. As discussed above, the benefits of deterrence and social justice on crimes such as murder, murder for hire and attempts to assassinate the President are obvious under the death penalty.

Drug-related murders are on the rise and the death penalty could be particularly effective in combatting this murder-for-profit trend. Law enforcement officers who are often required to work undercover in the drug community would be protected to a degree under the deterrence effect of the death penalty. In order to support President Bush's plan to combat the drug problem nationally and internationally, it seems obvious that drug kingpins should know that they are subject to the death penalty. What group of individuals create more chaos and death than these?

Other heinous crimes which pose a threat of great magnitude are those of terrorism. Crimes such as explosions, air piracy, mailing bombs and taking hostages, all where death results, very simply and obviously demand the strongest punishment and deterrent the law can impose. The effects of terrorism are so potentially great and devastating that the death penalty is the only conceivable punishment. The death penalty is not merely an alternative but a necessity for dealing with these large scale national problems.

One leading proponent of the death penalty, E. van den Haag, wrote "never to execute a wrongdoer, regardless of how depraved his acts, is to proclaim that no act can be so irredeemably vicious as to deserve death." In the question of deterrence this principle is exacerbated by a special group of sane murderers who, knowing that they will not be executed, will not hesitate to kill again. If opponents of the death penalty admit that there is a reasonable probability that such wrongdoers will murder again and/or attempt to murder again, and still insist they would never approve of capital punishment, I would conclude that they are indifferent to the lives of the human beings doomed to be the victims of the unexecuted criminals. "Charity for all human beings must not deprive us of our common sense." Hugo Adam Bedau. To those who could not impose the death penalty under any circumstances, van den Haag attributed what he called "a failure of nerve," a feeling that they themselves are incapable of rationally and justly making a life and death decision and that, therefore, everyone else is equally unqualified to decide life or death.

Such a view grossly and tragically underestimates our system of justice. I have always been impressed with the intelligence, compassion and common sense jurors display. Jurors really are the "conscience of the community." That is more than just a phrase lawyers bandy about in closing arguments. I have seen how seriously jurors take their oath to decide the issues, based on the law, regardless of their personal prejudices, and biases. The juries and the courts can evade decisions on life and death only by giving up paramount duties: those of serving justice, securing the lives of citizens and vindicating the norms that society holds inviolable. Justice requires that the punishment be proportional to the gravity of the crime. The death penalty comes closest to meeting this supreme standard while still falling short because those criminals sentenced to execution still had the luxury of choosing their fate when their victims did not.

POSTSCRIPT

Should the Death Penalty Be Abolished?

We are in a new era in the history of capital punishment. The death penalty is constitutional, and almost 3,000 persons are on death row, a larger number than at any time since a national count was begun. In the first edition of this book, published in 1982, I wrote, "Although only four persons have been executed in the past fifteen years, this situation seems certain to change in the next two years as appeals in many cases are exhausted." There has indeed been an increase in executions, although the rise has not been as fast as some had predicted. Three hundred thirty-eight persons had been executed through the middle of 1996.

Appeals are still time-consuming, a situation that some Supreme Court justices have complained about and that the Supreme Court looked at in its 1995–1996 term. As a result of the appeals process, the number of persons on death row is still growing by about 200 a year. In 1982 there were more than 1,000 people on death row, approximately a third of the number today. The increase in the death row population means that there are more people sentenced to death each year than there are executions. The slow pace of executions has been a source of great frustration to some Supreme Court justices and, as a result, the Court has restricted some appeals.

The Supreme Court has made several notable decisions in recent years involving the death penalty. These include *Penry v. Lyunaugh*, 109 S. Ct. 2934 (1989), in which the Court ruled that murderers with mental retardation may be executed, and *Stanford v. Kentucky*, 109 S. Ct. 2969 (1989), in which the Court ruled that persons as young as 16 years of age may be executed.

Interesting works on capital punishment include "Symposium on the Death Penalty," 23 *Hofstra Law Review* 627 (1995); "Symposium: The Death Penalty in the Twenty-first Century," 45 *American University Law Review* 239 (1995); M. Tushnet, *The Death Penalty* (1993); G. Russell, *The Death Penalty and Racial Bias* (1994); H. Bedau, *Death Is Different: Studies in the Morality, Law, and Politics of Capital Punishment* (Northeastern University Press, 1987); Bright, "Counsel for the Poor: The Death Sentence Not for the Worst Crime but for the Worst Lawyer," 103 *Yale Law Journal* 1835 (1994); J. M. Giarrantano, "To the Best of Our Knowledge, We Have Never Been Wrong: Fallibility vs. Finality in Capital Punishment," 100 *Yale Law Journal* 1005 (1991); and W. S. White, "The Death Penalty in the Nineties: An Examination of the Modern System of Capital Punishment," 53 *University of Pittsburgh Law Review* 251 (1991). Further information on the death penalty can be found on the Internet at http://members.magnet.at/k.sand/amnesty/usa/dp96/index.html and http://sun.soci.niu.edu/~critcrim/dp/dp.html.

ISSUE 15

Should the Exclusionary Rule Be Abolished?

YES: Malcolm Richard Wilkey, from "The Exclusionary Rule: Why Suppress Valid Evidence?" *Judicature* (November 1978)

NO: Yale Kamisar, from "The Exclusionary Rule in Historical Perspective: The Struggle to Make the Fourth Amendment More Than 'an Empty Blessing,'" *Judicature* (February 1979)

ISSUE SUMMARY

YES: U.S. Court of Appeals judge Malcolm Richard Wilkey raises objections to the exclusionary rule on the grounds that it may suppress evidence and allow the guilty to go free.

NO: Professor of law Yale Kamisar argues that the exclusionary rule is necessary to prevent abuses by police and to protect citizens' rights.

The Fourth Amendment to the Constitution provides that "the right of the people to be secure in their persons, houses, papers, and effects against unreasonable searches and seizures, shall not be violated, and no Warrants shall issue, but upon probable cause." Thus, if the police wish to search someone's property, they must first persuade a judge that probable cause exists that a crime has been committed and that the evidence sought will be found in the place to be searched. The warrant requirement is the key constitutional element restricting the power of the police to decide unilaterally to invade the privacy of someone's home.

What should happen if the police conduct an illegal search and, as a result, discover incriminating evidence? According to the exclusionary rule, such evidence may not be introduced at a trial or be considered by a jury in considering guilt or innocence. If no other evidence of guilt exists, therefore, the defendant will go free. If there is enough other evidence of the defendant's guilt, he may still be convicted.

The exclusionary rule is over 70 years old. It is not required by the Constitution nor mentioned in it. Rather, courts have imposed it because they felt it was the most workable and feasible way to deter illegal police conduct and maintain an honest system of law enforcement. In the following selections, Judge Malcolm Richard Wilkey asserts that society can no longer bear the costs that the rule brings, that guilty persons escape prosecution because of it, and that illegal police conduct is not deterred. Yale Kamisar, a noted criminal law scholar, argues that the rule's rationale is still valid and that the rule should be maintained.

The selections mention a number of legal cases that should be understood since they describe the historical development of the rule:

1. *Weeks v. United States*, 232 U.S. 383 (1914)—The U.S. Supreme Court imposed the exclusionary rule for the first time and ruled that illegally seized evidence could not be used in the federal courts. Such evidence, however, could still be used in criminal cases in state courts unless the state decided on its own to require the exclusionary rule in its courts. Although a few states did impose the exclusionary rule, most did not. The New York Court of Appeals, for example, rejected the rule, with Judge Benjamin N. Cardozo refusing to accept the proposition that "the criminal is to go free because the constable has blundered" (*People v. Defore*, 150 N.E. 585, 1926).

2. *Wolf v. Colorado*, 338 U.S. 25 (1949)—The Supreme Court ruled that due process of law under the Fourteenth Amendment is denied individuals who are illegally searched. But the Court refused to require state courts to impose or apply the exclusionary rule. Thus, the Court held that "in a prosecution in a State court for a State crime the Fourteenth Amendment does not forbid the admission of evidence obtained by an unreasonable search and seizure."

3. *Rochin v. California*, 342 U.S. 165 (1952) and *Irvine v. California*, 347 U.S. 128 (1954)—These two cases involved particularly blatant Fourth Amendment violations by the police. The defendants were convicted, but the Supreme Court refused, as in *Wolf*, to require states to follow the exclusionary rule. Rochin's conviction, however, was reversed because the police action was "shocking to the conscience."

4. *Mapp v. Ohio*, 367 U.S. 643 (1961)—Dollree Mapp was convicted of possession of obscene materials after the police conducted a search of her home without a search warrant. The Supreme Court decided to overrule the *Wolf* decision and require state courts to apply the exclusionary rule. The Court cited a well-known statement by Justice Louis D. Brandeis that "if the government becomes a lawbreaker, it breeds contempt for the law; it invites every man to become a law unto himself; it invites anarchy." As you read the following selections, consider whether or not Justice Brandeis's statement is still valid. (A fascinating description of the facts of the *Mapp* case is contained in Friendly and Elliot's *The Constitution: That Delicate Balance* [Random House, 1984].)

YES
Malcolm Richard Wilkey

WHY SUPPRESS VALID EVIDENCE?

America is now ready to confront frankly and to examine realistically both the achievements and social costs of the policies which have been so hopefully enacted in the past 40 years. That reappraisal has made the most headlines in regard to economic and fiscal matters. It is imperative that this honest reappraisal include the huge social costs which American society—alone in the civilized world—pays as a result of our unique exclusionary rule of evidence in criminal cases.

We can see that huge social cost most clearly in the distressing rate of street crimes—assaults and robberies with deadly weapons, narcotics trafficking, gambling and prostitution—which flourish in no small degree simply because of the exclusionary rule of evidence. To this high price we can rightfully add specific, pernicious police conduct and lack of discipline—the very opposite of the objectives of the rule itself....

Though scholars have been shedding more and more light on this problem, few people have considered the enormous social cost of the exclusionary rule, and fewer still have thought about possible alternatives to the rule. I propose to do both those things in this article.

THE RULE'S MYSTIQUE

What is the exclusionary rule? It is a judge-made rule of evidence, originated in 1914 by the Supreme Court in *Weeks v. United States*, which bars "the use of evidence secured through an illegal search and seizure." It is not a rule required by the Constitution. No Supreme Court has ever held that it was. As Justice Black once said,

> [T]he Fourth Amendment does not itself contain any provision expressly precluding the use of such evidence and I am extremely doubtful that such a provision could properly be inferred from nothing more than the basic command against unreasonable searches and seizures.

The greatest obstacle to replacing the exclusionary rule with a rational process, which will both protect the citizenry by controlling the police and avoid rewarding the criminal, is the powerful, unthinking emotional attachment to the rule. The mystique and misunderstanding of the rule causes not only many ordinary citizens but also judges and lawyers to feel (not think) that the exclusionary rule was enshrined in the Constitution by the Founding Fathers, and that to abolish it would do violence to the whole sacred Bill of Rights. They appear totally unaware that the rule was not employed in U.S. courts during the first 125 years of the Fourth Amendment, that it was devised by the judiciary in the assumed absence of any other method of controlling the police, and that no other country in the civilized world has adopted such a rule.

Realistically, the exclusionary rule can probably never be abolished until both the public and the Supreme Court are satisfied that there is available in our legal system a reasonably workable alternative. Unfortunately, the converse may also be true—we will never have any alternative in operation until the rule is abolished. So long as we keep the rule, the police are not going to investigate and discipline their own men, and thus sabotage prosecutions by invalidating the admissibility of vital evidence.

HOW THE RULE WORKS

The impact of the exclusionary rule may not be immediately apparent from the simple phrase of the *Wolf* decision that it bars "the use of evidence seized through an illegal search and seizure." It may help to consider three examples to see how the exclusionary rule needlessly frustrates police and prosecutors trying to do a very difficult job on the streets of our cities.

In *U.S. v. Montgomery*, two police officers on auto patrol in a residential neighborhood at 6 P.M. on a winter day saw Montgomery driving his car in a way that suggested he was "sizing up" the area. When they stopped and identified him, they learned by radio that an arrest warrant was outstanding against him. Before taking him into custody, the officers searched him for weapons and found a .38 caliber bullet in his pants pocket, a magnum revolver loaded with six rounds and an unregistered, sawed-off shotgun with shells in the car.

A trial court convicted him of illegal possession of firearms, but the Court of Appeals (2–1) reversed, holding that no probable cause existed for stopping Montgomery in the first place, and that all evidence discovered thereafter was the product of an illegal search and seizure. Applying the exclusionary rule, the court suppressed as evidence the revolver and the sawed-off shotgun, which made it impossible to convict Montgomery or to retry the case.

Montgomery is an example of typical routine police work, which many citizens would think of as needed reasonable effort to prevent crime. But now look at *U.S. v. Willie Robinson*, a similar case with a different result. A policeman stopped Robinson for a minor traffic violation and discovered that license bureau records indicated his license was probably a forgery. Four days later, the same officer spotted Robinson about 2 A.M. and arrested him for driving with a forged credential.

Since police regulations required him to take Robinson into custody, the officer began a pat down or frisk for dangerous weapons. Close inspection of the cigarette package in the outer pocket of the man's jacket revealed heroin. Robinson was convicted of heroin possession but the Court of Appeals held 5–4 that, in light of the exclusionary rule, the search of Robinson was illegal and the heroin evidence must be suppressed. The Supreme Court reversed, holding that probable cause existed for the search, the evidence was legally obtained, and it could be offered in evidence. The High Court reinstated the original conviction.

This is one search and seizure case which turned out, in my view, correctly. But it took a U.S. District Court suppression hearing, a 2–1 panel decision in the Court of Appeals, a 5–4 decision in the court *en banc*, and a 6–3 decision of the Supreme Court to confirm the validity of the on-the-spot judgment of a lone police officer exercised at 2 A.M. on a Washington Street—five years and eight months earlier.

In *Coolidge v. New Hampshire*, a 14-year-old girl was found with her throat slit and a bullet in her head eight days after she had disappeared. Police contacted the wife of a suspect whose car was like one seen near the crime, and she gave them her husband's guns. Tests proved that one of the weapons had fired the fatal bullet.

Invoking his statutory authority, the attorney general of the state issued a warrant for the arrest of the suspect and the seizure of his car. Coolidge was captured and convicted. But the Supreme Court reversed the conviction on the grounds that the warrant was defective, the search of the auto unreasonable and vacuum sweepings from the auto (which matched the victim's clothing) were inadmissible. Why? Because the attorney general who issued the warrant had personally assumed direction of the investigation and thus was not a "neutral and detached magistrate."

Observe that here the conviction was reversed because of a defect in the warrant, not because of any blunder. Errors of law by either the attorney preparing the affidavit and application for the warrant or the magistrate in issuing the warrant frequently invalidate the entire search that the police officers make, relying in good faith on the warrant; those errors cause the suppression of the evidence and the reversal of the conviction. How does the exclusionary rule improve police conduct in such cases?

THE COURT'S RATIONALE

Deterrence: During the rule's development, the Supreme Court has offered three main reasons for the rule. The principal and almost sole theory today is that excluding the evidence will punish the police officers who made the illegal search and seizure or otherwise violated the constitutional rights of the defendant, and thus deter policemen from committing the same violation again. The flaw in this theory is that there is absolutely no empirical data that excluding evidence against a defendant has anything to do with either punishing police officers or thereby deterring them from future violations.

Chief Justice Burger has flatly asserted "...there is no empirical evidence to support the claim that the rule actually deters illegal conduct of law enforcement officials," and the Supreme Court has never sought to adduce such empirical evidence in support of the rule. Probably such a connection can never be proved, for as a matter of logical analysis "the exclusionary rule is well tailored to deter the prosecutor from illegal conduct. But the prosecutor is not the guilty party in an illegal arrest or search and seizure, and he rarely has any measure of control over the police who are responsible."

Privacy: From *Weeks* (1914) to *Mapp* (1961) the rule was also justified as protecting the privacy of the individual against illegal searches and seizures as guaranteed by the Fourth Amendment. The Supreme Court later downgraded the protection of privacy rationale, perhaps because of the obvious defect that the rule purports to do nothing to recompense innocent victims of Fourth Amendment violations, and the gnawing doubt as to just what right of privacy guilty individuals have in illegal firearms, contraband narcotics and policy betting slips—the frequent objects of search and seizure.

Judicial integrity: A third theme of the Supreme Court's justifying rationale, now somewhat muted, is that the use of illegally obtained evidence brings the court system into disrepute. In *Mapp* Justice Clark referred to "that judicial integrity so necessary in the true administration of justice," which was reminiscent of Justice Brandeis dissenting in *Burdeau v. McDowell*, " . . . respect for law will not be advanced by resort, in its enforcement, to means which shock the common man's sense of decency and fair play."

THE IMPACT OF THE RULE

It is undeniable that, as a result of the rule, the most valid, conclusive, and irrefutable factual evidence is excluded from the knowledge of the jury or consideration by the judge. As Justice Cardozo predicted in 1926, in describing the complete irrationality of the exclusionary rule:

> The criminal is to go free because the constable has blundered.... A room is searched against the law, and the body of a murdered man is found.... The privacy

of the home has been infringed, and the murderer goes free.

Fifty years later Justice Powell wrote for the Court:

> The costs of applying the exclusionary rule even at trial and on direct review are well known: . . .the physical evidence sought to be excluded is typically reliable and often the most probative evidence bearing on the guilt or innocence of the defendant.... Application of the rule thus deflects the truthfinding process and often frees the guilty. The disparity in particular cases between the error committed by the police officer and the windfall afforded the guilty defendant by application of the rule is contrary to the idea of proportionality that is essential to the concept of justice.

I submit that justice is, or should be, a truth-seeking process. The court has a duty to the accused to see that he receives a fair trial; the court also has a duty to society to see that all the truth is brought out; only if all the truth is brought out can there be a fair trial. The exclusionary rule results in a complete distortion of the truth. Undeniable facts, of the greatest importance, are forever barred—facts such as Robinson's heroin, Montgomery's sawed-off shotgun and pistol, the bullet fired from Coolidge's gun and the sweepings from his car which contained items from the dead girl's clothes.

If justice is a truth-seeking process, it is all important that *there is never any question of reliability* in exclusionary rule cases involving material evidence, as the three examples illustrate. We rightly exclude evidence whenever its reliability is questionable—a coerced or induced confession, for example, or a faulty line-up for identification of the suspect. We exclude it because it is inherently unreliable, not because of the illegality of obtaining it. An illegal search in no way reduces the reliability of the evidence.

There have been several empirical studies on the effects of the exclusionary rule in five major American cities—Boston, Chicago, Cincinnati, New York and Washington, D.C.—during the period from 1950 to 1971. These have been recently collected and analyzed, along with other aspects of the exclusionary rule and its alternatives, by Professor Steven Schlesinger in his book *Exclusionary Injustice: The Problem of Illegally Obtained Evidence.*

Three of these studies concluded that the exclusionary rule was a total failure in its primary task of deterring illegal police activity and that it also produced other highly undesirable side effects. The fourth study, which said the first three were too harsh in concluding that the rule was totally ineffective, still said: "Nonetheless, the inconclusiveness of our findings is real enough; they do not nail down an argument that the exclusionary rule has accomplished its task."

Schlesinger and others regard the study by Dallin Oakes as perhaps the most comprehensive ever undertaken, both in terms of data and the breadth of analysis of the rule's effects. Oakes concluded:

> As a device for directly deterring illegal searches and seizures by the police, the exclusionary rule is a failure.... The harshest criticism of the rule is that it is ineffective. It is the sole means of enforcing the essential guarantees of freedom from unreasonable arrests and searches and seizures by law enforcement officers, and it is a failure in that vital task.

Spiotto made a comparative study of both the American exclusionary rule and the existing Canadian tort alternative, taking Chicago and Toronto as comparable metropolitan areas. He found that an

> empirical study [of narcotics and weapons cases] indicates that, over a 20-year period in Chicago, the proportion of cases in which there were motions to suppress evidence allegedly obtained illegally increased significantly. This is the opposite result of what would be expected if the rule had been efficacious in deterring police misconduct.

Three studies conducted between 1950 and 1971 show a substantial increase in motions to suppress in both narcotics and gun offenses. The increase from 1950 to 1971 can fairly be attributed to the impact of *Mapp* (1961) on search and seizure in the state courts.

CRITICISMS OF THE RULE

By this point, we should be able to see that the exclusionary rule actually produces many effects opposite from those that the Court intended to produce. No matter what rationale we consider, the rule in its indiscriminate workings does far more harm than good and, in many respects, it actually prevents us from dealing with the real problems of Fourth Amendment violations in the course of criminal investigations.

In the eyes of the Supreme Court, the first and primary rationale of the exclusionary rule is deterrence. I submit that all available facts and logic show that excluding the most reliable evidence does absolutely nothing to punish and thus deter the official wrongdoer, but the in-

YES Malcolm Richard Wilkey / 293

evitable and certain result is that the guilty criminal defendant goes free.

The second—now rather distant second—rationale in the eyes of the Court has been the protection of privacy. I submit a policy of excluding incriminating evidence can never protect an innocent victim of an illegal search against whom no incriminating evidence is discovered. The only persons protected by the rule are the guilty against whom the most serious reliable evidence should be offered. It cannot be separately argued that the innocent person is protected *in the future* by excluding evidence against the criminal *now*, for this is only the deterrent argument all over again.

The third rationale found in the past opinions of the Court is that the use of illegally obtained evidence brings our court system into disrepute. I submit that the exclusion of valid, probative, undeniably truthful evidence undermines the reputation of and destroys the respect for the entire judicial system.

Ask any group of laymen if they can understand why a pistol found on a man when he is searched by an officer should not be received in evidence when the man is charged with illegal possession of a weapon, or why a heroin package found under similar circumstances should not be always received in evidence when he is prosecuted for a narcotics possession, and I believe you will receive a lecture that these are outrageous technicalities of the law which the American people should not tolerate. If you put the same issue to a representative group of lawyers and judges, I predict you would receive a strong preponderance of opinions supporting the lay view, although from those heavily imbued with a mystique of the exclusionary rule as of almost divine origin you would doubtless hear some support.

The rationale of protecting judicial integrity is also inconsistent with the behavior of the courts in other areas of the criminal law. For example, it is well settled that courts will try defendants who have been illegally seized and brought before them. In *Ker v. Illinois*, a defendant kidnapped in Peru was brought by force to Illinois for trial; in *Mahon v. Justice* the accused was forcibly abducted from West Virginia for trial in Kentucky; and in *Frisbie v. Collins*, the defendant was forcibly seized in Illinois for trial in Michigan.

Said the *Frisbie* court:

> This court has never departed from the rule announced in *Ker v. Illinois* ... that the power of the court to try a person for crime is not impaired by the fact that he had been brought within the court's jurisdiction by reason of 'forcible abduction.'

Why should there be an exclusionary rule for illegally seized evidence when there is no such exclusionary rule for illegally seized people? Why should a court be concerned about the circumstances under which the murder weapon has been obtained, while it remains unconcerned about the circumstances under which the murderer himself has been apprehended? It makes no sense to argue that the admission of illegally seized evidence somehow signals the judiciary's condonation of the violation of rights when the judiciary's trial of an illegally-seized *person* is not perceived as signaling such condonation.

OTHER DEFECTS OF THE RULE

The rule does not simply fail to meet its declared objectives; it suffers from five other defects, too. One of those defects is that it uses an undiscriminating, meat-ax approach in the most sensitive areas of the administration of justice. It totally fails to discriminate between the degrees of culpability of the officer or the degrees of harm to the victim of the illegal search and seizure.

It does not matter whether the action of the officer was grossly willful and flagrant or whether he was conscientiously using his very best judgment under difficult circumstances; the result is the same: the evidence is out. The rule likewise fails to distinguish errors of judgment which cause no harm or inconvenience to the individual whose person or premises are searched, except for the discovery of valid incriminating evidence, from flagrant violations of the Fourth Amendment as in *Mapp* or *Rochin*. Chief Justice Burger's point in *Bivens* is undeniable:

> ... society has at least as much right to expect rationally graded responses from judges in place of the universal 'capital punishment' we inflict on all evidence when police error is shown in its acquisition.

Another defect is that the rule makes no distinction between minor offenses and more serious crimes. The teenage runner caught with policy slips in his pocket and the syndicate hit man accused of first degree murder are each automatically set free by operation of the exclusionary rule, without any consideration of the impact on the community. Customarily, however, we apply different standards to crimes which vary as to seriousness, both in granting bail before trial and in imposing sentence afterwards.

A third problem is that, strangely, a rule which is supposed to discipline and improve police conduct actually results in encouraging highly pernicious police behavior. A policeman is supposed to tell the truth, but when he knows that describing the search truthfully will taint the evidence and free the suspect, the policeman is apt to feel that he has a "higher duty" than the truth. He may perjure himself to convict the defendant.

Similarly, knowing that evidence of gambling, narcotics or prostitution is hard to obtain under the present rules of search and seizure, the policeman may feel that he can best enforce the law by stepping up the incidence of searches and seizures, making them frequent enough to be harassing, with no idea of ultimate prosecution. Or, for those policemen inclined *ab initio* to corruption, the exclusionary rule provides a fine opportunity to make phony raids on establishments, deliberately violating the standards of the Fourth Amendment and immunizing the persons and premises raided—while making good newspaper headlines for active law enforcement.

Fourth, the rule discourages internal disciplinary action by the police themselves. Even if police officials know that an officer violated Fourth Amendment standards in a particular case, few of them will charge the erring officer with a Fourth Amendment violation: it would sabotage the case for the prosecution before it even begins. The prosecutor hopes the defendant will plea bargain and thus receive some punishment, even if the full rigor of the law cannot be imposed because of the dubious validity of the search. Even after the defendant has been convicted or has pleaded guilty, it would be dangerous to discipline the officer—months or years later—because the offender might come back seeking one of the now popular post-conviction remedies.

Finally, the existence of the federally imposed exclusionary rule makes it virtually impossible for any state, not only the federal government, to experiment with any other methods of controlling police. One unfortunate consequence of *Mapp* was that it removed from the states both the incentive and the opportunity to deal with illegal search and seizure by means other than suppression. Justice Harlan, in commenting on the evil impact of the federal imposition of the exclusionary rule on the states, observed:

> Another [state], though equally solicitous of constitutional rights, may choose to pursue one purpose at a time, allowing all evidence relevant to guilt to be brought into a criminal trial, and dealing with constitutional infractions by other means.

ALTERNATIVES TO THE RULE

The excuse given for the persistence of the exclusionary rule in this country is that there is no effective alternative to make the police obey the law in regard to unreasonable searches and seizures. If this excuse did not come from such respected sources, one would be tempted to term it an expression of intellectual bankruptcy.

"No effective alternative"? How do all the other civilized countries control their police? By disciplinary measures against the erring policeman, by effective civil damage action against both the policeman and the government—not by freeing the criminal. Judging by police conduct in England, Canada and other nations, these measures work very well. Why does the United States alone rely upon the irrational exclusionary rule?

It isn't necessary. Justice Frankfurter in *Wolf* (1949) noted that none of the 10 jurisdictions in the British Commonwealth had held evidence obtained by an illegal search and seizure inadmissible, and "the jurisdictions which have rejected the *Weeks* doctrine have not left the right to privacy without other means of protection...." Justice Harlan in his dissent in *Mapp* noted the wisdom of allowing all evidence to be brought in and "dealing with constitutional infractions by other means." Justice Black, concurring in *Mapp*, noted that the Fourth Amendment did not itself preclude the use of illegally obtained evidence.

In his dissent in *Bivens*, Chief Justice Burger suggested that Congress provide that Fourth Amendment violations be made actionable under the Federal Tort Claims Act, or something similar. Senator Lloyd Bentsen and other members of Congress have put forward proposals to abolish the rule and substitute the liability of the federal government toward the victims of illegal searches and seizures, both those innocent and those guilty of crimes.

THE PURPOSES OF AN ALTERNATIVE

Before examining what mechanism we might adopt in place of the exclusionary rule as a tool for enforcing the rights guaranteed by the Fourth Amendment, let us see clearly what objectives we desire to achieve by such alternatives.

The *first* objective, in sequence and perhaps in the public consciousness of those who are aware of the shortcomings of the rule, is to prevent the unquestionably guilty from going free from all punishment for their crime—to put an end to the ridiculous situation that the murderer goes free because the constable has blundered. Let me reiterate: the exclusionary rule, as applied to tangible evidence, has never prevented an innocent person from being convicted.

Second, the system should provide effective guidance to the police as to proper conduct under the Fourth Amendment. When appellate courts rule several years after the violation, their decisions are not only years too late, but usually far too obscure for the average policeman to understand. They are remote in both time and impact on the policeman at fault. Immediate guidance to the policeman as to his error, with an appropriate penalty, is obviously more effective, in contrast to simply rewarding the criminal.

Third sequentially, but first in value, the mechanism should protect citizens from Fourth Amendment violations by law enforcement officers. (I say sequentially, because it is necessary first to abolish the exclusionary rule and then to provide guidance to the police.) If police receive immediate and meaningful rulings, accompanied by prompt disciplinary penalties, they will be effectively deterred from future wrongful action and citizens will thus be effectively protected.

Fourth, the procedure should provide effective and meaningful compensation to those citizens, particularly innocent victims of illegal searches and seizures. This the present exclusionary rule totally fails to do. Only the guilty person who has suffered an illegal search and seizure receives some form of compensation—an acquittal, which is usually in gross disproportion to the injury inflicted on him by an illegal search and seizure. Thus, under the present irrational exclusionary rule system, the guilty are over-rewarded by a commutation of all penalties for crimes they did commit and the innocent are never compensated for the injuries they suffered.

THE MAGNITUDE OF THE OFFENSE

Fifth, it should be an objective of any substitute for the exclusionary rule to introduce comparative values into what is now a totally arbitrary process and inflexible penalty Under the exclusionary rule, the "penalty" is the same irrespective of the offense. If an officer barely oversteps the line on probable cause and seizes five ounces of heroin from a peddler on the street corner, or an officer without a warrant and without probable cause barges into a home and seizes private papers, the result is automatic—the evidence is barred, the accused is freed, and this is all the "punishment" the officer receives.

Surely the societal values involved in the two incidents are of a totally different magnitude. The error of the officer in dealing with narcotics peddlers should not be overlooked, his misapprehension of the requirement of probable cause should be called to his attention quickly in a way which he will remember, but actual punishment should be relatively minimal. In the instance of an invalid seizure of private papers in the home, the officer should be severely punished for such a gross infraction of Fourth Amendment rights.

The exclusionary rule is applied automatically now when there is no illegal action by investigative officers and hence no possible deterrence to future police misconduct. For example, where government agents have dutifully applied to a judge or magistrate for a search warrant, and executed the warrant in strict conformity with its terms, a warrant which later proves defective will force the judge later to exclude the evidence illegally seized. All that is involved in these instances is a legal error on the part of the judge, magistrate, or perhaps the attorney who drew the papers. It is absurd to say that the court subsequently is "punishing" or attempting to "deter" the judge, magistrate, or attorney who made the legal error by suppressing the evidence and letting the accused go free, but this is what happens now.

If these are valid objectives in seeking a substitute procedure for the exclusionary rule as a method of enforcing Fourth Amendment rights, there seem to be two general approaches which might well be combined in one statute—internal discipline by the law enforcement authorities themselves, and external control by the courts or an independent review board.

INTERNAL DISCIPLINE

Disciplinary action against the offending law enforcement officer could be initiated by the law enforcement organization itself or by the person whose Fourth Amendment rights had been allegedly violated. The police could initiate action either within the regular command structure or by an overall disciplinary board outside the hierarchy of command. Many law enforcement organizations have such disciplinary boards now and they could be made mandatory by statute in all federal law enforcement agencies. Wherever they may be located, the organization would require action to be taken following the seizure of material evidence, if the criminal trial or an independent investigation showed a violation of the Fourth Amendment standards.

The person injured could also initiate action leading to internal discipline of the offending officer by complaint to the agency disciplinary board. Each enforcement agency or department could establish a process to hear and decide the complaint, providing both a penalty for the offending officer (if the violation were proved) and government compensation to the injured party.

This procedure would cover numerous cases in which citizens suffer violations of Fourth Amendment rights, but in which no court action results. The injured party could choose this administrative remedy in lieu of court action, but any award in the administrative proceedings would be taken into account by a court later if a citizen, dissatisfied with the award, instituted further legal action.

The penalty against the officer would be tailored to fit his own culpability; it might be a reprimand, a fine, a delay in promotion, a suspension, or discharge. Factors bearing upon the extent of the penalty would include the extent to which the violation was willful, the manner in which it deviated from approved conduct, the degree to which it invaded the privacy of the injured party, and the extent to which human dignity and societal values were breached.

Providing compensation to the injured party from the government is necessary, for it is simply realistic to make the government liable for the wrongful acts of its agent in order to make the prospect of compensation meaningful. Policemen traditionally are not wealthy and the government has a deep purse. Moreover, higher administrative officials and irate taxpayers may be expected to react adversely to losses resulting from the misconduct of policemen and to do something about their training and exercise of responsibilities.

EXTERNAL CONTROL

When a prosecutor tries a defendant in the wake of a violation of Fourth

Amendment rights, the court could conduct a mini-trial of the offending officer after the violation is alleged and proof outlined in the principal criminal case. This mini-trial would be similar to a hearing on a motion to suppress now, but it would be conducted after the main criminal case. The burden would be on the injured party to prove, by preponderance of the evidence, that the officer violated his Fourth Amendment rights. The policeman could submit his case to either the judge or the jury who heard the main criminal case.

By initiating the "trial" of the officer immediately following the criminal case in which he was charged with misconduct, the court could determine the question of his violation speedily and economically. Presumably both the judge and jury have been thoroughly familiarized with the facts of the main case and are able to put the conduct of the officer in perspective.

Such a mini-trial would provide an outside disciplinary force that the injured party could utilize in lieu of internal discipline by the agency. Any previous administrative action taken against the officer would be considered by the judge and jury, if a penalty were to be assessed as a result of the mini-trial. The same factors bearing on the penalty to the officer and compensation to the injured party as discussed under the administrative remedy would be relevant in the mini-trial.

In those instances where police violate Fourth Amendment rights but the prosecutor does not bring charges against the suspect, the wronged party should be able to bring a statutory civil action against the government and the officer. Both would be named as defendants: the officer to defend against any individual penalty, the government to be able to respond adequately in damages to the injured party if such were found. Many instances of Fourth Amendment violation now go unnoticed because no criminal charge is brought and the injured party is not in position to bring a *Bivens*-type suit for the alleged constitutional violation. The burden of proof on the factors in regard to penalty and compensation would be the same as in a mini-trial following the principal criminal case, as discussed above.

The creation of this civil remedy could be accomplished by simple amendment to the present Federal Tort Claims Act. This is the procedure followed in many other countries, among them Canada.

> ... the remedy in tort has proved reasonably effective; Canadian juries are quick to resent illegal activity on the part of the police and to express that resentment by a proportionate judgment for damages.

Disciplinary punishment and civil penalties directly against the erring officer involved would certainly provide a far more effective deterrent than the Supreme Court has created in the exclusionary rule. The creation of a civil remedy for violations of privacy, whether or not the invasion resulted in a criminal prosecution, would provide a remedy for the innocent victims of Fourth Amendment violations which the exclusionary rule has never pretended to give. And the rationale that the "government should not 'profit' from its own agent's misconduct" would disappear completely if erring officers were punished and injured parties compensated when there was a Fourth Amendment violation. If such a law and procedure were enforced, there would be no remaining objection to the subject of search and seizure still receiving his appropriate punishment for his crime.

CONCLUSION

All of the above was written before I read Professor Kamisar's ["Is the exclusionary rule an 'illogical' or 'unnatural' interpretation of the Fourth Amendment?" 62 Judicature 66.] It is apparent that our respective positions are widely divergent. After pondering his statement, I believe it fair to say that he must attempt to defend his position on one of two grounds, and that on analysis neither is defensible.

First, if Professor Kamisar believes that the Fourth Amendment necessarily mandates the exclusionary rule, then he ought to cite Supreme Court authority for this position. Nowhere in his article does he do so. It is undeniable that at no time in the Court's history has a majority in any case ever so held, and I do not believe that any more than two individual justices in the Court's history have so expressed themselves. In contrast, numerous justices, both favoring and opposing the rule, have stated that the rule itself is *not* mandated by the Fourth Amendment.

Second, if Professor Kamisar's article is intended only to say that under the Constitution we have a choice of methods to enforce the ban against "unreasonable searches and seizures," and that the exclusionary rule is a good choice only because of "the imperative of judicial integrity," then I submit both logic and experience in this country and all other countries refutes this. If the Supreme Court or the Congress has a choice of methods under the Constitution, then it simply will not do to rest the choice of exclusionary rule solely on the high principle of "judicial integrity" and to ignore the pragmatic result, the failure to achieve the objective of enforcement and the other pernicious side effects discussed above, which themselves strongly discredit judicial integrity.

If we have a choice, to attempt to justify the continuation of the exclusionary rule on this basis is to be stubbornly blind to 65 years of experience. If we have a choice, to insist on continuing a method of enforcement with as many demonstrated faults as the exclusionary rule is to be blindly stubborn. If we have a choice, let us calmly and carefully consider the available alternatives, draw upon the experience of other nations with systems of justice similar to our own, and by abolishing the rule permit in the laboratories of our 51 jurisdictions the experimentation with various possible alternatives promising far more than the now discredited exclusionary rule.

NO

Yale Kamisar

THE STRUGGLE TO MAKE
THE FOURTH AMENDMENT
MORE THAN "AN EMPTY BLESSING"

In the 65 years since the Supreme Court adopted the exclusionary rule, few critics have attacked it with as much vigor and on as many fronts as did Judge Malcolm Wilkey in his recent *Judicature* article, "The exclusionary rule: why suppress valid evidence?" (November 1978).

According to Judge Wilkey, there is virtually nothing good about the rule and a great deal bad about it. He thinks the rule is partly to blame for "the distressing rate of street crimes." He tells us that it "discourages internal disciplinary action by the police themselves"; actually results in "encouraging highly pernicious police behavior" (e.g., perjury, harassment and corruption); "makes it virtually impossible for any state, not only the federal government, to experiment with any methods of controlling police"; and "undermines the reputation of and destroys the respect for the entire judicial system."

Judge Wilkey claims, too, that the rule "dooms" "every scheme of gun control ... to be totally ineffective in preventing the habitual use of weapons in street crimes." Until we rid ourselves of this rule, he argues, "the criminal can parade in the street with a great bulge in his pocket or a submachine gun in a blanket under his arm" and "laugh in the face of the officer who might wish to search him for it."

UNTHINKING, EMOTIONAL ATTACHMENT?

Why, then, has the rule survived? "The greatest obstacle to replacing the exclusionary rule with a rational process," Judge Wilkey maintains, is "the powerful, unthinking emotional attachment" to the rule. If you put the issue to a representative group of lawyers and judges, he concedes, "you would doubtless hear some support" for the rule, but only from those "heavily imbued with a mystique of the exclusionary rule as of almost divine origin."

It is hard to believe that nothing more substantial than "unthinking emotional attachment" or mystical veneration accounts for support for the rule

From Yale Kamisar, "The Exclusionary Rule in Historical Perspective: The Struggle to Make the Fourth Amendment More Than 'an Empty Blessing,' " *Judicature* (February 1979). Copyright © 1979 by Yale Kamisar. Reprinted by permission of the author.

by Justices Holmes and Brandeis [and,] more recently, by such battlescarred veterans as Roger Traynor, Earl Warren and Tom Clark.

In the beginning, Judge Traynor was not attached to the rule, emotionally or otherwise. Indeed, in 1942 he wrote the opinion of the California Supreme Court reaffirming the admissibility of illegally seized evidence. But by 1955, it became apparent to Traynor that illegally seized evidence "was being offered and admitted as a routine procedure" and "it became impossible to ignore the corollary that illegal searches and seizures were also a routine procedure, subject to no effective deterrent."

[W]ithout fear of criminal punishment or other discipline, law enforcement officers... casually regard [illegal searches and seizures] as nothing more than the performance of their ordinary duties for which the City employs and pays them.

In light of these circumstances, Traynor overruled the court's earlier decision.

And consider Earl Warren. During the 24 years he spent in state law enforcement work in California (as deputy district attorney, district attorney and attorney general), California admitted illegally seized evidence. Indeed, Warren was the California Attorney General who successfully urged Judge Traynor and his brethren to reaffirm that rule in 1942. In 1954, during his first year as Chief Justice of the United States, he heard a case involving police misconduct so outrageous as to be "almost incredible if it were not admitted" (the infamous *Irvine* case), but he resisted the temptation to impose the exclusionary rule on the states, even in such extreme cases. It was not until 1961 that he joined in the opinion

for the Court in *Mapp*, which imposed the rule on the states.

Chief Justice Warren knew the exclusionary rule's limitations as a tool of judicial control, but at the end of an extraordinary public career—in which he had served more years as a prosecutor than any other person who has ascended to the Supreme Court—Warren observed:

[I]n our system, evidentiary rulings provide the context in which the judicial process of inclusion and exclusion approves some conduct as comporting with constitutional guarantees and disapproves other actions by state agents. A ruling admitting evidence in a criminal trial, we recognize, has the necessary effect of legitimizing the conduct which produced the evidence, while an application of the exclusionary rule withholds the constitutional imprimatur.

The author of the *Mapp* opinion, Tom Clark, was, of course, U.S. Attorney General for four years before he became a Supreme Court justice and he was assistant attorney general in charge of the criminal division before that. Evidently, nothing in his experience gave Clark reason to believe that the rule had "handcuffed" federal officials or would cripple state law enforcement. And he never changed his views about the need for the exclusionary rule during his 18 years on the Court or the 10 years he spent in the administration of justice following his retirement. Indeed, shortly before his death, he warmly defended *Mapp* and *Weeks*.

Moreover, nothing in Justice Clark's career suggests that he endorsed *Mapp* out of "sentimentality" or in awe of the "divine origins" of the exclusionary rule. More likely, he was impressed with the failure of *Wolf* and *Irvine* to stimulate any meaningful alternative to the exclusionary rule in the more than 20 states that still admitted illegally seized evidence at the time of *Mapp.*

I do not mean to suggest that Judge Wilkey's views on the exclusionary rule are aberrational among lawyers and judges; many members of the bench and bar share his deep distress with the rule. Indeed, when Judge Wilkey asks us to abolish the exclusionary rule now—without waiting for a meaningful alternative to emerge—he but follows the lead of Chief Justice Burger, who recently maintained:

> [T]he continued existence of the rule, as presently implemented, inhibits the development of rational alternatives.... It can no longer be assumed that other branches of government will act while judges cling to this Draconian, discredited device in its present absolutist form.

Because so many share Judge Wilkey's hostility to the exclusionary rule, it is important to examine and to evaluate Wilkey's arguments at some length. Only then can we determine whether the rule is as irrational and pernicious as he and other critics maintain—and whether we can abolish it before we have developed an alternative.

CRIME AND THE RULE

A year before the California Supreme Court adopted the exclusionary rule on its own—and years before the "revolution" in American criminal procedure began—William H. Parker, the Chief of the Los Angeles Police Department, said:

> [O]ur most accurate crime statistics indicate that crime rates rise and fall on the tides of economic, social, and political cycles with embarrassingly

little attention to the most determined efforts of our police.

Almost as soon as the California Supreme Court adopted the exclusionary rule, though, Chief Parker began blaming the rule for the high rate of crime in Los Angeles, calling it "catastrophic as far as efficient law enforcement is concerned," and insisting "that the imposition of the exclusionary rule has rendered the people powerless to adequately protect themselves against the criminal army."

Such criticism of the *Cahan* rule was only a preview of the attack on *Mapp.* Chief Justice Traynor, speaking about the debate following the *Mapp* decision, rightly observed that: "Articulate comment about [*Mapp*]...was drowned out in the din about handcuffing the police.

Thus, it is not surprising that Judge Wilkey would claim on his very first page that "[w]e can see [the] huge social cost [of *Weeks* and *Mapp*] most clearly in the distressing rate of street crimes...which flourish in no small degree simply because of the exclusionary rule." Nevertheless, it is disappointing to hear a critic repeat this charge, because after 65 years of debate, there was reason to hope that this criticism, at least, would no longer be made. As Professor James Vorenberg pointed out, shortly after he completed his two years of service as Executive Director of the President's Commission on Law Enforcement and Administration of Justice:

> What the Supreme Court does has practically no effect on the amount of crime in this country, and what the police do has far less effect than is generally realized.

Even Professor Dallin Oaks (now a university president), upon whose work

Judge Wilkey relies so heavily, advised a decade ago:

> The whole argument about the exclusionary rule 'handcuffing' the police should be abandoned. If this is a negative effect, then it is an effect of the constitutional rules, not an effect of the exclusionary rule as the means chosen for their enforcement.
>
> Police officials and prosecutors should stop claiming that the exclusionary rule prevents effective law enforcement. In doing so they attribute far greater effect to the exclusionary rule than the evidence warrants, and they are also in the untenable position of urging that the sanction be abolished so that they can continue to violate the [constitutional] rules with impunity.

A WEAK LINK

Over the years, I have written about the impact of *Cahan, Mapp* and other decisions on crime rates and police-prosecution efficiency. I will not restate my findings again, especially since Judge Wilkey has presented no statistical support for his assertion. I would, however, like to summarize a few points:

• Long before the exclusionary rule became law in the states—indeed, long before any of the procedural safeguards in the federal Constitution was held applicable to the states —invidious comparisons were made between the rate of crime in our nation and the incidence of crime in others.

Thus, in 1911, the distinguished ex-president of Cornell University, Andrew D. White, pointed out that, although London's population was two million larger than New York's, there were 10 times more murders in New York. And in 1920, Edwin W. Sims, the first head of the Chicago Crime Commission, pointed out that "[d]uring 1919 there were more murders in Chicago (with a population of three million) than in the entire British Isles (with a population of forty million)." This history ought to raise some doubts about the alleged causal link between the high rate of crime in America and the exclusionary rule.

• England and Wales have not experienced anything like the "revolution" in American criminal procedure which began at least as early as the 1961 *Mapp* case. Nevertheless, from 1955–65 (a decade which happened to be subjected to a most intensive study), the number of indictable offenses against the person in England and Wales increased 162 percent. How do opponents of the exclusionary rule explain such increases in countries which did not suffer from the wounds the Warren Court supposedly inflicted upon America?

• In the decade before *Mapp*, Maryland admitted illegally seized evidence in all felony prosecutions; Virginia, in all cases. District of Columbia police, on the other hand, were subject to both the exclusionary rule and the *McNabb-Mallory* rule, a rule which "hampered" no other police department during this period. Nevertheless, during this decade the felony rate per 100,000 population increased much more in the three Virginia and Maryland suburbs of the District (69 percent) than in the District itself (a puny one percent).

• The predictions and descriptions of near-disaster in California law enforcement which greeted the 1955 *Cahan* decision find precious little empirical support. The percentage of narcotics convictions did drop almost 10 points (to 77 percent), but only possession cases were significantly affected. Meanwhile, both the rate of arrests and felony complaints filed for narcotics offenses actually increased! Thus, in 1959–60, 20 percent more persons were convicted of narcotics offenses in California superior courts than in the record conviction percentage years before *Cahan*.

The overall felony conviction rate was 84.5 percent for the three years before *Cahan*, 85.4 percent for the *Cahan* year and 86.4 percent in the three years after *Cahan* (even including the low narcotic percentages). Conviction rates for murder, manslaughter, felony assault, rape, robbery and burglary remained almost the same, though the number of convicted felons rose steadily.

The exclusionary rule, to be sure, does free some "guilty criminals" (as would an effective tort remedy that inhibited the police from making illegal searches and seizures in the first place), but very rarely are they robbers or murderers. Rather they are "offenders caught in the everyday world of police initiated vice and narcotics enforcement...."

Though critics of the exclusionary rule sometimes sound as though it constitutes the main loophole in the administration of justice, the fact is that it is only a minor escape route in a system that filters out far more offenders through police, prosecutorial, and judicial discretion than it tries, convicts and sentences....

Moreover, the critics' concentration on the formal issue of conviction tends to overlook the very real sanctions that are imposed even on defendants who 'escape' via the suppression of evidence [e.g., among the poor, most suffer at least several days of imprisonment, regardless of the ultimate verdict; many lose their jobs as a result and have a hard time finding another]....

When one considers that many convictions in the courts that deal with large numbers of motions to suppress often amount to small fines, suspended sentences, and probation, the distinction between conviction and escape becomes even more blurred.

AN UNDEMONSTRATED CONNECTION

... Judge Wilkey hints darkly that there is a "connection" between America's high crime rate and its "unique" exclusionary rule. So far as I am aware, no one has been able to demonstrate such a connection on the basis of the annual *Uniform Crime Reports* or any other statistical data. In Michigan, for example, the rate of violent crime seems to have fluctuated without regard to the life and death of the state's "anti-exclusionary" proviso.

From 1960–64, the robbery rate increased only slightly in the Detroit Metropolitan Statistical Area but it quadrupled from 1964 to 1970 (from 152.5 per 100,000 to 648.5). When the Michigan Supreme Court struck down the state's "anti-exclusionary" proviso in 1970, the robbery rate fell (to 470.3 per 100,000 in 1973), climbed (to 604.2 in 1975), then dropped again (to 454.3 in 1977, the lowest it has been since the 1960's).

From 1960–64, the murder and nonnegligent manslaughter rate remained almost the same in the Detroit area, but it rose extraordinarily the next six years (5.0 in 1964 to 14.7 in 1970). In the next four years it continued to climb (but less sharply) to 20.2 in 1974. Then it dropped to 14.1 in 1977, the lowest it has been since the 1960's.

Finally, I must take issue with Judge Wilkey's case of the criminal who "parade[s] in the streets with a great bulge in his pocket or a submachine gun in a blanket under his arm," "laugh[ing] in the face of the officer who might wish to search him for it." If American criminals "know the difficulties of the police in making a valid search," as Judge Wilkey tells us, they know, too, that the exclusionary rule has "virtually no applicability" in "large areas of police activity which do not result in criminal prosecutions" and that confiscation of weapons is one of them. (The criminal might get back his blanket, but not the submachine gun).

Moreover, it is not at all clear that an officer who notices a "great bulge" in a person's pocket or, as in the recent *Mimms* case, a "large bulge" under a person's sports jacket, lacks lawful authority to conduct a limited search for weapons. Indeed, *Mimms* seems to say that a policeman *does* have the authority under such circumstances. Even if I am wrong, however, even if the Fourth Amendment does not permit an officer to make such a limited search for weapons, *abolishing the exclusionary rule wouldn't change that.* If an officer now lacks the lawful authority to conduct a "frisk" under these circumstances, he would still lack the lawful authority to do so if the rule were abolished. This is a basic point, one that I shall focus on in the next section.

A BASIC CONFUSION

In my earlier *Judicature* article, I pointed out how police and prosecutors have treated the exclusionary rule as if it were itself the guaranty against unreasonable search and seizure (which is one good

reason for retaining the rule). At several places Judge Wilkey's article reflects the same confusion.

He complains, for example, that if a search or frisk turns up a deadly weapon, that weapon cannot be used in evidence if the officer lacked the constitutionally required cause for making the search or frisk in the first place. But this is really an attack on the constitutional guaranty itself, not the exclusionary rule. Prohibiting the use of illegally seized evidence may be poor "public relations" because by then we know who the criminal is, but an *after-the-fact* prohibition

> prevents convictions in no greater degree than would effective prior direction to police to search only by legal means...[T]he maintenance of existing standards by means of exclusion is not open to attack unless it can be doubted whether the standards themselves are necessary.

If we replace the exclusionary rule with "disciplinary punishment and civil penalties directly against the erring officer involved," as Judge Wilkey proposes, and if these alternatives "would certainly provide a far more effective deterrent than...the exclusionary rule," as the judge assures us, the weapon still would not be brought in as evidence in the case he poses because the officer would not *make* the search or frisk if he lacked the requisite cause to do so.

Judge Wilkey points enviously to England, where "the criminals know that the police have a right to search them *on the slightest suspicion,* and they know that if a weapon is found they will be prosecuted" (emphasis added). But what is the relevance of this point in an article discussing the exclusionary rule and its alternatives? Abolishing the rule would not confer a *right* on our police to search "on the slightest suspicion"; it would not affect lawful police practices in any way. Only a change in the substantive law of search and seizure can do that.... And replacing the exclusionary rule with a statutory remedy against the government would not bring about an increase in unlawful police activity if the alternative were equally effective—and Judge Wilkey expects it to be "a far more effective deterrent."

I venture to say that Judge Wilkey has confused the *content* of the law of search seizure (which proponents of the exclusionary rule need not, and have not always, defended) with the *exclusionary rule*—which "merely states the consequences of a breach of whatever principles might be adopted to control law enforcement officers." The confusion was pointed out more than 50 years ago by one who had the temerity to reply to the great Wigmore's famous criticism of the rule. Every student of the problem knows Wigmore's views on this subject, but very few are familiar with Connor Hall's reply. It is worth recalling:

> When it is proposed to secure the citizen his constitutional rights by the direct punishment of the violating officer, we must assume that the proposer is honest, and that he would have such consistent prosecution and such heavy punishment of the offending officer as would cause violations to cease and thus put a stop to the seizure of papers and other tangible evidence through unlawful search.
>
> If this, then, is to be the result, no evidence in any appreciable number of cases would be obtained through unlawful searches, and the result would be the same, so far as the conviction of criminals goes, as if the constitutional right was enforced by a return of the evidence.

Then why such anger in celestial breasts? Justice can be rendered inefficient and the criminal classes coddled by the rule laid down in *Weeks* only upon the assumption that the officer will not be directly punished, but that the court will receive the fruits of his lawful acts, will do no more than denounce and threaten him with jail or the penitentiary and, at the same time, with its tongue in its cheek, give him to understand how fearful a thing it is to violate the Constitution. This has been the result previous to the rule adopted by the Supreme Court, and that is what the courts are asked to continue.

... If punishment of the officer is effective to prevent unlawful searches, then equally by this is justice rendered inefficient and criminals coddled. It is only by violations that the great god Efficiency can thrive.

WAITING FOR ALTERNATIVES

Judge Wilkey makes plain his agreement with Chief Justice Burger that "the continued existence of [the exclusionary rule] ... inhibits the development of rational alternatives" and that "incentives for developing new procedures or remedies will remain minimal or nonexistent so long as the exclusionary rule is retained in its present form."

Thus, Judge Wilkey warns that "we will never have any alternative in operation until the rule is abolished. So long as we keep the rule, the police are not going to investigate and discipline their men, and thus sabotage prosecutions by invalidating the admissibility of vital evidence...." He argues that *Mapp* "removed from the states both the incentive and the opportunity to deal with illegal search and seizure by means other than suppression." And he concludes his first article with these words:

> [L]et us ... by abolishing the rule permit in the laboratories of our 51 jurisdictions the experimentation with the various possible alternatives promising far more than the now discredited exclusionary rule.

In light of our history, these comments (both the Chief Justice's and Judge Wilkey's) are simply baffling. First, the fear of "sabotaging" prosecutions has never inhibited law enforcement administrators from disciplining officers for committing the "many unlawful searches of homes and automobiles of innocent people which turn up nothing incriminating, in which no arrest is made, about which courts do nothing, and about which we never hear."

Second, both defenders of the rule and its critics recognize that

> there are large areas of police activity which do not result in criminal prosecutions [e.g., arrest or confiscation as a punitive sanction (common in gambling and liquor law violations), illegal detentions which do not result in the acquisition of evidence, unnecessary destruction of property]—hence the rule has virtually no applicability and no effect in such situations.

Whatever the reason for the failure to discipline officers for "mistakes" in these "large areas of police activities," it cannot be the existence of the exclusionary rule.

Finally, and most importantly, *for many decades* a majority of the states had no exclusionary rule but *none of them* developed any meaningful alternative. Thirty-five years passed between the time the federal courts adopted the exclusionary rule and the time *Wolf* was decided in 1949, but none of the 31 states which still admitted illegally seized evidence had established an alternative method of controlling the police. Twelve more years passed before *Mapp* imposed the rule on the state courts, but none of the 24 states which still rejected the exclusionary rule had instituted an alternative remedy. This half-century of post-*Weeks* "freedom to experiment" did not produce any meaningful alternative to the exclusionary rule anywhere.

DISPARITY BETWEEN FACT AND THEORY

Of course, few critics of the exclusionary rule have failed to suggest alternative remedies that *might be devised* or that *warranted study.* None of them has become a reality.

In 1922, for example, Dean Wigmore maintained that "the natural way to do justice" would be to enforce the Fourth Amendment directly "by sending for the high-handed, overzealous marshal who had searched without a warrant, imposing a 30-day imprisonment for his contempt of the Constitution, and then proceeding to affirm the sentence of the convicted criminal." Nothing ever came of that proposal. Another critic of the rule suggested that a civil rights office be established, independent of the regular prosecutor, "charged solely with the responsibility of investigating and prosecuting alleged violations of the Constitution by law-enforcement officials." Nothing came of that proposal either.

Judge Wilkey recognizes that "policemen traditionally are not wealthy," but "[t]he government has a deep purse." Thus, as did Chief Justice Burger in his *Bivens* dissent, Judge Wilkey proposes that in lieu of the exclusion of illegally seized evidence there be a statutory remedy against the government itself to afford meaningful compensation and restitution for the victims of police illegality. Two leading commentators, Caleb Foote and Edward Barrett, Jr., made the same suggestion 20 years ago, but none of the many states that admitted illegally seized evidence at the time seemed interested in experimenting along these lines.

Indeed, the need for, and the desirability of, a statutory remedy against the government itself was pointed out at least as long ago as 1936. In a famous article published that year, Jerome Hall noted that the prospects of satisfying a judgment against a police officer were so poor that the tort remedy in the books "collapses at its initial application to fact." Said Hall:

> [W]here there is liability (as in the case of the policeman), the fact of financial irresponsibility is operative and, presumably, conclusive; while, where financial responsibility exists (as in the case of a city), there is no liability.

"This disparity between theory and fact, between an empty shell of relief and substantial compensation," observed Professor Hall—43 years ago—"could not remain unnoticed."

This disparity—no longer unnoticed, but still uncorrected—has troubled even the strongest critics of the rule. Thus, more than 35 years ago, J. A. C. Grant suggested "implement[ing] the law covering actions for trespass, even going so far as to hold the government liable in damages for the torts of its agents." And William Plumb, Jr., accompanied his powerful attack on the rule with a similar suggestion.

MAPP'S TRAUMATIC EFFECTS

At the time of Plumb's article, the admissibility of illegally seized evidence had "once more become a burning question in New York." Delegates to the 1938 constitutional convention had defeated an effort to write the exclusionary rule into the constitution, but only after a long and bitter debate. The battle then moved to the legislature, where bills were pending to exclude illegally obtained, or at least illegally wiretapped, evidence.

Against this background, Plumb offered a whole basketful of alternatives to the rule and he said the state legislature "should make a thorough study of the problem of devising effective direct remedies [such as those he had outlined] to make the constitutional guarantee 'a real, not an empty blessing.' " But nothing happened.

Otherwise why would a New York City Police Commissioner say of *Mapp* some 20 years later:

> I can think of no decision in recent times in the field of law enforcement which had such a dramatic effect as this.... I was immediately caught up in the entire problem of reevaluating our procedures which had followed the *Defore* rule, and modifying, amending, and creating new policies and new instructions for the implementation of *Mapp*. The problems were manifold. [Supreme Court decisions such as *Mapp*] create tidal waves and earthquakes which require rebuilding of our institutions sometimes from their very foundations upward. Retraining sessions had to be held from the very top administrators down to each of the thousands of foot patrolmen....

In theory, *Defore*, which rejected the exclusionary rule in New York, had not expanded lawful police powers one iota.

Nor, in theory, had *Mapp* reduced these powers. What was an illegal search before *Defore* was still an illegal search. What was an unlawful arrest before *Mapp* was still an unlawful arrest.

The *Defore* rule, of course, was based largely upon the premise that New York did not need to adopt the exclusionary rule because existing remedies were adequate to effectuate the guaranty against illegal search and seizure. Cardozo said that:

> The officer might have been resisted[!], or sued for damages or even prosecuted for oppression. He was subject to removal or other discipline at the hands of his superiors.

Why, then, did *Mapp* have such a "dramatic" and "traumatic" effect? Why did it necessitate "creating new policies"? What were the old policies like? Why did it necessitate retraining sessions from top to bottom? What was the *old* training like? What did the commissioner mean when he said that before *Mapp* his department had "followed the *Defore* rule"?

> On behalf of the New York City Police Department as well as law enforcement in general, I state unequivocally that every effort was directed and is still being directed at compliance with and implementation of *Mapp*....

Isn't it peculiar to talk about police "compliance with" and "implementation of" a *remedy* for a violation of a body of law the police were supposed to be complying with and implementing all along? Why did the police have to make such strenuous efforts to comply with *Mapp* unless they had not been complying with the Fourth Amendment?

Flowing from the *Mapp* case is the issue of defining probable cause to constitute a lawful arrest and subsequent search and seizure.

Doesn't this issue flow from the Fourth Amendment itself? Isn't that what the Fourth Amendment is all about?

The police reaction to *Mapp* demonstrates the unsoundness of the underlying premise of *Defore*. Otherwise why, at a post-*Mapp* training session on the law of search and seizure, would Leonard Reisman, then the New York Deputy Police Commissioner in charge of legal matters, comment:

> The *Mapp* case was a shock to us. We had to reorganize our thinking, frankly. Before this, nobody bothered to take out search warrants. Although the U.S. Constitution requires warrants in most cases, the U.S. Supreme Court had ruled [until 1961] that evidence obtained without a warrant—illegally if you will —was admissible in state courts. So the feeling was, why bother?

NO INCENTIVE FOR CHANGE

As I have already indicated, critics of the exclusionary rule have often made proposals for effectuating the Fourth Amendment by means other than the exclusionary rule—but almost always as a *quid pro quo* for rejecting or repealing the rule. Who has ever heard of a police-prosecution spokesman urging— or a law enforcement group supporting —an effective "direct remedy" for illegal searches and seizures in a jurisdiction which *admitted* illegally seized evidence? Abandoning the exclusionary rule without waiting for a meaningful alternative (as Judge Wilkey and Chief Justice Burger would have us do) will not furnish an incentive for devising an alternative, but *re-*

lieve whatever pressure there now exists for doing so.

I spoke in my earlier article of the great symbolic value of the exclusionary rule. Abolition of the exclusionary rule, after the long, bitter struggle to attain it, would be even more important as a symbol.

During the 12-year reign of *Wolf*, some state judges

> remained mindful of the cogent reasons for the admission of illegally obtained evidence and clung to the fragile hope that the very brazenness of lawless police methods would bring on effective deterrents other than the exclusionary rule.

Their hope proved to be in vain. *Wolf* established the "underlying constitutional doctrine" that "the Federal Constitution, by virtue of the Fourteenth Amendment, prohibits unreasonable searches and seizures by state officers" (though it did not require exclusion of the resulting evidence); *Irvine* warned that if the state "defaulted and there were no demonstrably effective deterrents to unreasonable searches and seizures in lieu of the exclusionary rule, the Supreme Court might yet decide that they had not complied with 'minimal standards' of due process." But neither *Wolf* nor *Irvine* stimulated a single state legislature or a single law enforcement agency to demonstrate that the problem could be handled in other ways.

The disappointing 12 years between *Wolf* and *Mapp* give added weight to Francis Allen's thoughtful commentary on the *Wolf* case at the time it was handed down:

> This deference to local authority revealed in the *Wolf* case stands in marked contrast to the position of the court in other cases arising within the last decade involving rights 'basic to a free society.' It seems safe to assert that in no other area of civil liberties litigation is there evidence that the court has construed the obligations of federalism to require so high a degree of judicial self-abnegation.
>
> ... [I]n no other area in the civil liberties has the court felt justified in trusting to public protest for protection of basic personal rights. Indeed, since the rights of privacy are usually asserted by those charged with crime and since the demands of efficient law enforcement are so insistent, it would seem that reliance on public opinion in these cases can be less justified than in almost any other....

Now Judge Wilkey asks us to believe that the resurrection of *Wolf* (and evidently the overruling of the 65-year-old *Weeks* case as well) will permit "the laboratories of our 51 jurisdictions" to produce meaningful alternatives to the exclusionary rule. His ideological ally, Chief Justice Burger, is even more optimistic. He asks us to believe that a return to the pre-exclusionary rule days "would inspire a surge of activity toward providing some kind of statutory remedy for persons injured by police mistakes or misconduct."

And to think that Judge Wilkey accuses *defenders* of the exclusionary rule of being "stubbornly blind to 65 years of experience"!

POSTSCRIPT

Should the Exclusionary Rule Be Abolished?

Wilkey is not the only federal judge to have opposed the exclusionary rule. The most famous judicial critic was former Supreme Court chief justice Warren E. Burger. Burger's opposition to the rule, however, did not lead to an overturning of *Mapp* or *Weeks*. But during the past several decades, there have been a substantial number of cases in which the Court considered the rule and restricted its scope. Thus, while the rule can still be invoked by a defendant at a criminal trial, it cannot be used at a grand jury proceeding (see *United States v. Calandra*, 414 U.S. 338, 1974), in a *habeas corpus* proceeding by a state prisoner (see *Stone v. Powell*, 428 U.S. 465, 1976), when the illegal search is conducted on someone other than the defendant (see *United States v. Payner*, 447 U.S. 727, 1980), or when the illegal search was conducted outside the United States (see *U.S. v. Verdugo-Urguidez*, 110 S. Ct. 1056, 1990). Many cases have involved automobiles, the most recent being *California v. Acevedo*, 111 S. Ct. 1982 (1991).

The Court has approved a good faith exception to the rule in cases where the police officer believed that he was acting lawfully, even though the warrant may have been defective or procured illegally (*Massachusetts v. Sheppard*, 104 S. Ct. 3424, 1984). It has also ruled that search warrants are not required for school officials to search school lockers if there are reasonable grounds for believing the search will reveal evidence of criminal behavior (*New Jersey v. T. L. O., A Juvenile*, 105 S. Ct. 733, 1985). A recent case involving good faith and computers is *Arizona v. Evans*, 115 S. Ct. 1185 (1995). The Rehnquist court has generally been lenient in upholding police law enforcement practices, and the policy of limiting the defendant's opportunities for invoking the exclusionary rule seems likely to continue.

In part, the resistance to the exclusionary rule is based on a belief that it does not deter illegal police conduct. Interesting articles about the exclusionary rule include Crocker, "Can the Exclusionary Rule Be Saved?" 84 *Journal of Criminal Law and Criminology* 310 (1993); LaFave, "Pinguitudinous Police, Pachydermatous Prey: Whence Fourth Amendment 'Seizures'?" 1991 *University of Illinois Law Review* 729 (1991); C. Slobogin, "The World Without a Fourth Amendment," 39 *UCLA Law Review* 1 (1991); and Note, "Cameras in Teddy Bears: Electronic Visual Surveillance and the Fourth Amendment," 58 *University of Chicago Law Review* 1045 (1991). For more information on issues of privacy and the law, see the following Internet sites: http://www.epic.org/; http://www.privacy.org/ipc/; http://www.cdt.org/; and http://www.eff.org/.

ISSUE 16

Will Waiting Periods Control Gun Purchases?

YES: Sarah Brady, from Statement Before the Subcommittee on Crime, Committee on the Judiciary, U.S. House of Representatives (February 24, 1988)

NO: James Jay Baker, from Statement Before the Subcommittee on Crime and Criminal Justice, Committee on the Judiciary, U.S. House of Representatives (March 21, 1991)

ISSUE SUMMARY

YES: Sarah Brady, head of a citizens' lobby for gun control, argues that a waiting period for purchasing a weapon does not change who is lawfully allowed to buy a gun, that it would not impose an undue burden on law enforcement agencies, and that it would prevent many crimes.

NO: James Jay Baker, director of federal affairs for the National Rifle Association, claims that waiting periods do not work, that criminals would still be able to obtain weapons, and that an additional burden would be placed on law enforcement authorities.

Unlike previous assassinations or attempted assassinations, the attempt on former president Ronald Reagan's life in 1981 did not lead to a widespread debate about gun control. The issue that captured public discussion was the insanity defense raised by his would-be assassin, John Hinckley. Probably because Reagan opposed gun control legislation, Hinckley's act did little, at least at first, to further the cause of gun control on the federal level.

Much more seriously injured than Reagan was his press secretary, James Brady. As a result of the attempted assassination, gun control became a major concern of James and Sarah Brady. For many years, the Bradys lobbied in Congress for stronger gun control measures. Finally, in 1993, the Brady Bill was passed and went into effect in early 1994. The bill provides for a mandatory waiting period before one can purchase a gun.

Can a measure such as the Brady Bill reduce illegal gun use and the violence associated with guns? Are more restrictive measures desirable, such as the regulation of the manufacture of weapons or a complete ban?

Both proponents and opponents of gun control come "armed" with statistics. Proponents point out that in Great Britain, where gun owners must be certified and their weapons stored at gun clubs, handguns killed only 22 people in 1990. In Australia, which requires a background check and a license to buy a handgun, they killed 10. In Japan, which bans most private ownership of handguns, they took 87 lives. In the United States, they killed 10,567. Yet there are already over 200 million guns held by citizens, and regulation of sales will not really affect these weapons or their owners.

One of the most frequently mentioned legal justifications for permitting individuals to possess handguns is the Second Amendment to the Constitution. This amendment states, "A well regulated Militia, being necessary to the security of a free State, the right of the people to keep and bear Arms, shall not be infringed." Yet due to court interpretations of the meaning of these words, the amendment has become almost irrelevant to the issue of gun control. Certainly, one convicted of violating a firearms statute is unlikely to win his or her case by relying on the Second Amendment.

Although many people are familiar with the last half of the amendment, the crucial words are contained in the first part. The right to bear arms is not absolute. Rather, it is a right related to the need for a state militia. This was the ruling of the Supreme Court in the case of *United States v. Miller*, 307 U.S. 174 (1939), the only case interpreting the Second Amendment as it relates to the federal government. In that case, two men were charged in federal court with transporting an unregistered sawed-off shotgun and violating the National Firearms Act. The defendants claimed that they were protected by the Second Amendment and won in the trial court. The Supreme Court, however, interpreted the rights granted by the Second Amendment differently. Justice James C. McReynolds wrote,

> In the absence of any evidence tending to show that possession or use of a "shotgun having a barrel of less than eighteen inches in length" at this time has some reasonable relationship to the preservation or efficiency of a well regulated militia, we cannot say that the Second Amendment guarantees the right to keep and bear such an instrument....
>
> The Constitution as originally adopted granted to the Congress power—"To provide for calling forth the Militia to execute the Laws of the Union, suppress Insurrections and repel Invasions."... With obvious purpose to assure the continuation and render possible the effectiveness of [the Militia] the declaration and guarantee of the Second Amendment were made. It must be interpreted and applied with that end in view.

In the following selections, Sarah Brady, wife of James Brady and a gun control lobbyist, argues for legislation to institute a waiting period for the purchase of guns. James Jay Baker, of the National Rifle Association, opposes such legislation and contends that waiting periods are ineffective in achieving their stated purposes and are not a good idea.

YES

Sarah Brady

STATEMENT OF SARAH BRADY

Thank you for the opportunity to testify once again before this distinguished Subcommittee. My name is Sarah Brady. I am Vice-Chair of Handgun Control, Inc., a national citizens organization working to keep handguns out of the wrong hands. I am here today in strong support of H.R. 975, introduced by Representative Edward Feighan.... This legislation establishes a seven-day waiting period and allows for a background check on handgun purchasers.

Having previously testified before this Subcommittee, I know many of you are familiar with my personal experience and my involvement with this issue. It seems odd to me that it is in question whether we should act to keep handguns out of the wrong hands. For that is what this debate is about —whether we allow convicted felons to simply walk into gun stores and immediately walk out with handguns.

We already have a federal law prohibiting convicted felons, minors, people who have been adjudicated mentally ill, illegal aliens, and drug addicts from acquiring handguns. But what does that mean if we do not have the tools to enforce that law? And so I ask you today, do you believe that a convicted felon should be able to walk into a gun store and get a handgun instantly? I cannot believe that anyone could sanction that. Yet as long as we do not have a reasonable waiting period and give police the opportunity to run background checks, a convicted felon will have our seal of approval. That is why I am here today. I am making a very personal appeal to you because I believe you have a responsibility to act to keep handguns out of the hands which would misuse them. Handguns in the wrong hands result in tragedy. I do not say that theoretically. I speak from experience.

I know that you are familiar with what happened on March 30, 1981. At 2:30 P.M. that day, my husband, Jim Brady, was shot through the head by a deranged young man. Jim nearly died. The President nearly died, and two of his security men were seriously wounded.

It has been almost seven years now. March 30th marks the anniversary of the shooting. I often think about the other handgun tragedies which have taken place in these seven years that could have been prevented if there were a national waiting period. We must not wait another seven years for other

From U.S. House of Representatives. Committee on the Judiciary. Subcommittee on Crime. *In Support of H.R. 975*. Hearing, February 24, 1988. Washington, DC: Government Printing Office, 1988.

tragedies to occur. We must not wait any longer. We need a national waiting period now.

John Hinckley's handguns were confiscated in October 1980 as he tried to board an airplane in Tennessee, where he was stalking President Jimmy Carter. Hinckley, a drifter, then gunless, needed to replenish his arsenal. In possession of a Texas driver's license and knowing that Texas had no waiting period or background check, Hinckley made the trip to Dallas to purchase the handgun he used to shoot my husband and the President of the United States. Hinckley no longer lived at the address he listed on the federal form he was required to complete. A simple check might have stopped him. Had police been given an opportunity to discover that Hinckley lied on the federal form, Hinckley might well have been in jail instead of on his way to Washington. Now Jim lives daily with the consequence of Hinckley's easy access to a handgun.

This bill does not change who is legally permitted to purchase a handgun. Nor does it impose a major burden on law-abiding citizens. This legislation also provides that if an individual has a legitimate, immediate need for a handgun, the waiting period can be waived by local law enforcement. Is seven days too much to ask a responsible citizen to wait when we know that so many lives are at stake? I don't think so.

Public support for a waiting period and background check is strong. A 1981 Gallup Poll found that more than 90% of Americans want such a law. This legislation is supported by every major law enforcement organization in the nation, many representatives of which are here today to testify in support of this bill. The American Bar Association, the American Medical Association, the

AFL-CIO, and other organizations too numerous to mention, all support a federal seven-day waiting period. The 1981 Reagan Administration Task Force on Violent Crime recommended such a law. A 1985 Justice Department report states that "at minimum, the acquisition of a firearm by a felon should be somewhat more complicated than just walking into a gun shop and buying one."

While the National Rifle Association opposes this bill, it is important to note that several years ago in its own publication, the NRA stated that a waiting period would be effective as a means of "reducing crimes of passion and in preventing people with criminal records or dangerous mental illness from acquiring guns."

The NRA has flip-flopped on waiting periods and recently taken extreme positions on machine guns, cop-killer bullets, and plastic guns. Considering these extreme positions, I find it incomprehensible that any Member of Congress could trust the judgment of the NRA on a national waiting period or any legislation affecting American lives and public safety, especially when the NRA is in direct opposition to America's law enforcement community which is charged with the responsibility of protecting us.

The NRA argues that proscribed persons do not purchase their handguns over the counter and certainly will not do so if they have to submit to a waiting period. Yet, a 1985 Department of Justice study entitled "The Armed Criminal in America" found that over 20 percent of criminals obtain their handguns through gun dealers. In fact, in states with waiting period laws, many criminals and others disqualified from buying handguns have been caught trying to purchase their handguns over the counter. Law enforcement officials from across the nation report tremendous success where waiting periods are in effect.

For example, according to a police official in Memphis, Tennessee, the state's fifteen-day waiting period screens out about 50 applicants a month, most of whom have criminal records.

According to the California Department of Justice, the state's fifteen-day waiting period screened out more than 1500 prohibited handgun purchasers in 1986. In that same year, Maryland's seven-day waiting period caught more than 700 prohibited handgun buyers.

States with waiting periods have been effective in stopping criminals before tragedy occurs, but it is unfortunate that in states without waiting periods or background checks, police do not have the same tools to prevent such tragedy.

One of the most shocking and disturbing cases of 1987 occurred in Florida in the wake of the October stock market crash. Arthur Kane purchased a handgun only forty-five minutes before murdering his Florida stock broker and wounding another. If police had been able to conduct a background check, they could have discovered that Kane was a convicted felon.

In another well-publicized event, Dwain Wallace, who had a history of mental illness, was able to instantly purchase a handgun from a Youngstown, Ohio pawnshop. Just two days later, he brandished the handgun in the Pentagon and was immediately gunned down by a Pentagon guard.

A convicted felon, Larry Dale, purchased a handgun at a Tulsa, Oklahoma gun shop, and within 24 hours opened fire at a grocery store, killing one customer and wounding another.

I have described a few of the many well-known cases of proscribed persons who instantly purchased their handguns over the counter without having to undergo a waiting period or background check. But for each well-known case, there are many, many more which never make the front page.

While I am not suggesting that a waiting period will stop all crime, it is obvious from these examples that we can save many lives if we want to.

The NRA claims that waiting periods do not prevent criminals from obtaining handguns because criminals will get them from other sources. But in reality, it is the states without waiting periods that are a significant source of handguns for criminals.

The Treasury's Bureau of Alcohol, Tobacco and Firearms' study of handguns used in crime found that of all the handguns used in crime in New York City, only four percent were purchased in New York State which requires a background check. Virtually all the rest were from states without waiting periods or background checks. In addition, the study found that in states without waiting periods or background checks, an overwhelming majority of handguns used in crime were purchased within the same state. For example, of all the handguns used in crime in Dallas, almost 90 percent were purchased in Texas which has no waiting period.

The NRA argues that waiting periods should be left up to the states, not the federal government. While individual states, many counties and municipalities have passed local waiting periods, a national law is critical because it will ensure that handguns are not purchased over the counter in states without waiting periods and then sold on the street in states requiring waiting periods and/or background checks.

I am ashamed that my own state of Virginia, which has no waiting period or background check, is a major source of handguns used in crime elsewhere. Just a few weeks ago, police arrested one Richmond man who reportedly purchased more than seventy guns in Virginia and then brought them into Washington, D.C. to sell on the street. Another man from the District was charged with using false identification, purchasing more than two dozen semi-automatic handguns in Virginia and selling them to District drug dealers. Unfortunately, these examples represent only the tip of the iceberg of this criminal traffic in handguns.

We can prevent needless tragedy. We can make it more difficult for criminals to get handguns. I hope that the day will come when no American family has to go through what my family has suffered. Again I ask, do you really believe that a convicted felon should be able to walk into a gun store and instantly purchase a handgun? The American people do not believe that. But until action is taken on this bill, a convicted felon purchasing a handgun will have our seal of approval.

The NRA would like to turn back the clock to the days before passage of the 1968 Gun Control Act, which has served our nation well for nearly two decades....

I ask that you stand with our law enforcement community and provide the leadership that will save lives by keeping handguns out of the wrong hands.

NO

James Jay Baker

STATEMENT OF JAMES JAY BAKER

Mr. Chairman, I am here today as the Representative of the National Rifle Association of America to comment on H.R. 7, the "Brady Handgun Violence Prevention Act." H.R. 7 is virtually identical to legislation the NRA opposed in the 101st Congress. The reason for our opposition is based on an objective analysis of the facts, which when stripped of the emotionalism and sentimentality which has almost completely overshadowed the reality of this issue, indicate that imposing further restrictions on the firearms ownership rights of law-abiding citizens will not only be ineffective, but counter-productive to the stated goals of its proponents. We firmly believe the need for H.R. 7 to be unsubstantiated by circumstance, logic, or the form and factual content of the debate between responsible and criminal firearms ownership and is antithetical to the rights of every law-abiding citizen under the Bill of Rights.

Before proceeding to a more specific discussion of our substantive disagreements with the issues surrounding H.R. 7, the National Rifle Association Institute for Legislative Action (NRA-ILA) would like to, once again, attempt to lay to rest one of the linchpin myths used to argue in favor of a national waiting period and background check before purchase of a pistol or revolver. It is unfortunate that we must spend so much time belaboring this point; it is equally unfortunate that advocates of "gun control" continue to misrepresent the facts concerning the tragic assassination attempt on President Ronald Reagan.

In much of the propaganda produced in support of waiting periods, the allegation is made that, if such a waiting period/background check system had been in place, "John Hinckley would have been caught" because "he lied on a federal form" when he purchased the revolver used in his attack on President Reagan. It is further claimed that Hinckley "would have been in jail, instead of on his way to Washington, D.C." had such a background check been conducted. These allegations are irrefutably false.

John Hinckley purchased a total of eight firearms—two .38 cal. and four .22 cal. revolvers, as well as two rifles—from August 1979 to January 1981. The .22 cal. revolver used in his assault on President Reagan was one of two he purchased in October 1980, more than six months before he left for

From U.S. House of Representatives. Committee on the Judiciary. Subcommittee on Crime and Criminal Justice. Hearing, March 21, 1991. Washington, DC: Government Printing Office, 1991.

Washington, D.C. Federal law was so diligently complied with in this case by the seller that multiple purchase forms were quickly filed with the regional office of ATF after the purchase.

Indeed, this purchase, and all previous purchases, were legal. And they would have been legal under this or any other "waiting period" scheme ever devised. At the time of his purchase, and until his attack on the President, John Hinckley had no felony record, he had no recorded history of mental illness or commitment, (as no check currently involves police inspection of private conversations with a psychiatrist) and he was using a *valid* Texas driver's license issued May 23, 1979, to make this firearms purchases. The contention that a background check would have "uncovered" the fact that he did not physically reside at the address listed on his license is a willful distortion of the criminal record check made by local police. To the contrary, had a check been run and all criminal records been thorough and completely available, they would have confirmed that Hinckley was not a prohibited person and that his last known address was in Lubbock, Texas.

Simply put, no detection system ever proposed or ever devised has mindreading capabilities. Advocates of the waiting period do a gross disservice to the nation by asserting that the tragic assassination attempt on President Reagan would have been prevented by the imposition of any regulatory "gun control" scheme. I urge this Committee to look carefully at other arguments made by those who continue to make that claim citing the case of John Hinckley as evidence.

The long history of waiting period schemes points up the failure of those systems in other criminal justice areas, as well. Waiting periods, permit-to-

purchase laws, and police background checks have been instituted around the country for most of the century. After the 1911 Sullivan law in New York, many were enacted in the 1920's and 1930's, about the same time that Uniform Crime Reporting system was implemented to facilitate the collection of crime data from cities and states throughout the nation. Thus, criminologists and other scholars have had ample time and abundant evidence with which to study and document the effectiveness of a waiting period in deterring violent crime. The results are a damning indictment of those who propose to control crime by regulating the behavior of law-abiding members of the community.

In October 1975, Douglas R. Murray of the University of Wisconsin published "Handguns, Gun Control Laws and Firearms Violence." Using the standard statistical methods—a multiple regression statistical framework—he compared the various state firearms laws —including purchase permit, waiting period, police notification, retail license, minimum age, permit to carry openly, and permit to carry concealed—to crime rates, while considering socio-economic conditions. Murray found that "gun control laws have no significant effect on rates of violence beyond what can be attributed to background social conditions." Secondly, he found that such laws do not effectively limit access to guns by the violence-prone; and, finally, accessibility to handguns "seems to have no effect on rates of violent crime and firearms accidents, another reason why gun control laws are ineffective."

Murray summarized: "On the basis of these data, the conclusion is, inevitably, that gun control laws have no individual or collective effect in reducing the rates of violent crime."

Murray's study was replicated by a self-proclaimed "gun control" advocate, Professor Matthew DeZee at Florida State University. His conclusion? "The results indicate that not a single gun control law, and not all the gun control laws added together, had a significant impact... in determining gun violence. It appears, then, that present legislation created to reduce the level of violence in society falls far short of its goals... Gun laws do not appear to affect gun crimes." Keep in mind that the types of laws studied by these scholars were identical to the legislation before you today.

Another study was conducted by two professors at the California State University at Long Beach. Professors Joseph Maggaddino and Marshall Medoff studied "waiting periods" and "cooling-off" periods and found them to be totally useless in curbing crime. They found no relationship between a waiting period or cooling-off period and any type of violent crime, except that they noted a slightly higher homicide rate and a slightly higher robbery rate in places with such laws.

Currently, there are twenty-four states with waiting periods or permit to purchase regulations required for the purchase of a pistol or revolver. Additionally, there are scores of cities and counties that have their own restrictive systems of this type. Again, the majority of these systems have been in place for decades, giving criminologists such as Murray, DeZee, Maggaddino and Medoff ample opportunity to unearth any supposed efficacy these systems have. Likewise, there has existed more than sufficient data for evaluation by those who are represented by Handgun Control Incorporated (HCI).

We find that, despite a great deal of sympathy, albeit short-lived, in the academic community for the idea of restrictive waiting periods scholars have failed to discern any benefits of the waiting period concept. A few, notably Massachusetts Professor James D. Wright, have been honest enough to change their position on this issue after their research revealed the facts.

In keeping with this criminological evaluation, which actually served to confirm common sense, the trend in this nation has been more towards rolling back or repealing existing waiting periods for handguns at the state and local level. Some states with handgun waiting periods have confirmed gun owners fears, not to mention their initial predictions, by increasing the length of waiting periods and including rifles and shotguns under waiting period strictures. In fact, voters in many states and cities have chosen to defeat attempts at imposing or lengthening existing waiting periods. The story at the state level in the recent past is of pro-gun initiatives, such as preemption and constitutional right to keep and bear arms amendments, passing overwhelmingly in reflection of the public's support of lawful, private firearms ownership. Waiting period proponents may quote as many simplistic polls as they choose, but it is these votes by duly elected state legislators, that should be viewed as the turn gauge of public opinion. Clearly, public opinion reflected at the ballot box is running strong and hard *against* restrictive gun laws.

Preemption represents an implicit rejection of waiting periods and justifiable claim for supremacy of the state legislative process in setting firearms regulatory law. Currently, forty states have preempted the field in firearms legislation, claiming for the state legislature the sole responsibility over the regulation of firearms. In Representative Feighan's own state of Ohio, Mr. Chairman, waiting periods have died in the 114th, 115th, 116th, 117th, and 118th, General Assemblies.

One of the more glaring deficiencies of H.R. 7 is that it would impose an additional burden of liability on law enforcement, if not de jure than de facto, without addressing the major problem in conducting a nation wide felon check— namely the lack of accurate [information]. The Attorney Generals Task Force on Felon Identification indicates that given the current state of criminal record keeping among the fifty states it is simply impossible to conduct a thorough and accurate background check on an individual on a state level. More to the point, Attorney General Thornburgh has said that to the extent criminal records are available for checking, the information is available on virtually an instantaneous basis, and that nothing is gained from the imposition of a seven-day waiting period.

Given this information we believe it is appropriate to restate our strong support for the implementation of a National Instantaneous Felon Identification system as embodied in H.R. 1412, the "Felon Handgun Purchase Prevention Act". H.R. 1412 was recently introduced by Representative Staggers, a member of the Judiciary Committee. Modeled on the very successful Virginia Firearms Transaction Program, H.R. 1412 addresses several key points which H.R. 7 either does not address, or worse, exacerbates rather than resolves.

First, it must be noted that H.R. 7 specifically exempts those states from the seven day waiting period which have in place, or implement an instantaneous

check system. While we hardly consider this a definitive endorsement for H.R. 1412, it certainly obviates any argument that the proponents of H.R. 7 might make that such a system is ineffectual. To the contrary, an explicit endorsement of the superiority of H.R. 1412 has already been given by Handgun Control Inc. and Sarah Brady when testifying in support of the Virginia system. That same testimony indicated that they believe it is legislation which could be used as a "model" for the nation. We agree. Moreover, based on the experience that Virginia has had, an instantaneous check system could be put into place in a relatively short period of time and at a reasonable cost. A strong argument can be made that a national felon identification system accessed directly by firearms dealers would be significantly cheaper than H.R. 7. At the very least, it will help to free law enforcement departments from the increasingly onerous burden of paperwork which so sorely impacts crime-fighting abilities. Then, too, the spillover benefits of upgrading the current national records keeping system are obviously applicable to many other areas in which certifying the lack of a criminal background may be a prerequisite for employment suitability. These include, but are not limited to" child care functions, banking, the securities and exchange industry, transportation, and the private security industry.

We are certainly not suggesting that this information should be widely accessible. To the contrary, we believe that the release of any information whatsoever must be strictly regulated and conveyed only on a legitimate need to know basis. We further believe that the penalties for the unlawful use or dispersal of such information should be clearly defined, and sufficiently stringent to discourage abuse. However, there are obvious advantages for implementing a system which encourages the respective states to comply with felon record keeping and conveyance systems which are already in place but are either deficient or misutilized....

One of the more obvious shortcomings of H.R. 7 is that it essentially mandates police compliance without enhancing capabilities. Although H.R. 7 does not specifically mandate a background check it does require law enforcement to sign off on all handgun purchases. Handgun Control Inc. has raised the threat of litigation against any law enforcement agency which approves the sale of a handgun on the basis of an incomplete or inaccurate background check from which subsequent harm would arise. In fact, in one of HCI's mass mailings they specifically cite a case in which a widow sued the City of Philadelphia and was awarded $350,000 as a result of a handgun sale which should not have been allowed. If H.R. 7 is enacted you can expect, at a minimum, that there will be a proliferation of litigation against law enforcement, regardless of the circumstances of the approval. As a result not only will there by every incentive to do an extensive background check on every individual when possible, there will also be every incentive for police departments to delay or deny a purchase for as long as possible when available information is incomplete. Again, the result of this will be that numerous suits will, no doubt, be brought against law enforcement agencies by those individuals who are denied lawful possession of their firearm after the seven day period has elapsed.

... [O]ne of the oft repeated questions asked in some form to most members of this Committee at some time or another, is "Why can't an individual wait seven days to purchase a handgun?" The obvious response is another question, "Why should a law-abiding citizen be denied a constitutional right?" There is no comparable waiting restriction levied on any of the other amendments, nor an unsupported invalidation or restriction placed on any other right based on an unsubstantiated presumption of guilt. By accepting other than the minimum criteria necessary to insure that those whom society has judged to be, by circumstances or behavior, unsuitable or in forfeiture of the legitimate exercise of the rights ordained by our Constitution, the American people will have adulterated and diminished not only their Second Amendment rights, but all other Constitutional protection in turn. Because H.R. 1412 provides for, essentially, the instant exercise of a constitutional right in keeping with the overall philosophy of the Founding Fathers, there is little question that it most clearly satisfies both the spirit and the letter of the Constitution. H.R. 7 fulfills neither criteria.

However, to specifically address the suitability of giving law enforcement the means to preclude an individual from taking possession of a handgun for a period of seven days, even were such a period necessary or desirable, highlights perhaps the most egregious, and in isolation, fatal flaw in H.R. 7. H.R. 7 specifically requires a firearms dealer to convey to local law enforcement the purchase request filled out by the customer within 24 hours. Yet, nowhere in H.R. 7 is there a similar mandate defined for law enforcement to return a purchaser's application to the gun store owner within the seven day time period the bill's supporters suppose to be reasonable, or penalty if law enforcement fails to do so. It takes but a small exercise of the imagination to envision the scenarios under which unreasonable delays well in excess of the seven day period could occur. Regardless, the effect will be that a law-abiding citizen will be precluded from taking possession of the firearm which he is lawfully entitled to own, and for which he may have imminent necessity or practical need.

H.R. 1412 is value neutral and specifically defines the rights of an individual and the responsibilities of the system. And, unlike H.R. 7, H.R. 1412 entails no needless infringement or proscription of individual constitutional rights based on the false assumption that firearms, and those who desire to possess them, are inherently deserving of societal suspicion. H.R. 1412 eliminates bias from the equation, H.R. 7 reinforces the circumstances under which biases can be exercised.

Perhaps the main reason there is no mandatory criminal records check by local law enforcement agencies is that those who support the concept embodied in H.R. 7 wish to have law enforcement support for the bill. Yet, a federal law which imposed duties on state and local law enforcement plainly might not be supported by state and local law enforcement; indeed, it might be actively opposed by them. Thus, the result is a bill which, by its express terms, "shall [not] be interpreted to require any action by a chief law enforcement officer which is not otherwise required." This places those in the law enforcement community who are supportive of any effort to prevent private acquisition and possession of firearms in a position where they can support legislation which appears to involve them in the acquisition process but which, in reality, requires them to do nothing.

Throughout its material, HCI misuses the word "caught" in reference to individuals denied lawful access to a handgun, for example, in saying that Columbus, Georgia or New Jersey police "catch" X number of convicted criminals under their system, or that Hinckley would "have been in jail instead of on his way to Washington." Rejection under the system does not equate with indictment, conviction, or incarceration for violation of firearms laws. In fact, our contacts with law enforcement around the country confirm that most individuals are not prosecuted, much less imprisoned, for violations of restrictive gun laws detected by background checks.

HCI's reference to New Jersey is especially interesting, in so far as it makes a stronger case against institution of their scheme than for its implementation. HCI alleged that New Jersey officials denied applications of "33,000 criminals." NRA-ILA and many others pointed out that, in fact, a majority of those rejections were not based on previous criminals records; that the system in question included applications for permits to carry a concealed firearm which are frequently denied solely because the issuing authority determines the "need" is insufficient; and that the system allowed denial based on the arbitrary and subjective standard that issuance would "not be in the interest of the public health, safety or welfare."

HCI has now apparently adopted a lower number of "rejections of criminals," by citing 10,000 most recently. But, according to the New Jersey State Police Firearm Licensing Division, this number is also misleading. The fact is that the "10,000" includes applicants rejected as drug addicts, for medical reasons: as alcoholics, for falsifying records and for the following three completely arbitrary reasons: "public health, safety and welfare; insufficient need, and, of course, other." The police officers we spoke with have completely rejected HCI's characterization of the denials, saying, "we don't keep records that way." This is hardly evidence of an efficient system weeding out criminals while protecting the rights of the law-abiding. And in the face of data showing that the level of firearms-related violent crime in New Jersey, has been rapidly rising, relative to the U.S. as a whole, it is obvious that the system is not preventing the criminal acquisition of firearms.

HCI then claims that the Chief of Police in Columbus, Georgia, believes their waiting period system to be working. NRA-ILA staff has followed up on this assertion and has found that the officers responsible for the waiting period system in Columbus do not share the Chief's view, as reported by HCI. In fact, HCI and/or the Chief appear to expand the level of rejections by more than four-fold. And again, denial does not necessarily indicate prevention of criminal acquisition of a firearm, nor does it relate to the level of violent crime in a community.

HCI also approvingly cites Memphis, Tennessee, and Atlanta, Georgia, as communities where restrictive gun laws are "working." They neglect to point out that those communities are two of the most crime-ridden within their respective states, and indeed within the South as a whole.

California's Attorney General may have been correct in his assessment of the effectiveness of their system in denying a constitutional right with frequency—even though the number of rejections which ultimately result from the California system given represents less than $1/2\%$ of the applicants—but that assertion is unrelated to any crime reductive effect. It should be noted that the homicide rate in California increased 126% as the state increased the length of its waiting period from 48 hours to 5 days to 15 days, even as the national rate rose by less than half as much.

HCI also misrepresents the Wright-Rossi felon study, conducted under a grant from the U.S. Department of Justice. That study found no difference in the methods of firearms acquisition by criminals regardless of the type of state "gun control" laws in place. Wright notes that criminals "obtain guns in hard-to-regulate sources... Swaps, purchases, and trades among private parties (friends and family members) represent the dominant pattern of acquisition within the illicit firearms market." HCI would have us believe that these private networks would suddenly dry up, or that they would suddenly participate in a law enforcement effort aimed at them.

Finally, it is instructive to once again note that waiting periods, police background checks, and permit-to-purchase systems have been in existence at the state and local level for most of this century. HCI alleges that these laws work, and contend that they have examples in x number of states and dozens, if not hundreds, of cities and counties. Yet when called upon to produce evidence of this efficacy, all that they can muster are three states and a few localities. And, upon further examination, even this scant "evidence" is usually found to be completely lacking, outright deceitful, or distorted beyond the recognition of truth.

Mr. Chairman, and members of the Subcommittee, I thank you once again for the opportunity to present the views of millions of NRA members on the legislation proposed here today, H.R. 7. The timely disposal of this proposal would free this Congress to address issues providing hope for real reductions in our nation's rate of violent crime, such as the implementation of the instantaneous handgun check system proposed by H.R. 1412, the streamlining of our criminal justice system and the imposition of swift and certain punishment for criminal offenders. Above all else we need to abandon the skewed logic of H.R. 7 and its ilk which mistakenly targets not the criminal elements in our society, but rather those who already obey the law. This is the wrong approach in the short term, and a long-term prescription for disaster. The Founding Fathers of our Nation sought to create a structure of government not to rule the individual, but rather that the individual might to the fullest extent possible be free to rule his own action. This is exactly why they were careful to specifically describe the inviolate rights of the first Ten Amendments to the U.S. Constitution apart from the restrictions which might be lawfully imposed under the general rubric of the preamble and body of the U.S. Constitution. H.R. 7 is inimical to these protections. Thank you.

POSTSCRIPT

Will Waiting Periods Control Gun Purchases?

The Brady Bill requires local officials to check the background of handgun buyers. Sheriffs in a number of states claim that this provision is an unconstitutional intrusion into local government. In June 1996 the Supreme Court agreed to consider the issue. It will hear arguments in the cases and issue a ruling during its 1996–1997 term.

The United States has about 20,000 gun control laws, the vast majority of which are state or local ordinances. There is considerable variation, therefore, from place to place. There have been several federal statutes enacted to control firearms in addition to the Brady Bill. The Federal Firearms Act of 1934 regulated possession of submachine guns, silencers, and several other weapons. In 1938 the National Firearms Act was passed, requiring the licensing of firearms manufacturers and dealers. As a result, all new weapons sold in the United States since 1938 have been registered and can be traced. The most important federal action was taken with the passage of the Gun Control Act of 1968. The act prohibited the interstate retailing of all firearms. Its purpose was to prevent individuals who cannot legally own a gun from ordering guns by mail under phony names.

There has been renewed attention to the issue of gun control lately as a result of rising drug-related violence and fear of violent crime generally. Is the Brady Bill merely a first step in a plan for a more comprehensive model of gun control? Or if the Brady Bill does not have an impact on violent crime, will gun control legislation generally be perceived as unworkable?

Public opinion polls suggest that a majority of the public wants more regulation. Yet membership in the National Rifle Association is also growing, and gun purchases are increasing. It is highly likely that gun control will continue to be an area of intense political conflict.

The power and influence of the National Rifle Association was recently examined in O. G. Davidson, *Under Fire: The NRA and the Battle for Gun Control* (1993). The meaning and history of the Second Amendment is discussed in Levinson, "The Embarrassing Second Amendment," 99 *Yale Law Journal* 637 (1989); Brown, "Guns, Cowboys, Philadelphia Mayors, and Civic Republicanism: On S. Levinson's 'The Embarrassing Second Amendment,'" 99 *Yale Law Journal* 661 (1989); Hardy, "Armed Citizens, Citizen Armies: Toward a Jurisprudence of the Second Amendment," 9 *Harvard Journal of Law and Public Policy* 559 (1986); and S. Halbrook, *That Every Man Be Armed* (University of New Mexico Press, 1984). On the Internet, see http://www.lib.uchicago.edu/~llou/guncont.html.

ISSUE 17

Should the Insanity Defense Be Abolished?

YES: Jonathan Rowe, from "Why Liberals Should Hate the Insanity Defense," *The Washington Monthly* (May 1984)

NO: Richard Bonnie, from Statement Before the Committee on the Judiciary, U.S. Senate (August 2, 1982)

ISSUE SUMMARY

YES: Editor Jonathan Rowe examines the insanity defense as it is now administered and finds that it is most likely to be used by white middle- or upper-class defendants and that its application is unfair and leads to unjust results.

NO: Professor of law Richard Bonnie argues that the abolition of the insanity defense would be immoral and would leave no alternative for those who are not responsible for their actions.

There is rarely a year in which the insanity defense is not raised in a high-profile case. When a crime is committed that raises questions about humanity and responsibility, defense lawyers may raise (or threaten to raise) the insanity defense. The success rate of such a defense strategy is quite low, and it is certainly lower than the public believes it to be. Yet the insanity defense remains a controversial issue.

In 1843 Daniel McNaughtan, suffering from delusions of persecution, fired a shot at a man he believed was British prime minister Robert Peel. Actually, the victim was the prime minister's secretary and the bullet killed him. Englishmen were outraged, since three other attempted assassinations of political officials had recently taken place, and Queen Victoria was prompted to send her husband, Prince Albert, to the trial as an observer. When McNaughtan was found not guilty by reason of insanity, Victoria sent a letter to the House of Lords, complaining that McNaughtan and the other assassins were "perfectly conscious and aware of what they did." The Lords summoned 15 judges who, after considering the matter, pronounced the McNaughtan rule (commonly referred to as the M'Naghten rule) as the most appropriate formulation of the insanity defense. This test requires that a jury must find that the defendant, when the act was committed, did not know the nature and quality of his act or that he could not tell right from wrong.

One of the problems with the insanity defense is in defining insanity. If one argues in favor of the defense, one should be able to define insanity with reasonable precision and in a way that can be applied consistently. The great difficulty in providing a definition is the basic argument against the insanity defense. The insanity defense issue has caused great controversy between lawyers and psychiatrists over the meaning of insanity and mental illness and over the ability of psychiatrists reliably to diagnose the problems of defendants.

A frequent objection to the M'Naghten rule was that there were persons who could distinguish between good and evil but still could not control their behavior. One response to this critique was the "irresistible impulse" test. Using this standard, a defendant would be relieved of responsibility for his or her actions even if he or she could distinguish right from wrong but, because of mental disease, could not avoid the action in question. A somewhat broader and more flexible version of the combined M'Naghten–irresistible impulse test was recommended by the American Law Institute in 1962. Under this formulation, people are not responsible for criminal conduct if they lack *substantial capacity* to appreciate the criminality of their conduct or to conform their conduct to the requirements of the law.

The most noteworthy and radical experiment with the reformulation of the insanity defense occurred in *Durham v. United States*, 214 F.2d 862 (1954). The District of Columbia Court of Appeals ruled that an accused was not criminally responsible if his act was the product of mental disease or defect. The effect of this rule was to increase the amount of expert psychiatric testimony presented in court about whether or not mental disease was present and whether or not the act was a product of the disease. While welcomed by many since it allowed for a more complete psychiatric picture to be presented to the jury, the rule proved to be too vague and led to too much power being given to psychiatric experts. As a result, in *United States v. Brawner*, 471 F.2d 969 (1972), the Durham experiment was abandoned.

Examination of the insanity defense opens up some extremely important issues of law. For example, what are the purposes of punishment? What assumptions does the law make about human nature, free will, and personal responsibility? What should be the role of the jury and what authority should be given medical and psychiatric experts in evaluating deviant behavior? How should we deal with the often competing goals of rehabilitation, retribution, and deterrence? These are among the questions raised in the following arguments presented by Jonathan Rowe and Richard Bonnie on the need for reforming or abolishing the insanity defense.

YES

Jonathan Rowe

WHY LIBERALS SHOULD HATE THE INSANITY DEFENSE

"It's the fallacy of your legal system," said Gary Trapnell, a bank robber who not long afterwards would hijack a TWA 707 flying from Los Angeles to New York. "Either the man falls under this antiquated psychiatric scheme of things, or he doesn't." Trapnell was talking about the insanity defense, which he had used with great acumen to avoid jail for his innumerable crimes over the years. "I have no right to be on the streets," he added.

The insanity defense has been much in the news of late. We read cases such as that of the Michigan ex-convict who pleaded insanity after seven killings, won an acquittal, but returned to the streets two months later when he was declared sane. In a month, he was charged with murdering his wife. Or take the 23-year-old Connecticut man who left the state hospital three months after an insanity acquittal for stabbing a man. The acquittee's mother pleaded to have him recommitted, but to no avail. Shortly thereafter, he repeatedly stabbed a man whose home he was burglarizing. Once again he was declared not guilty by reason of insanity.

It sounds like the warmup for a right-wing tirade against the coddlers of criminals. But the much publicized trials of John Hinckley and others have cast the issue in a somewhat different light. In a strange way, by jumbling liberal and conservative loyalties, these have made debate on the subject not only necessary, but possible as well. Take the "Twinkie Defense," which enabled former San Francisco City Supervisor Dan White to get off with a light eight-year sentence after shooting, with obvious deliberation, San Francisco Mayor George Moscone and his city administrator, Harvey Milk. As Milk was both liberal and openly homosexual, thousands who probably never before identified with the cause of law and order were outraged that this brutal act of (at least symbolic) homophobia should go lightly punished. John Hinckley, for his part, was the son of a wealthy upper-middle-class family, and not the sort of fellow who evoked sympathies usually reserved for the downtrodden. His trial prompted even *The Nation*, which rarely concedes the cops an inch, to suggest some mild reforms in the insanity defense.

From Jonathan Rowe, "Why Liberals Should Hate the Insanity Defense," *The Washington Monthly*, vol. 16, no. 4 (May 1984). Copyright © 1984 by The Washington Monthly Company, 1611 Connecticut Avenue, NW, Washington, DC 20009; (202) 462–0128. Reprinted by permission of *The Washington Monthly*.

In the wake of the Hinckley trial, a number of reforms have been suggested. *The Nation*, along with many others, advocates that we put the burden of proof upon the defendant. (In the Hinckley case, the prosecutors actually had to prove him sane, which is no mean feat.) Others have called for a tighter legal definition of insanity itself. Such changes might be helpful, but they amount to fiddling. The only way to resolve the injustices of the insanity defense is to do away with it entirely. This may sound cruel, but it is not. Nor is it a proposal to "lock 'em up and throw away the key." To the contrary, the injustices of this defense go much deeper than a few criminals getting off the hook. They go close to the core of our current practices regarding punishment and correction. Getting rid of the insanity defense would help to make us confront the need for humane reform in the way we sentence and confine those who break the law.

SUCH A DEAL

The insanity defense looms a good deal larger in our minds than it does in actual life. Somewhere between 1,000 and 2,000 criminals make use of it each year, or about 1 percent to 2 percent of felonies that go to trial (over 90 percent in many jurisdictions are plea-bargained before trial). The issue is important not because it arises frequently, but because it tends to arise in the most serious crimes: think of Son of Sam, for example, or the Hillside Strangler. Such people tend to be dangerous, and their trials attract so much publicity that they put our entire system of justice to a test. What single event of the last two years affected your view of the criminal justice system more than the Hinckley trial did?

It is hard to read about such trials without getting the impression that something is fundamentally wrong. Take the case of Robert H. Torsney, the New York City policeman who shot a 15-year-old black youth in the head from two feet away in November of 1978. In an article in the *Journal of Legal Medicine*, Abraham Halpern, director of psychiatry at the United Hospital, Port Chester, New York, tells the case in salient detail.

At first, Torsney's lawyer resisted any suggestion of psychological observation or treatment for his client. Such treatment for an officer who was only acting in the line of duty was "worse than putting him in the electric chair," the attorney said. As public indignation rose, however, and acquittal became more and more unlikely, the attorney decided that Torsney might have deep-seated psychological problems after all. At a hearing on Torsney's insanity defense, his paid psychiatrist explained the policeman's errant account of the incident, which was contradicted by other witnesses as an "involuntary retrospective falsification." Not a lie, mind you. The psychiatrist went on to explain that Torsney shot the kid because of an "organic psychomotor seizure" arising from a "mental defect."

The jury found Torsney not guilty by reason of insanity. After a year, however, the staff at the mental hospital recommended that he be released because they could find nothing wrong with him. When the lower court balked—such hasty releases are unseemly if nothing else—Torsney's attorney indignantly filed an appeal. "It can't be seriously argued," he wrote, "that the record in this case establishes that Mr. Torsney is either seriously mentally ill or presently dangerous. At most he may be said to have a personality flaw, which certainly does not distinguish him from the rest of society."

What really distinguished Torsney, it seemed, was that he had shot somebody and deserved to be punished. That such simple observations can become so obscured is largely the result of the wholesale invasion of psychiatry into the courtroom that has been underway since the 1950s. Back then, the stars of psychiatry and psychoactive drugs were shining bright. To many, we were on the threshold of a new age, in which psychiatrists could measure such things as responsibility and mental disease down to minute calibrations and effect cures with the precision of engineers. If only we could let these new wizards into the courtroom, to bring their expertise to bear upon the processes of justice.

The main opening came in 1954, when federal appeals Judge David Bazelon, of the Washington, D.C., District Court, declared the so-called "Durham Rule." Under the old "M'Naghten Rule," a criminal could be judged insane only if he or she didn't know right from wrong. This crimped the psychiatrists somewhat, since they tend to shrug their shoulders on questions of values. In the *Durham* case Judge Bazelon set them free, declaring that henceforth in the District of Columbia an accused was not criminally responsible "if his unlawful act was the product of mental disease or defect." Bazelon received a special award from the American Psychiatric Association, but not everyone was that enthused. The American Law Institute (ALI) produced a sort of compromise, declaring that a person wouldn't be responsible for a misdeed if he couldn't appreciate the wrongfulness of it or if he "lacked a substantial capacity... to conform his conduct to the requirements of the law." Though somewhat stiffer on paper, this ALI rule didn't vary from the Durham Rule in practice all that much. Adopted by a majority of the states, its various permutations have given the psychiatrists virtual free rein in the courtroom ever since.

The Hinckley trial demonstrated what the heavenly city of courtroom psychiatry has become. Three teams of psychiatrists—11 in all—picked over Hinckley's mind for hours in an exercise that 200 years from now will no doubt seem much the way that the heated debates over the medieval heresies seem to us today. The resulting trial dragged on for 52 excruciating days. One defense psychiatrist, Thomas C. Goldman, told the jury with a straight face that Hinckley saw actress Jody Foster as an "idealized mother who is all-giving and endowed with magical power," while President Reagan was an "all evil prohibitive figure who hates him, seeks to destroy him, and deny access to the idealized mother figure." No wonder he tried to shoot the man.

Or take the comments of Richard Delman, a psychiatrist who testified for the defense in the Dan White trial. As Lee Coleman, also a psychiatrist, tells it in his new book, *The Reign of Error*, Delman concluded on the basis of inkblot and other tests that it was White's deep concern for others that led him to sneak into San Francisco City Hall through a window rather than walk in through the front door. "He didn't want to embarrass the officer who was operating the metal detector [and would have discovered his gun]," Delman said.

On at least one occasion this kind of analysis has been more than even the defendant could take. Coleman cites the case of Inez Garcia, who was raped by two men in Soledad, California;

afterwards, she went home, got a rifle, and shot one of her attackers. At her trial she sat listening to defense psychiatrist Jane Olden go on and on about her "reactive formations" and her self-image as a "saint-like idealized virgin." "If you trigger her negative feelings, which would be provoked by such an act as rape," Olden explained, "being a hysterical person who was striving always to express this sensuality and aggression, then you could indeed throw her into a state where she is emotionally relating to her own conflict."

Garcia stood up and yelled at the judge, "I killed [him] because I was raped and I'd kill him again."

If you smell a fish in such psychologizing, it is with good reason. There is a cadre of so-called "forensic psychiatrists," who show up in these insanity trials again and again, plying their offensive or defensive specialties. Dr. Alan Stone of Harvard, former head of the American Psychiatric Association, describes the kind of trial that results as a "three-ring circus, in which lawyers are the ringmasters and the psychiatric witnesses are the clowns, and if they are carefully trained, then they will be trained clowns." Another Harvard psychiatrist, David Baer, was a defense witness in the Hinckley trial but does not regularly participate in these affairs, and he revealed some of the details to a reporter from *Harper's*. He spent, he said, at least 20 to 25 hours rehearsing his testimony with the lawyers, who admonished him, among other things, not to "weaken your answers with all the qualifications you think you ought to make." They said, "Oh, don't mention the exploding bullets. My God, that's so damaging to the case," he recalls. Baer, who was paid $35,000 for his efforts, added

that he was "determined never to tell a lie."

That may be. But what happens to most psychiatrists who resist the "training" of the defense lawyers? "If a man doesn't testify the right way, he is not rehired," said one defense attorney in a study published in the *Rutgers Law Journal*. (Section 6 of the "Principles of Medical Ethics" of the American Psychiatric Association, by the way, reads: "A physician should not dispose of his services under terms or conditions which tend to interfere with or impair the free and complete exercise of his medical judgment.")

DID YOU HEAR VOICES?

The theory behind our "adversary" system is that when you pit one group of experts like these against another the truth will somehow emerge. When the hired-gun psychiatrists do their act, however, the result is not information, but confusion. "None of them had the same conclusion," complained Nathalia Brown, a shop mechanic at the local electric utility and a Hinckley juror. "All of them said he had this illness, that illness, so how are we to know what illness he has? I felt on the brink of insanity myself going through this, you know."

This, of course, is precisely what defense lawyers seek. As far back as 1945, Julian Carroll, the New York attorney who handled poet Ezra Pound's famous insanity defense against treason charges, wrote a friend that insanity trials are a "farce" in which the "learned medicos for each side squarely contradict each other and completely befuddle the jury." What was true then is even more true today, and all it took was confusion and nagging doubts in the minds of the jurors to gain Hinckley's acquittal.

In the nation's prisons, fooling the shrinks is getting to be a science. Inkblot tests offer fertile ground for displays of psychosis, and inmates who have successfully pleaded insanity have instructed their cohorts on what to see—sexual acts, genitalia, and the like. Ken Bianchi, the Hillside Strangler, studied books on psychology and hypnosis before convincing a number of psychiatrists he had a dual personality, and only an especially alert one found him out. An experiment at Stanford University suggested that conning these psychiatrists may not be all that hard. Eight subjects, all without any record of mental illness, feigned hearing voices and thereby gained admission to 12 different mental hospitals. They did not falsify any details of their lives other than that they heard voices. Eleven of the 12 were diagnosed as "schizophrenic" while the 12th was diagnosed "manic depressive."

"I probably know more about psychiatry . . . than your average resident psychiatrist," boasted Gary Trapnell, who had some justification for his claim. "I can bullshit the hell out of one in ten minutes."

It's not that psychiatry has nothing to tell us, nor that many of its practitioners are not dedicated to helping others. The problem is the way this specialty is used in insanity trials: the endeavor itself is in many ways absurd. These psychiatrists are interviewing criminals who know that if they come off seeming a little bananas, they might get off the hook. The notion that something resembling scientific data will always result from such subjective encounters is, well, a little bananas itself. On top of that, the courtroom psychiatrists are not purporting to

inform us of a defendant's *present* mental state, though even that can be elusive enough. They are claiming to divine the defendant's mental state when he committed the crime, which probably was months before. "I can't even tell you what *I* was thinking about a week ago, or a year ago, let alone what someone else was thinking," says criminal psychologist Stanton Samenow, author of *Inside the Criminal Mind*, whose eight years working at St. Elizabeths hospital in Washington made him deeply skeptical of traditional attempts to understand and catalogue criminals according to Freudian concepts. Indeed, how would you begin to *prove* an assertion such as the one that John Hinckley tried to shoot Reagan because he saw the president as an "all evil prohibitive figure"? This is not evidence. It is vaporizing. Coleman testifies at criminal trials with delightful iconoclasm that psychiatrists such as himself have no more ability than anyone else to inform the jury as to what was going on in a criminal's mind at any given time.

POOR RELATIONS

But one should not conclude that the only thing wrong with the insanity defense is that it lets the felons free on the basis of recondite psychiatric excuses. The injustice goes much deeper. Some psychiatrists, for example, lend their courtroom aura and mantle of expertise to the prosecution. Jim Grigson, the so-called "Hanging Shrink" of Texas, will tell a jury after a 90-minute interview with a defendant that this individual "has complete disregard for another human being's life" and that "no treatment, no medicine, nothing is going to change this behavior." Psychiatric opinionizing can cut both ways.

There's the further problem that psychiatrists, the gatekeepers of this defense, have their greatest rapport with the problems of those closest to their own social status. A few years ago, Dr. Daniel Irving, a psychiatrist in Washington, demonstrated this attitude in an article Blain Harden wrote for *The Washington Post.* "I hate to say this," Irving confided, "but I don't like to work with poor people.... They are talking about stuff that doesn't interest me particularly. They are the kind of people who don't interest me." Over 95 percent of all psychiatric patients are white, and James Collins, a black psychiatrist who is chairman of the Howard University Medical School Department of Psychiatry, told Harden that "[the] biggest problem is that many psychiatrists cannot relate to poor people."

In fact, the insanity defense itself can be weighted heavily towards those who are well-off. This is not just because a Hinckley family can muster upwards of a million dollars to mount a prodigious legal and psychiatric defense. On a subtler level, someone from a "nice" upper-middle-class background who commits a heinous crime is more readily seen as off his rocker than is someone from a poorer background in which crime is closer to the norm (or is at least perceived to be). During the Hinckley trial the jury witnessed his family sitting behind him, the "perfect couple," as one observer said later. "Hinckley's father was sitting there with a pondering look on his face; his mother was wearing red, white, and blue outfits; and his sister was a former cheerleader and homecoming queen. Real Americans." Surely there must be something wrong with a young man who could enjoy such advantages and still go out and shoot a president. It was the sort of tableau that a black felon from, say,

East St. Louis, might have some trouble assembling.

Such, considerations may help explain why Henry Steadman of the New York State Department of Mental Hygiene found that while whites account for only 31 percent of the prison population in his state, they were a full 65 percent of those found not guilty by reason of insanity. "Racial discrimination favoring whites in successful insanity defenses is strongly suggested by these figures," writes Abraham Halpern.

This in turn points to something even more fundamentally unjust about the insanity defense: the way it draws arbitrary and culture-bound distinctions between defendants with different kinds of life burdens and afflictions. A John Hinckley may well harbor anger against his parents and anguish at his unrequited love for actress Jody Foster. Such problems can be very real for those who go through them. But they are no *more* real, no *more* inclined to affect behavior, than are the problems of a teenager of lesser means, who may be ugly, or kept back in school two or three times, or whose parents may not love him and who may have been "passed around" among relatives and older siblings for as long as he can remember, or who may find doors closed to him because he is not blond and blue-eyed the way Hinckley is. If a Hinckley merits our compassion, then surely those with hard life circumstances do also. Under the insanity defense, we absolve Hinckley totally of responsibility, while we label his hypothetical counterpart a bad person and send him to jail.

So arbitrary is the line that the insanity defense invites us to draw that all sorts of prejudices and vagaries can enter, of which racial and class bias are just two. "The actual psychological state of the defendant may be a rather minor factor" in the decision even to use the insanity defense, writes C. R. Jeffrey in his book, *Criminal Responsibility and Mental Disease*. Rather, this decision is based on such factors as "the economic position of the defendant, the nature of the criminal charges, the medical facilities in the community," and the like.

BIG DIFFERENCE

This is not to say that you won't find any poor people or non-Caucasians in the maximum-security hospitals in which insanity acquittees are kept. You will, but it's important to understand how they got there. It probably wasn't through the kind of circus trial that John Hinckley could afford. Very likely, it was a plea bargain, in which a prosecutor decided it was better to put a dangerous person away, even if just for a short time, than to devote scarce resources to a trial that he or she might lose. One study, published in the *Rutgers Law Review*, found at least two jurisdictions in which the prosecutors actually raised the insanity defense more frequently than the defense attorney did. "Clearly the prosecutor saw the [insanity] defense as a means to lock defendants up without having their guilt proved beyond a reasonable doubt," the study concludes.

Given such realities, it should not be surprising that there is often not much difference between those who end up in maximum security mental hospitals and those who end up in their penal counterparts. "Lots of people could have ended up in either one or the other," says E. Fuller Torrey, a psychiatrist at St. Elizabeths mental hospital in Washington. Samenow goes further. On the basis of his own experience studying insanity acquittees at St. Elizabeths, he declares flatly that "neither [his colleague Dr. Samuel] Yochelson nor I found that any of the men we evaluated were insane unless one took tremendous liberties with that word."

That may be a bit of an exaggeration. But the similarities between criminals we call "insane," and those we call simply "criminals," cannot be dismissed. Take recidivism. There is evidence that criminals released from mental hospitals tend to repeat their crimes with about the same frequency as their counterparts released from prison. This point is crucial because the purpose of a criminal justice system is not just to punish offenders; it is to protect the rest of us from dangerous people as well. Through the insanity defense, we go to lengths that are often ridiculous to make a distinction that in many cases is without a difference.

Sometimes the experts are the last to see what needs to be done. Listen to Lawrence Coffey, one of the Hinckley jurors who was unhappy with the verdict for which he himself voted. "I think it [the law] should be changed," he told a Senate hearing, "in some way where the defendant gets mental help enough that where he's not harmful to himself and society, and then be punished for what he has done wrong." Maryland Copelin, also one of the jurors, agreed. "I think they [defendants] should get the help they need and also punishment for the act they did." In other words, Hinckley needed treatment, but he deserved punishment, too. Who could argue with that? Well, the law, for one. It said that Hinckley was either guilty or not guilty by reason of insanity. "We could not do any better than what we did," Copelin said, "on account of your forms," which gave the jury only these two options.

In short, the insanity defense cuts the deck the wrong way. I makes no provision for the vast middle ground in which offenders have problems but should bear responsibility too. Instead of persisting in making this artificial distinction between "normal" criminals (whatever that means) and "insane" ones, we should ask first a very simple question: did the individual commit the crime? That established in a trial, we should then, in a sentencing phase, take all relevant factors into account in deciding what combination of punishment and treatment is appropriate. "Either you did it or you didn't do it," says Samenow, who supports the abolition of the insanity defense. "I think we should try the criminal first, and then worry about treatment." In other words, don't expect the jury to make Talmudic distinctions on which even the experts cannot agree. Get the psychiatrists out of the courtroom, where they cause confusion, and put them into the sentencing and treatment process, where they may be able to help.

In this sentencing phase, which would take on a new importance, Hinckley's infatuation with Jody Foster, and Dan White's overindulgence in junk food, would be given due regard. So too would the incapacity of one who was totally deranged. The crucial difference from current practice is that the examination would be done by court-appointed psychiatrists (or other professionals) instead of by hired guns proffered by either side. Since psychiatrists are as human as the rest of us, this system would not be perfect. It would, however, be better than what we have today.

In almost all cases, some punishment would be in order. You don't have to believe that retribution is the whole purpose of the law to acknowledge that something very basic in us requires that when someone causes serious harm to someone else, he should pay. This approach would eliminate perhaps the most dangerous absurdity of the present insanity defense. When a criminal wins acquittal on this ground, the criminal justice system has no more claim on him. The only way he can be kept in confinement is if he is declared insane and committed to a mental institution through a totally separate procedure. (Some states require an automatic confinement for one or two months, ostensibly to "observe" the acquittee.) No Problem, you say. They've just been declared insane. The problem is, that insanity was at the time of the crime, which may have been a year or more before. By the time of the commitment hearing, the old problem may have miraculously cleared up. The commitment authorities are then faced with two bad options. Either they tell the truth and let a dangerous person out or they fill a bed in a crowded mental hospital with someone who will be there not for treatment, but only to be kept off the streets. Eliminating the insanity defense would eliminate such charades.

Once punishment is completed, the question of danger to society would come to the fore. First offenders committing nonviolent crimes generally pose little such threat, and in most cases could be safely paroled. At the other extreme, violent repeat offenders would be locked up for a very long time. While reform is always possible, the sad fact is that most repeat offenders will keep on repeating until they reach a "burn-out" period sometime after they reach age 40. Since the recidivism rates cut across the categories we call "normal" and "insane" criminality, the insanity defense simply doesn't help us deal with reality in this regard.

Hot-blooded crimes, such as the Dan White shooting, should be seen for what they are. Such people generally don't pose a great threat because the circumstances of their crime are not likely to happen again. It costs between $10,000 and $20,000 a year to keep a prisoner in jail, and that money would be better spent on those for whom it's really needed. In other words, White's eight-year sentence was not necessarily wrong. The wrong was in the psychiatric speculation through which that result was justified. We can achieve justice in such cases through simpler and more honest means.

WHAT A TIME

But isn't the insanity defense necessary to protect the infirm? "People who are mentally ill deserve treatment," says Flora Rheta Schreiber, whose book *The Shoemaker* details the sad story of a troubled murderer. "They don't deserve to be locked up in prison."

Fair enough. The trouble is, virtually all criminals have mental problems. The difference between a bank robber and yourself is not in your shirt size or the shape of your hands. Is there any such thing as a "sane" rape or a "sane" axe murder? If anyone did such deeds with calm and rational deliberation, would that individual not be the most insane—and dangerous—of all? Samenow, moreover, says that for the vast majority of criminals, the kind of treatment that might be effective is pretty much the same. The secret scandal of the insanity defense is the way it justifies our atrocious penal system by purporting to show kindness for one group that is

selected arbitrarily in the first place. We deny treatment to the many under the pretext of providing it for a few.

And a pretext it often is. Talk to someone who has visited a maximum-security hospital for the criminally insane. To be sure, there are good ones here and there. But in his book *Beating the Rap*, Henry Steadman describes a reality that is probably more common than not. Such hospitals in his state are "prisonlike," he writes, with "locked wards, security officers, and barbed wire fences. . . . There is a substantial level of patient-patient assault; homosexuality, both consenting and nonconsenting, is common, and guards are sometimes unnecessarily brutal . . . *It is simply doing time in a different setting.*" (Emphasis added.) Barbara Weiner, who heads a special outpatient program for insanity acquittees in Chicago—one of the few programs of its kind in the country —told a Senate hearing that "few states have specialized programs for treating mentally ill offenders." (Those of means, of course, can often arrange a transfer to private facilities at which conditions are more genteel.)

So averse are American psychiatrists to helping people in life's lower stations that over half the staffs of this country's public mental hospitals are graduates of foreign medical schools, where standards may not be awfully high. In 11 states, including Illinois and Ohio, the figure is over 70 percent. Just try to imagine a psychiatrist from, say, India, trying to understand a felon from the South Bronx. Torrey cites a psychiatrist who left the Illinois state hospital system telling of a colleague in charge of prescribing drugs who did not know that .8 and .80 were the same number.

Much of the problem is that most of us prefer to keep a comfortable arm's length from such realities. The people who run our criminal justice system are no exception. After observing a year's worth of mental incompetency hearings in New York, Steadman observed that "of about 35 judges, 12 attorneys, six district attorneys, and 12 psychiatrists, not one had ever seen or been inside either of the two facilities to which incompetent defendants are committed." A former public defender in Washington, D.C., who had pleaded before the Supreme Court the case of an insanity-acquittee who was trying to get out of St. Elizabeths, told me he had never met the individual for whose release he was pleading.

Getting rid of the insanity defense would help to break the spell and make us confront the deficiencies in our correctional systems. No longer could we congratulate ourselves that we are being humane and just when we are being neither. If eliminating the defense would help get a few dangerous felons off the street, so much the better. But a great deal more is at stake.

NO

Richard Bonnie

STATEMENT OF RICHARD BONNIE

The effect of most of the proposals now before you would be to abolish the insanity defense as it has existed for centuries in Anglo-American criminal law. I urge you to reject these sweeping proposals. The insanity defense should be retained, in modified form, because some defendants afflicted by severe mental disorder cannot justly be blamed for their criminal conduct and do not, therefore, deserve to be punished. The defense, in short, is essential to the moral integrity of the criminal law.

I realize that the figure of John Hinckley looms before us today. Doubts about the moral accuracy of the jurors' verdict in this sad case have now been turned on the insanity defense itself. I do not want to second guess the verdict in the Hinckley case, but I do urge you to keep the case in proper perspective.

The highly visible insanity claim, pitting the experts in courtroom battle, is the aberrational case. The plea is raised in no more than 2% of felony cases and the defense is rarely successful when the question is contested in a jury trial. Most psychiatric dispositions in the criminal process are arranged without fanfare, without disagreement among the experts, and without dissent by the prosecution. In short, the exhaustive media coverage of cases like Hinckley's gives the public a distorted picture of the relative insignificance of the insanity defense in the day-to-day administration of justice.

In another way, however, the public debate about the aberrant case is highly to be desired because the trial of insanity claims keeps the community in touch with the moral premises of the criminal law. The legitimacy of the institution of punishment rests on the moral belief that we are all capable of rational choice and therefore deserve to be punished if we choose to do wrong. By acknowledging the exception, we reaffirm the rule. I have no doubt that the Hinckley trial and verdict have exposed the fundamental moral postulates of the criminal law to vigorous debate in every living room in the Nation. Thus, in a sense, whether John Hinckley was or was not legally insane may be less important than the fact that the question was asked at all.

These are the reasons I do not favor abolition of the insanity defense. However, I do not discount or dismiss the possibility that the defense occasionally may be successfully invoked in questionable cases. There is, in fact, some

From U.S. Senate. Committee on the Judiciary. *Insanity Defense.* Hearing, August 2, 1982. Washington, DC: Government Printing Office, 1982. (Y4.J89/2:J-97-126.)

evidence that insanity acquittals have increased in recent years. However, I am persuaded that the possibility of moral mistakes in the administration of the insanity defense can be adequately reduced by narrowing the defense and by placing the burden of proof on the defendant.

THE OPTIONS

You have basically three options before you.

The Existing (Model Penal Code) Law

One option is to leave the law as it now stands, by judicial ruling, in all of the federal courts (and, parenthetically, as it now stands in a majority of the states). Apart from technical variations, this means the test proposed by the American Law Institute in its Model Penal Code. Under this approach, a person whose perceptual capacities were sufficiently intact that he had the criminal "intent" required in the definition of the offense can nonetheless be found "not guilty by reason of insanity" if, by virtue of mental disease or defect, he lacked substantial capacity *either* to understand or appreciate the legal or moral significance of his actions, *or* to conform his conduct to the requirements of law. In other words, a person may be excused if his thinking was severely disordered—this is the so-called volitional prong of the defense.

Revival of M'Naghten

The second option is to retain the insanity defense as an independent exculpatory doctrine—independent, that is, of mens rea—but to restrict its scope by eliminating the volitional prong. This is the approach that I favor, for reasons I will outline below. Basically, this option is to restore the *M'Naghten* test—although I do not think you should be bound by the language used by the House of Lords in 1843—as the sole basis for exculpation or ground of insanity. Although this is now distinctly the minority position in this country—it is used in less than one third of the states—it is still the law in England.

Abolition: The Mens Rea Approach

The third option is the one I have characterized as abolition of the defense. Technically, this characterization is accurate because the essential substantive effect of the so-called "mens rea" approach (or "elements" approach) would be to eliminate any criterion of exculpation, based on mental disease, which is independent of the elements of particular crimes. To put it another way, the bills taking this approach would eliminate any separate exculpatory doctrine based on proof of mental disease; instead mentally ill (or retarded) defendants would be treated just like everyone else. A normal person cannot escape liability by proving that he did not know or appreciate the fact that his conduct was wrong, and—under the mens rea approach—neither could a psychotic person.

THE CASE AGAINST THE MENS REA APPROACH

Most of the bills now before you would adopt the mens rea option, the approach recently enacted in Montana and Idaho. As I have already noted, this change, abolishing the insanity defense, would constitute an abrupt and unfortunate departure from the Anglo-American legal tradition.

If the insanity defense were abolished, the law would not take adequate account of the incapacitating effects of severe mental illness. Some mentally ill defendants may be said to have "intended" to do what they did—that is, their technical guilt can be established—but they nonetheless may have been so severely disturbed that they were unable to appreciate the significance of their actions. These cases do not frequently arise, but when they do, a criminal conviction—signifying the societal judgment that the defendant *deserves* punishment—would offend the basic moral intuitions of the community. Judges and juries would then be forced either to return a verdict which they regard as morally obtuse or to acquit the defendant in defiance of the law. They should be spared such moral embarrassment.

Let me illustrate this point with a real case evaluated at our Institute's Forensic Clinic in 1975. Ms. Joy Baker, a thirty-one-year-old woman, admitted killing her aunt. She had no previous history of mental illness, although her mother was mentally ill and had spent all of Ms. Baker's early years in mental hospitals. Ms. Baker was raised by her grandparents and her aunt in a rural area of the state. After high school graduation Ms. Baker married and had two children. The marriage ended in divorce six years later and Ms. Baker remarried. This second marriage was stressful from the outset. Mr. Baker was a heavy drinker and abusive to his wife. He also was extremely jealous and repeatedly accused his wife of seeing other men.

The night before the shooting Mr. Baker took his wife on a ride in his truck. He kept a gun on the seat between them and stopped repeatedly. At each place he told listeners that his wife was an adultress. He insisted his wife throw her wedding ring from the car, which she did because she was afraid of her husband's anger. The Bakers didn't return home until three in the morning. At that time Ms. Baker woke her children and fed them, then stayed up while her husband slept because she was afraid "something terrible would happen."

During this time and for the three days prior to the day of the shooting Ms. Baker had become increasingly agitated and fearful. Her condition rapidly deteriorated and she began to lose contact with reality. She felt that her dogs were going to attack her and she also believed her children and the neighbors had been possessed by the devil.

On the morning of the shooting, Ms. Baker asked her husband not to leave and told him that something horrible was about to happen. When he left anyway she locked the doors. She ran frantically around the house holding the gun. She made her children sit on the sofa and read the Twenty-Third Psalm over and over. She was both afraid of what they might do and of what she might do but felt that reading the Bible would protect them. Shortly afterwards, Ms. Baker's aunt made an unexpected visit. Ms. Baker told her to go away but the aunt persisted and went to the back door. Ms. Baker was afraid of the dog which was out on the back porch and repeatedly urged her aunt to leave. At this time the aunt seemed to Ms. Baker to be sneering at her.

When her aunt suddenly reached through the screening to unlock the door Ms. Baker said, "I had my aunt over there and this black dog over here, and both of them were bothering me.... And then I had that black dog in front of me and she turned around and I was trying to kick the dog and my aunt was coming in the door and I just—took my hands I just went like this—right through the screen.... I shot her."

Ms. Baker's aunt fell backward into the mud behind the porch. Although she was bleeding profusely from her chest, she did not die immediately. "Why, Joy?" she asked. "Because you're the devil, and you came to hurt me," Joy answered. Her aunt said, "Honey, no, I came to help you." At this point, Ms. Baker said, she saw that her aunt was hurting and became very confused. Then, according to her statement, "I took the gun and shot her again just to relieve the pain she was having because she said she was hurt." Her aunt died after the second shot.

All the psychiatrists who examined Ms. Baker concluded that she was acutely psychotic and out of touch with reality at the time she shot her aunt. The police who arrested her and others in the small rural community concluded that she must have been crazy because there was no other explanation for her conduct. After Ms. Baker was stabilized on anti-psychotic medication, she was permitted to leave the state to live with relatives in a neighboring state. Eventually the case against her was dismissed by the court, with the consent of the prosecution, after a preliminary hearing at which the examining psychiatrists testified. She was never indicted or brought to trial.

It seems clear, even to a layman, that Ms. Baker was so delusional and regressed at the time of the shooting that she did not understand or appreciate the wrongfulness of her conduct. It would be morally obtuse to condemn and punish her. Yet, Ms. Baker had the state of mind required for some form of criminal homicide. If there were no insanity defense, she could be acquitted only in defiance of the law.

Let me explain. The "states of mind" which are required for homicide and other criminal offenses refer to various aspects of conscious awareness. They do not have any qualitative dimension. There is good reason for this, of course. The exclusive focus on conscious perceptions and beliefs enhances predictability, precision and equality in the penal law. If the law tried to take into account degrees of psychological aberration in the definition of offenses, the result would be a debilitating individualization of the standards of criminal liability.

At the time of the first shot, it could be argued that Ms. Baker lacked the "state of mind" required for murder because she did not intend to shoot a "human being" but rather intended to shoot a person whom she believed to be possessed by the devil. At common law, this claim would probably be characterized as a mistake of fact. Since the mistake was, by definition, an unreasonable one—i.e., one that only a crazy person would make—she would most likely be guilty of some form of homicide (at least manslaughter) if ordinary mens rea principles were applied. Even under the modern criminal codes..., she would be guilty of negligent homicide since an ordinary person in her situation would have been aware of the risk that her aunt was a human being. And she possibly could be found guilty of manslaughter since she was probably aware of the risk that her aunt was a human being even though she was so regressed that she disregarded the risk.

It might also be argued that Ms. Baker's first shot would have been justified if her delusional beliefs had been true since she would have been defending herself against imminent annihilation at the hands of the devil. Again, however, the application of ordinary common-law principles of justification... would indicate that she was unreasonably mistaken as to the existence of justificatory facts (the necessity for killing to protect one-self) and her defense would fail, although the grade of the offense would probably be reduced to manslaughter on the basis of her "imperfect" justification.

At the time of the second shot, Ms. Baker was in somewhat better contact with reality. At a very superficial level she "knew" that she was shooting her aunt and did so for the non-delusional purpose of relieving her aunt's pain. But euthanasia is no justification for homicide. Thus, if we look only at her legally relevant "state of mind" at the time of the second shot, and we do not take into account her highly regressed and disorganized emotional condition, she is technically guilty of murder.

I believe that Joy Baker's case convincingly demonstrates why, in theoretical terms, the mens rea approach does not take sufficient account of the morally significant aberrations of mental functioning associated with severe mental disorder. I readily concede, however, that these technical points may make little practical difference in the courtroom. If the expert testimony in Joy Baker's case and others like it were admitted to disprove the existence of mens rea, juries may behave as many observers believe they do now—they may ignore the technical aspects of the law and decide, very bluntly, whether the defendant was too crazy to be convicted. However, I do not believe that rational criminal law reform is served by designing rules of law in the expectation that they will be ignored or nullified when they appear unjust in individual cases.

IMPROVING THE QUALITY OF EXPERT TESTIMONY

I have tried to show that perpetuation of the insanity defense is essential to the moral integrity of the criminal law. Yet an abstract commitment to the moral relevance of claims of psychological aberration may have to bend to the need for reliability in the administration of the law.

I fully recognize that the litigation of insanity claims is occasionally imperfect. The defense is sometimes difficult to administer reliably and fairly. In particular, I recognize that we cannot calibrate the severity of a person's mental disability, and it is sometimes hard to know whether the disability was profound enough to establish irresponsibility. Nor can we be confident that every fabricated claim will be recognized. Yet these concerns are not unlike those presented by traditional defenses such as mistake, duress and other excuses which no one is seeking to abolish. Indeed, problems in sorting valid from invalid defensive claims are best seen as part of the price of a humane and just penal law. Thus, to the extent that the abolitionists would eradicate the insanity defense in response to imperfections in its administration, I would reply that a decent respect for the moral integrity of the criminal law sometimes requires us to ask questions that can be answered only by approximation. Rather than abolishing the defense we should focus our attention on ways in which its administration can be improved.

Some of the abolitionist sentiment among lawyers seems to be responsive to doubts about the competence—and, unfortunately, the ethics—of expert witnesses. The cry for abolition is also raised by psychiatrists and psychologists who believe that the law forces experts to "take sides" and to offer opinions on issues outside their sphere of expertise. These are all legitimate concerns and I have no doubt that the current controversy about the insanity defense accurately reflects a rising level of mutual professional irritation about its administration. However, the correct solution is not to abolish the insanity defense but rather to clarify the roles and obligations of expert witnesses in the criminal process. Some assistance in this effort can be expected from the American Bar Association's Criminal Justice-Mental Health Standards now being drafted by interdisciplinary panels of experts in the field.

A properly trained expert can help the judge or jury to understand aberrations of the human mind. However, training in psychiatry or psychology does not, by itself, qualify a person to be an expert witness in criminal cases. Specialized training in forensic evaluation is necessary, and a major aim of such special training must be to assure that the expert is sensitive to the limits of his or her knowledge.

THE CASE FOR TIGHTENING THE DEFENSE

I do not favor abolition of the "cognitive" prong of the insanity defense. However, I do agree with those critics who believe the risks of fabrication and "moral mistakes" in administering the defense are greatest when the experts and the jury are asked to speculate whether the defendant had the capacity to "control" himself or whether he could have "resisted" the criminal impulse.

Few would dispute the moral predicate for the control test—that a person who "cannot help" doing what he did is not blameworthy. Unfortunately, however, there is no scientific basis for measuring a person's capacity for self-control or for calibrating the impairment of such capacity. There is, in short, no objective basis for distinguishing between offenders who were undeterrable and those who were merely undeterred, between the impulse that was irresistible and the impulse not resisted, or between substantial impairment of capacity and some lesser impairment. Whatever the precise terms of the volitional test, the question is unanswerable—or can be answered only by "moral guesses." To ask it at all, in my opinion, invites fabricated claims, undermines equal administration of the penal law, and compromises its deterrent effect....

The sole test of legal insanity should be whether the defendant, as a result of mental disease, lacked "substantial capacity to appreciate the wrongfulness of his conduct." This language, drawn from the Model Penal Code, uses clinically meaningful terms to ask the same question posed by the House of Lords in *M'Naghten* 150 years ago. During the past ten years, I have not seen a single case at our Clinic involving a claim of irresponsibility that I personally thought was morally compelling which would not be comprehended by this formulation. Thus, I am convinced that this test is fully compatible with the ethical premises of the penal law, and that results reached by judges and juries in particular cases ordinarily would be congruent with the community's moral sense. In sum, then, I believe that the insanity defense, as I have defined it, should be narrowed, not abandoned, and that the burden of persuasion may properly be shifted to the defendant. Like the mens rea proposal, this approach adequately responds to public concern about possible misuse of the insanity defense. Unlike the mens rea proposal, however, I believe this approach is compatible with the basic doctrines and principles of Anglo-American penal law.

POSTSCRIPT

Should the Insanity Defense Be Abolished?

After the verdict—not guilty by reason of insanity—in the trial of John Hinckley, Jr., for the attempted assassination of President Ronald Reagan in 1981, some changes were made in the federal insanity defense standard. As part of a major anticrime bill passed in 1984, Congress requires the defendant to have the burden of proving that he or she was insane. In the Hinckley trial, the prosecution was required to prove beyond a reasonable doubt that Hinckley was sane. The defendant in such a case must now persuade a jury that, as a result of a severe mental disease or defect, he or she was unable to appreciate the nature and wrongfulness of the act.

In addition to raising questions about the diagnosis of mental illness, the insanity defense also requires consideration of treatment, of sentencing, and of institutionalization. Those advocating its retention argue not only that blameless people should not be punished but also that such individuals need care and treatment for their problems. The fact that many mental institutions have failed to provide adequate treatment or are, by their nature, inappropriate places for some individuals who need help but not institutionalization has been recognized recently in various lawsuits. As a result, the number of people in institutions has been declining. The ineffectiveness of prisons and mental institutions in reducing recidivism or promoting treatment should be considered in the debate over the insanity defense, since even those who wish to abolish the defense are willing to take the mental state of the defendant into account at the time of sentencing. There is, in addition, a possible relationship between the increase in the number of defendants invoking the insanity defense and the deinstitutionalization trend. The reason for this is that the insanity defense becomes more appealing as the expectation of a long stay in a mental institution decreases.

Recommended readings on the insanity defense and mental health law include Perlin, *The Jurisprudence of the Insanity Defense* (1994); Appelbaum, *Almost a Revolution: Mental Health Law and the Limits of Change* (1994); Steadman, *Before and After Hinckley: Evaluating Insanity Defense Reform* (1993); Smith and Meyer, *Law, Behavior, and Mental Health* (New York University Press, 1987); Eisner, "Returning the Not Guilty by Reason of Insanity to the Community: A New Scale to Determine Readiness," 17 *Bulletin of the American Academy of Psychiatry and the Law* 401 (1989); Klofas and Yandrasits, " 'Guilty But Mentally Ill' and the Jury Trial: A Case Study," 24 *Criminal Law Bulletin* 424 (1988); Symposium, "The Insanity Defense," *The Annals* (January 1985); and Moran, *Knowing Right from Wrong: The Insanity Defense of Daniel McNaughtan* (Free

Press, 1981), which provides an interesting look at McNaughtan's trial and at the central figure in the history of the insanity defense. Other books about particular cases include Kaplan and Waltz, *The Trial of Jack Ruby* (Macmillan, 1965); Gaylin, *The Killing of Bonnie Garland* (Simon & Schuster, 1982); and Caplan, *The Insanity Defense and the Trial of John W. Hinckley, Jr.* (David Godine, 1983). More discussion of the insanity defense can be found on the Internet at http://www.psych.org/public_info/INSANI~1.HTM.

ISSUE 18

Should Drug Use Be Legalized?

YES: Steven B. Duke, from "Drug Prohibition: An Unnatural Disaster," *Connecticut Law Review* (Winter 1995)

NO: Gregory A. Loken, from "The Importance of Being More Than Earnest: Why the Case for Drug Legalization Remains Unproven," *Connecticut Law Review* (Winter 1995)

ISSUE SUMMARY

YES: Steven B. Duke, a professor of law of science and technology, contends that the war on drugs has led to an increase in criminal behavior, including robberies, assaults with guns, and police corruption, and that the financial, health, and civil rights costs of drug prohibition are enormous. Therefore, he recommends decriminalization and government regulation of drugs.

NO: Associate professor Gregory A. Loken, directly responding to Duke, asserts that the war on drugs has successfully reduced crime and that legalization would have devastating consequences, particularly for children.

One can hardly miss the impact of illegal drugs on the fabric of American life. There is a continuing link between drugs and violent crime in urban neighborhoods, with most of the victims of violence being young. The lure of the "get very rich quick" lifestyle of drug dealers has tempted many poor teenagers into a life of violence, even against their own families. It is hard to believe that a child would turn the family apartment into a "shooting gallery" or sell all the family possessions for money to purchase drugs, but it happens.

The drug problem invades every institution in society. It touches some children even before they are born. In one urban hospital, it was estimated that one-fifth of the 3,000 babies that are born each year are born to addicted mothers. That is a staggering figure, particularly because these children will be among hundreds of other similarly afflicted children born in other urban hospitals across the nation.

The drug problem touches everyone. One poll indicated that Americans are far more worried about the impact of drugs on their lives than about problems of international peace or terrorism abroad. And so they should be, because the drug problem is not just the problem of the poor teenager in Detroit or Philadelphia. In Massachusetts a mother was tried for leaving her two small children alone in an apartment, which they set fire to and in which they died. Her defense was astonishing—she asked for leniency because she was a drug addict and had to leave her home to get a fix.

What is the solution to this situation, which is ripping apart American society? Should we legalize drugs, or should we continue with the traditional approach of criminalizing drug use? In the following selections, law professor Steven B. Duke argues that there is only an illusion of prohibition in the United States and that only through legalization of drugs can we get a grip on the situation. He claims that present approaches, relying heavily on the police and court systems, are not putting much of a dent in either the rate of use or the supply of drugs. Furthermore, the present system is draining the government coffers of billions of dollars while urban street crime increases.

Gregory A. Loken is skeptical of Duke's arguments. He takes issue with Duke's conclusions about links between drug use and crime, points out several areas where Duke's conclusions may be unwarranted, and argues that Duke minimizes the worst harms that drugs pose for children.

The question of whether or not illicit drugs should be legalized is an extremely difficult one that will continue to confront us. Current public opinion surveys find that the "legalizing" option has insignificant public support. But another few years of drug-related violence and complaints by judges and court administrators that drug cases are clogging the courts could bring about a shift in public attitudes. Drug cases account for 4 percent of criminal trials and 50 percent of criminal appeals in the U.S. federal courts. (See Martin, "Drugs, Crime, and Urban Trial Court Management: The Unintended Consequences of the War on Drugs," 8 *Law and Policy Review* 117, 1990.)

YES

Steven B. Duke

DRUG PROHIBITION: AN UNNATURAL DISASTER

The idea that government should determine for its people which psychoactive drugs they are free to consume and jail them for using others is a fairly recent arrival in the United States. Except for an occasional fling with prohibition at the state level, Americans were free until 1914 to consume any drugs they chose and to buy from anyone who chose to sell them. Those rights were widely exercised. In addition to alcohol, tobacco, and caffeine, tens of millions of Americans consumed cocaine and opiates in the nineteenth century. Cocaine was even an ingredient in Coca Cola until 1905, and opium was included in nostrums fed to colicky babies. Heroin was originally sold as a cough suppressant. Although dependence on these drugs was not uncommon, it was never as serious a problem as alcoholism. Indeed, although the proportions of the population using these drugs in the late nineteenth century was probably higher than it is now, the problems associated with their use were less serious than they are today.

In 1914, Congress enacted the Harrison Act, which was designed to medicalize cocaine and heroin by confining their distribution to health professionals. In 1919, on the eve of alcohol prohibition and doubtless influenced by prohibitionist fervor, the Supreme Court converted the Harrison Act into a ban on the distribution of such drugs, holding that prescribing drugs to addicts was not the practice of medicine and was therefore criminal. Drug and alcohol prohibition then proceeded to wreck the country. Crime, corruption, and disrespect for law grew at unprecedented rates. Because of alcohol prohibition, many Americans replaced their appetite for beer with a newly discovered preference for the cocktail, containing distilled spirits, which poisoned thousands.

Thirteen years of alcohol prohibition was enough. It was repealed in 1933 by the Twenty-first Amendment, which left alcohol regulation to the states. The repeal of alcohol prohibition coincided with the depth of the depression, when unemployment reached record levels and millions of Americans were without food, shelter, welfare, or hope. Despite this widespread misery and despair, crime rates dropped precipitously after the repeal, as did alcohol poi-

From Steven B. Duke, "Drug Prohibition: An Unnatural Disaster," *Connecticut Law Review*, vol. 27, no. 2 (Winter 1995). Copyright © 1995 by The Connecticut Law Review Association. Reprinted by permission. Notes omitted.

soning and contempt for law. Hardly anyone considers the repeal of alcohol prohibition to have been a mistake. Why, then, did we not repeal the Harrison Act at the same time? Why don't we repeal its modern sequelae? We are addicted to drug prohibition. A manifestation of that addiction is "denial" of the harms we are inflicting upon ourselves by prohibition.

A sober analysis of prohibition requires us to acknowledge that the use of psychoactive drugs, be they tobacco, alcohol, heroin, cocaine, or any of hundreds of others, has adverse effects on the physical or mental health of *some* users. The nature and seriousness of adverse effects vary greatly among both drugs and drug users. Many people can consume almost any popular drug, legal or illegal, without adverse physical or psychological effects, while others become horribly addicted to almost any drug they use. Because of the terrible consequences of drug abuse to some users, it is hard to make a positive case for the increased consumption of any pleasure drug. One who believes that we should repeal prohibition so that more people will enjoy a wider variety of drugs does not speak for me nor would such a person have a sympathetic audience among a large segment of the American population. Rather, I assume *arguendo* that the consumption of psychoactive drugs for other than medical reasons is, on the whole, undesirable.

We must also acknowledge, however, that most Americans use psychoactive drugs on a daily basis, as did their ancestors for thousands of years, and that they will continue to do so, no matter what the state of the law. Most Americans insist, often at great personal cost, on the right to consume substances that they desire. Many of those same Americans are just as insistent that

others be denied their own drug of choice. That is why tobacco, alcohol, and caffeine are permitted while only much less popular drugs are banned. The appetite for chemical intoxication is innate in humans (and most other animals as well) and indulging it has been a part of most cultures since the dawn of history. In addition to general notions of individual autonomy, a hunch that it could be dangerous to tamper with urges so "natural" may explain why we stayed out of the prohibition business for so long.

Reconsidering the problem compels us to compare the costs of drug prohibition as presently pursued with the costs of drug consumption in a hypothetical system in which prohibition has been repealed or in which enforcement is much less intense than is the case today. Most of the evils of drug prohibition would be drastically reduced if we simply took an attitude of benign neglect toward illicit drug consumption and distribution, which is largely what occurred until the early 1970s. The drug war is an indefensible disaster that harms almost everyone....

SOME COSTS OF "DRUG WAR" PROHIBITION

The Criminogenics of Drug Prohibition
Contrary to what our government told us when it imposed drug prohibition, most illegal recreational drugs have no pharmacological properties that produce violence or other criminal behavior. Heroin and marijuana diminish rather than increase aggressive behavior. Cocaine—or cocaine withdrawal—occasionally triggers violence but usually does not. Very little crime is generated by the mere use

of these drugs, especially in comparison to alcohol, which is causally related to thousands of homicides and hundreds of thousands of assaults annually. The major linkages between illegal drugs and crime must be found elsewhere-in prohibition.

Prohibition Creates Motivation to Steal and Rob

One of the main strategic goals of the drug war is to increase the costs of producing and distributing, and hence of buying, illicit drugs. As the price to the consumer is increased, demand can hopefully be curtailed and the number of users or the quantities of illicit drugs used can be reduced. The tactics for increasing producer and distributor costs include impeding production or distribution of the raw materials used in making drugs, attempting to interdict the products before they reach the consumer (with border searches, busts of stash houses, and the like), and putting smugglers and distributors of the illicit products in prison. Until recently, the strategy had considerable "success" in that prices for marijuana, heroin, cocaine, and other illicit drugs were quite high. A heroin addict would commonly need $200 or more per day to support a habit, and a cocaine user, before the era of cheap "crack," might need even more than that. Many cocaine users spent a thousand dollars a week on powder cocaine.

There is little evidence that demand is greatly reduced by jacking up the free market price of these drugs by a factor of 100 or more, but there is strong evidence that the consumers of these products increase their participation in acquisitive crimes in order to feed their habits. In a recent survey of persons in prison for robbery or burglary, one out of three said that they committed their crimes in order to get money to buy drugs. Those who commit crimes for drug money also seem to commit them at a much greater rate than less strongly motivated robbers, burglars, and thieves.

In a study of 356 heroin users in Miami, James Inciardi found that they admitted to committing nearly 120,000 crimes (an average of 332 per person) during a single year. In another study of 573 heroin users, Inciardi found them responsible for about 215,000 offenses during the previous year. Included were 25,000 shopliftings, 45,000 thefts and frauds, 6,000 robberies and assaults, and 6,700 burglaries. In another study of 459 nonnarcotic drug users (chiefly cocaine), Inciardi found them to have admitted to an average of 320 crimes apiece during the previous year. In a survey of callers to a cocaine hotline, 45% of the callers said they had stolen to buy cocaine. In a survey of adolescents, the 1.3% who admitted using cocaine accounted for 40% of the admitted crimes. In several studies of drug use by persons imprisoned, 65% to 80% have admitted regular or lifetime illicit drug use. All this data suggests that about 75% of our robberies, thefts, burglaries, and related assaults are committed by drug abusers. Some of the crimes committed by drug abusers—perhaps one-third—would be committed in any event, but numerous studies show that drug users commit far fewer crimes when undergoing outpatient treatment or even when the prices of drugs go down. Half of America's property crime, robberies, and burglaries are probably the result of the high costs of drug acquisition created by the drug war.

Systemic Causes

Creating an incentive to steal in order to buy drugs is only one of many crimino genic effects of drug prohibition. The illegal drug market is itself a cauldron of criminality. Murder is employed to protect or acquire drug-selling turf, to settle disputes among drug merchants and their customers, to enforce contracts, to remediate fraud, and to steal drugs and drug money from dealers. In many cities, such as New Haven, Connecticut, at least half of the killings are drug-business related. Nationwide, between 5,000 and 10,000 murders per year are systemic to the drug business. Thus, more people are killed by the prohibition of drugs than by the drugs themselves.

Drug money is also the lifeblood of criminal gangs, members of whom kill members of rival gangs, and innocent bystanders, for almost any reason, including showing off.

Victimogenics

Another way in which drug prohibition causes crime is by making victims vulnerable to predators. Many drug customers have to enter crime-infested territory to get their supplies. Since they are criminals themselves, obviously in the neighborhood to "score," they have strong disincentives to complain to the police about having been robbed or assaulted. As such, they are prime targets.

Proliferation of Deadly Weapons

Drug prohibition also accounts for much of the recent proliferation of handguns and assault rifles (which are doubling every twenty years). Guns are essential to carrying on the drug trade, since drug dealers must enforce their own contracts and provide their own protection from predators. Even "mules" who deliver drugs or money need weapons. Due in part to its association with the glamorous drug trade, packing a gun, like fancy clothing or costly jewelry, has become a status symbol among many adolescents. In such an atmosphere, other youngsters carry guns in the hope they will provide them with some protection. As a result, disputes that used to be settled with fists are now settled with guns. A decade ago only 15% of teenagers who got into serious trouble in New York City were carrying guns. Now the rate is 60% to 65%.

The more guns there are in the hands of drug dealers and others, the more the rest of the population feels the need to have guns for self-defense. So, partly as a result of the huge black-market drug business that creates a voracious appetite for guns, many ordinary citizens are arming themselves with guns. The more people who have guns, the more people get killed. Hence, many deaths by guns —intentional killings, accidental killings, even suicides—are causally linked to the drug trade in the sense that the guns would not be there but for the drug business. There is little that gun control laws can do about this problem. Unless we can greatly shrink the black-market drug business, we can do little about the proliferation of guns in this country.

Corruption Costs

Drug prohibition also fosters crime by producing police corruption. The news media are full of accounts of cops caught stealing money or drugs from drug dealers and reselling the drugs, simply taking money from drug dealers in exchange for looking the other way, or providing tips about police raids or other plans. The recently released report of New York City's Mollen Commission provides chilling accounts of drug-prohibition-related corruption in that city. Such corruption denigrates and demoralizes all police. It spreads like cancer into all phases of police work.

Distraction of Law Enforcement

The distractive effects of the drug war on the police are also indirectly but profoundly criminogenic. In many cities, half or more of the arrests are for drugs or other crimes related to drug trafficking. The energy expended by the police on drug criminals is not available to be focused on domestic violence, rape, and other nondrug offenses. As a consequence, criminals who are not directly involved in drug trafficking have a much better chance of escaping detection and punishment than they would have otherwise.

If, as the just enacted Violent Crime Control and Law Enforcement Act correctly presumes, the number of police available to detect and prosecute crimes has a strong effect on the number of crimes committed, then wasting half of our available police resources on drug and drug-related crimes—effectively cutting our police forces in half—clearly causes crime. Repeal of drug prohibition would in effect add 400,000 police officers—at no cost. On that account alone, it would surely eliminate one-fourth or more of our violent and property crimes.

Paralyzing Our Courts

Our court system is on the verge of collapse, mainly because of drug-related cases. Criminal cases are not decided on their merits. In many cities, most people who are indicted end up having their cases dismissed. Only a fraction of the people charged with felonies are ever convicted of those felonies. There are simply too many cases for the system to handle, and at least half of them, in many courts, are drug cases or drug-prohibition-caused cases.

Dilution of Incarceration Resources

The drug war deeply undercuts the role of imprisonment in dealing with non-drug related crimes, such as child molesting, rape, and homicide. We now jail or imprison 1.3 million Americans, the second highest rate of incarceration in the world. Our prisons are filled beyond capacity even as our rates of incarceration are increasing faster than ever before. Forty states are under court orders for overcrowding. Funds are not available to build prisons fast enough to provide the needed space. Child molesters and kidnappers are being paroled early or having their sentences cut to make prison space for drug users and drug dealers. Many dangerous criminals don't even make it to prison because there is no room for them. Because many drug users and dealers—most of them nonviolent —have mandatory sentences, they have priority for prison space. Repeal of drug prohibition would open up about 500,000 jail and prison spaces. The beneficial effects on crime rates can hardly be exaggerated....

Prohibition Wastes at Least $100 Billion Per Year

The federal, state, and local governments spend about $75 billion a year on law enforcement and criminal justice programs. About $20 billion of that is directly related to drug law enforcement. Roughly another $15 billion is related to crimes committed to obtain drug money or is systemically related in some way to drug commerce. Hence, about $35 billion per year spent on law enforcement can be saved by repeal of drug prohibition.

As Gore Vidal put it, "[F]ighting drugs is nearly as big a business as pushing them." Drug legalization threatens the jobs and careers of police officers and politician-drug warriors. Defense attorneys and prosecutors, who make their living on drug cases, will also lose from drug legalization. Former Drug Enforcement Administration (DEA) officer Michael Levine exaggerated when he told CBS News: "The whole drug war is a political grab bag, in that everybody has got their arm in looking for that political jackpot that will either win them an election, win them a lucrative position as a consultant or you name it." But serious de-escalation of the drug war does threaten tens of thousands of careers that the taxpayers would no longer need to support. That is a major impediment to repeal. Nonetheless, many law-enforcement officers are well ahead of politicians in recognizing the futility and economic wastefulness of the drug war. As Robert Stutman, previously a high-ranking DEA official, stated: "Those of us who carry a badge learned a long time ago we're not going to solve the problem, and yet an awful lot of policy makers continue to depend on us, and we keep telling them we can't do it."

Ralph Salerno, a famous organized crime expert and long-time drug warrior himself, goes further. He asserts not only that the drug war "will never work" but that police on the front line, risking their lives and their physical, psychological, and moral health, "are being lied to, just as I was lied to 20 years ago." ...

Adding the money squandered on the ineffective drug-suppression activities of state and federal governments to the money we all lose as a result of the unnaturally high price of drugs, the total would come to well over $100 billion per year.

Urban Blight

Drug prohibition is a major contributor to the destruction of our inner-cities. In America's most disadvantaged neighborhoods, open-air drug markets and gang violence related to drug-turf battles make life miserable. Residents of neighborhoods where drug trade is concentrated also suffer disproportionately from the crimes generated by drug prohibition, such as crimes to get drug money. When the drug business leaves the cities, our homes, streets, and schools will become much safer. It may even become possible to educate children in urban public schools....

Public Health Costs

Drug prohibition makes the inevitable use of psychotropic drugs far more dangerous than would be the case under regulation. Most overdoses and drug poisonings are attributable to the operation of the illicit market. Drug analyst James Ostrowski concludes that 80% of drug-use-deaths are caused by prohibition, only 20% by the inherent qualities of the drugs. That estimate does not include the fact that needle sharing by intravenous drug users now does as much or more to spread HIV, hepatitis, and other deadly diseases as do unsafe sexual practices. Our drug war mentality has widely blocked the implementation of clean-needle programs that clearly reduce the spread of AIDS and other deadly diseases. Drug prohibition also deters drug users from seeking treatment for a myriad of other medical conditions, many of which are communicable. Ironically, the criminal status of drugs even deters drug abusers from seeking treatment for drug addiction.

The "war" approach to drugs also makes health professionals afraid to prescribe legally controlled drugs, which are capable of curbing and controlling mental illness and making bearable much intractable pain. They fear that they will be suspected of "addicting" their patients or even of being drug dealers with a medical license. Physicians are also prohibited by law from prescribing marijuana, even though it is of unique medical utility in treatment of glaucoma, nausea resulting from chemotherapy, loss of appetite due to AIDS, and other serious medical conditions. . . .

Relegalizing heroin, cocaine, and marijuana would probably produce a net reduction in the use of tobacco and alcohol, saving thousands of lives every year, perhaps tens of thousands. This reduction would come from several sources. Our present demonization of illicit drugs permits us to avoid confronting the realities of alcohol and tobacco—that they are our two deadliest popular drugs. Prohibition of some drugs encourages consumption of permitted drugs. As prohibitionists commonly argue, relegalizing the illegal drugs would convey the "wrong" message—that the legal and illegal drugs are in the same socio-cultural-medical-moral family. Some of the billions of dollars that the government, and the tobacco and alcohol industries, have spent trying to convince us that illegal drugs are immoral, suicidal, treasonous, dumb, and so forth will be symbolically transferred to previously legal drugs, therefore, deterring some potential drinkers or smokers from using or abusing those drugs. Alcohol is nearly nine times as popular as all illegal drugs combined and tobacco is four times as popular. A significant decrement in favorable public perceptions of these two legal drugs can therefore have enormous health benefits. Any change in law that blurs distinctions in attitudes toward alcohol and tobacco on the one hand and illicit drugs on the other is likely to have positive effects on Americans' health. This would be true even if consumption of presently illicit drugs were to increase by several multiples—and even if the safety of those drugs were not to improve at all.

Wholly apart from how relegalization would affect attitudes toward alcohol and tobacco, increased availability (i.e. reductions in cost) of illicit drugs will, if it increases consumption of those drugs, almost certainly reduce consumption of alcohol, especially among alcohol abusers, with significant benefits to their health. Many of the illegal drugs are substitutes for alcohol, and vice versa. Studies demonstrate that when access to alcohol is restricted—as when the drinking age was raised from 18 to 21—there is a substantial corresponding increase in the consumption of marijuana, not otherwise explainable. This supports the reverse inference that increased consumption of marijuana would reduce alcohol consumption. Thus, if repeal of prohibition produced more consumption of marijuana, an offsetting benefit would be reduced consumption of alcohol—our second deadliest popular drug.

When heroin addicts are deprived of heroin, they become alcoholics. When drinkers are deprived of alcohol, they turn to opiates. If repeal were to cause more consumption of heroin (by no means certain), some of the increase would probably represent a substitution for alcohol. To the extent heavy alcohol drinkers were to substitute opiates for alcohol, that would create significant health benefits (opiates cause virtually no physical damage to the body). Despite common misconceptions about the relative health costs of using legal and illegal drugs, health benefits could even accrue if consumers were to switch from alcohol or tobacco to cocaine or heroin....

Drug Prohibition Destroys Civil Liberties

Each year, as some supposed "loophole" used by drug dealers is closed, we all lose important civil liberties. Many Americans are persuaded we must sacrifice any constitutional safeguard in order to keep drug felons from escaping on "technicalities." However, the "technicalities" are the substance of our liberty, which took a revolution to establish.

Under the pressure of drug war necessity, the Fourth, Fifth, Sixth, and Eighth Amendments of the Bill of Rights have been subverted and have lost much of their meaning. We permit police to enter and search our houses, cars, and effects on the flimsiest of suspicion. We allow them to arrest and search minorities in reliance on racist stereotypes, euphemistically called "profiles." We let them terrorize us in our homes and even kill our children without recourse. We have all but destroyed the right of property with expansive notions of forfeiture. We have become so inured to daily excesses that the drug war disease is spreading to other areas. Based on drug forfeiture precedents, we are now willing to confiscate the cars of persons who cruise for prostitutes or drive under the influence. As a result of drug war forfeiture precedents, we are now positioned in principle to take the homes and offices of anyone who commits, or permits others to commit, *any* crime on the premises, including tax evasion or neglect of pets. George Orwell would be astonished. Such is the effect of drug war morbidity. It is as destructive to

the Constitution as AIDS is lethal to the body.

Drug Prosecutions Destroy the Lives of Otherwise Productive Citizens

Most users of presently illegal drugs, like most users of tobacco and alcohol, are productive and generally law abiding people. But treating their drug consumption as a serious crime makes it harder for them to be so and makes it impossible for some to be so—those who are socially and economically marginal to begin with. Legalizing drugs would greatly increase the capacity of the users of presently illicit drugs to be productive citizens.

I estimate that about 500,000 of our 1.3 million jail and prison inmates are there for illegal drug or drug-related offenses, and as many as 300,000 would not be there if drug prohibition were repealed because they would not be criminals. They would be available to their families and would have an opportunity to be useful members of society rather than embittered criminals enraged over their unjust punishment. No one who gets a prison term of any duration for using drugs or selling drugs to a willing adult buyer is likely to be persuaded that his punishment was deserved. Hundreds of thousands of Americans who might otherwise be integrated into the mainstream of society have that possibility virtually eliminated by a combination of embitterment and stigma, rendering their acceptance of and by the mainstream unlikely. This appalling waste of human lives, which itself far exceeds any plausible cost of illegal drug use, would be eliminated by repeal.

Prohibition Creates and Sustains Racial Mistrust and Hostility

The greatest social problem plaguing the United States near the end of the twentieth century is the same one that has plagued the continent for five centuries: racial mistrust and hostility. The drug war did not cause that problem; however, the drug war widens the hostility and deepens the mistrust between the races. By almost any measure, blacks suffer disproportionately from drug prohibition. They are not only more drug-dependent than whites, they are more likely to get AIDS, syphilis, hepatitis, and other diseases in the course of taking drugs or interacting with infected drug abusers. They are far more often the victims of drug-systemic violence than whites....

A *New York Times/WCBS-TV* poll in late 1990 revealed that "[a] quarter of the blacks polled said that the government deliberately makes sure that drugs are easily available in poor black neighborhoods in order to harm black people." Another third of those surveyed believed that the availability of drugs might be the result of deliberate government activity.

Support for conspiracy theories, as they apply to drugs, seems to lie in the fact that racial minorities suffer from drugs and drug prohibition vastly out of proportion to their representation in the population, while drug dealing openly occurs on the streets of their neighborhoods, seemingly tolerated by the police....

African-Americans are incarcerated at a rate six times that of whites. There are twice as many black males in New York's prisons as there are in its colleges. Nationwide, one out of four black males in his twenties is in prison or under some form of court supervision, such as probation or parole. (Of black males aged 18–35, the court-enmeshed figure is 42% in Washington, D.C. and a mind-boggling 56% in Baltimore.) Fewer than one in sixteen white males of the same age is caught up in the criminal justice system.

As many as 70% of black men in Washington, D.C. are arrested by the time they turn 35. Although about 77% of current illegal drug users are white and less than 17% are black, of 13,000 drug arrests in Baltimore in 1991, 11,000, about 85%, were of blacks. Nationwide, about 45% of drug arrests are of African-Americans."...

APPROACHING REPEAL

Eliminating or greatly reducing almost any one of the costs associated with prohibition discussed above itself warrants a declaration of drug peace. When the benefits of reducing or ridding ourselves of all of them are combined, the case for repeal becomes overwhelming. If legalization is too large a leap, courageous governors and a courageous president could give us some of the benefits of repeal simply by deescalating the war. Cut the drug law enforcement budgets by two-thirds (as President Clinton cut the personnel of the "drug czar"), stop civil forfeitures, grant executive clemency to most of the nonviolent drug violators stuffing our prisons, and much of the evil of prohibition will disappear. When the benefits of de-escalation are experienced, the nation will then be ready for *de jure* reform.

The meekest among us must admit that the case for relegalizing marijuana is unanswerable. Jimmy Carter was right when he proposed decriminalization of marijuana during his presidency. All Americans would be better off if he had succeeded. Marijuana poses some health risks, but far fewer than any other pleasure drug, with the possible exception of caffeine, and it substitutes for and, therefore, competes with all psychoactive drugs. Pending the legalization of marijuana, our nation's chief executives and law enforcement officers should end all prosecution for marijuana possession or trafficking and open the prison doors for all who are there solely for such offenses. Even an ardent prohibitionist ought to join in this proposal. Everyone agrees that cocaine and heroin are worse drugs, by any standards, than marijuana. If marijuana is legalized, drug warriors can then focus their resources on the war against "hard" drugs.

Should we retain the prohibition of hard drugs but reduce the penalties for distributing them, treating drug trafficking as just another vice, like prostitution or illegal gambling? That would be a great improvement over our drug war approach, but I don't think it is the answer. The slight benefits we might get from such a parsimonious retention of prohibition—deterring those whose consumption patterns are highly responsive to legal norms—would not be worth what we would give up—regulation of the distribution of drugs and control over the content of the product, the packaging, the distributors, and the informational flow about them. What we gain in a safer, less addictive product would greatly exceed the minor deterrent value of a largely symbolic prohibition. Moreover, if we were to roll back drug prohibition to something defensible, ignorant or unprincipled politicians would soon seize the opportunity to escalate the drug war all over again. Drugs are too convenient a scapegoat for demagogues to resist.

Drug prohibition has clearly eclipsed alcohol prohibition as the nation's costliest, most catastrophic social program. It has been such a colossal failure that even to question it has become political heresy. Too much has been spent, too much crime created, and too many lives destroyed by it to allow us to consider its merits. We have fried our brains not with drugs but with their prohibition.

NO

Gregory A. Loken

THE IMPORTANCE OF BEING MORE THAN EARNEST: WHY THE CASE FOR DRUG LEGALIZATION REMAINS UNPROVEN

DRUGS AND CRIME

Reducing crime, for most Americans, is a matter of the highest priority. [Professor Steven] Duke's case for legalization shrewdly presents itself as a response to that concern with a series of empirical assertions that all carry at least a scent of plausibility: (1) that crime has "nearly doubled" since Richard Nixon declared the war on drugs in 1973; (2) that "simultaneous ascents in drug war budgets and crime rates are not coincidental," because the "drug war causes crime"; (3) that because drugs are illegal, they cost more to buy, and the "motivation to steal and rob" leads to a vast increase in theft and other "acquisitive crimes" in order to "feed [drug consumers'] habits"; and (4) that "Systemic Violence" and "Proliferation of Deadly Weapons" are also caused, not cured, by our prohibition regime. Furthermore, Duke declares the fear that ingestion of heroin, marijuana, or cocaine causes crime to be greatly exaggerated, with "[v]ery little crime ... generated by the mere use of these drugs"—though Duke does acknowledge that cocaine "occasionally triggers violence." He argues that none of these illicit drugs are as criminogenic as alcohol and that the prohibition of the former leads to increased consumption of the latter, thus generating, on balance, more crime. Above all, he urges that we should have learned our lesson about the inevitable increase in crime and violence resulting from criminal anti-drug strategies from the "unprecedented" increase in crime that marked our experiment with alcohol prohibition from 1920 to the end of 1933.

Before assessing any of these arguments, of course, it is important to acknowledge, as Duke appears only somewhat grudgingly to do, that assertions about causation of crime are notoriously difficult: for example, the debate over heredity versus environment as the primary "cause" of crime remains highly inconclusive. Likewise, human aggression has been blamed on gender, racism, erotica, drugs, and violent programming on television, while crime rates in general are hostage to simple fluctuations in the percentage of adolescents in the population along with unemployment and breakdowns in family life. In asserting that drug prohibition caused the crime which followed it, Duke risks, although pardonably, falling into a classic *post hoc propter hoc* ["after this, (therefore) on account of it"] fallacy. Occasionally it will be worth returning to the problem of rival causal factors, but for the sake of argument it is certainly worth examining our experience with prohibition of alcohol and other drugs to see whether it supports Duke's assertions.

Alcohol Prohibition and the Lessons of the 1920s

Central to Duke's historical account of drug prohibition is his characterization of the 1920s as a decade racked with violence and social disintegration, with the adoption of the Twenty-First Amendment bringing substantial benefits. Even more importantly, he uses the failure of the prohibition "experiment" as support for his analysis of the effects of prohibition of marijuana, heroin, and cocaine.

Yet the evidence of a crime epidemic fairly attributable to Prohibition is far weaker than Duke would have us suppose. It rests heavily on the assertion of James Ostrowski that "[t]he murder rate rose with the start of Prohibition,... then declined for eleven consecutive years when Prohibition ended." Yet that statement, while literally true, tells, as Ostrowski himself glancingly acknowledges, only a highly misleading part of the story of murder rates during this century. A careful look at the same historical statistics used by Ostrowski

suggests a remarkably different historical account of Prohibition's effects.

...As Ostrowski claims, the rate of both murders and assaults by firearm climbed during the period of Prohibition (from 1920 to 1933), with a 35 percent increase in the murder rate from the level of 1919. Yet compare those figures to the same ones for the decade immediately prior: in 1919 the murder rate stood 56 percent above the murder rate in 1910 and 500 percent higher than the rate in 1900. If Ostrowski and Duke wish to infer anything from these trends in homicide rates, then they should conclude that Prohibition dramatically *slowed* a radically increasing homicide rate in the early part of the century. Indeed, other scholars of the era have concluded simply that "[t]here is no convincing evidence that Prohibition brought on a crime wave."

Duke's analysis is all the more unpersuasive because of its failure to take into account two enormously important historical events that could easily explain changing crime rates. First, he neglects to mention that more than half of the increase in crime between 1919 and 1933 occurred in the years 1930 through 1933, during the deepest depths of the Great Depression. Perhaps even more important—because more relevant to crime rates throughout the entire first half of the century—he fails to consider the impact of the adoption of America's first highly restrictive laws on immigration in the early 1920s, and their final effectiveness in the 1930s. Thus the immigration rates (per 1000 residents) were 10.4 for the decade from 1901 to 1910, 5.7 from 1911 to 1920, 3.5 from 1921 to 1930, and only 0.4 for 1931 to 1940. This slowing rate of immigration coincides far better with changes in homicide rates than does adoption of Prohibition. Additionally, this suggests the danger of ignoring rival causal factors. It could be that changing crime rates in the first four decades of this century were attributable to enormous social changes—in particular, tumultuous economic fluctuations combined with record numbers of often destitute immigrants.

Even if we concede, however, that Prohibition "caused" an increase in crime, what exactly would it prove? Perhaps, as Duke implies, it shows that *all* government prohibition of *any* recreational drug is doomed. Or perhaps it suggests, as the Panel on Alternative Policies Affecting the Prevention of Alcohol Abuse and Alcoholism concluded in its 1981 report, that "[d]rinking customs in the United States are strongly held and resistant to frontal assault." If that is true, our nation's negative experience with alcohol control points to two possible conclusions very different from Duke's. First, even if history shows alcohol to be, as Duke repeatedly asserts, the worst of the popular recreational drugs, it has such a unique place in our national history and psyche that our experience with it provides little guide to current policymaking on other drugs. Alternatively, alcohol's stubborn presence may simply suggest that we must, if at all possible, avoid having the use of any other recreational drugs become so customary that direct controls on their distribution and abuse will become impossible.

The "War on Drugs" and Crime

If Duke's account of Prohibition as a "cause" of crime is unpersuasive for the 1920s, his argument becomes wholly insupportable in our own era. For once we have accepted his view that "benign neglect" of illicit drug use prevailed until 1973, when the war on drugs began in earnest, the kind of empirical evidence on which he relies points overwhelmingly in a direction he would likely find quite surprising—toward, if anything, the conclusion that the war on drugs has *suppressed* crime.

For example, the homicide-rate trends that Duke favors for judging the 1920s suggest a rather favorable view of recent drug policy. From 1960 to 1972, the last years prior to the drug war, murder and non-negligent manslaughter rates climbed 76 percent, including a 55 percent increase for the years 1965 to 1970 alone. By contrast, from 1972 to 1980, homicide rates rose only 13 percent and from 1980 to 1992, they declined 9 percent, to a level equivalent to that of 1972. Far from suggesting that the war on drugs was responsible for greater violence in our society, these rates whisper that such violence is a legacy of the "benign neglect" of drugs that occurred in the late 1960s.

Moreover, Duke's thesis does not appear to fare well when glancing at the evidence that he presents. Duke's assertion that "violent crime rates have nearly doubled" in the period since President Nixon declared the "war on drugs" in 1973 relies wholly on F.B.I. data that reports "offenses *known to police*" —data which, of course, is subject to a variety of confounding variables, in particular the willingness of the public to report crimes, which may in turn be a function of the number of police and other criminal justice system employees available to take their reports. Worse, his evidence neglects the fact that this data shows a 150 percent increase in violent crime for the ten year period from 1963 to 1973. Duke never bothers to explain how such crime could increase more during the last ten years of "benign neglect" than it did in the twenty years thereafter. Finally, the F.B.I.'s "Total Crime Index" has actually shown a significant decrease since 1980, which, as I will shortly argue, is a better year for dating the beginning of the war on drugs.

Since 1973, happily, a better tool than the reported-to-police figures has been available: the annual National Crime Victimization Survey conducted by the Department of Justice. These annual surveys can hardly be considered definitive measures of crime; nevertheless, they do not suffer from the same reporting and resource limitations as the previously available statistics. A quick glance at the trends they reflect reveals how far Duke and other proponents of legalization must travel before their more-crime—because-of-drug-prohibition contentions can be supportable.

Again, it is important to recognize the extreme difficulty of correctly inferring anything about crime "causation" from broad statistical measures, but given Duke's reliance on those measures, it seems fair to examine them for whatever they might reveal about his thesis.

... [C]rime victimization has *decreased* across the board since the late 1970s. During the same period, the rate of removal of cocaine and heroin by law enforcement from the domestic market... indicates that the beginning of a "war" on illicit drugs only began in earnest in the early 1980s, at about the same time victimization rates began to fall rapidly. Most significantly, victimization of Americans by theft—the crime most commonly related (because of drug consumers' obvious need for cash under the prohibition regime) to the drug "war"— declined more than 35 percent from 1979 to 1992. Victimization by violent crime fell nearly 7 percent during this same

period—paralleling the fall in homicide rates. Overall, the risk of being victimized by any kind of personal crime fell nearly 28 percent from 1979 to 1992....

The Special Problem of Cocaine

Duke consistently rejects or minimizes evidence showing links between illicit drug use and violent behavior, except insofar as that violence is connected to the need for obtaining drug money. His treatment of cocaine is particularly disturbing in this respect, especially since it is currently the second most widely used illegal drug—far behind marijuana, but far ahead of other rivals such as heroin. In slighting the growing weight of scholarship linking the use of cocaine to aggression and crime, Duke seriously damages the credibility of his advocacy for legalization. He [does] concede, almost as an aside, that the drug "sometimes leads to violence against others," but declare[s] (with extraordinarily thin supporting authority) that it is "unclear" and "doubtful" that cocaine increases by any "substantial" amount the risk that a consumer will commit a crime. Yet a significant number of careful experiments have shown that regular administration of cocaine to normal human volunteers can produce otherwise unexplainable paranoid psychotic behavior, while others, including one in 1993 by researchers at the University of Virginia, have demonstrated a causal connection between ingestion of high doses of cocaine and increased aggression. Moreover, the clinical evidence is in accord: as one recent, comprehensive review concluded, there "are several lines of evidence that support a psychopharmacologic basis for cocaine-induced violent behavior in humans." The American Psychiatric Association now recognizes Cocaine-Induced

Psychotic Disorder (with either delusions or hallucinations) as a well-defined reality of clinical practice. So much a reality, in fact, that one recent study advised: "Given... [cocaine's] profound association with extreme anger, irritability, agitation, and aggressive behavior, cocaine intoxication must be suspected for any patient who comes for treatment with such symptoms." Indeed, of homicide victims testing positive for recent cocaine use, a study by the Los Angeles County Medical Examiner found that "20%... were found to have been acting violently themselves at the time of death," and a similar study in New York found that cocaine-using "[h]omicide victims may have provoked violence through irritability, paranoid thinking, or verbal or physical aggression, which are known to be pharmacologic effects of cocaine." In failing to confront fully and fairly the evidence of cocaine use and the danger it poses in the event of legalization, Duke does the debate over drug prohibition a disservice.

Furthermore, Duke does not grapple fully with the other highly dangerous feature of cocaine that links it intimately with the commission of crime: its addictive properties. Duke cites studies from the early 1980s, a period when cocaine was characterized by many as a "safe, nonaddicting euphoriant agent," for the propositions that there is little or no development of tolerance for cocaine, and no clear evidence of withdrawal symptoms. Oddly, those assertions are in direct conflict with the settled views both of the American Psychiatric Association and of academic physicians. Worse, according to Dr. Herbert Kleber, a national authority on substance abuse, "[c]ocaine is a much more addictive drug than alcohol," and its legalization might lead to a nine-fold increase in the number of compulsive cocaine users.

That Duke downplays the evidence of cocaine's aggression-producing and addictive properties is not wholly surprising, for they seriously compromise the ability of legalization proponents to promise benefits from the end of prohibition. How do we balance a promised reduction in drug-distribution-related violence against the potential for substantial increases in aggressive behavior by legions of new compulsive cocaine users? What difference in drug-related theft will reducing the price for cocaine make if cocaine addicts will spend *whatever* money they have for the drug, even to the neglect of food and shelter? Duke refreshingly declares that "[a]ny analysis of drug consumption that disregards the differences between [various drugs], and treats all drug consumption as equivalent, makes no sense outside the realm of theology," but in the case of cocaine he and other advocates of legalization seem to substitute faith for hard analysis.

Drug Law Enforcement and Racism
One problem Duke does attack with *some* success is the disparate impact of enforcement of drug laws on racial minorities. He argues that minority youths are at special risk of extraordinarily severe penalties for becoming involved in a drug culture that is an all too attractive alternative to the dreariness and squalor of urban ghettos. Surely it is plausible, as he asserts, that the presence of drug-enforcement efforts in the inner city will subject minorities to disproportionately higher rates of arrest and incarceration than those suffered by whites.

Nevertheless, Duke's assertion is not true. If Duke's thesis were correct, we would expect that from 1973 to 1992 (using his dates for the drug war), the overall arrest rate for blacks would have grown at a rate wholly disproportionate to that of whites, thereby causing the ratio of black arrest rates to white arrest rates to climb substantially. In fact, that ratio actually decreased significantly both for adults and juveniles. In 1973, blacks over the age of 18 were, relative to population, arrested at a ratio of 5.69 times that of whites and by 1992, that ratio had declined to 4.96. The comparable black-white arrest ratio for persons under 18 was 2.93 in 1973; by 1992, it had fallen to 2.34....

DRUG LEGALIZATION AND CHILDREN

... In a 1990 article focusing on cocaine, Dr. James Kennedy and I addressed the problems faced by one particular group of victims, children and adolescents, and reached three conclusions: (1) that cocaine abuse causes devastating harm to the young, whether through perinatal exposure, parental neglect, or direct, addictive consumption as adolescents; (2) that greater availability of hard drugs following legalization would lead to substantially greater exposure of the young to those drugs; and (3) that no adequate strategy has been developed to prevent that exposure upon legalization. Ultimately we proposed that discussion of drug legalization for *adults* be tabled until both proponents and opponents of legalization commit themselves to developing a strategy which would radically reduce cigarette and alcohol use by the young. Such a strategy could be used as a case study for possible drug legalization.

While not directly addressing our analysis or commenting on our proposal,

Duke does make a brief effort to confront the problem that drug legalization poses to children. With respect to the harms that hard drugs could cause to children, he does acknowledge that "distribution of drugs to children [is]... child abuse," thereby appearing to concede to our first point. However, Duke's discussion minimizes, or barely acknowledges, many of the worst harms that drugs threaten to inflict on children. As for the danger of increased drug use and exposure among the young after legalization, and the difficulty of devising legal barriers to such exposure, Duke is dismissive. Indeed, he advances the remarkable claim that we could be "far more successful" in protecting our children from drug use if drugs were legal for adults. The result is a blind alley, but one worth strolling down briefly.

DANGERS TO CHILDREN RESULTING FROM LEGALIZATION

Whether or not children obtain easier access to drugs after the repeal of prohibition, many children will suffer the consequences of substance abuse through their parents' increased drug use. For example, it is well documented that drug use during pregnancy substantially increases the risk that a child will be born with a low birthweight and a small head circumference, which, along with other factors, increases the infant mortality risk by a factor of three. Although some of the suffering endured by drug-exposed newborns may, as Duke notes, be attributed to their mothers' lifestyle, as opposed to the chemical effects of the drugs, much of it cannot. Duke's analysis neglects to mention, for example, that children born of mothers regularly using heroin must go through a full "abstinence syndrome" (i.e. withdrawal), which encompasses the certainty of enormous pain and the potential for death. Without even advocating a full-scale research effort to rule out heroin, cocaine, and marijuana use as major risks for children in utero, Duke simply proposes legalization followed by an unspecified "comprehensive policy" for "dealing with" substance-abusing pregnant women.

Beyond the womb, sadly, Duke does not appear to recognize any further risks to children from their parents' use of now-illicit drugs. He ignores substantial evidence that prenatal and postnatal drug exposure causes enormous damage to children for years after birth. In the words of one recent journal article, prenatal and postnatal exposure leaves children vulnerable to "a variety of physical, cognitive, emotional, motor, and social developmental difficulties." Perhaps more tellingly—because this extends to drug abuse by adults outside the context of pregnancy—Duke and other proponents of drug legalization consistently fail to reckon the consequences of drug dependence for the quality of parenting that children receive. As Dr. Judy Howard, professor of pediatrics at U.C.L.A. and a clinician who works with children in drug-abusing households, recently put it: "When a parent is chemically dependent, ... the pediatrician cannot be confident that parenting functions are not compromised." Chronic drug use can so "impair and distort a parent's thoughts and perceptions" that she will have "difficulty remembering [her] own children's birthdates;" worse, the child faces a substantially elevated risk of abuse and neglect.

Most damaging of all, though, is the failure of legalization proponents to face up to the dangers of greater drug abuse by children. Duke ignores altogether the strong association between substance abuse and homelessness among adolescents, which leads thousands of kids every year into a desperately destructive life "on the street." Likewise, drug use has been shown to be strongly related to suicidal behaviors among high school students, as well as HIV-related sexual behaviors—facts not explicitly counted in Duke's cost-benefit analysis.

The most surprising omission from Duke's analysis, considering how heavily it focuses on the nexus between drugs and crime, is any discussion of the literature exploring the links between drugs and delinquency—in particular, evidence that substance abuse leads to delinquency. Indeed, the most substantial longitudinal study of at-risk youths ever conducted recently presented strong evidence that, "if substance use [by the adolescents studied] increased in seriousness this was accompanied by an increase in delinquency seriousness," but that increases in delinquency did not much affect substance abuse. This pattern tends to contradict the picture presented by Duke of youths becoming involved in the violent drug culture because it offers the chance for high illicit earnings under prohibition. Moreover, the drug that currently leads youths most directly toward delinquency is alcohol, which of course offers no black market reward for traffickers. If other now-illicit drugs became legal, and as readily available to teenagers as alcohol is, we should expect crime rates for that age group to rise, not fall, along with all the suffering that increased drug use can cause youths.

Preventing Youth Access

Why worry about harm to children when, as Duke declares, we can "treat the distribution of drugs to children like the child abuse that it is and put flagrant violators in prison for it," and when "adults who encourage children to engage in such 'adult' activities can[] be condemned"? At first these words seem strong, but then doubts creep in. Do the quotation marks around "adult" betray a recognition that it is adolescence, not comfortable middle age, when the urge to experiment with drugs is at its peak? And does that adjective "flagrant" inadvertently reveal just how little a post-prohibition state is likely to invest in nabbing casual, non-"flagrant" distributors of hard drugs who now give kids alcohol? . . .

How do we persuade young people to avoid substances that we adults embrace? And how do we expect the same drug traffickers who survive the war on drugs to neglect the only black market remaining to them once drugs are legal for adults?

Duke's answer, incredibly, appears to be that we can protect the young from drugs in the same way we have "severely condemned" sex between adults and children. No doubt sexual abuse is universally condemned, but it is nevertheless epidemic. The recent National Health and Social Life Survey, which comprehensively studied the sex life of Americans, found that 17 percent of women reported having been sexually touched before the age of 14, usually involving genital contact by men over the age of 18. And at least one study has found an association between drug abuse by a parent and sexual abuse of a child: the authors of the study conclude that this "suggests that . . . [the parents'] chemical dependence rendered them inadequate protectors of their daughters." What kind of child protectors will we be if we adopt legalization?

Drug Substitution
Even if no effective barriers can be raised to prevent juvenile access to drugs, Duke has one last line of defense for drug legalization. He asserts that any increase in juvenile use of marijuana, heroin, or cocaine might well be matched by a corresponding decrease in the use of alcohol, cigarettes, or inhalants, all of which he believes to be more dangerous. The assumption that cocaine, in particular, is a more benign substance than any of these drugs is highly questionable—especially given the limited knowledge we have regarding successful cocaine treatment. Nevertheless, it is worth lingering briefly to consider the claimed negative relationship between licit and illicit drug use.

On its face, this claim seems improbable and careful inspection does not improve its plausibility. For example, cigarettes are highly addictive, and as one recent longitudinal study found, "students who smoke are increasingly unlikely to quit as they get older." Even adolescents enrolled in model drug-prevention programs cannot be easily weaned from tobacco. So why would we expect kids to *substitute* cocaine and heroin for cigarettes, as opposed simply to adding them? As for inhalants, Duke is wrong to paint them either as "popular" or as an increasing threat to kids. Less than three percent of twelfth graders use inhalants regularly, and from 1976 to 1992 fluctuations in this rate have been statistically insignificant. And again, what, other than speculation, supports Duke's view that adolescents would be better off smoking crack than sniffing glue, or indeed would not do both *together* if given the chance.

Alcohol presents a more intriguing problem, for it is used more than any other drug by adolescents; at the same time, the percentage of young people who use it has tended to vary more than other "licit" drugs. As a result, it is possible to put Duke's substitution theory to a rough test. For if adolescents who use marijuana or cocaine do so instead of using alcohol, we would expect that in years with a higher percentage of students using those illicit drugs we would find a lower percentage of alcohol users. However,... there is a strong *positive* correlation between rates of marijuana and cocaine use and rates of alcohol use. That is, in years when more kids use marijuana or cocaine, we can expect that more kids will also be using alcohol. Such correlations do not show that one kind of substance abuse causes another, but it does indicate the improbability of Duke's theory. Furthermore, these correlations must cause a small shiver of fear that drug legalization would make under-age abuse of alcohol even worse....

BENEFITS, COSTS, AND IRREDUCIBLE VALUES

Because Duke and other proponents of drug legalization fail to take seriously the extremely knotty problem of protecting children from parental substance abuse and personal addiction, they cannot present us with a realistic estimate of the costs of legalization. And because their promise of less crime upon repeal of prohibition seems unlikely, the principle benefit they hold out is questionable. But one final aspect of their case against prohibition—the offense to fundamental notions of personal autonomy—is not lightly dismissed. Although this aspect of the debate is not the focus of Duke's commentary here, it merits at least brief consideration in conclusion.

Placed in a "rights" framework, the legalization debate can become uncomfortable for those defending prohibition. How is it, exactly, that a person wishing simply to enhance her private feelings in her own home can be punished by the state for doing so in the absence of a demonstrated harm to another? Why, as Duke asks, should we not ban swimming, motorcycles, and obesity, all of which put our lives and health at risk? Is not drug prohibition, as he calls it, a " 'gross usurpation' of [John Stuart] Mill's concept of liberty"?

Those of us who remain skeptical of legalization must, of course, quickly take refuge in Mill's famous proviso that "[a]cts injurious to others require a totally different treatment." We can return to the vulnerabilities of children and the problems this poses for drug legalization. We can point out how incapable the young are of defending themselves against the ravages of a drug culture or of making rational choices about drug use. We can argue that widespread drug use will increase the risks everyone faces while driving their cars or out in public. We can maintain that simply because we tolerate some risks, and some risky behavior (such as alcohol consumption), we do not have to tolerate all risks and any behavior. And even if the attack on prohibition has answers for these arguments, we still may view the legalization alternative, when dressed in the garb of "rights," as fundamentally incoherent, proving too little and too much all at once.

The case for legalization proves too little in failing to give clear shape to its agenda. Thus, Duke is wholly unwilling to follow a "rights" perspective to its logical conclusion and propose the elimination of *all* controls on drugs—he would retain prohibition against highly dangerous *and unpopular drugs*. While certainly an understandable qualification, this seemingly minor reservation is a gaping hole in the "liberty" rationale for legalization. Are only *unpopular* rights the ones to be suppressed? If so, what is the point, in a democracy anyway, of having "rights" at all? Likewise, what is the moral basis in "liberty" for Duke's generous, but undeveloped, dictum that "[w]e should make treatment available at no cost to any abuser who wants it"?

That last question perhaps points most properly to a sense in which the libertarian underpinnings of the case for legalization prove too much. For why should taxpayers, and not the person who has exercised her privacy right to choose drug abuse, pay for any necessary treatment? Fear of just this kind of question caused advocates for the homeless to suppress for years any suggestion that many of their clients might be chemically dependent.

Indeed, why should the government ever intervene against any personal choice, whether it is to buy uninspected meat, spoiled cheese, or unsafe medicines? Specifically, how is it that Duke wants the Food and Drug Administration to continue to exist and yet have no authority over recreational drugs?

More insidiously, though, the case for legalization, in seeking to rehabilitate "popular" illicit drugs through a narrow libertarianism yoked to a myopic cost-benefit analysis, seems to be "proving" a new corollary to Mill's harm principle. It will now read: I cannot exercise my liberty in a way that will cause you serious harm, *unless* I do so with so determinedly malevolent an intent and so viciously efficient a means that I make life cheap, neighborhoods ugly, children expendable, and law enforcement all but impossible. *Then* you will see that your "costs" of denying my "right" are simply too high and the "benefits" of generous surrender will be great, indeed. But this generosity—slavish to miscreants, blind to victims, just, ultimately, only to the unjust—is generosity misplaced.

POSTSCRIPT

Should Drug Use Be Legalized?

It should be emphasized that one choice is not necessarily the easy one and the other the hard one. The "legalizers" are occasionally depicted as advocates of a free market of drugs, of letting individuals make decisions about personal use of drugs, and of letting the market regulate the price of a product that now has an artificially elevated price. But most "legalizers" are, in fact, asking that government involvement in dealing with the drug problem continue. To suggest a noncriminal approach to drugs is not to advocate a hands-off approach. Treatment and education are needed. It is not all that clear that this would be cheaper than the current approach.

It would also not necessarily be easier. Other than complete legalization, where drugs might be as readily available as aspirin, most approaches call for some regulation by the state. Choices would have to be made among alternatives ranging from outlawing sales to minors to requiring medical prescriptions for some drugs to establishing clinics that would distribute the drugs. Each of these alternatives would raise questions about free access and about effects on the black market for drugs.

Recent writings on the legalization question include Duke, *America's Longest War: Rethinking Our Tragic Crusade Against Drugs* (1993); Bayer and Oppenheimer, *Confronting Drug Policy: Illicit Drugs in a Free Society* (1993); Trebach, *Legalize It? Debating American Drug Policy* (1993); Moire, "Drugs: Getting a Fix on the Problem and the Solution," 8 *Yale Law and Policy Review* 8 (1990); and Wilson, "Against the Legalization of Drugs," *Commentary* (February 1990). Cloud, in "Cocaine, Demand, and the Addiction: A Study of the Possible Convergence of Rational Theory and National Policy," 42 *Vanderbilt Law Review* 725 (1989), discusses the legislative history of prevention and treatment programs. Packer, in *The Limits of the Criminal Sanction* (1968), analyzes problems associated with legal enforcement of moral norms. The myths and realities of the Prohibition era are examined in Clark, *Deliver Us from Evil* (1976) and Kyvig, ed., *Law, Alcohol and Order: Perspectives on National Prohibition* (1985).

More information on drug legalization can be found on the Internet at http://www.cato.org/pubs/pas/pa121es.html and http://www.futurenow.com/campaign/legalize_drugs.html.

CONTRIBUTORS
TO THIS VOLUME

EDITOR

M. ETHAN KATSH, is a professor of legal studies at the University of Massachusetts–Amherst. A graduate of Yale Law School, his main area of expertise is law and computer technology, and he is the author of two books on the subject, *Law in a Digital World* (Oxford University Press, 1995) and *The Electronic Media and the Transformation of Law* (Oxford University Press, 1989), as well as many articles. He is also active in the field of dispute resolution and is codirector of the Online Ombuds Office (on the World Wide Web at `http://www.ombuds.org`), a project designed to assist in the resolution of disputes arising out of on-line activities. Professor Katsh may be reached by e-mail at `Katsh@legal.umass.edu`.

STAFF

David Dean   List Manager
David Brackley   Developmental Editor
Tammy Ward   Administrative Assistant
Brenda S. Filley   Production Manager
Juliana Arbo   Typesetting Supervisor
Diane Barker   Proofreader
Lara Johnson   Graphics
Richard Tietjen   Systems Manager

AUTHORS

JAMES C. ANDERS is solicitor of the Fifth Judicial Circuit of the State of South Carolina.

JAMES JAY BAKER is director of federal affairs for the National Rifle Association of America, an association of firearm enthusiasts headquartered in Washington, D.C., that promotes firearm safety, marksmanship, hunting, and collecting.

ROBERT BEESER is a judge on the U.S. Court of Appeals for the Ninth Circuit in Seattle, Washington.

HARRY A. BLACKMUN is a former associate justice of the U.S. Supreme Court. He received an LL.B. from Harvard Law School in 1932 and worked in a law firm in Minneapolis, Minnesota, where he specialized in taxation, litigation, wills, trusts, and estate planning. He was nominated to the U.S. Court of Appeals by President Dwight Eisenhower in 1959, and he served in that capacity until he was nominated to the Supreme Court by President Richard Nixon in 1970. He served as an associate justice of the Supreme Court for 24 years until his retirement in 1994.

RICHARD BONNIE is the John S. Battle Professor of Law at the University of Virginia School of Law and director of the university's Institute of Law, Psychiatry, and Public Policy. He has written extensively on the legal aspects of mental disability and behavioral health, and he was elected to the National Academy of Sciences Institute of Medicine. He is also a member of the MacArthur Foundation Research Network on Mental Health and the Law.

SARAH BRADY is vice chair of Handgun Control, Inc., in Washington, D.C., a public citizens' lobby working for legislative controls and government regulations on the manufacture, importation, sale, and civilian possession of handguns.

WILLIAM J. BRENNAN, JR., is a former associate justice of the U.S. Supreme Court. He served on the Supreme Court from 1956 to 1990, when he retired at the age of 84.

PENELOPE E. BRYAN is an associate professor at the University of Denver School of Law in Denver, Colorado. She works extensively in the fields of civil procedure, federal courts, family law, and alternative dispute resolution. She received her J.D. from the University of Florida in 1981.

DEPARTMENT OF JUSTICE employs thousands of lawyers, investigators, and agents to protect U.S. citizens through efforts for effective law enforcement, crime prevention, crime detection, and prosecution and rehabilitation of criminal offenders. The department serves as counsel for U.S. citizens and represents them in enforcing the law in the public interest. It conducts all suits in the U.S. Supreme Court in which the United States is concerned, and it represents the government in legal matters and offers legal advice to the president and heads of the executive departments.

STEVEN B. DUKE is a professor of law of science and technology at the Yale University School of Law in New Haven, Connecticut. He is coauthor, with Albert Gross, of *America's Longest War: Rethinking Our Tragic Crusade Against Drugs* (Putnam, 1993).

STEPHEN K. ERICKSON is a mediator for and director of the Erickson Mediation Institute in Minneapolis, Minnesota, an institute where lawyers and therapists train to be mediators. A founding board member of the Academy of Family Mediators, he was one of the first individuals in the United States to begin practicing as a divorce mediator.

YALE KAMISAR is a lawyer and a professor of law at the University of Michigan Law School. He is the author of *Police Interrogation and Confessions: Essays in Law and Policy* (University of Michigan Press, 1980).

ANTHONY KENNEDY is an associate justice of the U.S. Supreme Court. He received his LL.B. from Harvard Law School in 1961 and worked for law firms in San Francisco and Sacremento, California, until he was nominated by President Gerald Ford to the U.S. Court of Appeals for the Ninth Circuit in 1975. He was nominated by President Ronald Reagan to the Supreme Court in 1988.

KENNETH KIPNIS is chairman of the philosophy department at the University of Hawaii at Manoa. He is the editor of several volumes on legal, social, and political philosophy and the author of *Legal Ethics* (Prentice Hall, 1986).

SUSAN M. LISS is deputy assistant attorney general of the U.S. Department of Justice and a former director and counsel of the Citizens' Commission on Civil Rights.

GREGORY A. LOKEN is an associate professor at the Quinnipiac College School of Law. He received his J.D. from Harvard Law School in 1977.

JOHN B. MITCHELL is a clinical professor of law at the University of Puget Sound School of Law in Tacoma, Washington. He has authored or coauthored numerous articles on lawyer's ethics, and he is coauthor, with Marilyn J. Berger and Ronald H. Clark, of *Trial Advocacy: Planning, Analysis, and Strategy* (Little, Brown, 1989).

SANDRA DAY O'CONNOR is an associate justice of the U.S. Supreme Court. She worked in various legal capacities both in the United States and in Germany until she was appointed to the Arizona state senate in 1969. She served as a state senator for four years and served in the Arizona judiciary for six years before she was nominated to the Supreme Court by President Ronald Reagan in 1981.

WILLIAM H. REHNQUIST became the 16th chief justice of the U.S. Supreme Court in 1986. He engaged in a general practice of law with primary emphasis on civil litigation for 16 years before being appointed assistant attorney general, Office of Legal Counsel, by President Richard Nixon in 1969. He was nominated by Nixon to the Supreme Court in 1972.

STEPHEN REINHARDT is a judge on the U.S. Court of Appeals for the Ninth Circuit in Seattle, Washington.

WM. BRADFORD REYNOLDS is a senior litigation partner with the Washington, D.C., law firm of Collier, Shannon, Rill, and Scott. He served as assistant attorney general, Civil Rights Division, for the Reagan administration's Department of Justice, and he was counselor to former attorney general Edwin Meese from 1987 to 1988. He has been in private practice for 17 years.

JONATHAN ROWE is a contributing editor for *The Washington Monthly*.

ANTONIN SCALIA is an associate justice of the U.S. Supreme Court. He taught law at the University of Virginia, the American Enterprise Institute, Georgetown University, and the University of Chicago before being nominated to the U.S. Court of Appeals by President Ronald Reagan in 1982. He served in that capacity until he was nominated by Reagan to the Supreme Court in 1986.

NICK SCHWEITZER is an assistant district attorney for Rock County, Wisconsin. He has been a member of the Wisconsin Bar Association since 1985.

DOLORES K. SLOVITER is a judge in the Court of Appeals for the Third Circuit in Philadelphia, Pennsylvania.

DAVID H. SOUTER is an associate justice of the U.S. Supreme Court and a former judge for the U.S. Court of Appeals for the First Circuit in Boston, Massachusetts. He was nominated by President George Bush to the Supreme Court in 1990.

JOHN PAUL STEVENS is an associate justice of the U.S. Supreme Court. He worked in law firms in Chicago, Illinois, for 20 years before being nominated by President Richard Nixon to the U.S. Court of Appeals in 1970. He served in that capacity until he was nominated to the Supreme Court by President Gerald Ford in 1975.

HARRY I. SUBIN is a professor of law and head of the State Prosecution Clinic program at the New York University School of Law in New York City. He is the author of *Criminal Justice in Metropolitan Court* (Da Capo, 1973) and *The Criminal Process: Prosecution and Defense Functions* (West, 1993).

WILLIAM L. TAYLOR is a lawyer specializing in civil rights and education issues and an adjunct professor of law at the Georgetown University Law Center in Washington, D.C. He is also vice chair of the Citizen's Commission on Civil Rights and a former staff director of the U.S. Commission on Civil Rights.

CLARENCE THOMAS is an associate justice of the U.S. Supreme Court. A former judge on the U.S. Court of Appeals for the District of Columbia, he was nominated by President George Bush to the Supreme Court in 1991. He received his J.D. from the Yale University School of Law in 1974.

MALCOLM RICHARD WILKEY, a former judge in the U.S. Court of Appeals for the District of Columbia Circuit, served as special counsel in the House of Representative's bank scandal investigations. He is a fellow of the American Bar Foundation and a member of the American Bar Association.

INDEX